12/04

Ford Mustang & Mercury Capri Owners Workshop Manual

by Mike Lewis, Larry Warren and John H Haynes

Member of the Guild of Motoring Writers

Models covered

Ford Mustang and Mercury Capri with 170 cu in (2.8 liter) V6, 232 cu in (3.8 liter) V6, 255 cu in (4.2 liter) V8 or 302 cu in (5.0 liter) V8 engine — 1979 thru 1987

ISBN 1 85010 391 7

ABCDE
FGHIJ

Printed in England *(5P4 — 558)*

Haynes Publishing Group
Sparkford Nr Yeovil
Somerset BA22 7JJ England

Haynes Publications, Inc
861 Lawrence Drive
Newbury Park
California 91320 USA

Library of Congress

Catalog card number

87-80070

Acknowledgements

We wish to thank the Ford Motor Company for the supply of technical manuals and information as well as some of the illustrations which were used in the production of this manual. Special thanks to the Ford Parts and Service Division's Publications Section and the Training and Publications Department, whose employees lent invaluable help on several occasions.

Introduction to the Mustang/Capri

Originally introduced in 1964 as a sporty-type car, the 1979 version carries on the Mustang/Capri tradition. Available in 2- and 3-door versions, these models feature as standard equipment MacPherson strut-type front and coil spring rear suspension, rack and pinion steering, high-back bucket seats, halogen headlights, 4-speed manual transmission and 2.3 liter 4-cylinder engine.

Options include power steering and brakes, various trim packages, air conditioning, automatic transmission and radio. Also available is a 2.8 and 3.8 liter V6, 4.2 and 5.0 liter V8 as well as an in-line 6-cylinder engine. The 2.3 liter 4-cylinder and 3.3 liter 6-cylinder in-line engines are covered in another Haynes manual.

The Mustang/Capri is of conventional design, with the engine mounted at the front of the car and the transmission directly behind. The engine power is transmitted to the solid rear axle by a driveshaft. All models are equipped with disc front and self-adjusting rear brakes.

About this manual

Its aim

The aim of this book is to enable you to get the best value from your car. It can do so in two ways. First, it can help you decide what work must be performed, saving you the cost of diagnostic work by a mechanic, should you decide to have a dealer or garage perform the work. The routine maintenance, troubleshooting, and the text will help you pinpoint random faults and discuss their correction when they occur. It is hoped that you will use this manual for its second, fuller, purpose and perform the work yourself. This will not only provide you the satisfaction of a job well done, but will save you the time and aggravation of arranging rides and all of the other problems which occur when dealing with a dealer or garage. On many simpler tasks, it will be actually cheaper to perform the work yourself.

To reduce ever-rising labor costs, many dealerships and garages replace entire sub-assemblies, when a single component fix may be all that is needed. This book is intended to help the home mechanic determine which small part may be at fault and repair just that problem at lower cost.

This manual has drawings and descriptions to show the function and operation of the various components so that their layout can be understood. The repair tasks are described with the novice home mechanic in mind and every attempt has been made to simplify complicated functions and tasks.

In describing the various tasks, it is assumed that the home mechanic has a normal set of tools available to him (or her), and no special tools are recommended or used unless absolutely necessary. Most special tools are designed to enable dealership and garage mechanics to perform certain tasks faster and have no bearing on the actual performance of the task other than that one thing. On a small number of occasions, a special tool is required to prevent damage to components or to limit access to particular parts. Where this is the case, use of the special tool is described. If the tool cannot be borrowed or purchased, the work must be entrusted to a dealership or garage.

Using the manual

This manual is divided into thirteen Chapters. Each Chapter is divided into numbered Sections which are headed in bold-face type and separated from the surrounding text with horizontal lines. In some Chapters, the format is broken into Parts which are identified by italic headings, but do not interrupt the serial order of the Sections. Each Section is divided into serially numbered paragraphs.

There are two types of illustrations:

1) **Figures** – which are numbered according to Chapter then according to appearance order (eg, Fig. 1.3 means "first Chapter, third figure")

2) **Photographs** – which are referenced by Section number then according to the paragraph in which the action is described (eg, 4.5 means "Section 4, fifth paragraph"). A cross referencing is provided in the appropriate paragraph with the notation '(photo)'.

Once a task is described in the text, it is seldom repeated. If it is necessary to refer to another Chapter, reference will be given as (for example) 'Chapter 3'. References to another Section within the same Chapter will be given as (for example) 'Section 16'.

References to the right, left, forward and rear directions are given according to the location when seen by the driver seated in the driver's seat.

Contents

1980 Ford Mustang with optional 'convertible-look' roof

1980 Mercury Capri 3-door

General dimensions and capacities

Refer to Chapter 13 for specifications related to 1981 thru 1987 models

Dimensions

Overall length	179.1 in
Overall width	67.4 in
Overall height	51.4 in
Wheelbase	100.4 in

Curb weight

2-door	2530 lb
3-door	2560 lb

Capacities

Fuel tank	11.5 US gal
Coolant*	**US quarts**
2.8L without air conditioning	9.4
2.8L with air conditioning	9.4
4.2L without air conditioning	13.4
4.2L with air conditioning	13.7
5.0L without air conditioning	13.4
** figures are actual, but may vary ± 15% due to system variations*	
Engine oil	
2.8L without filter change	4.5
2.8L with filter change	5.0
4.2L and 5.0L without filter change	4.0
4.2L and 5.0L with filter change	4.5
Manual transmission oil	4.5
Automatic transmission fluid	
C3	8.0
C4	8.5
Rear axle oil	3.5

Buying spare parts and vehicle identification numbers

Buying spare parts

Spare parts are available from many sources, for example: Ford dealers, parts houses and accessory stores. Our advice regarding spare part sources is as follows:

Official Ford dealers – This is the best source of parts which are peculiar to your car and are otherwise not generally available (eg; complete cylinder heads, internal gearbox components, badges, interior trim, etc). It is also the only place at which you should buy parts if your car is still under warranty – non-Ford components may invalidate the warranty. To be sure of obtaining the correct parts it will always be necessary to give the counterman your car's vehicle identification number, and if possible, to take the 'old' part along for positive identification. Remember that many parts are available on a factory exchange system – any parts returned should always be clean! It obviously makes good sense to go straight to the specialists on your car for this type of part for they are best equipped to supply you.

Other repair stations and accessory shops – These are often very good places to buy materials and components needed for the maintenance of your car (eg; oil filters, spark plugs, bulbs, fan belts, oils and greases, touch-up paint, filler paste, etc). They also sell general accessories, usually have convenient opening hours, charge lower prices and can often be found not far from home.

Parts houses – These will stock all the more important components, pistons, valves, exhaust systems, brake cylinders/pipes/hoses/ seals/ shoes and pads etc). Parts houses will often provide new or reconditioned components on a part exchange basis – this can save a considerable amount of money.

Vehicle identification numbers

The *Vehicle Identification Number* will be found on a metal tag fastened to the top of the instrument panel. It is on the driver's side and visible from outside the car.

If it becomes necessary to obtain new parts for your car, make a note of the identification number and take it along to your Ford dealer.

A *Vehicle Certification Label* is attached to the left door pillar. The label is made of special material to guard against alteration. If an attempt is made to deface or remove it the word "void" will appear. Vehicle loading limits and tire pressures are shown on a label attached to the rear face of the right-hand door.

An *Emission Control Information decal* is located inside the engine compartment. In addition to displaying engine adjustment information it also gives the *maintenance schedule code letter* for your car (see example).

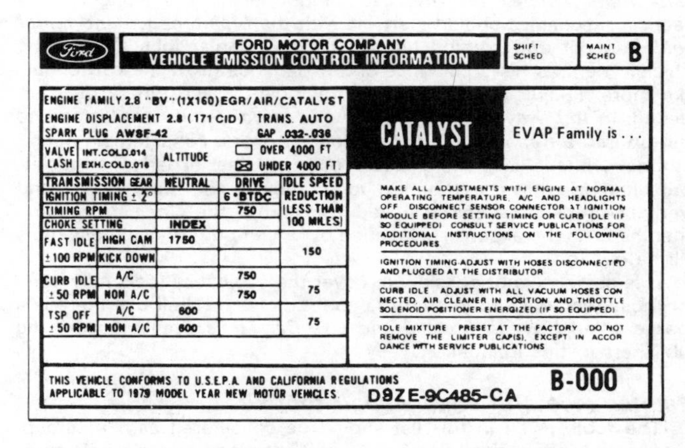

The Vehicle Emission Control label is located under the hood. The Evaporative Family letter is in the upper right hand corner of the label

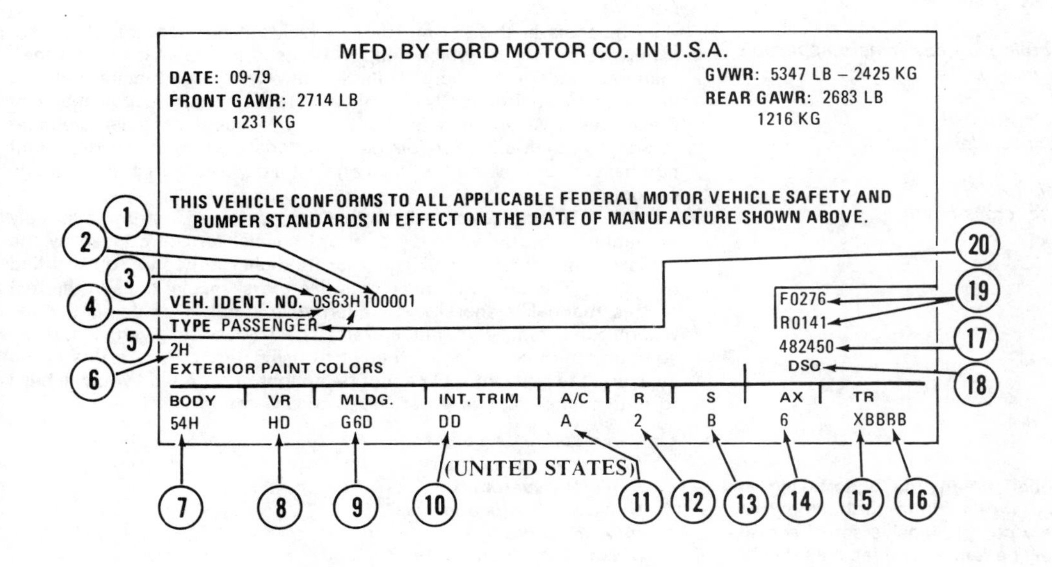

Located on the front left door post, the vehicle certification decal contains important information

1 *Consecutive unit number*
2 *Body serial code*
3 *Model year code*
4 *Assembly plant code*
5 *Engine code*
6 *Paint*
7 *Body type code*
8 *Vinyl roof*
9 *Body side moulding*
10 *Trim code – (First code letter = fabric and seat type, second code = color)*
11 *Air conditioning*
12 *Radio*
13 *Sun/moon roof*
14 *Axle ratio*
15 *Transmission*
16 *Springs – front L. and R. rear L. and R. (4 codes)*
17 *District sales office*
18 *PTO/SPL order number*
19 *Accessory reserve load*
20 *Vehicle type*

Tools and working facilities

Introduction

A selection of good tools is a fundamental requirement for anyone contemplating the maintenance and repair of a motor vehicle. For the owner who does not possess any, their purchase will prove a considerable expense, offsetting some of the savings made by doing-it-yourself. However, provided that the tools purchased are of good quality, they will last for many years and prove an extremely worthwhile investment.

To help the average owner to decide which tools are needed to carry out the various tasks detailed in this manual, we have compiled three lists of tools under the following headings: *Maintenance and minor repair, Repair and overhaul,* and *Special.* The newcomer to practical mechanics should start off with the *Maintenance and minor repair* tool kit and confine himself to the simpler jobs around the vehicle. Then, as his confidence and experience grow, he can undertake more difficult tasks, buying extra tools as, and when, they are needed. In this way, a *Maintenance and minor repair* tool kit can be built-up into a *Repair and overhaul* tool kit over a considerable period of time without any major cash outlays. The experienced do-it-yourselfer will have a tool kit good enough for most repair and overhaul procedures and will add tools from the *Special* category when he feels the expense is justified by the amount of use these tools will be put to.

It is obviously not possible to cover the subject of tools fully here. For those who wish to learn more about tools and their use there is a book entitled *How to Choose and Use Car Tools* available from the publishers of this manual.

Maintenance and minor repair tool kit

The tools given in this list should be considered as a minimum requirement if routine maintenance, servicing and minor repair operations are to be undertaken. We recommend the purchase of combination wrenches (ring one end, open-ended the other); although more expensive than open-ended ones, they do give the advantages of both types of wrench.

Combination wrenches - $\frac{3}{8}$, $\frac{7}{16}$, $\frac{1}{2}$, $\frac{9}{16}$, $\frac{5}{8}$ ins. A.F.
Adjustable wrench - 9 inch
Engine sump/gearbox/rear axle drain plug key (where applicable)
Spark plug wrench (with rubber insert)
Spark plug gap adjustment tool
Set of feeler gauges
Brake adjuster wrench (where applicable)
Brake bleed nipple wrench
Screwdriver - 4 in long x $\frac{1}{4}$ in dia (plain)
Screwdriver - 4 in long x $\frac{1}{4}$ in dia (cross head)
Combination pliers - 6 inch
Hacksaw (junior)
Tire pump
Tire pressure gauge
Grease gun (where applicable)
Oil can
Fine emery cloth (1 sheet)
Wire brush (small)
Funnel (medium size)

Repair and overhaul tool kit

These tools are virtually essential for anyone undertaking any major repairs to a motor vehicle, and are additional to those given in the basic list. Included in this list is a comprehensive set of sockets. Although these are expensive they will be found invaluable as they are so versatile - particularly if various drives are included in the set. We recommend the $\frac{1}{2}$ in square-drive type, as this can be used with most proprietary torque wrenches. If you cannot afford a socket set, even bought piecemeal, then inexpensive tubular box wrenches are a useful alternative.

The tools in this list will occasionally need to be supplemented by tools from the Special list.

Sockets (or box wrenches) to cover range $\frac{1}{4}$ in to $1\frac{1}{8}$ AF
Reversible ratchet drive (for use with sockets)
Extension piece, 10 inch (for use with sockets)
Universal joint (for use with sockets)
Torque wrench (for use with sockets)
'Vise grip' - 8 inch
Ball pein hammer
Soft-faced hammer, plastic or rubber
Screwdriver - 6 in long x $\frac{5}{16}$ in dia (plain)
Screwdriver - 2 in long x $\frac{5}{16}$ in square (plain)
Screwdriver - $1\frac{1}{2}$ in long x $\frac{1}{4}$ in dia (crosshead)
Screwdriver - 3 in long x $\frac{1}{8}$ in dia (electricians)
Pliers - electricians side cutters
Pliers - needle nosed
Pliers - circlip (internal and external)
Cold chisel - $\frac{1}{2}$ inch
Scriber (this can be made by grinding the end of a broken hacksaw blade
Scraper (this can be made by flattening one end of a piece of copper pipe
Center punch
Pin punch
Hacksaw
Valve grinding tool
Steel rule/straight edge
Allen keys
Selection of files
Wire brush (large)
Axle-stands
Jack (strong scissor or hydraulic type)

Special tools

The tools in this list are those which are not used regularly, are expensive to buy, or which need to be used in accordance with their manufacturers' instructions. Unless relatively difficult mechanical jobs are undertaken frequently, it will not be economic to buy many of these tools. Where this is the case, you could consider clubbing together with friends (or joining a motorists' club) to make a joint purchase, or borrowing the tools against a deposit from a local garage or tool rental specialist.

The following list contains only those tools and instruments freely available to the public, and not those special tools produced by the vehicle manufacturer specifically for its dealer network. You will find occasional references to these manufacturers' special tools in the text of this manual. Generally, an alternative method of doing the job without the vehicle manufacturers' special tool is given. However, sometimes, there is no alternative to using them. Where this is the case and the relevant tool cannot be bought or borrowed you will have to entrust the work to a franchised repair station.

Valve spring compressor
Piston ring compressor
Balljoint separator
Universal hub/bearing puller
Impact screwdriver
Micrometer and/or vernier gauge
Carburetor flow balancing device (where applicable)
Dial gauge
Stroboscopic timing light

Dwell angle meter/tachometer
Universal electrical multi-meter
Cylinder compression gauge
Lifting tackle
Trolley jack
Light with extension lead

Buying tools

For practically all tools, a tool supply or catalogue department store is the best source since they will have a very comprehensive range compared with the average garage or accessory shop. Having said that, accessory shops often offer excellent quality tools at discount prices, so it pays to shop around.

Remember, you don't have to buy the most expensive items on the shelf, but it is always advisable to steer clear of the very cheap tools. There are plenty of good tools around at reasonable prices, so ask the proprietor or manager of the shop for advice before making a purchase.

Care and maintenance of tools

Having purchased a reasonable tool kit, it is necessary to keep the tools in a clean serviceable condition. After use, always wipe off any dirt, grease and metal particles using a clean, dry cloth, before putting the tools away. Never leave them lying around after they have been used. A simple tool rack on the garage or workshop wall, for items such as screwdrivers and pliers is a good idea. Store all normal wrenches and sockets in a metal box. Any measuring instruments, gauges, meters, etc, must be carefully stored where they cannot be damaged or become rusty.

Take a little care when tools are used. Hammer heads inevitably become marked and screwdrivers lose the keen edge on their blades from time to time. A little timely attention with emery cloth or a file will soon restore items like this to a good serviceable finish.

Working facilities

Not to be forgotten when discussing tools, is the workshop itself. If anything more than routine maintenance is to be carried out, some form of suitable working area becomes essential.

It is appreciated that many an owner mechanic is forced by circumstances to remove an engine or similar item, without the benefit of a garage or workshop. Having done this, any repairs should always be done under the cover of a roof.

Wherever possible, any dismantling should be done on a clean flat workbench or table at a suitable working height.

Any workbench needs a vise; one with a jaw opening of 4 in (100 mm) is suitable for most jobs. As mentioned previously, some clean dry storage space is also required for tools, as well as the lubricants, cleaning fluids, touch-up paints and so on which become necessary.

Another item which may be required, and which has a much more general usage, is an electric drill with a chuck capacity of at least $\frac{5}{16}$ in (8 mm). This, together with a good range of twist drills, is virtually essential for fitting accessories such as wing mirrors and back-up lights.

Last, but not least, always keep a supply of old newspapers and clean, lint-free rags available, and try to keep any working area as clean as possible.

Wrench jaw gap comparison table

Jaw gap (in)	Wrench size
0.250	$\frac{1}{4}$ in AF
0.275	7 mm AF
0.312	$\frac{5}{16}$ in AF
0.315	8 mm AF
0.340	$\frac{11}{32}$ in AF
0.354	9 mm AF
0.375	$\frac{3}{8}$ in AF
0.393	10 mm AF
0.433	11 mm AF
0.437	$\frac{7}{16}$ in AF
0.472	12 mm AF
0.500	$\frac{1}{2}$ in AF
0.512	13 mm AF
0.551	14 mm AF
0.562	$\frac{9}{16}$ in AF
0.590	15 mm AF
0.625	$\frac{5}{8}$ in AF
0.629	16 mm AF
0.669	17 mm AF
0.687	$\frac{11}{16}$ in AF
0.708	18 mm AF
0.748	19 mm AF
0.750	$\frac{3}{4}$ in AF
0.812	$\frac{13}{16}$ in AF
0.866	22 mm AF
0.875	$\frac{7}{8}$ in AF
0.937	$\frac{15}{16}$ in AF
0.944	24 mm AF
1.000	1 in AF
1.023	26 mm AF
1.062	$1\frac{1}{16}$ in AF; 27 mm AF
1.125	$1\frac{1}{8}$ in AF
1.181	30 mm AF
1.250	$1\frac{1}{4}$ in AF
1.259	32 mm AF
1.312	$1\frac{5}{16}$ in AF
1.417	36 mm AF
1.438	$1\frac{7}{16}$ in AF
1.500	$1\frac{1}{2}$ in AF
1.574	40 mm AF
1.614	41 mm AF
1.625	$1\frac{5}{8}$ in AF
1.687	$1\frac{11}{16}$ in AF
1.811	46 mm AF
1.812	$1\frac{13}{16}$ in AF
1.875	$1\frac{7}{8}$ in AF
1.968	50 mm
2.000	2 in AF
2.165	55 mm AF
2.362	60 mm AF

Fastening systems

The Ford Motor Company has made extensive use of metric fasteners in the construction of your car. Since there are specific torque wrench settings it is essential that fasteners be properly identified, as many of these settings will not be given elsewhere in this manual.

As shown in the illustrations, bolts have four specific characteristics which may be readily determined: bolt strength, length, thread pitch, and nominal diameter. The latter three are determined by simple measurement, while the former is determined by markings on the bolt head.

Whenever you remove a number of bolts from any part of your car, make sure that the strength characteristic markings are the same, or that you know where the stronger bolts are to be replaced. The illustrations also show all strength characteristic markings used in your car's fasteners. Note that the 'M'- sizes mentioned in the general torque wrench settings chart are determined by measuring the diameter of the bolt head between the centers of opposing flats. If this measurement, for instance, is 14 mm, the bolt is then an M-14 bolt and must be torqued to between 80 and 140 ft-lb (109 to 154 Nm).

Nuts are also marked for strength and different strength nuts should not be mixed on reassembly of any component.

Finally, the illustrations show the more common fasteners and their strength characteristic markings, when applicable.

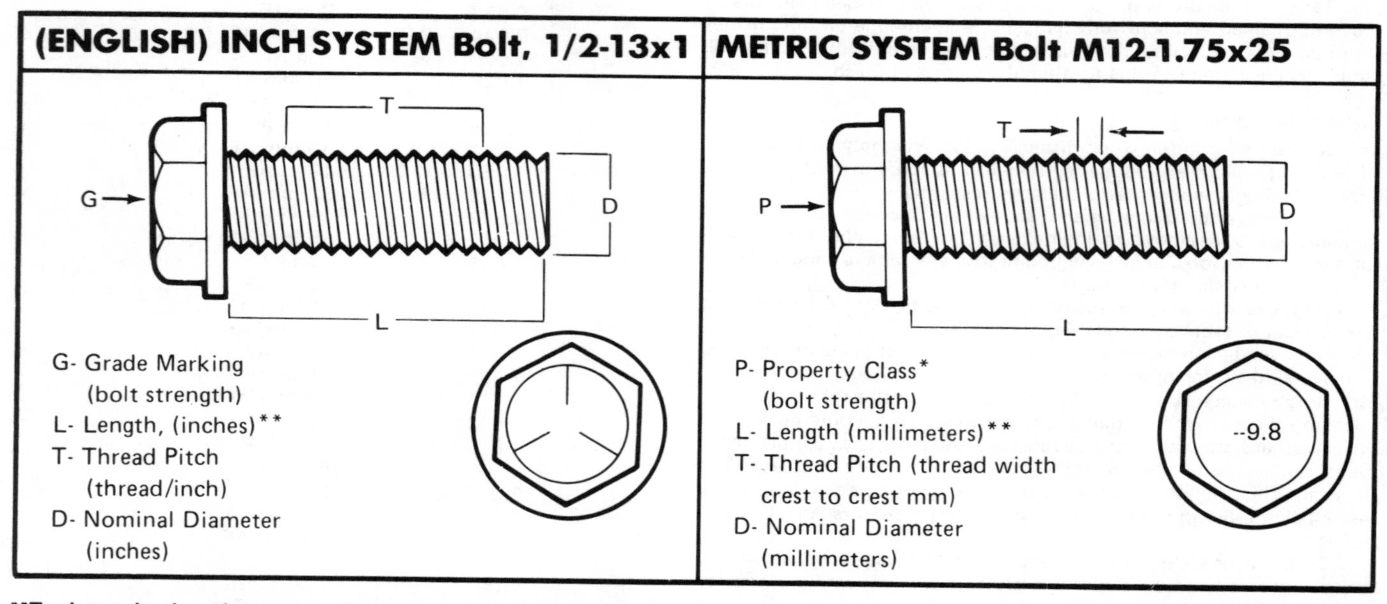

To determine length, measure from the underside of the head to the end of the bolt

***The property class is an Arabic numeral which distinguishes it from the SAE slash system**

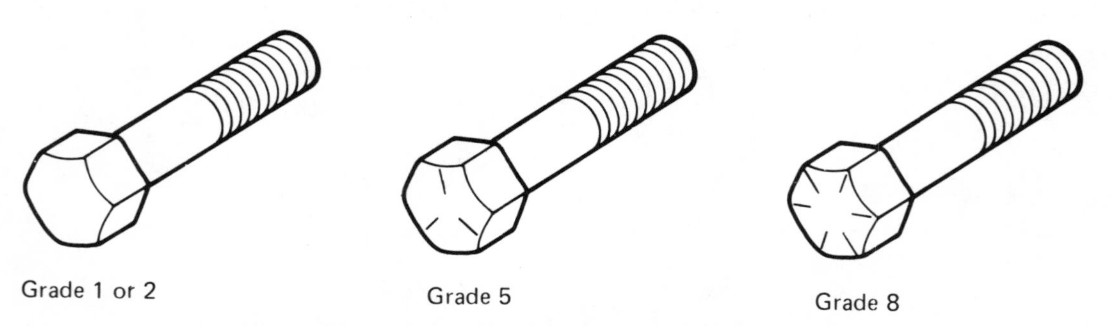

On English (inch) bolts, the number of marks (slashes) indicates the strength rating

METRIC SYSTEM

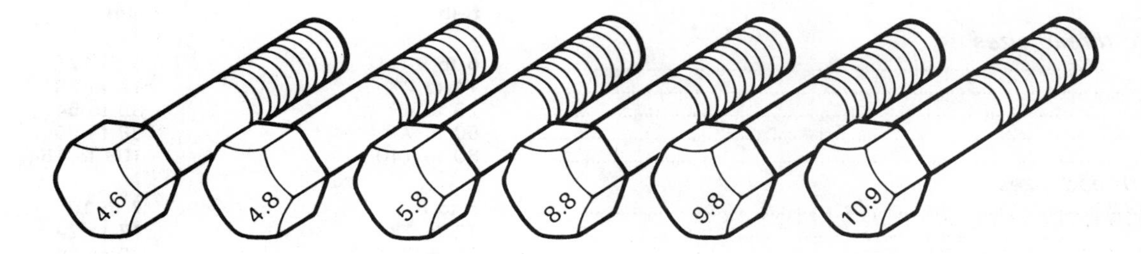

On metric bolts, the numbers on the head indicate bolt strength

(ENGLISH) INCH SYSTEM		METRIC SYSTEM	
Grade	Identification	Class	Identification
Hex Nut Grade 5	3 Dots	Hex Nut Property Class 9	Arabic 9
Hex Nut Grade 8	6 Dots	Hex Nut Property Class 10	Arabic 10
Increasing dots represent increasing strength.		May also have blue finish or paint daub on hex flat. Increasing numbers represent increasing strength.	

English and metric nuts are marked as to strength rating

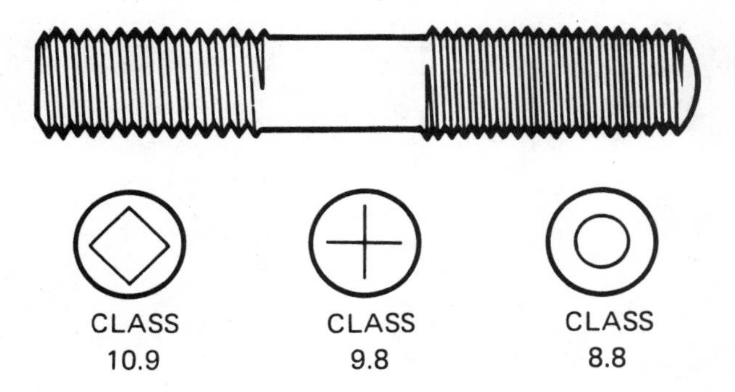

Large studs often have their strength rating embossed on the end

General torque wrench settings

The only torque wrench settings listed in this manual are those which differ from the norm, as given below, or are given to bring special attention to them. All nuts and bolts have a specific torque loading at which they must be set for safe operation of the car. If the bolt torque is not listed in the 'Torque wrench settings' section of the 'Specifications' torque the bolt to the setting appropriate as listed below. A similar listing is included in 'Specification' section of each Chapter, also.

	ft-lb	Nm
Metric thread sizes		
M-6	6 to 9	9 to 12
M-8	14 to 21	19 to 28
M-10	28 to 40	38 to 54
M-12	50 to 71	68 to 96
M-14	80 to 140	109 to 154
Pipe thread sizes		
$\frac{1}{8}$	5 to 8	7 to 10
$\frac{1}{4}$	12 to 18	17 to 24
$\frac{3}{8}$	22 to 33	30 to 44
$\frac{1}{2}$	25 to 35	34 to 47
U.S. thread sizes		
$\frac{1}{4}$ – 20	6 to 9	9 to 12
$\frac{5}{16}$ – 18	12 to 18	17 to 24
$\frac{5}{16}$ – 24	14 to 20	19 to 27
$\frac{3}{8}$ – 16	22 to 32	30 to 43
$\frac{3}{8}$ – 24	27 to 38	37 to 51
$\frac{7}{16}$ – 14	40 to 55	55 to 74
$\frac{7}{16}$ – 20	40 to 60	55 to 81
$\frac{1}{2}$ – 13	55 to 80	75 to 108

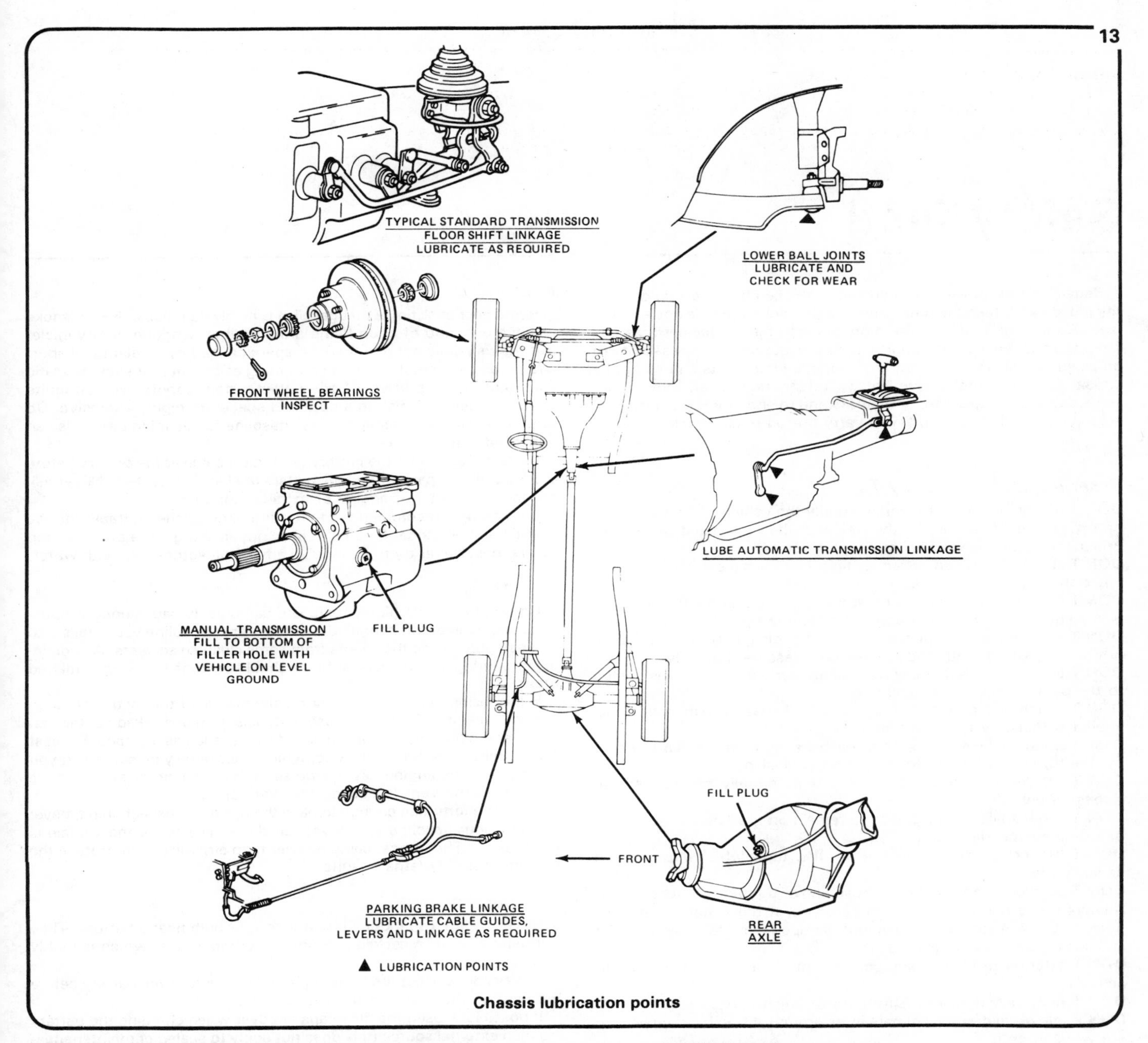

Chassis lubrication points

Recommended lubricants and fluids

Component	Description	Ford Specification
Hinges, hinge check, and pivots	Polyethylene grease	ESB-M1C106-B
Brake master cylinder	Extra Heavy Duty Brake Fluid (or DOT 3 fluid)	ESA-M6C25-A
Front suspension balljoints, front wheel bearings, and clutch linkage	Balljoint and Multi-purpose grease	ESA-M1C75-B
Hood latch and auxiliary catch	Polyethylene grease	ESB-M1C106-B
Lock cylinders	Lock lubricant	ESB-M2C20-A
Rear axle and differential:		
Standard	Hypoid Gear Oil	ESW-M2C-154-A
Limited slip	Hypoid Gear Oil	ESW-M2C-119-A
Power steering pump reservoir	Automatic Transmission Fluid	ESW-M2C33-F, Type F
Automatic transmission	Automatic Transmission Fluid	ESW-M2C33-F, Type F
Manual transmission, RAD and ET types	Hypoid Transmission Gear Oil	ESW-M2C83-C
Engine	Engine oil* (type SE or SF)	ESE-M2C101C
Engine coolant	Ford Cooling System Fluid	ESE-M97B18-C
Door weatherstrip	Silicone Lubricant	ESR-M1314-A

**Viscosity of the oil used depends on ambient temperature in your area. Check your Owner's Manual, supplied with the car, for further information.*

Safety first!

Regardless of how enthusiastic you may be about getting on with the job at hand, take the time to ensure that your safety is not jeopardized. A moment's lack of attention can result in an accident, as can failure to observe certain simple safety precautions. The possibility of an accident will always exist, and the following points should not be considered a comprehensive list of all dangers. Rather, they are intended to make you aware of the risks and to encourage a safety conscious approach to all work you carry out on your vehicle.

Essential DOs and DON'Ts

DON'T rely on a jack when working under the vehicle. Always use approved jackstands to support the weight of the vehicle and place them under the recommended lift or support points.
DON'T attempt to loosen extremely tight fasteners (i.e. wheel lug nuts) while the vehicle is on a jack — it may fall.
DON'T start the engine without first making sure that the transmission is in Neutral (or Park where applicable) and the parking brake is set.
DON'T remove the radiator cap from a hot cooling system — let it cool or cover it with a cloth and release the pressure gradually.
DON'T attempt to drain the engine oil until you are sure it has cooled to the point that it will not burn you.
DON'T touch any part of the engine or exhaust system until it has cooled sufficiently to avoid burns.
DON'T siphon toxic liquids such as gasoline, antifreeze and brake fluid by mouth, or allow them to remain on your skin.
DON'T inhale brake lining dust — it is potentially hazardous (see *Asbestos* below)
DON'T allow spilled oil or grease to remain on the floor — wipe it up before someone slips on it.
DON'T use loose fitting wrenches or other tools which may slip and cause injury.
DON'T push on wrenches when loosening or tightening nuts or bolts. Always try to pull the wrench toward you. If the situation calls for pushing the wrench away, push with an open hand to avoid scraped knuckles if the wrench should slip.
DON'T attempt to lift a heavy component alone — get someone to help you.
DON'T rush or take unsafe shortcuts to finish a job.
DON'T allow children or animals in or around the vehicle while you are working on it.
DO wear eye protection when using power tools such as a drill, sander, bench grinder, etc. and when working under a vehicle.
DO keep loose clothing and long hair well out of the way of moving parts.
DO make sure that any hoist used has a safe working load rating adequate for the job.
DO get someone to check on you periodically when working alone on a vehicle.
DO carry out work in a logical sequence and make sure that everything is correctly assembled and tightened.
DO keep chemicals and fluids tightly capped and out of the reach of children and pets.
DO remember that your vehicle's safety affects that of yourself and others. If in doubt on any point, get professional advice.

Asbestos

Certain friction, insulating, sealing, and other products — such as brake linings, brake bands, clutch linings, torque converters, gaskets, etc. — contain asbestos. *Extreme care must be taken to avoid inhalation of dust from such products since it is hazardous to health.* If in doubt, assume that they *do* contain asbestos.

Fire

Remember at all times that gasoline is highly flammable. Never smoke or have any kind of open flame around when working on a vehicle. But the risk does not end there. A spark caused by an electrical short circuit, by two metal surfaces contacting each other, or even by static electricity built up in your body under certain conditions, can ignite gasoline vapors, which in a confined space are highly explosive. Do not, under any circumstances, use gasoline for cleaning parts. Use an approved safety solvent.

Always disconnect the battery ground (–) cable *at the battery* before working on any part of the fuel system or electrical system. Never risk spilling fuel on a hot engine or exhaust component.

It is strongly recommended that a fire extinguisher suitable for use on fuel and electrical fires be kept handy in the garage or workshop at all times. Never try to extinguish a fuel or electrical fire with water.

Fumes

Certain fumes are highly toxic and can quickly cause unconsciousness and even death if inhaled to any extent. Gasoline vapor falls into this category, as do the vapors from some cleaning solvents. Any draining or pouring of such volatile fluids should be done in a well ventilated area.

When using cleaning fluids and solvents, read the instructions on the container carefully. Never use materials from unmarked containers.

Never run the engine in an enclosed space, such as a garage. Exhaust fumes contain carbon monoxide, which is extremely poisonous. If you need to run the engine, always do so in the open air, or at least have the rear of the vehicle outside the work area.

If you are fortunate enough to have the use of an inspection pit, never drain or pour gasoline and never run the engine while the vehicle is over the pit. The fumes, being heavier than air, will concentrate in the pit with possibly lethal results.

The battery

Never create a spark or allow a bare light bulb near a battery. They normally give off a certain amount of hydrogen gas, which is highly explosive.

Always disconnect the battery ground (–) cable *at the battery* before working on the fuel or electrical systems.

If possible, loosen the filler caps or cover when charging the battery from an external source (this does not apply to sealed or maintenance-free batteries). Do not charge at an excessive rate or the battery may burst.

Take care when adding water to a non maintenance-free battery and when carrying a battery. The electrolyte, even when diluted, is very corrosive and should not be allowed to contact clothing or skin.

Always wear eye protection when cleaning the battery to prevent the caustic deposits from entering your eyes.

Household current

When using an electric power tool, inspection light, etc., which operates on household current, always make sure that the tool is correctly connected to its plug and that, where necessary, it is properly grounded. Do not use such items in damp conditions and, again, do not create a spark or apply excessive heat in the vicinity of fuel or fuel vapor.

Secondary ignition system voltage

A severe electric shock can result from touching certain parts of the ignition system (such as the spark plug wires) when the engine is running or being cranked, particularly if components are damp or the insulation is defective. In the case of an electronic ignition system, the secondary system voltage is much higher and could prove fatal.

Routine maintenance

Introduction

Routine maintenance instructions are those recommended by the manufacturer, supplemented by other tasks shown to be necessary over time.

When performing any adjustments on the carburetor, emission control system, or the ignition, remember that these three systems are interrelated and that an adjustment to one may affect the performance of the others.

Make sure that all adjustments you make to your car are not items which might cause problems with your vehicle warranty at a later date. Be familiar with all warranty terms and conditions to save problems later.

Another problem which arises when performing adjustments is the possibility of making adjustments which will cause the engine to become in violation of emissions and pollutions standards. If you are in doubt, and feel that your car may be in violation of these laws after you have performed necessary maintenance tasks, have the final settings checked by a competent garage or your dealer.

Some of the tasks which follow require specialized tools or knowledge. We suggest that you review the appropriate sections of this manual and decide which tasks you feel qualified to perform. Should you decide that any of these tasks are outside your skill, or if you lack the tools, your dealer or a qualified garage should be capable of performing these for you.

Routine maintenance intervals

Every 250 miles (400 km), weekly, and before long trips

Steering

Check tire pressures (cold)
Check steering for smooth and accurate operation
Examine tires for wear and damage

Brakes

Check the level in the brake fluid reservoir, If the amount of fluid has dropped noticeably since the last check, inspect all brake lines and hoses for leakage and condition
Check for satisfactory brake operation
Check the operation of windshield wipers and washer
Check the windshield wiper blade condition
Check the operation of the horn
Check the operation of all instruments
Check radiator level and add coolant as required
Check battery electrolyte level and add distilled water as required

5000 miles (8000 km) or 5 months

Check engine idle speeds and adjust as required
Check and adjust automatic transmission bands as required

10 000 miles (16 000 km) or 10 months

Change engine oil
Change engine oil filter
Check clutch pedal free play and adjust as required
Check and adjust automatic transmission bands as required

20 000 miles (32 000 km) or 20 months

Change engine oil
Change engine oil filter
Check clutch pedal free play and adjust as required
Drain and refill automatic transmision fluid (severe conditions only)

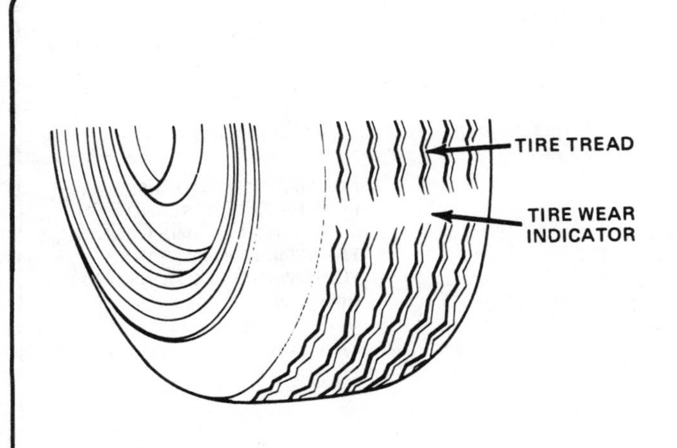

When checking tires, look for the tread wear indicator bands which appear as solid bars when the tire is almost worn down

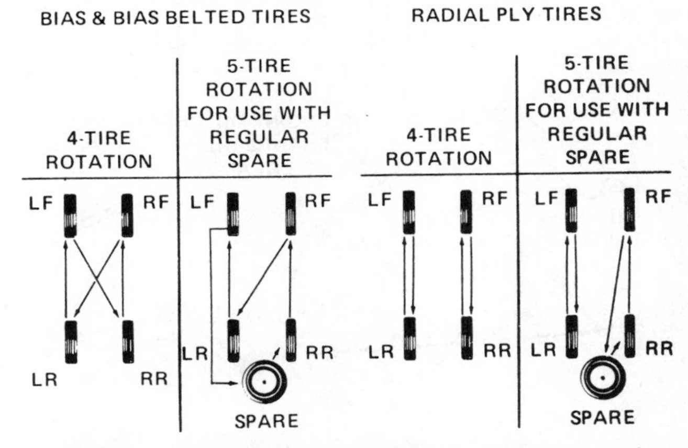

Tire rotation patterns. The temporary type spare is not to be included in this sequence, and is only to be used until a flat tire is fixed or replaced

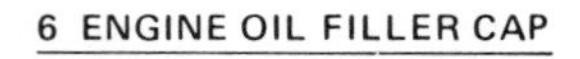

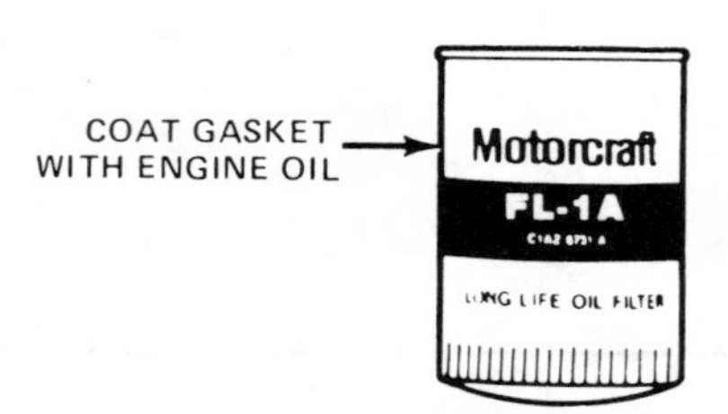

5 ENGINE OIL FILTER. CHANGE AT RECOMMENDED INTERVALS

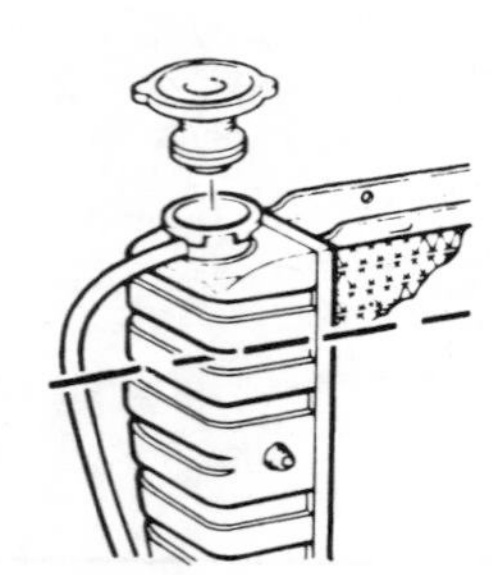

7 CROSSFLOW RADIATOR LEVEL SHOULD BE 2-1/2 INCHES (63.5) BELOW NECK WHEN COLD

9 DRIVE BELT USE DRIVE BELT TENSION GAUGE TO CHECK BELT TENSION AT RECOMMENDED INTERVALS

4 COOLANT EXPANSION RESERVOIR

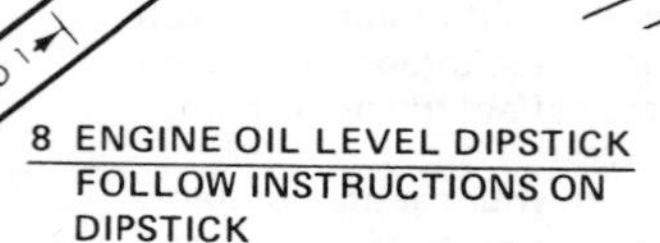

8 ENGINE OIL LEVEL DIPSTICK FOLLOW INSTRUCTIONS ON DIPSTICK

3 WINDSHIELD WASHER RESERVOIR

10 BATTERY

2 POWER STEERING PUMP DIPSTICK FLUID LEVEL SHOULD BE BETWEEN FULL HOT AND FULL COLD MARKS DEPENDING ON FLUID TEMPERATURE

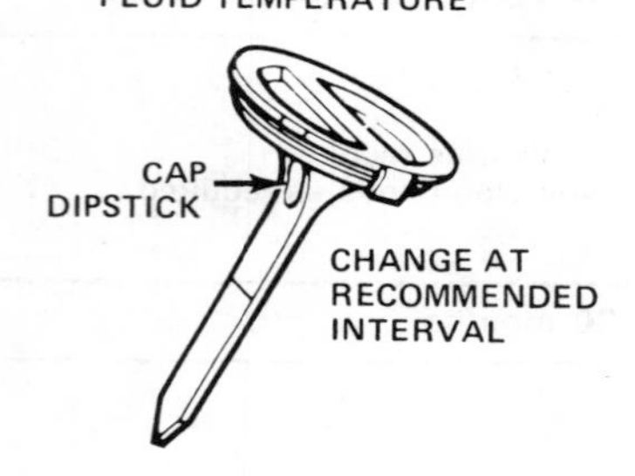

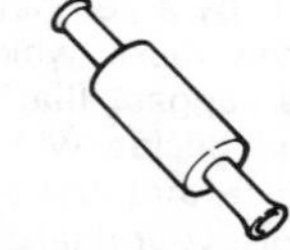

11 IN-LINE FUEL FILTER CHANGE ELEMENT AT RECOMMENDED INTERVAL

12 AIR CLEANER CHANGE ELEMENT AT RECOMMENDED INTERVAL

1 BRAKE MASTER CYLINDER FLUID SHOULD BE 1/4 INCH (6.4 mm) FROM TOP

13 CRANKCASE VENTILATION FILTER CHANGE AT RECOMMENDED INTERVALS

16 CRANKCASE VENTILATION PCV VALVE

15 ENGINE OIL DRAIN PLUG CHANGE OIL AT RECOMMENDED INTERVAL

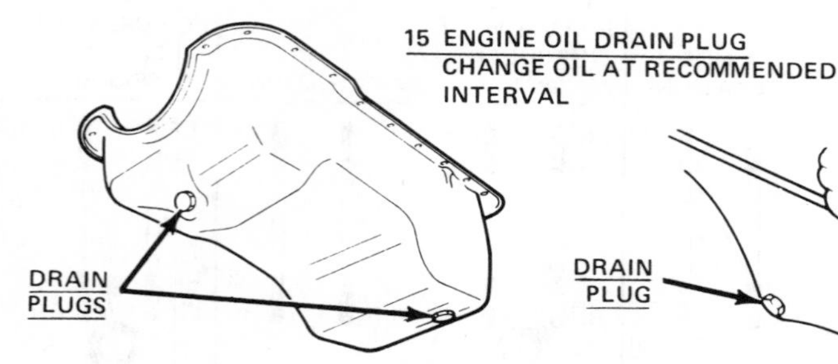

14 AUTOMATIC TRANSMISSION FLUID DIPSTICK (STANDARD) CHECK WITH ENGINE RUNNING, TRANSMISSION IN "PARK" FOLLOW INSTRUCTIONS ON DIPSTICK

V8 engine service points

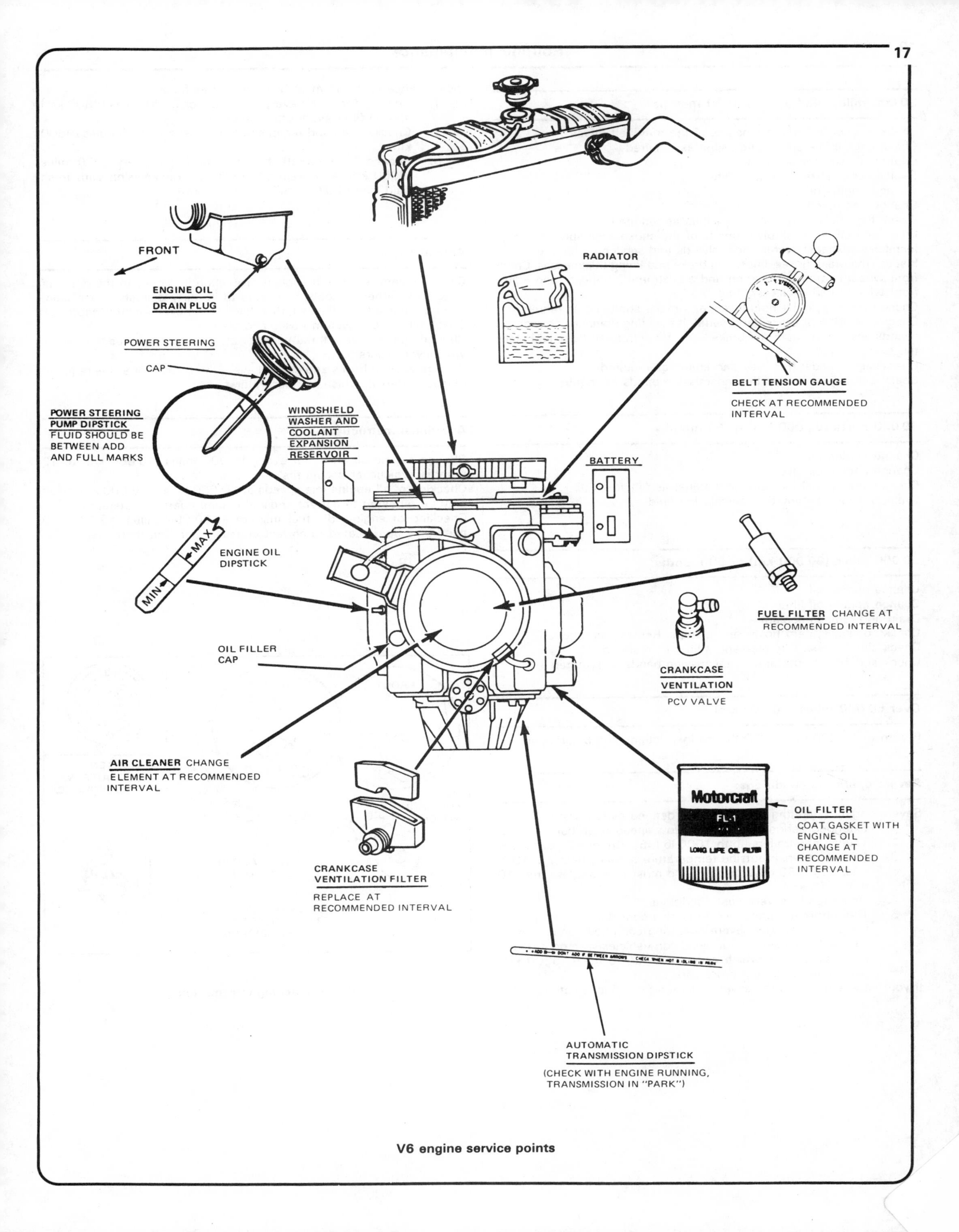

V6 engine service points

30 000 miles (48 000 km) or 30 months

Check the condition and tensions of the multibelt drives
Check engine idle speed and asjust as required
Change air cleaner element
Replace crankcase emissions filter
Change engine oil
Change engine oil filter
Check the choke assembly and adjust as required
Clean and lubricate all pivot points of the choke assembly
Inspect all exhaust system heat shields and service as required
Inspect the brake hoses, lines, and brake pad lining thicknesses. Check front wheel bearing lubrication and adjustment. Lubricate and adjust front wheel bearings as required
Check master cylinder fluid levels and make additions as required
Check operation of brakes and pedal. If bleeding does not correct any sponginess noted, drain the brake lines, fill with fresh fluid, and bleed the system again
Check clutch pedal free play and adjust as required
Check and adjust automatic transmission bands as required

40 000 miles (64 000 km) or 40 months

Change engine oil
Change engine oil filter
Check clutch pedal free play and adjust as required
Drain and refill automatic transmission fluid

50 000 miles (80 000 km) or 50 months

Change engine oil
Change engine oil filter
Drain and replace coolant
Check cooling system hoses and clamps. Replace as required
Check clutch pedal free-play and adjust as required
Check and adjust automatic transmission bands as required

Over 50 000 miles (80 000 km)

Return to 10 000 mile (16 000 km) instructions and begin again

Severe operating conditions:

Severe engine operating conditions are defined as follows:

1. Extended periods of idling or slow speed operation
2. Towing any trailers up to 1000 lb (450 kg) for long distances
3. Operation when outside temperature remains below + 10°F (-12°C) for 60 days or more and most trips are less than 10 miles (16 km)
4. Operation in severe dust conditions
5. The automatic transmission is also considered to be part of the systems under severe operating conditions and must be serviced at closer time intervals on vehicles with no auxiliary coolers, vehicles which accumulate 2000 miles (3200 km) per month, and fleet order cars.

If your vehicle falls into the severe operating conditions category, the maintenance schedule must be amended as follows:

1. Change engine oil every 3 months or 3000 miles (4800 km) and oil filter every other oil change
2. Check, clean and regap spark plugs every 6000 miles (9600 km)
3. Service the automatic transmission bands every 5000 miles (8000 km) and drain and refill the transmission with fresh fluid every 20 000 miles (32 000 km).

Annual checks

Check coolant levels and coolant protection just prior to the onset of freezing weather. If coolant appears to be dirty or rusty, the system must be drained and flushed, then filled with new coolant (Chapter 2).
Check all coolant system hoses and clamps
Change coolant every three years or at the required mileage interval, whichever occurs first.
Change coolant hoses and clamps every three years or at the required mileage interval, whichever occurs first.

Additional instructions

Change engine oil and filter every 10 000 miles (16 000 km) or 12 months, whichever occurs first
Checking of all engine idle speeds at 10 000 miles (16 000 km) need only be repeated to correct unusual engine operation thereafter
Checking of engine idle fuel mixture at 30 000 miles (48 000 km) need only be repeated to correct unusual operation thereafter.

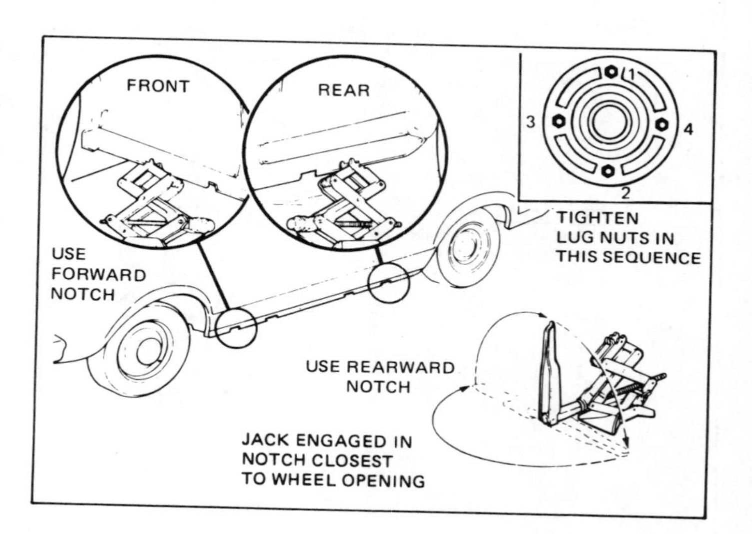

Chassis jacking information

Troubleshooting

Contents

Engine

1 Engine will not rotate when attempting to start

1 Battery terminal connections loose or corroded. Check the cable terminals at the battery; tighten or clean corrosion as necessary.
2 Battery discharged or faulty. If the cable connectors are clean and tight on the battery posts, turn the key to the 'On' position and switch on the headlights and/or windshield wipers. If these fail to function, the battery is discharged.
3 Automatic transmission not fully engaged in 'Park' or manual transmission clutch not fully depressed.
4 Broken, loose or disconnected wiring in the starting circuit. Inspect all wiring and connectors at the battery, starter solenoid (at lower right side of engine) and ignition switch (on steering column).
5 Starter motor pinion jammed on flywheel ring gear. If manual transmission, place gearshift in gear and rock the car to manually turn the engine. Remove starter (Chapter 11) and inspect pinion and flywheel (Chapter 11) at earliest convenience.
6 Starter solenoid faulty (Chapter 11).
7 Starter motor faulty (Chapter 11).
8 Ignition switch faulty (Chapter 11).

2 Engine rotates but will not start

1 Fuel tank empty.
2 Battery discharged (engine rotates slowly). Check the operation of electrical components as described in previous Section (see Chapter 1).
3 Battery terminal connections loose or corroded. See previous Section.
4 Carburetor flooded and/or fuel level in carburetor incorrect. This will usually be accompanied by a strong fuel odor from under the hood. Wait a few minutes, depress the accelerator pedal all the way to the floor and attempt to start the engine.
5 Choke control inoperative (Chapter 3).
6 Fuel not reaching carburetor. With ignition switch in 'Off' position, open hood, remove the top plate of air cleaner assembly and observe the top of the carburetor (manually move choke plate back if necessary). Have an assistant depress accelerator pedal fully and check that fuel spurts into carburetor. If not, check fuel filter (Chapters 1 and 3), fuel lines and fuel pump (Chapter 3).
7 Excessive moisture on, or damage to, ignition components (Chapter 4).
8 Worn, faulty or incorrectly adjusted spark plugs (Chapter 1).
9 Broken, loose or disconnected wiring in the starting circuit (see previous Section).
10 Distributor loose, thus changing ignition timing. Turn the distributor body as necessary to start the engine, then set ignition timing as soon as possible (Chapter 4).
11 Ignition condenser faulty (Chapter 4).
12 Broken, loose or disconnected wires at the ignition coil, or faulty coil (Chapter 4).

3 Starter motor operates without rotating engine

1 Starter pinion sticking. Remove the starter (Chapter 11) and inspect.
2 Starter pinion or engine flywheel teeth worn or broken. Remove the inspection cover at the rear of the engine and inspect.

4 Engine hard to start when cold

1 Battery discharged or low. Check as described in Section 1.
2 Choke control inoperative or out of adjustment (Chapter 3).
3 Carburetor flooded (see Section 2).
4 Fuel supply not reaching the carburetor (see Section 2).
5 Carburetor worn and in need of overhauling (Chapter 3).

5 Engine hard to start when hot

1 Choke sticking in the closed position (Chapter 3).
2 Carburetor flooded (see Section 2).
3 Air filter in need of replacement (Chapter 3).
4 Fuel not reaching the carburetor (see Section 2).

6 Starter motor noisy or excessively rough in engagement

1 Pinion or flywheel gear teeth worn or broken. Remove the inspection cover at the rear of the engine and inspect.
2 Starter motor retaining bolts loose or missing.

7 Engine starts but stops immediately

1 Loose or faulty electrical connections at distributor, coil or alternator.
2 Insufficient fuel reaching the carburetor. Disconnect the fuel line at the carburetor and remove the filter (Chapter 3). Place a container under the disconnected fuel line. Observe the flow of fuel from the line. If little or none at all, check for blockage in the lines and/or replace the fuel pump (Chapter 3).
3 Vacuum leak at the gasket surfaces or the intake manifold and/or carburetor. Check that all mounting bolts (nuts) are tightened to specifications and all vacuum hoses connected to the carburetor and manifold are positioned properly and are in good condition.

8 Engine 'lopes' while idling or idles erratically

1 Vacuum leakage. Check mounting bolts (nuts) at the carburetor and intake manifold for tightness. Check that all vacuum hoses are connected and are in good condition. Use a doctor's stethoscope or a length of fuel line hose held against your ear to listen for vacuum leaks while the engine is running. A hissing sound will be heard. A soapy water solution will also detect leaks. Check the carburetor and intake manifold gasket surfaces.
2 Leaking EGR valve or plugged PCV valve (see Chapter 3).
3 Air cleaner clogged and in need of replacement (Chapter 3).
4 Fuel pump not delivering sufficient fuel to the carburetor (see Section 7).
5 Carburetor out of adjustment (Chapter 3).
6 Leaking head gasket. If this is suspected, take the car to a repair shop or dealer where this can be pressure checked without the need to remove the heads.
7 Timing chain or gears worn and in need of replacement (Chapter 1).
8 Camshaft lobes worn, necessitating the removal of the camshaft for inspection (Chapter 1).

9 Engine misses at idle speed

1 Spark plugs faulty or not gapped properly (Chapter 4).
2 Faulty spark plug wires (Chapter 4).
3 Carburetor choke not operating properly (Chapter 3).
4 Sticking or faulty emissions systems (see Troubleshooting in Chapter 3).
5 Clogged fuel filter and/or foreign matter in fuel. Remove the fuel filter (Chapter 3) and inspect.
6 Vacuum leaks at carburetor, intake manifold or at hose connections. Check as described in Section 8.
7 Incorrect idle speed (Chapter 4) or idle mixture (Chapter 3).
8 Incorrect ignition timing (Chapter 4).
9 Uneven or low cylinder compression. Remove plugs and use compression tester as per manufacturer's instructions.

10 Engine misses throughout driving speed range

1 Carburetor fuel filter clogged and/or impurities in the fuel system (Chapter 4). Also check fuel output at the carburetor (see Section 7).
2 Faulty or incorrectly gapped spark plugs (Chapter 4).
3 Incorrectly set ignition timing (Chapter 4).
4 Check for a cracked distributor cap, disconnected distributor wires, or damage to the distributor components (Chapter 4).

5 Leaking spark plug wires (Chapter 4).
6 Emission system components faulty (Chapter 3).
7 Low or uneven cylinder compression pressures. Remove spark plugs and test compression with gauge.
8 Weak or faulty EEC ignition system (see Chapter 4).
9 Vacuum leaks at carburetor, intake manifold or vacuum hoses (see Section 8).

11 Engine stalls

1 Carburetor idle speed incorrectly set (Chapter 3).
2 Carburetor fuel filter clogged and/or water and impurities in the fuel system (Chapter 3).
3 Choke improperly adjusted or sticking (Chapter 3).
4 Distributor components damp, points out of adjustment or damage to distributor cap, rotor, etc. (Chapter 4).
5 Emission system components faulty (Troubleshooting section, Chapter 3.
6 Faulty or incorrectly gapped spark plugs. (Chapter 4). Also check spark plug wires (Chapter 4).
7 Vacuum leak at the carburetor, intake manifold or vacuum hoses. Check as described in Section 8.
8 Valve lash incorrectly set (Chapter 1).

12 Engine lacks power

1 Incorrect ignition timing (Chapter 3).
2 Excessive play in distributor shaft. At the same time check for worn or maladjusted contact rotor, faulty distributor cap, wires, etc. (Chapter 3).
3 Faulty or incorrectly gapped spark plugs (Chapter 4).
4 Carburetor not adjusted properly or excessively worn (Chapter 3).
5 Weak coil or condensor (Chapter 4).
6 Faulty EEC system coil (Chapter 4).
7 Brakes binding (Chapter 9).
8 Automatic transmission fluid level incorrect, causing slippage (Chapter 7).
9 Manual transmission clutch slipping (Chapter 7).
10 Fuel filter clogged and/or impurities in the fuel system (Chapter 3).
11 Emission control system not functioning properly (Chapter 3).
12 Use of sub-standard fuel. Fill tank with proper octane fuel.
13 Low or uneven cylinder compression pressures. Test with compression tester, which will also detect leaking valves and/or blown head gasket.

13 Engine backfire

1 Emission system not functioning properly (Chapter 3).
2 Ignition timing incorrect (Section 3).
3 Carburetor in need of adjustment or worn excessively (Chapter 3).
4 Vacuum leak at carburetor, intake manifold or vacuum hoses. Check as described in Section 8.
5 Valve lash incorrectly set, and/or valves sticking (Chapter 1).

14 Pinging or knocking engine sounds on hard acceleration or uphill

1 Incorrect grade of fuel. Fill tank with fuel of the proper octane rating.
2 Ignition timing incorrect (Chapter 4).
3 Carburetor in need of adjustment (Chapter 3).
4 Improper spark plugs. Check plug type with that specified on tune-up decal located inside engine compartment. Also check plugs and wires for damage (Chapter 4).
5 Worn or damaged distributor components (Chapter 4).
6 Faulty emission system (Chapter 3).
7 Vacuum leak (Check as described in Section 8).

15 Engine 'diesels' (continues to run) after switching off

1 Idle speed too fast (Chapter 4).
2 Electrical solenoid at side of carburetor not functioning properly (not all models, see Chapter 3).
3 Ignition timing incorrectly adjusted (Chapter 4).
4 Air cleaner valve not operating properly (Chapter 3).
5 Excessive engine operating temperatures. Probable causes of this are: malfunctioning thermostat, clogged radiator, faulty water pump (See Chapter 2).

Engine electrical

16 Battery will not hold a charge

1 Alternator drivebelt defective or not adjusted properly (Chapter 11).
2 Electrolyte level too low or too weak (Chapter 11).
3 Battery terminals loose or corroded (Chapter 11).
4 Alternator not charging properly (Chapter 11).
5 Loose, broken or faulty wiring in the charging circuit (Chapter 11).
6 Short in vehicle circuitry causing a continual drain on battery.
7 Battery defective internally.

17 Ignition light fails to go out

1 Fault in alternator or charging circuit (Chapter 11).
2 Alternator drivebelt defective or not properly adjusted (Chapter 11).

18 Ignition light fails to come on when key is turned

1 Ignition light bulb faulty (Chapter 11).
2 Alternator faulty (Chapter 11).
3 Fault in the printed circuit, dash wiring or bulb holder (Chapter 11).

Engine fuel system

19 Excessive fuel consumption

1 Dirty or choked air filter element (Chapter 3).
2 Incorrectly set ignition timing (Chapter 4).
3 Choke sticking or improperly adjusted (Chapter 3).
4 Emission system not functioning properly (not all cars, see Chapter 3).
5 Carburetor idle speed and/or mixture not adjusted properly (Chapter 3).
6 Carburetor internal parts excessively worn or damaged (Chapter 3).
7 Low tire pressure or incorrect tire size (Chapter 10).

20 Fuel leakage and/or fuel odor

1 Leak in a fuel feed or vent line (Chapter 3).
2 Tank overfilled. Fill only to automatic shut-off.
3 Emission system filter in need of replacement (Chapter 3).
4 Vapor leaks from system lines (Chapter 3).
5 Carburetor internal parts excessively worn or out of adjustment (Chapter 3).

Engine cooling system

21 Overheating

1 Insufficient coolant in system (Chapter 2).
2 Fan belt defective or not adjusted properly (Chapter 2).
3 Radiator core blocked or radiator grille dirty and restricted (Chapter 2).
4 Thermostat faulty (Chapter 2).
5 Fan blades broken or cracked (Chapter 3).
6 Radiator cap not maintaining proper pressure. Have cap pressure tested by gas station or repair shop.
7 Ignition timing incorrect (Chapter 4).

22 Overcooling

1 Thermostat faulty (Chapter 2).
2 Inaccurate temperature gauge (Chapter 11).

23 External water leakage

1 Deteriorated or damaged hoses. Loose clamps at hose connections (Chapter 2).
2 Water pump seals defective. If this is the case, water will drip from the 'weep' hole in the water pump body (Chapter 2).
3 Leakage from radiator core or header tank. This will require the radiator to be professionally repaired (see Chapter 2 for removal procedures).
4 Engine drain plugs or water jacket freeze plugs leaking (see Chapters 1 and 2).

24 Internal water leakage

Note: *Internal coolant leaks can usually be detected by examining the oil. Check the dipstick and inside of valve cover for water deposits and an oil consistency like that of a milkshake.*
1 Faulty cylinder head gasket. Have the system pressure-tested professionally or remove the cylinder heads (Chapter 1) and inspect.
2 Cracked cylinder bore or cylinder head. Dismantle engine and inspect (Chapter 1).

25 Water loss

1 Overfilling system (Chapter 2).
2 Coolant boiling away due to overheating (see causes in Section 15).
3 Internal or external leakage (see Sections 22 and 23).
4 Faulty radiator cap. Have the cap pressure tested.

26 Poor coolant circulation

1 Inoperative water pump. A quick test is to pinch the top radiator hose closed with your hand while the engine is idling, then let loose. You should feel a surge of water if the pump is working properly (Chapter 2).
2 Restriction in cooling system. Drain, flush and refill the system (Chapter 2). If it appears necessary, remove the radiator (Chapter 2) and have it reverse-flushed or professionally cleaned.
3 Fan drivebelt defective or not adjusted properly (Chapter 2).
4 Thermostat sticking (Chapter 2).

Clutch

27 Fails to release (pedal pressed to the floor – shift lever does not move freely in and out of reverse)

1 Improper linkage adjustment (Chapter 6).
2 Clutch fork off ball stud. Look under the car, on the left side of transmission.
3 Clutch disc warped, bent or excessively damaged (Chapter 6).

28 Clutch slips (engine speed increases with no increase in road speed)

1 Linkage in need of adjustment (Chapter 6).
2 Clutch disc oil soaked or facing worn. Remove disc (Chapter 6) and inspect.
3 Clutch disc not seated in. It may take 30 or 40 normal starts for a new disc to seat.

29 Grabbing (juddering) on take-up

1 Oil on clutch disc facings. Remove disc (Chapter 6) and inspect. Correct any leakage source.
2 Worn or loose engine or transmission mounts. These units may move slightly when clutch is released. Inspect mounts and bolts.
3 Worn splines on clutch gear. Remove clutch components (Chapter 6) and inspect.
4 Warped pressure plate or flywheel. Remove clutch components and inspect.

30 Squeal or rumble with clutch fully engaged (pedal released)

1 Improper adjustment; no lash (Chapter 6).
2 Release bearing binding on transmission bearing retainer. Remove clutch components (Chapter 6) and check bearing. Remove any burrs or nicks, clean and relubricate before reinstallation.
3 Weak linkage return spring. Replace the spring.

31 Squeal or rumble with clutch fully disengaged (pedal depressed)

1 Worn, faulty or broken release bearing (Chapter 6).
2 Worn or broken pressure plate springs (or diaphragm fingers) (Chapter 6).

32 Clutch pedal stays on floor when disengaged

1 Bind in linkage or release bearing. Inspect linkage or remove clutch components as necessary.
2 Linkage springs being over-traveled. Adjust linkage for proper lash. Make sure proper pedal stop (bumper) is installed.

Manual transmission

Note: *All the following Sections contained within Chapter 7 unless noted.*

33 Noisy in neutral with engine running

1 Input shaft bearing worn.
2 Damaged main drive gear bearing.
3 Worn countergear bearings.
4 Worn or damaged countergear anti-lash plate.

34 Noisy in all gears

1 Any of the above causes, and/or:
2 Insufficient lubricant (see checking procedures in Chapter 7).

35 Noisy in one particular gear

1 Worn, damaged or chipped gear teeth for that particular gear.
2 Worn or damaged synchronizer for that particular gear.

36 Slips out of high gear

1 Transmission loose on clutch housing.
2 Shift rods interfering with engine mounts or clutch lever.
3 Shift rods not working freely.
4 Damaged mainshaft pilot bearing.
5 Dirt between transmission case and clutch housing, or misalignment of transmission (Chapter 6).
6 Worn or improperly adjusted linkage (Chapter 6).

37 Difficulty in engaging gears

1 Clutch not releasing fully (see clutch adjustment, Chapter 6).
2 Loose, damaged or maladjusted shift linkage. Make a thorough inspection, replacing parts as necessary. Adjust as described in Chapter 6.

38 Fluid leakage

1 Excessive amount of lubricant in transmission (see Chapter 7 for correct checking procedures. Drain lubricant as required).
2 Side cover loose or gasket damaged.
3 Rear oil seal or speedometer oil seal in need of replacement (Section 6).

Automatic transmission

Note: *Due to the complexity of the automatic transmission, it is difficult for the home mechanic to properly diagnose and service this component. For problems other than the following, the vehicle should be taken to a reputable mechanic.*

39 Fluid leakage

1 Automatic transmission fluid is a deep red color, and fluid leaks should not be confused with engine oil which can easily be blown by air flow to the transmission.
2 To pinpoint a leak, first remove all built-up dirt and grime from around the transmission. Degreasing agents and/or steam cleaning will achieve this. With the underside clean, drive the car at low speeds so the air flow will not blow the leak far from its source. Raise the car and determine where the leak is coming from. Common areas of leakage are:

a) Fluid pan: tighten mounting bolts and/or replace pan gasket as necessary (see Chapter 7).
b) Rear extension: tighten bolts and/or replace oil seal as necessary (Chapter 7).
c) Filler pipe: replace the rubber oil seal where pipe enters transmission case.
d) Transmission oil lines: tighten connectors where lines enter transmission case and/or replace lines.
e) Vent pipe: transmission over-filled and/or water in fluid (see checking procedures, Chapter 7).
f) Speedometer connector: replace the O-ring where speedometer cable enters transmission case.

40 General shift mechanism problems

1 Chapter 7 deals with checking and adjusting the shift linkage on automatic transmissions. Common problems which may be attributed to maladjusted linkage are:

a) Engine starting in gears other than 'P' (Park) or 'N' (Neutral).
b) Indicator on quadrant pointing to a gear other than the one actually being used.
c) Vehicle will not hold firm when in 'P' (Park) position.

Refer to Chapter 7 to adjust the manual linkage.

41 Transmission will not downshift with accelerator pedal pressed to the floor

1 Chapter 7 deals with adjusting the downshift cable or downshift switch to enable the transmission to downshift properly.

42 Engine will start in gears other than 'P' (Park) or 'N' (Neutral)

1 Chapter 7 deals with adjusting the neutral start switches used with automatic transmissions.

43 Transmission slips, shifts rough, is noisy or has no drive in forward or reverse gears

1 There are many probable causes for the above problems, but the home mechanic should concern himself only with one possibility: fluid level.
2 Before taking the vehicle to a specialist, check the level of the fluid and condition of the fluid as described in Chapter 7. Correct fluid level as necessary or change the fluid and filter if needed. If problem persists, have a professional diagnose the probable cause.

Driveshaft

44 Leakage of fluid at front of driveshaft

1 Defective transmission rear oil seal. See Chapter 7 for replacing procedures. While this is done, check the splined yoke for burrs or a rough condition which may be damaging the seal. If found, these can be dressed with crocus cloth or a fine dressing stone.

45 Knock or clunk when transmission is under initial load (just after transmission is put into gear)

1 Loose or disconnected rear suspension components. Check all mounting bolts and bushings (Chapter 10).
2 Loose driveshaft bolts. Inspect all bolts and nuts and tighten to torque specifications (Chapter 8).
3 Worn or damaged universal joint bearings. Test for wear (Chapter 8).

46 Metallic grating sound consistent with road speed

1 Pronounced wear in the universal joint bearings. Test for wear (Chapter 8).

47 Vibration

Note: *Before it can be assumed that the driveshaft is at fault, make sure the tires are perfectly balanced and perform the following test.*
1 Install a tachometer inside the car to monitor engine speed as the car is driven. Drive the car and note the engine speed at which the vibration (roughness) is most pronounced. Now shift the transmission to a different gear and bring the engine speed to the same point.
2 If the vibration occurs at the same engine speed (rpm) regardless of which gear the transmission is in, the driveshaft is NOT at fault since the driveshaft speed varies.
3 If the vibration decreases or is eliminated when the transmission is in a different gear at the same engine speed, refer to the following probable causes.
4 Bent or dented driveshaft. Inspect and replace as necessary (Chapter 8).
5 Undercoating or built-up dirt, etc, on the driveshaft. Clean the shaft thoroughly and test.
6 Worn universal joint bearings. Remove and inspect (Chapter 8).
7 Driveshaft and/or companion flange out of balance. Check for missing weights on the shaft. Remove driveshaft (Chapter 8) and reinstall 180° from original position. Retest. Have driveshaft professionally balanced if problem persists.

Rear axle

48 Noise – same when in drive as when vehicle is coasting

1 Road noise. No corrective procedures available.
2 Tire noise. Inspect tires and tire pressures (Chapter 10).
3 Front wheel bearings loose, worn or damaged (Chapter 10).

49 Vibration

1 See probable causes under 'Driveshaft'. Proceed under the guidelines listed for the driveshaft. If the problem persists, check the rear wheel bearings by raising the rear of the car and spinning the wheels by hand. Listen for evidence of rough (noisy) bearings. Remove and inspect (Chapter 8).

50 Oil leakage

1 Pinion oil seal damaged (Chapter 8).
2 Axle shaft oil seals damaged (Chapter 8).
3 Differential inspection cover leaking. Tighten mounting bolts or replace the gasket as required (Chapter 8).

Brakes

Note: *Before assuming a brake problem exists, check: that the tires are in good condition and are inflated properly (see Chapter 10); the front end alignment is correct; and that the vehicle is not loaded with weight in an unequal manner.*

51 Vehicle pulls to one side under braking

1 Defective, damaged or oil contaminated disc pad on one side. Inspect as described in Chapter 9.
2 Excessive wear of brake pad material or disc on one side. Inspect and correct as necessary.
3 Loose or disconnected front suspension components. Inspect and tighten all bolts to specifications (Chapter 10).
4 Defective caliper assembly. Remove caliper and inspect for stuck piston or damage (Chapter 9).

52 Noise (high pitched squeak without brake applied)

1 Front brake pads worn out. This noise comes from the wear sensor rubbing against the disc. Replace pads with new ones immediately (Chapter 9).

53 Excessive brake pad travel

1 Partial brake system failure. Inspect entire system (Chapter 9) and correct as required.
2 Insufficient fluid in master cylinder. Check (Chapter 9) and add fluid and bleed system if necessary.
3 Rear brakes not adjusting properly. Make a series of starts and stops while the vehicle is in 'R' (Reverse). If this does not correct the situation remove drums and inspect self-adjusters (Chapter 9).

54 Brake pedal appears spongy when depressed

1 Air in hydraulic lines. Bleed the brake system (Chapter 9).
2 Faulty flexible hoses. Inspect all system hoses and lines. Replace parts as necessary.
3 Master cylinder mountings insecure. Inspect master cylinder bolts (nuts) and torque-tighten to specifications.
4 Master cylinder faulty (Chapter 9).

55 Excessive effort required to stop vehicle

1 Power brake servo not operating properly (Chapter 9).
2 Excessively worn linings or pads. Inspect and replace if necessary (Chapter 9).
3 One or more caliper pistons (front wheels) or wheel cylinders (rear wheels) seized or sticking. Inspect and rebuild as required (Chapter 9).
4 Brake linings or pads contaminated with oil or grease. Inspect and replace as required (Chapter 9).
5 New pads or linings fitted and not yet 'bedded in'. It will take a while for the new material to seat against the drum (or rotor).

56 Pedal travels to floor with little resistance

1 Little or no fluid in the master cylinder reservoir caused by: leaking wheel cylinder(s); leaking caliper piston(s); loose, damaged or disconnected brake lines. Inspect entire system and correct as necessary.

57 Brake pedal pulsates during brake application

1 Wheel bearings not adjusted properly or in need of replacement (Chapter 10).
2 Caliper not sliding properly due to improper installation or obstructions. Remove and inspect (Chapter 9).
3 Rotor not within specifications. Remove the rotor (Chapter 9) and check for excessive lateral run-out and parellelism. Have the rotor professionally machined or replace it with a new one.

Suspension and steering

58 Car pulls to one side

1 Tire pressures uneven (Chapter 10).
2 Defective tire (Chapter 10).
3 Excessive wear in suspension or steering components (Chapter 10).
4 Front end in need of alignment. Take car to a qualified specialist.
5 Front brakes dragging. Inspect braking system as described in Chapter 9.

59 Shimmy, shake or vibration

1 Tire or wheel out of balance or out of round. Have professionally balanced.
2 Loose, worn or out of adjustment wheel bearings (Chapter 10).
3 Shock absorbers and/or suspension components worn or damaged (Chapter 10).

60 Excessive pitching and/or rolling around corners or during braking

1 Defective shock absorbers. Replace as a set (Chapter 10).
2 Broken or weak springs and/or suspension components. Inspect as described in Chapter 10.

61 Excessively stiff steering

1 Lack of lubricant in steering box (manual) or power steering fluid reservoir (Chapter 10).
2 Incorrect tire pressures (Chapter 10).
3 Lack of lubrication at steering joints (Chapter 10).
4 Front end out of alignment.
5 See also Section 62 'Lack of power assistance'.

62 Excessive play in steering

1 Loose wheel bearings (Chapter 10).
2 Excessive wear in suspension or steering components (Chapter 10).
3 Steering gear out of adjustment (Chapter 10).

63 Lack of power assistance

1 Steering pump drivebelt faulty or not adjusted properly (Chapter 10).
2 Fluid level low (Chapter 10).
3 Hoses or pipes restricting the flow. Inspect and replace parts as necessary.
4 Air in power steering system. Bleed system (Chapter 10).

64 Excessive tire wear (not specific to one area)

1 Incorrect tire pressures (Chapter 10).
2 Tires out of balance. Have professionally balanced.
3 Wheels damaged. Inspect and replace as necessary.

4 Suspension or steering components excessively worn (Chapter 10).

65 Excessive tire wear on outside edge

1 Inflation pressures not correct (Chapter 10).
2 Excessive speed on turns.
3 Front end alignment incorrect (excessive toe-in). Have professionally aligned.
4 Suspension arm bent or twisted.

66 Excessive tire wear on inside edge

1 Inflation pressures incorrect (Chapter 10).
2 Front end alignment incorrect (toe-out). Have professionally aligned.
3 Loose or damaged steering components (Chapter 10).

67 Tire tread worn in one place

1 Tires out of balance. Balance tires professionally.
2 Damaged or buckled wheel. Inspect and replace if necessary.
3 Defective tire.

Chapter 1 Part A 2.8L V6 engine

Contents

Specifications

Engine – general

Type	60° V6 pushrod-operated OHV
Compression ratio	8.7 : 1
Bore and stroke	3.65 x 2.70 in
Displacement	2.8L (170 cu in)
Oil pressure (hot @ 2000 rpm)	40 to 50 psi
Firing order	1-4-2-5-3-6

Cylinder head and valve train

Valve guide bore diameter	0.3174 to 0.3184 in
Valve seats	
Width – Intake	0.060 to 0.079 in
Width – Exhaust	0.060 to 0.079 in
Angle	45°
Runout Limit	0.0015 in
Valve arrangement (front to rear)	
LH	I-E-E-I-E-I
RH	I-E-I-E-E-I
Valve stem-to-guide clearance	
Intake	0.0008–0.0025 in
Exhaust	0.0018–0.0035 in
Service clearance limit	0.0055 in
Valve head diameter	
Intake	1.562–1.577 in

Exhaust	1.261–1.276 in
Valve face runout limit	0.002 max. in
Valve face angle	44°
Valve stem diameter (std)	
Intake	0.3159–0.3156 in
Exhaust	0.3149–0.3156 in
Valve stem diameter (0.008 in oversize)	
Intake	0.3239–0.3245 in
Exhaust	0.3228–0.3235 in
Valve stem diameter (0.016 in oversize)	
Intake	0.3318–0.3324 in
Exhaust	0.3307–0.3314 in
Valve stem diameter (0.032 in oversize)	
Intake	0.3475–0.3481 in
Exhaust	0.3461–0.3468 in
Valve springs	
Free length	1.91 in
Assembled height	$1\frac{37}{64} - 1\frac{39}{64}$ in
Rocker arm	
Shaft diameter	0.7799–0.7811 in
Bore diameter	0.7830–0.7842 in
Ratio	1.46:1
Pushrod runout	0.020 in
Valve tappet, lifter or adjuster	
Diameter (std)	0.8736–0.8741 in
Clearance to bore	0.0009–0.0024 in
Service limit	0.005 in
Valve lash clearance (cold)	
Intake	0.014 in
Exhaust	0.016 in

Camshaft

Lobe Lift	
Intake	0.2555 in
Exhaust	0.2555 in
End play	0.0008–0.004 in
Service limit	0.006 in
Camshaft gear backlash	0.006–0.010 in
Journal diameter	
No 1	1.6497–1.6505 in
No 2	1.6347–1.6355 in
No 3	1.6197–1.6205 in
No 4	1.6047–1.6055 in
Runout	0.005 in Max.
Out-of-round	0.0003 in Max.
Bearing inside diameter	
No 1	1.6515–1.6523 in
No 2	1.6365 – 1.6373 in
No 3	1.6215–1.6223 in
No 4	1.6065–1.6073 in
Front bearing location	0.040–0.060 in. Distance in inches that the front edge of bearing is installed below front face of cylinder block.

Cylinder block

Head gasket surface flatness	0.003 inches in any 6 inches–0.006 in overall
Cylinder bore	
Diameter	3.6614–3.6630 in
Out-of-round	0.0015 in
Service limit	0.005 in
Taper service limit	0.010 in
Main bearing bore diameter	2.3966–2.3874 in

Crankshaft and flywheel

Main bearing journal diameter	2.2433–2.441 in
Out-of-round	0.0006 in
Taper limit	0.0006 in per inch
Journal runout limit	0.002 in max.
Runout service limit	0.005 in
Thrust bearing journal	
Length	1.039–1.041 in
Connecting rod journal	
Diameter	2.1252–2.1260 in
Out-of-round	0.0006 in
Taper limit	0.0006 per inch
Main bearing thrust face	
Runout	0.001 in max.
Flywheel clutch face	
Runout	0.005 in

Flywheel ring gear lateral runout	
Standard transmission	0.025 in
Automatic transmission	0.060 in
Crankshaft free end play	0.004–0.008 in
Service limit	0.012 in
Connecting rod bearings (clearance-to-crankshaft)	
Desired	0.0006–0.0016 in
Allowable	0.0005–0.0022 in
Bearing wall thickness (standard)	
Coded red	0.0548–0.0552 in
Coded blue	0.0552–0.0556 in
Main bearings (clearance-to-crankshaft)	
Desired	0.0008–0.0015 in
Allowable	0.0005–0.0019 in
Bearing wall thickness (standard)	
Coded red	0.0707–0.0710 in
Coded blue	0.0711–0.0714 in

Connecting rod, piston and rings

Connecting rod	
Piston pin bore diameter	0.9450–0.9452 in
Crankshaft bearing bore	
Diameter	2.2370–2.2378 in
Out-of-round	0.0004 in
Taper	0.0004 in
Length (center to center)	5.1386–5.1413 in
Alignment (bore-to-bore max. dif)	
Twist	0.006 in
Bend	0.002 in
Side clearance (assembled to crankshaft)	
Standard	0.004–0.011 in
Service limit	0.014 in
Piston	
Diameter (measured at the pin bore centerline at 90° to the pin)	
Coded red	3.6605–3.6615 in
0.020 in oversize	3.6802–3.6812 in
Piston-to-bore clearance	0.0011–0.0019 in
Pin bore diameter	0.9450–0.9452 in
Ring groove width:	
Compression (top)	0.0803–0.811 in
Compression (bottom)	0.1197–0.1205 in
Oil	0.1579–0.1587 in
Piston pin	
Length	2.835–2.866 in
Diameter (standard)	0.9446–0.9450 in
Pin-to-piston clearance	0.0003–0.0006 in
Pin-to-rod clearance	Interference fit
Piston rings	
Ring width	
Compression (top)	0.0778–0.0783 in
Compression (bottom)	0.1172–0.1177 in
Side clearance	
Compression (top)	0.0020–0.0033 in
Compression (bottom)	0.0020–0.0033 in
Oil ring	snug fit
Service limit	0.006 in
Ring gap	
Compression (top)	0.015–0.023 in
Compression (bottom)	0.015–0.023 in
Oil ring (steel rail)	0.015–0.055 in

Lubricating system

Oil pump	
Relief valve spring tension (lbs. at spec. length)	13.6–14.7 @ 1.39 in
Driveshaft-to-housing bearing clearance	0.0015–0.0030 in
Relief valve-to-bore clearance	0.0015–0.0030 in
Rotor assembly end clearance (assembled)	0.004 in max.
Outer race-to-housing clearance	0.001–0.013 in
Oil capacity	4½ US qts

Torque specifications

	ft-lb	Nm
Camshaft gear bolt	30 to 36	41 to 49
Camshaft thrust plate bolt	12 to 15	16 to 20
Carburetor spacer (stud)	3 to 5	4 to 7
Carburetor adapter-to-manifold (stud)	3 to 5	4 to 7
Connecting rod nut	21 to 25	28 to 34

	ft-lb	Nm
Crankshaft damper pulley bolt	92 to 103	125 to 140
Cylinder head bolts – In sequence		
Step 1	29 to 40	39 to 54
Step 2	40 to 51	54 to 69
Step 3	65 to 80	88 to 108
Distributor clamp hold-down bolt	12 to 15	16 to 20
Exhaust manifold	20 to 30	27 to 49
Flywheel-to-crankshaft	47 to 51	63 to 69
Front cover-to-cylinder block	12 to 15	16 to 20
Fuel pump	17 to 21	23 to 28
Intake manifold-to-cylinder block (bolt/nut) – In sequence		
Step 1	3 to 6	4 to 8
Step 2	6 to 11	8 to 15
Step 3	11 to 15	15 to 20
Step 4	15 to 18	20 to 24
Intake manifold-to-cylinder block (stud)	10 to 12	14 to 16
Main bearing cap bolt	65 to 75	88 to 102
Oil pump pick-up tube-to-pump	7 to 9	9 to 12
Oil pump pick-up tube-to-main bearing cap	12 to 15	16 to 20
Oil pan drain plug	21 to 38	28 to 52
Oil pan-to-cylinder block	7 to 10	9 to 14
Rocker arm cover bolt	3 to 5	4 to 7
Rocker arm shaft support bolt	43 to 49	58 to 66
Water outlet connection bolt	12 to 15	16 to 20
Water pump-to-cylinder block	7 to 9	9 to 12
Spark plug	10 to 15	14 to 20
Alternator mounting bracket-to-cylinder head	18 to 25	24 to 34
Alternator bracket-to-cylinder block	28 to 40	32 to 54
Alternator pivot bolt	45 to 60	61 to 81
Alternator adjusting arm-to-front cover	50 to 71	68 to 96
Alternator adjusting arm-to-alternator	24 to 40	33 to 54
Crankshaft pulley-to-damper	18 to 25	24 to 34
Fan-to-water pump hub	14 to 20	19 to 27
Thermactor pump mounting bracket-to-cylinder block	28 to 40	38 to 54
Thermactor pump mounting bracket-to-cylinder head	18 to 25	24 to 34
Thermactor pump adjusting arm-to-pump	22 to 32	30 to 50
Thermactor pump pivot bolt	30 to 45	41 to 65

All fasteners not listed, use the following torque wrench settings:

Metric thread sizes		
M-6	6 to 9	9 to 12
M-8	14 to 21	19 to 28
M-10	28 to 40	38 to 54
M-12	50 to 71	68 to 96
M-14	80 to 140	109 to 154
Pipe thread sizes		
$\frac{1}{8}$	5 to 8	7 to 10
$\frac{1}{4}$	12 to 18	17 to 24
$\frac{3}{8}$	22 to 33	30 to 44
$\frac{1}{2}$	25 to 35	34 to 47
US thread sizes		
$\frac{1}{4}$ by 20	6 to 9	8 to 12
$\frac{5}{16}$ to 18	12 to 18	16 to 24
$\frac{5}{16}$ by 24	14 to 20	19 to 27
$\frac{3}{8}$ by 16	22 to 32	30 by 43
$\frac{3}{8}$ by 24	27 to 38	37 to 52
$\frac{7}{16}$ by 14	40 to 55	55 to 75
$\frac{7}{16}$ by 20	40 to 60	55 to 81
$\frac{1}{2}$ by 13	55 to 80	75 to 108

1 General information

The engine described in this part of the Chapter is a 6-cylinder ohv gasoline type with the cylinders arranged in a 60° 'V' formation.

The cylinder bores are machined directly into the cast iron cylinder block. The cylinder block is cast integral with the crankcase and incorporates full length water jackets. There are four large diameter main bearings each having removable caps.

A cast-iron crankshaft runs in the main bearings which are fitted with detachable steel-backed copper-lead bearing shells. The endfloat of the crankshaft is controlled by thrust washers fitted on either side of the front intermediate bearing.

Pressed-in oil seals are incorporated in the front cover and rear carrier so as to prevent oil leaks from either the front or the rear of the crankshaft. The rear oil seal in the carrier runs directly onto the crankshaft flange.

A gear on the end of the camshaft is in direct mesh with a gear on the end of the crankshaft and is driven by the crankshaft at half-engine speed. The camshaft runs in steel-backed white-metal bearings. Incorporated on the camshaft in front of the rearmost bearing journal is a skew gear and this drives the oil pump and distributor. The camshaft also drives, through an eccentric and a pushrod, the fuel pump, which is bolted to the lower left-hand side of the block.

The valves are mounted overhead and are operated by a system of rockers, pushrods and tappets from the camshaft that is placed in the valley between the two banks of cylinders. The inlet valves are of a larger diameter than those of the exhaust, to improve engine breathing. The rocker arms are mounted on a rocker shaft located on the top of each cylinder head. The valve springs are of an unusual form with close coils at one end, with the close coils fitted adjacent to the cylinder head.

The connecting rods are H-section forgings and the connecting rod caps are located by bolts and secured with two nuts. Similar to the crankshaft main bearing the connecting rod bearings are steel-backed and copper-lead lined.

The little end, sometimes called the small, is not bearing lined but is shrunk onto the piston to secure the latter in position.

Mounted onto the rear end of the crankshaft is a cast-iron flywheel machined to accept the clutch.

A steel starter ring gear is shrunk onto the outer periphery of the flywheel and engages with the starter motor driver during engine starting conditions. If an automatic transmission is fitted, the ring gear is shrunk onto an inertia ring which is attached to the torque converter. The torque converter is driven via a drive plate to the rear crankshaft flange instead of the normal flywheel.

The engine oil pan is a steel pressing having a rear well. The drain plug is on the right-hand side of the pressing.

The hexagonal driveshaft from the distributor drives a bi-rotor type oil pump. Incorporated into the design of the pump is an oil pressure relief valve. Oil under pressure is directed via a full flow oil filter to the main, connecting rod, and camshaft bearings and to the valve lifters. As the valve lifters are hollow they control the amount of oil through the hollow pushrods to the rocker arms and valves.

There is a drilling in the cylinder block front face which supplies oil to the timing gears.

The oil from the rocker arms drains from the cylinder head and into the valve lifter chamber so lubricating the cams and distributor drive gear as it returns to the oil pan at the base of the engine.

The cylinder bores are lubricated by one squirt of oil every crankshaft revolution emitting from a small drilling in each connecting rod web. The piston pins are continuously lubricated by oil mist created by internal engine activity and also on the downward strokes by oil scraped by the oil control rings from the cylinder bores.

Located on the left-hand rocker cover top is the oil filler cap and this incorporates a filter for the positive crankcase ventilation system. Any crankcase fumes are discharged into the intake manifold under the control of an emission valve located in the left-hand rocker cover.

2 Major operations with engine in place

The following major operations may be carried out without taking the engine from the car:

1 *Removal and replacement of the cylinder heads.*
2 *Removal and replacement of the timing gear.*
3 *Removal and replacement of the front engine mountings.*
4 *Removal and replacement of the engine – transmission rear mounting.*
5 *Removal and replacement of the camshaft.*

3 Major operations with engine removed

Although it would be possible to carry out some of the following operations with the engine in the car if the transmission and clutch were removed, it is deemed inadvisable.

1 *Removal and replacement of the flywheel.*
2 *Removal and replacement of the rear main bearing oil seal.*
3 *Removal and replacement of the oil pan.*
4 *Removal and replacement of the connecting rod bearings.*
5 *Removal and replacement of the pistons and connecting rods.*
6 *Removal and replacement of the oil pump.*
7 *Removal and replacement of the crankshaft and crankshaft main bearings.*
8 *Removal and replacement of the camshaft and camshaft bearings.*

4 Methods of engine removal

The engine may be lifted out together with the transmission or separated from the transmission and lifted out by itself. If the transmission is left attached the disadvantage is that the engine has to be tilted to a very steep angle to get it out, particularly when automatic transmission is fitted. Unless both the engine and transmission are being repaired or overhauled together there is no other reason for removing them as a unit.

5 Engine removal without transmission

1 This task takes about three hours. It is essential to have a good hoist. If an inspection pit is not available, two axle stands will also be required. In the later stages, when the engine is being separated from the transmission and lifted, the assistance of another person is most useful.
2 Open the hood.
3 Place a container of suitable size under the radiator and one under the engine and drain the cooling system, as described in Chapter 2. Do not drain the water in the garage or the place where the engine is to be removed if receptacles are not at hand to catch the water.
4 Place a container of 12 US pints (6 liters) under the oil pan and remove the drain plug. Let the oil drain for 10 minutes and then replace the plug.
5 Place old blankets over the fenders and across the cowl to prevent damage to the paintwork.
6 It is easier if two assistants are available so that hood can be supported while the hinges are being released.
7 Using a pencil, mark the outline of the hinges on the hood.
8 Undo and remove the four nuts and washers and bolt plates that secure the hinges to the hood.
9 Release the hood stay and carefully lift the hood up and over the front of the engine compartment.
10 Disconnect the battery, release the battery clamp and lift away from its tray. Remove the battery heat shield.
11 Remove the air cleaner and intake duct assembly.
12 Loosen the clips that secure the upper and lower radiator hoses and carefully remove the hoses.
13 Refer to Chapter 2 and remove the radiator and its shroud.
14 Detach the terminal connector at the rear of the alternator. Loosen the mounting bolts and push the alternator towards the engine. Lift away the fanbelt. Remove the alternator mounting bolts and lift away the alternator.

Note: *On cars fitted with a power steering and thermactor pump and/or an air-conditioning compressor, the drivebelts for these units will have to be removed first, (refer to Chapter 2).*

15 Remove the alternator bracket securing bolts and spring washers and lift away the bracket and ground cable from the side of the cylinder block.

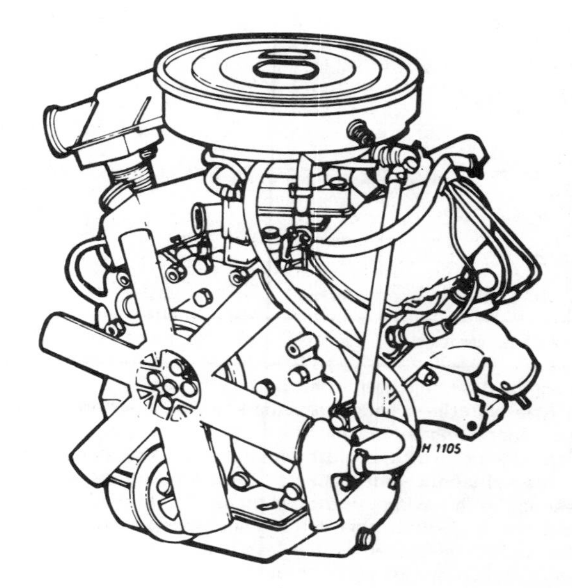

Fig. 1.1 2.8L V6 engine (Sec 5)

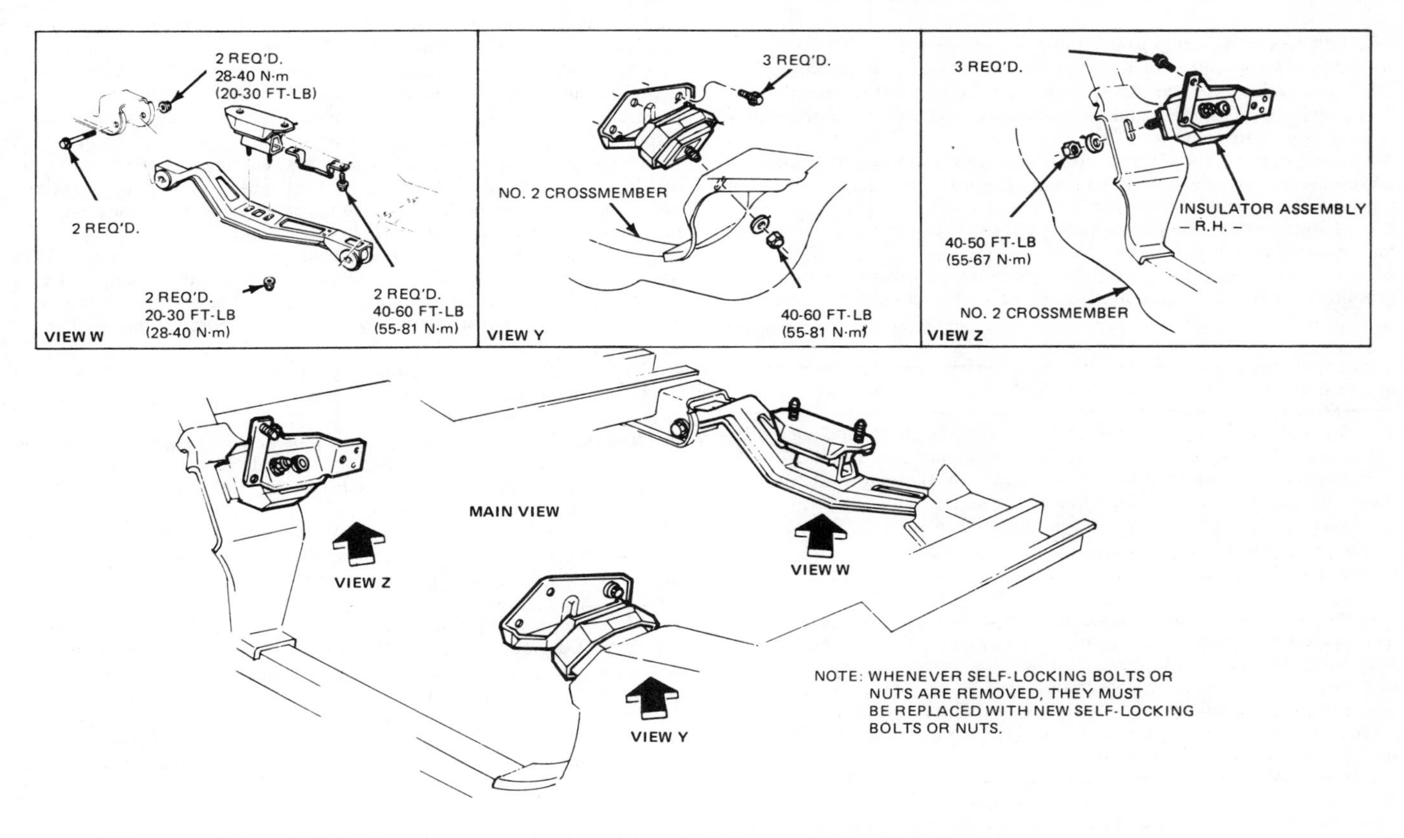

Fig. 1.2 Engine supports and components (Sec 5)

16 Loosen the heater hose clips at the cylinder block and water pump unions and detach the hoses.
17 Remove the engine ground cable securing bolt from the engine and move the ground cable to one side.
18 Disconnect the main fuel line from the inlet side of the fuel pump and plug the end of the line to prevent syphoning of gasoline.
19 Detach the accelerator cable or linkage at the carburetor installation and intake manifold. Further information will be found in Chapter 3.
20 When an automatic transmission is fitted, disconnect the downshift linkage.
21 Make a note of the cable connections to the ignition coil, and water temperature sender unit and detach from the terminals. Also release the oil pressure gauge pressure pipe.
22 Detach the vacuum hose to the brake servo unit from the inlet manifold.
23 Disconnect the emission control pipes and electrical connections from the carburetor and inlet manifold.
24 Remove the two hoses and electrical connector from the choke thermostat housing.
25 Undo and remove the nuts that secure each exhaust downpipe to the exhaust manifolds, release the clamp plates and move the downpipes to the side of the engine compartment.
26 Chock the rear wheels, jack-up the front of the car and support on firmly based axle stands. To give better access, remove the front wheels.
27 Make a note of the cable connections to the starter motor. Detach the cables from the starter motor terminals.
28 Undo and remove the bolts and spring washers that secure the starter motor to the engine. Lift away the starter motor.
29 Undo and remove the engine front mounting through-bolts at the cylinder block, and remove the rear engine mounting crossmember.

Automatic transmission

30 Undo and remove the bolts and spring washers that secure the converter inspection cover to the housing. Lift away the inspection cover.

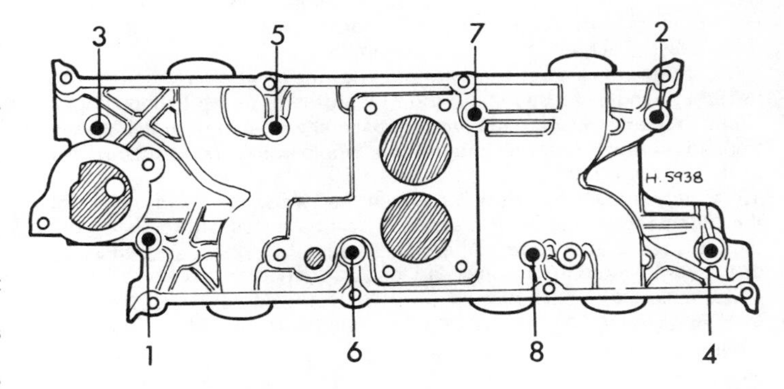

Fig. 1.3 Intake manifold bolt tightening diagram (Secs 10 and 47)

31 Undo and remove the bolts that secure the torque converter to the flywheel/adaptor plate. It will be necessary to rotate the crankshaft using a large wrench on the crankshaft pulley securing bolt.
32 Undo and remove the converter housing to engine block securing bolts and spring washers.
33 Detach the downshift rod from its bracket.
34 Pull back the clutch release arm rubber boot, if fitted. Loosen the locknut and adjustment nut. Detach the inner cable from the release arm and withdraw the cable assembly.
35 Undo and remove the bolts and spring washers securing the bellhousing to the engine.

All models

36 Refit the wheels and lower the front of the car.
37 Attach the lifting chains to the engine. Take up the slack.
38 Place jack under the transmission unit to support its weight.
39 Check that all cables and controls have been detached and safely tucked out of the way.
40 Raise the engine slightly and then draw it forwards. When an automatic transmission is fitted make sure that the torque converter remains attached to the transmission unit.
41 Continue lifting the engine taking care that the backplate does not foul the bodywork.
42 With the engine away from the engine compartment lower to the ground or bench and suitably support so that it does not roll over.

6 Engine removal with manual transmission attached

1 Proceed exactly as described in Section 5 up to and including paragraph 19 then 21 to 29 inclusive and finally paragraph 34.
2 Unscrew the transmission drain plug and allow the oil to drain away for five minutes. Replace the drain plug.
3 From inside the car remove the gearshift lever, (see Chapter 7).
4 Support the weight of the transmission using a small jack located adjacent to the drain plug.
5 Undo and remove the center bolt which locates the transmission extension housing into the support member. Then making sure the transmission support jack is firmly in position, undo and remove the four bolts and washers that secure the crossmember to the underside of the body. Lift away the crossmember.
6 With the crossmember removed it is now an easy task to disconnect the speedometer cable from the transmission by removing the circlip and withdrawing the cable.
7 Detach the back-up lamp cable connector at its snap-connector.
8 Attach the lifting chains to the engine. Take up the slack.
9 Check that all cables and controls have been detached and safely tucked out of the way.
10 With the jack under the gearbox still in position start lifting and at the same time, once the front mountings have been cleared, move the engine forward until the driveshaft is withdrawn from the end of the transmission. Support the shaft on a wooden block.
11 Due to the face that the transmission is attached, the engine will have to be lifted out at a much steeper angle than for removing the engine on its own. As the weight is more towards the rear, it will be fairly easy to achieve the necessary angle.
12 Continue to raise the engine and move it forwards at the necessary angle. At this stage the forward edge of the bellhousing is likely to catch against the front crossmember and the tail of the transmission will need raising until the whole unit is forward and clear of it.
13 Finally the whole unit will rise clear and if the maximum height of the lifting tackle has been reached, it will be necessary to swing the unit so that the tail can be lifted clear while the hoist is moved away or the car lowered from its axle stands and pushed from under the unit.
14 The whole unit should be lowered to the ground (or bench) as soon as possible and the transmission may then be separated from the engine.

7 Engine removal with automatic transmission a1ttached

1 It is recommended that the engine should not be removed while still attached to the automatic transmission, because of the weight involved. If it is necessary to remove both units refer to Chapter 7 and remove the transmission unit first. Then remove the engine as described in Section 5 but disregarding information on detachment from the transmission unit.

8 Engine dismantling – general

1 Ideally, the engine is mounted on a proper stand for overhaul but it is anticipated that most owners will have a strong bench on which to place it. If a sufficiently large strong bench is not available then the work can be done at ground level. It is essential, however, that some form of substantial wooden surface is available. Timber should be at least $\frac{3}{4}$ inch thick, otherwise the weight of the engine will cause projections to punch holes straight through it.
2 It will save a great deal of time later if the exterior of the engine is thoroughly cleaned down before any dismantling begins. This can be done by using kerosene and a stiff brush or, more easily, by the use of a proprietary water soluble solvent which can be brushed on and then the dirt washed off with a water jet. This will dispose of all the heavy muck and grit once and for all so that later cleaning of individual components will be a relatively clean process and the solvent bath will not become contaminated with abrasive material.
3 As the engine is stripped down, clean each part as it comes off. Try to avoid immersing parts with oilways in solvent as pockets of liquid could remain and cause oil dilution in the critical first few revolutions after reassembly. Clean oilways with pipe cleaners, or, preferably, an air jet.
4 Where possible avoid damaging gaskets on removal, especially if new ones have not been obtained. They can be used as patterns if new ones have to be specially cut.
5 It is helpful to obtain a few blocks of wood to support the engine while it is in the process of being dismantled. Start dismantling at the top of the engine and then turn the block over and deal with the oil pan and crankshaft etc., afterwards.
6 Nuts and bolts should be replaced in their locations where possible to avoid confusion later. As an alternative keep each group of nuts and bolts (all the timing gear cover bolts for example) together in a jar or can.
7 Many items dismantled must be re-installed in the same position, if they are not being replaced. These include valves, rocker arms, valve lifters, pistons, pushrods, bearings and connecting rods. Some of these are marked on assembly to avoid any possibility of mixing them up during overhaul. Others are not, and it is a great help if adequate preparation is made in advance to classify these parts. Suitably labelled cardboard boxes or trays should be used. The time spent in this preparation will be amply repaid later.

9 Engine accessories – removal

1 Before beginning a complete overhaul, or if the engine is being exchanged for a reconditioned unit, the following items should be removed:

Fuel system components:
- *Carburetor*
- *Intake and exhaust manifolds*
- *Fuel pump*
- *Fuel lines*

Ignition system components:
- *Spark plugs*
- *Distributor*
- *Coil*

Electrical system components (if not removed already):
- *Alternator and mounting brackets*
- *Starter motor*

Cooling system components:
- *Fan and fan pulley*
- *Water pump thermostat housing and thermostat*
- *Water temperature sender unit*

Engine:
- *Crankcase ventilation tube*
- *Oil filter element*
- *Oil pressure sender unit (if fitted)*
- *Oil level dipstick*
- *Oil filler cap*
- *Engine mounting brackets*

Clutch:
- *Clutch pressure plate and total assembly*
- *Clutch friction plate and total assembly*

Optional equipment:
- *Air-conditioning compressor*

Power steering pump
Thermactor pump

10 Cylinder heads – removal with engine in car

1 For safety reasons disconnect the battery.
2 Remove the air cleaner from the carburetor.
3 Disconnect the accelerator linkage from the carburetor.
4 Refer to Chapter 2 and drain the cooling system.
5 Detach the HT leads from the spark plugs, release the distributor cap securing clips and remove the distributor cap.
6 Loosen the clips and disconnect the hose from the water pump to the water outlet.
7 Detach the vacuum pipe from the distributor body and carburetor installation.
8 Refer to Chapter 3, and remove the carburetor and intake manifold assembly. This will necessitate removal of the distributor. Be sure to mark the distributor location so that ignition timing will be maintained at reassembly.
9 Remove the two rocker covers by undoing and removing the securing screws and lifting away together with their respective gaskets.
10 Undo and remove the three bolts and washers that secure each rocker shaft assembly to the top of each cylinder head. This must be done in a progressive manner. When the bolts are free lift away the rocker shaft assembly and oil baffles. Note to which cylinder head each rocker shaft assembly was fitted.
11 With the rocker shaft assemblies away, remove the pushrods. Keep them in order and the right way up by pushing them through a piece of stiff paper or cardboard with the valve numbers marked.
12 Detach the exhaust downpipes from the exhaust manifold and move the downpipes to the sides of the engine compartment. Leave the manifolds in place as they will act as a lever to assist removal of the heads.
13 Taking each cylnder head in turn, loosen the eight bolts in the order shown in Fig. 1.6. When all are free of tension remove all the bolts.
14 On occasions the heads may have stuck to the head gasket and cylinder block, in which case if pulling up on the exhaust manifolds does not free them they should be struck smartly with a soft faced hammer in order to break the joints. Do not try to pry them off with a blade of any description or damage will be caused to the faces of the head or block, or both.
15 Lift the heads off carefully. Note which side each head comes from as they are identical, and it is essential to replace them on th same bank of cylinders. Place them where they cannot be damaged. Undo the bolts holding the exhaust manifold to each head if not previously removed.
16 Remove the cylinder head gaskets. New ones will be required for reassembly.

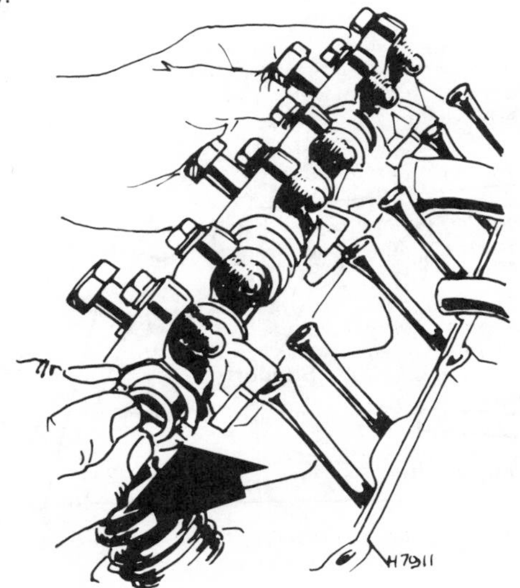

Fig. 1.4 Rocker shaft assembly removal (Secs 10 and 46)

11 Cylinder heads – removal with engine out

1 Follow the sequence given in Section 10, paragraphs 5 to 16 inclusive, disregarding information on parts mentioned that have been previously removed.

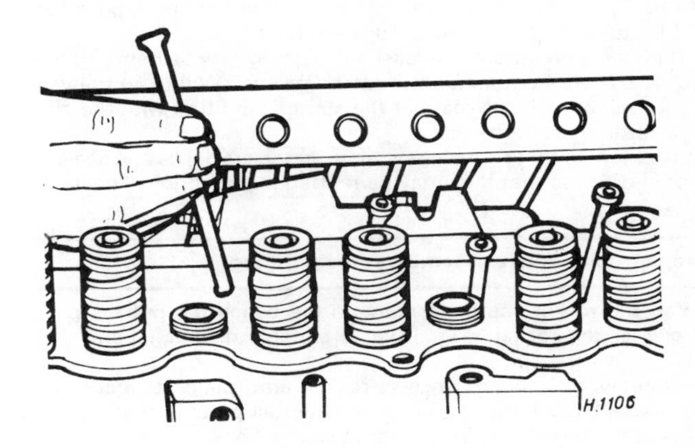

Fig. 1.5 Removing pushrods (Sec 10)

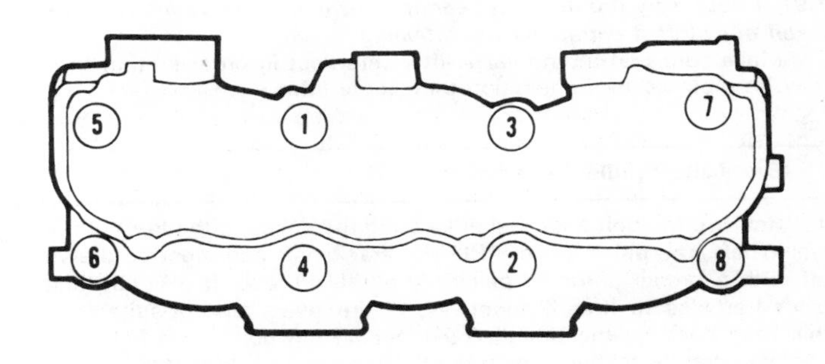

Fig. 1.6 Head bolt loosening or tightening diagram (Secs 10 and 47)

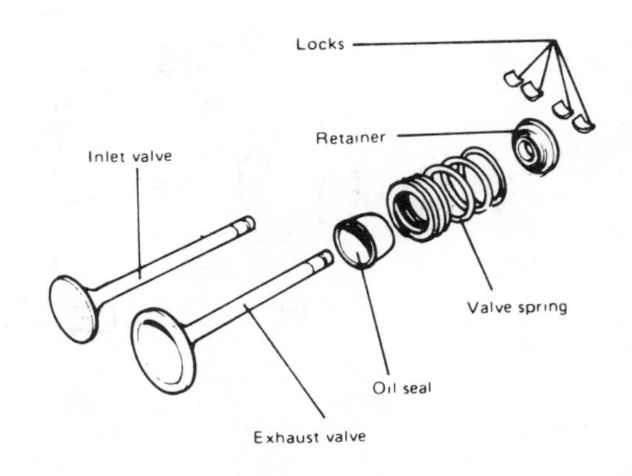

Fig. 1.7 Valves and components (Sec 12)

12 Cylinder heads – dismantling of valves and springs

1 Lay the cylinder head on its side and using a proper valve spring compressor place the 'U' shaped end over the spring retainer and screw on the valve head so as to compress the spring.
2 Sometimes the retainer will stick, in which case the end of the compressor over the spring should be tapped with a hammer to release the retainer from the locks (collets).
3 As the spring is compressed two tapered locks will be exposed and should be taken from the recess in the retainer.
4 When the compressor is released the spring may be removed from the valve. Lift off the retainer, spring and oil seal. Withdraw the valve from the cylinder head. Note that the sprngs are fitted with the close coils towards the cylinder head.
5 It is essential that the valves, springs, retainers, locks and seals are all kept in order so that they may be refitted in their original positions.

13 Valve rocker shaft assembly – dismantling

1 With the rocker shaft assembly on the bench tap out the pin at each end of the rocker shaft using a suitable diameter parallel pin punch.
2 Withdraw the spring washer, rocker arm, support, rocker arm spring and subsequent parts in order. Keep all parts in that order so that they may be refitted in their original positions.

14 Valve lifters – removal

1 The valve lifters may now be removed fro the cylinder block by pushing them up from the camshaft and lifting them out. **Note:** *with the engine in the car a magnet may be required to withdraw them (Fig. 1.9). If necessary the pushrod bearing caps in each valve lifter can be taken out by first extracting the retaining circlip.*
2 Make sure that all the valve lifters are kept in order so that they may be replaced in the location they came from.

15 Crankshaft pulley – removal

1 Remove the bolt and washer locating the pulley to the front of the crankshaft. The pulley is keyed to the crankshaft and must be drawn off with a proper sprocket puller. Attempts to lever it off with long bladed articles such as screwdrivers or tire levers are not suitable in this case because the timing cover behind the pulley is a light and relatively fragile casting. Any pressure against it could certainly crack it and possibly break a hole in it.
2 The pulley may be removed with the engine in the car but it will be necessary to remove the radiator, and drivebelts.
3 Recover the Woodruff key fro the crankshaft nose.

16 Flywheel – removal

1 Remove the clutch assembly, as described in Chapter 5.
2 The flywheel is held in position to the crankshaft by six bolts. One of these bolts is spaced unevenly so that the flywheel will only fit one position.
3 Remove the six bolts, taking care to support the weight of the flywheel as they are slackened off in case it slips off the flange. Secure it carefully, taking care not to damage the mating surfaces of the crankshaft and flywheel.

17 Oil pan – removal

1 With the engine out of the car, first invert the engine and then remove the bolts which hold the pan in place.

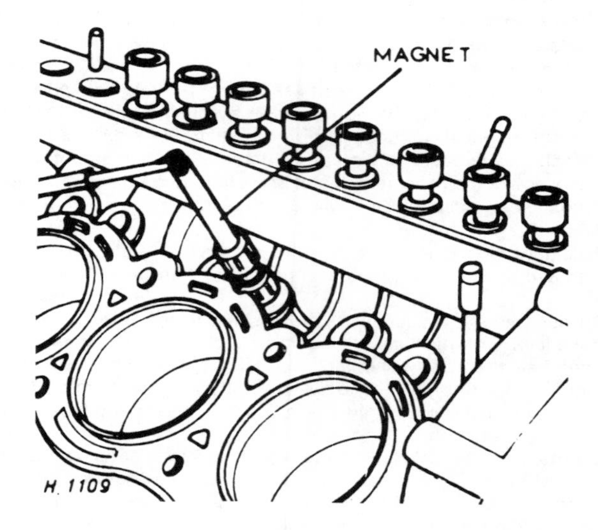

Fig. 1.9 Using a magnet to remove tappets (Sec 14)

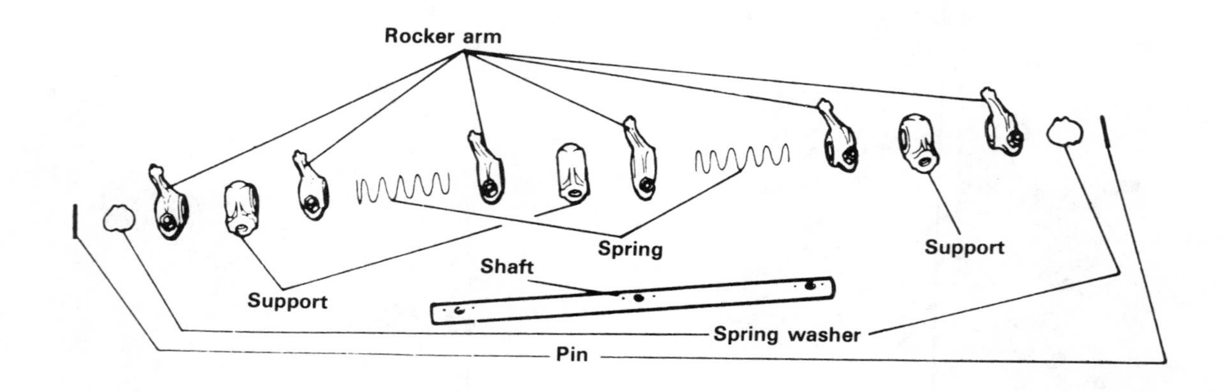

Fig. 1.8 Rocker shaft and components (Secs 13 and 47)

2 The pan may be stuck quite firmly to the engine if sealing compound has been used on the gasket. It is in order to lever it off in this case. The gasket should be removed and discarded in any case.
3 It is possible to remove the pan with the engine in the car. First withdraw the oil level dipstick.
4 Remove the bolts that secure the fan shroud to the radiator. Place the shroud over the fan.
5 Detach the battery ground cable.
6 Loosen the alternator mounting bolts and remove the fan belt.
7 Chock the rear wheels, jack up the front of the car and support on firmly based stands.
8 Drain the oil pan after placing a container of at least 12 US pints (5.7 liters) under the drain plug and removing the plug. Allow to drain for five minutes and refit the plug.
9 Note the electrical cable connections to the starter motor and detach from their terminals.
10 Undo and remove the starter motor securing bolts and spring washers. Lift away the starter motor.
11 Undo and remove the bolts and spring washers that secure the splash shield.
12 Support the engine using an overhead hoist or crane and then undo and remove the engine front support nuts.
13 Raise the engine and place some wood blocks between the engine front supports and chassis brackets.
14 Remove the rear 'K' braces. Undo and remove the bolts and spring washers that secure the clutch or converter housing cover. Lift away the cover.
15 Undo and remove the oil pan retaining bolts and lift away the oil pan. If stuck, refer to paragraph 2. Remove the oil pump bolts and lower the pump into the pan. It may be necessary to rotate the crankshaft so the pan will clear the counterweights. Remove the pan gasket.

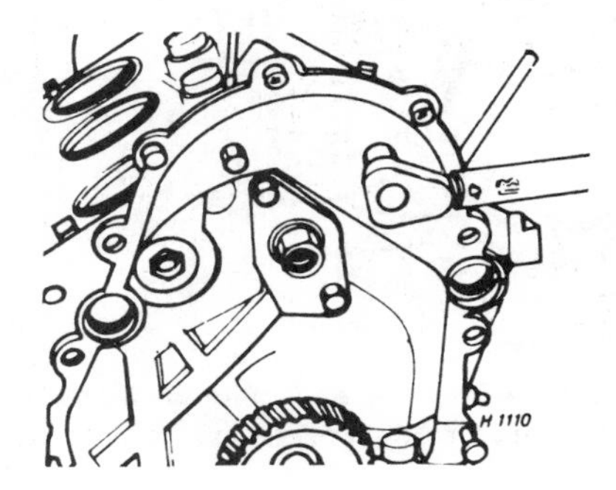

Fig. 1.10 Removing front cover securing bolts (Sec 18)

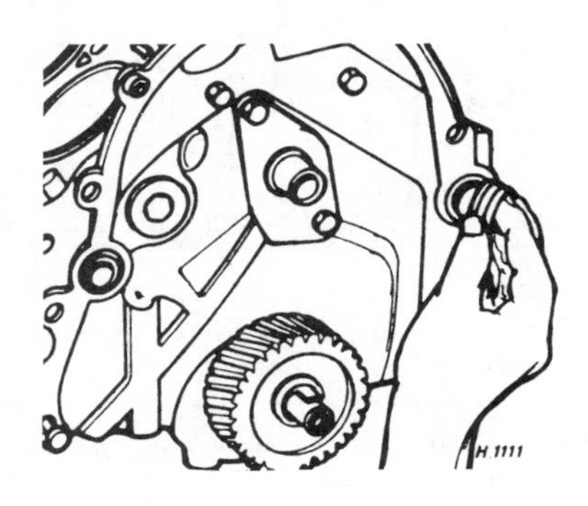

Fig. 1.11 Removing front cover plate sleeves (Sec 18)

18 Front cover – removal

1 With the engine out of the car, remove the oil pan and crankshaft pulley. Drain the coolant.
2 Undo and remove the water pump retaining bolts and lift the water pump from the front cover. It may be necessary to tap it with a soft-faced hammer if a jointing compound has been used.
3 Undo and remove the front cover securing bolts and lift away. If stuck, carry out the instructions in paragraph 2. Remove the front cover gasket.
4 If the engine is still in the car it will be necessary to remove the front oil pan bolts which run through the timing cover. It will also be necessary to remove the fanbelt, crankshaft pulley and fuel pump.

19 Timing gears – removal

1 Undo and remove the bolt and washer that secures the timing gear to the camshaft.
2 To remove the gear lightly tap it at the rear, so releasing it from the camshaft. Lift away the gear and then the Woodruff key.
3 To remove the crankshaft gear use a universal puller and draw it from the end of the crankshaft. This is only necessary when the gear is to be replaced.
4 Recover the Woodruff key.

20 Camshaft – removal

1 The camshaft can be removed with the engine in the car. (Should camshaft replacement be necessary it will probably be necessary to overhaul other parts of the engine too. If this is the case engine removal should be considered).
2 Refer to Chapter 2 and remove the radiator.
3 Detach the spark plug leads from the spark plugs, release the cap securing clips and place the cap to one side.
4 Detach the distributor vacuum line and then remove the distributor as described in Chapter 4.
5 Remove the alternator and Thermactor pump.
6 Undo and remove the screws that secure each rocker cover to the cylinder heads. Lift away the rocker covers and gaskets.
7 Refer to Chapter 3 and remove the intake manifold and carburetor installation.
8 Undo and remove the three bolts and washers that secure each rocker shaft assembly to the cylinder heads. This should be done in a progressive manner to avoid straining the shaft. Lift away each rocker shaft assembly noting from which head each was fitted.
9 Remove the pushrods and note the location from where they came and also which way up. Keep them in order and the right way up by pushing them through a piece of stiff paper with valve numbers marked.
10 Refer to Section 17 and remove the oil pan.
11 Refer to Section 18 and remove the front cover.
12 Refer to Section 19 and remove the camshaft timing gear.

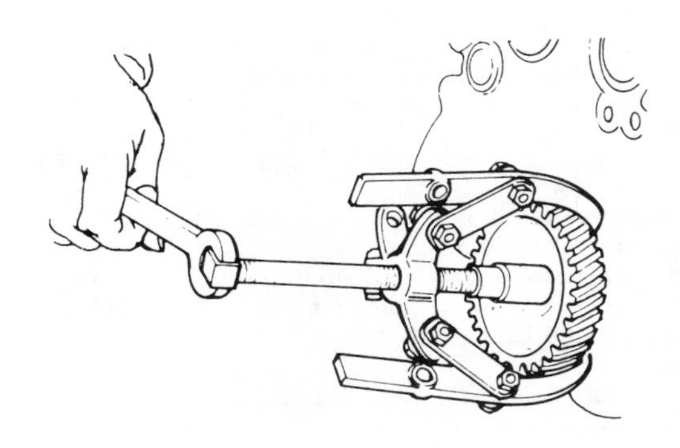
Fig. 1.12 Removing the timing gear using a gear puller (Sec 19)

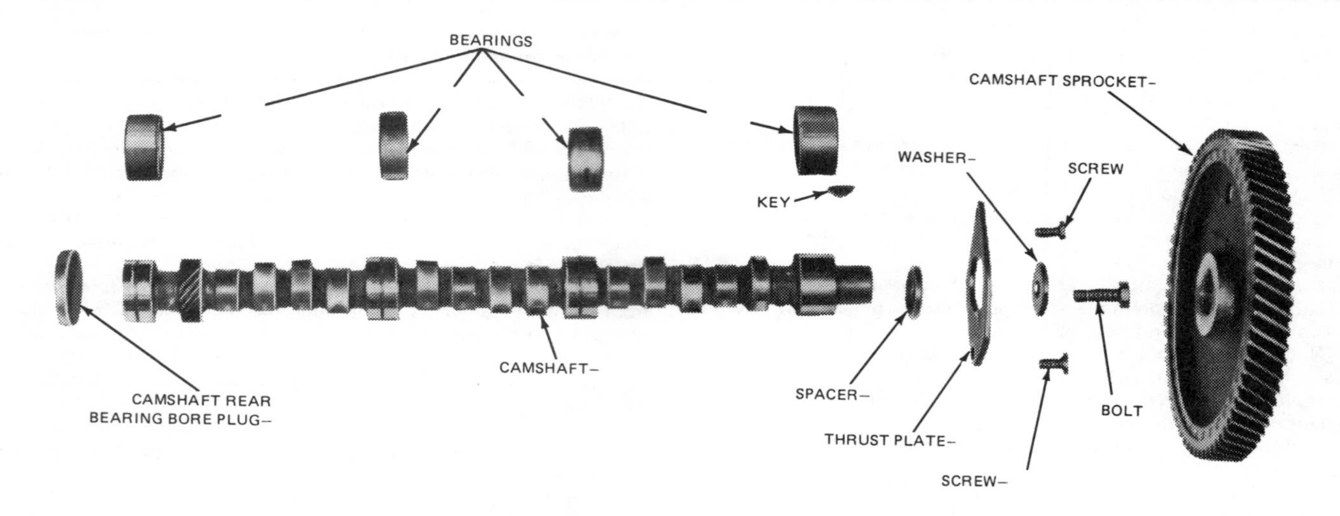

Fig. 1.13 Camshaft components and sprocket (Sec 20)

13 Undo and remove the two screws which secure the camshaft thrust plate to the cylinder block face. Lift away the plate and spacer.
14 Using a magnet recover the valve lifters from the 'Vee' in the cylinder block. Keep in order as they must be refitted in their original positions.
15 If any valve lifters cannot be removed, retain in their maximum height positions with clips.
16 The camshaft may now be drawn forwards through the cylinder block. Take care that the sharp edges of the cam do not damage the bearings.

21 Oil pump – removal

1 Refer to Section 17 and remove the oil pan.
2 Undo and remove the two bolts that secure the pump to the crankcase. Lift away the pump and recover the gasket.
3 The long hexagonal section driveshaft will come out with the pump. This is driven by the distributor shaft.

22 Pistons, connecting rods and bearings – removal

1 Pistons and connecting rods may be removed with the engine in the car, provided the oil pan and cylinder heads are first removed. The bearing shells may be removed with the heads on.
2 Loosen the two nuts holding each bearing cap to the connecting rod. Use a good quality socket wrench for this work. A ring wrench may be used for removal only – not replacement which calls for a special torque wrench. Having loosened the nuts two or three turns tap the caps to dislodge them from the connecting rods. Completely remove the nuts and lift away the end caps.
3 Each bearing cap normally has the cylinder number etched on one end as does the connecting rod. However, this must be verified and if in doubt the cap should be marked with a dab of paint or punch mark to ensure that its relationship with the connecting rod and its numerical position in the cylinder block is not altered.
4 The piston and connecting rod may then be pushed out of the top of each cylinder.
5 The connecting rod bearing shells can be removed from the connecting rod and cap by sliding them round in the direction of the notch at the end of the shell and lifting them out. If they are not being replaced it is vital they are not interchanged – either between pistons or between cap and connecting rod.

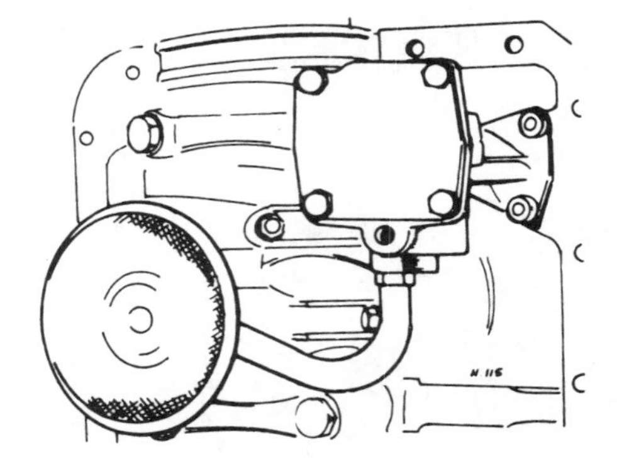

Fig. 1.14 Oil pump and inlet tube Sec 21)

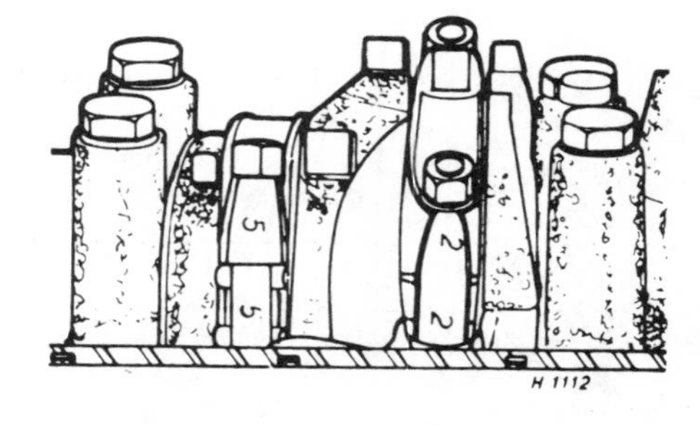

Fig. 1.15 Connecting rod bearing identification marks (Sec 22)

23 Piston rings – removal

1 Remove the pistons from the engine.
2 The rings come off over the top of the piston. Starting with the top one, lift one end of the ring out of the groove and gradually ease it out all the way round. With the second and third rings an old feeler blade is useful for sliding them over the other grooves. However, as rings are only normally removed if they are going to be replaced it should not matter if breakages occur.

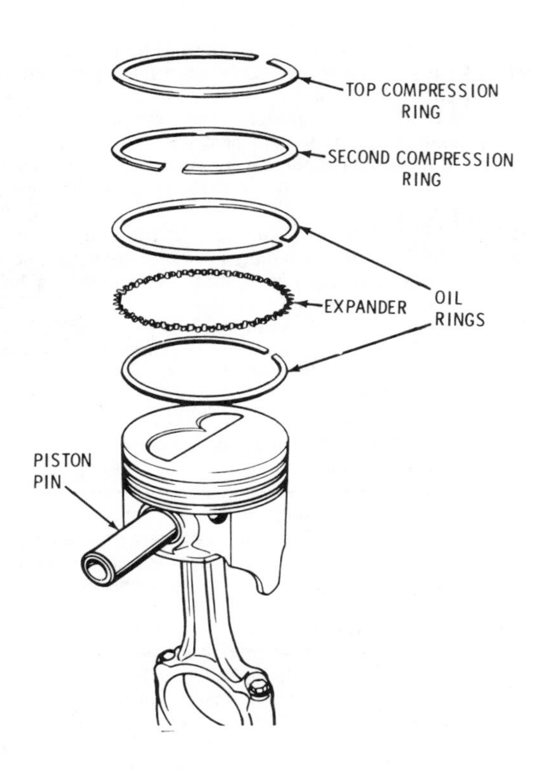

Fig. 1.16 Piston, connecting rod and components (Sec 22)

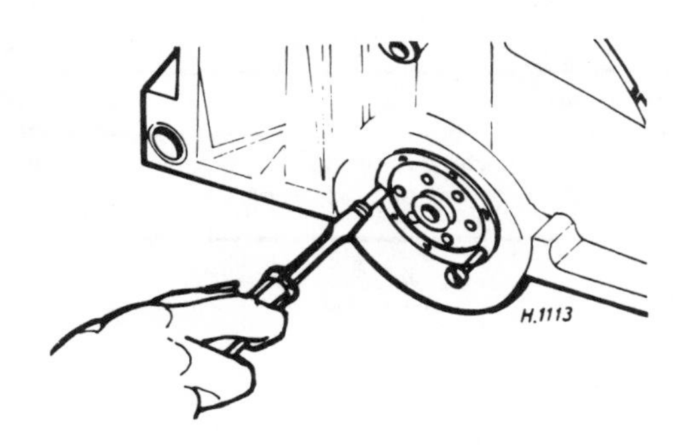

Fig. 1.17 Removing crankshaft rear oil seal (Sec 25)

24 Piston pin – removal

1 The piston pins need removing if the pistons are being replaced. New pistons are supplied with new pins for fitting to the existing connecting rods. The piston pin is semi-floating – that is, it is a tight shrink fit with the connecting rod and a moving fit in the piston. To press it out requires considerable force and under usual circumstances a proper press and special tools are essential. Otherwise piston damage will occur. If damage to the pistons does not matter, then the pins may be pressed out using suitable diameter pieces of rod and tube between the jaws of a vise. However, this is not recommended as the connecting rod might be damaged also. It is recommended that piston pins and pistons are removed from, and refitted to, connecting rods, by dealers with the necessary facilities.

25 Crankshaft rear oil seal – removal

It is possible to remove the crankshaft rear oil seal with the engine in or out of the car. Where the engine is being completely removed, refer to Section 26 and remove the crankshaft. The seal can then be drawn from the end of the crankshaft. With the engine in the car proceed as follows:

1 Refer to Chapter 6 and remove the transmission.
2 Manual transmission: Refer to Chapter 5 and remove the clutch assembly.
3 Refer to Section 16 and remove the flywheel.
4 Undo and remove the bolts and spring washers that secure the flywheel housing and rear plate where fitted.
5 Using an awl make two holes in the crankshaft rear oil seal. Punch holes on opposite sides of the crankshaft and just above the rear bearing cap to cylinder block split line.
6 Screw two long self-tapping screws into the two holes and with pliers pull or lever out the oil seal. If tight it may be necessary to place small blocks of wood against the cylinder block to provide a fulcrum for the pliers when levering out.
7 Take extreme caution not to scratch the crankshaft oil seal surface.

26 Main bearings and crankshaft – removal

Note: *Keep bearing caps separated so that they can be installed in their original locations.*

1 The engine should be taken from the car and the oil pan, cylinder heads, timing gears and pistons removed.
2 With a good quality socket wrench undo the eight bolts holding the four main bearing caps.
3 When all the bolts are removed lift out the caps. If they should be tight, tap the sides gently with a piece of wood or soft mallet to dislodge them.
4 Lift out the crankshaft.
5 Slide out the bearing shells from the caps and from the crankcase seats. Also take away the thrust washers on each side of the center main bearing. The half which is on each side of the center bearing cap is fitted with a tang to prevent rotation.

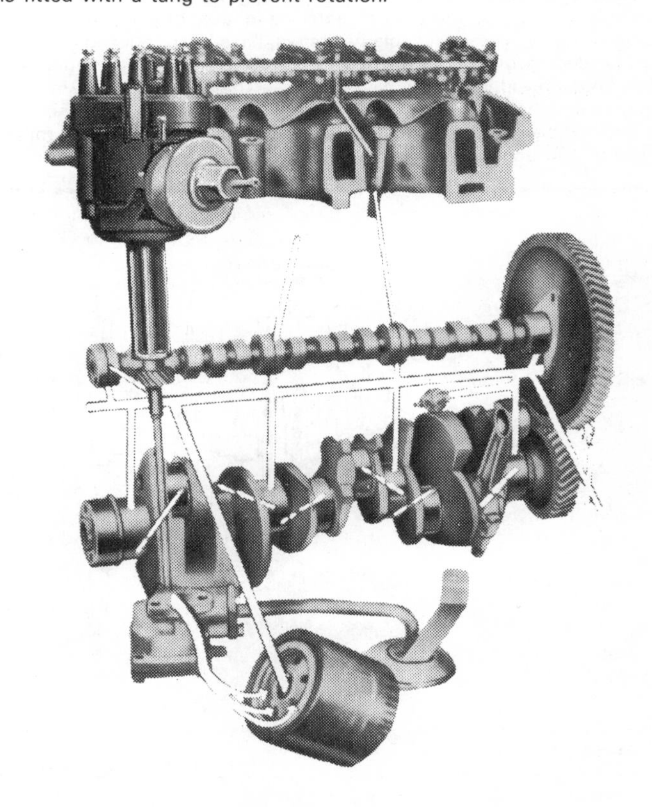

Fig. 1.18 V6 engine lubrication system (Sec 27)

27 Lubrication and crankcase ventilation system – description

1 A general description of the oil circulation system is given in Section 1 of this Chapter.
2 The oil pump is of the eccentric bi-rotor type.
3 The oil is drawn through a gauze screen and tube which is below the oil level in the well of the oil pan. It is then pumped via the full flow oil filter to the system of oil galleries in the block as previously described. The oil filter cartridge is mounted externally on the left-hand side of the block.
4 The crankcase is positively ventilated. Air enters through the oil filler cap in the left-hand rocker cover which is fitted with a washable gauze filter. Air enters directly under the rim of the cap or as in the closed system, the cap is connected to the carburetor air filter by a pipe so that filtration of the air is by existing air filter.
5 Air passes through the pushrod and oil drain channels in the tappet chamber and up the right-hand bank of the block to the right-hand rocker cover. The right-hand rocker cover is fitted with an outlet connected by a pipe to the engine intake manifold. A tapered valve in the rocker cover outlet controls the outlet of fumes so that when manifold depression is high the valve closes partially, thus reducing the flow proportionally.

28 Oil filter – removal and replacement

1 The oil filter is a complete throwaway cartridge screwed into the left-hand side of the engine block. Simply unscrew the old unit, clean the seating on the block and screw the new one in, taking care not to cross the thread. Continue until the sealing ring just touches the block face. Then tighten one half turn. Always run the engine and check for signs of leaks after installation.

29 Engine components – inspection for wear

1 When the engine has been stripped down and all parts properly cleaned decisions have to be made as to what needs replacement and the following Sections tell the examiner what to look for. In any border-line case it is always best to decide in favor of a new part. Even if a part may still be serviceable its life will have been reduced by wear and the degree of trouble needed to replace it in the future must be taken into consideration. However, these things are relative and it depends on whether a quick 'survival' job is being done or whether the car as a whole is being regarded as having many thousands of miles of useful and economical life remaining.

30 Crankshaft – inspection and overhaul

1 Look at the three main bearing journals and the four crankpins and if there are any scratches or score marks then the shaft will need grinding. Such conditions will nearly always be accompanied by similar deterioration in the matching bearing shells.
2 Each bearing journal should also be round and can be checked with a micrometer or caliper gauge around the periphery at several points. If there is more than 0.001 in (0.0254 mm) of ovality regrinding is necessary.
3 A Ford/Lincoln-Mercury dealer or engine rebuilder will be able to decide to what extent regrinding is necessary and also supply the special under-size shell bearings to match whatever may need grinding off the journals.
4 Before taking the crankshaft for regrinding, check also the cylinder bores and pistons as it may be more convenient to have the machining operations performed at the same time.

31 Crankshaft (main) bearings and connecting rod bearings – inspection and overhaul

1 With careful servicing and regular oil and filter changes bearings will last for a very long time but they can still fail for unforeseen reasons. With connecting rod bearings the indications are regular rhythmic loud knocking from the crankcase, the frequency depending on engine speed. It is particularly noticeable when the engine is under load. This symptom is accompanied by a fall in oil pressure although this is not normally noticeable unless an oil pressure gauge is fitted. Main bearing failure is usually indicated by serious vibration, particularly at higher engine revolutions, accompanied by a more significant drop in oil pressure and a 'rumbling' noise.
2 Bearing shells in good condition have bearing surfaces with a smooth, even, matt silver/grey color all over. Worn bearings will show patches of a different color where the bearing metal has worn away and exposed the underlay. Damaged bearings will be pitted or scored. It is nearly always well worthwhile fitting new shells as their cost is relatively low. If the crankshaft is in good condition it is merely a question of obtaining another set of standard size. A reground crankshaft will need new bearing shells as a matter of course.

32 Cylinder bores – inspection and overhaul

1 A new cylinder is perfectly round and the walls parallel throughout its length. The action of the pistons tends to wear the walls at right

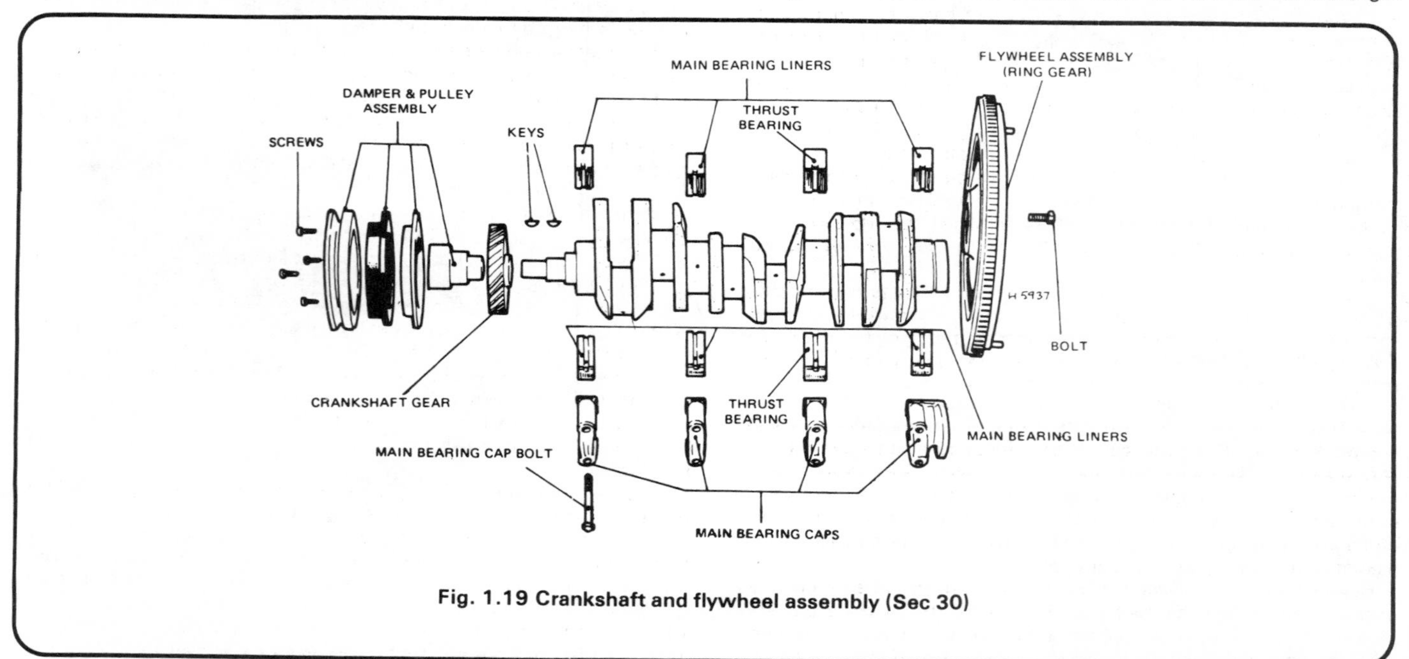

Fig. 1.19 Crankshaft and flywheel assembly (Sec 30)

angles to the piston pin due to side thrust. This wear takes place principally on that section of the cylinder swept by the piston rings.
2 It is possible to get an indication of bore wear by removing the cylinder heads with the engine still in the car. With the piston down in the bore first signs of wear can be seen and felt just below the top of the bore where the top piston ring reaches and there will be a noticeable lip. If there is no lip it is fairly reasonable to expect that bore wear is low and any lack of compression or excessive oil consumption is due to worn or broken rings or pistons (see next Section).
3 If it is possible to obtain a bore-measuring micrometer, measure the bore in the thrust plane below the lip and again at the bottom of the cylinder in the same plane. If the difference is more than 0.010 inch, then a rebore is necessary. Similarly, a difference of 0.005 inch or more across the bore diameter is a sign of ovality calling for a rebore.
4 Any bore which is significantly scratched or scored will need reboring. This symptom usually indicates that the piston or rings are damaged in that cylinder. In the event of only one cylinder being in need of reboring it will still be necessary for all six to be bored and fitted with new oversize pistons and rings. Your Ford/Lincoln-Mercury dealer or local engine rebuilder will be able to rebore and obtain the necessary matched pistons. If the crankshaft is undergoing regrinding it is a good idea to let the same firm renovate and reassemble the crankshaft and pistons to the block. A reputable firm normally gives a guarantee for such work. In cases where engines have been rebored already to their maximum, new cylinder liners are available which may be fitted. In such cases the same reboring processes have to be followed and the services of a specialist engineering firm are required.

33 Pistons and piston rings – inspection and overhaul

1 Worn pistons and rings can usually be diagnosed when the symptoms of excessive oil consumption and low compression occur and are sometimes, though not always, associated with worn cylinder bores. Compression testers that fit into the spark plug holes are available and these can indicate where low compression is occurring. Wear usually accelerates the more it is left so when the symptoms occur early action can possibly save the expense of a rebore.
2 Anther symptom of piston wear is piston slap – a knocking noise from the crankcase not to be confused with connecting rod bearing failure. It can be heard clearly at low engine speed when there is no load (idling for example) and the engine is cold, and is much less audible when the engine speed increases. Piston wear usually occurs in the skirt or lower end of the piston and is indicated by vertical streaks in the worn area which is always on the thrust side. It can also be seen where the skirt thickness is different.
3 Piston ring wear can be checked by first removing the rings from the pistons, as described in Section 23. Then place the rings in the cylinder bores from the top, pushing them down about 1.5 inches (38.1 mm) with the head of a piston (from which the rings have been removed) so that they rest square in the cylinder. Then measure the gap at the ends of the ring with a feeler gauge. If it exceeds 0.023 in (0.584 mm) for the two top compression rings, or 0.055 in (1.397 mm) for the oil control ring then they need replacement.
4 The groove in which the rings locate in the piston can also become enlarged in use. The clearance between ring and piston, in the groove, should not exceed 0.006 inch (0.1524 mm) for the top two compression rings and 0.003 inch (0.0762 mm) for the lower oil control ring.
5 However, it is rare that a piston is only worn in the ring grooves and the need to replace them for this fault alone is hardly ever encountered. Wherever pistons are replaced the weight of the six piston/connecting rod assemblies should be kept within the limit variation of 8 gms to maintain engine balance.

34 Connecting rods and piston pins – inspection and overhaul

1 Piston pins are a shrink fit into the connecting rods. Neither of these components would normally need replacement unless the pistons were being changed, in which case the new pistons would automatically be supplied with new pins.
2 Connecting rods are not subject to wear but in extreme circumstances such as engine seizure, they could be distorted. Such conditions may be visually apparent but where doubt exists they should be changed. The bearing caps should also be examined for indications of filing down which may have been attempted in the mistaken idea that bearing looseness could be remedied in this way. If there are such signs then the connection rods should be replaced.

35 Camshaft and camshaft bearings – inspection and overhaul

1 The camshaft bearings should be examined for signs of scoring and pitting. If they need replacement they will have to be dealt with professionally as, although it may be relatively easy to remove the old bearings, the correct fitting of new ones requires special tools. If they are not fitted evenly and square from the very start they can be distorted, thus causing localised wear in a very short time. See your Ford dealer or local engine rebuilder for this work.
2 The camshaft itself may show signs of wear on the bearing journals, cam lobes or the skew gear. The main decision to take is what degree of wear justifies replacement, which is costly. Any signs of scoring or damage to the bearing journals must be rectified and as under-size bearings are not supplied the journals cannot be reground. Replacement of the whole camshaft is the only solution. Similarly excessive wear on the skew gear which can be seen where the distributor driveshaft teeth mesh, will mean replacement of the whole camshaft.
3 The cam lobes themselves may show signs of ridging or pitting on the high points. If the ridging is light then it may be possible to smooth it out with fine emery. The cam lobes, however, are surface hardened and once this is penetrated wear will be very rapid thereafter. The cams are also offset and tapered to cause the valve lifters to rotate – thus ensuring that wear is even – so do not mistake this condition for wear.

36 Valve lifters – inspection and overhaul

1 The faces of the valve lifters which bear on the camshaft should show no signs of pitting, scoring or other forms of wear. They should also not be a loose fit in their housing. Wear is only normally encountered at very high mileages or in cases of neglected engine lubrication. Replace with new parts if necessary.

37 Valves and valve seats – inspection and overhaul

1 With the valves removed from the cylinder heads examine the heads for signs of cracking, burning away and pitting of the edge where it seats in the port. The seats of the valves in the cylinder head should also be examined for the same signs. Usually it is the valve that deteriorates first but if a bad valve is not rectified the seat will suffer and this is more difficult to repair.
2 The inlet valve heads are coated with diffused aluminum to increse their resistance to oxidation and to give a hard wear-resistant surface on the valve seat area. These valves should in no circumstances be ground as this will remove the aluminum coating. If the valves are worn or pitted they should be replaced with a new set. The exhaust valve seats can however, be lapped with an old or dummy valve in the way described below.
3 As far as the exhaust valves are concerned, provided there are no obvious signs of serious pitting the valve should be ground with its seat. This may be done by placing a smear of carborundum paste on the edge of the valve, and, using a suction type valve holder, grinding the valve in place. This is done with a semi-rotary action, twisting the handle of the valve holder between the hands and lifting it occasionally to redistribute the paste. Use a coarse paste to start with and finish with a fine paste. As soon as a matt grey unbroken line appears on both the valve and the seat the valve is 'ground-in'. All traces of carbon should also be cleaned from the head and the neck of the valve stem. A wire brush mounted in a power drill is a quick and effective way of doing this.
4 If an exhaust valve requires replacement it should be ground into the seat in the same way as an old valve.
5 Another form of valve wear can occur on the stem where it runs in the guide in the cylinder head. This can be detected by trying to rock the valve from side to side. If there is any movement at all it is an indication that the valve stem or guide is worn. Check the stem first with a micrometer at points all along and around its length and if they are not within the specified size new valves will probably solve the

problem. If the guides are worn, however, they will need reboring for oversize valves or for fitting guide inserts. The valve seats will also need recutting to ensure they are concentric with the stems. This work should be given to your Ford/Lincoln-Mercury dealer or local engine rebuilder.

6 When all valve grinding is completed it is essential that every trace of grinding paste is removed from the valves and ports in the cylinder head. This should be done with thorough washing in solvent or kerosene and blowing out with a jet of air. If particles of carborundum should work their way into the engine they would cause havoc with bearings or cylinder walls.

38 Timing gears – inspection and overhaul

1 Carefully inspect the gear teeth for signs of excessive wear which will cause noisy operation. When assembled to the engine the backlash must not exceed 0.004 in (0.1016 mm).

39 Flywheel ring gear – inspection and overhaul

1 If the ring gear is badly worn or has missing teeth it should be replaced. The old ring can be removed from the flywheel by cutting a notch between two teeth with a hacksaw and then splitting it with a cold chisel.

2 To fit a new ring gear requires heating the ring to 400°F (204°C). This can be done by polishing four equally spaced sections of the gear, laying it on a suitable heat resistant surface (such as fire bricks) and heating it evenly with a torch until the polished areas turn a light yellow tint. Do not overheat or the hard wearing properties will be lost. The gear has a chamfered inner edge which should go against the shoulder when put on the flywheel. When hot enough place the gear in position quickly, tapping it home if necessary and let it cool naturally without quenching in any way.

40 Oil pump – overhaul

1 The oil pump maintains a pressure of around 45 lb sq in. An oil pressure gauge is fitted to give earlier warning of falling oil pressures due either to overheating, pump or bearing wear.

2 At a major engine overhaul it is as well to check the pump and exchange it for a reconditioned unit if necessary. The efficient operation of the oil pump depends on the finely machined tolerances between the moving parts of the rotor and the body and reconditioning of these is generally not within the competence of the non-specialist owner.

3 To dismantle the pump, first remove it from the engine, as described in Section 21.

4 Remove the two bolts holding the end cover to the body and remove the cover and relief valve parts which will be released.

5 The necessary clearances may now be checked using a machined straight edge (a good steel rule) and a feeler gauge.

6 On bi-rotor type pumps the critical clearances are between the lobes of the center rotor and convex faces of the outer rotor, between the outer rotor and the pump body, and between both rotors and the end cover plate.

7 The rotor lobe clearances may be checked as shown in Fig. 1.20. The clearances should not exceed 0.006 in (0.152 mm). The clearance between the outer rotor and pump body should not exceed 0.010 in (0.254 mm).

8 The endfloat clearance can be measured by placing a steel straight edge across the end of the pump and measuring the gap between the rotors and the straight edge. The gap on either rotor should not exceed 0.005 in (0.127 mm). See Fig. 1.21.

9 If any clearances are out of specification, the oil pump must be replaced.

10 When reassembling the pump and refitting the end cover make sure that the interior is scrupulously clean and that the pressure relief valve parts ar assembled in the correct positions.

41 Cylinder heads and piston crowns – cleaning

1 When cylinder heads are removed either in the course of an overhaul or for inspection of bores or valve condition when the engine is in the car, it is normal to remove all carbon deposits from the piston crowns and heads.

2 This is best done with a cup shaped wire brush and an electric drill and is fairly straightforward when the engine is dismantled and the pistons removed. Sometimes hard spots of carbon are not easily removed except by a scraper. When cleaning the pistons with a scraper take care not to damage the surface of the piston in any way.

3 When the engine is in the car certain precautions must be taken when cleaning the piston crowns, in order to prevent dislodged pieces of carbon falling into the interior of the engine which would cause damage to cylinder bores, pistons and rings – or if allowed into the water passages – damage to the water pump. Turn the engine, therefore, so that the piston being worked on is at the top of its stroke and then mask off the adjacent cylinder bore and all surrounding water jacket orifices with paper and adhesive tape. Press grease into the gap

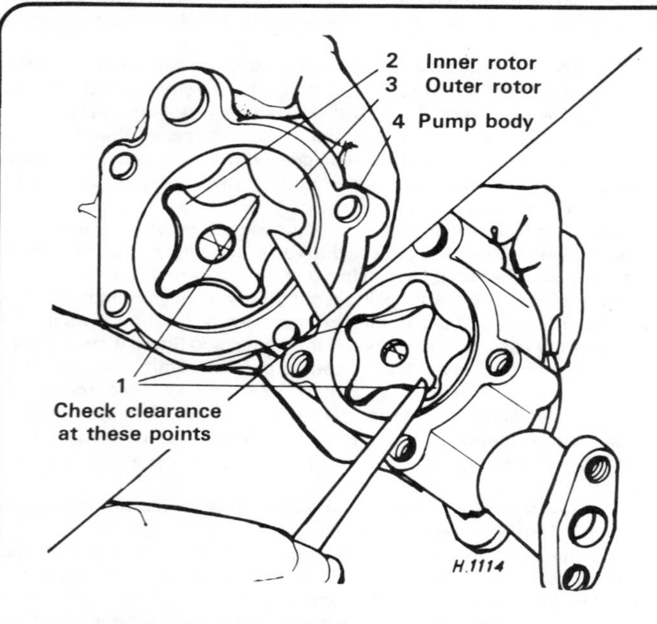

Fig. 1.20 Checking oil pump rotor clearances (Sec 40)

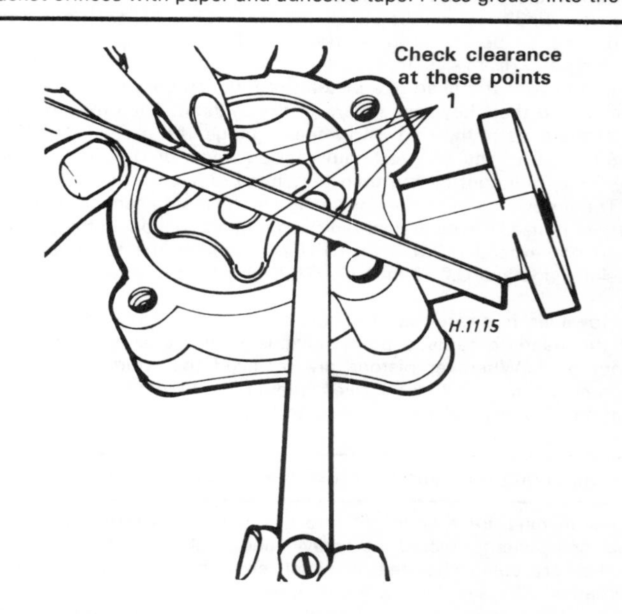

Fig. 1.21 Checking oil pump endfloat clearances (Sec 40)

all round the piston to keep carbon particles out and then scrape all carbon away by hand carefully. Do not use a power drill and wire brush when the engine is in the car as it will be virtually impossible to keep all the carbon dust clear of the engine. When completed carefully clear out the grease round the rim of the piston with a matchstick or something similar – bringing any carbon particles with it. Repeat the process on the other five piston crowns. It is not recommended that a ring of carbon is left round the edge of the piston on the theory that it will reduce oil consumption. This was valid in the earlier days of long stroke low revving engines but modern engines, fuels and lubricants cause less carbon deposits anyway and any left behind tends merely to cause hot-spots.

42 Rocker gear – inspection and overhaul

1 Check the shaft for straightness by rolling it on a flat surface. It is most unlikely that it will deviate from normal, but if it does, then a judicious attempt may be made to straighten it. If this is not successful purchase a new shaft. The surface of the shaft should be free from any worn ridges caused by the rocker arms. If any wear is evident replace the rocker shaft. Wear is likely to have occurred only if the rocker shaft oil holes have become blocked.
2 Check the rocker arms for wear of the rocker bushings, for wear at the rocker arm face which bears on the valve stem, and for wear of the adjusting ball ended screws. Wear in the rocker arm bushing can be checked by gripping the rocker arm tip and holding the rocker arm in place on the shaft, noting if there is any lateral rocker arm shake. If any shake is present, and the arm is loose on the shaft, remedial action must be taken. It is recommended that any worn rocker arm be taken to the local Ford/Lincoln-Mercury dealer or engine rebuilder to have the old bush drawn out and a new bushing fitted.
3 Check the tip of the rocker arm where it bears on the valve stem, for cracking or serious wear on the case hardening. If none is present the rocker arm may be refitted. Check the pushrods for straightness by rolling them on a flat surface.

43 Engine reassembly – general

1 All components of the engine must be cleaned of oil sludge and old gaskets and the working area should also be clear and clean. In addition to the normal range of good quality socket wrenches and general tools which are essential, the following must be available before reassembly begins:

(a) Complete set of new gaskets
(b) Supply of clean rags
(c) Clean oil can full of clean engine oil
(d) Torque wrench
(e) All new spare parts as necessary

44 Engine reassembly – camshaft, crankshaft and oil pump

1 Insert the camshaft carefully into the block, taking care not to let any of the cam lobes damage the bearings.
2 Install the camshaft thrust plate and secure it with the two screws. These screws must be tightened firmly.
3 Select the halves of the four main bearing shells which have the oil hole and grooves and place them in position in the crankcase. The notches on the ends of the shells should locate in the cut-outs in the housings. It is essential tht the two surfaces coming together are scrupulously clean.
4 Lubricate the bearings generously with clean engine oil.
5 Make sure that the crankshaft is scrupulously clean and lower it carefully into place on the bearings with the gearwheel towards the front of the engine.
6 Take the two halves of the thrust washers which do not have tangs on and very carefully slide them into position round the side of the first intermediate main bearing. The grooves in the washers should face outwards from the bearing.
7 The end of the top half of the thrust washer can easily be pushed finally into position with a finger.
8 Fit the plain halves of the main bearing shells into the caps, with

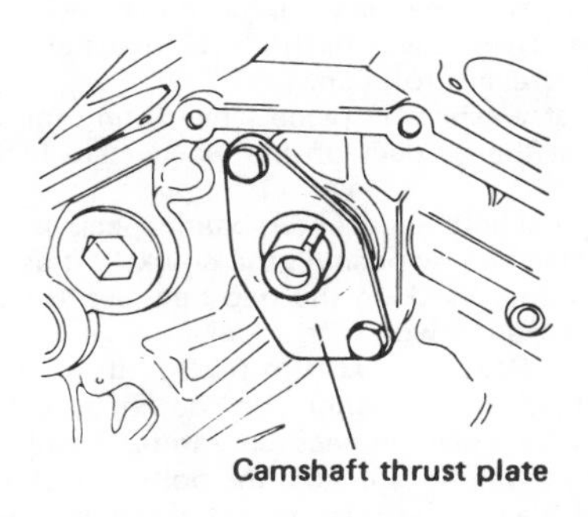

Fig. 1.22 Camshaft thrust plate installed (Sec 44)

Fig. 1.23 Inserting rear bearing wedge seals (Sec 44)

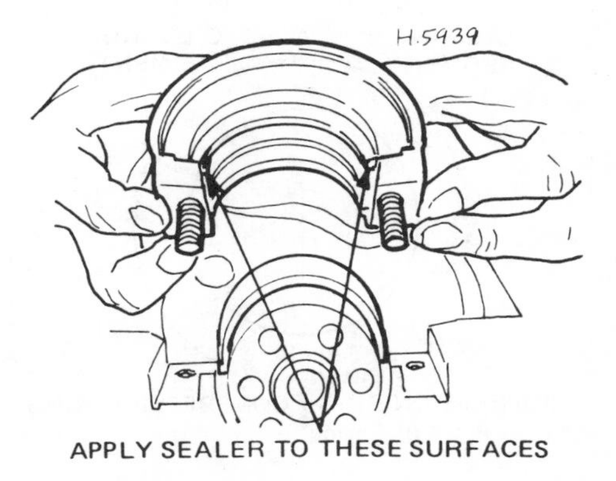

Fig. 1.24 Installing crankshaft rear oil seal (Sec 44)

the notches in the shells corresponding with the grooves in the caps.

9 The first intermediate bearing cap has machined recesses on each side to accept the lower halves of the thrust washers which have the tangs on them to prevent rotation.

10 Hold the thrust washers in place while fitting the center bearing cap and check that the grooves on the washer are facing away from the cap.

11 When the crankshaft and center bearing cap is in position the endfloat may be checked by pushing the crankshaft as far as it will go in either direction and checking the gap between the relevant thrust washer and the crankshaft web with a feeler gauge. The gap should be between 0.003 and 0.011 in (0.08 to 0.28 mm).

12 The front and rear main bearing caps do not automatically line up for bolting down and it may be necessary to tap them with a hammer handle or other soft weight to enable the bolts to pick up the threads.

13 Make sure tht the bolts are clean and tighten them all down evenly to the specified torque setting.

14 Place the new crankshaft rear oil seal squarely in position with the open lip facing away from the shoulder in the bore. The seal can be tapped home squarely with a soft metal drift.

15 It is important to make sure that the seal is driven in squarely from the very start, otherwise it will buckle; so if one side tends to go in too far to start with pull it out and start afresh until it is squarely and firmly 'started' all round.

16 Lubricate the crankshaft flange well so that the seal will not run on a dry surface to start with and heat up.

17 Make sure the hexagonal driveshaft is located in the oil pump and replace the pump; tighten the two mounting bolts evenly to the specified torque setting.

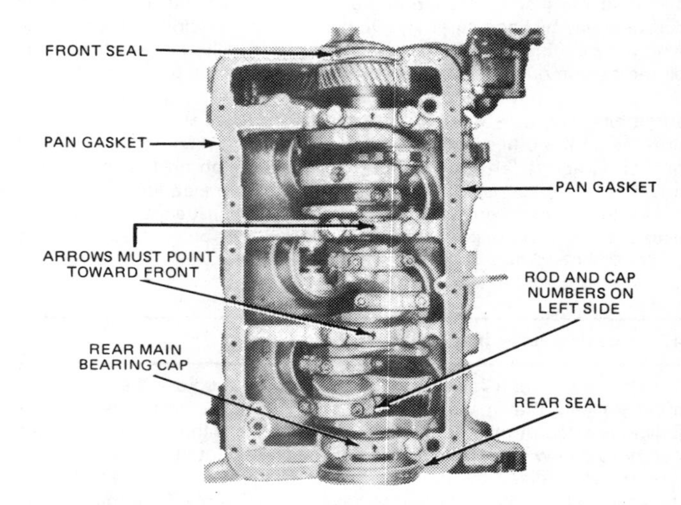

Fig. 1.25 Oil pan seals and gaskets (Sec 44)

45 Engine reassembly – pistons, piston rings, connecting rods, bearings, endplates, timing gear and front cover

1 The subsequent paragraphs on assembly assume that all the checks described in Sections 33 and 34 have been carried out. Also the engine has been partially assembled as described in Section 44.

2 The assembly of new pistons to connecting rods should have been carried out as detailed in Section 24. The new pistons should be supplied with rings already fitted.

3 If new rings are being fitted to existing pistons the following procedure should be followed. Having removed the old rings make sure that each ring groove in the piston is completely cleaned of carbon deposits. This is done most easily by using a special groove cleaning tool or by breaking one of the old rings and using the sharp end as a scraper. Be careful not to remove any metal from the groove by mistake!

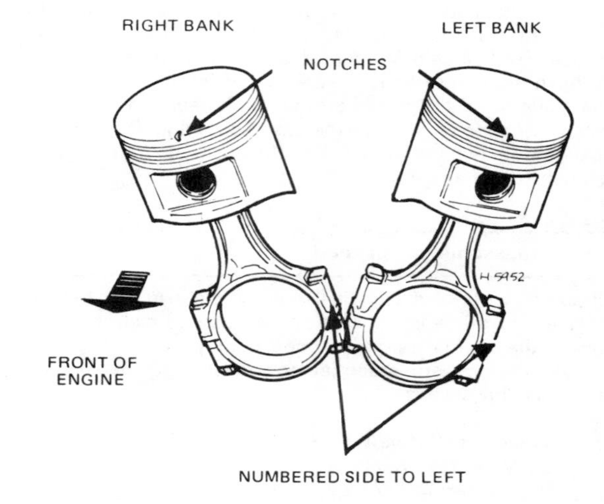

Fig. 1.26 Correct locations of pistons and connecting rods (Sec 45)

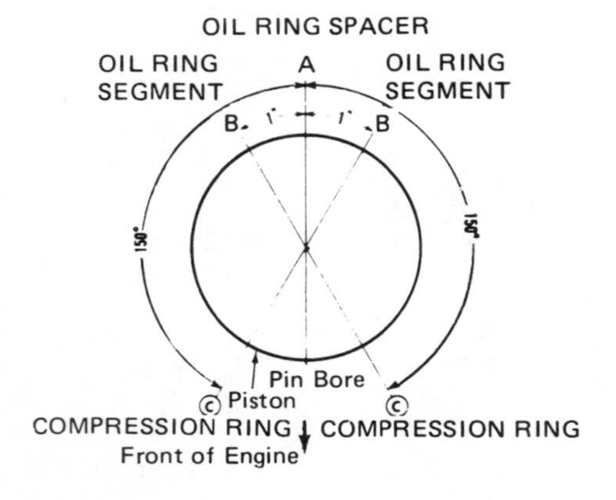

Fig. 1.27 Piston ring end gap diagram (Sec 45)

Fig. 1.28 Installing piston using ring compressor tool (Sec 45)

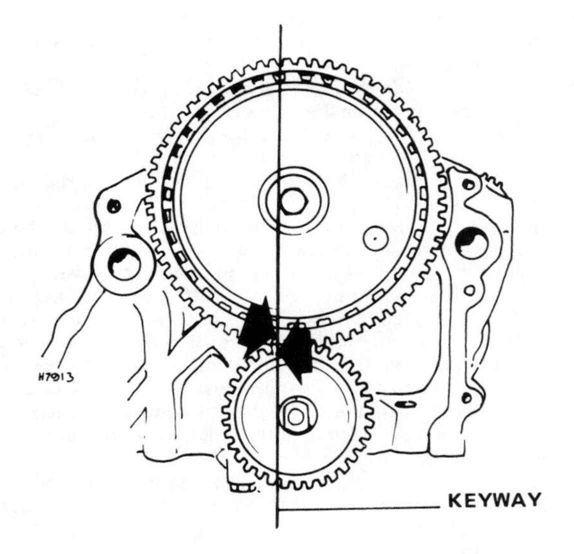

Fig. 1.29 Alignment of timing marks (Sec 45)

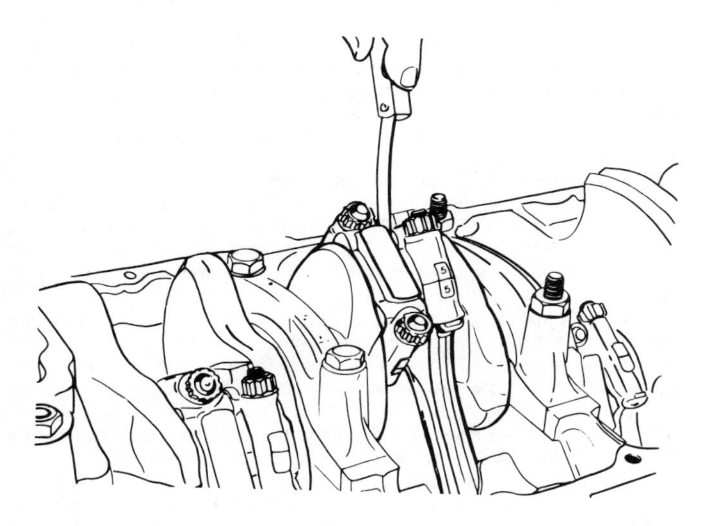

Fig. 1.30 Checking connecting rod side clearances (Sec 45)

4 The end-gap of the new piston rings – three for each piston – must be checked in the cylinder bores as described in Section 33. It is assumed that the gap at the ends could meet when normal operating temperatures are reached and the rings would then break.

5 The minimum gap for all three rings is 0.015 in (0.38 mm). If the gap is too small, one end of the ring must be filed to increase the gap. To do this the ring should be gripped in a vise between two thin pieces of soft metal in such a way that only the end to be filed is gripped and so that it only protrudes above the jaws of the vise a very small distance. This will eliminate the possibility of bending and breaking the ring while filing the end. Use a thin, fine file and proceed in easy stages – checking the gap by replacing the ring in the bore until the necessary minimum gap is obtained. This must be done with every ring, checking each one in the bore to which it will eventually be fitted. To avoid mistakes it is best to complete one set of rings at a time and replace the piston in the cylinder bore before proceeding to the next.

6 To replace the rings on to the pistons calls for patience and care if breakages are to be avoided. The three rings for each piston must all be fitted over the crown, so obviously the first one to go on is the slotted oil control ring. Hold the ring over the top of the piston and spread the ends just enough to get it around the circumference. Then, with the fingers ease it down, keeping it parallel to the ring grooves by 'walking' the ring ends alternately down the piston. Being wider than the compression rings no difficulty should be encountered in getting it over the first two grooves in the piston.

7 The lower compression ring, which goes on next, must only be fitted one way up. It is marked 'TOP' to indicate its upper face.

8 Start fitting this ring by spreading the ends to get it located over the top of the piston.

9 The lower compression ring has to be guided over the top ring groove and this can be done by using a suitably cut piece of tin which can be placed so as to cover the top groove under the ends of the ring.

10 As an alternative, a feeler gauge blade may be slid around under the ring to guide it into its groove.

11 The top ring may be fitted either way up as it is barrel faced.

12 With the rings fitted, the piston/connecting rod assembly is ready for replacement in the cylinder.

13 Each connecting rod and bearing cap should have been marked on removal but in any case the cylinder number is etched lightly on the end of the cap and connecting rod alongside. The piston and connecting rod are also marked to show which side faces the front of the engine.

14 Start with No 1 cylinder and remove the existing oil 'glaze' from the bore by using a cylinder hone or rubbbing it down with very fine emery. This will break down the hardened skin and permit the new piston rings to bed down more quickly.

15 Fit a new shell bearing half into the connecting rod of No 1 piston so that the notch in the bearing shell locates in the groove in the connecting rod.

16 Push the piston into the cylinder bore (the correct way round) until the oil control ring abuts the face of the block. Then, using a piston ring compressor contract the rings and tap the piston into the cylinder. Take great care to be sure that a ring is not trapped on the top edge of the cylinder bore and when tapping the piston in do not use any force. If this is not done the rings could easily be broken.

17 When the piston has been fully located in the bore push it down so that the end of the connecting rod seats on the journal on the crankshaft. Make sure the journal is well lubricated with engine oil.

18 Maintaining absolute cleanliness all the time fit the other shell bearing half into the cap, once again with the notches in the bearing and cap lined up. Lubricate it with engine oil and fit it onto the connecting rod so that the holes in the cap fit to the dowels in the connecting rod.

19 Replace all pistons and connecting rods in a similar manner and do not make any mistakes locating the correct number piston in the correct bore. Numbers 1, 2 and 3 cylinders are on the right-hand bank and numbers 4, 5 and 6 on the left-hand bank starting from the front of the engine. However, due to the 'Vee' formation of the engine the big-end journals on the crankshaft starting at the front run 1, 4, 2, 5, 3, and 6. This is different again from the firing order so make sure you have it all clear in your mind to start with!

20 When all caps are correctly fitted tighten down the bolts to the correct torque (see Specifications).

21 The timing gears are easily fitted but care must be taken to ensure that the marks line up properly. The camshaft and crankshaft gears are keyed to their respective shafts. The timing marks are in the form of a single dimple on one tooth of each gearwheel (see Fig. 1.29).

22 Before replacing the camshaft timing gear, the front engine plate must be replaced. Select the new gasket and coat the clean face of the block with suitable sealing compound and stick the gasket to it in position. Then install the cover plate.

23 Bolt the cover plate up tight to the block, not forgetting to fit the support plate behind the three center bolts.

24 Fit the camshaft and crankshaft gears so that the timing marks line up. Replace the camshaft gear locking bolt and washer. Tighten the bolt to the specified torque setting.

25 If the crankshaft pulley oil seal is being replaced in the front cover it will be necessary to take care in driving out the old one as the cover is a light alloy casting which will not stand rough treatment. As the old seal must be driven out from the front it is essential to find two pieces of wood thicker than the depth of the cover so that the immediate area near the seal ring may be supported.

26 With the cover firmly supported inside, it can be laid on the bench and the old seal driven out with a punch.

27 Turn the cover over and carefully tap in the new seal evenly with

the inner lip facing away from the shoulder in the bore.
28 Tap the seal home finally with a block of wood.
29 Select the front cover gasket and using a suitable sealing compound position it on the engine front plate and install the cover.
30 Place the front cover bolts in position and screw them up loosely. Then fit the crankshaft pulley onto the keyway of the crankshaft. See that the boss of the pulley is lubricated where the oil seal runs.
31 The replacement of the crankshaft pulley, before tightening the cover bolts, centers the seal to the pulley. The bolts holding the cover may then be tightened to the specified torque setting.

46 Engine reassembly – rear plate, crankshaft pulley, oil pan and flywheel

1 If the engine rear plate has been removed it should now be replaced. Make sure that both metal faces are quite clean before refitting. No gasket is used.
2 Replace the bolt and washer which locate the crankshaft pulley, block the crankshaft with a piece of wood against the side of the crankcase and tighten the bolt to the specified torque setting.
3 Trim the projecting pieces of the front cover and backplate gaskets at the oil pan face of the block and front cover.
4 Trim the projecting edge of the rear oil seal carrier on the sump face at the rear of the crankcase.
5 Clean all traces of old gasket which may remain from the oil pan joint faces and cover the faces of both the crankcase and pan with sealing compound. The oil pan gasket is in four sections which dovetail together and these should be carefully positioned and the joints interlocked.
6 The engine is then ready for the oil pan to be replaced.
7 Clean the interior of the pan thoroughly, apply sealer to the joint edge and place it in position.
8 Replace all the oil pan bolts and tighten them evenly to the specified torque setting (Fig. 1.31).
9 The flywheel may now be replaced. Make sure that the mating flanges are clean and free from burrs and line up the bolt holes correctly. They are so positioned that they will only line up in one position. Do not hammer the flywheel into position if it should be difficult to get it fully onto the flange. Support it squarely and replace the bolts, tightening them evenly so as to draw the flywheel squarely onto its seat. There are no washers and the bolts should be tightened evenly and progressively to the specified torque setting.

47 Engine reassembly – valve gear, cylinder heads and intake manifold

1 When the cylinder heads have been cleaned and the valves ground in as described in Sections 37 and 41, the cylinder heads may be reassembled. If the valves have been removed as described in Section 12 there will be no confusion as to which valve belongs in which position.

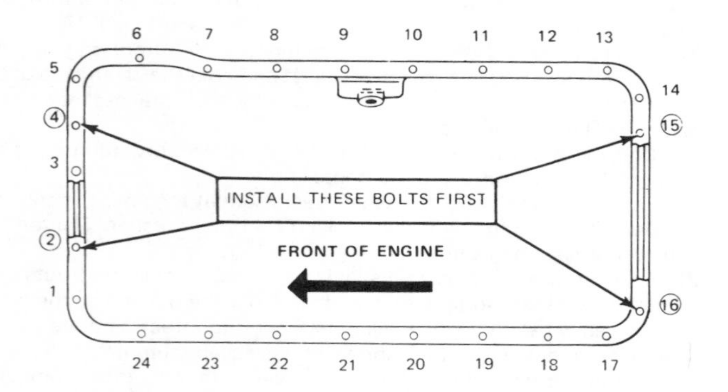

Fig. 1.31 Oil pan bolt tightening sequence (Sec 46)

2 Make sure all traces of carbon and grinding paste have been removed, lubricate the valve stem with engine oil and place it in the appropriate guide.
3 It will then protrude through the top of the cylinder head.
4 Fit a new seal cup over the valve stem.
5 Place the valve spring over the valve stem with the close coils of the spring nearest the cylinder head.
6 Fit the circular retainer over the spring with the protruding center boss retainer downwards.
7 Using a proper valve spring compressor tool, compress the spring down the valve stem sufficiently far to enable the two halves of the locks (collets) to be fitted into the groove in the valve stem. If necessary the locks should be smeared with grease to keep them in position. The spring compressor may then be released. Watch to ensure that the locks stay together in position as the retainer comes past them. If the retainer is a little off center it may force one lock out of its groove in which case the spring must be recompressed and the lock repositioned. When the compressor is finally released, tap the head of the valve stem with a soft mallet to make sure the valve assembly is securely held in position.
8 Stand the engine the right way up on the bench and replace the valve lifters if they have been removed from the block. If these have been kept in order on removal, as suggested, it will be a simple matter to replace them.
9 The two cylinder heads are identical so if they were marked left and right on removal they can be replaced on the same bank. If they have been mixed up no real harm will result but the pushrods will not be matched to their correct rocker arms. As they normally 'run in' together excessive wear could occur until such time as the two unfamiliar surfaces have bedded in again.
10 Select a new cylinder head gasket and place it in position on the block on one bank. These gaskets are identical and can fit either bank but they can only go on the bank one way – which is obvious from the way the bolt holes and cooling jack holes line up.
11 Locate the gasket over the protruding spigots in the block and then place the cylinder head in position.
12 Make sure the cylinder head bolts are clean and lightly oiled and replace them. Install the bolts finger-tight and then tighten them in the sequence shown in Fig. 1.6. The bolts should be tightened down to progressive torque loadings – all to 50 ft-lb (6.9 kg m) then all to 60 ft-lb (8.30 kg m) and finally to the specified requirement of 65 - 80 ft-lb.
13 Now fit the pushrods into position, making sure that they are replaced the same way up as they came out and according to the original valve position. This will not be difficult if they have been kept in order. Reassemble the rocker shaft assemblies in the order shown in Fig. 1.8.
14 Refit the rocker shaft assemblies to the cylinder heads and secure to the cylinder heads with the three bolts and washers.
15 The inlet manifolds may now be refitted to the cylinder heads. In view of the large area to be sealed for both air and water it is a safety measure – if not essential – to use a sealing compound in addition to the gasket on the mating surfaces.
16 Place the intake manifold gasket in position in the Vee so that the single square hole is on the left-hand cylinder head. The gasket is obviously incorrect if put on any other way but this is a positive guide.
17 Apply sealing compound to the mating faces of the intake manifold. Note the square port which matches the gasket hole and port in the left-hand cylinder head.
18 Place the manifold in position taking care not to disturb the gasket.
19 Replace the manifold securing bolts, ensuring that the gasket is lined up to permit them to pick up the threads in the cylinder heads, and screw them up lightly.
20 With a torque wrench tighten the bolts down evenly to 15 -18 ft-lb. This tightening should be done in stages – all being tightened to 5 ft-lb then to 10 ft-lb before finally reaching the specified figure. Any uneven or excessive tightening may crack the manifold casting so take care (Fig. 1.3).

48 Valve lash – adjustment

1 The valve stem to rocker clearance, which is in effect the mechanical free play between the camshaft and the end of the valve stem, is important to the correct operation and performance of the

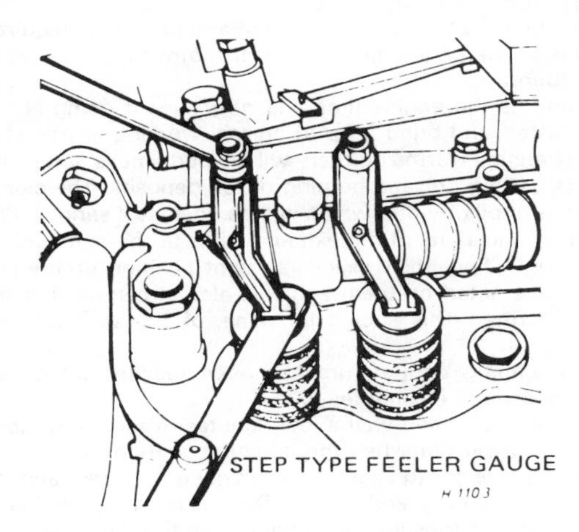

Fig. 1.32 Adjusting valve clearance (Sec 48)

engine. If the clearance is too great the valve opening is reduced with consequent reduction in gas flow – and is also very noisy. If the clearance is too little the valve could open too much with the danger of hitting the crown of the piston. The clearance is checked when the tappet is on the heel of the cam (opposite the highest point) and the valve therefore closed. This position coincides with certain other valves being fully open with their tappets on the high point of the cam. This can be seen easily when the valve spring is fully compressed.

2 The table below shows the relationship between the fully open valves and the closed valves which are to be checked.

Valves open	Adjust valves
No 5 cylinder	*No 1 cylinder*
No 3 cylinder	*No 4 cylinder*
No 6 cylinder	*No 2 cylinder*
No 1 cylinder	*No 5 cylinder*
No 4 cylinder	*No 3 cylinder*
No 2 cylinder	*No 6 cylinder*

3 For valve stem to rocker clearance dimensions, refer to the Specifications Section at the beginning of this Chapter.

4 The actual adjustment procedure is straightforward. With the appropriate valve ready for checking, place a feeler gauge of the required thickness (for exhaust or inlet valve) between the top of the valve stem and the rocker arm. If it will not go in or it is too loose, screw the lash adjuster in or out until the correct setting is obtained.

49 Engine reassembly – installing accessory components

1 The exhaust manifolds are best replaced before putting the engine back into the car as they provide very useful holds if the engine has to be manhandled at all. Note that no gaskets are used on the exhaust manifolds.

2 Replace each manifold and tighten the bolts evenly.

3 The accessory engine components must be replaced and the method of doing this is detailed in the appropriate Chapters. Section 9 of this Chapter gives a full list of the items involved. When this has been done the engine is ready to be put back in the car.

50 Engine replacement – without transmission

1 The engine must be positioned suitably so tht the sling used to remove it can be easily refitted and the lifting tackle hooked on. Positiion the engine the right way round in front of the car and then raise it so that it may be brought into position over the car, or the car rolled into position underneath it.

2 The transmission should be jacked up to its approximately normal position.

3 Lower the engine steadily into the engine compartment, keeping all ancillary wires, pipes and cables well clear of the sides. It is best to

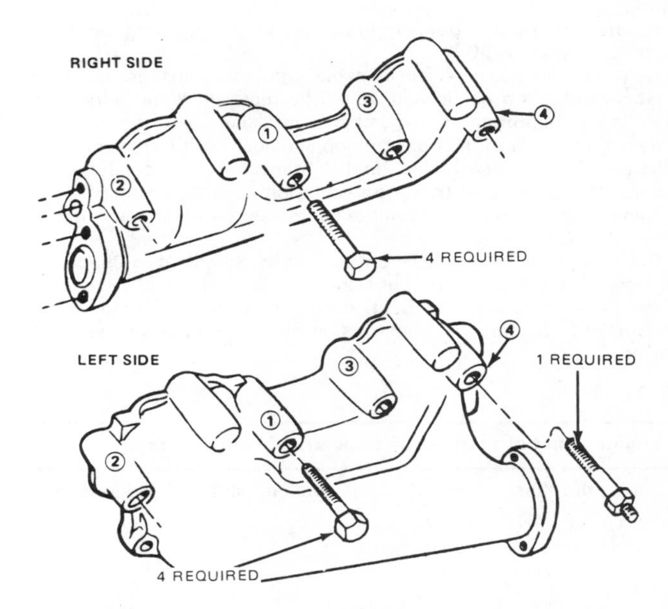

Fig. 1.33 Exhaust manifold installation (Sec 49)

have a second person guiding the engine while it is being lowered.

4 The tricky part is finally mating the engine to the transmission, which involves locating the input shaft into the clutch housing and flywheel. Provided that the clutch friction plate has been centered correctly as described in Chapter 5, there should be little difficulty. Grease the splines of the transmission input shaft first. It may be necessary to rock the engine from side to side in order to get the engine fully home. Under no circumstances let any strain be imparted onto the input shaft. This could occur if the shaft was not fully located and the engine was raised or lowered more than the amount required for very slight adjustment of position.

5 As soon as the engine is fully up to the transmission bellhousing replace the bolts holding the two together.

6 Now finally lower the engine onto its mounting brackets at the front and replace and tighten down the nuts, and washers.

7 Replace all electrical connections, the fuel lines and carburetor linkages, cooling system hoses and radiator in the reverse order to that described in Section 5.

8 Reconnect the clutch cable as described in Chapter 5, replace the exhaust pipes and reconnect them to the manifold extensions, replace the plate covering the lower half of the bellhousing and remove the supporting jack.

9 Fill the engine with fresh oil and replace the coolant.

51 Engine replacement – with manual transmission

1 The transmission should be refitted to the engine, taking the same precautions as regards the input shaft as mentioned in Section 50.

2 The general principles of lifting the engine/transmission assembly are the same as for the engine above but the transmission will tilt everything to a much steeper angle. Replacement will certainly require the assistance of a second person.

3 Lift the transmission end of the unit into the engine compartment (unless you are fortunate enough to have a hoist with a very high lift) and then lower and guide the unit down. One of the first things to be done is to reconnect the driveshaft into the transmission rear extension casing so someone should be ready to lift and guide the driveshaft into position as soon as the transmission is near enough. This cannot be done after the unit has been lowered beyond a certain position.

4 If a trolley jack is available this is the time to place it under the transmission so that as the engine is lowered further the rear end can be supported and raised as necessary – at the same time being able to roll back as required. Without such a jack, support the rear in such a way that it can slide if possible. In any case the transmission will

have to be jacked and held up in position when the unit nears its final position.

5 Locate the front mounting brackets on the locating bolts as described in Section 50.

6 Refit the speedometer drive cable with the transmission drive socket and refit the circlip and bolt. This must be done before the transmission supporting crossmember is in place.

7 Jack up the rear of the transmission and position the crossmember to the bodyframe. Then replace and tighten down the four retaining bolts and the center bolt to the transmission extension.

8 Replace the transmission remote control shift lever and housing as described in Chapter 6.

9 Reconnect the clutch cable and adjust as described in Chapter 5 and reconnect the back-up light wire. The final connections should then be made as described in Section 50 and in addition to the engine lubricant and coolant, the transmission should also be refilled with fresh oil.

52 Engine – initial start-up after overhaul or major repair

1 Make sure that the battery is fully charged and that all lubricants, coolants and fuel are replenished.

2 If the fuel system has been dismantled it will require several revolutions of the engine on the starter motor to get the gasoline up to the carburetor.

3 As soon as the engine fires and runs keep it going at a fast idle only (no faster) and bring it up to normal working temperature.

4 As the engine warms up there will be odd smells and some smoke from parts getting hot and burning off oil deposits. The signs to look for are leaks of oil or water which will be obvious if serious. Check also the clamp connections of the exhaust pipes to the manifolds as these do not always 'find' their exact gas-tight position until warmth and vibration have acted on them and it is almost certain that they need tightening further. This should be done, of course, with the engine stopped.

5 When running temperature has been reached adjust the idling speed as described in Chapter 3.

6 Stop the engine and wait a few minutes to see if any lubricants or coolant is dripping out when the engine is stationary.

7 Road test the car to check tht the timing is correct and giving the necessary smoothness and power. Do not race the engine – if new bearings and/or pistons and rings have been fitted it should be treated as a new engine and run in at reduced revolutions for 500 miles (800 km).

Chapter 1 Part B: 4.2L and 5.0L V8 engines

Refer to Chapter 13 for specifications and information related to 1981 thru 1987 models

Contents

Specifications

Engine, general

Engine type	90° V8 pushrod operated OHV
Compression ratio	
4.2 L	8.8 : 1
5.0L	8.4 : 1
Displacement	4.2L (255 cu in) or 5.0L (302 cu in)
Bore and stroke	
4.2L	3.68 x 3.00 in
5.0L	4.0 x 3.00 in
Firing order	1-5-4-2-6-3-7-8

Cylinder head and valve train

Valve guide bore diameter	0.3433 to 0.3443 in
Valve seats	
Width – Intake	0.060 to 0.080 in
Width – Exhaust	0.060 to 0.080 in
Angle	45°
Runout limit	0.002 in
Valve arrangement (front to rear)	L.H. E-I-E-I-E-I-E-I R.H. I-E-I-E-I-E-I-E
Valve stem-to-guide clearance	
Intake	
4.2L	0.0010 in
5.0L	0.0027 in
Exhaust	
4.2L	0.0015 in
5.0L	0.0032 in
Service clearance limit	0.0055 in
Valve head diameter	
4.2L	1.770 in
5.0L	1.794 in
Exhaust	
4.2L	1.439 in
5.0L	1.463 in

Valve face runout limit	0.002 in
Valve face angle	44°
Valve stem diameter (standard)	
Intake	0.3416 to 0.3423 in
Exhaust	0.3411 to 0.3418 in
Valve stem diameter (0.015 in oversize)	
Intake	0.3566 to 0.3568 in
Exhaust	0.3561 to 0.3568 in
Valve stem diameter (0.030 in oversize)	
Intake	0.3716 to 0.3723 in
Exhaust	0.3711 to 0.3718 in
Valve springs	
Free length (approximate)	
Intake	2.04 in
Exhaust	1.85 in
Assembled height	
Intake	1.6719 to 1.7031 in
Exhaust	1.5781 to 1.6094 in
Out-of-square limit	0.0781 in
Rocker arm ratio	1.58 : 1
Pushrod runout	0.015 in
Valve tappet, lifter or adjuster	
Diameter (standard)	0.8740 to 0.8745 in
Clearance to bore	0.0007 to .0027 in
Service limit	0.005 in
Out-of-service limit	$\frac{5}{64}$ in
Hydraulic tappet clearance (collapsed)	
Allowable	
4.2L	0.098 to 0.198 in
5.0L	0.071 to 0.193 in
Desirable	
4.2L	0.123 to 0.173 in
5.0L	0.096 to 0.163 in
Camshaft end play	0.001 to 0.007 in
Service limit	0.009 in
Journal to bearing clearance	0.001 to 0.003 in
Service limit	0.006 in
Camshaft gear backlash	0.006 to 0.101 in
Journal diameter	
Number 1	2.0805 to 2.0815 in
Number 2	2.0655 to 2.0665 in
Number 3	2.0505 to 2.0515 in
Number 4	2.0355 to 2.0365 in
Number 5	2.0205 to 2.0215 in
Runout limit	0.005 max.
Out-of-round limit	0.005 max.
Bearing inside diameter	
Number 1	2.0825 to 2.0835 in
Number 2	2.0675 to 2.0685 in
Number 3	2.0525 to 2.0535 in
Number 4	2.0375 to 2.0385 in
Number 5	2.0225 to 2.0235 in
Front bearing location	0.005 to 0.020 in – Distance front edge of bearing is below front face of cylinder block

Cylinder block

Head gasket surface flatness	0.003 inches in any 6 inches – 0.006 in overall
Cylinder bore	
Diameter	
4.2L	3.6800 to 3.6835 in
5.0L	4.004 to 4.0052 in
Out-of-round limit	0.0015 in
Out-of-round service limit	0.005 in
Taper service limit	0.010 in
Tappet bore diameter	0.8752 to 0.8767 in
Main bearing bore diameter	2.4412 to 2.4420 in

Crankshaft and flywheel

Main bearing journal diameter	2.2490 to 2.2482 in
Out-of-round limit	0.0006 in max.
Taper limit	0.006 in max.
Journal runout limit	0.002 in
Runout service limit	0.005 in
Thrust bearing journal	
Length	1.137 to 1.139 in

Connecting rod journal	
Diameter	2.1328 to 2.1236 in
Out-of-round limit	0.0006 in
Taper limit	0.0006 per in max.
Main bearing thrust face	
Runout limit	0.001 in max.
Flywheel clutch face	
Runout limit	0.010 in
Flywheel ring-gear lateral runout limit	
Standard transmission	0.030 in
Automatic transmission	0.060 in
Crankshaft free end play	0.004 to 0.008 in
Service limit	0.012 in max.
Crankshaft runout to rear face of block	0.005 in max.

Connecting rod bearings

Clearance to crankshaft	
Desired	0.0008 to 0.0015 in
Allowable	
4.2L	0.0008 to 0.0024 in
5.0L	0.0007 to 0.0025 in
Bearing wall thickness (standard)	0.0572 to 0.0577 in (for 0.002 in under size, add 0.001 in to standard thickness)

Main bearings

Clearance-to-crankshaft	
Desired	Number 1, 0.0001 to 0.0015 in – Others, 0.0004 – 0.0015 in
Allowable	Number 1, 0.0001 to 0.0017 in – Others, 0.0004 – 0.0021 in

Connecting rod

Piston pin bore diameter	0.9096 to 0.9127 in
Crankshaft bearing bore diameter	2.2390 to 2.2398 in
Out-of-round limit	0.0004 in max.
Taper limit	0.0004 in max.
Length (center to center)	5.0885 to 5.0915 in
Alignment (bore to bore maximum difference)	
Twist	0.024 in
Bend	0.012 in
Side clearance (assembled to crankshaft)	
Standard	0.010 to 0.020 in
Service limit	0.023 in

Piston

Diameter (measure at piston pin bore centerline, at 90° to the pin)	
Coded red	
4.2L	3.6784 to 3.6790 in
5.0L	3.9978 to 3.9984 in
Coded blue	
4.2L	3.6798 to 3.6804 in
5.0L	3.9990 to 3.9996 in
0.0003 in oversize	
4.2L	3.6812 to 3.6818 in
5.0L	4.0002 to 4.0008 in
Piston-to-bore clearance	0.0018 to 0.0026 in
Pin bore diameter	0.9127 to 0.0127 in
Ring groove width	
Compression (top)	0.080 to 0.081 in
Compression (bottom)	0.080 to 0.081 in
Oil	0.199 to 0.189 in

Piston pin

Length	3.010 to 3.040 in
Diameter	
Standard	0.9119 to 0.0124 in
0.001 in oversize	0.9130 to 0.0124 in
0.002 in oversize	0.9140 to 0.9143 in
Piston-to-pin clearance	0.0002 to 0.0004 in
Pin-to-rod clearance	Interference fit

Piston rings

Ring width	
Compression (top)	0.077 to 0.078 in
Compression (bottom)	0.077 to 0.078 in
Oil ring	Snug fit
Service limit	0.006 in max.

Ring gap	
Compression (top)	0.010 to 0.020 in
Compression (bottom)	0.010 to 0.020 in
Oil ring (steel rail)	0.015 to 0.055 in

Lubrication system

Oil pump	
Relief valve spring tension (lbs at specified length)	10.6 to 12.2 @ 1.704 in
Drive shaft-to-housing bearing clearance	0.0015 to 0.0030 in
Relief valve to bore clearance	0.0015 to 0.0030 in
Rotor assembly end clearance (assembled)	0.004 max
Outer race-to-housing clearance	0.001 to 0.013 in
Oil capacity (U.S. qts)	4

Torque specifications

	ft-lb	N-m
Alternator adjustment arm-to-alternator bolt	24 to 40	32 to 54
Alternator adjustment arm-to-engine block	12 to 18	16 to 24
Alternator bracket-to-engine block	12 to 18	16 to 24
Camshaft sprocket-to-camshaft bolt	40 to 45	54 to 61
Camshaft thrust plate-to-engine block bolts	9 to 12	12 to 16
Carburetor mounting nuts	12 to 15	16 to 20
Connecting rod nuts	19 to 24	26 to 32
Cylinder head bolts		
Step 1	55 to 65	75 to 88
Step 2	65 to 72	88 to 97
Damper-to-crankshaft bolt	70 to 90	95 to 122
Distributor hold-down bolt	18 to 26	24 to 35
EGR valve-to-carburetor spacer	12 to 18	16 to 24
Engine block front cover bolts	12 to 18	16 to 24
Exhaust manifold-to-cylinder head	18 to 24	24 to 32
Fan-to-water pump hub	12 to 18	16 to 24
Flywheel-to-crankshaft bolts	75 to 85	102 to 115
Fuel pump-to-engine block	19 to 27	26 to 37
Intake manifold-to-cylinder head	20 to 22	28 to 30
Main bearing cap bolts	60 to 70	81 to 95
Oil inlet tube-to-main bearing cap nut	22 to 32	32 to 43
Oil inlet tube-to-oil pump bolt	10 to 15	14 to 20
Oil pan drain plug	15 to 25	20 to 34
Oil pan-to-engine block bolts	9 to 11	12 to 15
Oil pump-to-engine block bolts	22 to 32	30 to 43
Pulley-to-damper bolts	35 to 50	47 to 68
Rocker arm stud bolts	18 to 25	24 to 34
Spark plugs	10 to 15	14 to 22
Thermactor pump adjustment arm-to-pump	22 to 32	30 to 43
Thermactor pump bracket-to-engine block	30 to 45	41 to 61
Thermactor pump pivot bolt	22 to 32	30 to 43
Thermactor pump pulley-to-hub bolts	13 to 18	15 to 20
Valve cover bolts	3 to 5	4 to 7
Water outlet housing bolts	9 to 12	12 to 16
Water pump-to-front cover bolts	12 to 18	16 to 24

All fasteners not listed, use the following torque wrench setting:

Metric thread sizes		
M-6	6 to 9	9 to 12
M-8	14 to 21	19 to 28
M-10	28 to 40	38 to 54
M-12	50 to 71	68 to 96
M-14	80 to 140	109 to 154
Pipe thread sizes		
1/8	5 to 8	7 to 10
1/4	12 to 18	17 to 24
3/8	22 to 33	30 to 44
1/2	25 to 35	34 to 47
U.S. thread sizes		
1/4 by 20	6 to 9	8 to 12
5/16 by 18	12 to 18	16 to 25

	ft-lb	Nm
$\frac{5}{16}$ by 24	14 to 20	19 to 27
$\frac{3}{8}$ by 16	22 to 32	30 by 43
$\frac{3}{8}$ by 24	27 to 38	37 to 52
$\frac{7}{16}$ by 14	40 to 55	55 to 75
$\frac{7}{16}$ by 20	40 to 60	55 to 81
$\frac{1}{2}$ by 13	55 to 80	75 to 108

1 General information

The V8 engines covered in this Chapter are of 5.0 liter (302 CID) (1979 models) and 4.2 liter (255 CID) (1980 models) displacement. Both engines are very similar in design, varying mainly in some detail and dimensions (see Specifications).

The cylinder bores are machined directly into the cast cylinder block which is integral with the crankcase. The one-piece crankshaft is supported within the crankcase on five replaceable shell-type bearings.

The valve gear is actuated by a five bearing camshaft located in the 'V' section of the two cylinder banks, and is chain driven from a sprocket on the front of the crankshaft. A gear on the front of the camshaft drives the distributor which in turn drives the oil pump via an intermediate shaft.

The intake manifold is bolted between the cylinder heads and has internal water passages and exhaust gas crossover to help in vaporizing the fuel. The fuel is fed into each bank through two separate passages.

All engines have hydraulically-operated valve lifters which are quiet in operation and do not require frequent adjustment.

All models use a replaceable spin-on oil filter. Some models use a dual sump oil pan with two drain plugs and both plugs must be removed when draining the pan to avoid an incorrect oil level reading after filling.

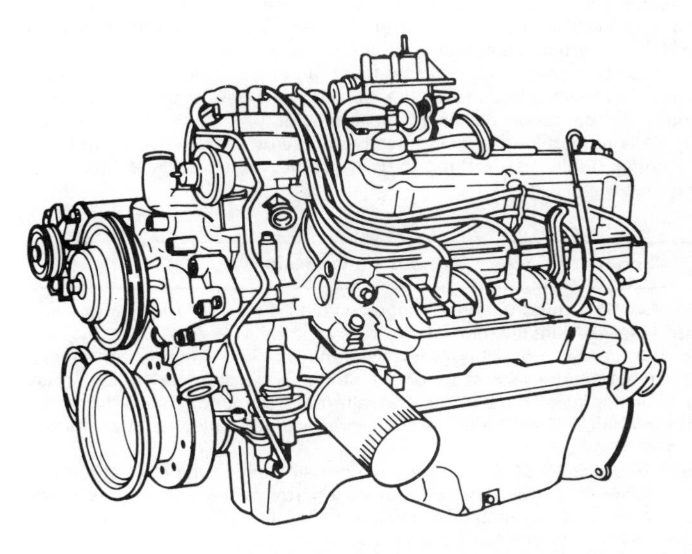

Fig. 1.34 4.2L (255 cu in) V8 engine (Sec 1)

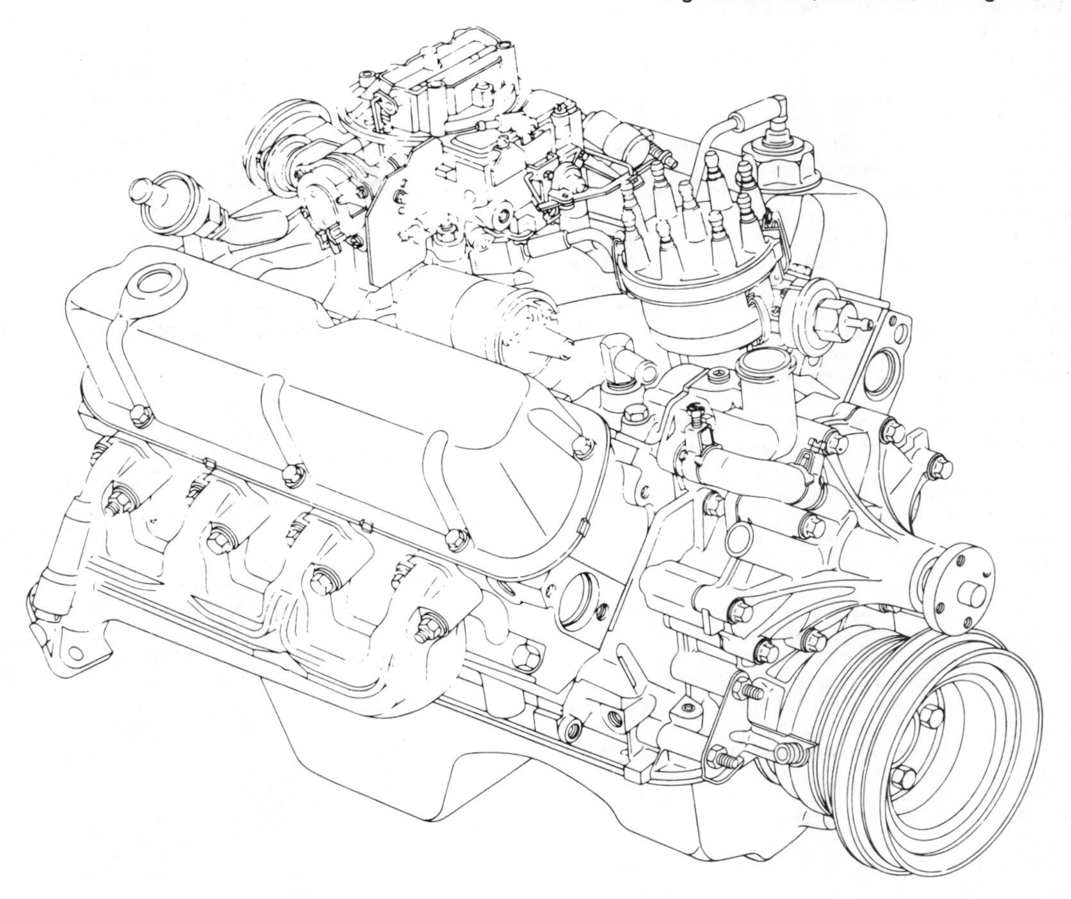

Fig. 1.35 5.0L (302 cu in) V8 engine (Sec 1)

A positive type crankcase ventilation (PCV) system is used to direct crankcase fumes back into the engine via the intake manifold. Various additional emissions systems are used depending on model and year to meet emissions laws (refer to Chap. 3).

2 Engine removal – general

1 The engine can be lifted out by itself or with the transmission attached. If the engine and transmission are removed as a unit they have to be lifted out at an extreme angle so make sure that there is sufficient vertical clearance and lifting capacity available.
2 You will need a good lifting hoist, a set of tools, a hydraulic jack and pair of jack stands to do the job. Also, the help of an assistant will make the operation easier, faster and safer.
3 It is a good idea to plan ahead and have the proper containers for catching fluids and for the orderly collection of parts as they are removed.

3 Engine removal – without transmission

1 Scribe around the hood hinges with a pencil to mark their position for ease of re-installation and remove the hood.
2 Drain the cooling system and crankcase into suitable containers.
3 Place fender protectors or old blankets over the fenders and cowl.
4 Disconnect the battery and alternator ground cables from the engine block. Remove the ground strap from the block and position it out of the way.
5 Referring to Chapter 3, remove the air cleaner and duct assembly.
6 Disconnect the upper and lower radiator hoses and remove them. On automatic transmission-equipped vehicles, disconnect the transmission oil cooler lines from the radiator.
7 Remove the radiator, fan, spacer, pulley and shroud.
8 Disconnect all of the thermactor belts, hoses and lines and unbolt and remove the Thermactor.
9 Unplug the connector at the rear of the alternator, unbolt and remove the alternator.
10 Disconnect the oil pressure sending unit wire and the flexible fuel line, making sure to plug the line.
11 Remove the power steering drive belt, unbolt the power steering pump and position it out of the way so that the fluid will not drain out.
12 Disconnect the accelerator cable from the carburetor. Remove the speed control cable, if equipped.
13 Disconnect the throttle valve vacuum line at the intake manifold and unbolt the automatic transmission filler tube from the cylinder block.
14 If the vehicle is equipped with air conditioning, unbolt the compressor and secure it out of the way. *Do not attempt to remove any of the hoses as the system is pressurized.*
15 Disconnect the brake booster vacuum line if so equipped, at the intake manifold.
16 Disconnect the heater hoses from the water pump and intake manifold and remove the coolant temperature sending unit wire from the unit.
17 Remove the bolts securing the flywheel or converter housing to the engine. Disconnect the downshift rod.
18 Unplug the primary wiring connector from the ignition coil and remove the wiring harness from the left valve cover.
19 Disconnect any remaining emissions or electrical connectings still attached to the engine which may interfere with removal.
20 After chocking the rear wheels, jack up the front of the vehicle and support it on jack stands. For better access, remove the front wheels.
21 Disconnect the starter cable and remove the starter.
22 Unbolt the muffler inlet pipes at the exhaust manifolds and move the pipes out of the way.
23 On manual transmission-equipped vehicles, remove the clutch release cable from the release lever.
24 On automatic transmission-equipped vehicles, disconnect the transmission cooler lines from the converter inspection cover and remove the cover.
25 Remove the bolts securing the torque converter to the flywheel, using a larger wrench to turn the crankshaft pulley bolt to rotate the engine. After all the bolts are removed, secure the converter assembly to the housing as it will be lifted out with the engine.
26 On manual transmission-equipped vehicles, remove the bolts securing the bellhousing to the engine block.
27 Replace the front wheels and lower the vehicle to the ground.
28 Support the transmission with a jack and attach lifting chains to the exhaust manifolds.
29 Raise the engine slightly with the lifting hoist and remove the engine mount through-bolts and insulators.
30 Lift the engine and pull it forward from the transmision. Make sure that the converter remains attached to the engine on automatic transmission equipped vehicles.
31 Lift the engine carefully, making sure that the rear cover plate does not contact the body.
32 Once the engine is clear of the engine compartment, lower it onto a workbench or the floor and support it with blocks of wood so that it doesn't fall over.

4 Engine removal – transmission attached

1 It is not recommended that the engine be removed with the automatic transmission attached, due to the weight involved. Should it be necessary to remove both units, refer to Chapter 7 and remove the transmission first. The engine can then be removed as described in Section 3.

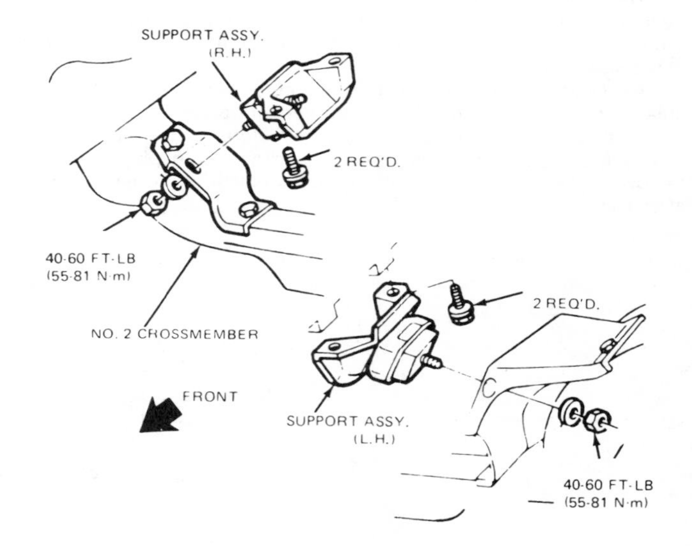

Fig. 1.36 Front engine supports (Secs 3 and 4)

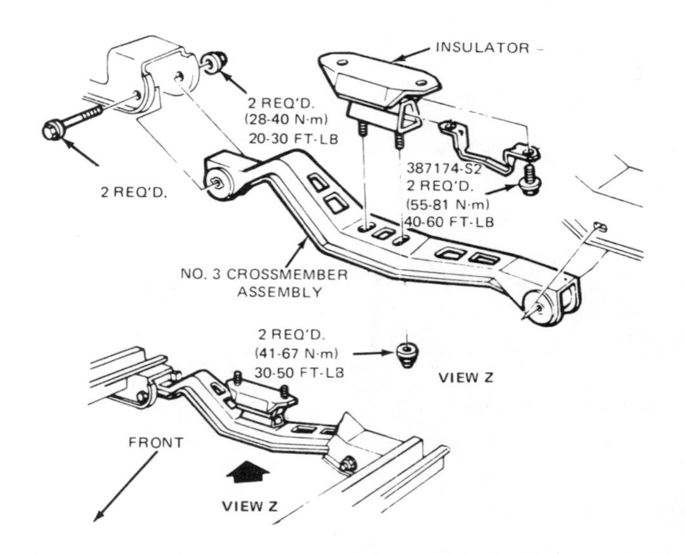

Fig. 1.37 Rear crossmember and engine supports (Secs 3 and 4)

2 To remove the engine with manual transmission attached, follow the procedure described in Section 3, paragraphs 1 through 23, except for those having to do with the automatic transmission.
3 Remove the gearshift lever, referring to Chapter 7.
4 From beneath the car, remove the transmission drain plug and allow the oil to drain for five minutes. Replace the plug.
5 After marking its position, remove the driveshaft (refer to Chapter 7).
6 Support the weight of the transmission with a small jack.
7 Remove the bolts attaching the crossmember to the transmission extension and the body and remove the crossmember.
8 Check that all cables and controls have been detached and are out of the way.
9 With the jack still in position under the transmission, start lifting and moving the engine forward.
10 Because the transmission is attached, the engine will have to be lofted out at an extreme angle. As the weight is toward the rear, it will be fairly easy to achieve this angle.
11 Continue to raise the engine and move it forward at the necessary angle. At this stage the forward edge of the bellhousing is likely to catch against the front crossmember and the tail of the gearbox will need raising until the whole unit is forward and clear of it.
12 As the maximum height of the lifting tackle is reached, it will be necessary to switch the entire engine/transmission unit so that the tail can be lifted clear while the hoist is moved away or the vehicle is lowered from the jack stands and rolled rearward.
13 The whole unit should be lowered to the ground or work bench as soon as possible and the transmission separated from the engine.

5 Engine dismantling – general

1 Ideally, the engine should be mounted on a proper stand for overhaul but it is anticipated that most owners will have a strong bench on which to place it instead. If a sufficiently large strong bench is not available, then the work can be done at ground level. It is essential, however, that some form of substantial wooden surface is available. Timber should be at least ¾ inch thick, otherwise the weight of the engine will cause projections to punch holes straight through it.
2 It will save a great deal of time later if the exterior of the engine is thoroughly cleaned down before any dismantling begins. This can be done by using a proprietary solvent which can be brushed on and then the dirt sprayed off with a water jet. This will dispose of all the heavy muck and grit once and for all so that later cleaning of individual components will be a relatively clean process.
3 As the engine is stripped down, clean each part as it comes off. Try to avoid immersing parts with oilways in solvent as pockets of liquid could remain and cause oil dilution in the critical first few revolutions after reassembly. Clean oilways with pipe cleaners, or, preferably, an air jet.
4 Where possible avoid damaging gaskets on removal, especially if new ones have not been obtained. They can be used as patterns if new ones have to be specially cut.
5 It is helpful to obtain a few blocks of wood to support the engine while it is in the process of being dismantled. Start dismantling at the top of the engine and then turn the block over and deal with the oil pan and crankshaft etc., afterwards.

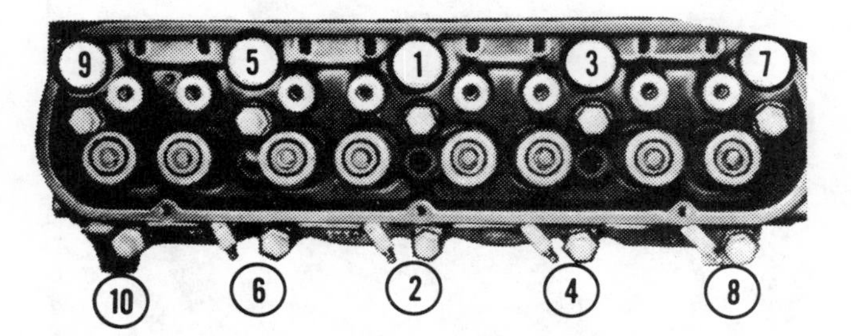

Fig. 1.38 Cylinder head bolt loosening or tightening sequence (Secs 7 and 44)

6 Nuts and bolts should be refitted in their locations where possible to avoid confusion later. As an alternative keep each group of nuts and bolts (all the timing gear cover bolts for example) together in a jar or can.
7 Many items when dismantled must be refitted in the same position, if they are not being replaced. These include valves, rocker arms, valve lifters, pistons, pushrods, bearings and connecting rods. Some of these are marked on assembly to avoid any possibility of mixing them up during overhaul. Others are not, and it is a great help if adequate preparation is made in advance to classify these parts. Suitably labelled cardboard boxes or trays should be used. The time spent in this preparation will be amply repaid later.

6 Engine accessories – removal

1 Before beginning a complete overhaul, or if the engine is being exchanged for a rebuilt unit, the following items should be removed:

Fuel system components:
  Carburetor
  Intake and exhaust manifolds
  Fuel pump
  Fuel lines
  Ignition system components:
  Spark plugs
  Distributor
  Coil
Electrical system components (if not removed already):
  Alternator and mounting brackets
  Starter motor
Cooling system components:
  Fan and fan pulley
  Water pump thermostat housing and thermostat
Engine:
  Crankcase ventilation tube
  Oil filter element
  Oil pressure sender unit (if fitted)
  Oil level dipstick
  Oil filler cap
  Engine mounting brackets
Clutch:
  Clutch pressure plate and total assembly
  Clutch friction plate and total assembly
Optional equipment:
  Air conditioning compressor
  Power steering pump
  Thermactor pump

7 Cylinder heads – removal withh engine in vehicle

1 Open the hood.
2 For safety reasons disconenct the battery.
3 Remove the air cleaner from the carburetor installation, as described in Chapter 3.
4 Disconnect the accelerator linkage from the carburetor.
5 Refer to Chapter 2 and drain the cooling system.
6 Detach the HT leads from the spark plugs, release the distributor cap securing clips and remove the distributor cap.
7 Loosen the clips and disconnect the hose from the water pump to the water outlet.
8 Detach the vacuum pipe from the distributor body and carburetor installation.
9 Refer to Chapter 3, and remove the carburetor and inlet manifold assembly.This will necessitate removal of the distributor.
10 Remove the two rocker covers by undoing and removing the securing screws and lifting away together with their respective gaskets.
11 Loosen the alternator adjusting arm bolt and remove the alternator mounting bracket bolt and spacer. Push the alternator down out of the way.
12 Remove the accelerator shaft bracket from the left-hand cylinder head and position it out of the way.
13 Loosen the rocker arm studs nuts just enough to enable the rocker arms to be rotated to one side.

14 Lift out the pushrods and keep them in the correct order of removal by pushing them through a piece of cardboard with the valve numbers marked on it (1 to 16).
15 Detach the exhaust downpipes from the exhaust manifold and move the downpipes to the sides of the engine compartment. Leave the manifolds in place as they will act as a lever to assist removal of the heads.
15 Taking each cylinder head in turn, loosen the eight holding down bolts in the order shown in Fig. 1.38. When all are free of tension remove all the bolts.
17 On occasions the heads may have stuck to the head gasket and cylinder block, in which case if pulling up on the exhaust manifolds does not free them they should be struck smartly with a soft faced hammer in order to break the joints. **Do not** try to pry them off with a blade of any description or damage will be caused to the faces of the head or block, or both.
18 With the help of an assistant, lift off the cylinder heads, remove them from the vehicle and place them on the workbench. Remove the exhaust manifolds.
19 Remove the cylinder head gaskets. New ones will be required for reassembly.

8 Cylinder heads – removal with engine out

Follow the sequence given in Section 7, paragraphs 6 to 19 inclusive, disregarding information on parts mentioned that have been previously removed.

9 Cylinder heads – dismantling of valves and springs

1 Remove the rocker arm retaining nuts and lift off the fulcrum seats and rocker arms.
2 Lay the cylinder head on its side and using a proper valve spring compressor place the 'U' shaped end over the spring retainer and screw on the valve head so as to compress the spring.
3 Sometimes the retainer will stick, in which case the end of the compressor over the spring should be tapped with a hammer to release the retainer from the locks (collets).
4 As the spring is compressed two tapered locks will be exposed and should be taken from the recess in the retainer.
5 When the compressor is released the spring may be removed from the valve. Lift off the retainer, spring and oil seal. Withdraw the valve from the cylinder head.
6 It is essential that the valves, springs, retainer, locks and seals are alll kept in order so that they may be refitted in the original positions

10 Valve lifters – removal

1 Remove the valve lifters and lay them out in the correct order of removal so that they may be refitted in their original bores.
2 Use a magnet to remove the tappets from the bores (Fig. 1.41).

11 Crankshaft damper – removal

1 Remove the retaining bolts and remove the pulley wheel from the front of the damper.
2 Remove the bolt and washer locating the damper to the front of the crankshaft. The damper is keyed to the crankshaft and must be drawn off with a proper sprocket puller. Attempts to lever it off with long bladed articles such as screwdrivers or tire levers are not suitable in this case because the timing cover behind the damper is a light and relatively fragile casting. Any pressure against it could certainly crack it and possibly break a hole in it.
3 The damper may be removed with the engine in the car but it will be necessary to remove the radiator, and drivebelts.
4 Recover the Woodruff key from the crankshaft nose.

12 Flywheel – removal

1 Remove the clutch assembly, as described in Chapter 6.

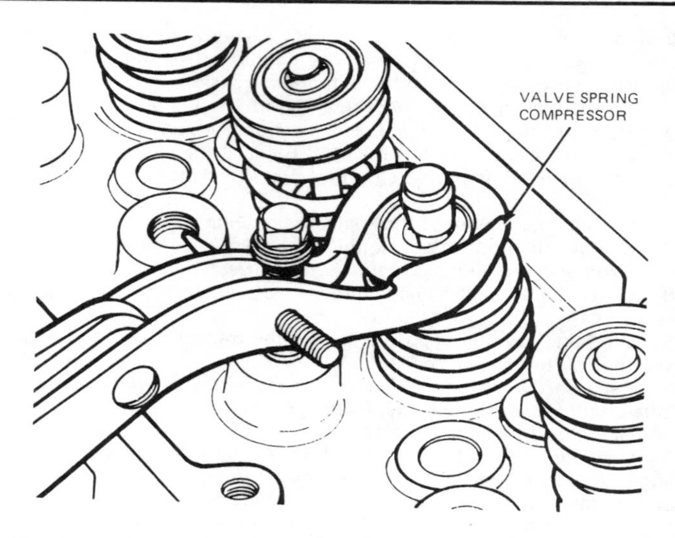

Fig. 1.39 Using a valve spring compressor to release the retainer (Sec 9)

Fig. 1.40 Removing the valve seal (Sec 9)

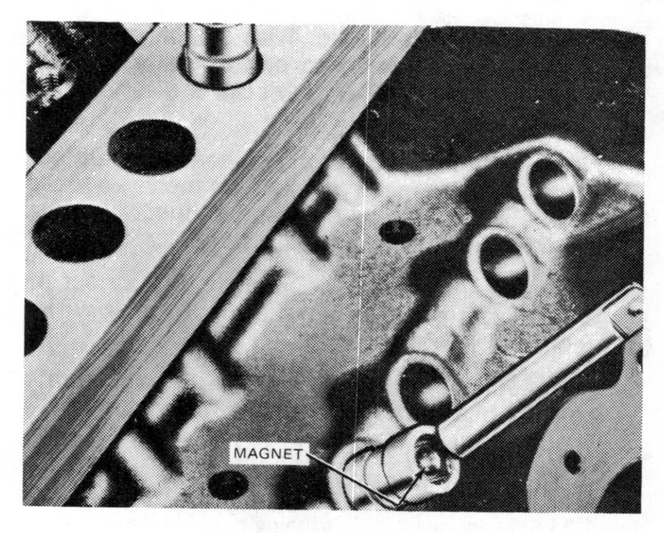

Fig. 1.41 Removing the valve tappet with a magnet (Sec 10)

Fig. 1.42 Removing the crankshaft damper (Sec 11)

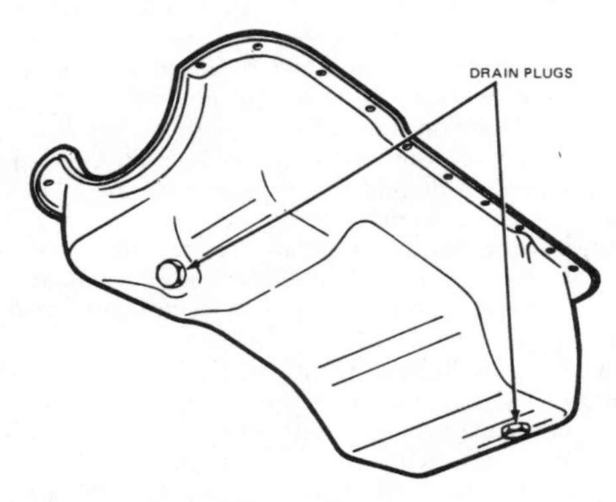

Fig. 1.43 Dual sump oil pan (Sec 13)

Fig. 1.44 Removing timing sprocket and chain (Sec 15)

2 The flywheel is held in position to the crankshaft by six bolts and a locating dowel.
3 Remove the six bolts, taking care to support the weight of the flywheel as they are slackened off in case it slips off the flange. Remove it carefully, taking care not to damage the mating surfaces on the crankshaft and flywheel.

13 Oil pan – removal

1 With the engine out of the car, first invert the engine and then remove the bolts which hold the pan in place.
2 The pan may be stuck quite firmly to the engine if sealing compound has been used on the gasket. It is in order to lever it off in this case. The gasket should be removed and discarded in any case.
3 The oil pan can be removed with the engine still fitted in the vehicle but it is first necessary to raise the engine within the engine compartment approximately 4 inches to provide the necessary clearance.
4 Open the hood and drain the cooling system as described in Chapter 2.
5 Jack up the front of the vehicle, support it on jack stands and drain the engine oil into a suitable container. If vehicle is equipped with a dual sump oil pan, both drain plugs must be removed to thoroughly drain the crankcase.
6 Refer to Section 3 and disconnect all controls and components that will impede the upward movement of the engine; this will include the radiator shroud and hoses, the two front exhaust pipes, the air cleaner and carburetor linkage, alternator and transmission linkage etc. Disconnect the steering flex coupling and remove the 2 bolts attaching the steering gear to the frame crossmember. Rest the steering gear on the frame away from the oil pan.
7 Remove the converter inspection cover and the front engine mounting securing nuts. Place a jack and wooden block under the oil pan and slowly raise the engine at least 4 inches. Place wooden blocks between the engine and crossmember to hold it in the raised position. Remove the jack.
8 Remove all the retaining bolts and lower the oil pan as far as possible, unbolt the oil pump assembly from inside the crankcase. Allow it to drop into the oil pan and withdraw the oil pan complete with pump.
9 Remove the oil pan gasket. A new one must be obtained for reassembly.

14 Front cover – removal

1 With the engine out of the car, remove the oil pan, crankshaft pulley wheel and damper. Disconnect the fuel pump outlet line, unbolt the fuel pump and move it to one side with the fuel line still attached.
2 Remove the water pump retaining bolts and lift the water pump from the front cover. It may be necessary to tap it with a soft-faced mallet if a jointing compound has been used.
3 Remove the front cover securing nuts and lift it away. If it is stuck, cary out the instructions in paragraph 2. Remove the front cover gasket.
4 If the engine is still in the vehicle it will be necessary to remove the front oil pan bolts which run through the timing cover. It will also be necessary to remove the fan belt, crankshaft pulley wheel and fuel pump.

15 Timing chain and sprockets – removal

1 Remove the front timing chain cover as described in th previous Section and withdraw the oil slinger from the front of the crankshaft.
2 Remove the camshaft sprocket securing bolt and remove the fuel pump eccentric from the sprocket. Replace the front damper bolt and use a wrench to rotate the engine until the sprocket timing marks are aligned.
3 Using a suitable puller, withdraw the crankshaft sprocket and, if necessary the camshaft sprocket; remove both sprockets and chain as a complete assembly (Fig. 1.44).
4 Recover the Woodruff key from the groove in the crankshaft.
5 To test the chain for wear, refer to Section 34 of this Chapter.

16 Camshaft – removal

1 The camshaft can be removed with the engine in the vehicle. (Should camshaft replacement be necessary it will probably be necessary to overhaul other parts of the engine too. If this is the case engine removal should be considered).
2 Refer to Chapter 2 and remove the radiator.
3 Detach the spark plug leads from the spark plugs, release the cap securing clips and place the cap to one side.
4 Detach the distributor vacuum line and then remove the distributor as described in Chapter 4.
5 Remove the alternator as described in Chpater 11.
6 Remove the screws that secure each rocker cover to the cylinder heads. Lift away the rocker covers and gaskets.
7 Refer to Chapter 3 and remove the intake manifold and carburettor installation.
8 Loosen the rocker arm retaining nuts just enough to enable the rocker arms to be rotated to one side.
9 Remove the pushrods and note each rod's original location, and also which way up they are fitted. Keep them in order and the right way up by pushing them through a piece of stiff card with valve numbers marked.
10 Refer to Section 14 and remove the front cover.
11 Refer to Section 15 and remove the camshaft timing sprocket and chain.
12 Remove the two screws which secure the camshaft thrust plate to the cylinder block face. Lift away the plate and spacer.
13 Using a magnet, recover the valve lifters from the 'Vee' in the cylinder block. Keep in order as they must be replaced in their original positions.
14 If any valve lifters cannot be removed, retain in their maximum height positions with clips.
15 The camshaft may now be drawn forwards through the cylinder block. Take care that the sharp edges of the cams do not damage the bearings.

17 Oil pump – removal

1 Refer to Section 13 and remove the oil pan.
2 Remove the two bolts that secure the pump to the crankcase. Lift away the pump and recover the gasket.
3 The long hexagonal section driveshaft will come out with the pump. This is driven by the distributor shaft.

18 Pistons, connecting rods and bearings – removal

1 Pistons and connecting rods may be removed with the engine in the vehicle, provided the oil pan and cylinder heads are first removed. The bearing shells may be removed with the heads on.
2 Loosen the two nuts holding each bearing cap to the connecting rod. Use a good quality socket wrench for this work. A box wrench may be used for removal only – not replacement which calls for a special torque wrench. Having slackened the nuts two or three turns tap the caps to dislodge them from the connecting rods. Completely remove the nuts and lift away the end caps.
3 Each bearing cap normally has the cylinder number etched on one end as does the connecting rod. However, this must be verified and if in doubt the cap should be marked with a dab of paint or punch mark to ensure that its relationship with the connecting rod and its numerical position in the cylinder block is not altered.
4 The piston and connecting rod may then be pushed out of the top of each cylinder.
5 The connecting rod bearing shells can be removed from the connecting rod and cap by sliding them round in the direction of the notch at the end of the shell and lifting them out. If they are not being replaced it is vital they are not interchanged – either between pistons or between cap and connecting rod.

19 Piston rings – removal

1 Remove the pistons from the egine.
2 The rings come off over the top of the pistons. Starting with the top one, lift one end of the ring out of the groove and gradually ease it out all the way round. With the second and third rings an old feeler blade is useful for sliding them over the other grooves. However, as rings are only normally removed if they are going to be replaced it should not matter if breakages occur.

20 Piston pin – removal

The piston pins need removing if the pistons are being replaced. New pistons are supplied with new pins for fitting to the existing connecting rods. The piston pin is semi-floating, that is, it is a tight shrink fit with the connecting rod and a moving fit in the piston. To press it out requires considerable force and under usual circumstances a proper press and special tools are essential, otherwise piston damage will occur. If damage to the pistons does not matter, then the pins may be pressed out using suitable diameter pieces of rod and tube between the jaws of a vise. However, this is not recommended as the connecting rod might be damaged also. It is recommended that piston pins and pistons are removed from, and refitted to, connecting rods, by Ford dealers with the necessary facilities.

21 Crankshaft rear oil seal – removal and installation

1 It is possible to remove the crankshaft rear oil seal with the engine in or out of the vehicle. Where the engine is being completely removed, refer to Section 22 and remove the crankshaft. Remove the two halves of the seal from the upper rear main bearing and cap.
2 With the engine in the vehicle, drain the engine oil and remove the oil pan and pump as described in Section 13.
3 Undo the two bolts and carefully pry the rear main bearing cap from the crankshaft. Remove the oil seal from the cap and if a locating pin is fitted in the bottom of the groove in the cap, drive it out using a pin punch.
4 Loosen all the main bearing cap bolts to enable the crankshaft to drop down slightly, but **not** more than $\frac{1}{32}$ in (0.79 mm).
5 Using a piece of brass rod, push one end of the upper half of the oil seal upwards to rotate it around the crankshaft. When the other end of the seal is protruding sufficiently, grip it with a pair of pliers and carefully pull it out while continuing to push on the other end with the piece of wire. Great care must be taken not to scratch the crankshaft oil seal surface.
6 Clean out the oil seal grooves in the cylinder block and cap using a suitable solvent.
7 Soak the new rubber seals in clean engine oil prior to fitting.
8 Fit the upper half of the seal in the cylinder block with the inner lip facing towards the front of the engine. Slide the seal around the crankshaft until $\frac{3}{8}$ in (9 mm) protrudes from the base of the block.

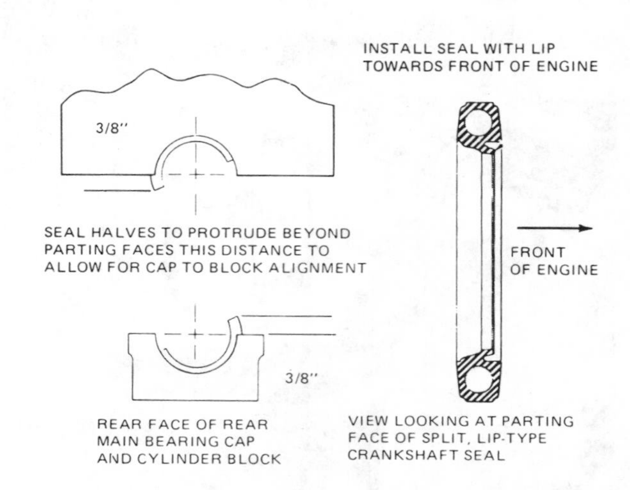

Fig. 1.45 Rear oil seal installation (Sec 21)

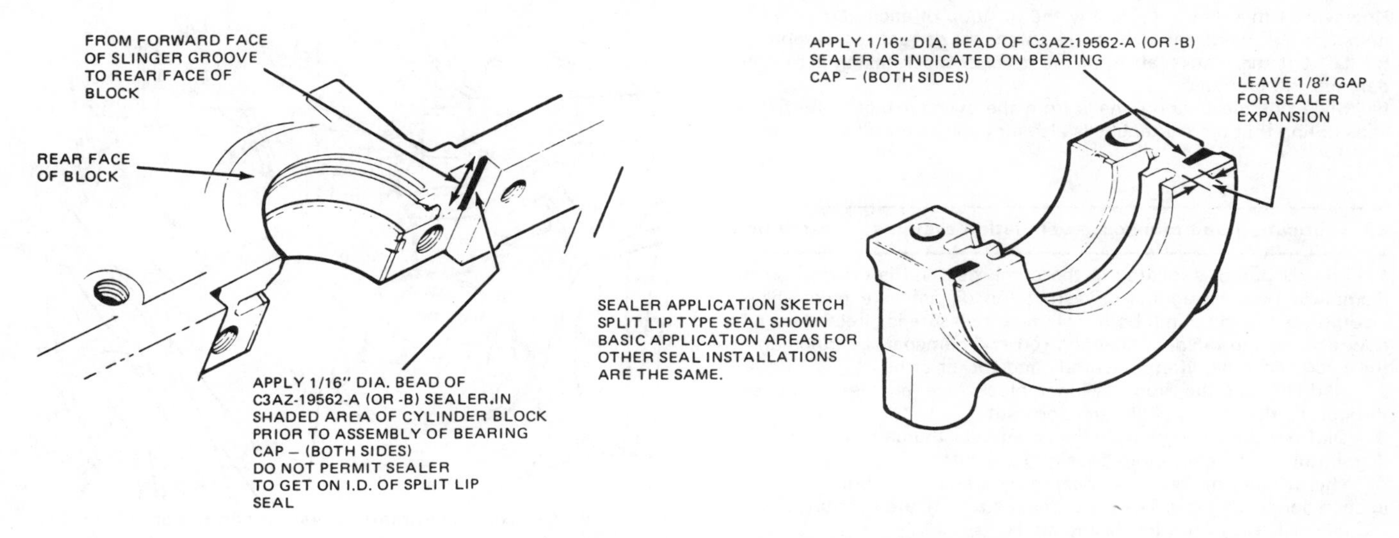

Fig. 1.46 Rear oil seal and bearing cap sealer application (Sec 21)

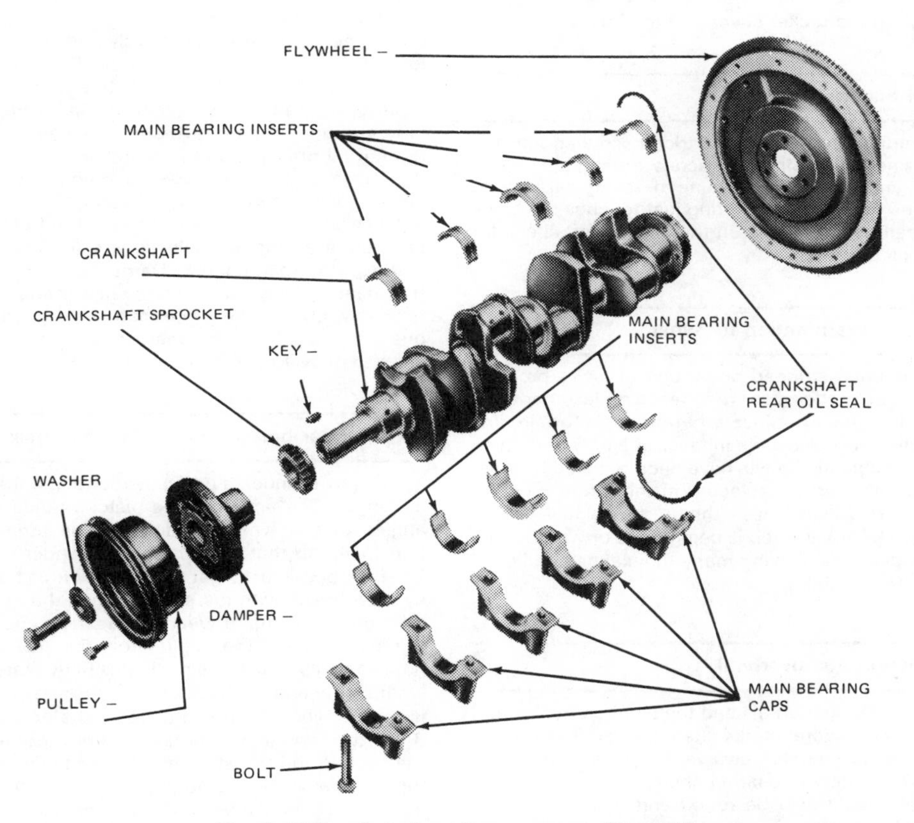

Fig. 1.47 Crankshaft and components (Sec 22)

9 Repeat the procedure for the lower half of the seal, allowing an equal amount of the seal to protrude beyond the opposite end of the bearing cap, (see Fig. 1.45).

10 Fit the rear bearing cap and seal ensuring the protruding ends of the seals correctly enter the respective grooves. Apply a bead of sealer to the rear corners of the block and sides of the cap as shown in Fig. 1.46.

11 Tighten all the main bearing cap bolts to the specified torque wrench setting.

12 Fit the new coil pan seals and gaksets and refit the oil pump and oil pan as described in Sections 41 and 43 respectively.

22 Main bearings and crankshaft – removal

1 The engine should be taken from the vehicle and the oil pan, cylinder heads, timing gears and pistons removed.

2 With a good quality socket wrench undo the ten bolts holding the five main bearing caps.

3 When all the bolts are removed lift out the caps. If the are tight, tap the sides gently with a piece of wood or soft mallet to dislodge them.

4 On some engines the main bearing caps are marked from 1 – 5.

However, if they are not, identify the position of each cap with paint marks or light center punch marks to ensure correct reassembly.
5 Lift out the crankshaft from the cylinder block taking care not to damage the journals.
6 Slide out the bearing shells from the cylinder block and bearing caps noting that the center shells also function as thrust bearings, (Fig. 1.47).

23 Lubrication and crankcase ventilation systems – description

1 The oil pump is located in the crankcase and is driven from the distributor by a hexagonal driveshaft. An oil pressure relief valve is incorporated in the pump body. Oil under pressure is directed via a full flow filter to the main, connecting rod and camshaft bearings and to the hydraulic valve lifters pushrods and rocker arms.
2 A drilling in the front cylinder block face enables oil to pass through to the timing chain and sprocket.
3 Oil from the valve gear drains down over the camshaft lobes and distributor drive gear before passing back into the oil pan.
4 The cylinder bores are lubricated by a squirt of oil from a drilling in each connecting rod. The piston pins are lubricated continuously by the oil mist thrown up inside the crankcase.
5 The crankcase has a positive ventilation system (PCV). Instead of allowing engine fumes to escape into the atmosphere they are drawn back into the engine via a hose and non-return valve connected between the oil filler cap on the rocker cover and the intake manifold.

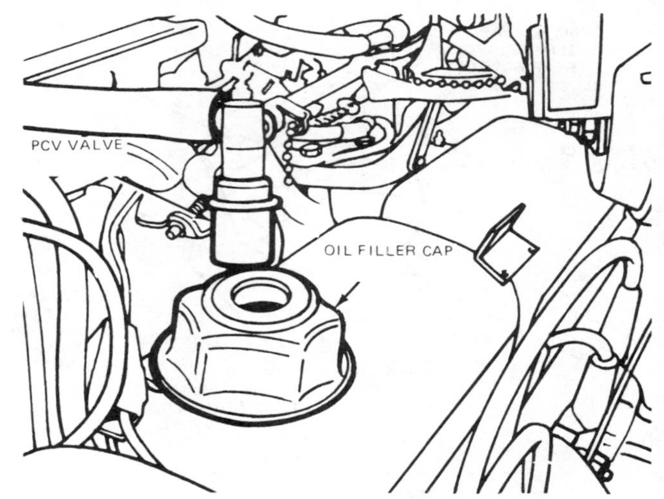

Fig. 1.48 Crankcase ventilation system components (Sec 23)

24 Oil filter – removal and installation

1 The oil filter is a complete throw-away cartridge screwed into the left-hand side of the engine block. Simply unscrew the old unit, clean the seating on the block and screw the new one in, taking care not to cross the thread. Continue until the sealing ring just touches the block face. Then tighten one half turn. Always run the engine and check for signs of leaks after installation.

25 Engine components – examination for wear

1 When the engine has been stripped down and all parts properly cleaned, decisions have to be made as to what needs replacement and the following Sections tell the examiner what to look for. In any border-line case it is always best to decide in favor of a new part. Even if a part may still be serviceable its life will have been reduced by wear and the degree of trouble needed to replace it in the future must be taken into consideration. However, these things are relative and it depends on whether a quick 'survival' job is being done or whether the car as a while is being regarded as having many thousands of miles of useful and economical life remaining.

26 Crankshaft – inspection and overhaul

1 Look at the five main bearing journals and the eight crankpins and if there are any scratches or score marks then the shaft will need grinding. Such conditions will nearly always be accompanied by similar deterioration in the matching bearing shells.
2 Each bearing journal should also be round and can be checked with a micrometer or caliper gauge around the periphery at several points. If there is more than 0.006 in (0.0152 mm) of ovality, regrinding is necessary.
3 A Ford dealer or engine rebuilder will be able to decide to what extent regrinding is necessary and also supply the special under-size shell bearings to match whatever may need grinding off the journals.
4 Before taking the crankshaft for regrinding, check also the cylinder bores and pistons as it may be more convenient to have the machining operations performed at the same time by the same rebuilder.

27 Crankshaft (main) bearings and connecting rod bearings – inspection and overhaul

1 With careful servicing and regular oil and filter changes bearings will last for a very long time but they can still fail for unforeseen reasons. With connecting rod bearings the indications are a regular rhythmic loud knocking from the crankcase, the frequency depending on engine speed. It is particularly noticeable when the engine in under load. This symptom is accompanied by a fall in oil pressure although this is not normally noticeable unless an oil pressure gauge is fitted. Main bearing failure is usually indicated by serious vibration, particularly at higher engine revolutions, accompanied by a more significant drop in oil pressure and a 'rumbling' noise.
2 Bearing shells in good condition have bearing surfaces with a smooth, even, matt silver/grey color all over. Worn bearings will show patches of a different color where the bearing metal has worn away patches of a different color where the bearing metal has worn away and exposed the underlay. Damaged bearings will be pitted or scored. It is nearly always well worthwhile fitting new shells as their cost is relatively low. If the crankshaft is in good condition it is merely a question of obtaining another set of standard size. A reground crankshaft will need new bearing shells as a matter of course.

28 Cylinder bores – inspection and overhaul

1 A new cylinder is perfectly round and the walls parallel throughout its length. The action of the pistons tends to wear the walls at right angles to the wrist pin due to side thrust. This wear takes place principally on that section of the cylinder swept by the piston rings.
2 It is possible to get an indication of bore wear by removing the cylinder heads with the engine still in the car. With the piston down in the bore fist signs of wear can be seen and felt just below the top of the bore where the top piston ring reaches and there will be a noticeable lip. If there is no lip it is fairly reasonable to expect that bore wear is low and any lack of compression or excessive oil consumption is due to worn or broken piston rings or pistons (see next Section).
3 If it is possible to obtain a bore measuring micrometer, measure the bore in the thrust plane below the lip and again at the bottom of the cylinder in the same plane. If the difference is more than 0.010 inch (0.254 mm) then a rebore is necessary. Similarly, a difference of 0.005 inch (0.127 mm) or more across the bore diameter is a sign of ovality calling for a rebore.
4 Any bore which is significantly scratched or scored will need reboring. This symptom usually indicates that the piston or rings are damaged in that cylinder. In the event of only one cylinder being in need of reboring it will still be necesary for all eight to be bored and fitted with new oversize pistons and rings. Your Ford dealer or local machine shop will be able to rebore and obtain the necessary matched pistons. If the crankshaft is undergoing regrinding it is a good idea to let the same firm renovate and reassemble the crankshaft and pistons to the block. A reputable firm normally gives a guarantee for such work. In cases where engines have been rebored already to their maximum, new cylinder liners are available which may be installed. In such cases the same reboring processes have to be followed and the services of a machine shop are required.

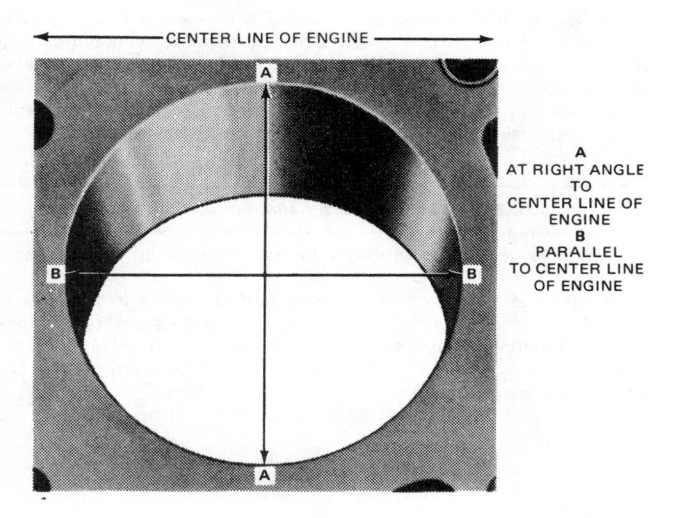

Fig. 1.49 Measuring cylinder bore for wear (Sec 28)

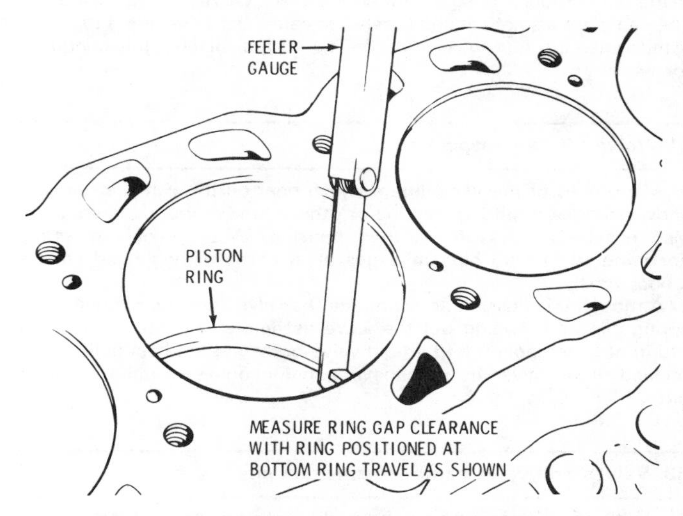

Fig. 1.50 Measuring piston ring end gap (Sec 29)

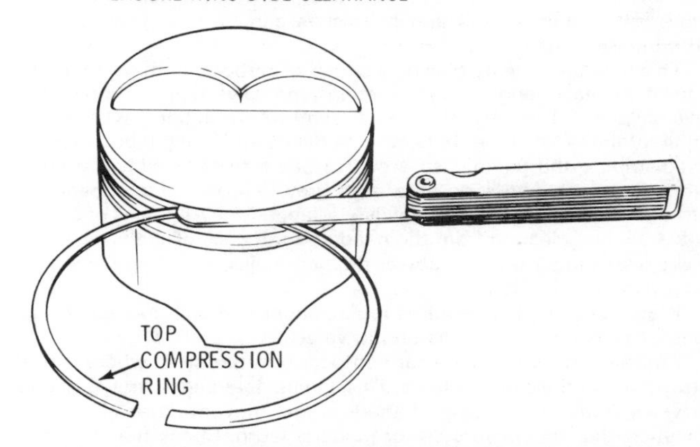

Fig. 1.51 Measuring piston ring side clearance (Sec 29)

29 Pistons and piston rings – inspection and overhaul

1 Worn pistons and rings can usually be diagnosed when the symptoms of excessive oil consumption and low compression occur and are sometimes, though not always, associated with worn cylinder bores. Compression testers that fit into the spark plug holes are available and these can indicate where low compresson is occurring. Wear usually accelerates the more it is left so when the symptoms occur, early action can possibly save the expense of a rebore.

2 Another symptom of piston wear is piston slap – a knocking noise from the crankcase not to be confused with connecting rod bearing failure. It can be heard clearly at low engine speed when there is no load (idling for example) and the engine is cold, and is much less audible when the engine speed increases. Piston wear usually occurs in the skirt or lower end of the piston and is indicated by vertical streaks in the worn area which is always on the thrust side. It can also be seen where the skirt thickness is different.

3 Piston ring wear can be checked by first removing the rings from the pistons, as described in Section 19. Then place the rings in the cylinder bores from the top, pushing them down about 1.5 inches (38 mm) with the head of a piston (from which the rings have been removed) so that they rest square in the cylinder. Then measure the gap at the ends of the ring with a feeler gauge. If it exceeds 0.020 in (0.508 mm) for the two top compression rings, or 0.055 in for the oil control ring then they need replacement.

4 The groove in which the rings locate in the piston can also become enlarged due to wear. The clearance between the ring and piston should not exceed 0.004 in (0.1016 mm) for the top and second ring. The bottom oil control ring should be a snug fit in the groove with no visible clearance (Fig. 1.51).

5 However, it is rare that a piston is only worn in the ring grooves and the need to replace them for this fault alone is hardly ever encountered.

30 Connecting rods and piston pins – insepction

1 Piston pins are a shrink fit into the connecting rods. Neither of these components would normally need replacement unless the pistons were being changed, in which case the new pistons would automatically be supplied with new pins.

2 Connecting rods are not subject to wear but in extreme circumstances such as engine seizure, they could be distorted. Such conditions may be visually apparent but where doubt exists they should be changed. The bearing caps should also be examined for indications of filing down which may have been attempted in the mistaken idea that bearing looseness could be remedied in this way. If there are such signs then the connecting rods should be replaced.

31 Camshaft and camshaft bearings – inspection

The camshaft bearing bushes should be examined for signs of scoring and pitting. If they need replacement they will have to be dealt with professionally as, although it may be relatively easy to remove the old bushes, the correct fitting of new ones requires special tools. If they are not fitted evenly and square from the very start they can be distorted, thus causing localized wear in a very short time. See your Ford dealer or local machine shop for this work.

2 The camshaft itself may show signs of wear on the bearing journals, cam lobes or the skew gear. The main decision to take is what degree of wear justifies replacement which is costly. Any signs of scoring or damage to the bearing journals must be rectified and as under-size bearing brushes are not supplied the journals cannot be reground. Replacement of the whole camshaft is the only solution. Similarly. excessive wear on the skew gear which can be seen where the distributor driveshaft teeth mesh, will mean replacement of the whole camshaft.

3 The cam lobes themselves may show signs of ridging or pitting on the high points. If the ridging is light then it may be possible to smooth it out with fine emery cloth. The cam lobes, however, are surface

hardened and once this penetrated wear will be very rapid thereafter. The cams are also offset and tapered to cause the valve lifters to rotate – thus ensuring that wear is even – so do not mistake this condition for wear.

32 Valve lifters – inspection

1 The faces of the valve lifters which bear on the camshaft should show no signs of pitting, scoring or other forms of wear. They should also not be a loose fit in their housing. Wear is only normally encountered at very high mileages or in cases of neglected engine lubrication.

2 Although it is possible to dismantle the valve lifters by removing the spring clip and tapping out the valve assembly, it is not worthwhile fitting new components to an old valve body and the best policy is to replace all the valve lifters whenever a major engine overhaul is carried out.

33 Valves and valve seats – inspection and overhaul

1 With the valve removed from the cylinder heads examine the heads for signs of cracking, burning away and pitting of the edge where it seats in the port. The seats of the valves in the cylinder head should also be examined for the same signs. Usually it is the valve that deteriorates first but if bad valve is not rectified the seat will suffer and this is more difficult to repair.

2 Providing the valve heads and seats are not cracked or badly pitted, minor burn marks and blemishes can be removed by using carborundum paste.

3 This may be done by placing a smear of carborundum paste on the edge of the valve and, using a suction type valve holder, lapping the valve in place. This is done with a semi-rotary action, twisting the handle of the valve holder between the hands and lifting it occasionally to redistribute the paste. Use a coarse paste to start with and finish with a fine paste. As soon as a matt grey unbroken line appears on both the valve and the seat the valve is 'lapped-in'. All traces of carbon should also be cleaned from the head and the neck of the valve stem; A wire brush mounted in a power drill is a quick and effective way of doing this.

4 If an exhaust valve requires replacement it should be lapped into the seat in the same way as an old valve.

5 Another form of valve wear can occur on the stem where it runs in the guide in the cylinder head. This can be detected by trying to rock the valve from side to side. If there is any movement at all it is an indication that the valve stem or guide is worn. Check the stem first with a micrometer at points all along and around its length and if they are not within the specified size new valves will probably solve the problem. If the guides are worn, however, they will need reboring for oversize valves or for fitting guide inserts. The valve seats will also need recutting to ensure they are concentric with the stems. This work should be given to your Ford dealer or local machine shop.

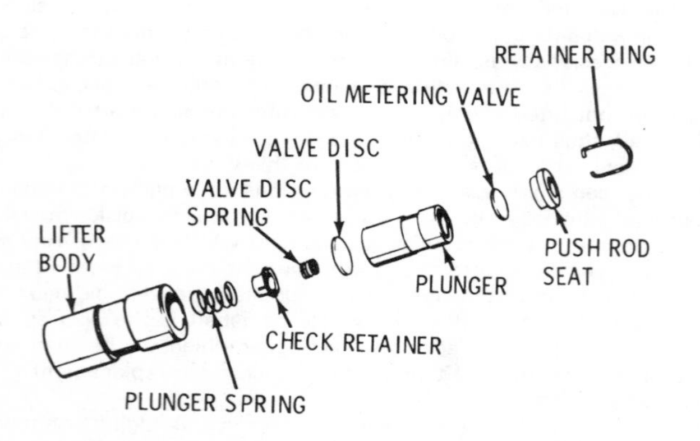

Fig. 1.52 Hydraulic valve lifter components (Sec 32)

6 When all valve lapping is completed it is essential that every trace of paste is removed from the valves and ports in the cylinder head. This should be done by a thorough washing in gasoline or kerosene and blowing out with a jet of air. If particles of carborundum paste should work their way into the engine they would cause havoc with bearings or cylinder walls.

34 Timing chain and sprockets – inspection and overhaul

1 Examine the sprocket teeth for excessive wear and replace if necessary.

2 Check the timing chain for wear and slackness in the pins and links. As a guide, temporarily refit the chain and sprockets and rotate the crankshaft so that one side of the chain in under tension. Now check that the maximum possible sideways movement of the slack side of the chain does not exceed $\frac{1}{2}$ in (12.5 mm).

3 If any doubt exists regarding the condition of the chain the most sensible policy is to replace it.

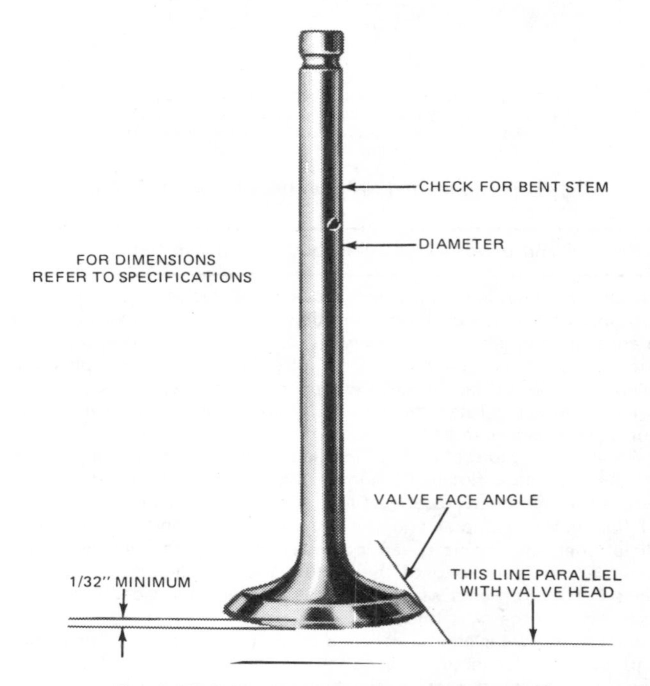

Fig. 1.53 Critical valve dimensions (Sec 33)

Fig. 1.54 Checking timing chain deflection (Sec 34)

35 Flywheel ring gear – inspection and overhaul

1 If the ring gear is badly worn or has missing teeth it should be replaced. The old ring can be removed from the flywheel by cutting a notch between two teeth with a hacksaw and then splitting it with a cold chisel.
2 To fit a new ring gear requires heating the ring to 400°F (204°C). This can be done by polishing four equally spaced sections of the gear, laying it on a suitable heat resistant surface (such as fire bricks) and heating it evenly with a torch until the polished areas turn a light yellow tint. Do not overheat or the hard wearing properties will be lost. The gear has a chamfered inner edge which should go against the shoulder when put on the flywheel. When hot enough place the gear in position quickly, tapping it home if necessary and let it cool naturally without quenching in any way.

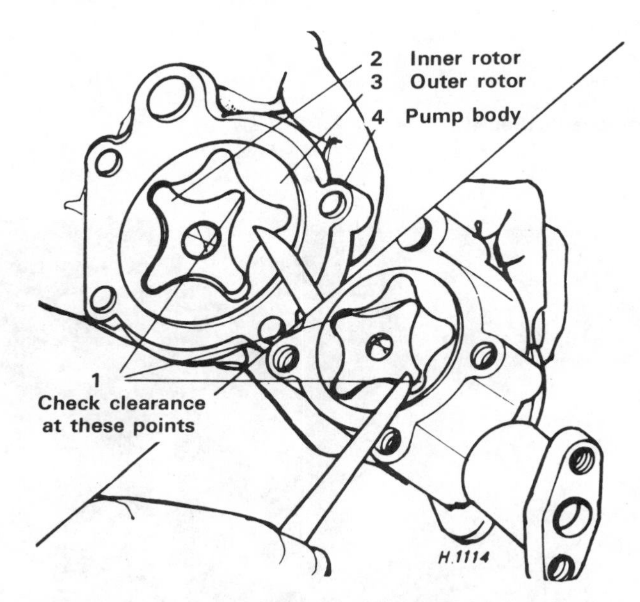

Fig. 1.55 Checking oil pump rotor side clearances (Sec 36)

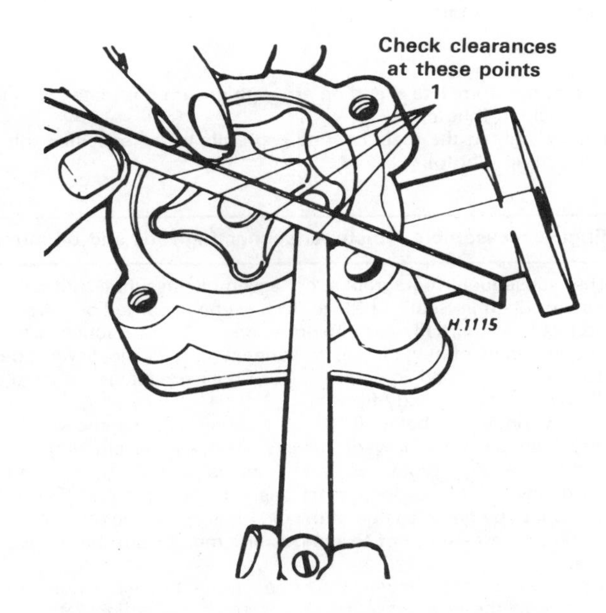

Fig. 1.56 Checking oil pump rotor endfloat (Sec 36)

36 Oil pump – inspection

1 The oil pump maintains a pressure of around 40 to 60 psi. An oil pressure gauge is fitted to give earlier warning of falling oil pressures due either to overheating, pump failure or bearing wear.
2 At a major engine overhaul it is as well to check the pump and exchange it for a reconditioned unit if necessary. The efficient operation of the oil pump depends on the finely machined tolerances between the moving parts of the rotor and the body and reconditioning of these is generally not within the competence of the non-specialist owner.
3 To dismantle the pump, first remove it from the engine, as described in Section 17.
4 Remove the two bolts holding the end cover to the body and remove the cover and relief valve parts which will be released.
5 Remove the four bolts securing the rotor end plate.
6 The necessary clearances may now be checked using a machined straight edge (a good steel rule) and a feeler gauge.
7 On bi-rotor type pumps the critical clearances are between the lobes of the center rotor and convex faces of the outer rotor, between the outer rotor and the pump body, and between both rotors and the end cover plate.
8 The rotor lobe clearances may be checked as shown in Fig. 1.55. The clearances should not exceed 0.006 in (0.152 mm). The clearance between the outer rotor and pump body should not exceed 0.013 in (0.33 mm).
9 The endfloat clearance can be measured by placing a straight edge across the end of the pump and measuring the gap between the rotors and the straight edge. The gap on either rotor should not exceed 0.005 in (0.127 mm). See Fig. 1.56.
10 If any clearances are out of specification, the oil pump must be replaced with a new one.
11 When reassembling the pump and replacing the end cover make sure that the interior is scrupulously clean and that the pressure relief valve parts are assembled in the correct positions.

37 Cylinder heads and piston crowns – cleaning

1 When cylinder heads are removed either in the course of an overhaul or for inspection of bores or valve condition when the engine is in the vehicle, it is normal to remove all carbon deposits from the piston crowns and heads.
2 This is best done with a cup-shaped wire brush and an electric drill and is fairly straightforward when the engine is dismantled and the pistons removed. Sometimes hard spots of carbon are not easily removed except by a scraper. When cleaning the pistons with a scraper take care not to damage the surface of the piston in any way.
3 When the engine is in the vehicle certain precautions must be taken when removing the piston crowns, in order to prevent dislodged pieces of carbon falling into the interior of the engine which could cause damage to cylinder bores, pistons and rings – or if allowed into the water passages – damage to the water pump. Turn the engine, therefore, so that the piston being worked on is at the top of its stroke and then mask off the adjacent cylinder bore and all surrounding water jacket orifices with paper and adhesive tape. Press grease into the gap all round the piston to keep carbon particles out and then scrape all carbon away by hand carefully. Do not use a power drill and wire brush when the engine is in the car as it will be virtually impossible to keep all the carbon dust clear of the engine. When completed carefully clear out the grease round the rim of the piston with a matchstick or something similar – bringing any carbon particles with it. Repeat the process on the other seven piston crowns. It is not recommended that a ring of carbon is left round the edge of the piston on the theory that it will reduce oil consumption. This was valid in the earlier days of long stroke low revving engines but modern engines, fuels and lubricants cause less carbon deposits anyway and any left behind tends merely to cause hot spots.

38 Oil pan – inspection

1 Wash out the oil pan with the proper solvent and wipe dry. Inspect the exterior for signs of damage or excessive rust. If evident, a new oil pan must be obtained. To ensure an oil tight joint scrape away all traces of the old gasket from the cylinder block mating face.

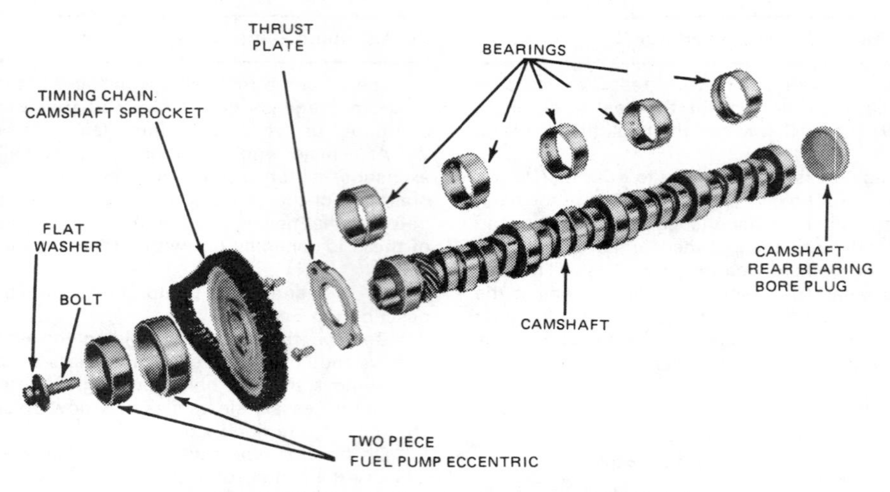

Fig. 1.57 Camshaft and components (Sec 40)

39 Engine reassembly – general

All components of the engine must be cleaned of oil, sludge and old gasket and the working area should also be cleared and clean. In addition to the normal range of good quality socket wrenches and general tools which are essential, the following must be available before reassembling begins:

a) Complete set of new gaskets
b) Supply of clean lint-free cloths
c) Clean oil can full of new engine oil
d) Torque wrench
e) All new spare parts as necessary

40 Engine reassembly – camshaft and crankshaft

1 Insert the camshaft carefully into the block, taking care not to let any of the cam lobes damage the bearing bushes (photo).
2 Replace the camshaft thrust plate and secure it with the two screws. These screws must be tightened firmly (photo).
3 Ensure that the crankcase is thoroughly clean and that all oilways are clear. A thin twist drill is useful for cleaning the oilways, or if possible they may be blown out with compressed air. Treat the crankshaft in the same fashion, and then inject engine oil into the oilways.
4 Select the halves of the five main bearing shells that have the oil slots and grooves and fit them into the crankcase bearing housings (photo). Ensure that the notches in the ends of the shells are correctly located in the cut-outs in the housings.
5 Note that the center main bearing shells have flanges, which act as thrust washers. These are available in various thicknesses in order to be able to set the crankshaft endfloat.
6 Push the upper half of the crankshaft oil seal into the recess at the rear of the crankcase. For further information on fitting the rear crankshaft oil seal refer to Section 21 (Fig. 1.45).
7 Lubricate the crankshaft journals with engine oil and carefully lower the crankshaft into position (photo).
8 Fit the lower (plain) shells into the main bearing caps (photo).
9 Push the lower half of the crankshaft oil seal into the recess in the rear main bearing cap (photo).
10 Fit the rear and main bearing caps over the crankshaft and temporarily tighten the retaining bolts (photos).
11 Check the crankshaft endfloat using feeler gauges (photo). If the endfloat is not within 0.004 – 0.008 in (0.101 – 0.202 mm) the crankshaft should be removed and the center thrust bearings replaced with ones of the necessary thickness to achieve this tolerance.
12 When the crankshaft endfloat is correct, fit all the main bearing caps and retaining bolts. Note that the bearing caps should be marked with a number from 1 to 5 and an arrow to ensure it is installed in the correct position (photo).
13 Finally, tighten the main bearing cap bolts to the specified torque wrench setting (photo).

40.1 When inserting the camshaft, make sure that the lobes do not contact the sides of the bearing bores

41 Engine reassembly – pistons, connecting rods and oil pump

1 The subsequent paragraphs on assembly assume that all the checks described in Sections 29 to 30 have been carried out. Also the engine has been partially assembled as described in Section 40.
2 The assembly of new pistons to connecting rods should have been carried out as detailed in Section 20. The new pistons should be supplied with rings already fitted.
3 If new rings are being fitted to existing pistons the following procedure should be followed. Having removed the old rings make sure that each ring groove in the piston is completely cleaned of carbon deposits. This is done most easily by using a special groove cleaner tool or by breaking one of the old rings and using the sharp end as a scraper. Be careful not to remove any metal from the groove by mistake.
4 The end-gap of the new piston rings – three for each piston – must be checked in the cylinder bores as described in Section 29.
5 Check Specifications for the minimum end gap for all three rings.

40.2 Camshaft thrust plate after installation

40.4 Upper main bearing in position (flanged center bearing shown)

40.7 Lowering the crankshaft into block

40.9 Groove (arrow) in the rear main bearing cap in which the oil seal is installed

40.10A Installing the rear main bearing cap

40.10B Installing the center main bearing cap

40.11 Checking crankshaft endfloat

40.12 Bearing cap identification markings which denote position and direction of installation

40.13 Tightening the main bearing cap bolts

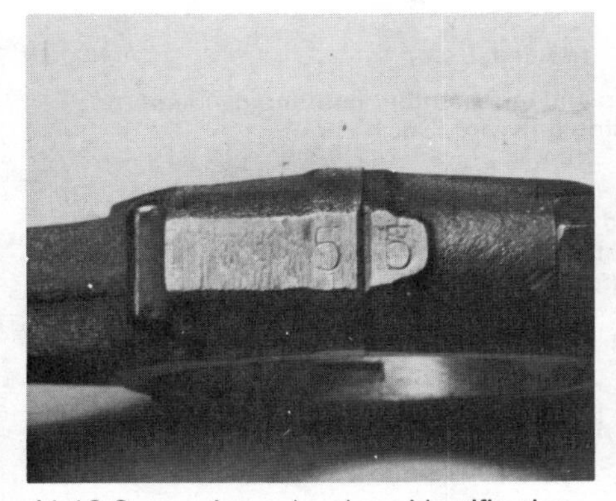

41.13 Connecting rod and cap identification numbers

41.14A The notches on the piston crown must face toward the front of the engine

41.14B Connecting rod and cap chamfered side

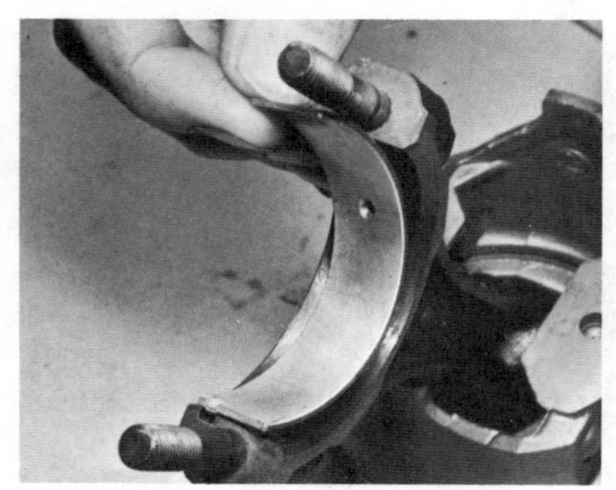
41.17 Installing the connecting rod bearing shell

41.18 Inserting a piston into the cylinder block

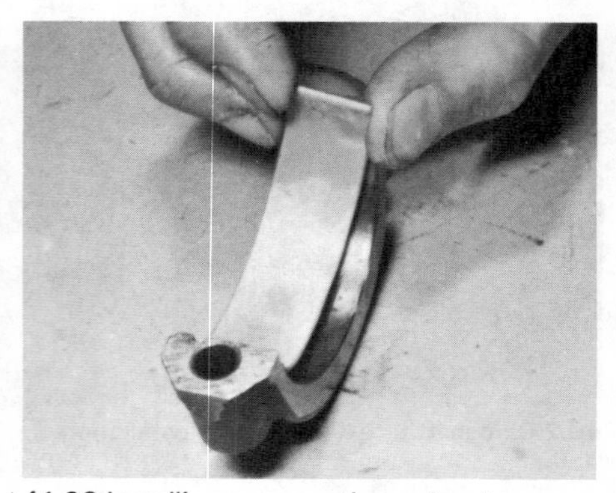
41.20 Installing a connecting rod end cap bearing shell

41.22 Tightening the connecting rod nuts

41.25 Inserting the oil pump and driveshaft

41.26 Installing the oil pump inlet pipe and filter assembly

If the gap is too small, one end of the ring must be filed to increase the gap. To do this the ring should be gripped in a vise between two thin pieces of soft metal in such a way that only the end to be filed is gripped and so that it only protrudes above the jaws of the vise a very small distance. This will eliminate the possibility of bending and breaking the ring while filing the end. Use a thin, fine file and proceed in easy stages – checking the gap by refitting the ring in the bore until the necessary minimum gap is obtained. This must be done with every ring, checking each one in the bore to which it will eventually be fitted. To avoid mistakes it is best to complete one set of rings at a time and refit the piston in the cylinder bore before proceeding to the next.

6 To fit the rings onto the pistons calls for patience and care if breakages are to be avoided. The three rings for each piston must all be fitted over the crown, so obviously the first one to go on is the slotted oil control ring. Hold the ring over the top of the piston and spread the ends just enough to get it around the circumference. Then, with the fingers, ease it down, keeping it parallel to the ring grooves by 'walking' the ring ends alternately down the piston. Being wider than the compression rings no difficulty should be encountered in getting it over the first two grooves in the piston.

7 The lower compression ring, which goes on next, must only be fitted one way up. It is marked 'TOP' to indicate its upper face.

8 Start fitting this ring by spreading the ends to get it located over the top of the piston.

9 The lower compression ring has to be guided over the top ring groove and this can be done by using a suitable cut piece of tin which can be placed so as to cover the top groove under the ends of the ring.

10 Alternatively, a feeler blade may be slid around under te ring to guide it into its groove.

11 The top ring may be fitted either way up as it is barrel faced.

12 With the rings fitted, the piston/connecting rod assembly is ready for refitment in the cylinder.

13 Each connecting rod and bearing cap should have been marked on removal but in any case the cylinder number is etched lightly on the end of the cap and connecting rod alongside (photo).

14 The connecting rod and bearing caps are numbered from 1 to 4 in the right bank of the cylinder block and from 5 to 8 in the left bank

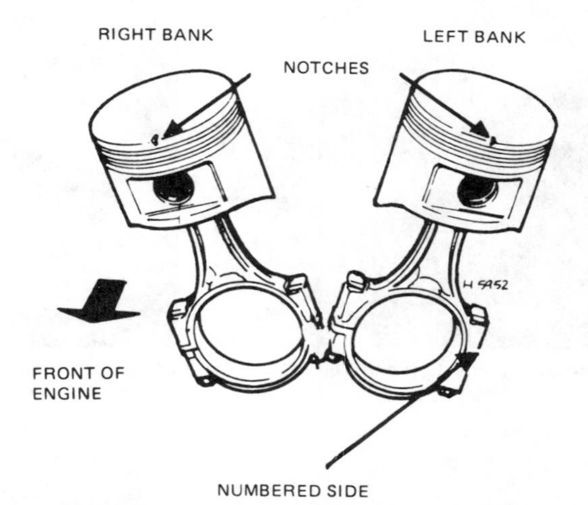

Fig. 1.58 Correct piston and rod position, numbered side of rods facing outward (Sec 41)

with the lower number commencing at the front of the block. The numbered side of the rod and cap must face toward the outside of the cylinder block and the notch in the top of the piston must dace toward the front of the engine (Fig. 1.59 and photo).

IMPORTANT: One side of the bearing cap and connecting rod is chamfered and this must be positioned toward the crankpin thrust face of the crankshaft to allow for the small radius between the journal and web (photo).

15 Before refitting the pistons, position the three rings around each piston so that the gaps are spaced from each other as shown in Fig. 1.60.

16 Clean the cylinder bores using a clean piece of lint-free cloth and lubricate the bores with some engine oil.

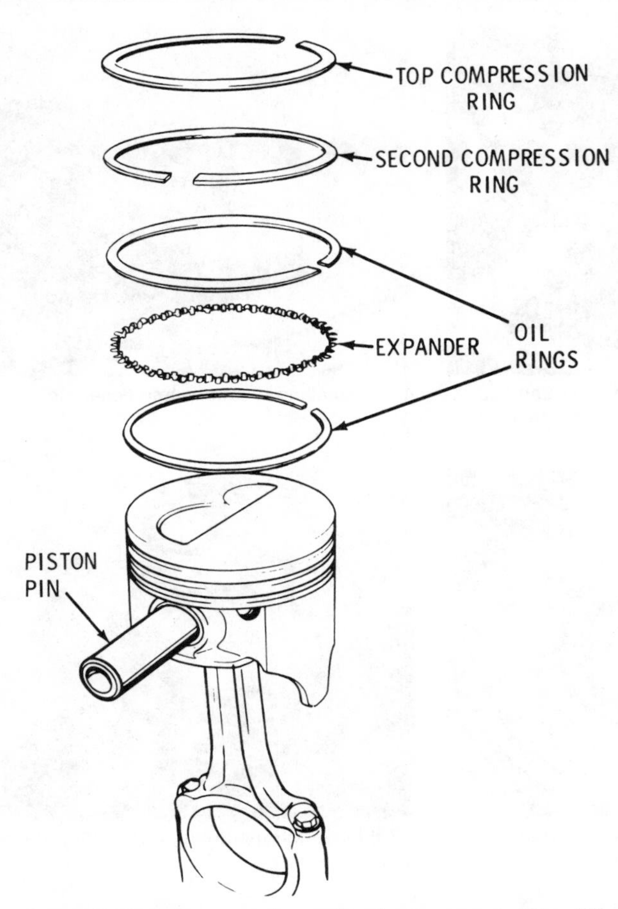

Fig. 1.59 Piston, connecting rod and components (Sec 41)

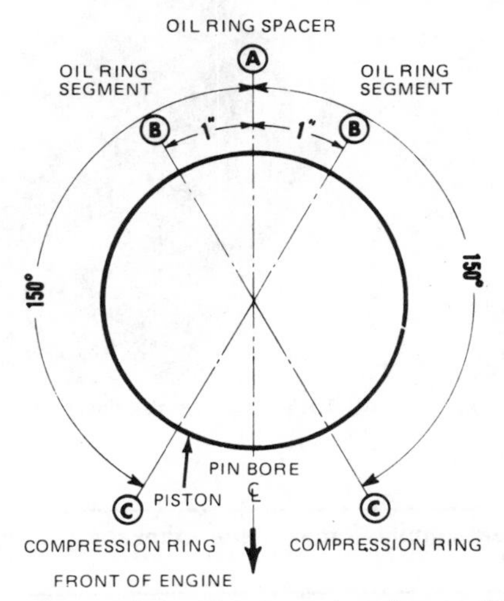

Fig. 1.60 Piston ring end gap spacing diagram (Sec 41)

17 Fit a new shell bearing half into the first connecting rod ensuring the oil feed hole in the shell lines up with the hole in the connecting rod (photo).

18 Push the piston into the cylinder bore (the correct way round) until the oil control ring touches the face of the block. Then, using a piston ring compressor contract the rings and tap the piston into the cylinder (photo). Take great care to be sure that a ring is not trapped on the top edge of the cylinder bore and when tapping the piston in do not use any force. If this is not done the rings could easily be broken.

19 When the piston has been fully located in the bore push it down so that the end of the connecting rod seats on the journal on the crankshaft. Make sure the journal is well lubricated with engine oil.

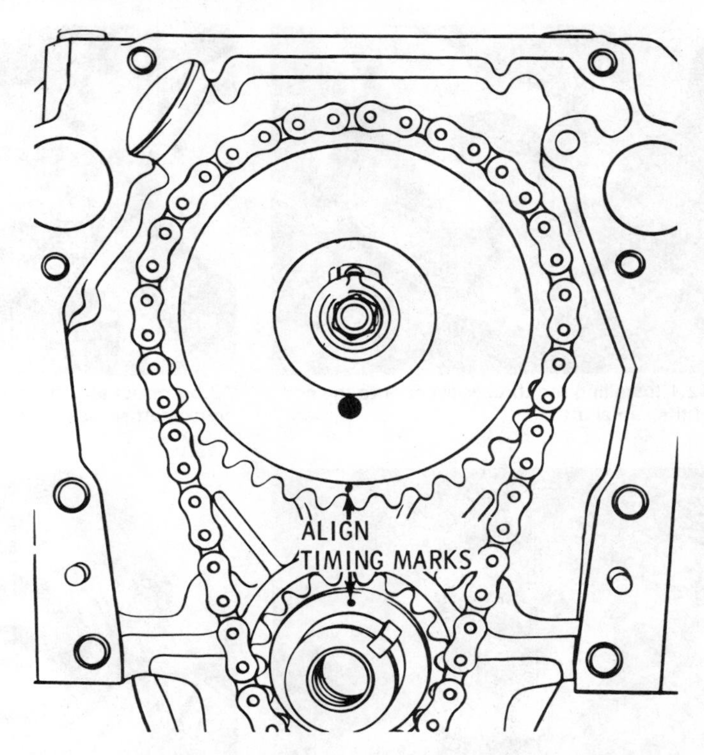

Fig. 1.61 Aligning sprocket timing marks (Sec 42)

20 Maintaining absolute cleanliness all the time, fit the other shell bearing half into the cap, once again with the notches in the bearing and cap lined up (photo). Lubricate it with engine oil and fit it onto the connecting rod so that the holes in the cap fit to the dowels in the connecting rod.

21 Refit all pistons and connecting rods in a similar manner and do not make any mistakes locating the correct number piston in the correct bore.

22 When all the connecting rod caps are correctly fitted tighten the securing nuts to the specified torque wrench setting (photo).

23 Before refitting the oil pump, prime it by filling the inlet port with engine oil and rotating the driveshaft to distribute it.

24 Fit the hexagonal driveshaft into the pump body noting that the end of the driveshaft fitted with the spring washer must be furthest away from the pump.

25 Carefully fit the driveshaft and pump into the block ensuring that the end of the shaft is correctly entered into the distributor aperture (photo).

26 Secure the pump in place with the two retaining bolts and fit the filter and pipe assembly (photo).

42 Engine reassembly – timing chain and timing cover

1 Fit the spacer onto the end of the camshaft ensuring the slot is correctly located over the dowel (photo).

2 Rotate the camshaft so that the dowel is facing downward and then rotate the crankshaft so that the keyway in the front end of the crankshaft is facing upward in line with the camshaft dowel.

Note: *If the task is being carried out with the engine in the vehicle and the distributor has not been removed, lift off the distributor cap and check that the rotor is pointing toward the No. 1 cylinder spark plug lead position. If it is not, rotate the camshaft a full 360° until it is.*

3 Lay the camshaft and crankshaft sprockets on the bench so that the single dot on the camshaft sprocket perimeter is directly opposite the mark on the crankshaft sprocket. Maintain them in this position and fit the timing chain around both sprockets.

4 Carefully fit both sprockets and the chain onto the camshaft and crankshaft and tap them onto the dowel and keyway respectively.

42.1 Installing the thrustwasher onto the end of the camshaft

42.5 Correct alignment of camshaft and crankshaft sprocket timing marks (arrows)

42.6 Installing the fuel pump eccentric

42.7 Crankshaft oil slinger installed

42.8 Installing the timing cover oil seal

42.9 Lowering the timing cover into position

42.10 Installing the crankshaft damper

43.3 Interlocking the oil pan gasket and seal joints

43.7 Re-installing the flywheel

5 Now make a careful check to ensure the timing marks are still correctly aligned (photo and Fig. 1.61).
6 Position the fuel pump eccentric on the camshaft dowel and secure it with the washer and bolt (photo). Tighten the bolt to the specified torque wrench setting.
7 Place the oil thrower in position on the end of the crankshaft (photo).
8 Fit a new seal in the timing cover aperture ensuring it is the correct way round (photo). Tap it fully home using a flat block of wood.
9 Select the front cover gasket and using a suitable sealing compound position it on the engine front plate and install the cover (photo).
10 Place the front cover bolts in position and screw them up loosely. Fit the crankshaft damper onto the keyway of the crankshaft (photo). See that the boss of the damper is lubricated where the oil seal runs.
11 Refitting the crankshaft damper before tightening the cover bolts, centralises the seal to the damper. The bolts holding the cover may then be tightened to the specified torque wrench settings.

43 Engine reassembly – rear plate, crankshaft damper, oil pan and flywheel

1 If the engine rear plate has been removed it should now be refitted. Make sure that both metal faces are quite clean before refitting. No gasket is used.
2 Install the bolt and washer which locates the crankshaft damper, block the crankshaft with a piece of wood against the side of the crankcase and tighten the bolt to the specified torque wrench setting.
3 Clean all traces of old gasket which may remain from the oil pan joint faces and cover the faces of both the crankcase and pan with sealing compound. The oil pan gasket is in four sections which dovetail together and these should be carefully positioned and the joints interlocked (photo).
4 The engine is then ready for the oil pan to be re-installed.
5 Clean the interior of the pan thoroughly, apply sealer to the joint edge and place it in position.

44.4 Correctly installed valve stem seal

44.5 Installing the valve stem spring and retainer

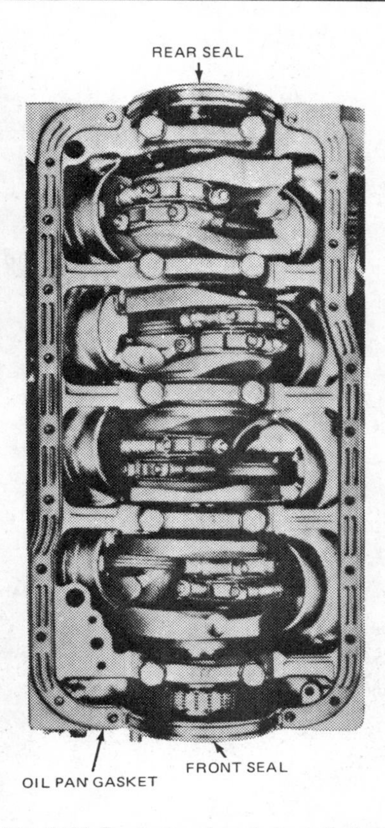

Fig. 1.62 Gasket and seals installed on engine (Sec 43)

44.8 Installing the valve lifters

44.9A Head gasket installed on block

44.9B The word FRONT ensures the correct positioning of the gasket

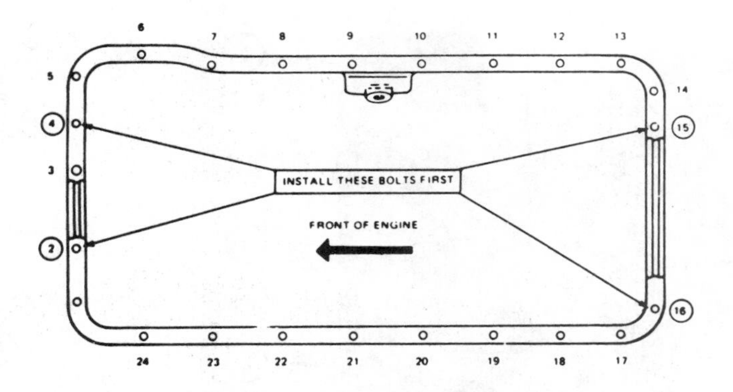

Fig. 1.63 Oil pan bolt tightening sequence diagram (Sec 43)

6 Refit all the oil pan bolts and tighten them evenly to the specified torque wrench setting (Fig. 1.63).
7 The flywheel may now be re-installed. Make sure that the mating flanges are clean and free from burrs and that the bolt holes line up correctly (photo).
8 Screw in six retaining bolts and tighten them evenly to the specified torque wrench setting.

44 Engine reassembly – valve gear, cylinder heads and intake manifolds

1 When the cylinder heads have been cleaned and the valves lapped in as described in Sections 37 and 33, the cylinder heads may be reassembled. If the valves have been removed as described in Section 9, there will no confusion as to which valve belongs in which position.
2 Make sure all traces of carbon and paste have been removed, lubricate the valve stem with engine oil and place it in the appropriate guide.
3 It will then protrude through the top of the cylinder head.
4 Fit a new seal cup over the valve stem (photo).
5 Place the valve spring over the valve stem.
6 Fit the circular retainer over the spring with the protruding center boss retainer downwards (photo).
7 Using a proper valve spring compressor tool, compress the spring down the valve stem sufficiently enough to enable the two halves of the locks (collets) to be fitted into the groove in the valve stem. If necessary the locks should be smeared with grease to keep them in psition. The spring compressor may then be released. Watch to ensure that the locks stay together in position as the retainer comes past them. If the retainer is a little off center it may force one lock out of its groove in which case the spring must be recompressed and the lock repositioned. When the compressor is finally released, tap the head of the valve with a soft mallet to make sure the valve assembly is securely held in position.
8 Stand the engine the right way up on the bench and refit the valve lifters if they have been removed from the block. If these have been kept in order on removal, as suggested, it will be simple matter to refit

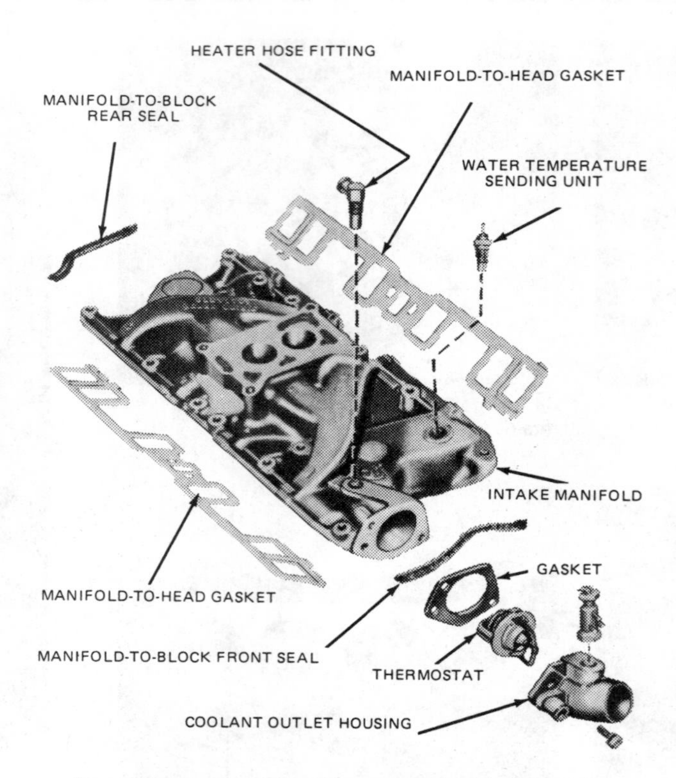

Fig. 1.64 Intake manifold and components (Sec 44)

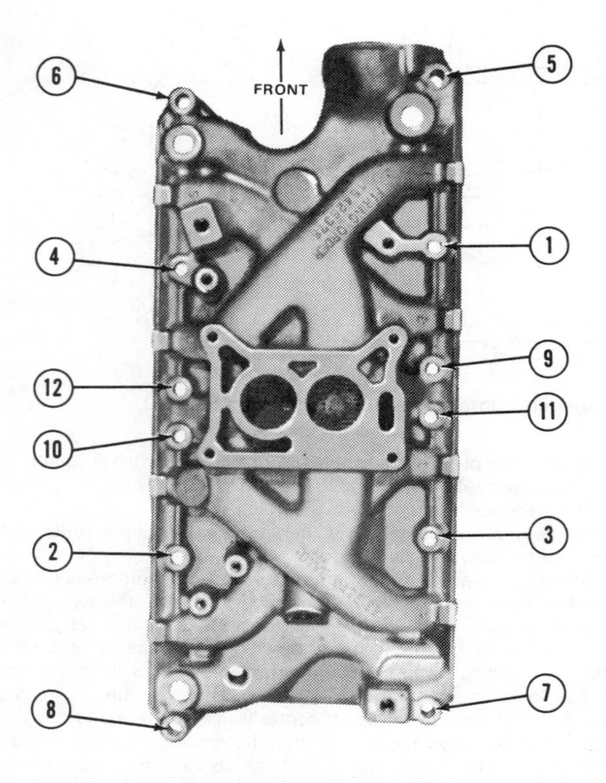

Fig. 1.65 Intake manifold bolt tightening sequence (Sec 44)

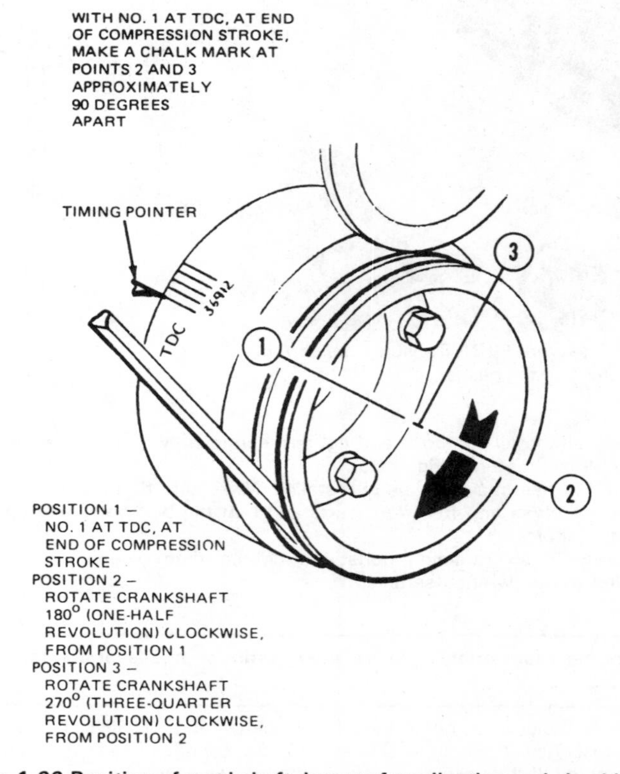

Fig. 1.66 Position of crankshaft damper for adjusting and checking valves (Sec 45)

44.10 Cylinder head in position

44.12 Installing pushrods

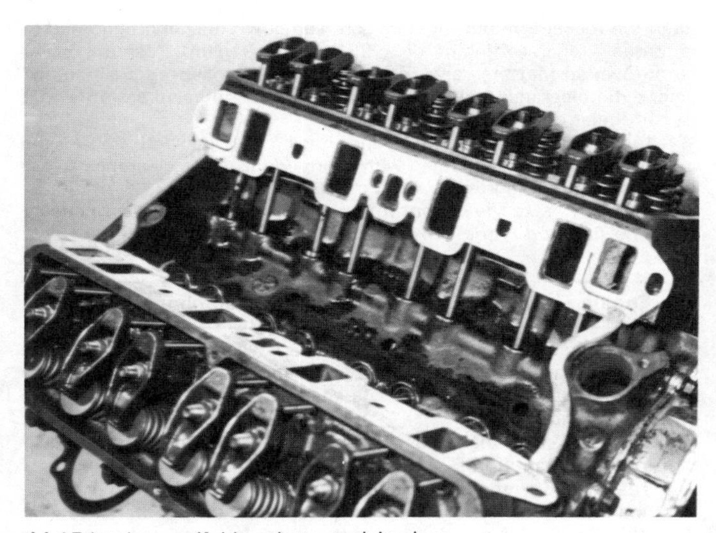
44.15 Intake manifold gaskets stuck in place

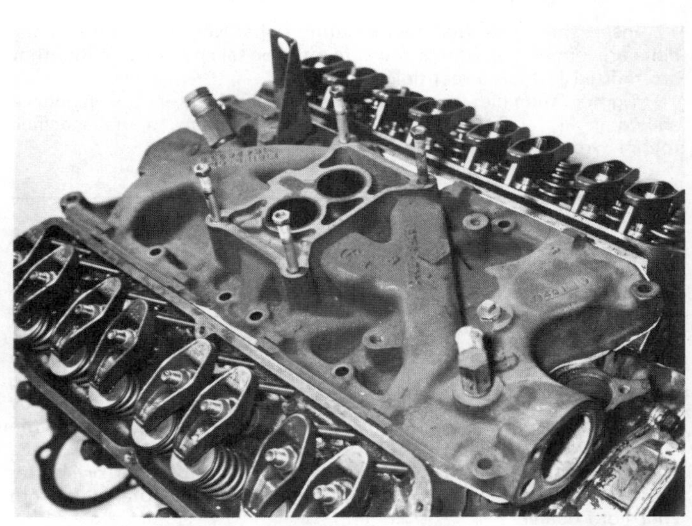
44.16 When installing the intake manifold, make sure that none of the gaskets are knocked out of place

them (photo).

9 Make sure that the cylinder head faces are clean and free from grease or oil and place the new head gaskets in position. To ensure correct location 'FRONT' is usually marked on the upper side of the gasket (photos).

10 Carefully place the cylinder heads in position on the block (photo).

11 Make sure the cylinder head bolts are clean and lightly oiled and refit them. Nip them alll down lightly and then tighten them in the sequence shown in Fig. 1.38. The bolts should be tightened down to progressive torque loadings – (see Specifications) and finally to the specified torque wrench setting.

12 Now fit the pushrods into position, makings sure that they are refitted the same way up as they came out and according to the original valve position. This will not be difficult if they have been kept in order (photo).

13 Position the rocker arms over the pushrods and valve stems and carefully tighten the remaining nuts just enough to retain the pushrods in their correct position. The valve clearances must be adjusted either now or at a later stage as described in the following Section.

14 To refit the inlet manifold first ensure that the cylinder head faces are clean and then lightly coat them with a suitable jointing compound.

15 Carefully stick the gaskets in place ensuring that the small front and rear pieces are interlocked with the two main gaskets (photo).

16 Lower the intake manifold into place and check that none of the gaskets have been pushed out of position (photo).

45.8 Setting the valve clearances

46.2A Install the exhaust manifolds before re-installing the engine

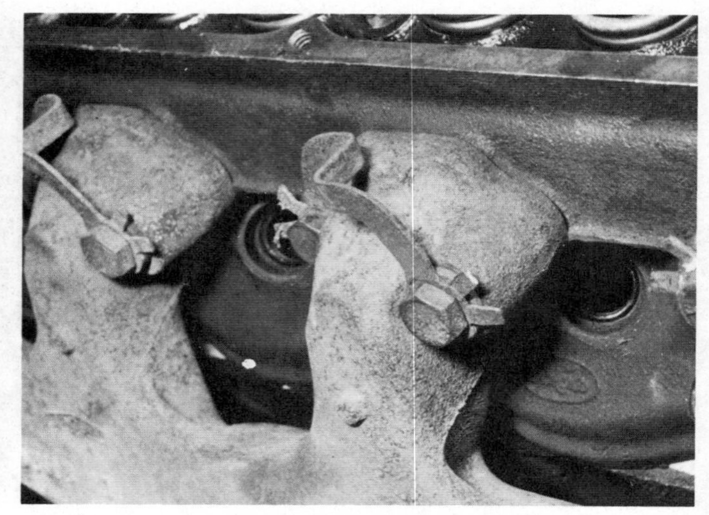

46.2B Exhaust manifold retaining bolts with locking tabs

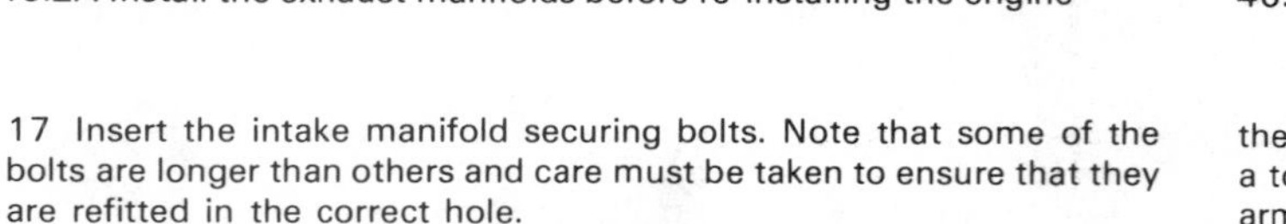

17 Insert the intake manifold securing bolts. Note that some of the bolts are longer than others and care must be taken to ensure that they are refitted in the correct hole.
18 Tighten the inlet manifold bolts progressively in the sequence shown in Fig. 1.65 and then finally tighten them to the specified torque wrench setting.

45 Valve lash – adjustment

1 The hydraulic valve fitters used on the V8 engines automatically compensate for valve gear wear and once the initial clearance has been correctly set no further adjustment will be required until a considerable mileage has been covered .
2 Some of the early 302 cu in engines are fitted with adjustable rockers but all later V8 engines have positive stop rocker mounting studs. On the former type the correct valve clearance is obtained by screwing the rocker arm locknut up or down as necessary, while on the latter type the nut is screwed right down until it stops. If the clearance is then found to be outside the specified limits, a longer or shorter pushrod must be installed as necessary. These are obtainable from your Ford dealer.
3 The later positive stop type rocker stud can be identified by the fact that the plain section of the stud nearest the cylinder head is larger in diameter that the threaded portion.
4 Before commencing adjustment ensure the rocker arm locknuts are in good condition and the fulcrum spacer slides easily on the rocker stud.
5 On the earlier 302 cu in engines with adjustable rocker arms, proceed by rotating the crankshaft until No. 1 piston is at TDC of the compression stroke. This can be ascertained by removing the spark plug and with a finger placed over the hole rotate the engine until pressure is felt. This indicates the piston is rising on the compression stroke. Continue to rotate the engine until the timer pointer on the front cover is aligned with the TDC mark on the crankshaft damper (Fig. 1.66).
6 Push down the No. 1 cylinder rocker arms so that the pushrod forces the valve lifter down into the completely collapsed position.
7 Using a set of feeler gauges, check that the clearance between the rocker arm and the valve stem is within the limits given in the Specifications at the beginning of this Chapter.
8 Adjust the clearance as necessary by turning the rocker nut up or down using a socket wrench (photo).
9 When the No. 1 cylinder valve clearances are correct, rotate the crankshaft until No. 5 piston is at the TDC position of the compression stroke and adjust the valve clearances as described for No. 1 cylinder. Continue to adjust the remaining valve clearances following the firing order sequence of 1, 5, 4, 2, 6, 3, 7, 8.
10 On later engines fitted with the positive stop rocker arm studs, the piston must be set to the TDC position as described previously and then the rocker arm nut must be screwed down fully and tightened to a torque wrench setting of 17 to 23 ft lb (24-31 Nm). Push the rocker arm down so that the valve lifter is in the fully collapsed position and check the clearance between the rocker arm and valve stem using a set of feeler gauges.
11 If the clearance exceeds the maximum specified figure, the pushrod should be exchanged with a longer one. If the clearance is less than specified a shorter pushrod must be fitted.
Note: *Always take the old pushrod along to your Ford dealer to ensure that the new rod is the correct size.*

46 Engine reassembly – installing auxiliary components

1 The exhaust manifolds are best re-installed before putting the engine back into the car as they provide very useful holds if the engine has been manhandled at all. Note that no gaskets are used on the exhaust manifolds.
2 Re-install each manifold, tighten the bolts evenly and bend over the locking tabs (photos).
3 The auxiliary engine components must be re-installed and the method of doing this is detailed in the appropriate Chapters. Section 9 of this Chapter gives a full list of the items involved. When this has been done the engine is ready to put back into the car.
4 For details on how to re-install the distributor and ignition timing refer to Chapter 5.

47 Engine – installation

1 The procedure for installing the engine into the vehicle is basically the reversal of the removal procedure described in Sections 3 and 4.
2 Using the same sling used for engine removal, raise the engine on the extended arm of the hoist and position it over the engine compartment.
3 Lower the engine steadily into the engine compartment, keeping all auxiliary wires, pipes and cables well clear of the sides. It is best to have a second person guiding the engine while it is being lowered.
4 The tricky part is finally mating the engine to the transmission, which involves locating the transmission input shaft into the clutch housing and flywheel. Provided that the clutch friction plate has been centered correctly as described in Chapter 6, there should be little difficulty. Grease the splines of the transmission input shaft first. It may be necessary to rock the engine from side to side in order to get the engine fully home. Under no circumstances let any strain be imparted onto the transmission input shaft. This could occur if the shaft was not fully located and the engine was raised or lowered more than the amount required for very slight adjustment of position.
5 As soon as the engine is fully up to the transmission bellhousing replace the bolts holding the two parts together.

6 Now, finally lower the engine onto its mounting brackets at the front and replace and tighten down the nuts, and washers.

7 Replace all electrical connections, the fuel lines and carburetor linkages, cooling system hoses and radiator in the reverse order to that described in Sections 3 and 4.

8 Reconnect the clutch cable as described in Chapter 5, re-install the exhaust pipes and reconnect them to the manifold extensions, re-install the plate covering the lower half of the bellhousing and remove the supporting jack.

9 Fill the engine with fresh oil and refill with coolant.

48 Engine – initial start-up after overhaul or major repair

1 Make sure that the battery is fully charged and that all lubricants, coolants and fuel are replenished.

2 If the fuel system has been dismantled, it will require several revolutions of the engine on the starter motor to get the gas up to the carburetor. It will help if the plugs are removed and the engine turned over on the starter motor. This will ensure that gas is delivered to the carburetor and also that oil is being circulated around the engine prior to starting.

3 As soon as the engine fires and runs keep it going at a fast idle only (no faster) and bring it up to normal working temperature.

4 As the engine warms up there will be odd smells and some smoke from parts getting hot and burning off oil deposits. The signs to look for are leaks of oil or water which will be obvious if serious. Check also the clamp connections of the exhaust pipes to the manifolds as these do not always 'find' their exact gas-tight position until warmth and vibration have acted on them and it is almost certain that they need tightening further. This should be done, of course, with the engine stopped.

5 When the running temperature has been reached adjust the idling speed as described in Chapter 3.

6 Stop the engine and wait a few minutes to see if any lubricant or coolant is dripping out when the engine is stationary.

7 Road test the vehicle to check that the timing is correct and giving the necessary smoothness and power. Do not race the engine – if new bearings and/or pistons and rings have been installed it should be treated as a new engine and run in at reduced revolutions for 500 miles (800 km).

Chapter 2 Cooling system

Refer to Chapter 13 for specifications and information related to 1981 thru 1987 models

Contents

Specifications

System type	Pressurized, belt driven pump and fan
Thermostat	
Type	Wax pellet
Operating temperature	
2.8L V6	192 ° to 199°, fully open at 226°
4.2L V8	fully open at 221°
5.0L V8	193° to 200°, fully open at 221°
Radiator	
Type	Corrugated fin, cross-flow
Pressure cap, operating pressure	13 psi
Lower limit	11 psi
Upper limit	17 psi
Water pump	Impeller-type, belt-driven
Cooling system capacities*	**US quarts**
2.8L V6, without air conditioning	9.2
2.8L V6, with air conditioning	9.4
4.2L V8, without air conditioning	13.4
4.2L V8, with air conditioning	13.7
5.0L V8, without air conditioning	14.0
5.0L V8, with air conditioning	14.6
* all figures are actual, but may vary ± 15% due to system variations	
Coolant type	50/50 mix of Ford Long Life Coolant ESE-M79B18-C or equivalent
Drivebelt tension	
¼ in V-belt	
new (A)	50 to 80 lb
used	40 to 60 lb (B)
All other V- and cogged belts	
new (A)	120 to 160 lb
used	75 to 120 lb (C)
V-ribbed	
new (A)	140 to 170 lb
used	110 to 130 lb (D)

(A) a new belt has been installed for less than one revolution of the pulley, a used belt for ten minutes of operation, or more
(B) if less than 40 lb, readjust to 40 to 60 lb
(C) if less than 75 lb, readjust to 90 to 120 lb
(D) if less than 100 lb, readjust to 90 to 120 lb

Torque specifications

	ft-lbs	in-lbs	Nm
Fan shroud-to-radiator	–	24 to 28	3 to 5
Fan pulley-to-hub	12 to 18	–	16 to 24
Radiator hose clamps	–	20 to 30	2 to 3
Automatic transmission oil cooler tubes	9 to 12	–	12 to 24
All fasteners not listed, use the following torque wrench settings:			
Metric thread sizes			
M-6	6 to 9		9 to 12
M-8	14 to 21		19 to 28
M-10	28 to 40		38 to 54
M-12	50 to 71		68 to 96
M-14	80 to 140		109 to 154
Pipe thread sizes			
1/8	5 to 8		7 to 10
1/4	12 to 18		17 to 24
3/8	22 to 33		30 to 44
1/2	25 to 35		34 to 47
U.S. thread sizes			
1/4 – 20	6 to 9		9 to 12
5/16 – 18	12 to 18		17 to 24
5/16 – 24	14 to 20		19 to 27
3/8 – 16	22 to 32		30 to 43
3/8 – 24	27 to 38		37 to 51
7/16 – 14	40 to 55		55 to 74
7/16 – 20	40 to 60		55 to 81
1/2 – 13	55 to 80		75 to 108

1 General information

The basic components of the cooling system consist of a radiator, which is connected to the engine by top and bottom hoses; a fan; and a belt-driven water pump. Small bore hoses transfer coolant to the heater and automatic choke control unit.

Vehicles equipped with automatic transmission use radiators which incorporate transmission oil coolers in their tanks.

The cooling system is pressurized so that higher coolant temperature may be maintained without boiling the coolant. Pressure is controlled by a spring-loaded radiator cap. If coolant pressure exceeds the preset limit of the spring, it releases and pressure is bled from the system.

Constant water temperature is controlled by the thermostat. The thermostat remains closed during startup, restricting coolant flow and allowing fast warmup to operating temperature. Once operating temperature is reached, the thermostat opens and allows a free flow of coolant throughout the system.

All models use a coolant recovery system consisting of a plastic reservoir connected to the radiator inlet by a hose. When the coolant in the radiator expands, it is released by the radiator pressure cap into the reservoir. When the coolant in the radiator cools, it contracts and pulls the coolant in the reservoir back into the radiator through a vacuum relief valve in the pressure cap.

Proper cooling depends on engine coolant passages which are free of restriction, hoses which are properly maintained and frequent checking and adjustment of drivebelts. These functions are covered in detail below.

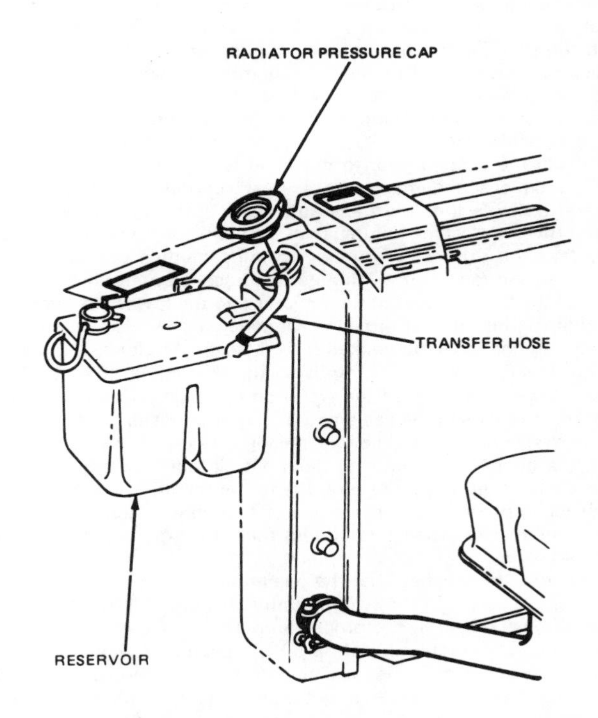

Fig. 2.1 Typical coolant recovery system (Sec 1)

2 Cooling system – draining, flushing, coolant mixing and filling

1 Do not perform the following tasks if the engine has been run to operating temperature. Hot steam and coolant can scald, and the pressures present in the system can force scalding liquid out causing widespread burning. If you wish to perform these tasks after operating your car, leave it in a shady spot for at least one hour, or until the temperature gauge registers a nearly-cold engine when the ignition is switched on, but the engine is not started.

2 The car must be parked on a level, flat spot. Run the engine only long enough to move the vehicle, then shut it off immediately.

3 Place the heater controls on their hottest setting.

4 Raise the hood of the car and remove the radiator cap. If the engine and radiator are warm enough to give off noticeable heat, do not remove the cap. Once heat cannot be felt or when the engine becomes cool enough to touch comfortably with the palm of your hand, the radiator cap may be removed. Turn the cap to its first detent position and allow any remaining pressure to dissipate, then twist it to the second position and remove.

5 Place a pan beneath the radiator to catch draining coolant. Coolant is poisonous and should not be poured into gutters or dumped into storm drains.

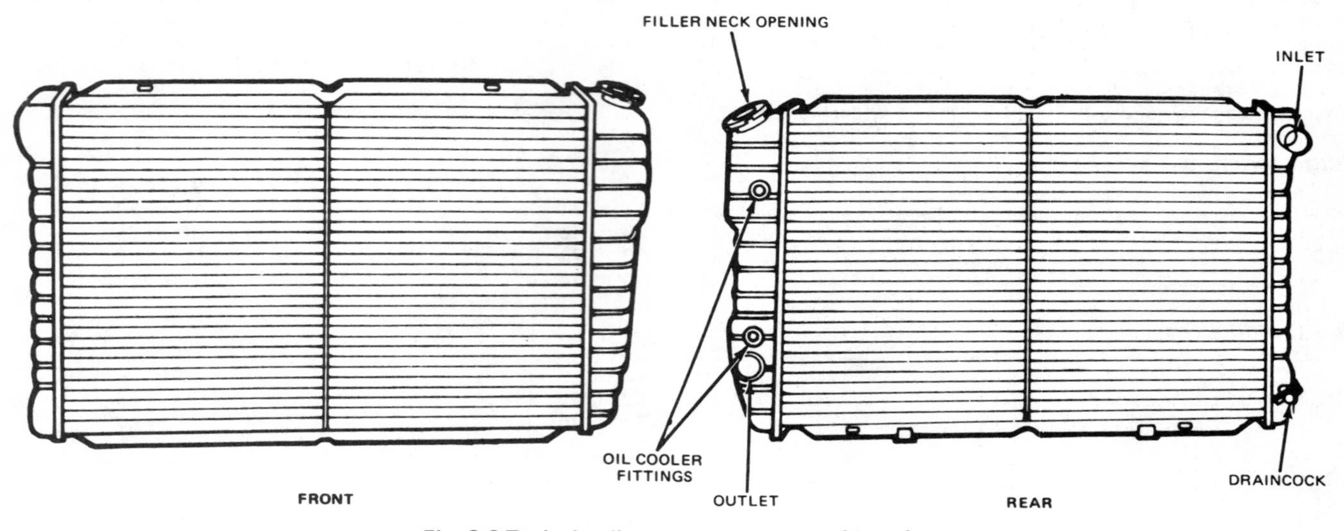

Fig. 2.2 Typical radiator and components (Sec 1)

6 Open the drain petcock. On crossflow radiators this is located at the bottom of the right side reservoir tank and faces the rear of the vehicle. On 2.8L engines it is necessary to remove the heater hose from the thermostat housing to drain the cooling system.
7 When the system has been drained, close the petcock and tighten it until it is snug. Before disposing of the used coolant, check to see if it is rusty in color. If it is, and the coolant is very cloudy, it is advisable to flush the radiator and engine coolant passages.
8 Flushing may be performed in a number of ways. The easiest method is to flush the system with a brand-name flushing fluid according to the manufacturer's directions. To remove the greatest amounts of scale and deposits, it is further recommended that you reverse-flush the system prior to filling. At least one manufacturer in the U.S. produces and markets a special adapter for this purpose. These are available through many auto parts stores.
9 If the reverse-flushing fixture is not available, or if you do not wish to undertake the expense, the most common method of flushing the engine block and radiator is with a garden hose adapter which can be installed in the lower spigot of the radiator and the lower hose adapter at the engine. This adapter provides a female garden hose coupling so that a garden hose may be hooked directly to the engine and radiator.
10 Begin reverse flushing by removing the thermostat (Section 12), then installing the hose. Turn the water on to a high pressure, then off several times to loosen the scale and all larger deposits. After this has been done several times, allow a steady stream of water to flow through the engine or radiator to flush out all loosened deposits.
11 If scale build-up is very severe due to the minerals in local water, consider using distilled water in place of tap water when refilling the cooling system. The expense is far less than the expense of replacing an engine block.
12 When you are satisfied that the engine block water passages and the radiator are clean, fill the system with a mixture of ethylene glycol-based antifreeze mixed in the proper proportions (see manufacturer's specifications) with water, or with a 50/50 mixture of water and Ford Long Life Coolant, which is available from all authorized dealers. Before filling the system, make sure that the hoses are tightly clamped (Section 3), the drain plug has been tightened, and that the thermostat has been replaced (if it was removed for flushing the engine). The system is filled by pouring coolant into the radiator filler neck opening, which is covered by the radiator cap when the car is in use.
13 When the system has been filled, start the engine and allow it to run until the thermostat opens. Fill the radiator again until the proper levels of coolant are reached. On crossflow radiators, fill with coolant until it is within $2\frac{1}{2}$ to 4 in below the radiator cap seal.
14 When proper fill levels have been reached, and brief acceleration of the engine does not cause the coolant level to drop, the system is properly filled. Replace the radiator cap and tighten it fully. Continue to run the engine until proper pressure is built up. Inspect all joints and connections for water-tightness.

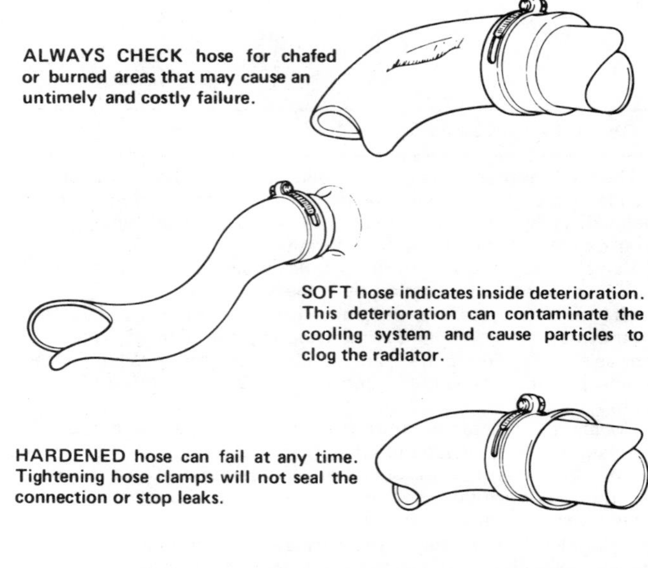

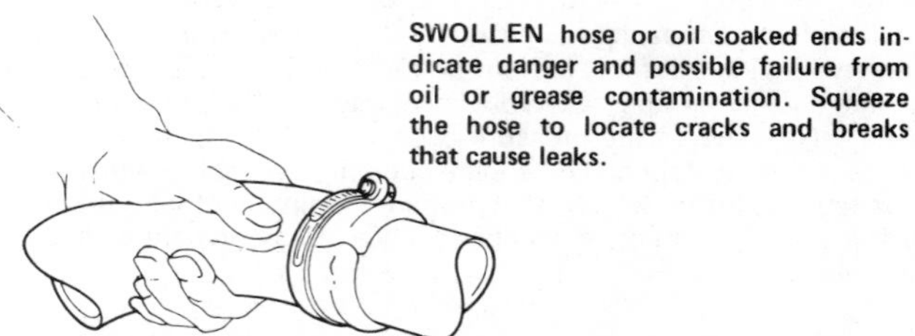

Fig. 2.3 Conditions to look for when inspecting the radiator hoses (Sec 3)

3 Hoses – removal, inspection, and installation

1 A key ingredient in the proper operation of the cooling system is the routine inspection of hoses and their connectors for condition. Another ingredient to long hose life is the proper removal and installation procedure, as incorrect methods will shorten the useful life of the hose and may also lead to the damaging of other engine components.

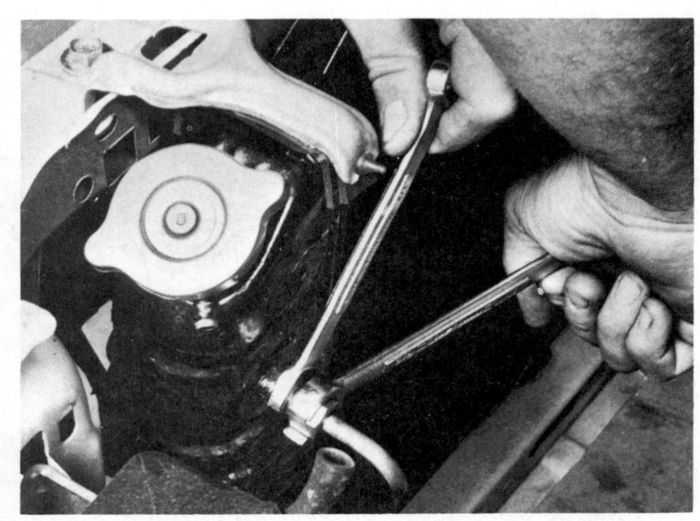

4.5 Use one wrench to lock the fitting while removing the transmission cooler lines with the other to avoid damaging the radiator

4.6A Removing the upper radiator mounting bolts

4.6B Lift the radiator upward carefully to avoid damaging the radiator

2 Routine inspection of hoses involves checking of all connections for watertight fit and all hoses for cracking. Squeeze each hose at several points along its length and closely inspect the surface for cracking, splitting, or breaks. If cracking is severe, replace the hose (Fig. 2.4).
3 To remove the hoses, first park the car on a flat, level surface.
4 Disconnect the negative lead from the battery.
5 It is necessary to drain only enough coolant from the system to allow removal of the hose. Upper hoses will require far less draining than lower. Use the instructions in Section 2 for draining.
6 Loosen the hose clamps at each end of the hose.
7 Grasp the hose firmly at the flange, twist and pull simultaneously. Discretion is required for this job. Do not 'muscle' the connectors on the radiator, for instance, as they are of soft, thin, alloy sheet and will deform or break very easily.
8 If the above procedure doesn't work, the hose will have to be cut from the flange to avoid the possibility of damaging flanges and other related parts.
9 Using a razor blade or art knife, carefully slit the hose in several shallow cuts. These cutting tools are manufactured of metal harder than the flanges and will gouge the flanges. These gouges will be the primary site of fatigue cracking later in the life of the engine, so take the time to cut the hose, only.
10 When the hose has been cut, carefully peel it away from the flange. Do not insert any tools or levers between the hose and the flange as these will also gouge or deform the flange, making sealing of the new hose difficult.
11 Inspect the inside surfaces of all removed hoses for evidence of mineral build-up and rust in the cooling system. If there is evidence of build-up, flush the system (Section 2).
12 Installation of the hoses is the reverse of removal.
13 Coat the flange surface with waterproof sealer.
14 Slide the hose over the flange and position the clamp.
15 Tighten the clamp until the hose is snug on the flange.
16 Fill the cooling system with fresh coolant mixed according to the directions in Section 2.
17 Start the engine and allow it to reach operating temperature. Check all connections for leakage.

4 Radiator – removal and installation

1 Park the car on a flat, level surface.
2 Disconnect the negative lead from the battery.
3 Drain the cooling system (Section 2).
4 Remove the cooling fan and shroud (Sections 7 or 10).
5 Remove the upper and lower hoses from the radiator. If your car is equipped with an automatic transmission, disconnect the hoses from the transmission oil cooler and plug the lines with rubber plugs. Place a pan beneath the radiator to catch any transmission fluid which may escape during the removal of the radiator (photo).
6 On cars with crossflow radiators, remove the two bolts which hold the radiator to its upper mounts. Remove the upper mounts. Lift the radiator from the car (photos).
7 Installation is the reverse of the removal procedure.
8 If a new radiator is to be installed, the draincock from the old radiator must be installed. On automatic transmission models, the oil line adapters must also be installed, using an oil resistant sealer.

5 Radiator – pressure testing, repair, and service

1 Aside from the tasks outlined in this Chapter, we recommend that you seek the services of a competent radiator repair shop for the performance of the above, and any other unlisted tasks. These shops are set up to perform this type of work on an efficient and low cost basis.

6 Radiator cap – pressure test

1 This task requires the use of several specialized tools which may be purchased from an authorized dealer. If you do not wish to undertake the expense of such equipment, have your dealer or a garage perform the following test.

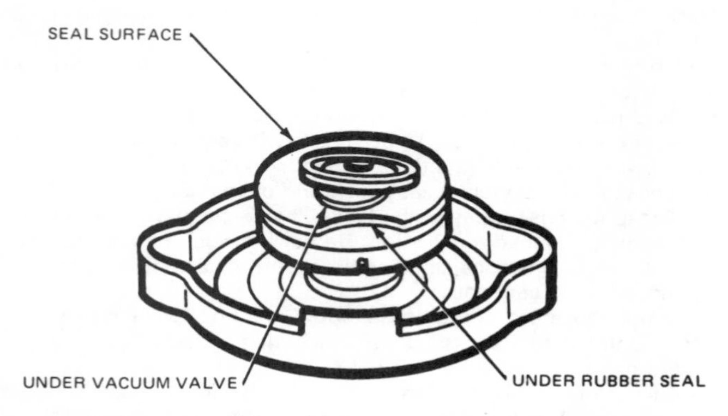

Fig. 2.4 Inspecting the radiator cap and components (Sec 6)

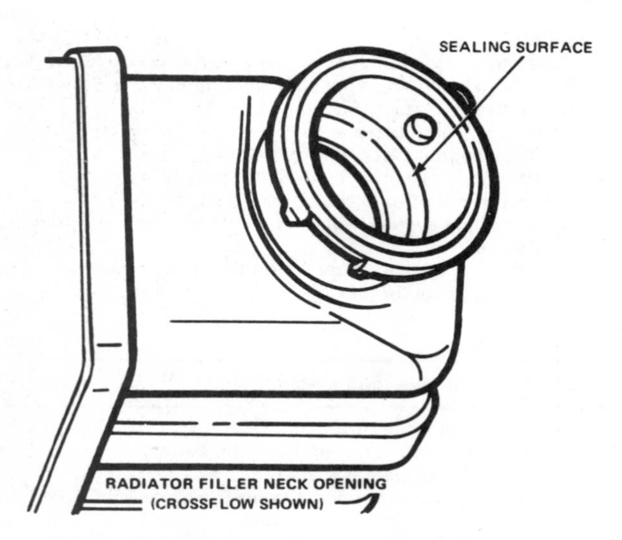

Fig. 2.5 Radiator filler neck sealing surfaces (Sec 6)

2 Remove the radiator cap from the radiator filler neck. The engine must be cool at this time.
3 Wash the cap with water, paying careful attention to the cleaning of the rubber seal and the vacuum relief valve (Fig. 2.4).
4 Immerse the cap in water and install it on the end of special tool 21-0012 (Radiator Cap Pressure Test Adapter) or an equivalent. Leave this assembly immersed in your container of water.
5 Immerse the filler neck seal from the testing kit and install it in the other end of the filler neck adapter.
6 Remove the assembly from the water and install it on the radiator filler neck adapter, pressure tester.
7 Connect the special pressure test pump (an air pump with pressure gauge installed) according to the directions in the testing kit.
8 Depress the plunger of the pressure test pump slowly and note the highest pressure obtained. Do not depress the plunger quickly or false readings will result.
9 Release the pressure by turning the pressure relief screw counter-clockwise. Perform this test at least twice more to be sure of the reading, then check your results with the pressure test specification at the beginning of this Chapter. If the readings are not within the acceptable limits given, replace the radiator cap. If they are within the limits, have an authorized garage perform a pressure test on your cooling system.

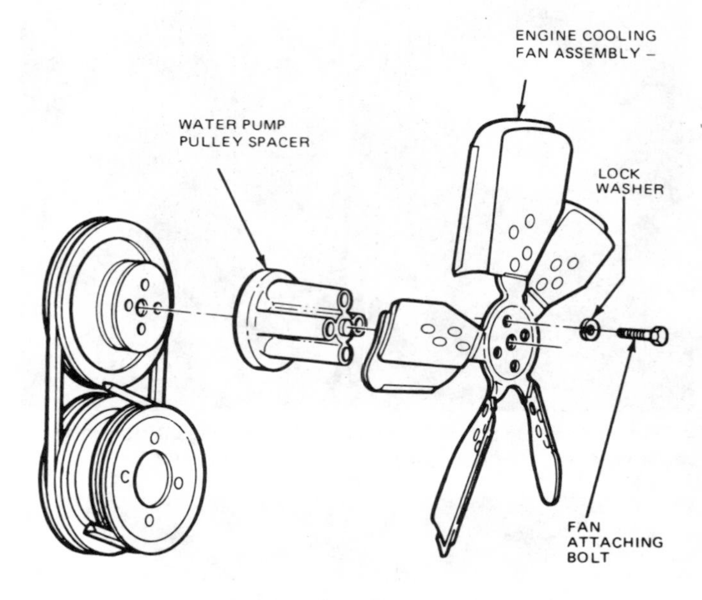

Fig. 2.6 Typical fan and components (Sec 6)

7 Cooling fan – removal and installation (except Turbo)

1 Disconnect the negative lead from the battery.
2 Remove the bolts which hold the fan shroud in place and remove the shroud.
3 Remove the bolts which hold the fan to the pulley and remove the fan (photo).
4 Installation is the reverse of the removal procedure.
5 Tighten the fan bolts in a cross pattern.
6 Tighten the fan shroud mounting bolts in a cross pattern.

8 Cooling fan – inspection (all models)

1 Carefully check each of the fan blades for signs of cracking, material separations, and breakage. Be especially watchful when checking around the root of each blade, particularly on molded nylon blades, as this is an area of great stress and is most likely to show signs of stress first.
2 If any breaks, cracks, bends, or other damage is noted, do not reinstall the same fan. If it is necessary to use the car you are working on to go to a dealer and purchase another fan, do not, under any circumstances, start the engine while the hood is open, nor should you open the hood while the engine is running. Replace the fan immediately.

9 Thermostat – removal and installation

1 All engines in this line share a common variation from normal automotive practice in that the thermostat is connected to the lower radiator hose instead of the upper and controls the flow of coolant out of the engine rather than into it. A further departure from standard practice on V8 engines is that the thermostat housing is designed to allow accurate placement of the thermostat by screwing it into the housing.
2 Park the car on a flat, level surface.

9.12 The thermostat ready for installation, with the gasket retained in place with grease or sealer

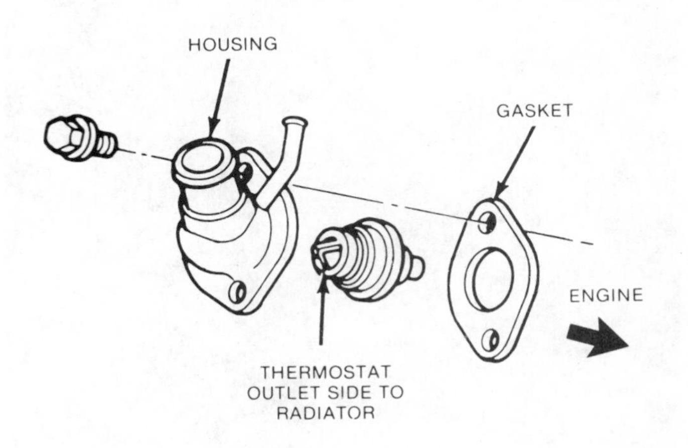

Fig. 2.7 Typical V8 thermostat installation (Sec 9)

3 Disconnect the negative lead from the battery.
4 Following the procedures in Section 2, drain about 2 quarts of coolant from the radiator.
5 Remove the two bolts which hold the thermostat housing to the engine block.
6 Carefully pull the housing from the block. There is a coating of gasket sealer whose grip must be broken. Do not insert any tools or other objects into the join between the housing and the block as damage to the sealing surfaces may result.
7 Remove the thermostat housing from the coolant hose by loosening the hose clamp and then twisting and pulling the housing from the hose at the same time. If removal is not possible in this way, follow the additional instructions provided in Section 3.
8 To remove the thermostat from the housing, hold the housing with the thermostat facing you. Turn the thermostat about $\frac{1}{4}$-turn or until the slots in the thermostat align with the tabs on the housing. Pull the thermostat toward you.
9 Check the thermostat to see if it is in the open position (piston is extended beyond the seat). If it is open dispose of it. If it is closed, perform the thermostat check outlined in Section 13, if you intend to reuse it.
10 Installation is the reverse of the removal procedure.
11 Clean all sealing surfaces with a gasket scraper or putty knife before assembling the thermostat and housing. Carefully clean all scraped material from the sealing surfaces.
12 Coat both sides of the gasket with a light coating of waterproof gasket sealer (photo).
13 Tighten both bolts evenly and allow the sealer to be squeezed flat, fill the cooling system with fresh coolant and water mixed according to the directions in Section 2.

10 Thermostat – testing

1 Remove the thermostat from its housing (Section 12).
2 Fill a pan with water and bring it to a boil.
3 Immerse the thermostat in the boiling water. The piston must raise at least $\frac{1}{8}$ in from the seat within one minute of immersion at 212°F (100°C). A greater extension is not cause for disposal, although a lesser extension will result in the thermostat needing replacement.

11 Water pump – description, removal, and installation

1 The water pump is of the impeller type and is driven by an accessory drivebelt off the oil pump. Operation of the pump is dependent upon proper drivebelt adjustment (Section 16) and proper condition of the pump. The water pump is located at the front of the engine block, just above the oil pump (photo).
2 The water pump need never be removed unless the engine block

11.1 Water pump location

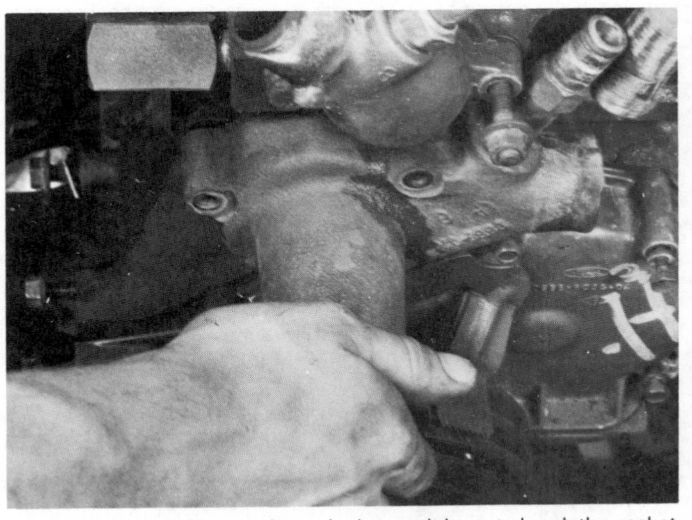
11.11 The water pump can be rocked up and down to break the gasket seal. Do not try to pry on the gasket surfaces with a screwdriver or other tool

11.14 The water pump ready for installation with the gasket retained with sealer

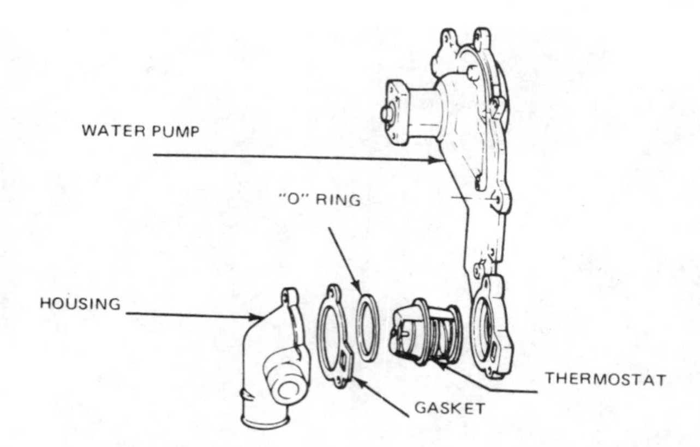

Fig. 2.8 Typical V6 water pump and thermostat installation (Secs 9 and 11)

is being stripped down for rebuilding, or if the pump itself proves defective. Signs of water pump failure include coolant leakage, noisy operation, and excess vibration of the cooling fan and driveshaft (upon which the fan is mounted and from which the impeller is driven [except Electrodrive models]). Do not confuse an out-of-balance fan with a defective water pump. Always remove the fan (Section 7) and check the radial play of the water pump shaft. This is accomplished by grasping the water pump pulley and attempting to rock the mounting shaft up and down and from side to side. If rocking is felt the problem is most likely with the water pump. Removal of the water pump is as follows:

3 Disconnect the negative lead from the battery.
4 Remove the fan and shroud (Section 7).
5 Drain the cooling system (Section 2).
6 Loosen and remove all drivebelts (Section 16).
7 On some models, one of the water pump mounting bolts is also a bracket for the alternator. Remove the nut which holds the bracket in place and move it out of your work area.
8 Remove the four bolts which hold the fan pulley to the water pump flange and remove the pulley.
9 Remove the hoses which are connected to the water pump.
10 Remove the four bolts which hold the water pump to the engine block.
11 The water pump is located by three locating pins which match up to holes in the engine block. In order to break the seal between the engine and the pump, it is necessary to rap on the water pump flange with a rubber mallet or a hammer and block of wood. Do not insert any tools or other levering devices between the engine block and the water pump in an attempt to pry them apart as damage to the sealing surfaces may result (photo).
12 Clean all sealing surfaces with a gasket removal tool or a putty knife. Do not use a razor blade as this may damage the sealing surfaces.
13 Installation is the reverse of the removal procedure.
14 Coat the water pump gasket with a thin coating of waterproof sealant before installing it on the seal surface of the water pump (photo).
15 Tighten the four water pump bolts evenly, wait about five minutes for the sealer to be pushed down, then retighten the bolts.
16 Fill the cooling system with fresh coolant when parts installation and belt adjustment is complete.

12 Water pump – rebuilding

1 Water pumps are not an item which can be rebuilt economically by the home mechanic. We suggest that you purchase a new unit or investigate the purchase of a rebuilt exchange unit from an auto parts store.

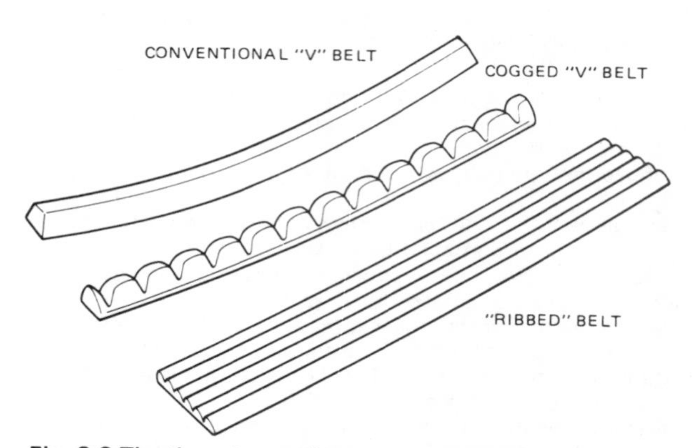

Fig. 2.9 The three types of accessory drive belts (Sec 13)

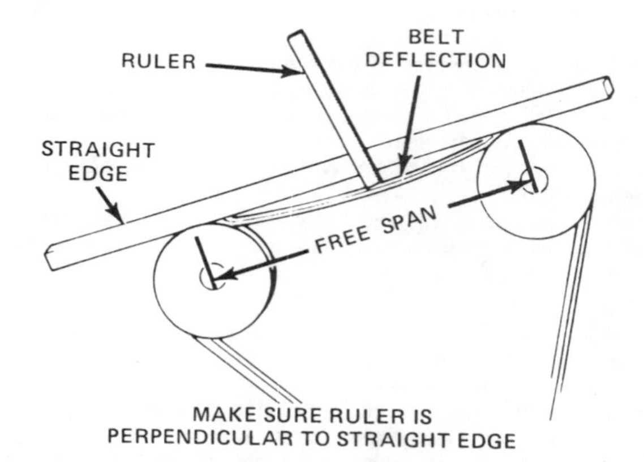

Fig. 2.10 Measuring belt deflection (Sec 13)

13 Drivebelts – description, removal and installation

1 Drivebelts are used to drive all ancillaries including the cooling fan, alternator, Thermactor pump, air conditioning pump, and power steering pump. The belts vary in size and design, according to function.
2 Belts are considered stretched after ten minutes of use and must be adjusted. Ford Motor Company and its subsidiaries do not use 'inches of belt deflection' as a means of determining belt adjustment,

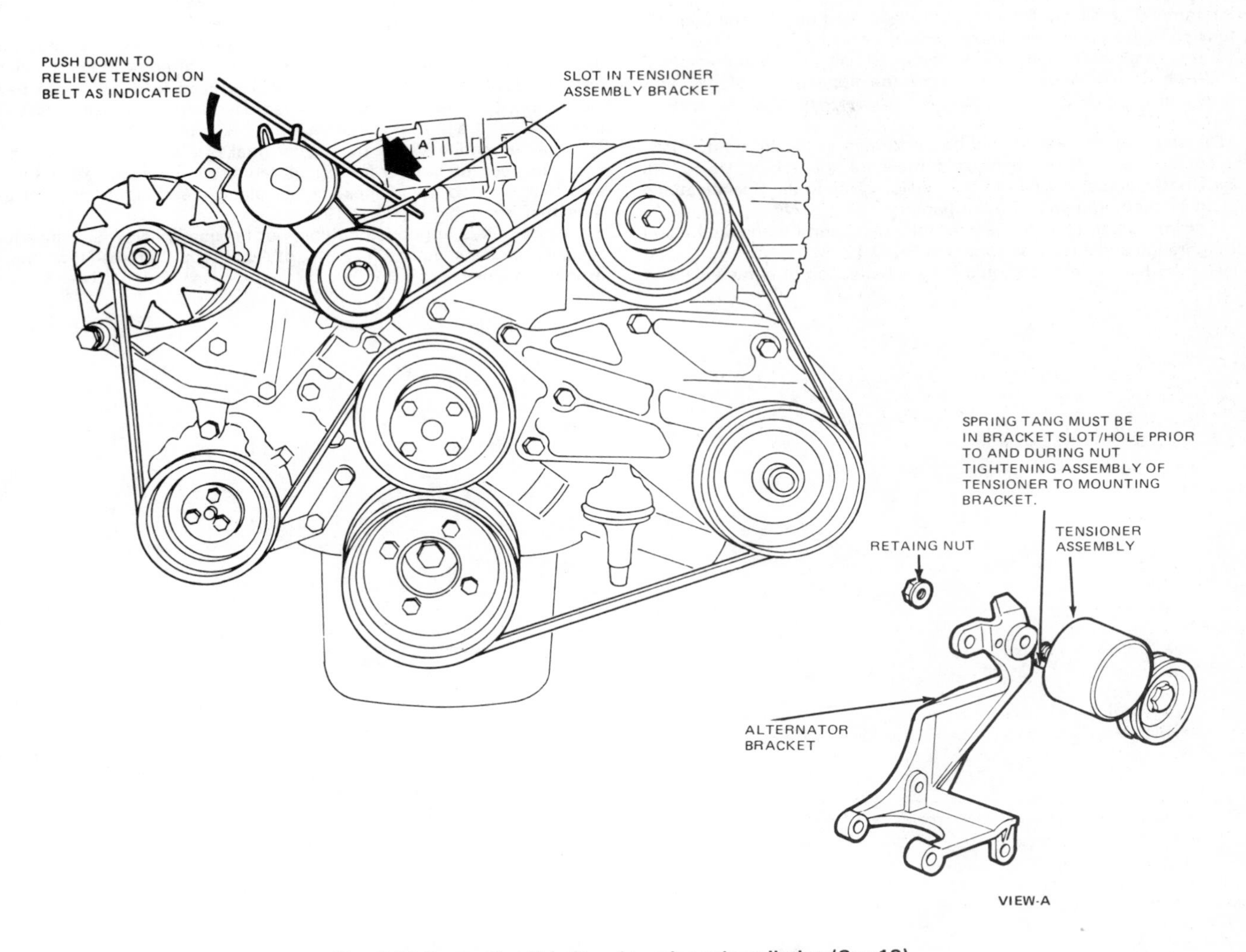

Fig. 2.11 Serpentine V-belt and tensioner installation (Sec 13)

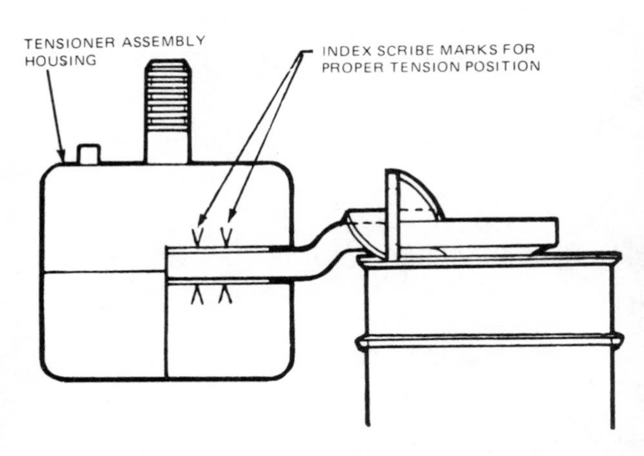

Fig. 2.12 Belt tensioner and alignment marks (Sec 13)

13.4 When adjusting drivebelts, maintain belt tension with a bar or large screwdriver while tightening the adjustment bolt

but refer to 'pounds of adjustment' This is determined by use of a tensionometer, available from an authorized Ford dealer. The 'pounds of tension' is based on the design of belt being tested.

3 Belts are of three types; V-belts, cogged belts, and V-ribbed belts. The V-ribbed belt is differentiated by the appearance of its inner surface which appears to be made up of several V-belts placed side by side.

4 Drivebelt adjustment should be performed in the following manner: Locate each of the belts and measure the width. Using the tensionmeter, adjust the belt to the tension given in the Specifications Section at the beginning of this Chapter.

5 If no tensionometer tool is available, belts can be adjusted using a straightedge and a ruler as shown in Fig. 2.10. Belts with a free span of less than twelve inches should have a deflection of between $\frac{1}{4}$ and $\frac{1}{8}$ inches (3-6 mm). The deflection of a belt with a span greater than twelve in should be between $\frac{1}{8}$ and $\frac{3}{8}$ inches (3-9.5 mm).

6 Some vehicles are equipped with ribbed serpentine V-belts and use an auto tensioner to maintain tension. A different model tensionometer (BT3386L or BT3386WK8-22) is used to check these belts because of the higher tension involved. The deflection testing method mentioned in Section 5 is not valid on these belts.

7 If a serpentine V-belt installation makes a squealing or rumbling noise, inspect the belt for fraying, glazed or burned appearance. Check also that the two index lines scribed along the circumference of the tensioner are aligned (Fig. 2.12).

8 If the belt is in good condition, but tension is below specification, replace the tensioner (Fig. 2.11) making sure that the new one is properly aligned.

Chapter 3 Fuel and exhaust systems

Refer to Chapter 13 for specifications and information related to 1981 thru 1987 models

Contents

Specifications

Fuel pump

Type	Mechanical, operated by the camshaft, diaphragm in pump provides vacuum
Static pressure	
Tested at	Normal operating temperature at curb idle, transmission in Neutral
2.8L V6	3.0 to 6.0 psi
4.2L and 5.0L V8	6.0 to 8.0 psi
Minimum volume flow	
Tested at	Same test conditions as above with smallest passage 0.220 in diameter
2.8L V6	1 US pt in 25 sec.
4.2L and 5.0L V8	1 US pt in 20 sec.

Carburetor

1979 2.8L V6 and 5.0L V8

49-state	Motorcraft 2150-2V
California	Motorcraft 2700VV-2V

1980 5.0L V8

49-state	Motorcraft 2150-2V
California	Motorcraft 7200VV-2V

1980 4.2L V8

All	Motorcraft 7200VV-2V

Engine speed setting
Refer to emission decal

Fuel tank capacity
12.5 US gal.

Filters

Fuel filter	Disposable in-line filter with paper element
Air filter	Replaceable paper element

Torque specifications

	ft-lb	Nm
Fuel pump-to-block		
2.8L V6	12 to 15	16 to 20
4.2L and 5.0L V8	19 to 27	26 to 37
All fasteners not listed, use the following torque wrench settings:		
Metric thread sizes		
M-6	6 to 9	9 to 12
M-8	14 to 21	19 to 28
M-10	28 to 40	38 to 54
M-12	50 to 71	68 to 96
M-14	80 to 140	109 to 154
Pipe thread sizes		
1/8	5 to 8	7 to 10
1/4	12 to 18	17 to 24
3/8	22 to 33	30 to 44
1/2	25 to 35	34 to 47
US thread sizes		
1/4 – 20	6 to 9	9 to 12
5/16 – 18	12 to 18	17 to 24
5/16 – 24	14 to 20	19 to 27
3/8 – 16	22 to 32	30 to 43
3/8 – 24	27 to 38	37 to 51
7/16 – 14	40 to 55	55 to 74
7/16 – 20	40 to 60	55 to 81
1/2 – 13	55 to 80	75 to 108

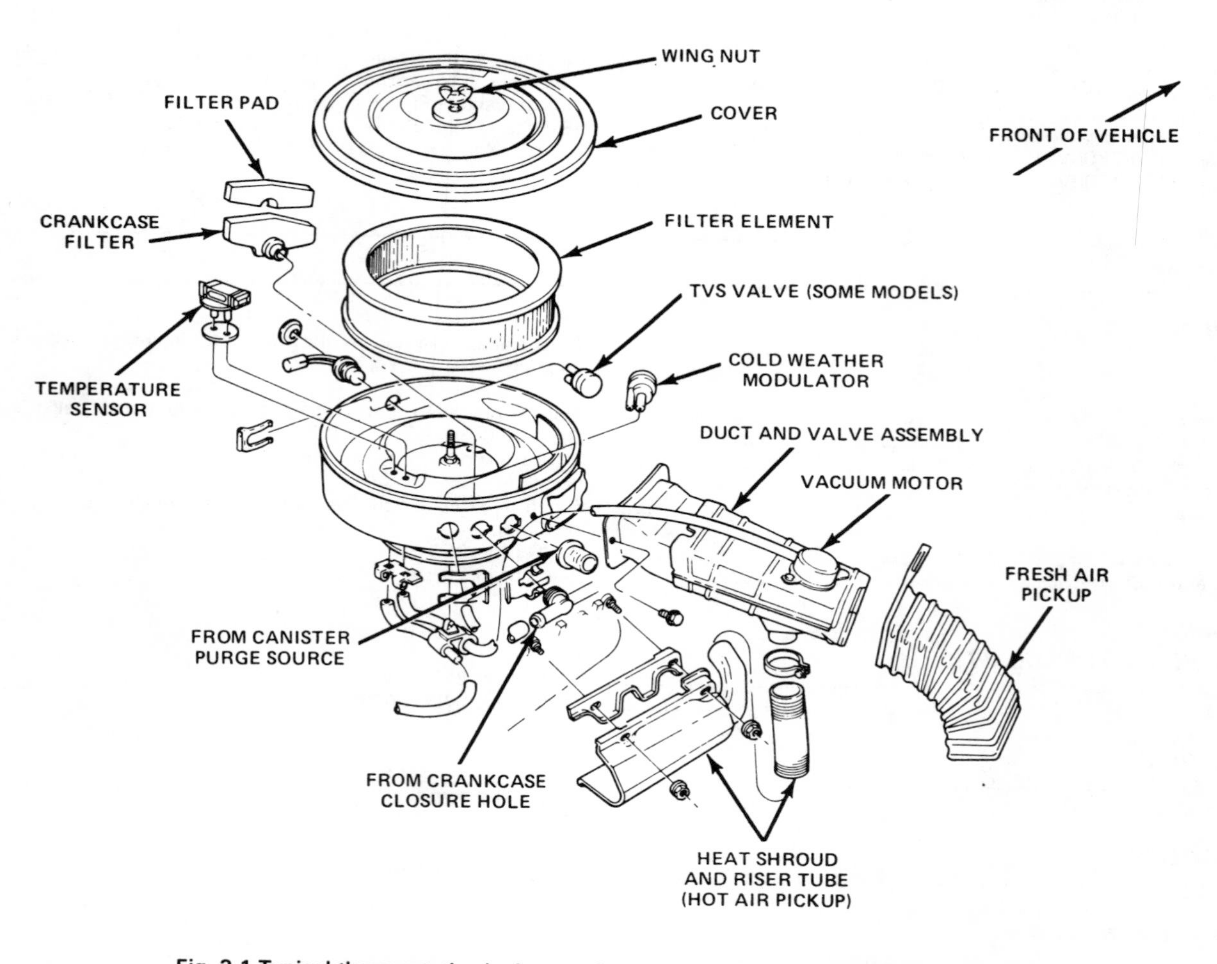

Fig. 3.1 Typical thermostatic air cleaner, duct system and elements (Secs 3, 4 and 5)

1 General information

The 2.8L V6 and 5.0L V8 engines are equipped with the Motorcraft 2150-2V carburetor in 49-state applications and the 2700VV (variable venturi) carburetor in California.

In 1980 the 4.2L V8 used the 7200VV carburetor as did some models of the 5.0L V8.

The 7200VV carburetor is basically a 2700VV with the difference that it uses a feedback central system in conjunction with an onboard electronic control computer (EEC). The EEC system is covered in Chapter 4.

All vehicles use a rear-mounted fuel tank and the fuel is drawn from the tank by means of a mechanical fuel pump actuated by the camshaft.

The exhaust systems of all vehicles incorporate a catalytic converter which requires that unleaded fuel be used.

2 U.S. Federal regulations – emission controls

The fuel system is designed so that the car will comply with all U.S.A. Federal regulations covering emission hydrocarbons and carbon monoxide. To achieve this, the ignition system must be accurately set using the proper equipment. Proper ignition timing is a must before attempting any other emission-related adjustments. The information in this Chapter is given to assist the reader to clean and/or replace certain components before taking the vehicle to the local Ford dealer or repair shop for final adjustments. Failure to do this could mean that the car will not comply with the regulations.

3 Thermostatic air cleaner and duct system – general description

The air cleaner is retained by a wingnut on a stud projecting from the top of the carburetor.

An additional feature is the control system for intake air to ensure that fuel atomization within the carburetor takes place using air at the correct temperature. This is effected by a duct system which draws in fresh air or pre-heated air from a heat shroud around the engine exhaust manifold.

Operation of the system can be summarized as follows:

When the engine is cold, heated air is directed from the exhaust manifold into the air cleaner, but as the engine warms up, cold air is progressively mixed with this warm air to maintain a carburetor air temperature of 105° to 130°F (40.5 to 76.8°C). At high ambient temperatures the hot air intake is closed off completely.

The mixing of air is regulated by a vacuum-operated motor on the air cleaner duct, which is controlled by a bi-metal temperature sensor and cold weather modulator valve.

An additional feature on cars with catalytic converters or Cold Temperature Actuated Vacuum (CATV) systems is an ambient temperature sensor mounted within the air cleaner. This switch is operated by ambient temperature changes and under certain conditions will override the cold weather modulator system.

4 Thermostatic air cleaner – testing

Vacuum motor and valve assembly

1 Check that the valve is open when the engine is switched off. Start the engine, and check that the valve closes when idling (except where the engine is hot). If this fails to happen, check for disconnected or leaking vacuum lines, and for correct operation of the bi-metal sensor (see below).

2 If the valve closes, open and close the throttle rapidly. The valve should open at temperatures above 55°F (12.7°C) during the throttle operation. If this does not happen, check the valve for binding.

Bi-metal switch

3 The bi-metal switch can be checked by subjecting it to heated air, either from the engine or from an external source (eg, a hair dryer). Do not immerse it in water or damage may occur.

Cold weather modulator valve

4 Without the use of a supply of refrigerant R-12 and a vacuum source, testing is impractical. If the modulator valve is suspected of being faulty it should be tested by your Ford dealer.

5 Air cleaner element – removal and installation

1 Remove the wing nut(s) attaching the air cleaner top plate to the air cleaner housing.

2 Remove the air cleaner top and take out the air filter element.

3 Installation is the reverse of removal.

6 Fuel pump – description

1 The 4.2L and 5.0L V8 engine fuel pump is bolted to the left side of the front cover. An eccentric bolted to the end of the camshaft operates the fuel pump actuator arm.

2 On the 2.8L V6, the fuel pump is mounted on the lower left side of the cylinder block. The pump is operated by a lobe of the camshaft by means of a pushrod.

3 Neither pump is repairable and should a fault be suspected, replacement is necessary.

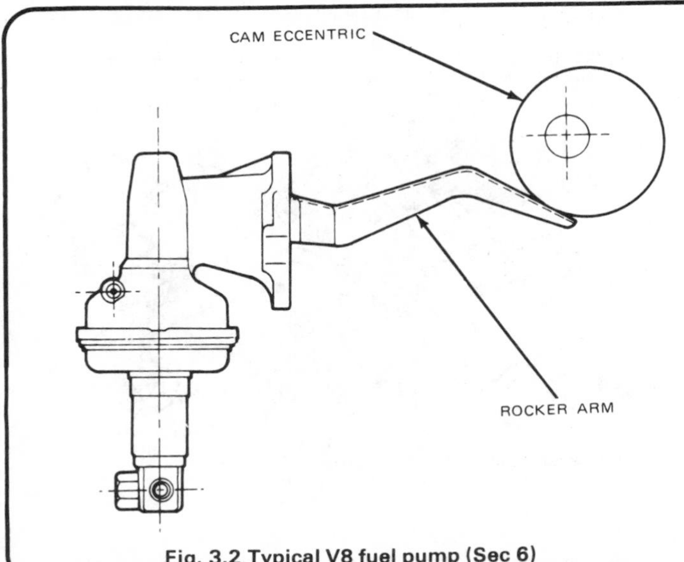

Fig. 3.2 Typical V8 fuel pump (Sec 6)

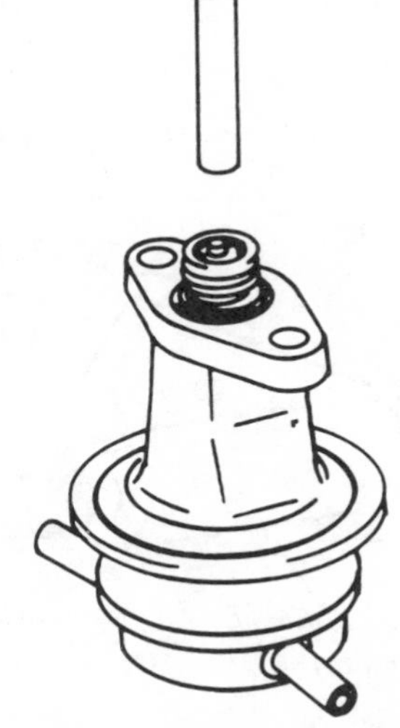

Fig. 3.3 V6 fuel pump and pushrod (Sec 6)

7 Fuel pump – removal and installation

1 Remove the inlet and outlet pipes at the pump and plug the ends to stop fuel loss or dirt finding its way into the fuel system.
2 Undo and remove two bolts and spring washers that secure the pump to the cylinder block.
3 Lift away the fuel pump and gasket.
4 Installing the fuel pump is the reverse sequence to removal but there are several additional points that should be noted:

(a) Tighten the pump securing bolts to the specified torque
(b) Before reconnecting the pipe from the fuel tank to the pump inlet, move the end to a position lower than the fuel tank so that fuel can syphon out. Quickly connect the pipe to the pump inlet
(c) Disconnect the pipe at the carburetor and turn the engine over until gasoline flows from the open end. Quickly connect the pipe to the carburetor union. This last operation will help to prime the pump
(d) On 2.8L V6 engines, make sure that the pushrod is riding on the camshaft. On V8 engines, check that the fuel pump activating arm contacts the eccentric on the front of the cam

8 Fuel pump – testing (all models)

1 Assuming that the fuel lines and unions are in good condition and that there are no leaks anywhere, check the performance of the fuel pump in the following manner. Disconnect the fuel pipe at the carburetor inlet union, and the high tension lead to the coil and, with a suitable container or large rag in position to catch the ejected fuel, turn the engine over. A good spurt of gasoline should emerge from the end of the pipe every second revolution.

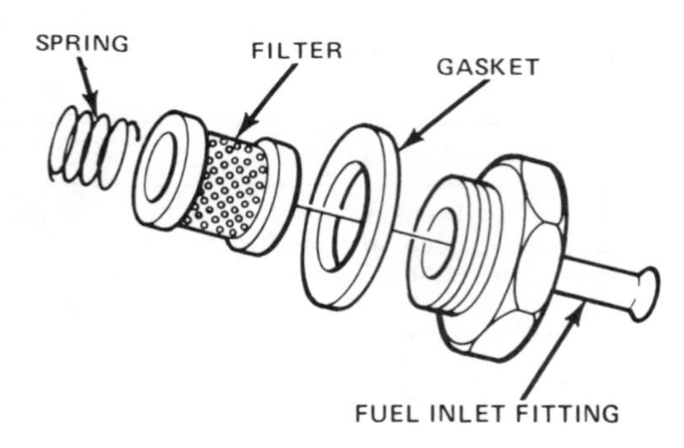

Fig. 3.4 2700VV and 7200VV fuel filter (Sec 9)

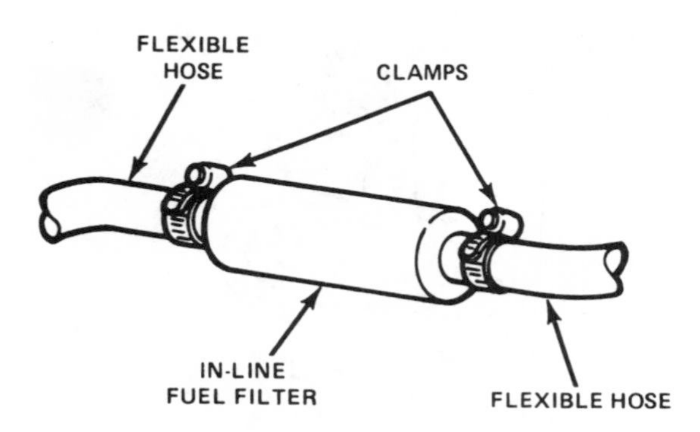

Fig. 3.5 Typical inline type fuel filter (Sec 9)

9 Fuel filter – replacement

1 Initially remove the carburetor air cleaner.
2 Loosen the fuel line clips at the filter, pull off the fuel lines and discard the clips. On later models, unscrew the filter from the carburetor.
3 Fit the replacement filter using new clips, start the engine and check for fuel leaks. **Note:** *If the replacement filter shows the direction of fuel flow, take care that it is installed in the correct direction.*
4 Install the air cleaner.

10 Carburetor (2150-2V) – general description

1 The Motorcraft 2150-2V carburetor is used on the 2.8L V6 and 5.0L V8 engines sold in all states except California.
2 The 2150-2V carburetor is comprised of two main assemblies; the main body and the air horn. The air horn assembly serves as the main body cover and contains the choke plate and fuel bowl vent valve. Also in this assembly is the pullover enrichment system which provides additional fuel flow when there is high air flow through the air horn.

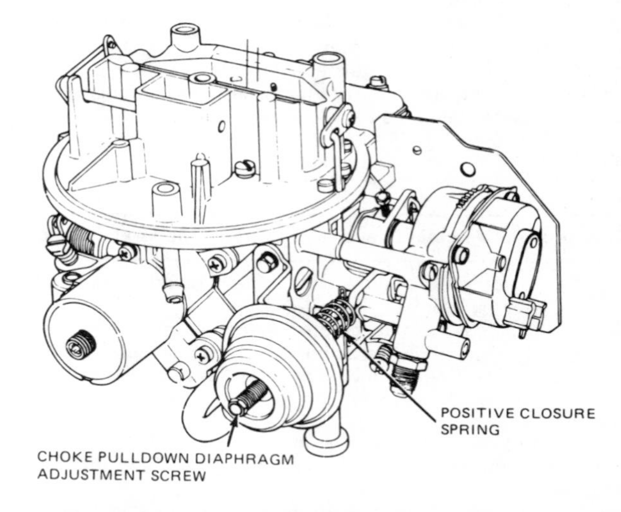

Fig. 3.6 Typical Motorcraft 2150-2V carburetor (Sec 10)

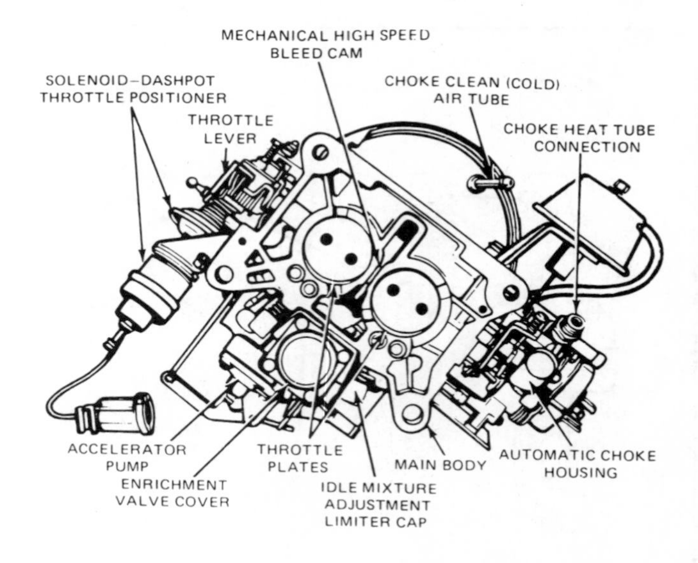

Fig. 3.7 Bottom view of 2150-2V carburetor (Sec 10)

3 Fuel is drawn from the fuel bowl into the air flow through bleeds in the metered orifice.
4 In the main body are the throttle plate, accelerator pump assembly, fuel bowl and mechanical high-speed bleed cam.
5 Some models are equipped with high altitude compensators which consist of a choke in the bypass air intake for improved high altitude cold starts.
6 On most vehicles the choke is electronically operated.

11 Choke plate vacuum pulldown (2150-2V) – adjustment

1 Run the engine until it is up to operating temperature (about 5 minutes) and then shut it off.
2 Remove the carburetor air cleaner to provide access to the carburetor.
3 Rotate the choke housing to the rich setting which will lightly close the choke plate. Rotate the housing an additional 90° (Fig. 3.9).
4 Push the choke pulldown diaphragm to the closed position.
5 Use a $\frac{1}{2}$ in drill bit shank to measure the clearance between the air horn wall and lower edge of the choke plate (Fig. 3.10).
6 To decrease the choke pulldown, turn the adjusting screw clockwise and to increase it, turn the screw counterclockwise (Fig. 3.11).
7 The fast idle cam must be adjusted after choke vacuum pulldown has been adjusted.

12 Fast idle cam (2150-2V) – adjustment

1 With the choke housing rotated to the rich position as described in Section 11, push the throttle open to set the fast idle cam.
2 Close the choke as described in step 4 of Section 11.
3 Open the throttle while watching the fast idle cam and idle speed screw. The cam should drop to the kickdown step and idle speed screw should be opposite the 'V' notch on the cam.
4 To align the fast idle speed screw with the 'V' notch, turn the hex head screw in the plastic fast idle cam lever (Fig. 3.12).
5 To de-choke after adjusting the choke vacuum pulldown fast idle cam, hold the throttle wide open.
6 Measure the clearance between the choke plate lower edge and the air horn wall as described in step 5, Section 11. To adjust the clearance, bend the metal tang on the fast idle speed lever (Fig. 3.13).
7 After all adjustments are made, reset the choke thermostat housing to the specifications on the emissions decal.

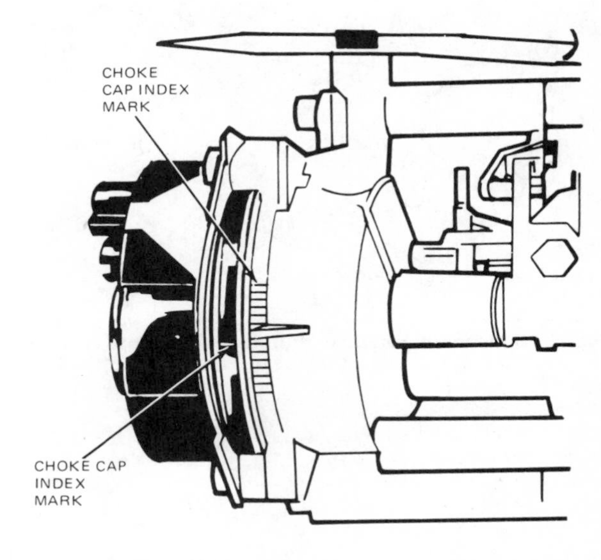

Fig. 3.8 2150 carburetor choke housing (Sec 11)

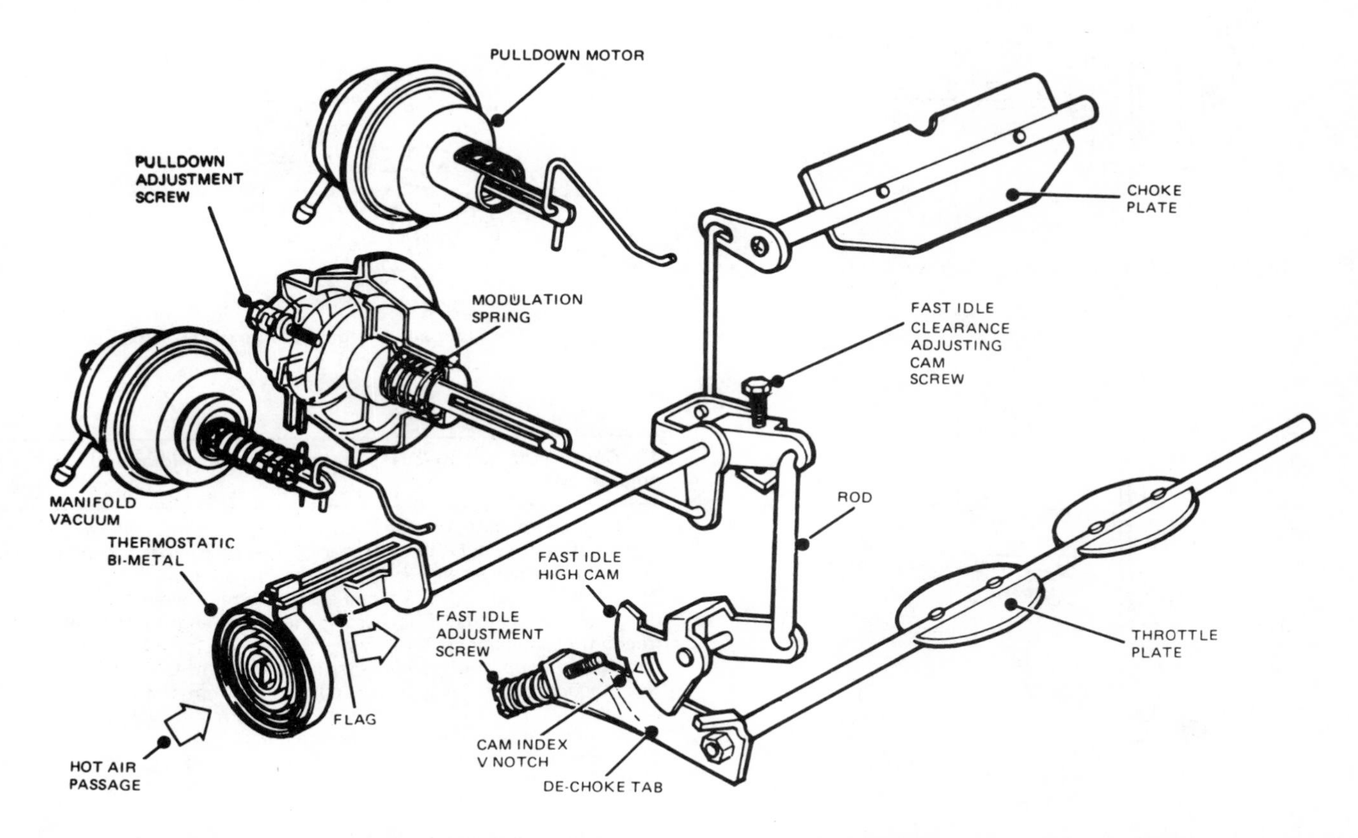

Fig. 3.9 Choke pulldown assemblies (2150-2V) (Sec 11)

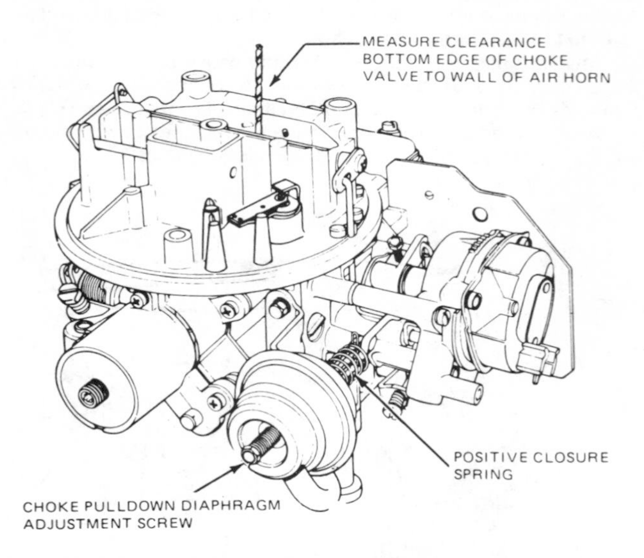

Fig. 3.10 Measuring 2150 carburetor choke plate clearance (Sec 11)

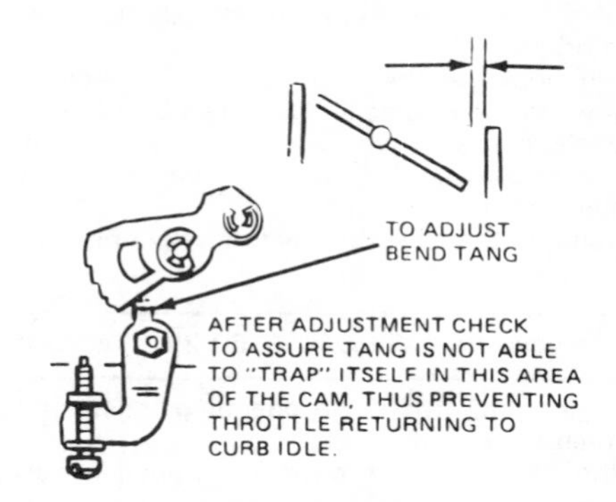

Fig. 3.13 Adjusting the fast idle speed lever tank (2150-2V) (Sec 12)

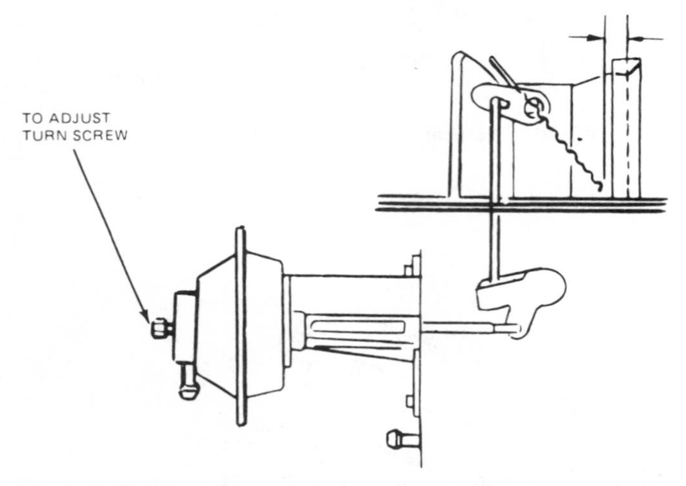

Fig. 3.11 Choke pulldown adjustment screw (2150-2V) (Sec 11)

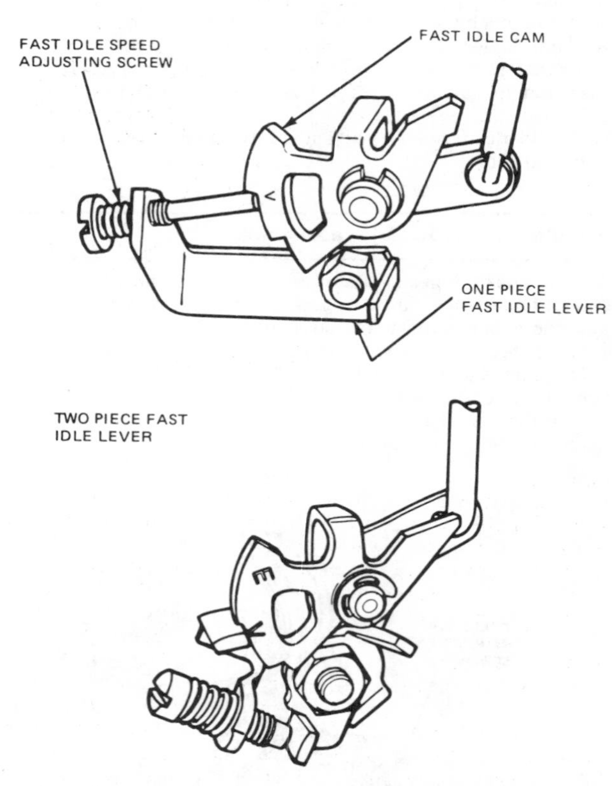

Fig. 3.14 Fast idle adjustment screws (2150-2V) (Sec 13)

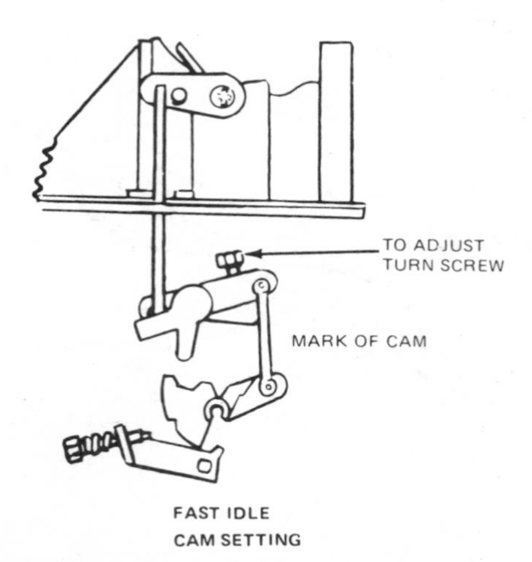

Fig. 3.12 Fast idle cam adjustment screw (2150-2V) (Sec 12)

13 Carburetor (2150-2V) – fast idle, curb idle and TSP off adjustment

1 Start the engine and run it up to operating temperature. Shut the engine off and remove the air cleaner. The air cleaner assembly must be in position when engine speeds are measured.
2 Apply the parking brake and block the rear wheels.
3 Check, and adjust if necessary, the choke and throttle linkage for freedom of movement.
4 Where applicable, turn the air conditioner to OFF.
5 Disconnect the evaporative purge line from the carburetor and plug it.
6 Connect a tachometer to the engine.
7 Disconnect the EGR vacuum hose and plug it. If the vehicle is equipped with a ported vacuum switch (PVS), do not disconnect the EGR line.
8 Disconnect the distributor vacuum hose from the advance side of the distributor and plug it.

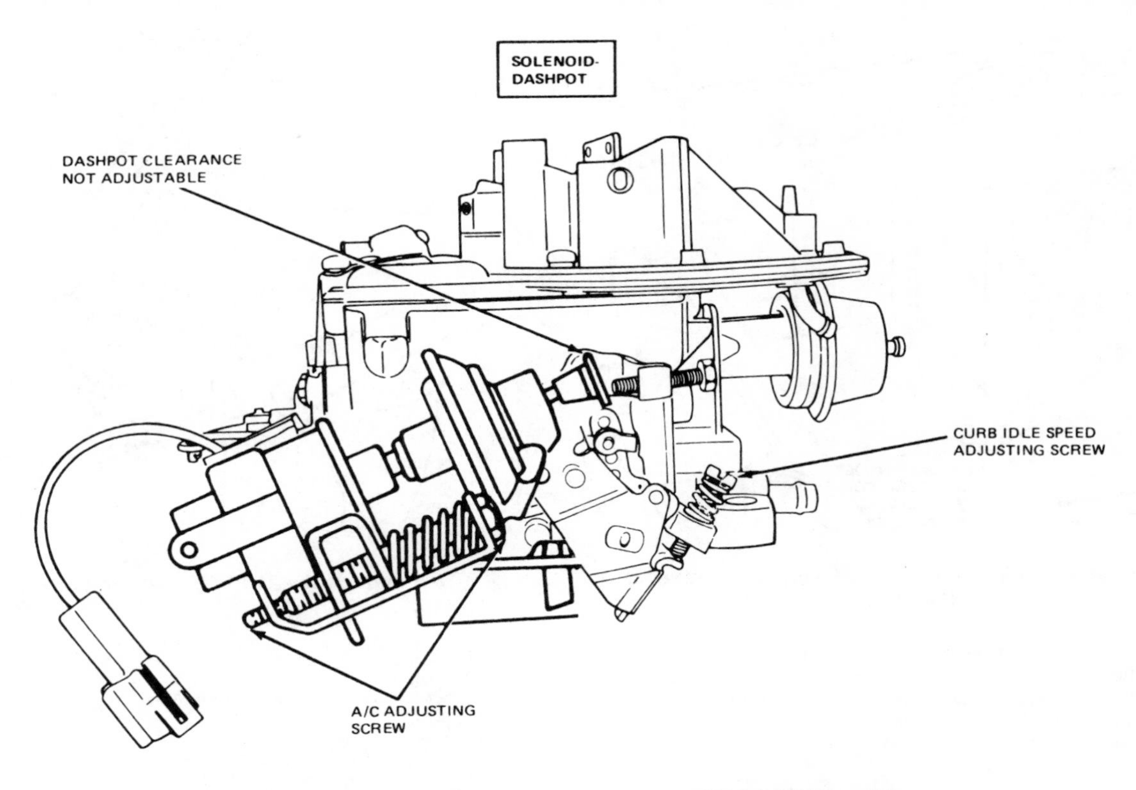

Fig. 3.15 Solenoid-dashpot throttle positioner (2150-2V) (Sec 13)

9 Follow the vacuum hose from the thermactor dump valve to the carburetor and disconnect the dump valve vacuum hose nearest the carburetor. Plug the original vacuum source and connect the dump valve directly to the manifold vacuum.
10 With the transmission in Park (automatic) or Neutral (manual) and the choke plate fully open, run the engine at 2500 rpm for 15 seconds. Place the fast idle lever on the step of the fast idle cam specified on the emissions decal. Allow the engine speed to stabilize (10 to 15 seconds) and measure the fast idle rpm.
11 Repeat this procedure three times and adjust the fast idle rpm if not specified (Fig. 3.14).
12 Before adjusting the curb idle, it is necessary to determine which of the various throttle positioners and engine speed control devices the carburetorr is equipped with (Figs. 3.15 and 3.16). Refer to Chapter 4 for a description of these devices.
13 Make all adjustments after determining the curb idle speed by following the procedure described in steps 1 through 11.
14 On vehicles without air conditioning or other solenoid devices, the curb idle is adjusted by turning the throttle screw.
15 If the carburetor is equipped with a dashpot to control the throttle closing, the dashpot plunger must be collapsed with the engine off. Check the clearance between the plunger and the throttle lever pad and adjust, if necessary, to the specifications on the emissions label. Each time the curb idle is adjusted, the dashpot clearance must also be adjusted.
16 On anti-diesel TSP-equipped vehicles, the curb idle is adjusted by collapsing the TSP plunger by forcing the throttle lever pad against the plunger. The curb idle is then adjusted by turning the throttle stop adjusting screw.
17 If equipped with air conditioning, dashpot and TSP, turn the air conditioning off and determine the curb idle rpm. Adjust to the specified air conditioning off curb idle by turning the throttle stop screw. Turn the engine off, collapse the TSP plunger and check the clearance between the plunger and throttle lever pad. To adjust, turn the long screw which is part of the assembly mounting bracket.
18 Reconnect all vacuum lines and Thermactor hoses to their proper locations and re-install the air cleaner.

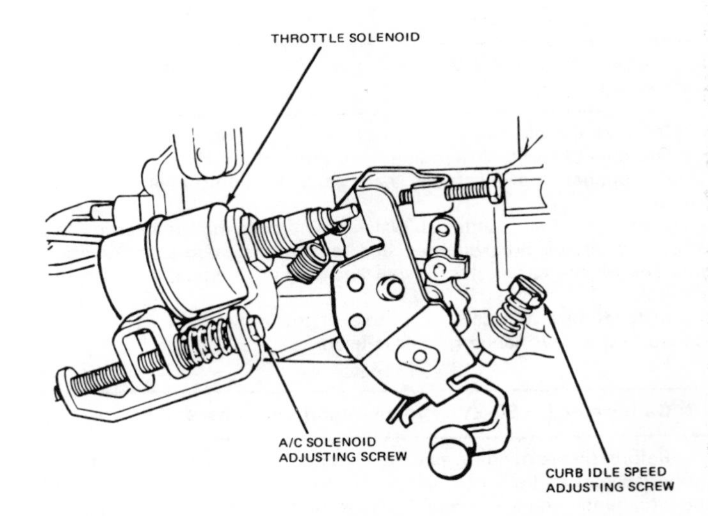

Fig. 3.16 2150-2V throttle solenoid throttle positioner (Sec 13)

14 Carburetor (2150-2V) – dry float setting

1 The dry float setting can only be checked at the appropriate stage of carburetor disassembly.
2 Remove the carburetor air horn, raise the float and seat the fuel inlet needle.
3 Remove the gasket and depress the float tab to assure seating of the fuel inlet needle while being careful not to damage the needle's Viton tip.

Fig. 3.17 Measuring dry float level with Ford gauge (2150-2V) (Sec 14)

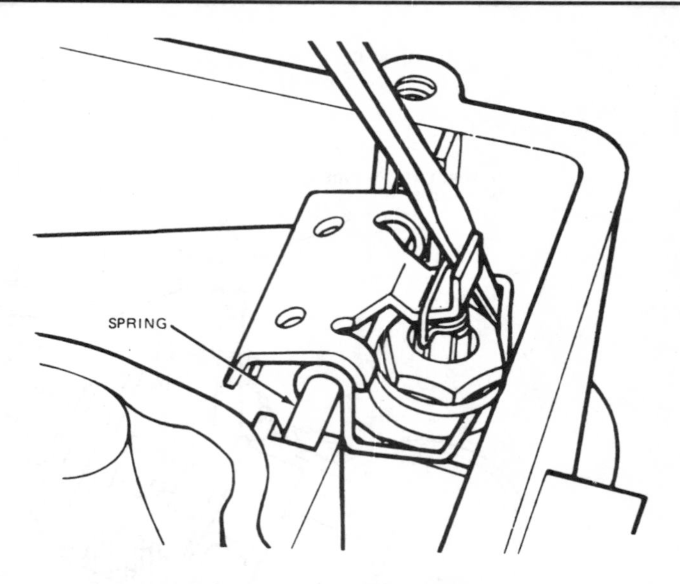

Fig. 3.18 Removing the 2150-2V float shaft retainer (Sec 17)

4 Measure from a point near the center, $\frac{1}{8}$ in (3.2 mm) from the free end of the float to the top surface of the carburetor body. This measurement must be $\frac{7}{16}$ in. Bend the tab on the float to adjust the level. Alternatively, the float level can be checked using a cardboard gauge available at your Ford dealer (Fig. 3.17).

15 Carburetor – idle mixture adjustment

Note: *Idle mixture adjustment can only be satisfactorily carried out by using special test equipment. Refer to your local dealer or repair shop for proper adjustment.*

16 Carburetor (2150, 2700VV and 7200VV) – removal and installation

1 Remove the air cleaner as described in Section 5.
2 Disconnect the fuel feed line from the carburetor.
3 Disconnect the electrical leads and vacuum lines from the carburetor.
4 Disconnect the throttle cable/kick-down cable from the carburetor.
5 Using suitable cranked wrenches, remove the carburetor mounting nuts and lift the carburetor, gasket and spacer (if equipped) from the manifold.
6 Installation is basically a reverse of the removal procedure, but ensure that a new flange gasket is used.

17 Carburetor (2150-2V) – dismantling and reassembly

1 Before dismantling, wash the exterior of the carburetor in the proper solvent and wipe off using a lint-free rag. Select a clean area of the workbench and lay several layers of newspaper on the top. Obtain several small containers to segregate the many small parts which will be removed from the carburetor.
2 Remove the air cleaner anchor screw and automatic choke control rod retainer.
3 Remove the air horn attaching screws, lockwashers, carburetor identification tag, air horn and gasket.
4 Loosen the screw securing the choke control rod to the choke shaft lever. Remove the choke control rod and slide out the plastic dust seal.
5 Remove the choke plate screws after removing the staking marks on their ends and remove the choke plate by sliding it out of the top of the air horn.
6 Remove the bypass air choke plate and screws and slide the choke shaft out of the air horn.

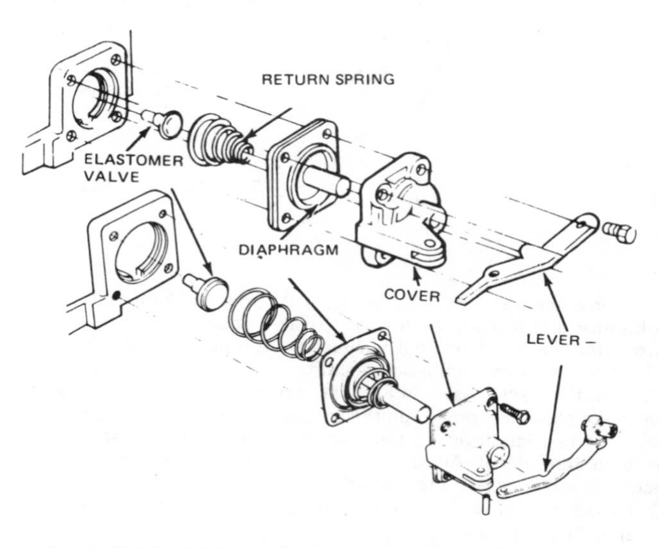

Fig. 3.19 2150-2V accelerator pump assembly (Sec 17)

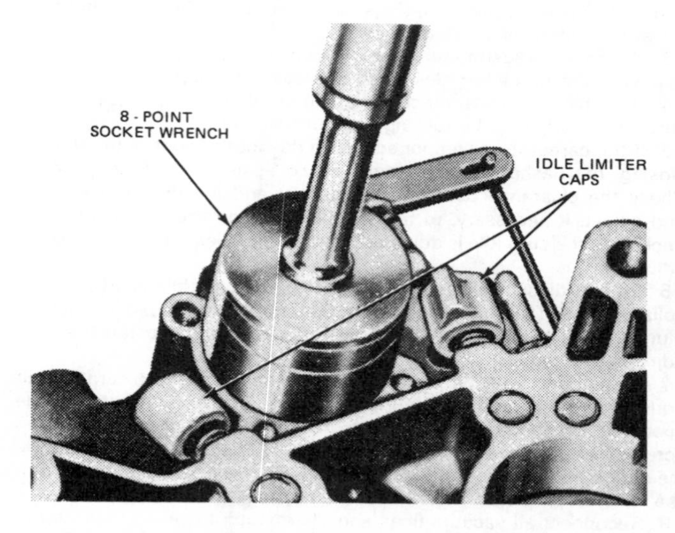

Fig. 3.20 2150-2V enrichment valve removal (Sec 17)

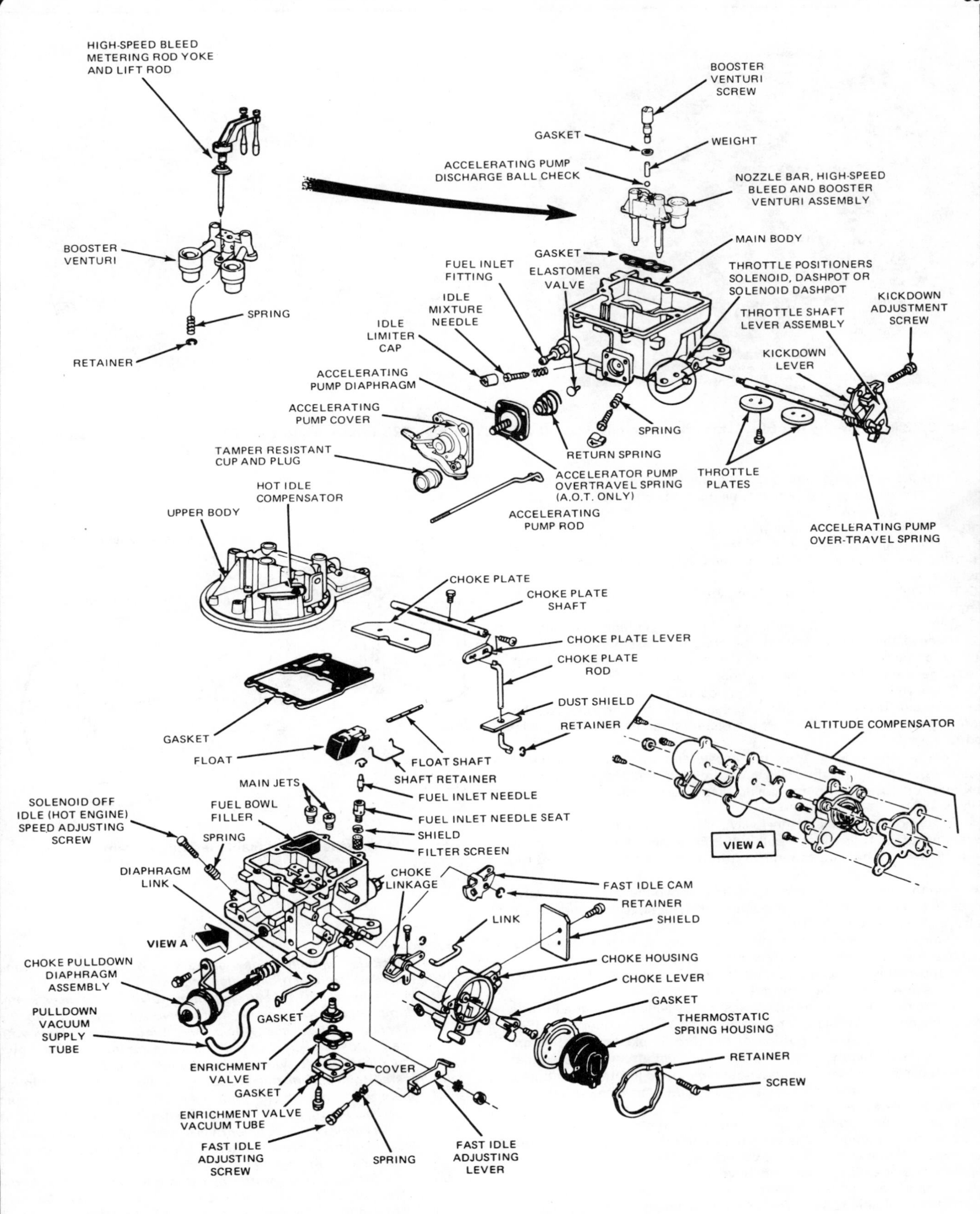

Fig. 3.21 Exploded view of Motorcraft 2150-2V carburetor (Sec 17)

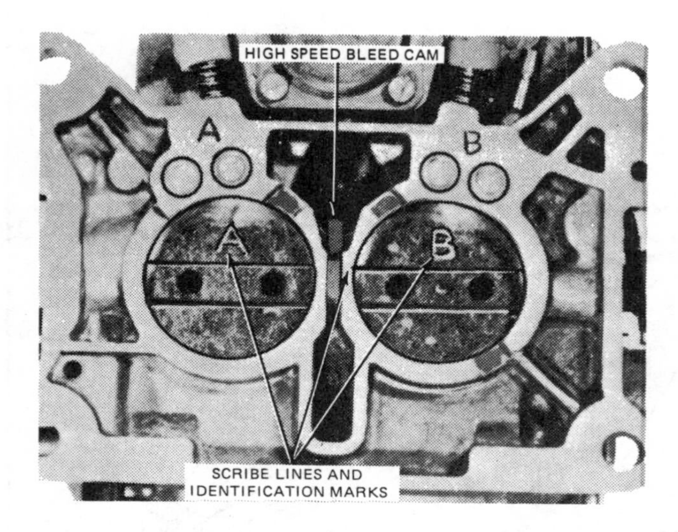

Fig. 3.22 Marking the throttle plates prior to removal (2150-2V) (Sec 17)

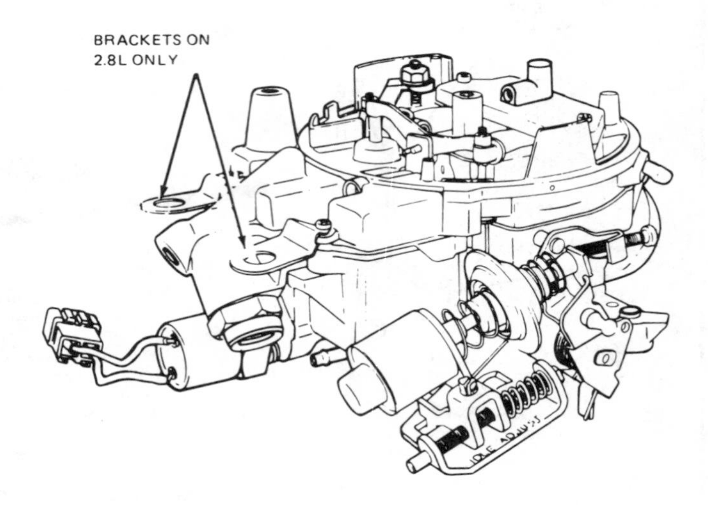

Fig. 3.23 Typical Motorcraft 2700/7200 variable venturi carburetor (Sec 18)

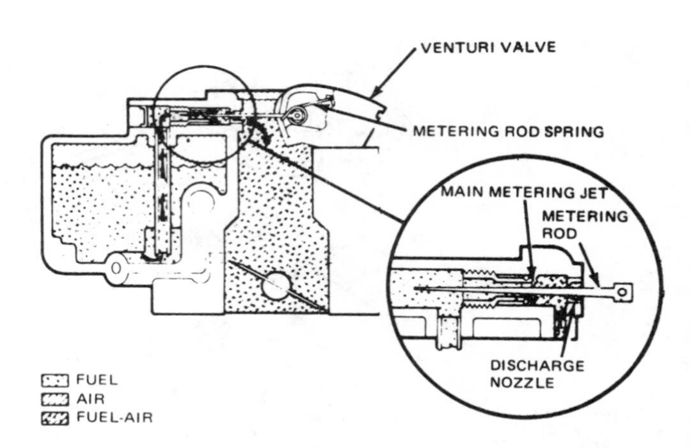

Fig. 3.24 Variable venturi main metering system (Sec 18)

7 From the automatic choke, remove the fast idle cam retainer, the thermostatic choke spring housing, clamp and retainer.

8 Remove the choke housing assembly, gasket and the fast idle cam and rod from the fast idle cam lever.

9 On the main body, use a screwdriver to pry the float shaft retainer from the fuel inlet seat (Fig. 3.18). Remove the float, float shaft and fuel inlet needle assembly.

10 Remove the retainer and float shaft from the float lever and remove the fuel filler bowl.

11 Remove the fuel inlet needle, seat filter screen and main jets.

12 Remove the booster venturi, metering rod assembly and gasket. Turn the main body upside down and let the accelerator pump, discharge weight and ball fall into your hand.

13 Disassemble the lift rod from the booster by removing the lift rod spring retaining clip and spring and separating the lift rod assembly from the booster. Do not remove the metering rod hanger from the lift rod.

14 Remove the roll pin from the accelerator pump cover, using a suitable punch. Retain the roll pin and remove the accelerator pump link and rod assembly, pump cover, diaphragm assembly and spring (Fig. 3.19).

15 To remove the elastomer valve from the accelerator pump assembly, grasp it firmly and pull it out. Examine the valve, and if the tip is broken off, be sure to remove it from the fuel bowl. Discard the valve.

16 Turn the main body upside down and remove the enrichment valve cover and gasket. Using an 8-point socket, remove the enrichment valve and gasket (Fig. 3.20).

17 Remove the idle fuel mixture adjusting screws and springs. Remove the idle screw limiter caps (Fig. 3.20).

18 Remove the fast idle adjusting lever assembly and then remove the idle screw and spring from the lever.

19 Before removing the throttle plates, lightly scribe along the throttle shaft and mark each plate for re-installation in the proper bore (Fig. 3.21). File off the staked portion of the throttle plate screws before removing them. Remove any burrs from the shaft after removal so that the shaft can be withdrawn without damage to the throttle shaft bores. Be ready to catch the mechanical high-speed cam located between the throttle plates when the shaft is removed.

20 If an altitude compensator is installed, remove the 4 screws attaching the assembly to the main body and remove the compensator assembly. Remove the 3 screws holding the aneroid valve and separate the aneroid, gasket and valve.

21 Dismantling is now complete and all parts should be thoroughly cleaned in a suitable solvent. Remove any sediment from the fuel bowl and passages, taking care not to scratch any of the passages. Remove all traces of gaskets with a suitable scraper.

22 Reassembly is basically a reversal of dismantling with attention paid to the following:

(a) Check that all holes in new gaskets are properly punched and that they are clean of foreign material

(b) When installing a new elastomer valve in the accelerator pump assembly, lubricate its tip before inserting it into the accelerator pump cavity hole. Reach into the fuel bowl with needle nosed pliers and pull the valve tip into the fuel bowl. Cut off the tip forward of the retainer shoulder

(c) Install the idle mixture adjusting screw needles by turning them with your fingers until they just contact the seat and then backing them off $1\frac{1}{2}$ turns. Do not install the limiter caps at this time. The enrichment valve cover and gasket must be installed next as the limiter stops on the cover provide a positive stop for the limiter caps

(d) After installing the throttle plates in the main body, hold the assembly up to the light. Little or no light should be seen between the throttle plates and bores. Fully tighten and stake the throttle plate screws at this time

(e) When checking the float setting, make sure that the elastomer valve in the accelerator pump does not interfere with the float

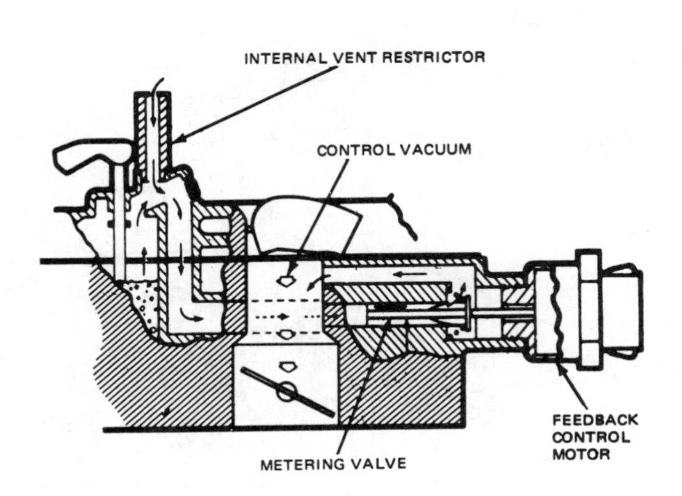

Fig. 3.25 7200VV backsuction feedback system (Sec 18)

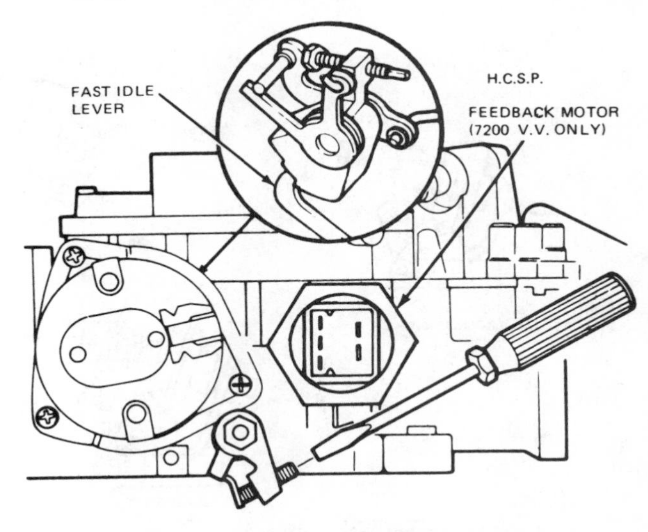

Fig. 3.26 Fast idle speed adjustment (2700/7200) (Sec 20)

18 Carburetor (2700VV-2V and 7200VV-2V) – general description

1 The Motorcraft 2700VV and 7200VV carburetors are unusual in that they don't have a fixed venturi area, the area instead varying according to load and speed.
2 The carburetor features dual venturi valves connected to two tapered main metering rods which ride in the main metering jets. The dual venturi valves are controlled by engine vacuum and the throttle position and when the venturi valve position is changed, the metering rods move along with them. This varies the fuel flow by changing the main metering jets (Fig. 3.24).
3 The speed of the air passing through the carburetor remains fairly constant with this design and maintains even fuel/air mixtures throughout the engine operating range.
4 Supplementary systems to adjust to varying air which are used in a fixed venturi carburetor are not necessary on the variable venturi design.
5 The Motorcraft 7200VV variable venturi carburetor is basically the same design as the 2700VV, the major difference being the addition of feedback control system designed to work in conjunction with an onboard electronic control system (EEC). The EEC system is described in Chapter 5.
6 The feedback system improves drivability, fuel economy and exhaust emissions by more precisely controlling the fuel/air ratio because of the continuous response to the flow of commands from the EEC system.
7 The 7200VV carburetor has no provision for vacuum adjustment as vacuum control is set at the factory.

19 Carburetor – adjustments, notes and precautions

1 When making any adjustments to the carburetor, make sure that all hoses and lines are connected to the air cleaner assembly even when the assembly is moved to clear the carburetor. The air cleaner assembly, including the filter, should be fitted for any adjustment governing engine speed.
2 Due to the interaction of emission controls and temperature changes, the engine speed may oscillate. If this is encountered, use the average engine speed.
3 Do not allow the vehicle to idle for long periods of time as overheating of the catalytic converter may result in excessive underbody temperatures.
4 Always apply the parking brake and block the wheels before making any underhood carburetor adjustments.
5 Except where otherwise noted, turn all accessories to OFF.
6 The fuel evaporative purge valve MUST be disconnected. Disconnect as follows: Trace the purge valve vacuum hose from the purge valve to the first place the vacuum hose can be disconnected from the underhood routing, eg: vacuum tee connection. Disconnect the hose and plug both the hose and the open connection.

20 Fast idle rpm (2700/7200VV) – adjustment and check

1 Connect a tachometer to the engine.
2 Disconnect the EGR hose from the valve and plug the hose.
3 With the choke off and the engine running at normal operating temperature, raise the speed of the engine to 2500 rpm for 15 seconds. Place the fast idle lever on the specified step of the fast idle cam (refer to the emission decal in the engine compartment).
4 Allow the engine speed to stabilize and measure the engine speed (rpm). Depending upon the engine and the state of tune, it may require anywhere from 15 seconds to 2 minutes for the engine speed (number of rpm) to stabilize.
5 Repeat the above step three times to ensure accuracy.
6 Adjust the fast idle screw as necessary.
7 Repeat the rpm check if an adjustment has been made.
8 Turn the engine off and reconnect the EGR hose.

21 Curb idle speed (2700/7200VV) – adjustment and check

1 Connect a tachometer to the engine.
2 Disconnect the EGR hose from the valve and plug the hose.
3 Disconnect the fuel evaporative purge hose as described in step 6, Section 19.
4 Check the engine curb idle as described in steps 1 through 5 of Section 20.
5 The method of adjustment of curb idle is determined by the type of throttle positioning device installed on the carburetor (Fig. 3.27). The adjustment procedures are as follows:

(a) 2700VV carburetors with solenoid positioners must be in Drive when the curb idle rpm is checked. The curb idle is adjusted by turning the adjustment screw in the bracket

(b) On vehicles with no solenoids or positioners, turn the throttle adjustment screw to obtain the specified curb idle rpm

(c) On dashpot equipped carburetors, adjust the curb idle with the throttle stop adjustment screw. Turn the engine off, collapse the dashpot plunger and measure the distance between the throttle lever pad and adjust to specifications if necessary. Start the engine and check the curb idle, repeating the procedure until the proper curb idle is obtained

(d) On 7200VV carburetors equipped with vacuum-operated throttle modulator (VOTM), turn the throttle stop screw counterclockwise and recheck. If the curb idle rpm is below

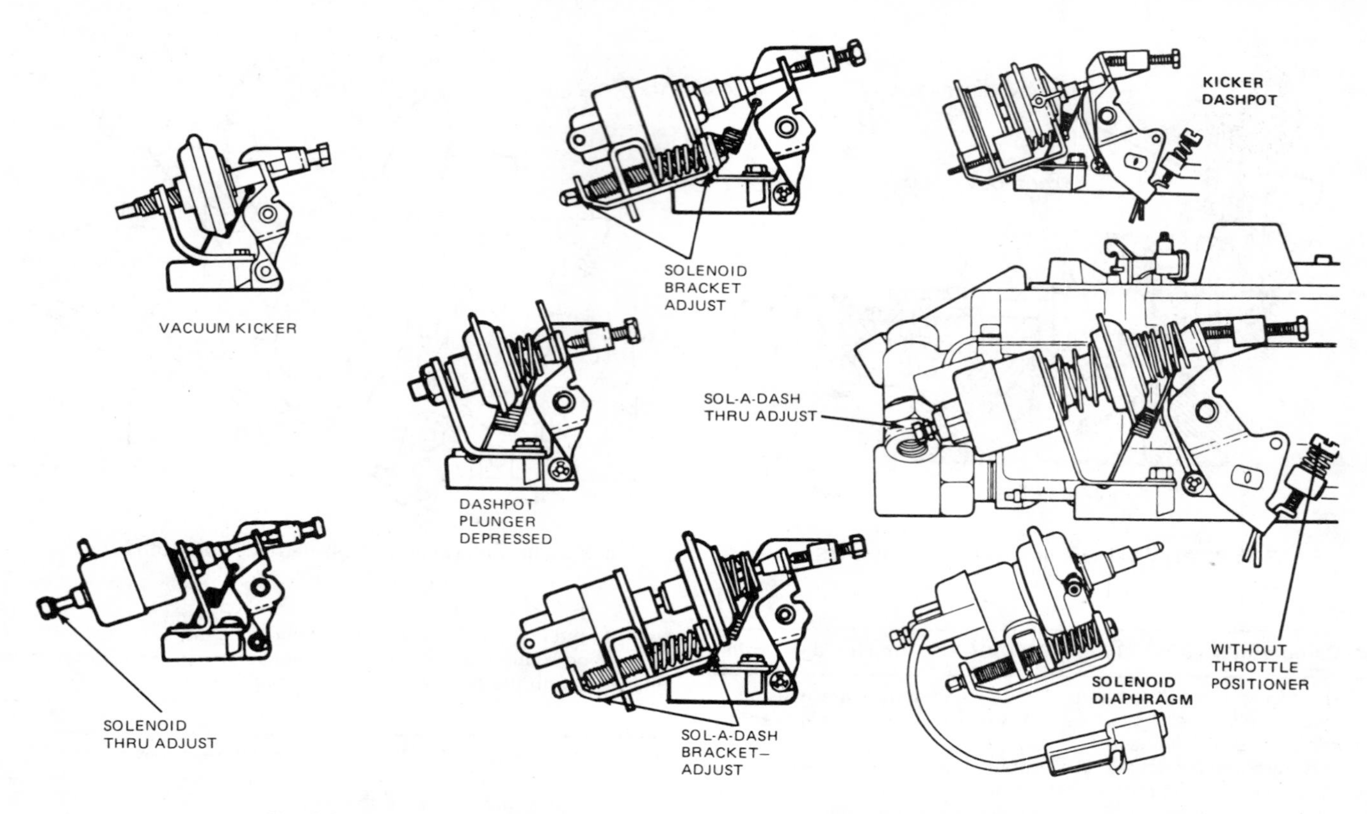

Fig. 3.27 The various types of throttle positioners on 2700/7200 carburetors (Sec 21)

specifications, shut off the engine and turn the throttle stop screw a full turn clockwise. Start the engine and recheck the curb idle, repeating the procedure until the idle is within specifications

22 Accelerator pump lever lash (2700VV and 7200VV) – checking and adjustment

1 Each time the curb idle is adjusted, the accelerator pump lever lash must be checked and if necessary, adjusted.
2 After setting curb idle adjustment as described in Section 21, take up the accelerator pump clearance by pushing down on the nylon nut on the top of the pump.
3 Use a feeler gauge to check the clearance between the accelerator pump stem and lever (Fig. 3.28).
4 Turn the nylon nut on the accelerator pump clockwise until the clearance is between 0.010 and 0.020 in.
5 To set the accelerator lever lash preload, turn the accelerator pump rod counterclockwise one turn.

23 Choke cap (2700/7200VV) – removal and installation

1 The choke cap on 2700/7200VV carburetors is held in place by 3 screws or in the case of California vehicles, 3 rivets.
2 To remove the choke cap, remove the 3 screws and lift the cap and gasket away from the carburetor. On California vehicles, the 2 top rivets are removed by drilling them out. The bottom rivet is located in a blind hole and must be tapped out, using a suitable punch and hammer. The choke cap, gasket and retainer can then be removed from the carburetor.
3 Re-installation is a reverse of removal on choke caps retained with screws. California vehicles require the use of a suitable rivet gun and three $\frac{1}{4}$ in by $\frac{1}{2}$ in rivets. It may be necessary to remove the carburetor when installing the rivets.

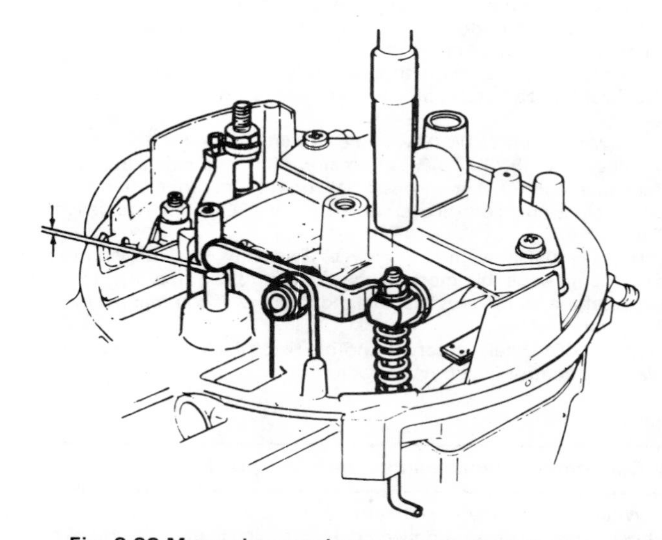

Fig. 3.28 Measuring accelerator pump stem clearance (2700/7200) (Sec 22)

24 Cold enrichment rod, control vacuum regulator (CVR) and choke control diaphragm (2700/7200VV) – adjustment

1 Remove the choke cap as described in Section 23.
2 Remove the choke pulldown diaphragm and spring.
3 Install a choke weight on the choke bimetal lever, Ford part T77L-9848-A or equivalent. Place the fast idle pick-up lever on the first highest step of the fast idle cam.

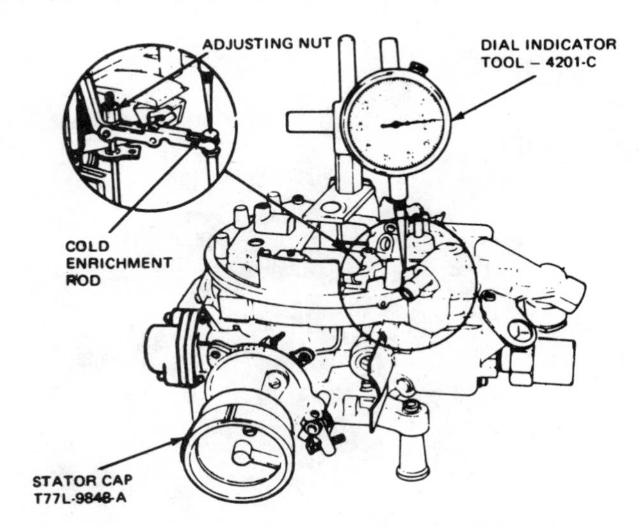

Fig. 3.29 Cold enrichment metering rod adjustment (2700/7200) (Sec 24)

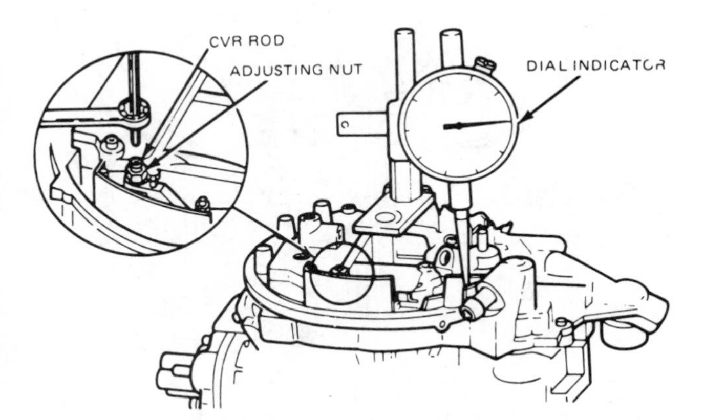

Fig. 3.30 Control vacuum regulator (CVR) adjustment (2700/7200) (Sec 24)

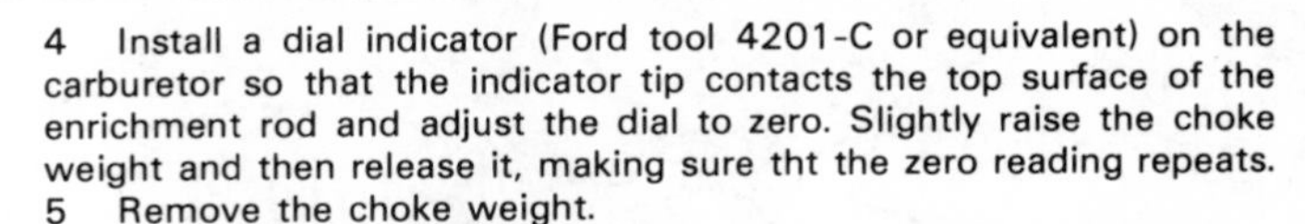

4 Install a dial indicator (Ford tool 4201-C or equivalent) on the carburetor so that the indicator tip contacts the top surface of the enrichment rod and adjust the dial to zero. Slightly raise the choke weight and then release it, making sure tht the zero reading repeats.
5 Remove the choke weight.
6 After installing the stator cap at the index position, the dial indicator should read to specification. If it doesn't, adjust the rod height by turning the adjusting nut clockwise to increase height and counterclockwise to decrease it (Fig. 3.29).
7 To check the setting, repeat steps 3 through 6.
8 To adjust the control vacuum regulator (CVR), remove the stator cap and leave the dial indicator installed but not reset to zero.
9 Set the fast idle on the highest step.
10 Press the CVR rod down until it bottoms in its seat and read the travel on the dial indicator.
11 If adjustment is necessary, place a $\frac{3}{8}$ in box wrench on the CVR adjusting nut to prevent it from turning (Fig. 3.30).
12 Using a $\frac{3}{32}$ in Allen wrench, turn the CVR rod counterclockwise to increase its travel or clockwise to decrease it.
13 With the stator cap removed and dial indicator still installed but not reset to zero, seat the choke diaphragm assembly in the direction of the fast idle cam.
14 If the dial indicator reading is not within specification, turn the choke diaphragm clockwise to decrease or counterclockwise to increase the height (Fig. 3.31).
15 The cold idle enrichment rod height must be checked after each adjustment of the CVR and choke control diaphragm.

25 Fast idle cam (2700/7200VV) – adjustment

1 Remove the choke cap as described in Section 23.
2 Counting the highest step as the first, install the fast idle lever in the corner of the step specified on the emissions label.
3 Install the stator cap and rotate it clockwise until the lever contacts the adjusting screw.
4 Line up the index mark on the stator cap with the specified mark on the choke casing by turning the fast idle cam adjusting screw. This screw may be hard to turn as it was coated with Loc-Tite at the time of manufacture.
5 Remove the stator cap and re-install the choke cap to the setting specified on the emissions label.

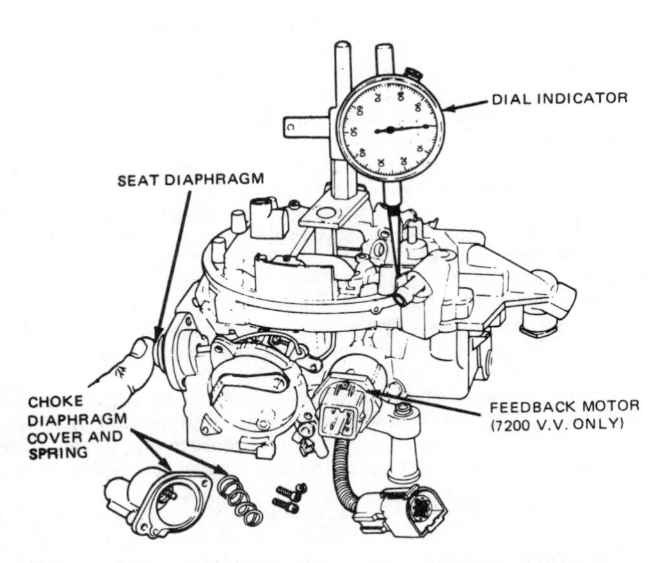

Fig. 3.31 Choke diaphragm adjustment (2700/7200) (Sec 24)

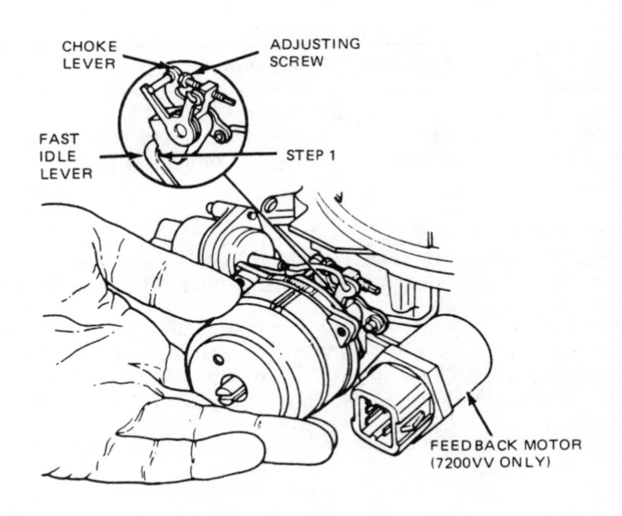

Fig. 3.32 Fast idle cam setting (2700/7200) (Sec 25)

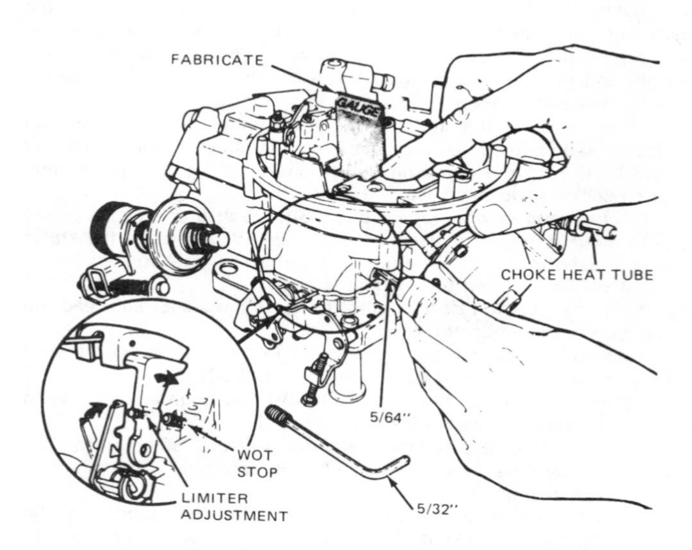

Fig. 3.33 Venturi valve limiter adjustment (2700/7200) (Sec 26)

Fig. 3.34 Removing the cold enrichment and CVR assembly (2700/7200) (Sec 27)

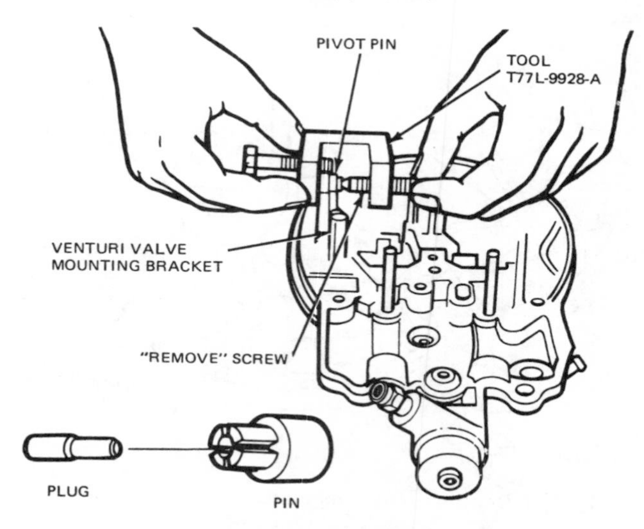

Fig. 3.35 Pressing out the tapered plugs (2700/7200) (Sec 27)

26 Venturi valve limiter (2700/7200VV) – adjustment

1 Remove the carburetor.
2 Remove the venturi valve cover, gasket and roller bearings.
3 Using a suitable punch, remove the expansion plug at the rear of the main body on the throttle side.
4 Remove the venturi valve limiter screw assembly, using a $\frac{5}{32}$ in Allen wrench (Fig. 3.33) and block the throttle plates open.
5 Lightly close the venturi valve and check the gap between the valve and the air horn wall. Adjust if necessary.
6 Move the venturi valve to the wide open position and insert an Allen wrench into the stop screw hole. To adjust the gap, turn the limiter adjusting screw counterclockwise to decrease the clearance and clockwise to increase it.
7 Remove the Allen wrench, lightly close the valve and re-check the gap.
8 Re-install the venturi valve limiter stop screw and turn it clockwise until it contacts the valve.
9 Open the venturi valve all the way and check the gap between the valve and the air horn. Adjust the stop screw to specification if necessary.
10 After installing a new expansion plug, re-install the venturi valve cover, gasket and bearing and re-install the carburetor.

27 Carburetor (2700/7200VV) – disassembly

1 Remove the carburetor as described in Section 16.
2 Place the carburetor on a clean working surface and obtain a variety of small containers for collecting and separating parts as they are removed.

Upper Body (refer to Fig. 3.34)

3 Remove the fuel inlet fitting (1), filter (2), gasket (3) and spring (4). Remove the E-rings on the accelerator pump rod and remove the rods (5, 6 and 7).
4 Remove the air cleaner stud (not shown) from the carburetor body.
5 Remove the 7 screws holding the upper body in place and remove the upper body. Mark the 2 long screws (8) for re-installation in their original location. Place the upper body upside down in a clean work area.
6 Remove the float hinge pin (10), float assembly (11) and gasket (12).
7 Remove the accelerator pump link retaining screw and nut (17 and 17A), adjusting nut and pump link (20 and 18). Remove the accelerator pump overtravel spring (6A), E-clip (6C) and washer (6B).
8 Remove the accelerator pump rod (6) and dust seal (16).
9 Remove the choke control rod (7) and carefully lift the retainer and slide the dust seal (16) out.
10 Remove the choke hinge pin E-ring (5) and slide the pin (21) out of the casting.
11 Remove the cold enrichment rod adjusting nut (22), lever (23), adjusting swivel control vacuum regulator (24) and adjusting nut (25) as an assembly as shown in Fig. 3.35. Slide the cold enrichment rod (26) out of the upper body.
12 Remove the 2 screws securing the venturi valve cover (27 and 28). Hold the cover in place as your turn the carburetor over and remove the cover, gasket (29) and bearings (30).
13 Press out the tapered plugs (32) from the venturi valve pivotal pins using Ford tool T77P-9928-A or equivalent (Fig. 3.36).
14 Push the venturi plugs (31) out as you slide the venturi valve (32) to the rear and clear of the casting. Remove the venturi valve pivot pin bushings (34).
15 Remove the metering rod pins (35) from the outboard sides of the venturi valve, the metering rods (36) and the springs (37). Mark the rods 'throttle' and 'choke' for ease of proper reassembly. Make sure to always block the venturi valve wide open whenever working on the jets.
16 Remove the cap plugs (38) recessed into the upper body casting using Ford tool T77L-9533-B or equivalent as shown in Fig. 3.37.
17 The main jet setting is crucial to the carburetors overall calibration so *the following sequence must be strictly adhered to:*

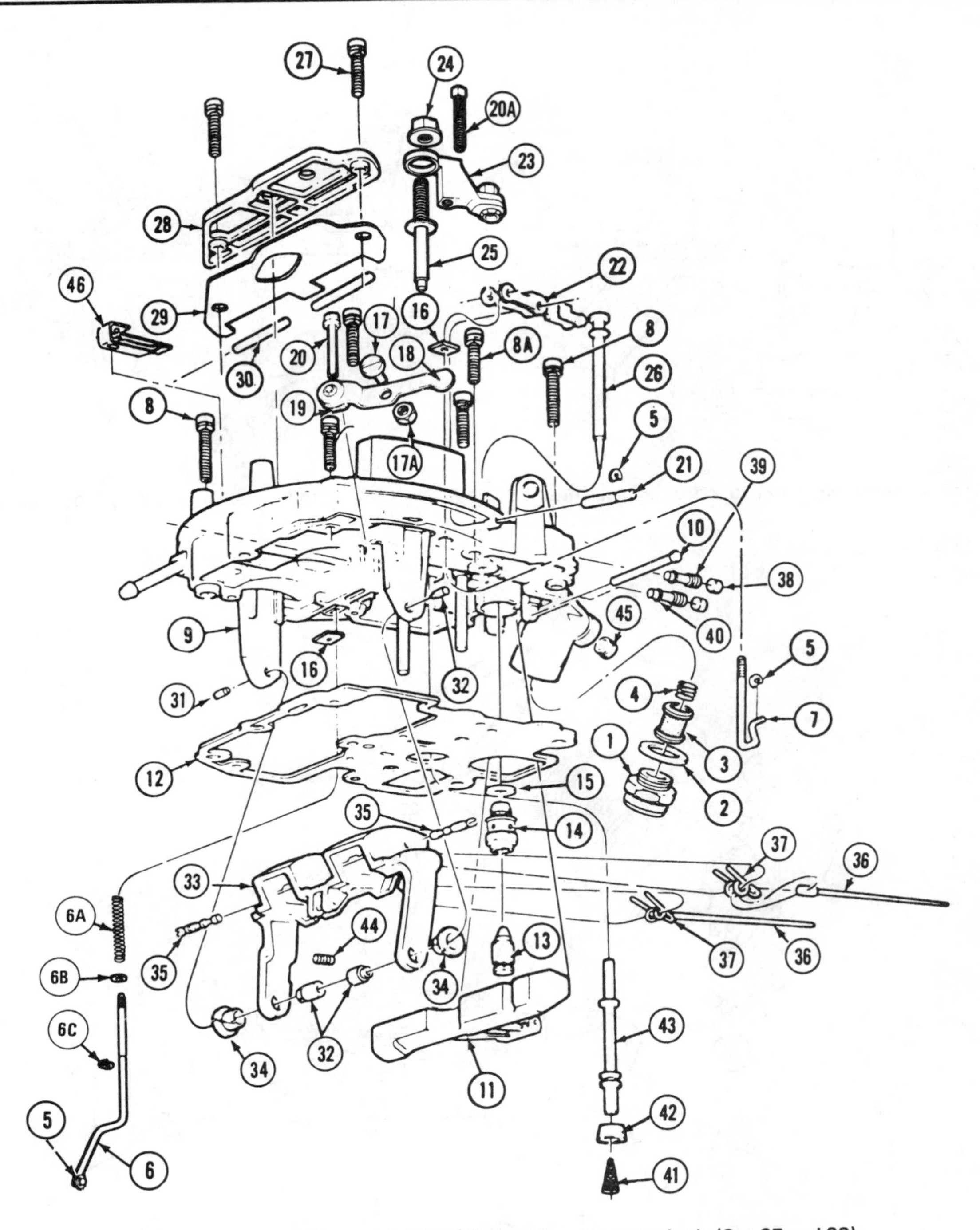

Fig. 3.36 Exploded view of the Motorcraft 2700/7200 carburetor upper body (Sec 27 and 28)

1 *Fuel inlet fitting*
2 *Fuel inlet fitting gasket*
3 *Fuel filter*
4 *Fuel filter spring*
5 *$\frac{1}{8}$ retaining E-ring*
6 *Accelerator pump rod*
6A *Spring-overtravel*
6B *Washer*
6C *Clip*
7 *Choke control rod*
8 *Screw (2) 8.32 x .88*
8A *Screw (5) 8.32 x .75*
9 *Upper body*
10 *Float hinge pin*
11 *Float assembly*
12 *Float bowl gasket*
13 *Fuel inlet valve*
14 *Fuel inlet seat*
15 *Fuel inlet seat gasket*
16 *Dust seal*
17 *Screw*
17A *Nut*
18 *Accelerator pump link and swivel assembly*
19 *Accelerator pump swivel (part of 18)*
20 *Nut – nylon adjusting*
20A *Choke travel stop adjusting screw*
21 *Choke hinge pin*
22 *Cold enrichment rod lever*
23 *Cold enrichment rod swivel*
24 *Control vacuum regulator adjusting nut*
25 *Control vacuum regulator*
26 *Cold enrichment rod*
27 *Screw (2) 8.32 x .75*
28 *Venturi valve cover plate*
28A *Plug*
29 *Gasket*
30 *Roller bearing*
31 *Venturi valve pivot plug*
32 *Venturi valve pivot pin*
33 *Venturi valve*
34 *Venturi valve pivot pin bushing*
35 *Metering rod pivot pin*
36 *Metering rod*
37 *Metering rod spring*
38 *Cup plug*
39 *Main metering jet assembly*
40 *"O" ring*
41 *Accelerator pump return spring*
42 *Accelerator pump cup*
43 *Accelerator pump plunger*
44 *Venturi valve limiter adjusting screw*
45 *Pipe plug*
46 *Hot idle compensator*

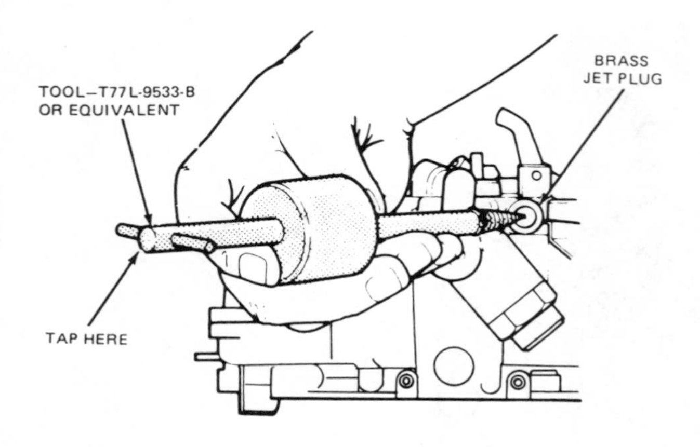

Fig. 3.37 Removing the 2700/7200 cap plugs (Sec 27)

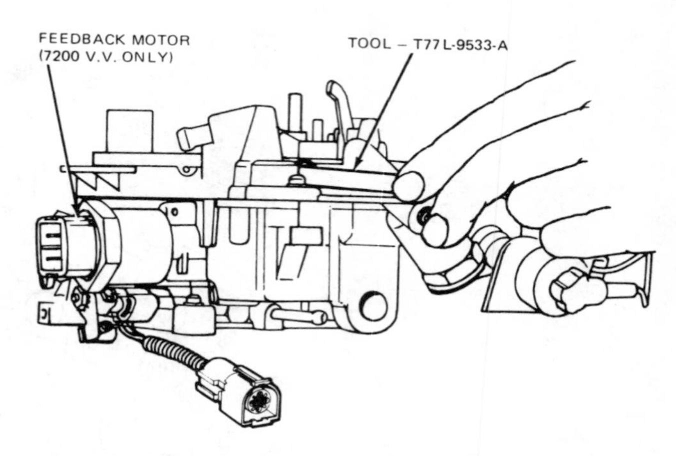

Fig. 3.38 Removing the 2700/7200 main jets (Sec 27)

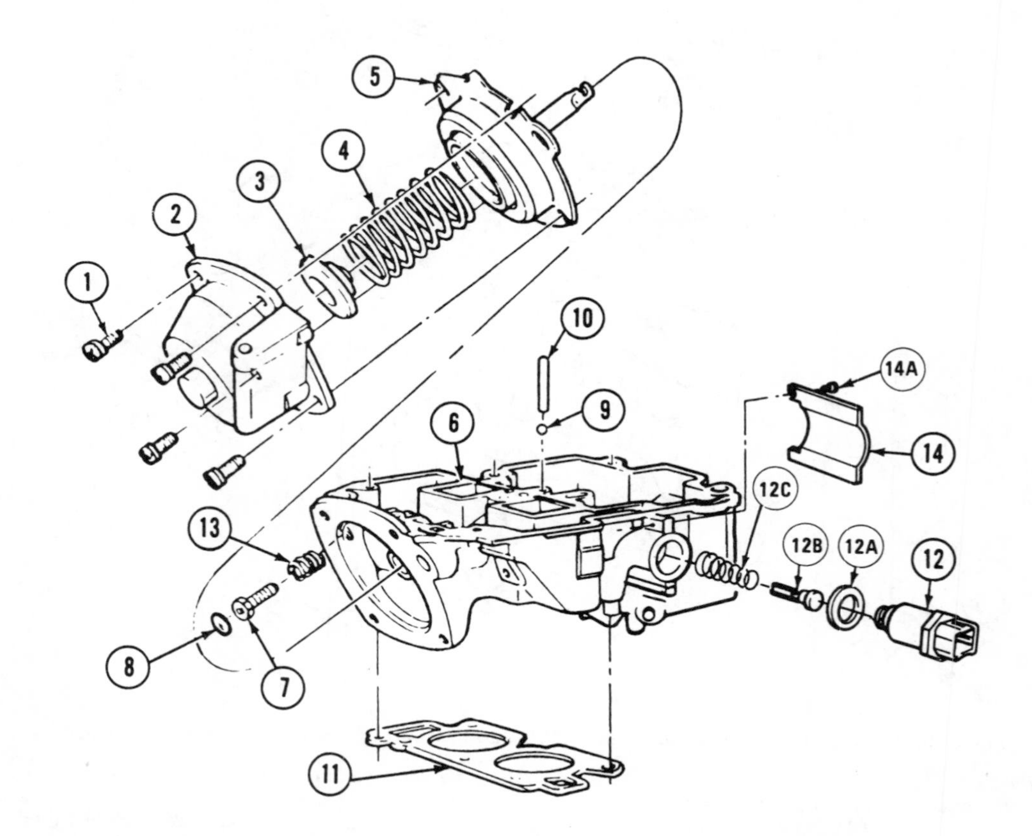

Fig. 3.39 2700/7200 carburetor main body (Secs 27 and 28)

1 *Screw (4) 8.32 x .56*
2 *Venturi valve diaphragm cover*
3 *Venturi valve diaphragm spring guide*
4 *Venturi valve diaphragm spring*
5 *Venturi valve diaphragm assembly*
6 *Main body*
7 *Venturi valve limiter stop screw and torque retention spring*
8 *Plug expansion*
9 *Accelerator pump check ball*
10 *Accelerator pump check ball weight*
11 *Throttle body gasket*
12 *Feedback stepper motor 7200VV only*
12A *Gasket – 7200VV only*
12B *Pintle valve – 7200 only*
12C *Pintle spring*
13 *Torque retention spring*
14 *Choke heat shield 2700VV only*
14A *Screw 6-32 x .38*

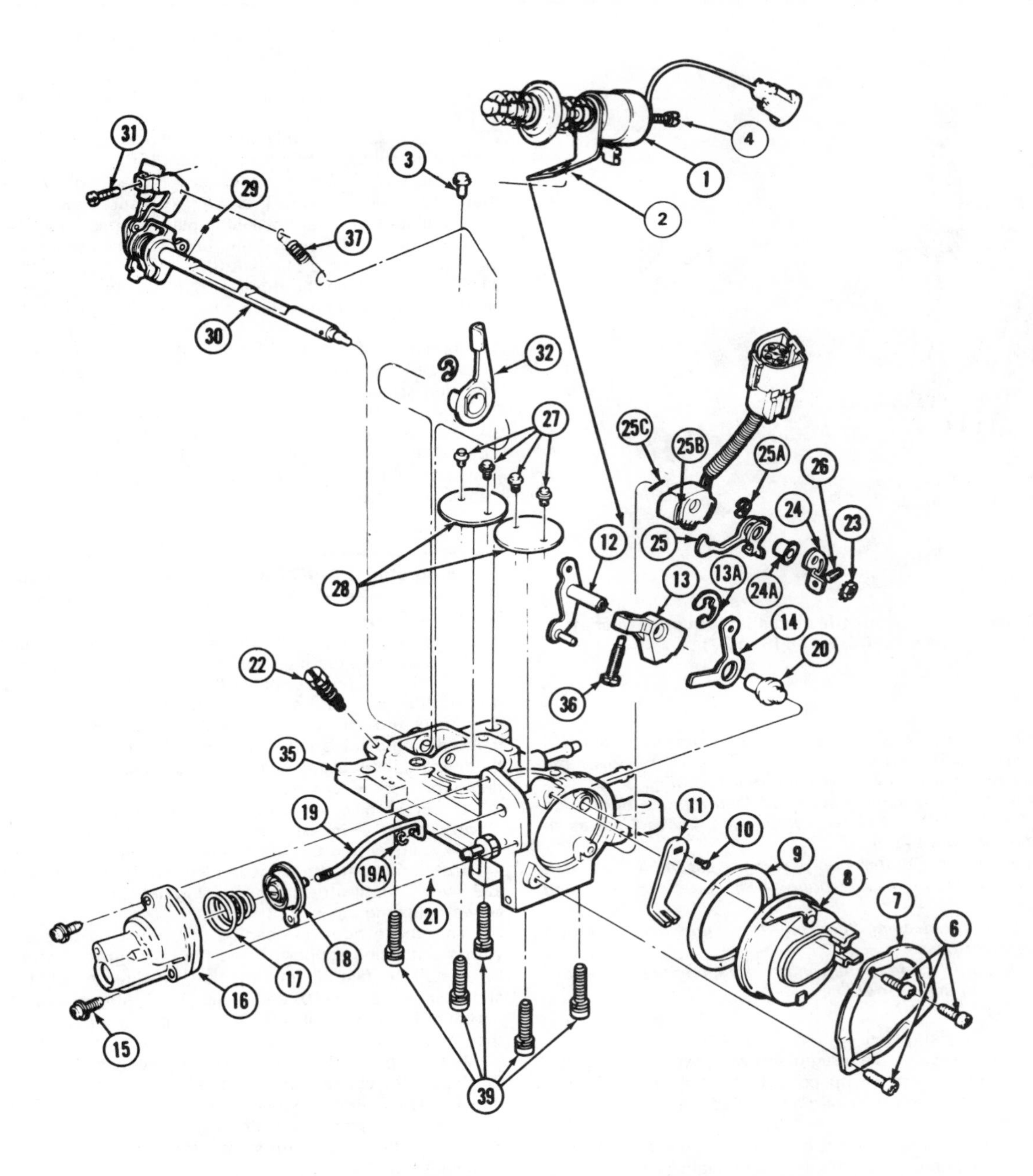

Fig. 3.40 2700/7200 carburetor throttle body (Secs 27 and 28)

1 Throttle return control device
2 Throttle return control device bracket
3 Mounting screw 10.32 x .50
4 Adjusting screw (TSP on)
5 (Not applicable)
6 Screw (3) 8.32 x .50
7 Choke thermostatic housing retainer
8 Choke thermostatic housing
9 Choke thermostatic housing gasket
10 Screw, 6.32 x .50
11 Choke thermostatic lever
12 Choke shaft lever and pin assembly
13 Fast idle cam
13A Large E-clip
14 Fast idle intermediate lever
15 Screw (2) 8.32 x .75
16 Choke control diaphragm cover
17 Choke control diaphragm spring
18 Choke control diaphragm assembly
19 Choke control diaphragm rod
19A Clip
20 Choke housing bushing
21 Choke heat tube (if equipped)
22 Curb idle adjusting screw (TSP OFF)
23 Retaining nut, 10.32
24 Fast idle adjusting lever
24A Nylon washer and bushing assembly
25 Fast idle lever
25A Large E-clip
25B Roll pin
25C Throttle position sensor (7200VV only)
26 Fast idle adjusting screw
27 Throttle plate screws (4)
28 Throttle plates
29 Venturi valve limiter stop pin
30 Throttle shaft assembly
31 Transmission kickdown adjusting screw
32 Venturi valve limiter lever and bushing assembly
33 E-clip
34 (Not applicable)
35 Throttle body
36 Fast idle cam adjusting screw
37 Transmission kickdown lever return spring (if equipped)
38 (Not applicable)
39 Screw (5) 8.32 x .75

Fig. 3.41 Positioning the throttle stop shaft pin prior to shaft removal (2700/7200) (Sec 27)

(a) *Using Ford tool T77L-9533-A, turn each main jet (39 and 40) clockwise, counting the turns as you go. Write down the number of turns to the nearest quarter turn (Fig. 3.38)*
(b) *Unscrew the jet assembly (39) and then remove the O-ring (40). For ease of proper reassembly, identify the jets as to 'throttle' or 'choke' side*
(c) *Remove the accelerator pump plunger assembly and then remove the pump return spring (41), pump cup (42) and plunger (43)*
(d) *If necessary for cleaning, remove the $\frac{1}{8}$ in pipe plug (45) from the fuel inlet boss*
(e) *From the throttle side of the venturi valve, remove the venturi valve limiting screw (44)*

Main Body (refer to Fig. 3.39)
18 Remove the venturi valve diaphragm screws, cover, spring guide and spring (1, 2, 3 and 4). Loosen the cover by tapping lightly. Do not pry. Carefully loosen the venturi valve diaphragm (5) and slide it from the main body.
19 Turn the carburetor upside down, holding your hand under it to catch the accelerator pump check ball (9) and weight (10).
20 Remove the five throttle body retaining screws and remove the throttle body and gasket (11).
21 On the 7200VV only, use a $\frac{5}{8}$ in socket to remove the feedback stepper motor (12), gasket (12A), pintle valve (12B) and spring (12C).
22 On the 2700VV only, remove the choke heat seal screw and shield (14 and 14A).

Throttle Body (refer to Fig. 3.40)
23 Remove the throttle return control device assembly (1, 2, 3, 4 and 37).
24 Remove the choke thermostatic spring and housing assembly (6, 7, 8 and 9). On California vehicles this housing is retained by rivets, refer to Section 23 for the removal procedure.
25 Remove the choke thermostatic lever (11) and screw (10) and slide the choke shaft and lever assembly (12) out of the casting. Remove the fast idle cam (13) and E-clip (13A) and the adjusting screw (36). Remove the fast idle intermediate lever (14).
26 Remove the choke control diaphragm lever assembly (15, 16 and 17). Remove the choke control diaphragm assembly (18) and rod (19).
27 Should the choke housing bushing (20) have to be removed, it will have to be pressed out, while the casting is being supported, so that it is not damaged. The bushing is staked in place and the staked areas will have to be ground off before pressing.
28 Remove the TSP Off idle speed screw (22), throttle shaft nut (23), nylon bushing (24A), fast idle lever (24), fast idle adjusting lever (25) and screw (26).
29 On the 7200VV only, remove the large E-clip (25A), throttle positioning sensor (25B) and roll pin (25C).
30 If the throttle plates are to be removed, lightly scribe along the shaft and mark the plate 'T' and 'C' to ensure proper reassembly. The throttle plate screws are staked in place so their staked areas must be filed or ground off. Remove the throttle plate screws (27) and discard them and remove the plates (28).
31 When removing the throttle shaft assembly, the limiter lever stop pin (29) will have to be driven down until it is flush with the shaft (Fig. 3.41).
32 Remove the E-clip (33) adjacent to the venturi valve limiter and slide the throttle shaft assembly (30) from the casting and remove the adjusting screw (31).
33 Remove the venturi valve limiter and bushing assembly.
34 Disassembly is now complete and all components should be cleaned in the proper solvent and inspected for wear. All traces of gasket should be removed from the carburetor body and all passages cleaned of dirt or gum deposits.

28 Carburetor (2700/7200VV) – reassembly and adjustment

Throttle Body (refer to Fig. 3.40)
1 After supporting the throttle shaft assembly, carefully drive out the venturi valve limiter stop pin and roll pin (if equipped). Place the venturi valve limiter assembly (32) in the throttle body (35) and insert the throttle shaft (30) and install the E-clips (33).
2 Install the throttle plates (28), according to the scribed marks made during disassembly. Close the throttle, tap the plates to center them and tighten the screws (27). Stake the ends of the screws so that they won't come loose.
3 Drive the new venturi valve limiter stop pin (29) into the shaft, leaving about $\frac{1}{8}$ in exposed. Install the roll pin (25B) and on the 7200VV, install the throttle positioner sensor (25C) and E-clip (25A).
4 Install the fast idle adjusting lever (24), nylon bushing (24A), fast idle lever (25), throttle shaft retaining nut (26). Install the TSP Off idle speed adjusting screw (22).
5 The choke housing bushing (20) must be pressed into position with the housing supported and the bushing then staked in place.
6 Install the fast idle intermediate diaphragm rod (18) into position and engage the rod (19) and E-clip (19A). After sliding the choke shaft pin and lever assembly (12) into the casting, install the choke thermostatic lever (11) and screw (12). Install the choke control diaphragm spring (17), cover (16) and screws (15).
7 Install the choke thermostat gasket (9), housing (8), and retaining ring (7). On California vehicles, follow the procedure in Section 23. Adjust the cap to the specified setting.
8 Install the throttle return control devices (1, 2, 3, 4 and 5), if equipped.

Main Body (refer to Fig. 3.39)
9 Place the throttle body gasket (11) on the main body (6) and install the main body to the throttle body.
10 Drop the accelerator pump check ball (9) and weight (10) into the pump discharge channel.
11 The venturi valve limiter stop screw, torque retention spring (7), and plug (8) are not to be installed at this time, but as one of the final steps of upper body assembly.
12 Slide the venturi valve diaphragm (5) into the main body and install the venturi valve spring (4), spring guide (3), cover (2) and screws (1).
13 On the 7200VV only, install the feedback motor (12), gasket (12A), pintle valve (12B) and pintle spring ((12C).
14 On the 2700VV only, install the choke heat shield.

Upper Body (refer to Fig. 3.34)
15 Install the $\frac{1}{8}$ in pipe plug (45) into the fuel inlet boss.
16 Install the venturi valve limiter screw (44) in the venturi valve (33).
17 Install the O-rings (40) on the main metering jets. Lubricate the O-rings with mild soapy solution prior to installation.

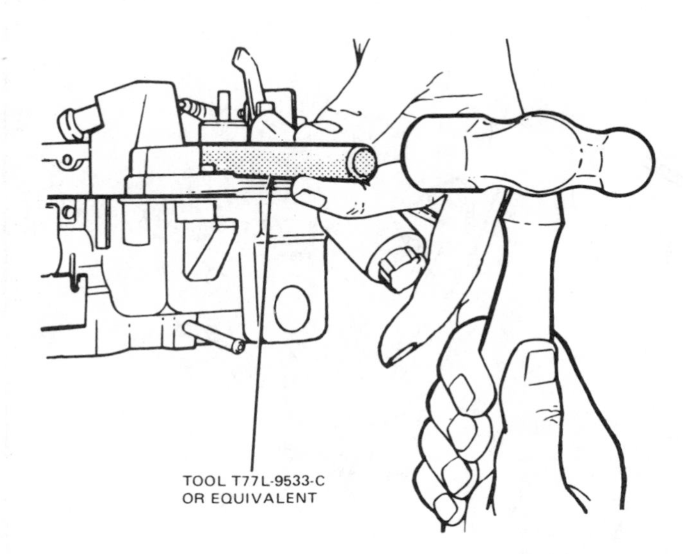

Fig. 3.42 Installing 2700/7200 main jet plugs (Sec 28)

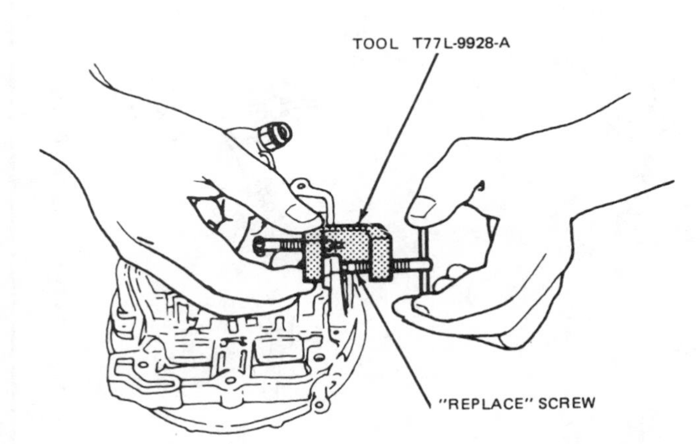

Fig. 3.43 Installing 2700/7200 tapered plugs (Sec 28)

18 Install each main metering jet by turning it clockwise with Ford tool T77L-9533-A or equivalent, until seated in the casting. At this point, turn each jet counterclockwise the same number of turns recorded in Step 18a of Section 27.
19 Install the jet plugs (38), using the Ford jet plug driver tool T77L-9533-C or equivalent. Tap lightly on the end of the tool until it bottoms against the face of the casting (Fig. 3.42).
20 Install the metering rods (36), springs (37) and pivot pins (35) on the venturi valve (33). Install the venturi valve and carefully guide the metering rods into the main metering jets. Press downward on the metering rods and if the springs are properly assembled, they will spring back.
21 Install the venturi valve pivot pin bushings (34) and pivot pins (35). Use Ford tool T77P-9928-A or equivalent to press the tapered plugs into the venturi valve pivot pins (Fig. 3.43).
22 Install the venturi valve cover plate (28), roller bearings (39), gasket (29) and attaching screws (27).
23 Install the accelerator pump operating rod (6) and dust seal (16). Attach the E-clip (6C) and washer (6B). Slide the overtravel spring (6A) over the accelerator pump operating rod.
24 Insert the accelerator pump lever and swivel assembly (18) into the pump link. Install the accelerator pump link screw (17), nut (17A) and the accelerator pump adjustment nut (20).
25 Install the fuel inlet valve seat gasket (15), the seat (14) and valve (13). Install the float gasket (12), float assembly (11) and hinge pin (10).
26 Assemble the accelerator pump return spring (41), cup (42) and plunger (43). Place the pump piston assembly in the hole in the upper body.
27 Assemble the upper body to the main body. Holding the pump piston with your finger, guide it into the main body pump cavity, making sure the venturi valve limiter diaphragm stem engages the venturi valve. Install screws (8 and 8A).
28 Install the fuel filter spring (4), filter (3), inlet filter gasket (2) and fitting (1).
29 Install the air cleaner stud.
30 Install the choke control rod dust seal (16). Tap it gently to straighten the retainer.
31 Slide the cold enrichment rod (26) into the upper body. Assemble the cold enrichment assembly consisting of lever (22), adjusting rod nut (20), swivel (23), control vacuum regulator (25) and adjusting nut (24) and install it.
32 Install the choke control rod (7). See Section 24 for final adjustment procedure.
33 Engage the accelerator pump operating rod (6) to the choke control rod (7) and install the E-ring retainers (5).
34 At this point, install the venturi valve limiter stop screw and torque retention spring (7, Fig. 33). Follow the adjustment procedure in Section 26, installing the plug after the adjustment is made.
35 Adjust the carburetor to the operating specifications on the emissions label.

29 Fuel tank – removal and installation

1 Disconnect the battery terminals.
2 Using a suitable length of pipe siphon out as much gas from the tank as possible. Do not use your mouth to start the flow.
3 Remove the four screws securing the filler pipe to the bodywork aperture and carefully ease the bottom end of the pipe out of the sealing ring in the side of the tank.
4 Jack up the rear of the car and suitably support it for access beneath.
5 Disconnect the fuel feed and vapor pipes at the tank and detach them from the clips along the tank front edge.
6 Disconnect the electrical leads from the sender unit.
7 Undo and remove the two support strap retaining nuts at the rear of the tank while supporting the weight of the tank.
8 Push the straps downwards and lift the tank out toward the rear of the car.
9 If it is necessary to remove the sender unit, this can be unscrewed from the tank using the appropriate special tool. A suitable C-wrench or drift can probably be used, but great care should be taken that the flange is not damaged and that there is no danger from sparks if a hammer has to be used.
10 Taking care not to damage the sealing washer, pry out the tank-to-filler pipe seal.
11 When installing, ensure that the rubber pads are stuck in position.
12 Install a new filler pipe seal.
13 Refit the sender unit using a new seal, as the orginal one will almost certainly be damaged.
14 The remainder of the installation procedure is the reverse of removal. A smear of engine oil on the tank filler pipe exterior will aid its installation.
15 Do not overtighten the tank retaining strap nuts.

30 Fuel tank – cleaning and repair

1 With time it is likely that sediment will collect in the bottom of the fuel tank. Condensation, resulting in rust and other impurities, will usually be found in the fuel tank of any car more than three or four years old.
2 When the tank is removed it should be vigorously flushed out with hot water and detergent and, if facilities are available, steam cleaned.
3 **Note:** *Never weld, solder or bring a naked light close to an empty fuel tank. All repairs should be done by a professional due to the extremely hazardous conditions.*

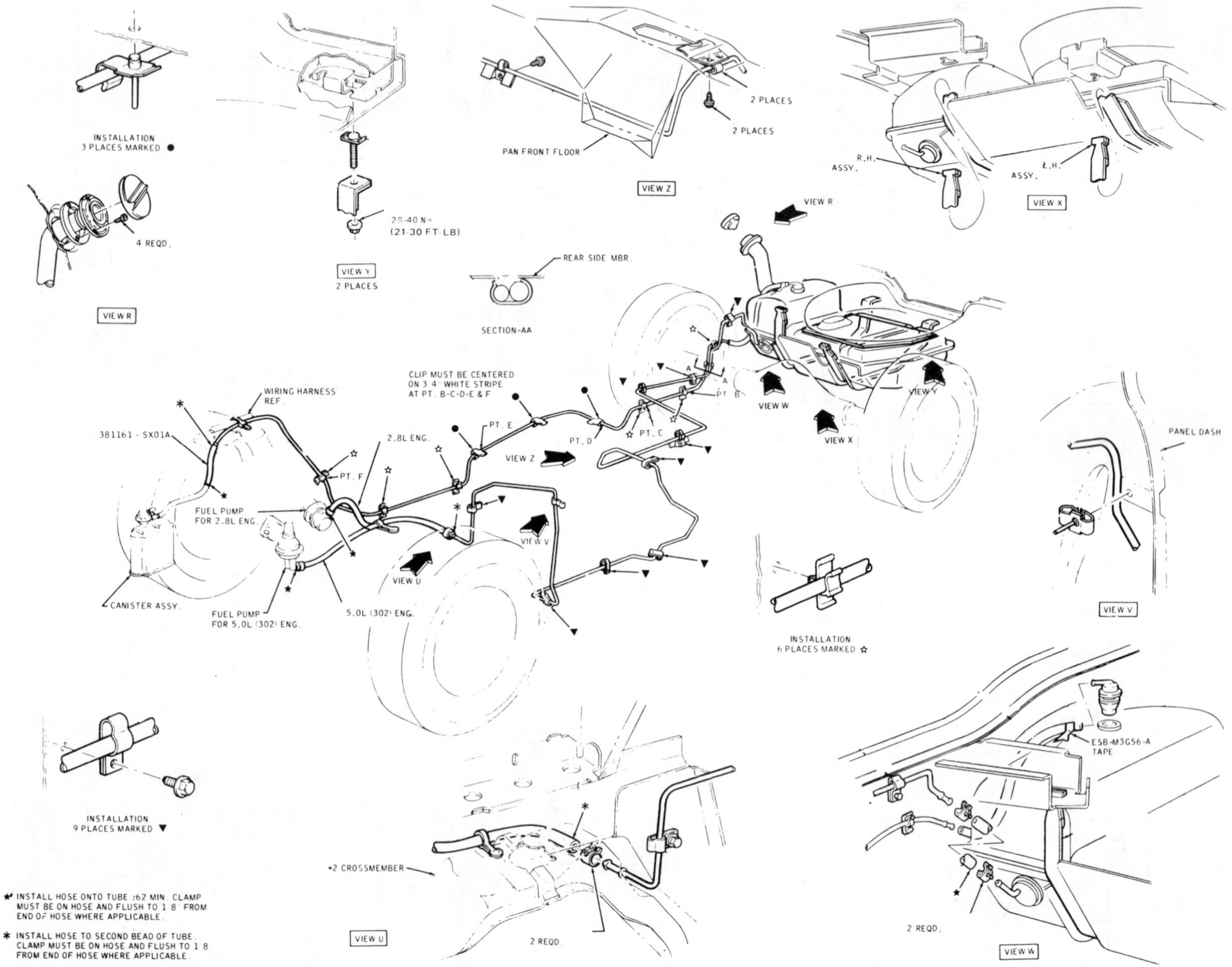

Fig. 3.44 Typical fuel system layout (Sec 29)

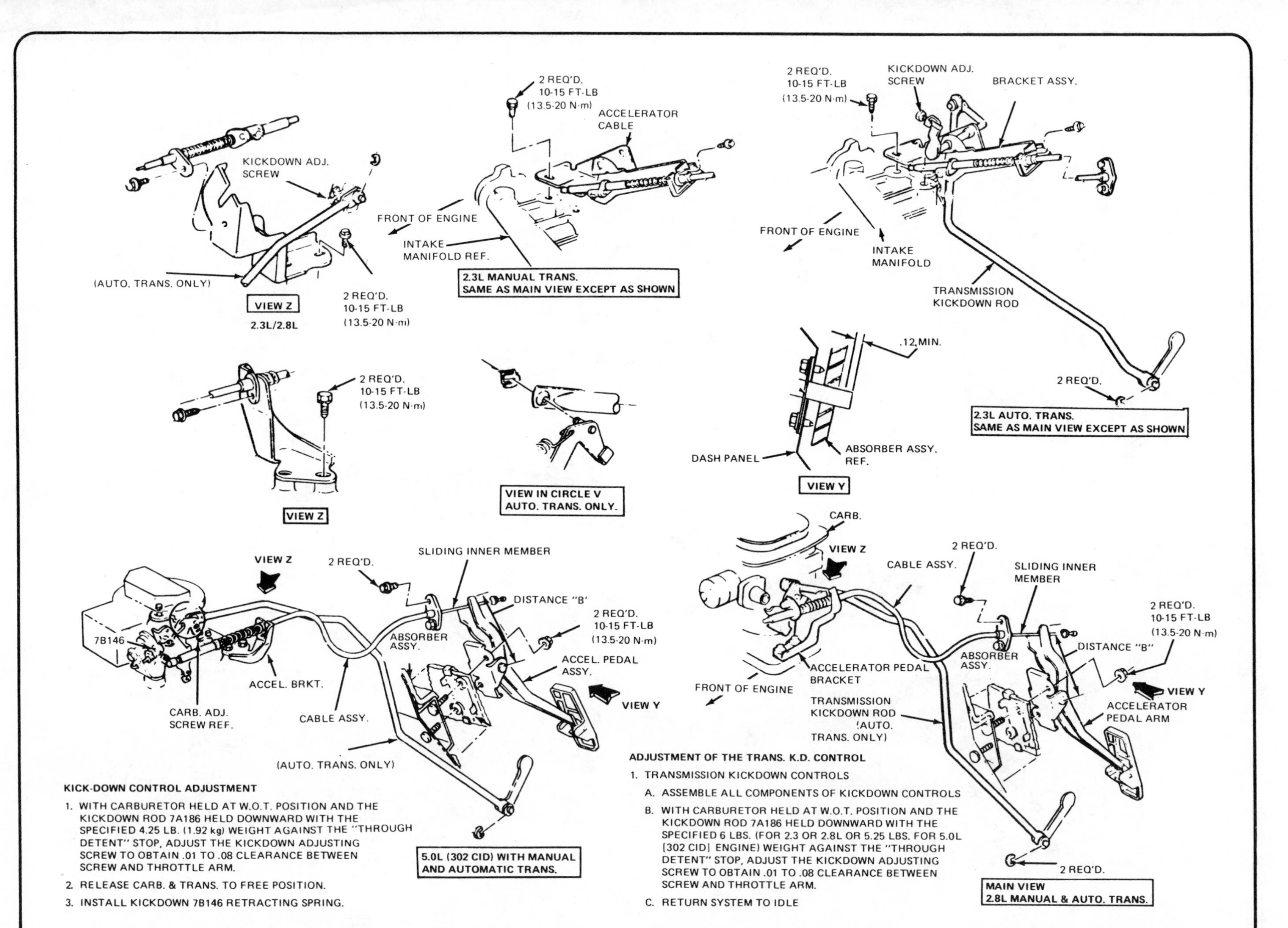

KICK-DOWN CONTROL ADJUSTMENT

1. WITH CARBURETOR HELD AT W.O.T. POSITION AND THE KICKDOWN ROD 7A186 HELD DOWNWARD WITH THE SPECIFIED 4.25 LB. (1.92 kg) WEIGHT AGAINST THE "THROUGH DETENT" STOP, ADJUST THE KICKDOWN ADJUSTING SCREW TO OBTAIN .01 TO .08 CLEARANCE BETWEEN SCREW AND THROTTLE ARM.
2. RELEASE CARB. & TRANS. TO FREE POSITION.
3. INSTALL KICKDOWN 7B146 RETRACTING SPRING.

ADJUSTMENT OF THE TRANS. K.D. CONTROL

1. TRANSMISSION KICKDOWN CONTROLS
   A. ASSEMBLE ALL COMPONENTS OF KICKDOWN CONTROLS
   B. WITH CARBURETOR HELD AT W.O.T. POSITION AND THE KICKDOWN ROD 7A186 HELD DOWNWARD WITH THE SPECIFIED 6 LBS. (FOR 2.3 OR 2.8L OR 5.25 LBS. FOR 5.0L [302 CID] ENGINE) WEIGHT AGAINST THE "THROUGH DETENT" STOP, ADJUST THE KICKDOWN ADJUSTING SCREW TO OBTAIN .01 TO .08 CLEARANCE BETWEEN SCREW AND THROTTLE ARM.
   C. RETURN SYSTEM TO IDLE

Fig. 3.45 Throttle and kickdown linkage layout (Secs 31 and 32)

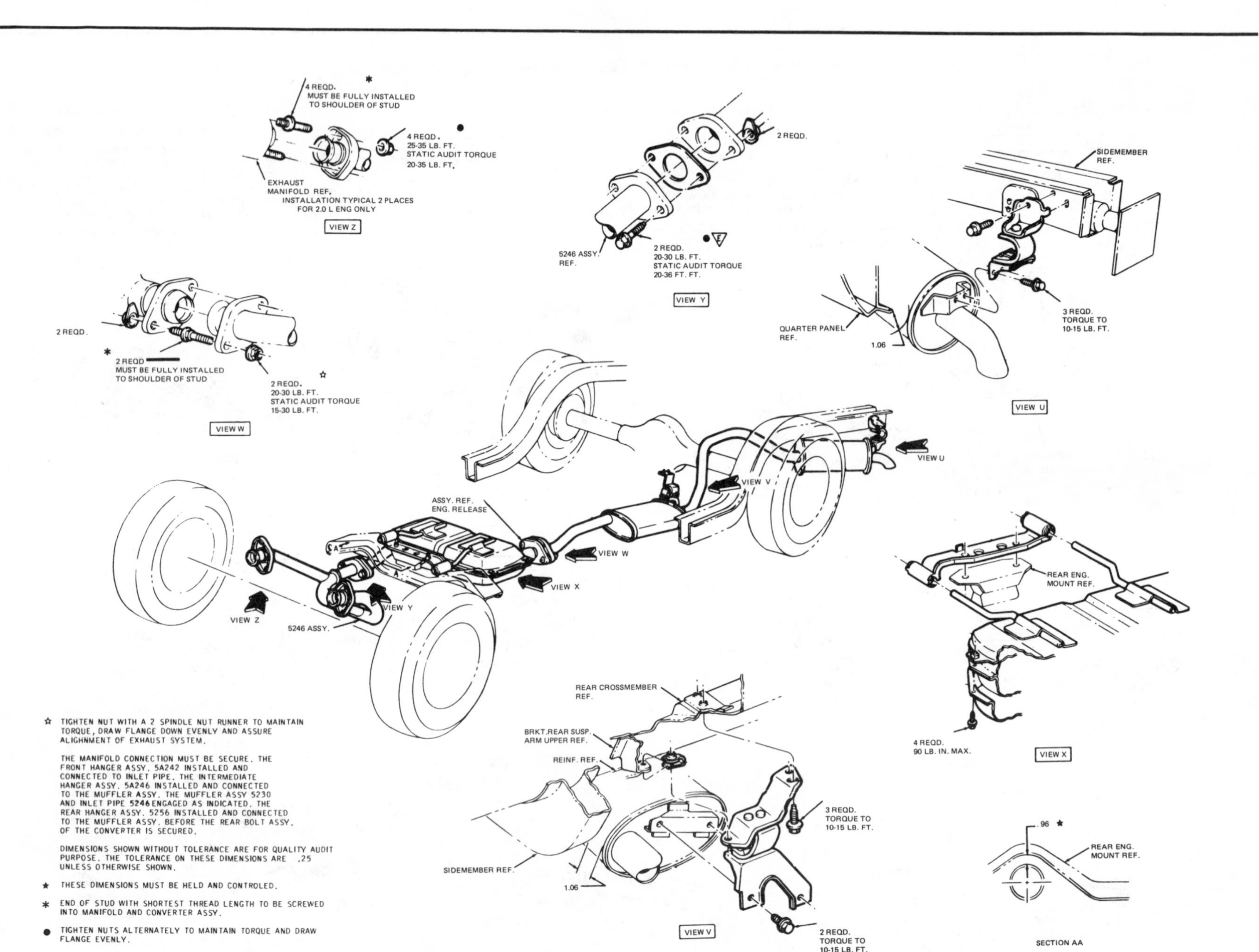

Fig. 3.46 Typical V6 exhaust system layout (Sec 33)

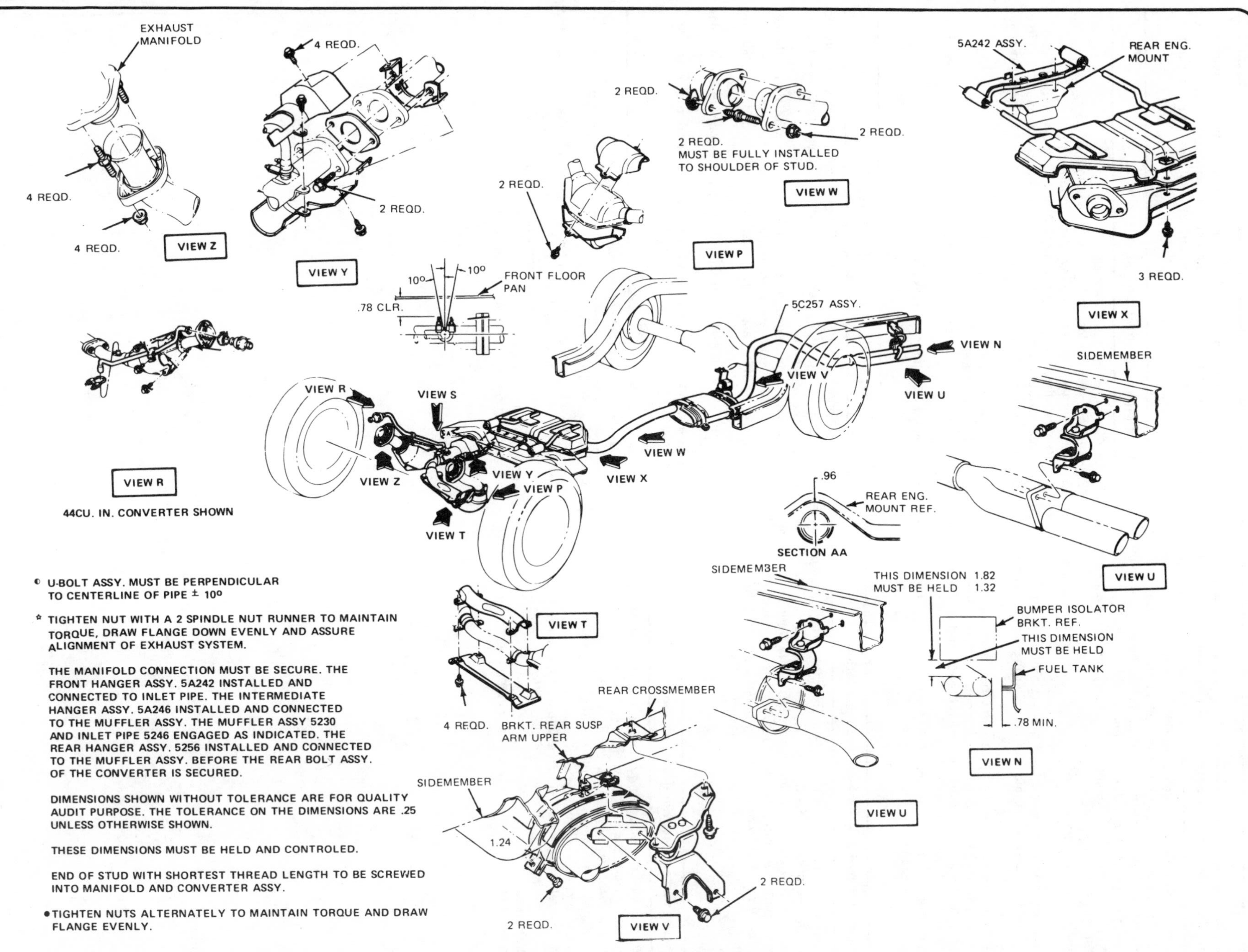

- U-BOLT ASSY. MUST BE PERPENDICULAR TO CENTERLINE OF PIPE ± 10°

* TIGHTEN NUT WITH A 2 SPINDLE NUT RUNNER TO MAINTAIN TORQUE, DRAW FLANGE DOWN EVENLY AND ASSURE ALIGNMENT OF EXHAUST SYSTEM.

THE MANIFOLD CONNECTION MUST BE SECURE. THE FRONT HANGER ASSY. 5A242 INSTALLED AND CONNECTED TO INLET PIPE. THE INTERMEDIATE HANGER ASSY. 5A246 INSTALLED AND CONNECTED TO THE MUFFLER ASSY. THE MUFFLER ASSY 5230 AND INLET PIPE 5246 ENGAGED AS INDICATED. THE REAR HANGER ASSY. 5256 INSTALLED AND CONNECTED TO THE MUFFLER ASSY. BEFORE THE REAR BOLT ASSY. OF THE CONVERTER IS SECURED.

DIMENSIONS SHOWN WITHOUT TOLERANCE ARE FOR QUALITY AUDIT PURPOSE. THE TOLERANCE ON THE DIMENSIONS ARE .25 UNLESS OTHERWISE SHOWN.

THESE DIMENSIONS MUST BE HELD AND CONTROLED.

END OF STUD WITH SHORTEST THREAD LENGTH TO BE SCREWED INTO MANIFOLD AND CONVERTER ASSY.

• TIGHTEN NUTS ALTERNATELY TO MAINTAIN TORQUE AND DRAW FLANGE EVENLY.

Fig. 3.47 Typical V8 exhaust system (Sec 33)

31 Throttle cable and kick-down rod – removal and installation

1 Pry the throttle cable retainer bushing from the top end of the accelerator pedal and remove the inner cable from the pedal assembly. **Note**: *On later model cars the cable is retained by a Tinnerman-type fastener which must be pried off the end of the cable.*
2 Remove the circular retaining clip holding the inner cable to the underside of the dash panel.
3 Remove the two screws retaining the outer cable to the dash panel.
4 Disconnect the control rod from the carburetor linkage.
5 Remove the screw or spring clip retaining the outer cable to the engine bracket.
6 The complete cable assembly can now be removed.
7 To remove the kick-down rod (automatic transmission only), remove the 'C' type spring clips and pins at each end of the rod and remove the rod.
8 Install the throttle cable and kick-down rod using the reverse procedure to removal.

32 Accelerator pedal – removal and installation

1 Remove the inner throttle cable from the pedal assembly as described in the previous Section.
2 Undo the two nuts retaining the pedal to the floor bracket and remove the pedal assembly. **Note**: *If a pedal extension pad is installed this will have to be uncrimped from the pedal prior to pedal removal.*
3 Install the accelerator pedal using the reverse procedure to removal.

33 Exhaust system – general description

Note: *Because of manufacturing changes, the exhaust system on your car may differ from those shown in this manual. If problems arise, consult your local dealer or repair shop.*
1 All 2.8L V6 engines use a single exhaust system consisting of a 'Y' pipe, catalytic converter, muffler and resonator.
2 The V8 systems are also single exhaust of the same basic design as the V6, varying in that there are two different sizes of catalytic converters used.
3 The exhaust system is usually serviced in 4 pieces: the rear section of the muffler inlet pipe, catalytic converter, inlet pipe and muffler.
4 Due to the high operating temperatures of the exhaust system, do not work on the exhaust system until at least one hour after use.

34 Inlet pipe – removal and installationn

1 Raise and support the vehicle.
2 Support the muffler assembly with a length of wire.
3 Remove the converter-to-inlet pipe mounting bolts.
4 Remove the front hanger mounting screws from the inlet pipe.
5 Remove the nuts securing the inlet pipe to the exhaust manifold.
6 Installation is the reverse of removal with the following precautions.
7 Clean all flange and gasket surfaces.
8 Use new gaskets.
9 Install the entire system loosely, aligning all components, then tighten.
10 Check for absence of leaks and noise.

35 Muffler assembly – removal and installation

1 Raise and support the vehicle. Support the vehicle allowing the rear axle to hang at full extension without the wheel assemblies touching the ground.
2 Remove the nuts securing the converter to the muffler pipe flange.
3 Remove the rear hanger to muffler support screws.
4 Pull the muffler assembly toward the rear and disconnect the catalytic converter.
5 Remove the screws securing the hanger assembly to the muffler support.
6 Installation is the reverse of removal. Refer to the installation precautions in Section 33.

36 Catalytic converter – removal and installation

1 Raise and support the vehicle.
2 Remove the screws securing the heat shields to the converter and carefully remove the shield. Be careful of sharp edges.
3 Remove the fasteners securing both ends of the catalytic converter, and lower the converter from the car.
4 Installation is the reverse of removal.

Chapter 4 Emissions systems

Contents

Specifications

Catalalytic converter mounting bolt size

Round converter, 4 in	
Outlet	⅜ x 2.83 in
Inlet	⅜ x 1.50 in
Round converter, 5 in	
Outlet	⅜ x 1.50 in
Oval converter, 4 x 7 in	
Outlet	⅜ x 3.25 in
Inlet	⅜ x 2.00 in

Torque specifications

	ft-lb	Nm
Thermactor pump pivot bolts	22 to 32	30 to 43
Thermactor adjusting arm bolt	24 to 30	32 to 54

1 General information

In order to meet Federal anti-pollution laws, each car is equipped with a variety of emission control systems, depending on the model and the state in which it was sold.

Since the emissions systems control so many engine functions, drivability, fuel consumption as well as conformance to the law can be affected should any faults develop. Consequently, keeping the emissions system operating at peak efficiency is very important.

This Chapter will describe all of the systems which may be installed in order to cover all models.

The emissions label located under the hood contains information important to properly maintaining the emissions control system as well as for keeping properly tuned.

Before beginning any work on the emission control system, read Section 2, Chapter 3 to avoid going contrary to any of the emission control regulations.

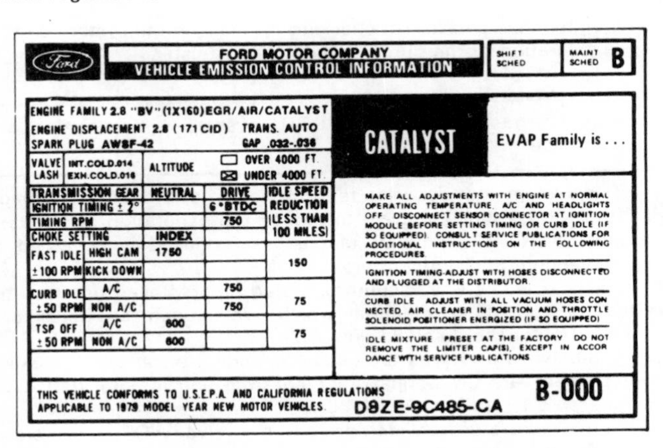

Fig. 4.1 Typical emissions label (Sec 1)

2 Electrically assisted choke heater – description and testing

1 Some carburetors have an electrically operated heater to aid in fast choke release and help reduce emissions during warm up.

2 The choke assist system consists of a choke cap, thermostatic spring, bimetal temperature sensing switch and positive temperature coefficient (PTC) heater. The system is grounded to the carburetor and receives from the center tap of the alternator.

3 At temperatures below 60° F (16°C), the sensing switch remains open and normal thermostatic spring action takes place. Above 60°F the sensing switch allows current from the alternator to activate the heater, warming the thermostatic spring so it opens faster. The thermostatic spring then pulls down the choke.

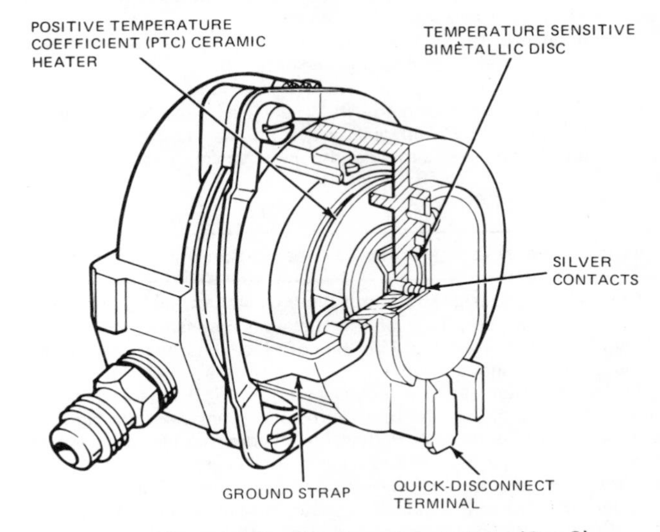

Fig. 4.2 Typical electrically-assisted choke (Sec 2)

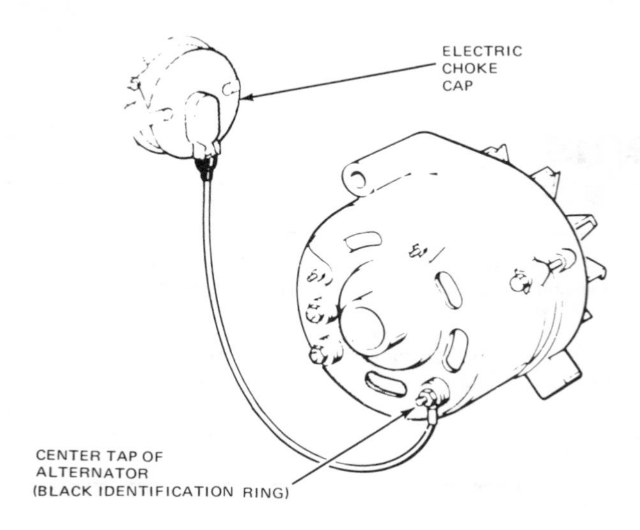

Fig. 4.3 Electric choke wiring (Sec 2)

4 A fast idle cam latch works in conjunction with the choke to hold the cam in the high position until the choke backs off, allowing the latch to rotate to the normal run position.
5 Fast idle cam and choke pulldown adjustment are described in Chapter 3.
6 The only test that can be carried out on this assembly, without special test equipment, is a continuity check of the heater coil. If an ohmmeter is available, check for specified resistance. If no ohmmeter is available, disconnect the stator lead from the choke cap terminal and connect it to one terminal of a 12 volt low wattage bulb (such as an instrument panel bulb). Ground the other terminal of the bulb and check that it illuminates when the engine is running. If it fails to illuminate, check the alternator output and the choke lead for continuity. If the bulb illuminates, disconnect the bulb ground terminal and reconnect it to the choke lead. If the bulb does not illuminate when the engine is warm, a faulty choke is indicated.

3 Positive crankcase ventilation (PCV) system – description and maintenance

1 The PCV system consists of the PCV valve, oil filler cap associated hoses.
2 The system operates by drawing vapors that escape past the piston rings back into the intake manifold, allowing fresh air to fliw through the oil filler cap into the crankcase.
3 Maintenance of the PCV system consists of periodically removing the hoses, valve and filler cap and cleaning them and checking for obstructions.
4 If a fault is suspected in the PCV valve, it is easily removed by grasping it at the elbow and pulling it from the engine valve cover. Replacement involves assembling the new valve to the elbow and installing it.

4 Evaporative emission control – description and maintenance

1 This system is designed to limit the emission of fuel vapors to the atmosphere. It is comprised of the fuel tank, pressure and vacuum sensitive fuel filler cap, a restrictor bleed orifice, charcoal canister and the associated connecting lines.
2 When the fuel tank is filled, vapors are discharged to the atmosphere through the filler tube, and a space between the inner fuel filler tube and the outer neck. When fuel covers the filler control tube, vapors can no longer escape and a vapor lock is created by the orifice, therefore, there can be no flow to the vapor charcoal canister.
3 When the thermal expansion occurs in the fuel tank, vapor is forced through the orifice and is drawn into the carburetor intake system as soon as the engine is started.

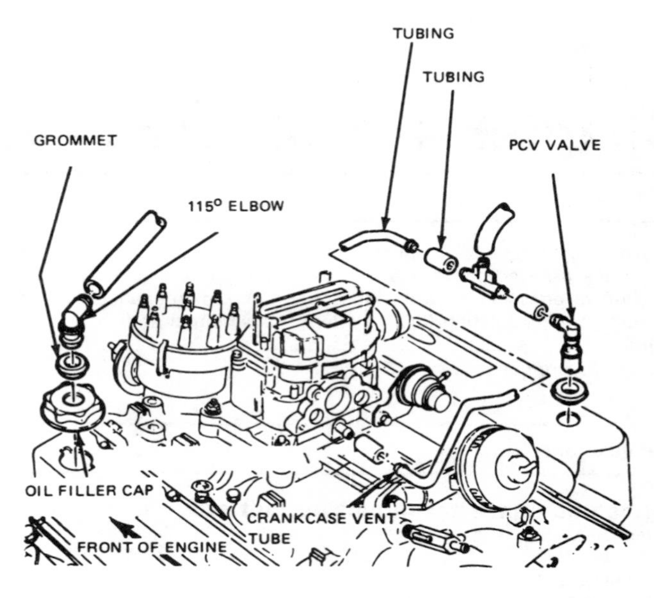

Fig. 4.4 Typical PCV system layout (Sec 3)

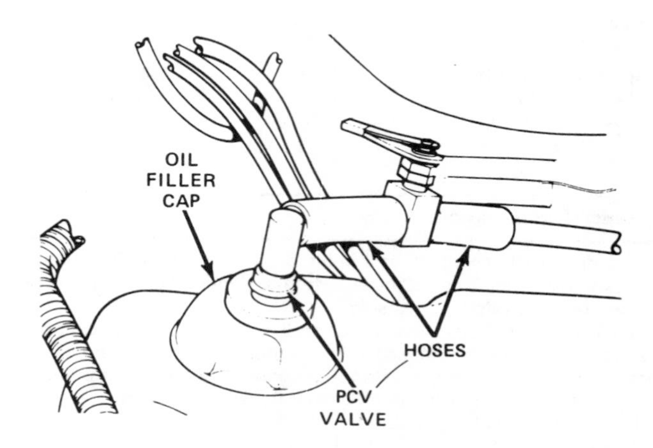

Fig. 4.5 PCV valve installation (Sec 3)

4 Some models incorporate a fuel bowl vent valve to direct vapors which collect in the carburetor back into the canister when the engine is off.
5 Maintenance consists of checking for leaks in the system and for proper operation of the purge valve on the canister.

5 Exhaust gas recirculation (EGR) system – description and maintenance

1 This system is designed to re-introduce small amounts of exhaust gas into the combustion cycle to reduce the generation of oxides of nitrogen (NOx). The amount of gas re-introduced is governed by engine vacuum and temperature.
2 The EGR valve is a vacuum-operated unit installed between the carburetor and intake manifold which, when open, allows exhaust gasses to enter the manifold (Fig. 4.7).
3 Three types of valves are used, depending on emission requirements. These are the poppet, tapered stem and integral transducer backpressure type (Figs. 4.9 through 4.11).
4 Some models use a wide-open throttle valve (WOT) which closes the EGR valve when the engine is at or near wide-open throttle.
5 Electronic ignition equipped (EEC) engines use a vacuum operated

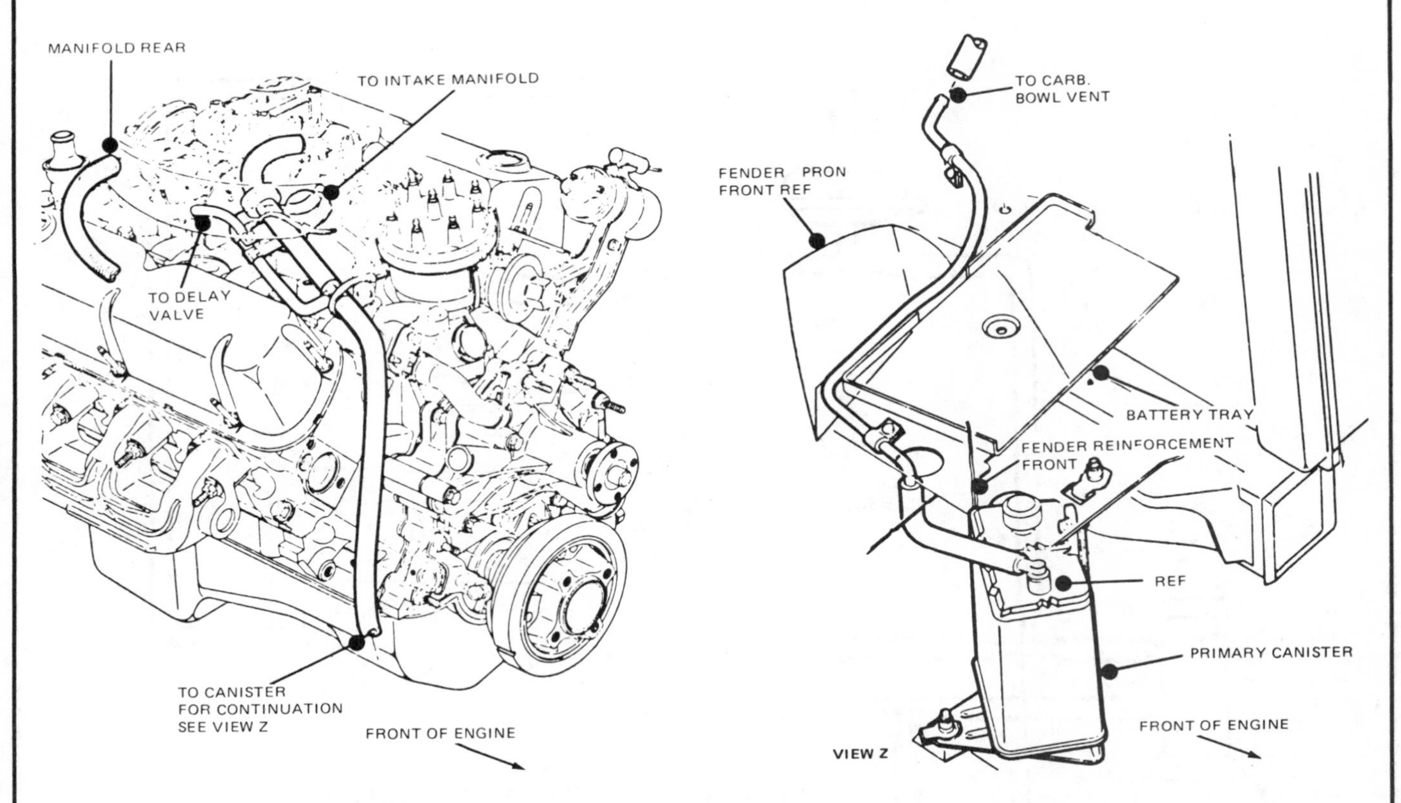

Fig. 4.6 Evaporative emissions system and charcoal canister layout (Sec 4)

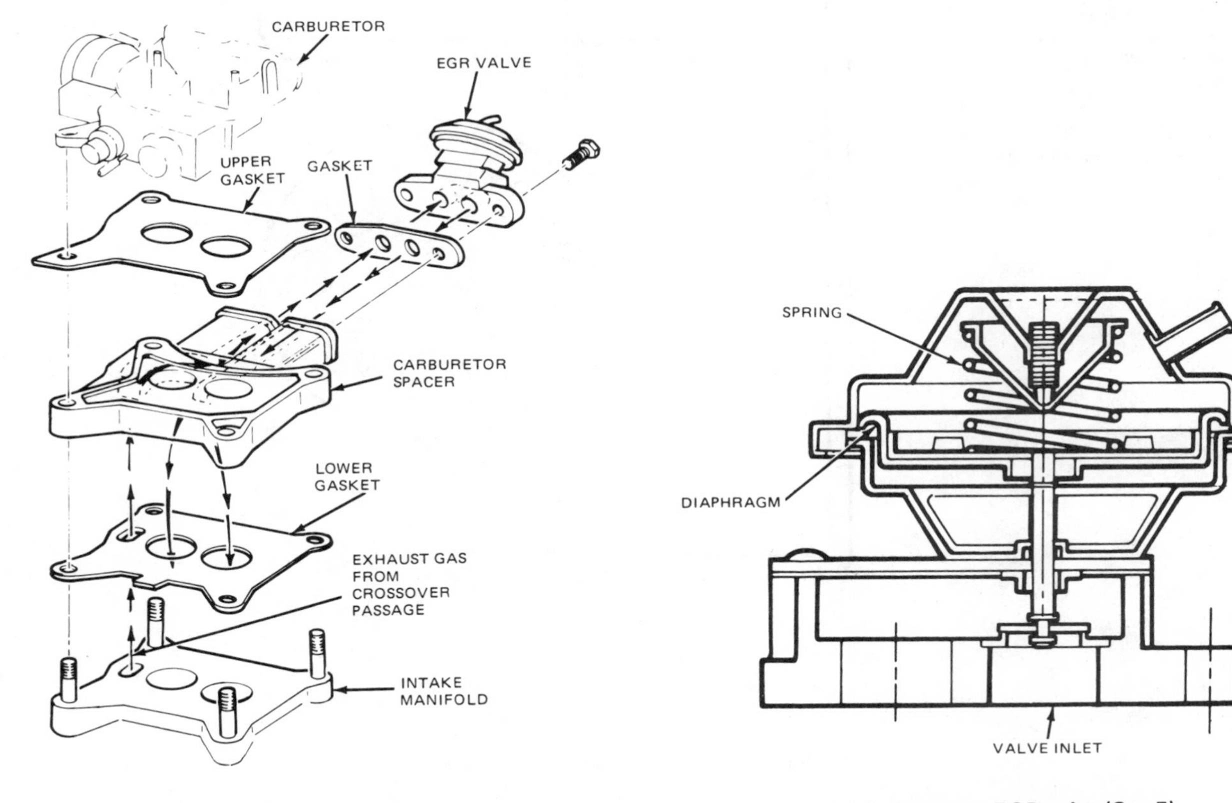

Fig. 4.7 Typical EGR valve installation (Sec 5)

Fig. 4.8 Poppet-type EGR valve (Sec 5)

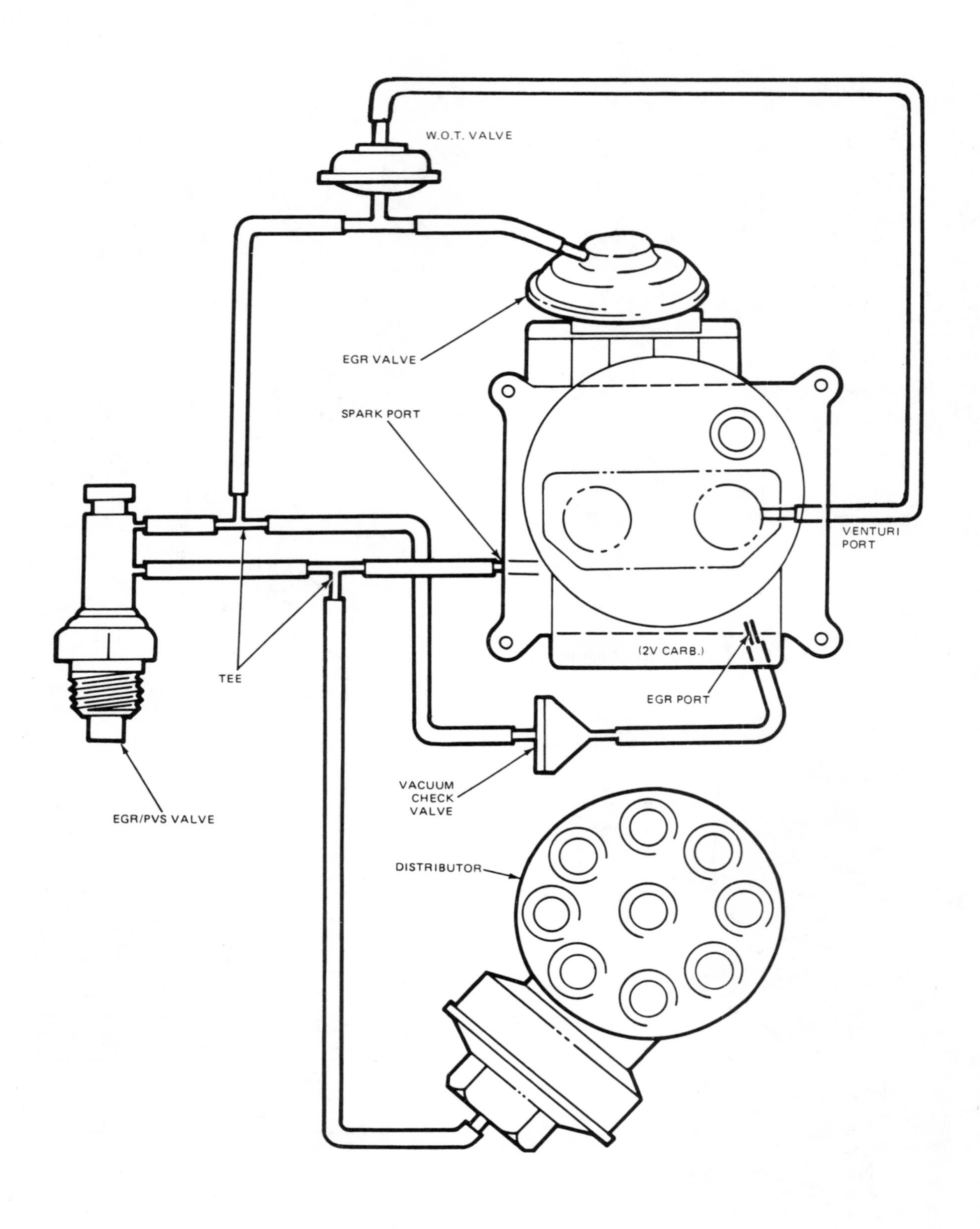

Fig. 4.9 Typical EGR system layout (Sec 5)

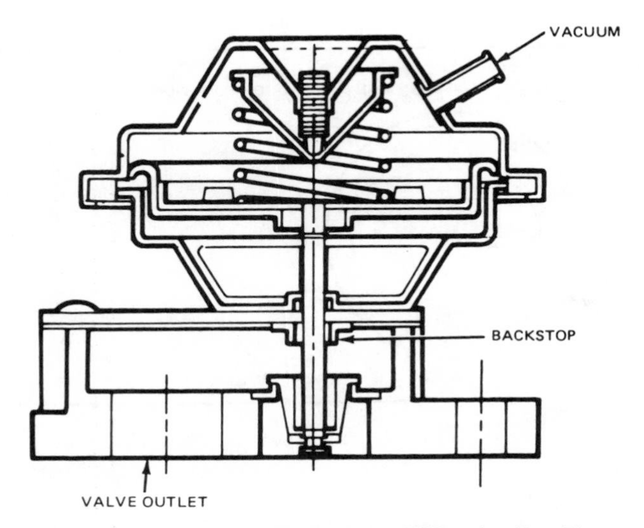

Fig. 4.10 Internal tapered stem-type EGR valve (Sec 5)

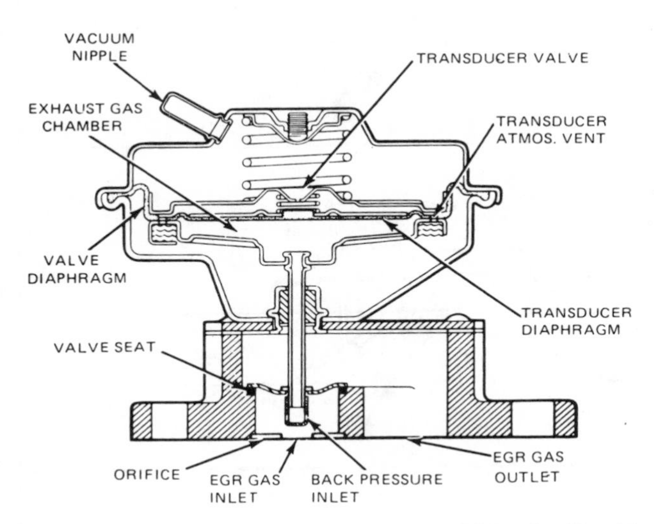

Fig. 4.11 Integral backpressure transducer EGR valve (Sec 5)

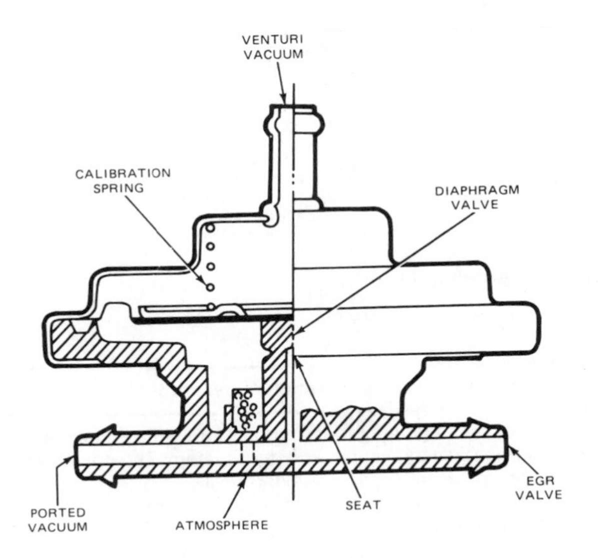

Fig. 4.12 Wide open throttle (WOT) valve (Sec 5)

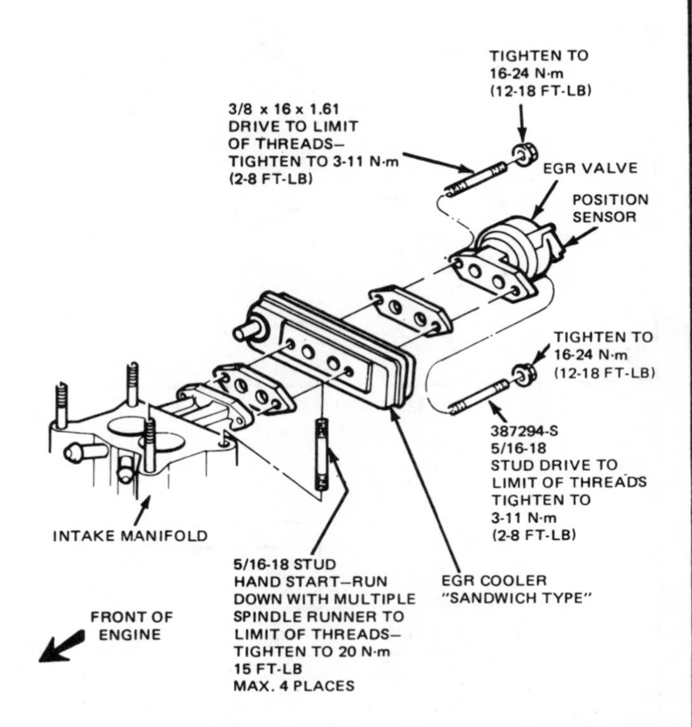

Fig. 4.13 EEC ignition EGR valve and cooler installation (Sec 5)

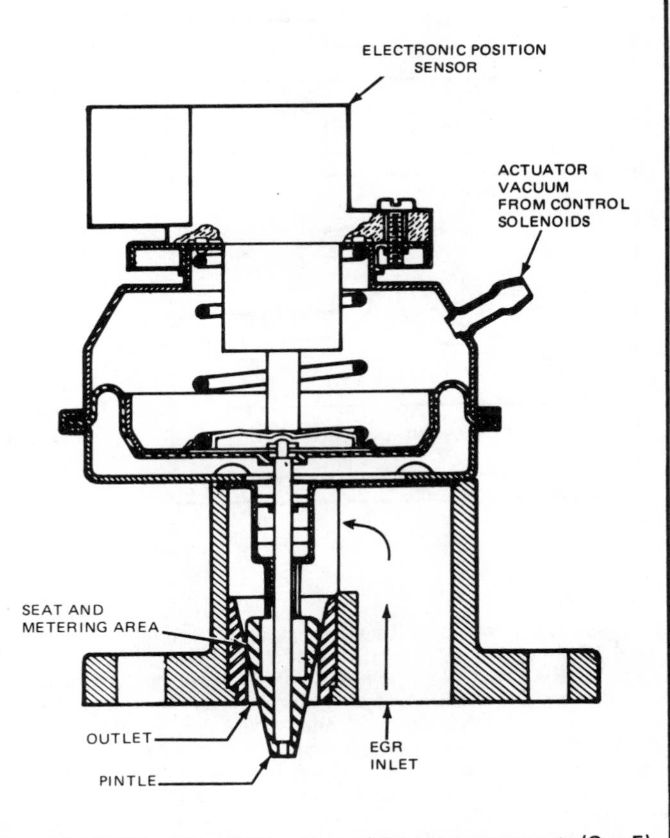

Fig. 4.14 EEC ignition EGR valve and sensor components (Sec 5)

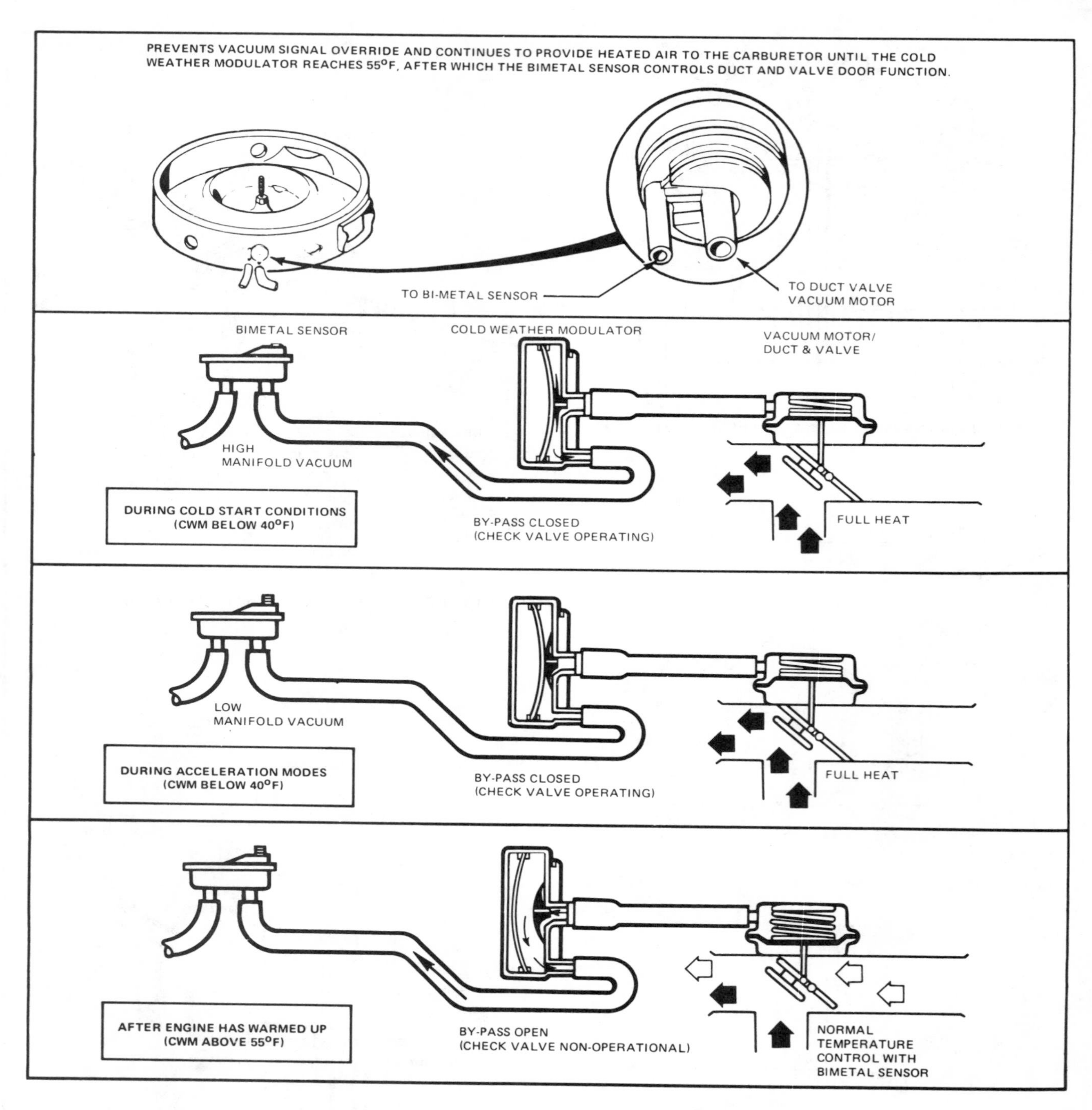

Fig. 4.15 Cold water modulator (CWM) operation (Sec 6)

EGR valves which incorporate a cooler assembly and position sensor (Figs. 4.13 and 4.14).

6 The EGR valve can be removed for cleaning, but where it is damaged, corroded or extremely dirty it is preferable to replace it with a new valve. If the valve is to be cleaned, check that the orifice in the body is clear and take care not to enlarge it. The internal deposits can be removed with a small power-driven rotary wire brush. Deposits around the valve stem and disc can be removed using a steel blade or ship approximately 0.029 in (0.7 mm) thick in a sawing motion around the stem shoulder at both sides of the disc. Clean the cavity and passages in the main body, ensuring that the poppet wobbles and moves axially before reassembly.

6 Inlet air temperature regulation – description

Control of the engine inlet air temperature is accomplished by the use of a thermostatic air cleaner and duct system. The operation of this system is described in Section 3, Chapter 3.

Some models incorporate a cold weather modulator (CWM) in the air cleaner assembly. At temperatures below 50° (13°C) the CWM prevents the air cleaner duct door from opening to non-heated intake air. At temperatures below 55°, the CWM does not operate. Under acceleration in cold conditions the CWM will hold the duct door open (Fig. 4.15).

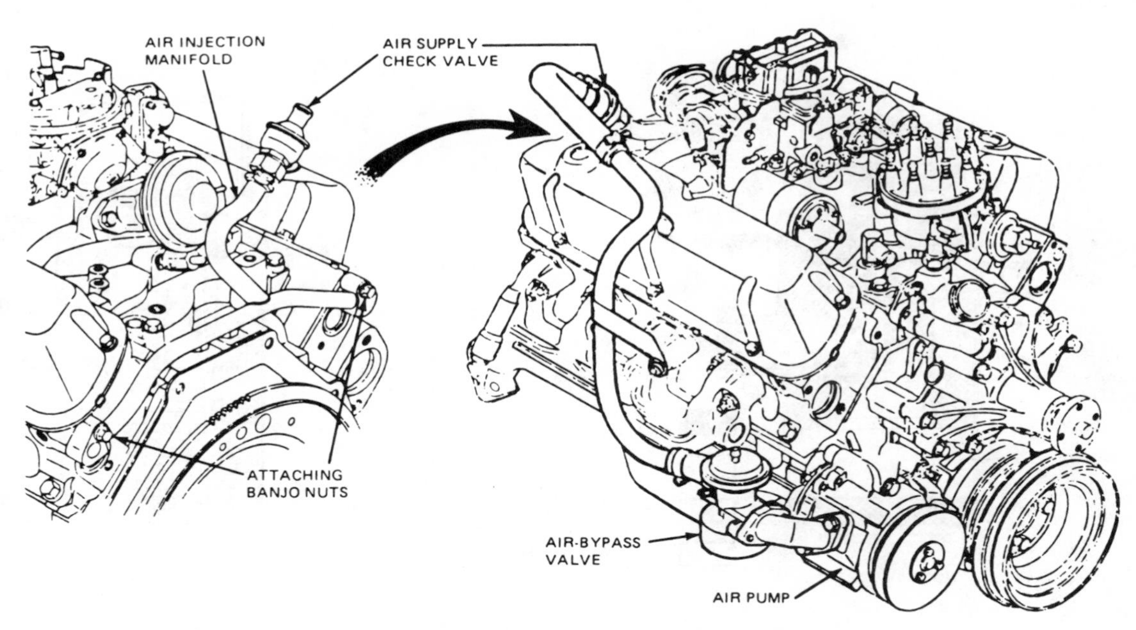

Fig. 4.16 Typical Thermactor system layout (Sec 7)

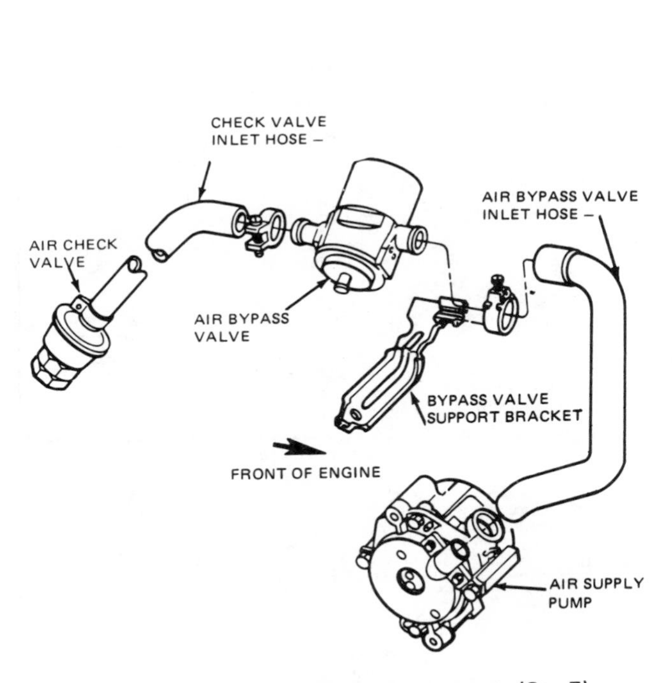

Fig. 4.17 Thermactor system components (Sec 7)

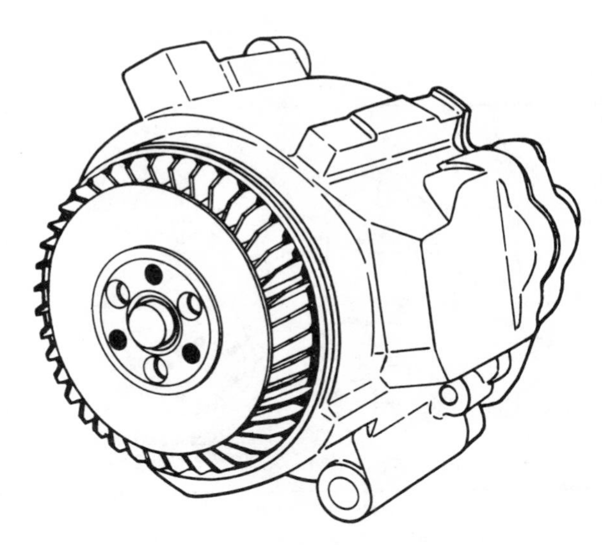

Fig. 4.18 Typical Thermactor pump (Sec 7)

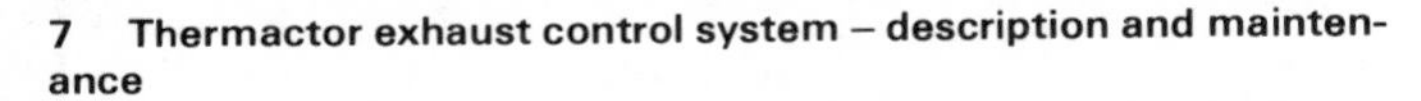

7 Thermactor exhaust control system – description and maintenance

1 This system is designed to reduce the hydrocarbon (HC) and carbon monoxide (CO) content of the exhaust gases by continuing the oxidation of the unburned gasses after they leave the combustion chamber. This air mixes with the hot exhaust gasses and promotes further oxidation, thus reducing their concentration and converting some of them into carbon dioxide and water. Some models also inject Thermactor air directly into the catalytic converter.

2 The air pump draws in air through an impeller-type, centrifugal fan and exhausts it from the exhaust manifold through a vacuum controlled air bypass valve and check valve. Under normal conditions Thermactor air passes straight through the bypass valve, but during deceleration, when there is a high level of intake manifold vacuum, the diaphragm check valve operates to shut off the Thermactor air to the air supply valve check valve and exhausts it to the atmosphere. The air supply check valve is a non-return valve which will allow Thermactor air to pass to the exhaust manifold but will not allow exhaust gasses to flow in the reverse direction.

3 Some models are equipped with an air injector system called Thermactor II which does not use an air pump. This system uses the

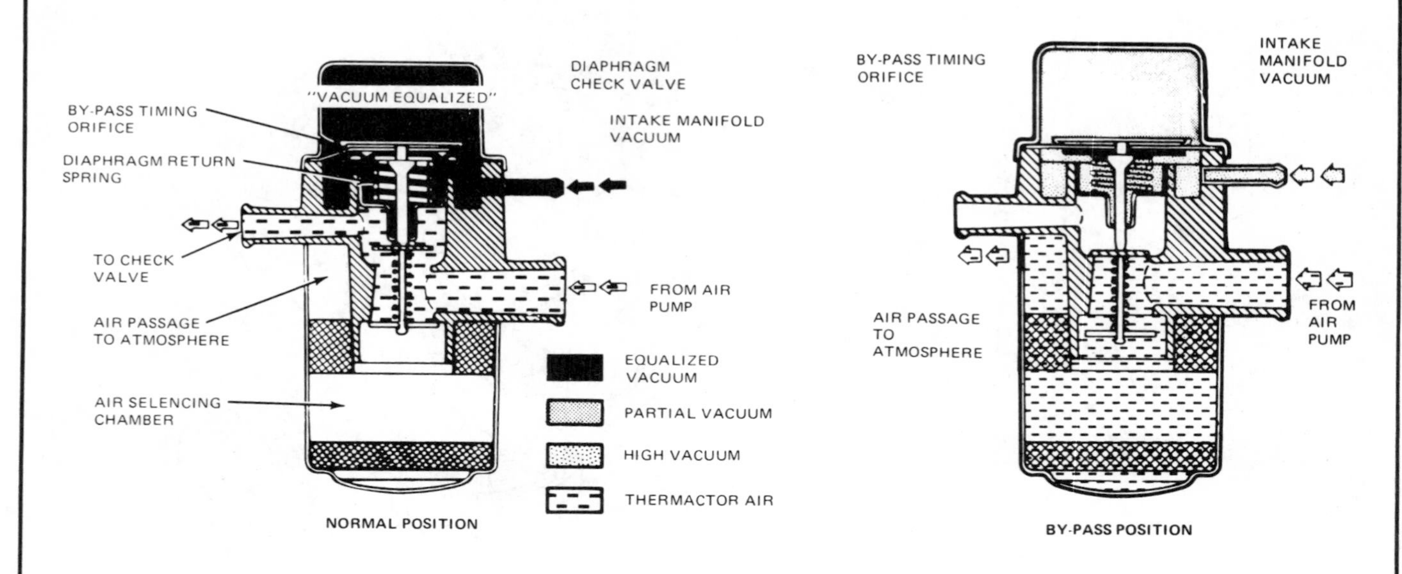

Fig. 4.19 Normally open Thermactor bypass valve (Sec 7)

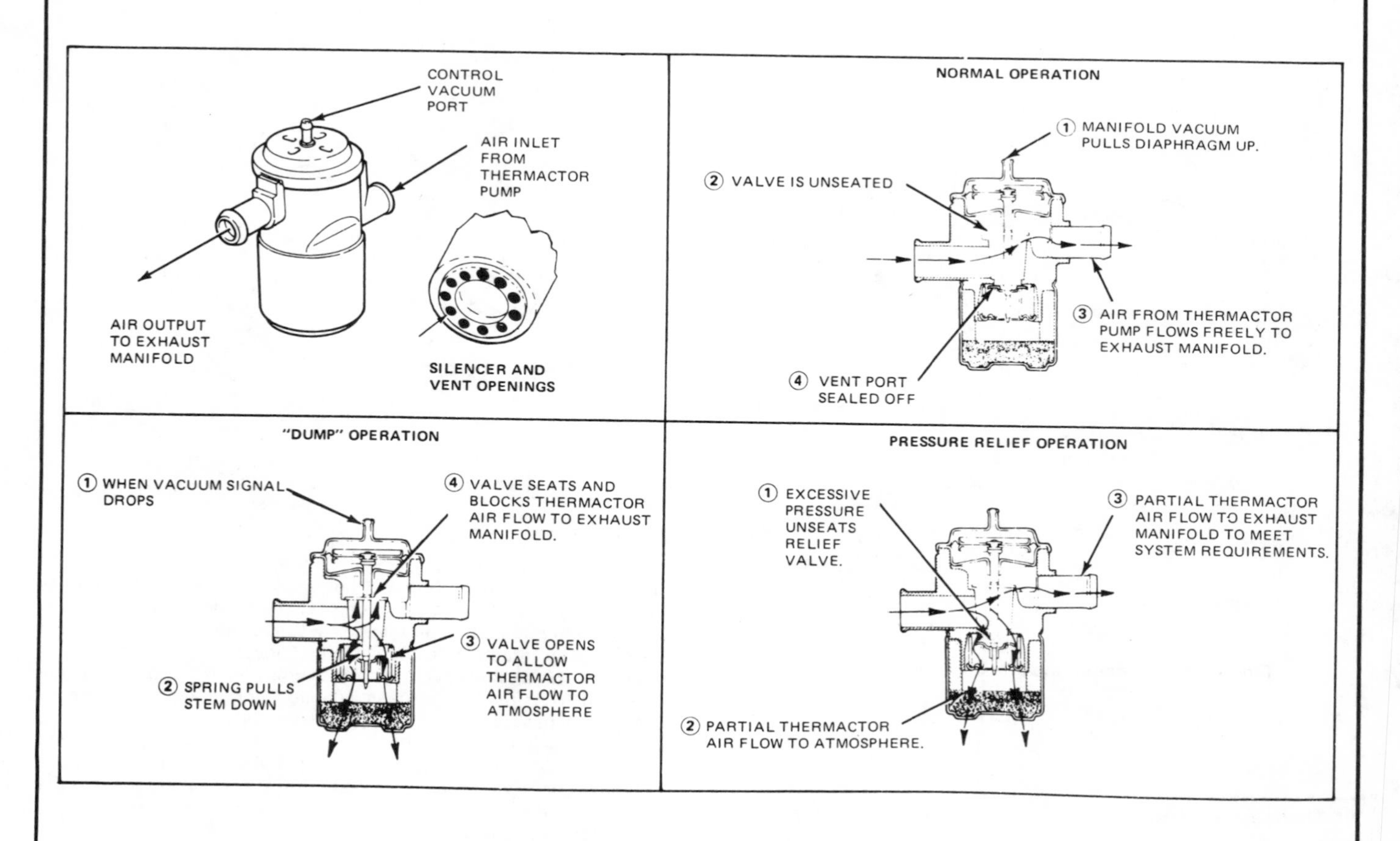

Fig. 4.20 Normally closed Thermactor bypass valve (Sec 7)

natural pulses of the exhaust system to pull the air into the exhaust system. The Thermactor II inlet valve incorporates a reed valve connected to the exhaust manifold and air cleaner by hoses (Fig. 4.19).
4 Several models of air bypass valves are used on the normal Thermactor system, but all are of two main types: normally open or normally closed.
5 Normally open bypass valves remain open because the vacuum is equal on both sides of the diaphragm. Under conditions of suddenly high intake manifold the diaphragm overcomes its return spring pressure, closing the valve and diverting the Thermactor air to the atmosphere momentarily (Fig. 4.19).
6 A normally closed bypass valve is held in the upwards or closed position by manifold pressure and Thermactor air flows to the cylinder heads, blocking the vent port. When the intake manifold fluctuates under acceleration or deceleration, the integral vacuum differential valve cuts off the vacuum, allowing the spring to pull the stem down. This cuts off Thermactor air to the exhaust manifold and diverts the air to the atmosphere (Fig. 4.20).
7 Apart from checking the condition of the drivebelt and hose connections, and checking the drivebelt tension, there is little that can be done without the use of special test equipment. Drivebelt tension should be checked by an authorized dealer with a special tensioning tool. The tensioning procedure is described in Chapter 2.
8 Special equipment is required to carry out a complete test on the bypass valve functions and it is recommended that the car is taken to an authorized dealer.

8 Catalytic converter – description

1 The catalytic converter is incorporated upstream of the exhaust front muffler. The converter is comprised of a ceramic honeycomb-like core housed in a stainless steel pipe. The core is coated with a platinum and palladium catalyst which converts unburned carbon monoxide and hydrocarbons into carbon dioxide and water by a chemical reaction. Converters of this type are called Conventional Oxidation Catalysts (COC) or 'two-way' catalysts because they control two of the three exhaust emissions.
2 'Three-way Catalysts' (TWC) control hydrocarbons (HC), carbon monoxide (CO) and oxides of nitrogen (NOx). Three-way catalysts consist of 2 converters in one shell, with a mixing chamber in between them. The front chamber is coated with rhodium and platinum for controlling NOx while the rear chamber is a two-way type (Fig. 4.22).
3 Air is injected from the Thermactor system into the mixing chamber to aid oxidation.
4 No special maintenance of the converter is required, but it can be damaged by the use of leaded fuels, engine misfire, excessive richness of the carburetor mixture, incorrect operation of the Thermactor system or running out of gasoline.

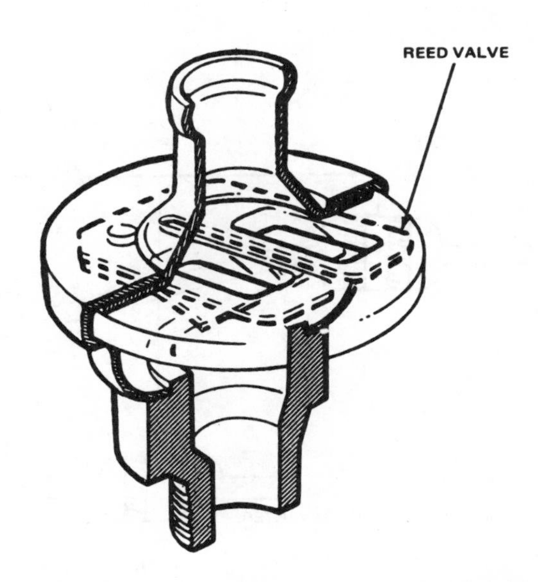

Fig. 4.21 Thermactor II air inlet valve (Sec 7)

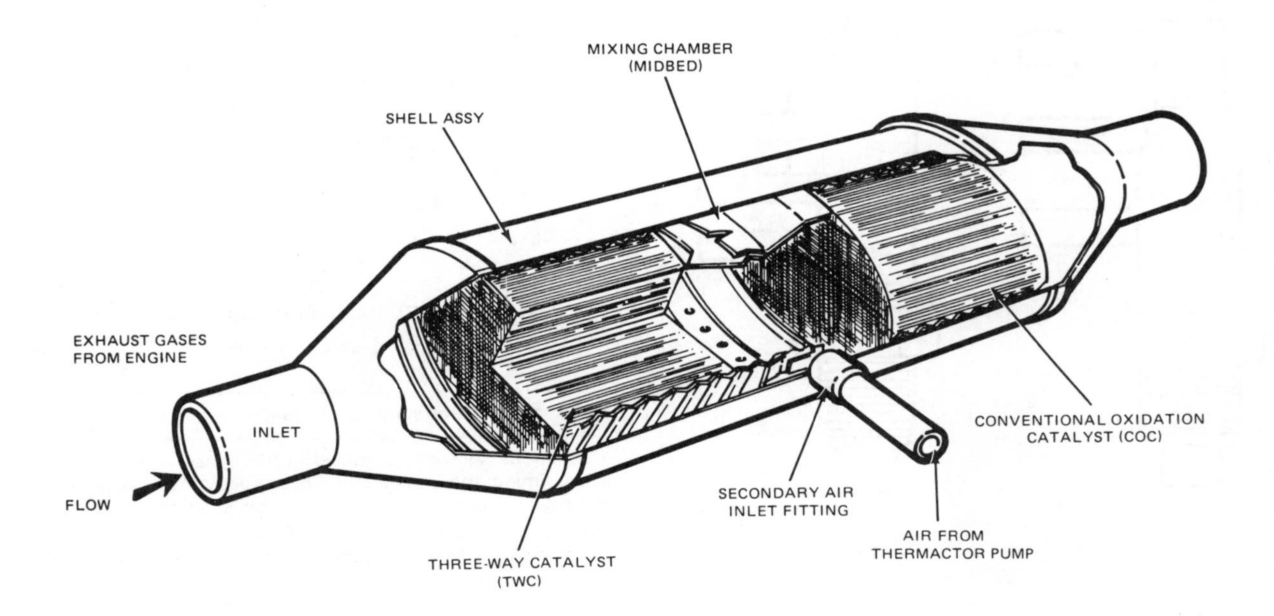

Fig. 4.22 Typical dual catalytic converter (Sec 8)

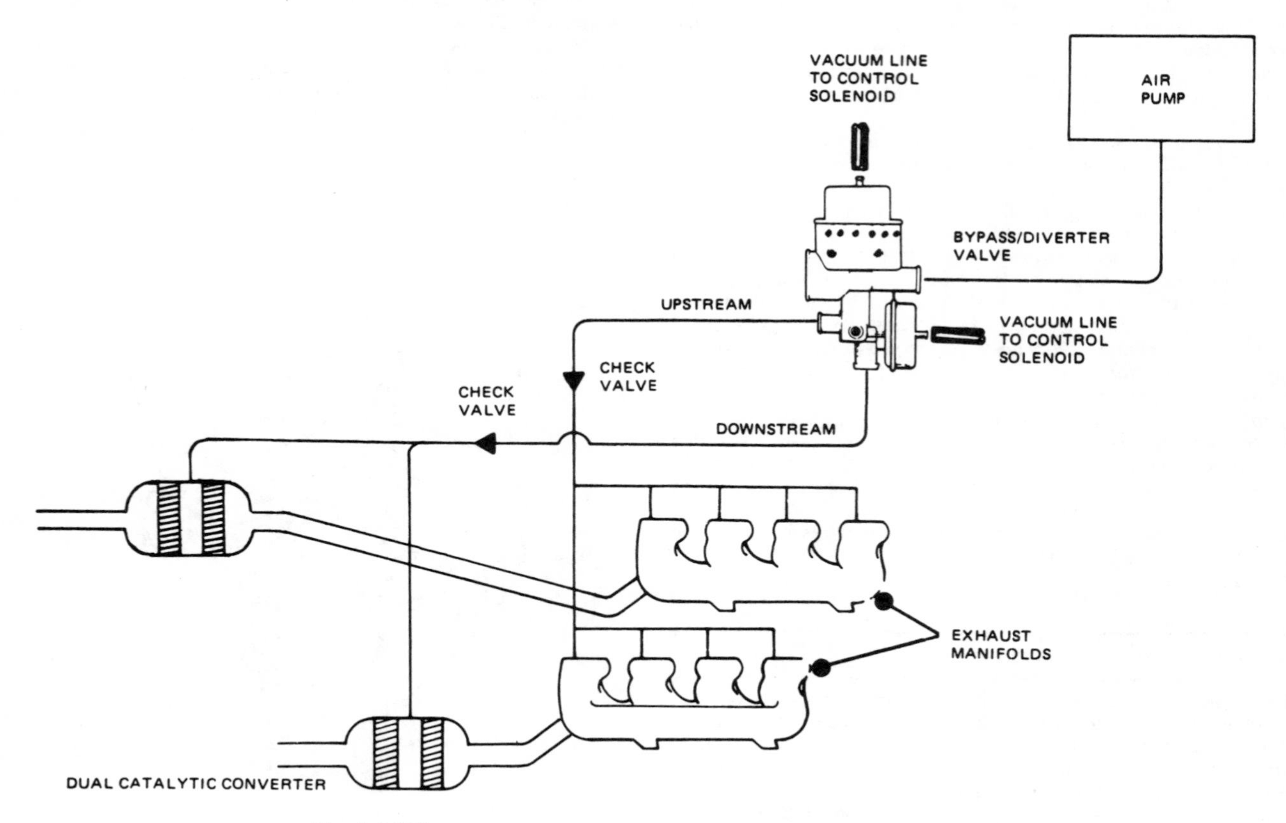

Fig. 4.24 Three-way catalytic system used with Thermactor (Sec 8)

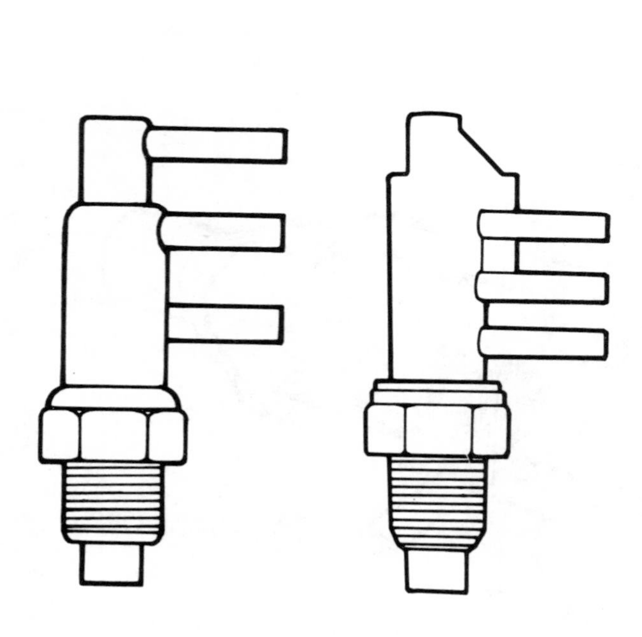

Fig. 4.24 Cooling ported vacuum switch (PVS) (Sec 9)

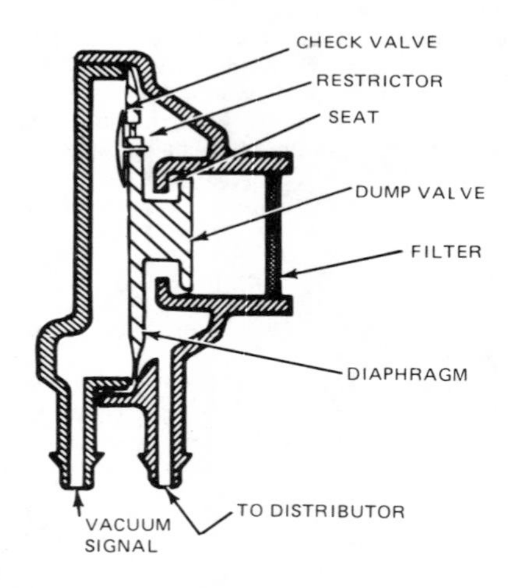

Fig. 4.25 Distributor vent valve (Sec 9)

9 Spark control switches – description

1 Various switches are used in the emission system for modifying spark timing and engine idle. These vacuum switches have anywhere from 2 to 4 ports, depending on their function.

Ported vacuum switches (PVS)

2 A typical ported vacuum switch is situated in the cooling system to increase idle rpm when the engine overheats. When the coolant is at normal temperature, the vacuum goes through the top and center ports of the PVS, providing the distributor with vacuum advance suitable for normal driving. When hot, the PVS center and bottom parts are connected so that the engine manifold vacuum allows the distributor to advance and increase idle.

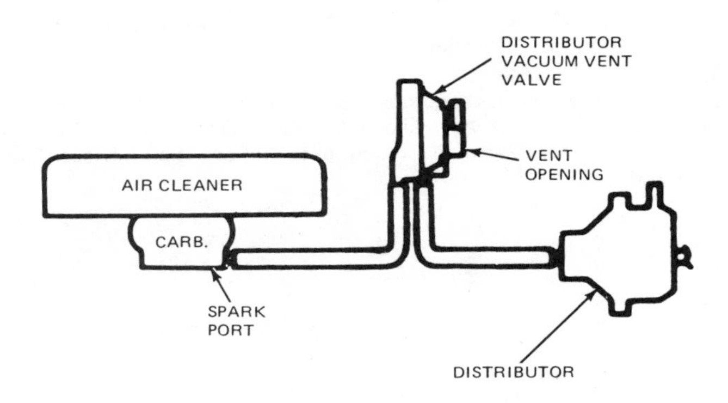

Fig. 4.26 Typical distributor vent valve installation (Sec 9)

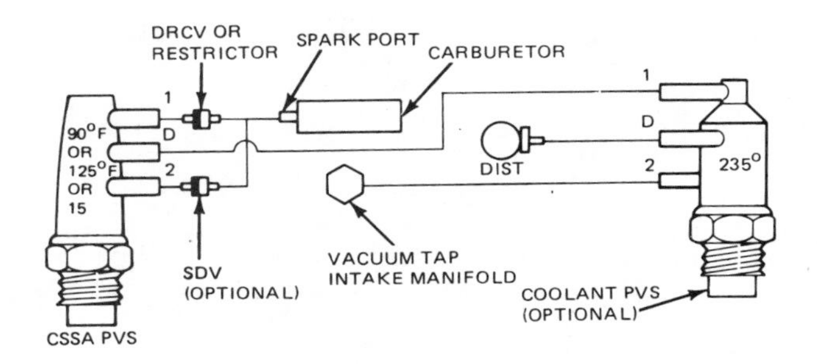

Fig. 4.27 Typical cold start spark advance (CSSA) system (Sec 9)

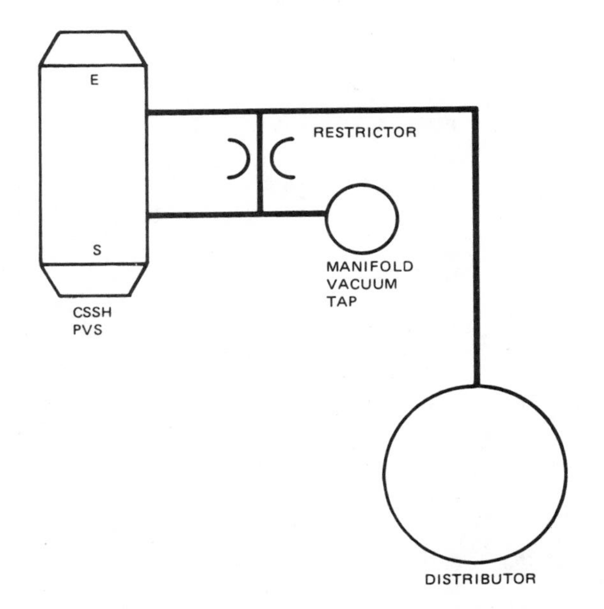

Fig. 4.28 Cold start spark hold (CSSH) system (Sec 9)

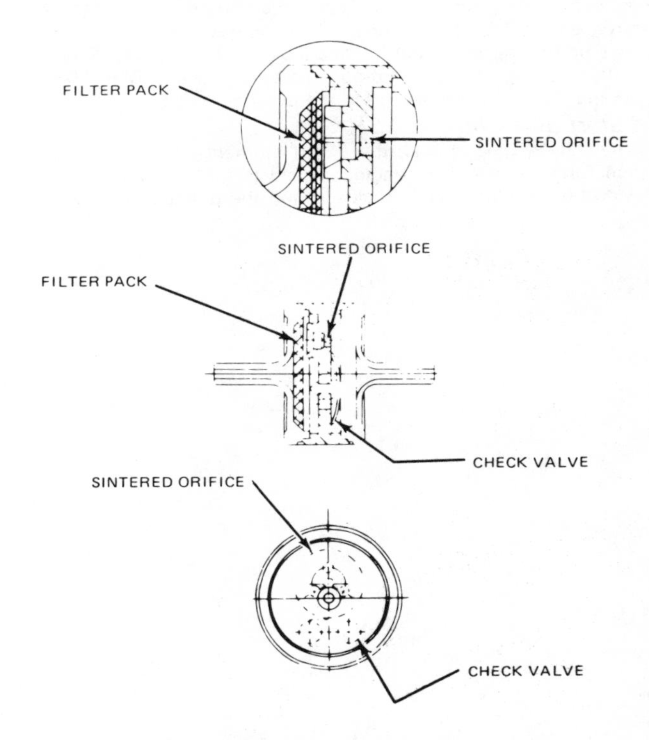

Fig. 4.29 Spark delay valve (SDV) (Sec 9)

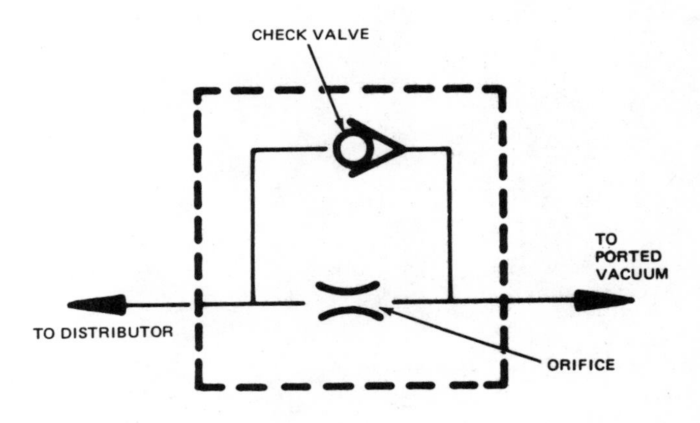

Fig. 4.30 Spark delay valve schematic (Sec 9)

Distributor vacuum vent valve

3 Some engines use a distributor vacuum vent valve to both prevent fuel from migrating into the distributor advance diaphragm and to act as a spark advance delay valve. During light acceleration deceleration, and idle, the vent valve dumps vacuum through a check valve (Figs. 4.25 and 4.26). This keep the distributor from advancing excessively for the load and evacuates the fuel in the spark port line.

Cold start spark advance (CSSA)

4 The CSSA system is located in the distributor spark control system. When coolant temperature is below 128° (53°), it momentarily traps the spark port vacuum at the distributor advance diaphragm. The vacuum follows a path through the carburetor vacuum tap, the distributor retard control valve (DRCV), the CSSA ported vacuum

switch, cooling vacuum switch to the distributor. At coolant temperatures above 128°F, the CSSA PVS operates and the vacuum follows a path from the carburetor spark port through the cooling PVS to the distributor. In an overheating condition, above 225°F (103°C), the cooling PVS operates as described in paragraph 2.

Cold start spark hold (CSSH)

5 When the engine is cold, the CSSH momentarily provides spark advance for improved cold engine acceleration. Below 128°F, the CSSH ported vacuum swtch is closed and the distributor vacuum is routed through a restrictor. Under cold starting conditions, the high vacuum present advances the distributor. During cold acceleration, the vacuum is slowly bled off through the restrictor, slowing the vacuum advance during initial acceleration.

Spark delay valve (SDV)

6 Spark delay valves are designed to slow the air flow in one direction while a check valve allows free flow in the opposite direction. This allows closer control of vacuum operated emission devices (Figs. 4.29 and 4.30).

Chapter 5 Ignition system

Refer to Chapter 13 for specifications and information related to 1981 thru 1987 models

Contents

Specifications

Distributor

Type	Solid state, breakerless
Automatic advance	Vacuum and centrifugal
Direction of rotation	
V6	Clockwise
V8	Counterclockwise
Static advance	Refer to Emission Control Decal

Coil

Coil	Motorcraft 8 volt, oil filled

Firing order

V6	1-4-2-5-3-6
V8	1-5-4-2-6-3-7-8

Spark plugs

2.8L V6	AWSF-42
4.2L V8	ASF-42
5.0L V8	ASF-52
5.0L V8, Calif.	ASF-52-6
Spark plug electrode gap	
2.8L V6	0.034 in
4.2L V8	0.050 in
5.0L V8	0.050 in
5.0L V8, Calif.	0.060 in

Note: *all adjustment figures given in these specifications should be double-checked against the vehicle's individual Emission Control Decal.*

Torque specifications

	ft-lb	Nm
Spark plugs		
V6	7 to 11	9 to 15
V8	10 to 15	14 to 20
Distributor clamp bolt		
V6	12 to 15	16 to 20
V8	5 to 10	6 to 13

1 General information

All models are equipped with an electronic (breakerless) type distributor. Mechanically, this system is similar to the contact breaker type with the exception that the distributor cam and contact breaker are replaced by an armature and magnetic pick-up. The coil primary circuit is controlled by an amplifier module.

The system is made up of a primary (low voltage) circuit and a secondary (high voltage) circuit (Fig. 5.3).

When the ignition is switched on, the ignition primary circuit is energized. When the distributor armature 'teeth' approach the magnetic coil assembly, a voltage is induced which signals the amplifier to turn off the coil primary current. A timing circuit in the amplifier module turns the coil current on after the coil field has collapsed.

When on, current flows from the battery through the ignition switch, through the coil primary winding, through the amplifier module and then to ground. When the current is off, the magnetic field in the ignition coil collapses, inducing a high voltage in the coil secondary winding. This is conducted to the distributor where the rotor directs it to the appropriate spark plug. This process is repeated for each power stroke of the engine.

The distributor is equipped with devices to control the actual point of ignition according to the engine speed and load. As the engine speed increases, two centrifugal weights move outwards and alter the position of the armature in relation to the distributor shaft to advance the spark slightly. As engine load increases (as when climbing hills or accelerating), a reduction in intake manifold vacuum causes the base plate assembly to move slightly in the opposite direction under the action of the spring in the vacuum unit, retarding the spark slightly and tending to counteract the centrifugal advance. Under light loading

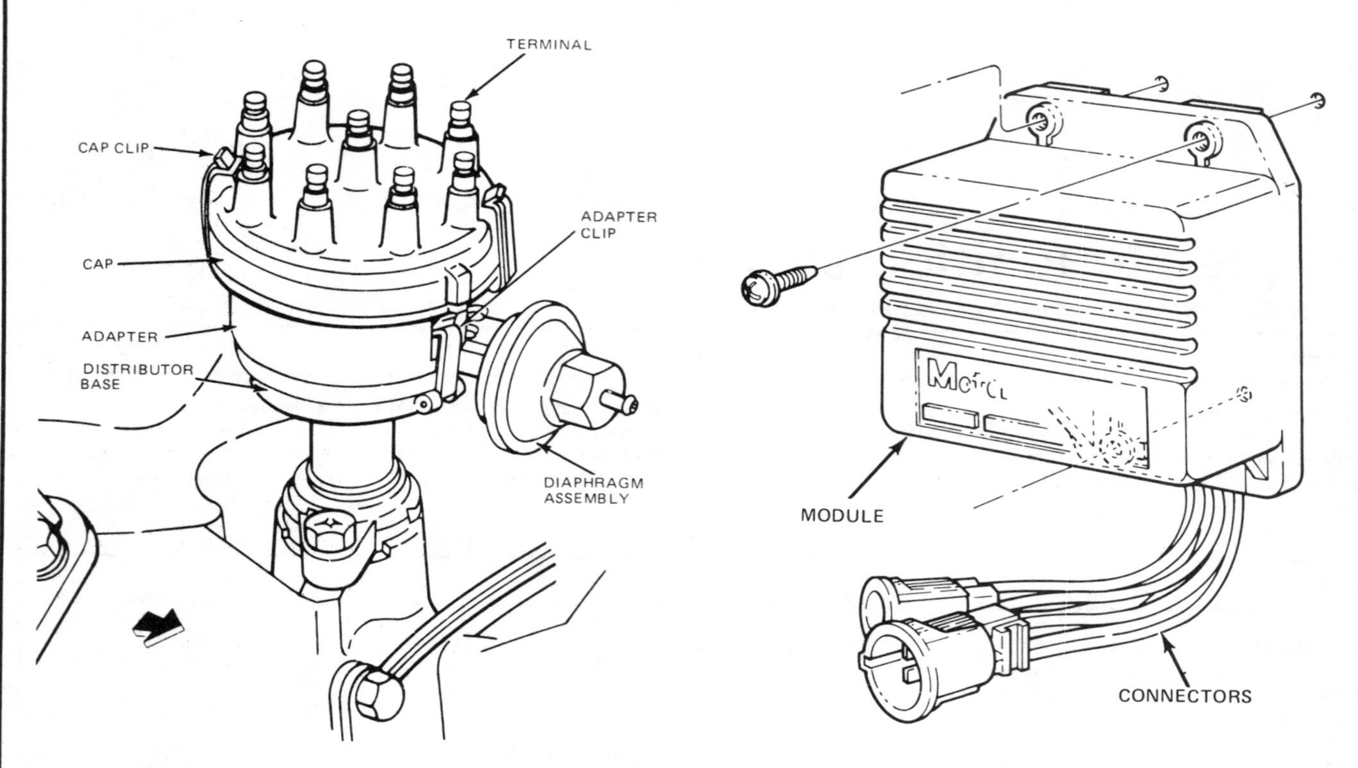

Fig. 5.1 Breakerless ignition distributor components (Sec 1)

Fig. 5.2 Amplifier module (Sec 1)

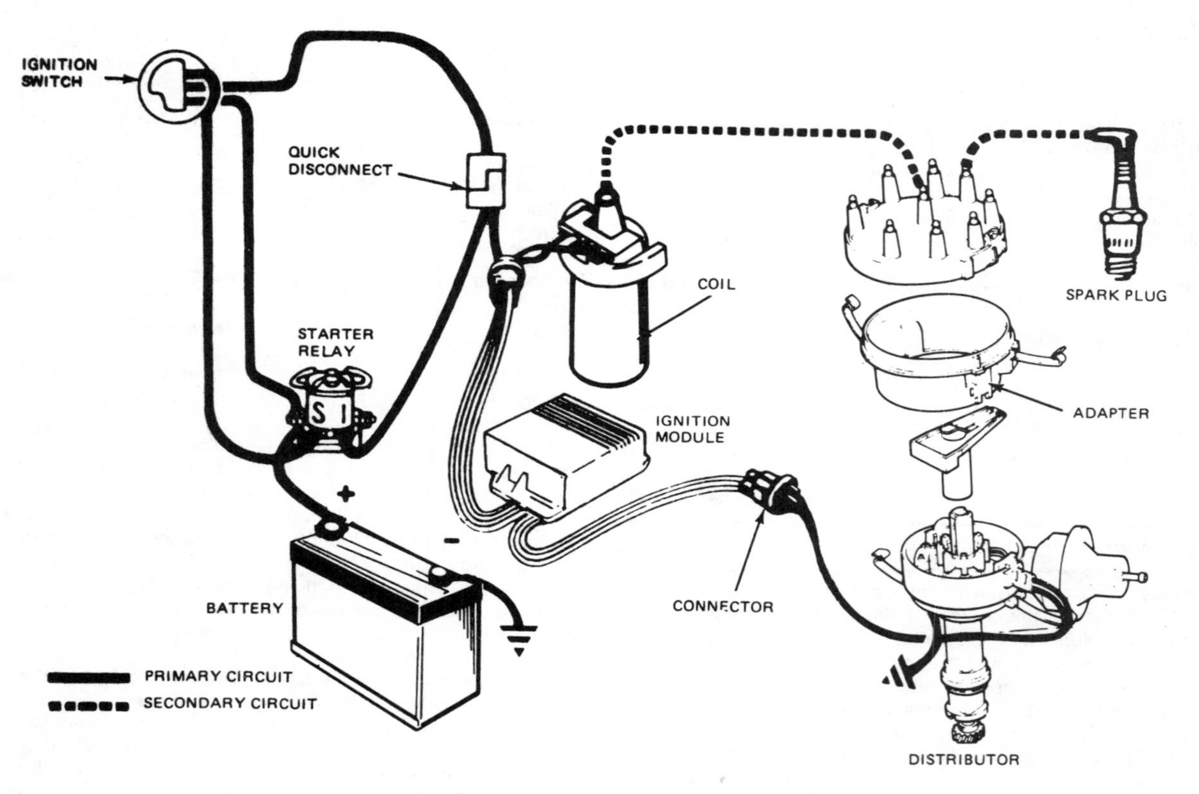

Fig. 5.3 Breakerless ignition system (Sec 1)

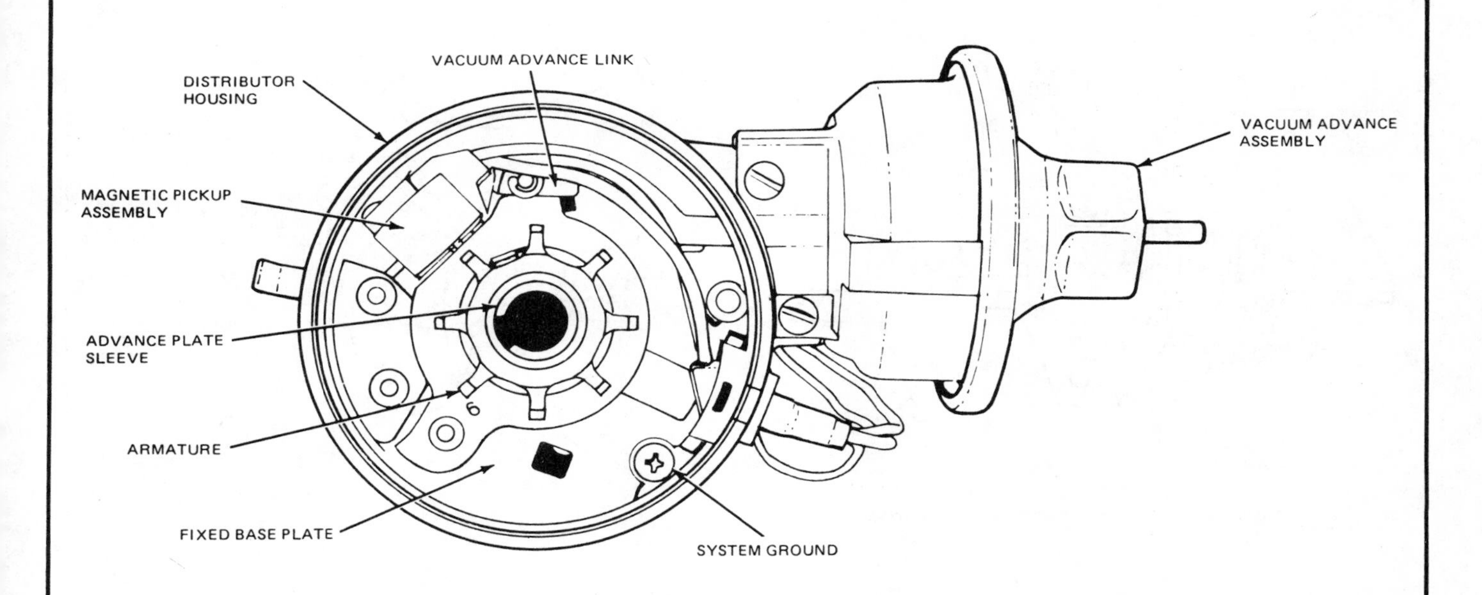

Fig. 5.4 Breakerless distributor components (Sec 1)

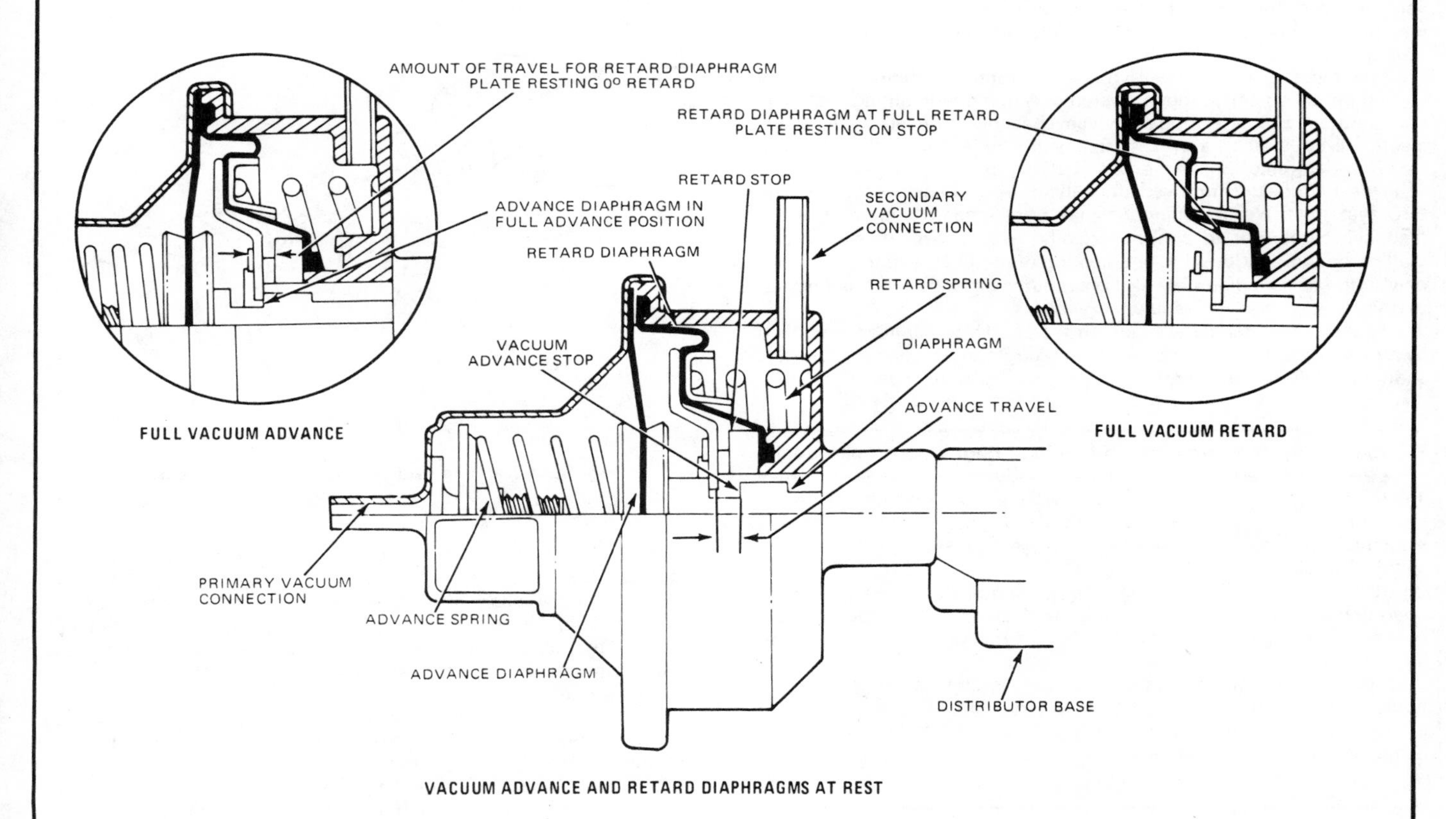

Fig. 5.5 Dual diaphragm vacuum advance (Sec 1)

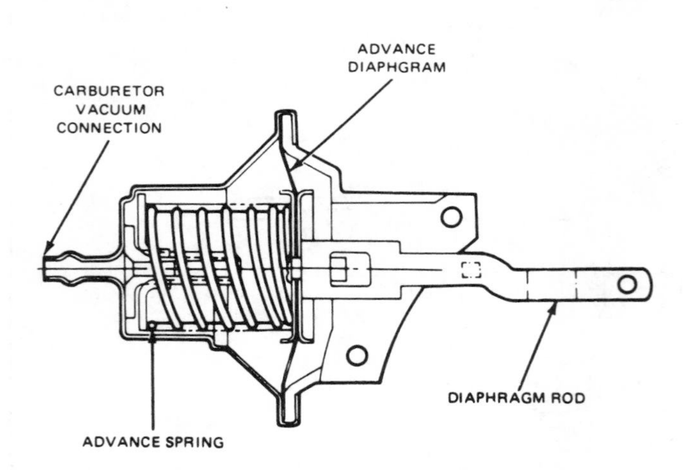

Fig. 5.6 Single diaphragm vacuum advance (Sec 1)

conditions (moderate, steady driving) the comparatively high intake manifold vacuum on the vacuum advance diaphragm causes the baseplate assembly to move in the opposite direction of the distributor shaft rotation, giving a larger amount of spark advance.

Some models are equipped with a dual diaphragm vacuum assembly which is operated by two different sources of vacuum. The outer (primary) diaphragm is operated by the carburetor venturi vacuum and provides timing advance. The inner (secondary) diaphragm is operated by intake manifold vacuum and retards ignition timing.

For most practical do-it-yourself purposes, ignition timing is carried out as on conventional systems. A monolithic timing system is incorporated on some models which can only be used with special electronic equipment, a procedure beyond the scope of this manual.

The Electronic Engine Control (EEC) system is installed on some vehicles to provide improved driveability and emission control. The EEC system works in conjunction with an onboard computer and a feedback carburetor to control virtually every aspect of engine and ignition operation. Checking or adjusting of the EEC system is possible only with special equipment and procedures described in this Chapter pertain only to non-EEC-equipped vehicles.

Faults in the breakerless ignition system which cannot be rectified by the substitution of parts or cleaning/tightening connections, etc. should be referred to a properly equipped dealer or repair shop.

2 Ignition system servicing and Federal Regulations (all models)

1 In order to conform with the Federal Regulations which govern the emission of hydrocarbons and carbon monoxide from car exhaust systems, the engine carburetion and ignition systems have been suitably modified.

2 It is critically important that the ignition system is kept in good operational order and to achieve this, accurate analytical equipment is needed to check and reset the distributor function. This will be found at a local repair shop or dealer.

3 Information contained in this Chapter is supplied to enable the home mechanic to set the ignition system roughly to enable you to start the engine. Thereafter the car must be taken to the local dealer or repair shop for final tuning.

3 Spark plugs – removal, checking and installation

Note: *During this operation, the end of your wrench may be near the battery. To avoid an electrical shock, either cover the top of the battery with a heavy cloth or disconnect the negative cable.*

1 Before removing any spark plug wires, check that they are properly numbered as to their original location. Mark the wires with tape if necessary or remove only one plug at a time so that the wires are always in order.

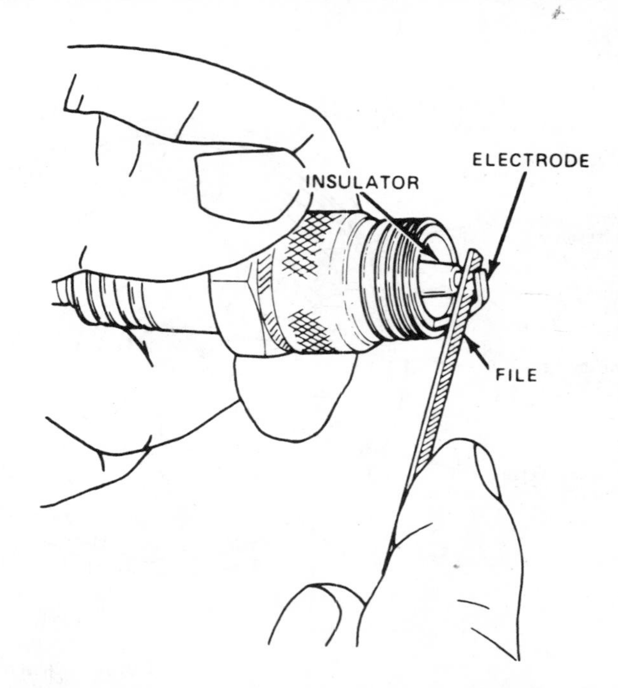

Fig. 5.7 Cleaning spark plug electrode with a file (Sec 3)

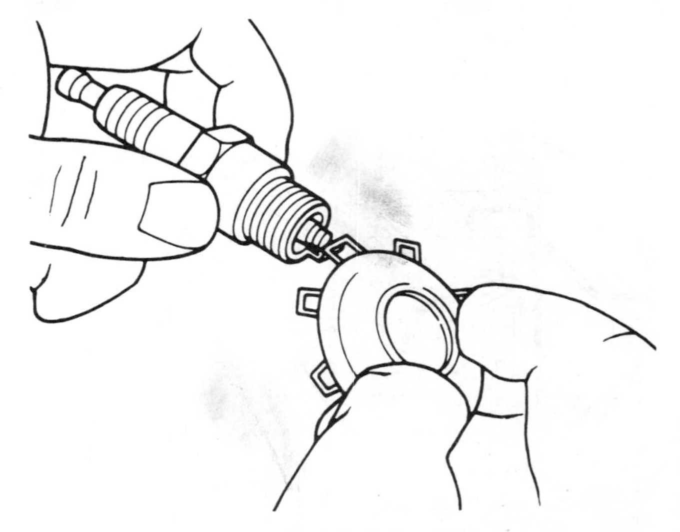

Fig. 5.8 Checking and setting plug gap (Sec 3)

2 Remove each spark plug wire by grasping the molded boot, twisting it slightly and then pulling it away from the end of the spark plug. Do not pull on the wire itself because it could separate the connector inside the boot. If this happens, the wire must be replaced with a new one.

3 Using an insulated spark plug socket, loosen each spark plug about two turns and carefully clean around the plug hole so that no dirt can enter when the plug is removed.

4 Fully remove each of the spark plugs by hand.

5 Inspect the firing ends of the plugs for deposits and electrode condition. Inspect the insulators for cracks and discoloration.

6 If the plug appears useable, clean it with a wire brush to remove carbon deposits from the electrodes and threads.

7 Use a small file to clean the electrode surfaces (Fig. 5.7).

8 Set the spark plug electrode gap to the setting on the emission control decal by bending the outer electrode, never the center one (Fig. 5.8).

Measuring plug gap. A feeler gauge of the correct size (see ignition system specifications) should have a slight 'drag' when slid between the electrodes. Adjust gap if necessary

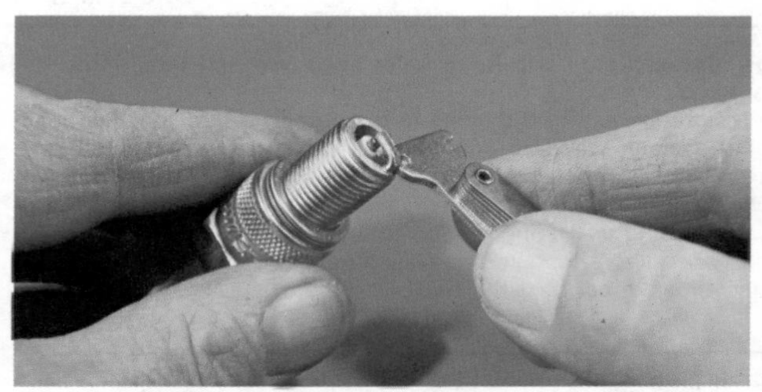

Adjusting plug gap. The plug gap is adjusted by bending the ground electrode inwards, or outwards, as necessary until the correct clearance is obtained. Note the use of the correct tool

Normal. Gray brown deposits, lightly coated core nose. Gap increasing by around 0.001 in (0.025 mm) per 1000 miles (1600 km). Plugs ideally suited to engine, and engine in good condition

Carbon fouling. Dry, black, sooty deposits. Will cause weak spark and eventually misfire. Fault: over-rich fuel mixture. Check: carburetor mixture settings, float level and jet sizes; choke operation and cleanliness of air filter. Plugs can be re-used after cleaning

Oil fouling. Wet, oily deposits. Will cause weak spark and eventually misfire. Fault: worn bores/piston rings or valve guides; sometimes occurs (temporarily) during running-in period. Plugs can be re-used after thorough cleaning

Overheating. Electrodes have glazed appearance, core nose very white – few deposits. Fault: plug overheating. Check: plug value, ignition timing, fuel octane rating (too low) and fuel mixture (too weak). Discard plugs and cure fault immediately

Electrode damage. Electrodes burned away; core nose has burned, glazed appearance. Fault: pre-ignition. Check: as for 'Overheating' but may be more severe. Discard plugs and remedy fault before piston or valve damage occurs

Split core nose (may appear initially as a crack). Damage is self-evident, but cracks will only show after cleaning. Fault: pre-ignition or wrong gap-setting technique. Check: ignition timing, cooling system, fuel octane rating (too low) and fuel mixture (too weak). Discard plugs, rectify fault immediately

9 Position each plug into its cylinder head port and thread into the hole by hand.
10 Fully tighten each of the plugs to the proper torque specifications.
11 Using a clean standard screwdriver, apply a thin film of silicone grease on the entire interior surface of the spark plug wire boot.
12 Push each of the spark plug wires into position on the ends of the plugs, again using a twisting motion to fully seat the boots. Make sure that the wires are re-installed in their original positions.
13 Uncover or re-connect the battery.

4 Spark plug wires – checking and replacement

1 The wires leading from the distributor cap to the spark plugs and the single wires from the center of the cap to the ignition coil are called the secondary, or high-tension wires. These play a very important role in the overall operation of the ignition system and should be periodically checked and/or replaced.

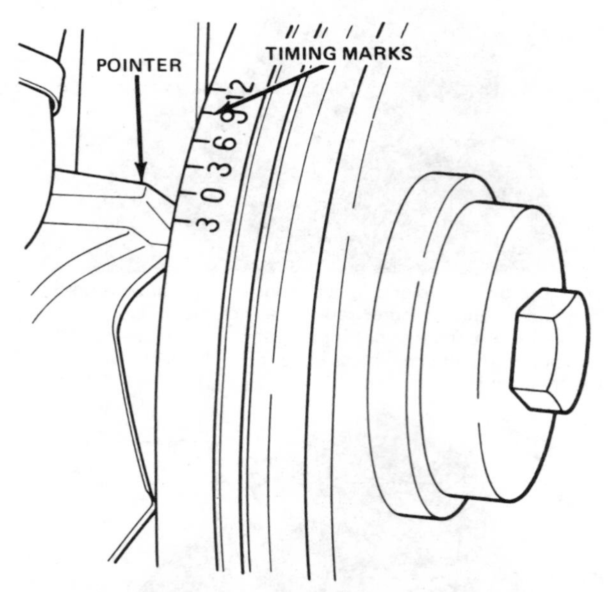

Fig. 5.9 Typical timing marks (Secs 5 and 6)

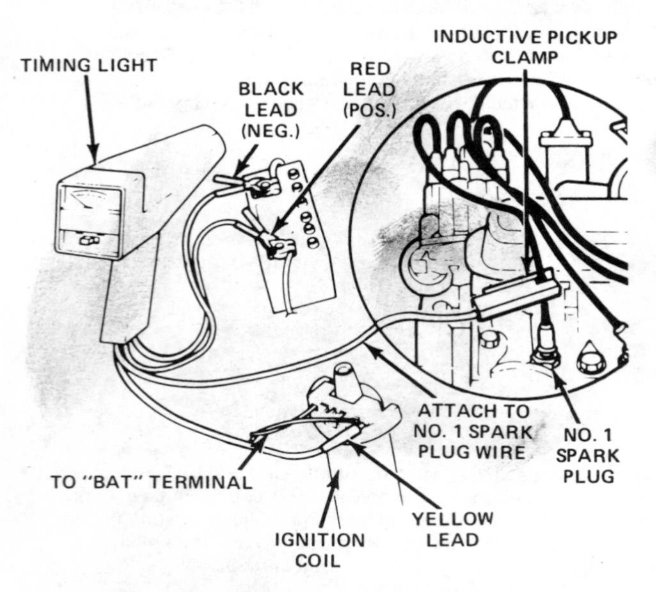

Fig. 5.10 Typical inductive timing light installation (Sec 6)

2 These wires are a radio resistance type designed to filter out electrical impulses which are the source of ignition noise interference. Make sure replacement wires are of this type.
3 Due to the high energy type ignition system, it is important to apply silicone grease to the inside boot surface whenever a high-tension wire is disconnected from a spark plug, the distributor cap or ignition coil.
4 To visually check the wires, use a clean rag to wipe all dirt and grime fron each plug wire, its entire length. As this is done, inspect for cracks, burns or any other obvious damage to the wire insulation.
5 The wires can be further checked using an ohmmeter.
6 Disconnect the distributor cap from the top of the distributor.
7 Disconnect one of the spark plug leads from its spark plug. Do this by using the special removal tool, or by grasping the molded boot, twisting, and then pulling the wire from the plug.
8 Place one of the ohmmeter probes inside the plug boot and the other touching the appropriate terminal inside the distributor cap.
9 If the resistance of the wires exceeds 5000 ohms per inch, the wire should be completely removed from the distributor cap and the resistance measured directly from the wire ends.
10 If the resistance still exceeds 5000 ohms, the wire should be replaced with a new one.
11 All wires should be checked in the same manner.
12 If the wires are in good shape, apply a thin film of silicone grease to the inside of each disconnected boot and reinstall. Push and twist to fully seat the wire boot on the end of the spark.
13 Whenever a new set of plug wires is purchased to replace the old, care must be taken to avoid mixing up the spark plug order. This is best done by replacing the wires one at a time. Due to the nature of these wires, the home mechanic should probably purchase replacement plug wire sets which are pre-cut to the proper length and ready to install.

5 Ignition timing – preparation

1 Before you begin the task of timing the engine or checking the timing, a few special tools must be gathered and some preparatory steps taken.
2 Engine timing requires the following tools:
- *a) Induction strobe light or Sun meter pickup probe*
- *b) Hand held dwell-tachometer*
- *c) Proper box end wrench to fit the distributor hold-down bolt*
- *d) White paint and thin brush*
- *e) Shop cloths and cleaning solvent*

With the items above readily at hand, perform the following:
3 Clean the surface of the front damper and the pointer with the solvent and cloths.
4 Turn the engine over until the proper timing mark, indicated on the engine decal, is aligned with the pointer. With the white paint and thin brush, carefully paint in the proper timing mark. (On some engines it may be necessary to mark both the proper degree line on the damper and the damper notch.)

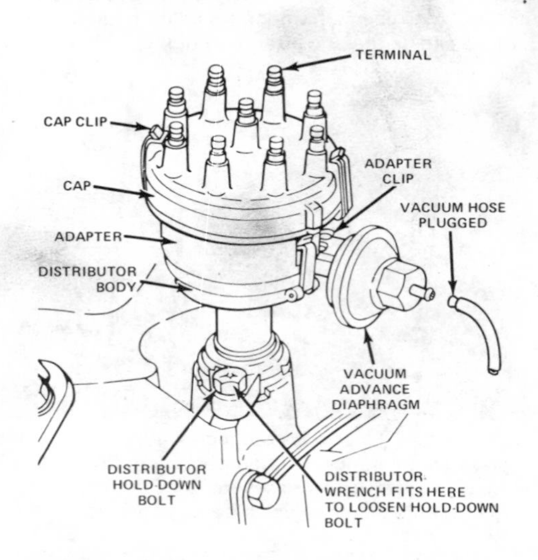

Fig. 5.11 Distributor vacuum plugged (Sec 6)

5 When the brush is cleaned and the paint put away, you can begin the timing checks and adjustments.

6 Engine initial timing – setting

1 Place the transmission in Park (automatic transmission) or Neutral (manual).
2 Start the engine and allow it to reach normal operating temperature.
3 Shut off the engine and connect a hand-held tachometer and inductive timing light to the engine, following the manufacturer's instructions.
4 Remove the vacuum hose from the distributor advance connection and plug the hose (Fig. 5.11).
5 With the engine at normal idle (consult emission decal), shine the beam of the timing light against the timing marks on the front marker and note whether timing mark (marked with paint as described in Section 3) is aligned with the pointer. If the timing mark is not aligned, loosen the hold-down bolt on the distributor and turn the distributor until the marks are in alignment. Tighten the bolt.
6 Shut off the engine and remove the plug from the distributor advance hose and reconnect the hose. Remove all of the timing check equipment.

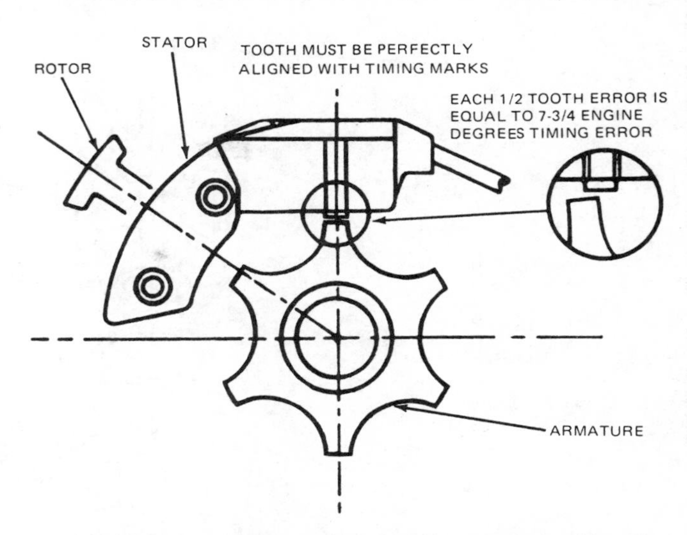

Fig. 5.12 Correct stator position for V6 static timing (Sec 7)

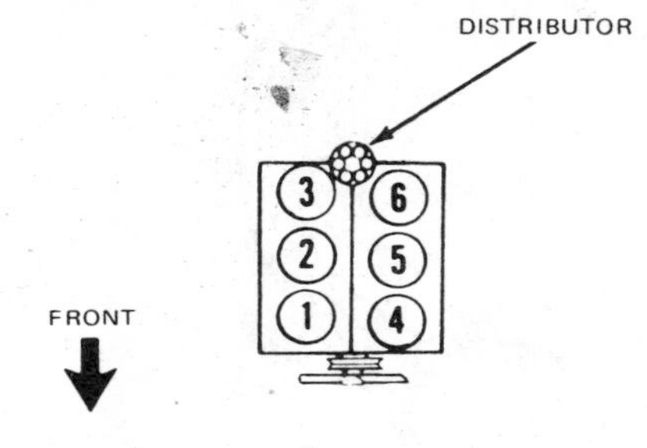

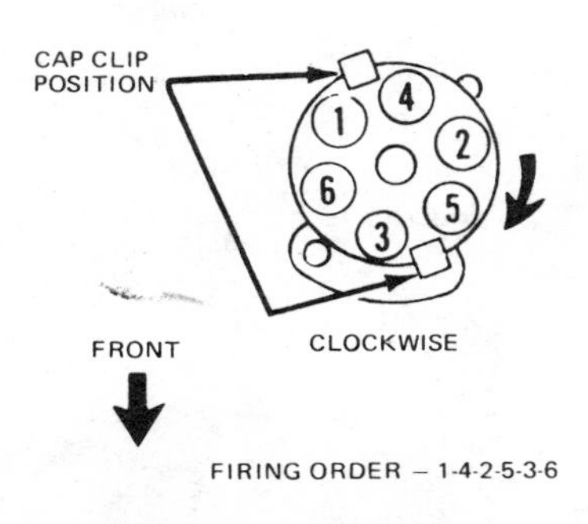

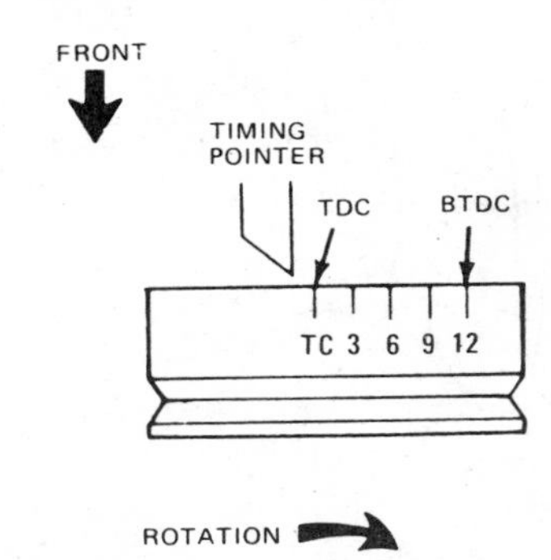

Fig. 5.13 Ignition timing marks, firing order and distributor location for 2.8L V6 (Sec 6)

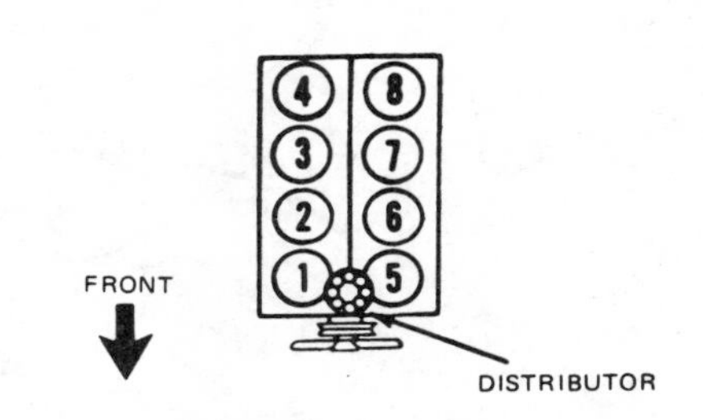

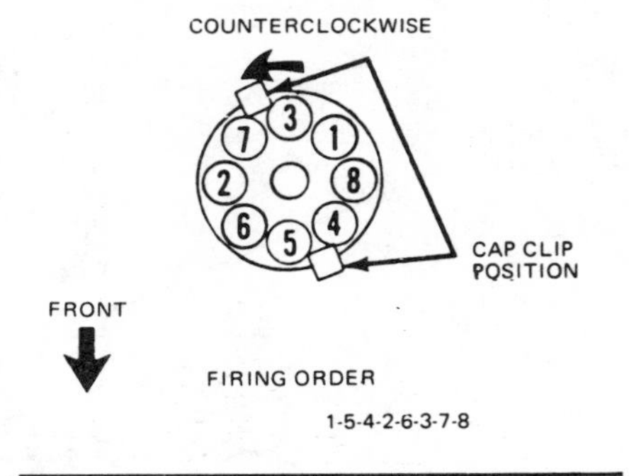

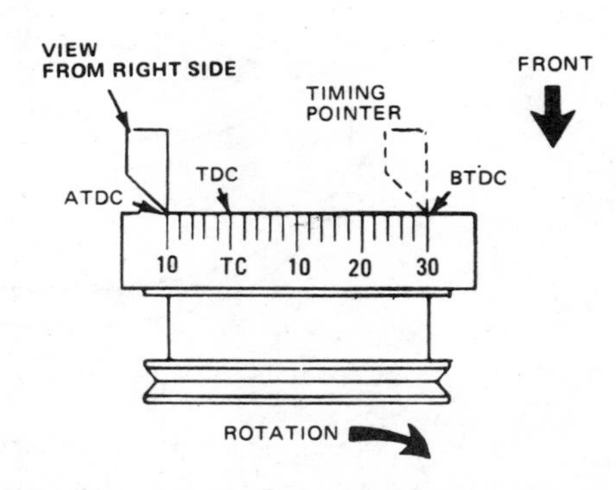

Fig. 5.14 Ignition timing marks, firing order and distributor location for V8 (Sec 6)

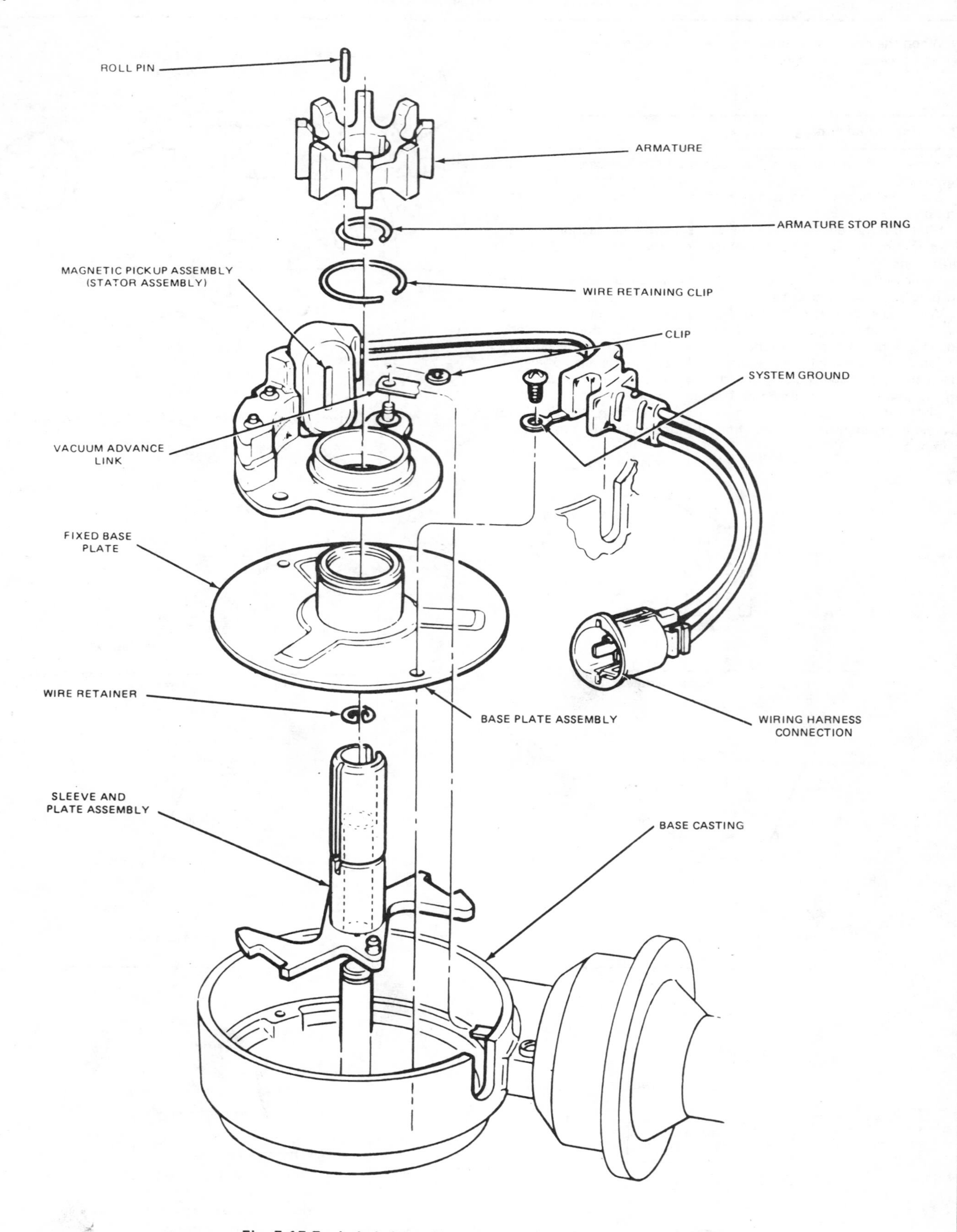

Fig. 5.15 Exploded view of breakerless ignition (Secs 7 and 8)

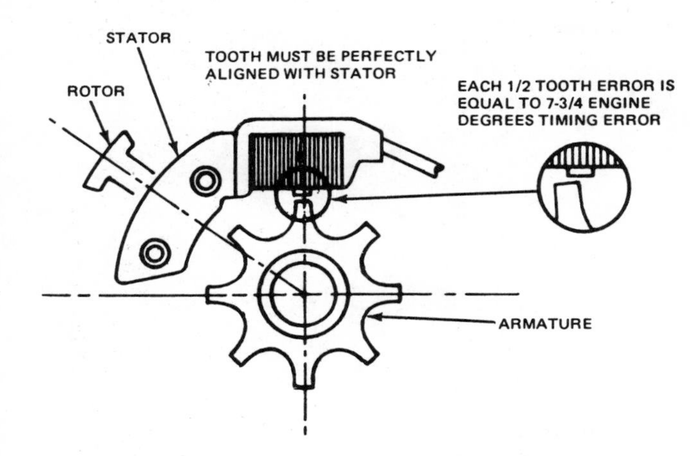

Fig. 5.16 Correct stator position for V8 static timing (Sec 7)

7 Distributor – removal and installation

1 Remove the air cleaner.
2 Disconnect the distributor harness and vacuum advance line.
3 Remove the distributor cap from the top of the distributor. Position the cap (with the wires attached) to one side. Use a length of wire or tape to hold the cap out of the way.
4 Remove the rotor and adaptor section from the top of the distributor. Reinstall the rotor to the top of the distributor shaft.
5 Scribe or paint a mark on the distributor body in a direct line with the rotor arm. A small dab of paint on the rotor is also a useful aid in alignment.
6 Scribe another mark in line with these two on the cylinder block. These marks are crucial to the re-installation of the distributor in the exact same direction and position.
7 Disconnect the wiring harness connector.
8 Remove the hold-down bolt at the base of the distributor and carefully withdraw the distributor from the engine. On V6 engines, the oil pump driveshaft may come out with the distributor.
9 If the engine has not been rotated, installation is basically a reversal of removal. If the oil pump shaft was removed with the distributor, coat one end of this shaft with heavy grease and insert it into the hex hole in the distributor shaft.
10 Align the rotor with the mark on the distributor body and the armature with the marks on the top of the magnetic pickup (Figs. 5.12 and 5.13).
11 Position the distributor into the cylinder block, aligning the rotor and distributor body markings with the mark on the cylinder block.
12 Install the distributor hold-down clamp and bolt. Do not tighten the bolt completely until the initial timing is checked later.
13 Connect the vacuum hose(s) and the wiring connector.
14 Install the adaptor, rotor and cap.
15 Install the air cleaner.
16 Check the ignition timing as described in Section 5 and tighten the distributor hold-down bolts to specification.

8 Distributor stator assembly – removal and installation

1 Remove the distributor cap, adapter and rotor from the top of the distributor.
2 Disconnect the electrical harness plug.
3 Using a small gear puller or two screwdrivers, pry the armature from the sleeve and plate assembly.
4 Remove the roll pin, using caution not to damage the pickup coil wires.
5 Remove the E-clip washer and wave washer which are used to secure the stator assembly to the lower plate.
6 Remove the ground screw and lift the stator assembly off the plate.
7 To install, place the stator assembly into position, inserting the post into diaphragm pull rod hole.
8 Slide the wiring grommet into the slot at the edge of the lower plate and secure the ground screw.
9 Install the washers and E-clip to secure the pick-up coil assembly. The wave washer should have the outer edges up.
10 Install the armature on the sleeve and plate assembly making sure the roll pin is engaged in the matching slots.
11 Install the rotor, adaptor and cap. Connect the wiring harness plug.

9 Distributor vacuum advance unit – removal and installation

1 Remove the distributor cap, rotor and adapter.
2 Disconnect the vacuum line(s).
3 Remove the attaching screws at the diaphragm unit and lift away the diaphragm unit and identification tag. The unit is best removed by tilting downward to disengage the link from the stator assembly.
4 Upon installation, hook the diaphragm link in position and place the unit against the distributor body.
5 Install the identification tag and tighten the attaching screws.
6 Connect the vacuum hose(s).
7 Install the adapter, rotor and cap.
8 Included with the new diaphragm will be approved method for calibrating the new diaphragm unit. Follow the instructions given.

Chapter 6 Clutch

Refer to Chapter 13 for information related to 1981 thru 1987 models

Contents

Specifications

Type	Single dry plate, diaphragm spring
Actuation	Cable
Friction plate diameter	10.0 in (254 mm)
Clutch pedal free travel	0.5 – 0.75 in (3.5 – 3.7 mm)

Torque specifications	**ft-lb**	**Nm**
Clutch-to-flywheel	12 to 20	17 to 27
Clutch housing-to-transmission case	38 to 55	52 to 74
All fasteners not listed, use the following torque wrench settings:		
Metric thread sizes		
M-6	6 to 9	9 to 12
M-8	14 to 21	19 to 28
M-10	28 to 40	38 to 54
M-12	50 to 71	68 to 96
M-14	80 to 140	109 to 154
Pipe thread sizes		
$\frac{1}{8}$	5 to 8	7 to 10
$\frac{1}{4}$	12 to 18	17 to 24
$\frac{3}{8}$	22 to 33	30 to 44
$\frac{1}{2}$	25 to 35	34 to 47
U.S. thread sizes		
$\frac{1}{4}$ to 20	6 to 9	9 to 12
$\frac{5}{16}$ to 18	12 to 18	17 to 24
$\frac{5}{16}$ to 24	14 to 20	19 to 27
$\frac{3}{8}$ to 16	22 to 32	30 to 43
$\frac{3}{8}$ to 24	27 to 38	37 to 51
$\frac{7}{16}$ to 14	40 to 55	55 to 74
$\frac{7}{16}$ to 20	40 to 60	55 to 81
$\frac{1}{2}$ 1to 13	55 to 80	75 to 108

1 General information

The diaphragm single dry disc type clutch, consisting of the clutch disc, pressure plate and clutch release bearing, is actuated by a pedal and mechanical linkage.

When the clutch pedal is in the up (released) position, the clutch disc is clamped between the friction surface of the engine flywheel and the face of the clutch pressure plate diaphragm, thus transmitting the drive of the engine through the disc which is splined to the transmission. Friction lining material is riveted to the clutch disc and the splined hub is spring-cushioned to absorb transmission shocks.

When the clutch pedal is depressed, the clutch release lever moves the release bearing against the clutch diaphragm, which in turn moves the pressure plate away from the clutch disc, disengaging the clutch and disconnecting the drive to the transmission.

Because the release bearing is in constant contact with the clutch fingers there is no freeplay adjustment on these vehicles. Consequently, adjustment is made to the clutch pedal travel whenever necessary, such as after the installation of a new clutch or when the clutch does not engage properly.

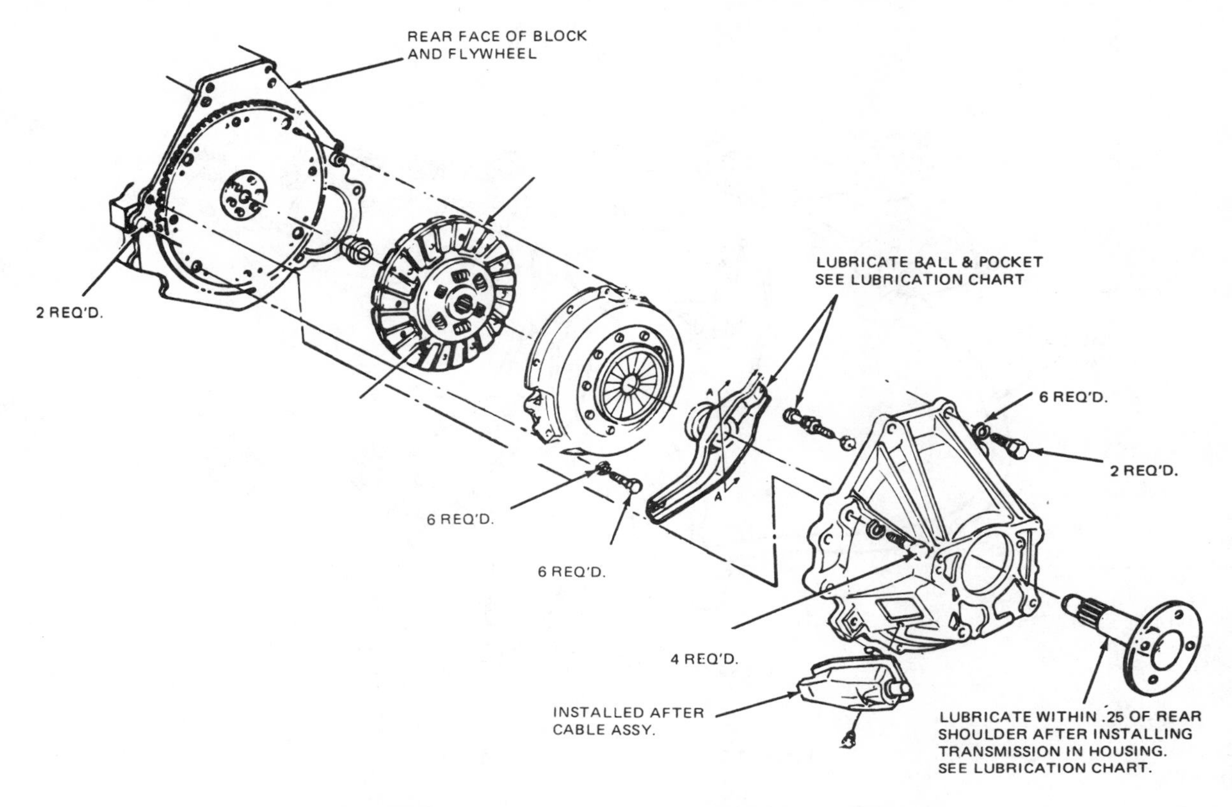

Fig. 6.1 Clutch assembly and components (Secs 1 and 6)

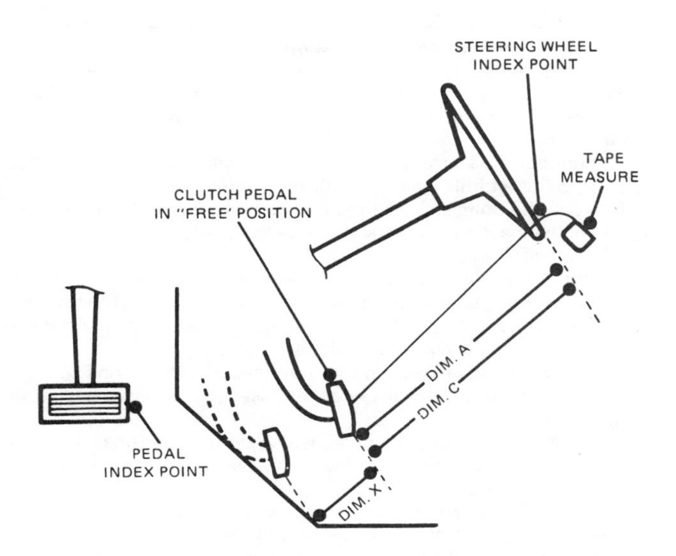

Fig. 6.2 Clutch pedal free travel measurement (Sec 2)

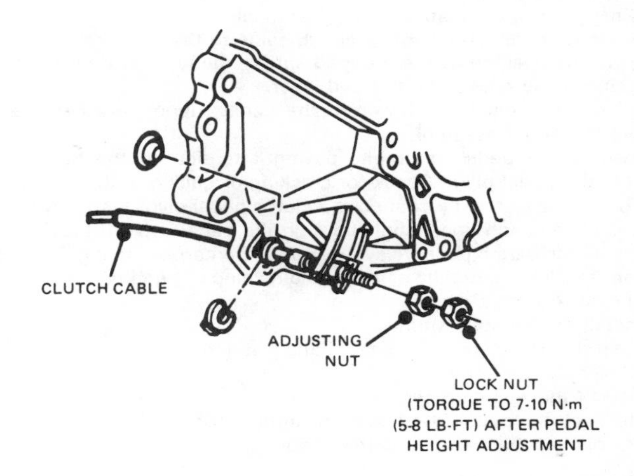

Fig. 6.3 Clutch pedal free travel adjustment (Sec 3 and 5)

2 Clutch pedal – free travel measurement

1 Measure and make a notation of the following distances:
2 Steering wheel rim-to-brake pedal, measuring to the flat off to the side of the ribbed contact patch.
3 Depress the clutch pedal to the floor and measure the distance between the steering wheel rim and the clutch pedal.
4 Subtract the two measurements (dimension X in Fig. 6.2). The difference in measurements should be $6\frac{1}{2}$ in. If it is not, adjust the clutch cable as described in Section 3.

3 Clutch pedal – free travel adjustment

1 Remove the dust shield covering the clutch cable-to-bellhousing junction.
2 Loosen the cable locknut (Fig. 6.3).
3 Adjust by lengthening or shortening the cable as required.
4 Tighten the locknut to 5 to 8 ft-lb (7 to 10 Nm).
5 Depress the clutch pedal to the floor several times and then re-check the pedal travel. Re-adjust as necessary.
6 Re-install the dust shield.

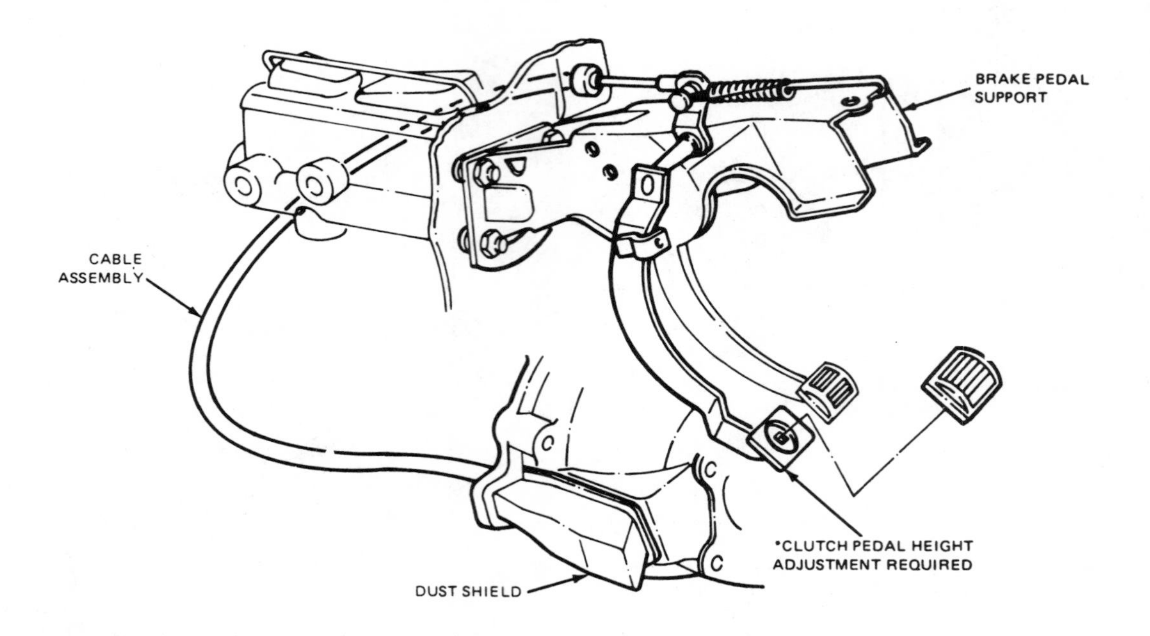

Fig. 6.4 Clutch pedal assembly (Sec 4)

4 Clutch pedal – replacement

1 Disconnect the negative battery terminal.
2 Remove the clip holding the clutch cable to the pedal relay lever.
3 Note the position of the pre-load spring, then remove the spring.
4 Remove the relay lever nut and lever.
5 Slide the pedal assembly from the pedal support bracket, then remove the entire assembly.
6 Inspect the pedal assembly, paying attention to the bushings found at the pedal pivot. Check for cracking or galling of the bushing.
7 To re-install, start by coating the clutch pedal pivot with 10W oil.
8 Slide the clutch pedal shaft through the pedal support bracket.
9 Install the clutch pedal relay lever over the corresponding 4-sided flats on the clutch pedal flats. Install the holding nut and tighten to 32 to 50 ft-lb (43 to 68 Nm).
10 Install the pre-load spring.
11 Hold the pedal against the stop, and install the clutch cable to the relay lever.
12 Attach the retaining clip.
13 Recheck the pedal free travel adjustment (Section 3).
14 Reconnect the negative battery cable.

5 Clutch cable – replacement

1 Disconnect the negative battery cable.
2 Loosen the cable adjusting nuts at the bellhousing and pull the cable assembly forward (Fig. 6.3).
3 Remove the cable retaining clip at the bellhousing.
4 Remove the retaining clip at the clutch pedal relay lever. Withdraw the cable from the vehicle.
5 Installation is the reverse of the removal with the following cautions:
6 Do not allow the cable to kink or bind. Check for a smooth arc through from the pedal relay to the bellhousing.
7 Recheck the clutch pedal free travel (Section 3).
8 Reconnect the negative battery cable.

6 Clutch – removal and installation

1 Remove the transmission as described in Chapter 7.
2 Disconnect the clutch release lever retaining spring from the release lever.
3 Disconnect the starter motor cable, then remove the starter motor attaching bolts and lift away the starter motor.
4 Remove the bolts securing the engine rear plate to the front lower part of the flywheel housing. Remove the flywheel housing lower cover (if so equipped).
5 Remove the flywheel housing securing bolts and move the housing back just far enough to clear the pressure plate, then move it to the right to free the pivot from the clutch equalizer bar. Take care not to disturb the linkage and assist spring.
6 Unscrew the six pressure plate cover securing bolts one turn at a time, to prevent distortion of the cover assembly, when releasing the spring tension.
7 If the same pressure plate and cover assembly is to be re-installed, mark the cover and flywheel so that the assembly can be installed in its original position.
8 Remove the clutch cover assembly and clutch disc from the flywheel. Make a note of which way round the clutch disc is installed.
9 It is important that no oil or grease gets on the clutch disc friction linings, or the pressure plate and flywheel faces. It is advisable to handle the parts with clean hands and to wipe down the pressure plate and flywheel faces with a clean dry rag before installing the clutch cover assembly.
10 Place the clutch disc and pressure plate assembly in position on the flywheel. If the same assembly is being re-installed, align the matching marks made at removal, and install the securing bolts. Tighten the bolts alternately a few turns at a time until the clutch disc is gripped lightly but can still be moved.
11 The clutch disc must now be centered so that when the transmission is installed, the input shaft splines will pass through the splines in the clutch disc hub.
12 Centering can be carried out by inserting a screwdriver through the clutch assembly and moving the clutch disc as necessary to obtain correct centering. Alternatively, if an old input shaft is available, this

can be used as an arbor to center the disc; this will eliminate all guesswork and achieve more accurate centering of the clutch disc.
13 After the clutch disc has been located correctly, tighten the securing bolts in an even and diagonal sequence to ensure the cover assembly is secured without distortion. Tighten the bolts to the specified torque wrench setting.
14 Using a lithium base grease, lightly lubricate the outside diameter of the transmission front bearing retainer, both sides of the release lever fork where it contacts the release bearing spring clips, and the release bearing surface that contacts the pressure plate release fingers. Fill the grease groove in the release bearing hub, then clean all excess grease from inside the bore, otherwise grease will be forced onto the splines by the transmission input shaft bearing retainer and will contaminate the clutch disc.
15 Install the release bearing and hub on the release lever.
16 Install the felt washer on the pivot in the flywheel housing and slip the pivot into the clutch equalizer shaft, taking care not to disturb the linkage, at the same time locate the housing on the dowels in the cylinder block. Install the securing bolts and tighten them to the specified torque.
17 Install the starter motor and connect the cable.
18 Install the transmission as described in Chapter 7.
19 Check and, if necessary, adjust the clutch pedal free-play as described in Section 3.

7 Clutch – inspection and renovation

1 Examine the machined surfaces of the flywheel and the pressure plate for scoring, ridges or burn marks. Minor defects can be removed by machining, but if any components are badly scored or burned they should be replaced with new ones.
2 Check the wear on the clutch fingers; if there is considerable difference in wear between the fingers, the excessively worn finger is binding and the pressure plate assembly must be replaced with a new one. Check the pressure plate for warpage using a steel rule.
3 Lubricate the pressure plate openings. Depress the pressure plate fingers fully, apply the grease and then move the fingers up and down until the grease is worked in.
4 Examine the clutch disc for worn or loose lining, distortion, loose nuts at the hub, and for broken springs. If any of these defects are found, replace the disc with a new or rebuilt unit.
5 Wipe all oil and dirt off the release bearing but do not clean it in solvent, as it is pre-lubricated. Inspect the bearing retainer for loose spring clips and rivets. Hold the bearing inner race and rotate the outer race. If it is noisy or rough, replace the bearing with a new one.

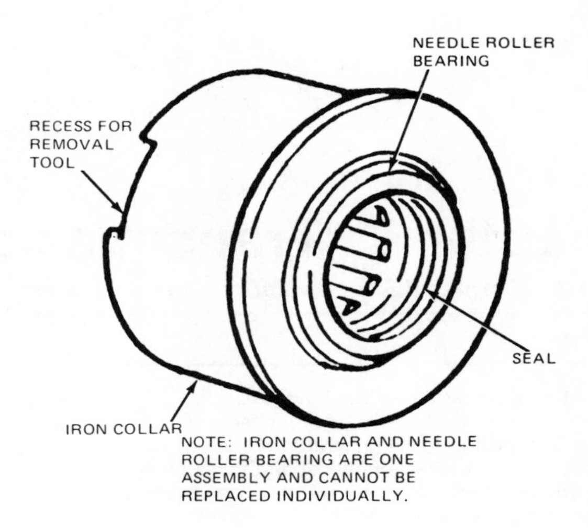

Fig. 6.5 Pilot bearing (Sec 8)

8 Pilot bearing – removal and installation

1 A needle roller bearing is used as a clutch pilot bearing on all vehicles. The bearings are pre-greased and require no lubrication.
2 Remove the transmission (Chapter 7), clutch, pressure plate and disc (Section 6).
3 Pull the bearing from the crankshaft using a slide hammer or Ford tool T50T-100A or T59L-100B with a puller attachment tool T58L-101-A.
4 To install the new bearing, coat the opening on the crankshaft with a small amount of lithium grease. Apply the grease sparingly as an excess could find its way to the clutch and cause slippage.
5 With the seal end facing the transmission, tap the bushing into the crankshaft. A 1 in, 12 point socket can be used to carefully tap the bearing squarely into the bore.
6 Check carefully for any damage during installation.

Chapter 7 Transmission

Refer to Chapter 13 for specifications and information related to 1981 thru 1987 models

Contents

Specifications

Manual transmission, SROD type

Number of gears	4 forward, 1 reverse
Type of gears	Helical, constant mesh
Synchromesh	All forward gears
Lubricant type	ESW-M2C83-C
Lubricant capacity	4.5 US pts
Component endplay	
Countershaft gear	0.004 to 0.018 in
1st gear	0.005 to 0.024 in
2nd gear	0.003 to 0.021 in
4th gear	0.009 to 0.023 in

Automatic transmission, type C3

Type	Fluid drive with hydrodynamic torque converter, 3 forward speeds, 1 reverse
Lubricant type	ESW-M2C33-F, Type F
Lubricant capacity	8 U.S. qts
Component endplay	
Transmission endplay	0.001 to 0.025 in
Turbine and stator – new	0.023 in maximum
Turbine and stator – used	0.050 in maximum

Automatic transmission, type C4

Type	Fluid drive with hydrodynamic torque converter, 3 forward speeds, 1 reverse
Lubricant type	ESW-M2C33-F, Type F
Lubricant capacity	8½ U.S. qts
Component endplay	
Transmission endplay	0.008 to 0.042 in
Turbine and stator – new	0.023 in maximum
Turbine and stator – used	0.050 in maximum

Torque specifications

Manual transmission, SROD type	ft-lb	Nm
Input shaft bearing retainer-to-case	11 to 25	15 to 33
Extension housing-to-case	42 to 50	54 to 67
Top cover-to-case	20 to 25	28 to 33
Filler plug	10 to 20	14 to 27
Detent bolt	10 to 15	14 to 20
Turret assembly bolts	8 to 12	11 to 16
Reverse gear pivot bolt	15 to 25	21 to 33
Back-up lamp switch	8 to 12	11 to 16

All fasteners not listed: use the chart at the end of this section

Automatic transmission, type C3	ft-lb	Nm
Converter housing-to-case	27 to 39	37 to 52
Extension housing-to-case	27 to 39	37 to 52
Oil pump to converter housing	7 to 10	10 to 13
Flywheel to converter housing	27 to 49	37 to 66
Main control to case	7 to 9	10 to 12
Plate to valve body	7 to 9	10 to 12
Servo cover to case	7 to 10	10 to 13
OWC inner race to case	7 to 10	10 to 13
Oil pan to case	12 to 17	17 to 23
Governor to collector body	7 to 10	10 to 13
Converter housing to engine	28 to 38	38 to 51
Outer downshift to lever nut	7 to 11	10 to 14
Inner manual lever nut	30 to 40	41 to 51
Neutral switch to case	12 to 15	17 to 20
Front band adjusting lock nut	35 to 45	48 to 61
Vacuum diaphragm retaining clip	15 to 23 (in-lb)	1.69 to 2.59
Oil cooler line/bypass tube	7 to 10	10 to 13
Connector to case	8 to 11	24 to 31
Converter drain plug	20 to 30	28 to 40
Flywheel to crankshaft	48 to 53	66 to 71
Filler tube to engine	28 to 38	38 to 51

All fasteners not listed: use the chart at the end of this section

Automatic transmission, type C4	ft-lb	Nm
End plates to body	25 to 40*	2.82 to 4.51
Separator plate to lower body	40 to 55*	4.51 to 6.21
Lower body to upper body	40 to 60*	4.51 to 6.77
Screen to upper body	40 to 60*	4.51 to 6.77
Governor to oil collector	80 to 120*	9.03 to 12.55
Pump assembly to case	20 to 35*	2.25 to 3.95
Main control to case	80 to 120*	9.03 to 12.55
Neutral switch to case	55 to 75*	6.21 to 8.47
Upper body to lower body	80 to 120*	9.03 to 12.55
$\frac{5}{16}$ in fitting, cooler line to transmission case	144 to 216*	17 to 24
Overrunning clutch race to case	13 to 20	18 to 27
Oil pan to case	12 to 16	17 to 21
Stator support to pump	12 to 20	17 to 27
Converter housing cover	12 to 16	17 to 21
Rear servo cover to case	12 to 20	17 to 27
Intermediate servo cover to case	16 to 22	22 to 29
Oil distributor sleeve to case	12 to 20	17 to 27
Extension housing to case	28 to 40	38 to 54
Front pump to case	28 to 38	38 to 51
Transmission to engine	28 to 38	38 to 51
Engine separator plate to converter housing	5 to 9	7 to 12
Downshift lever to shaft	12 to 16	17 to 21
Flywheel to converter	20 to 30	28 to 40
Band adjusting screws to case	35 to 45	48 to 61
Manual inner valve lever to shaft	30 to 40	41 to 54
Pipe plug, case front pump or line pressure	6 to 12	9 to 16
$\frac{5}{16}$ in fitting, cooler line to transmission case	12 to 18	17 to 24
Filler tube to oil pan	32 to 42	44 to 56
Intermediate band adjusting screw	10	13.55
Intermediate band adjusting screw lock nut	40	54.33
Low-reverse band adjusting screw	10	13.55
Low-reverse band adjusting screw lock nut	40	54.33

* in-lb, not ft-lb

All fasteners not listed, use the following torque wrench settings:

Metric thread sizes	ft-lb	Nm
M-6	6 to 9	9 to 12
M-8	14 to 21	19 to 28
M-10	28 to 40	38 to 54
M-12	50 to 71	68 to 96
M-14	80 to 140	109 to 154
Pipe thread sizes		
$\frac{1}{8}$	5 to 8	7 to 10
$\frac{1}{4}$	12 to 18	17 to 24
$\frac{3}{8}$	22 to 33	30 to 44
$\frac{1}{2}$	25 to 35	34 to 47
U.S. thread sizes		
$\frac{1}{4}$ – 20	6 to 9	9 to 12
$\frac{5}{16}$ – 18	12 to 18	17 to 24

	ft-lb	Nm
$\frac{5}{16}$ – 24	14 to 20	19 to 27
$\frac{3}{8}$ – 16	22 to 32	30 to 43
$\frac{3}{8}$ – 24	27 to 28	37 to 51
$\frac{7}{16}$ – 14	40 to 55	55 to 74
$\frac{7}{16}$ – 20	40 to 60	55 to 81
$\frac{1}{2}$ – 13	55 to 80	75 to 108

1 Manual transmission – general information, SROD type

The SROD type single rail overdrive transmission is equipped with four forward and one reverse gear.

All forward gears are engaged through synchro-hubs and rings to obtain smooth, silent gearchanges. All forward gears on the mainshaft and input shaft are in constant mesh with their corresponding gears on the countershaft gear cluster and are helically cut to achieve quiet running.

The countershaft reverse gear has straight-cut spur teeth and drives the toothed 1st/2nd gear synchro-hub on the mainshaft through an interposed sliding idler gear.

Gears are engaged by a single selector rail and forks. Control of the gears is from a floor mounted shift lever which connects with the single selector rail.

Fourth gear is an overdrive ratio for quieter running and better mileage at highway speeds.

2 Transmission (SROD type) – removal and installation

1 If the transmission alone is to be removed from the car, it can be taken out from below leaving the engine in position. It will mean that a considerable amount of working room is required beneath the car, and ideally ramps or an inspection pit should be used. However, provided that suitable jacks and supports are available, the task can be accomplished without the need for sophisticated equipment.

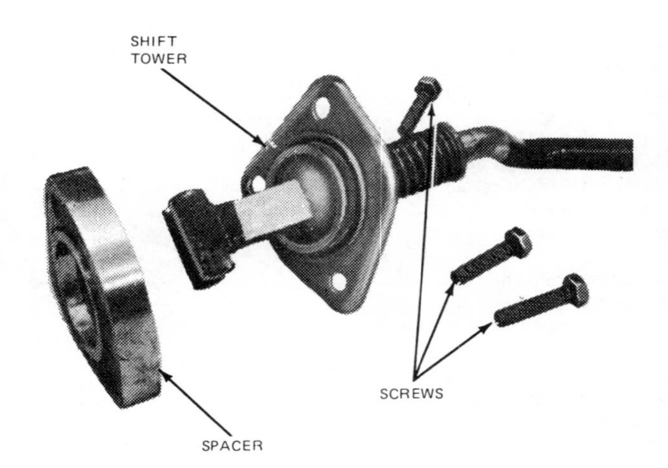

Fig. 7.1 Shift control assembly (SROD) (Sec 1)

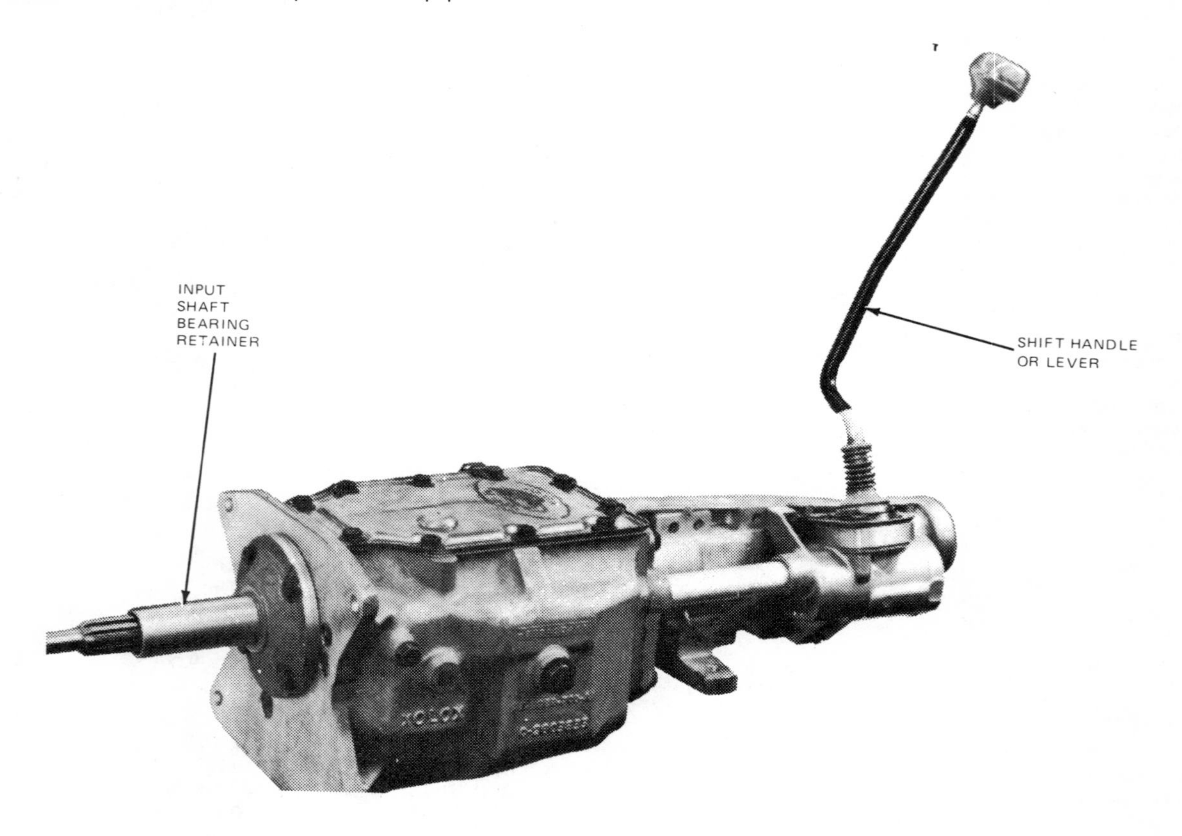

Fig. 7.2 Single rail overdrive transmission (SROD) (Sec 1)

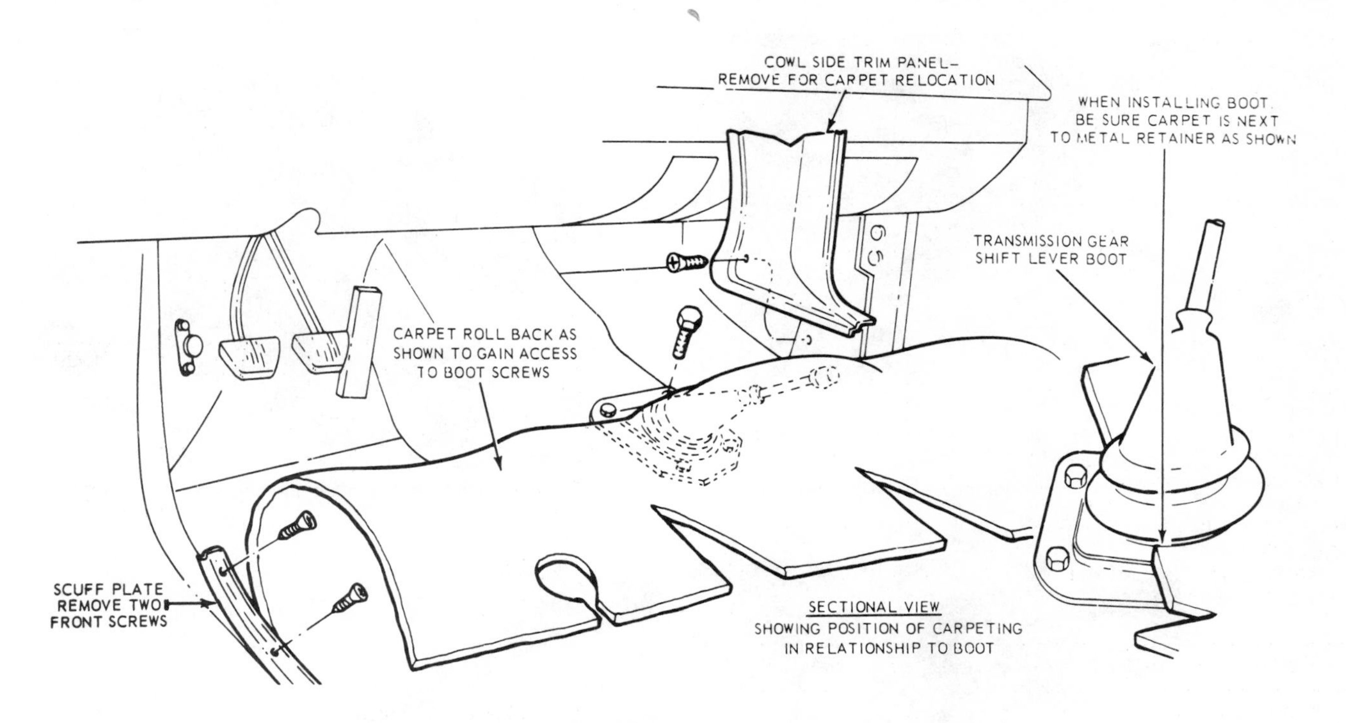

Fig. 7.3 Shift lever boot and carpet removal (Sec 2)

2 Disconnect the battery ground lead.
3 From inside the car remove the two front screws from each scuff plate and the side trim panel and pull the carpet back over the gear-shift lever.
4 Remove the four bolts holding the shift lever boot retaining plate and lift the plate and boot off the lever. Remove the shift lever knob if necessary.
5 Undo and remove the three shift lever retaining bolts and remove the lever assembly.
6 Drain the transmission oil into a suitable container.
7 Mark the driveshaft so that it can be re-installed in the same relative position. Remove the propeller shaft as described in Chapter 8.
8 Remove the front exhaust pipe section from the manifold flange and the front of the resonator box or converter, if fitted.
9 Disconnect the clutch cable from the clutch release lever and the side of the clutch housing (see Chapter 6).
10 Remove the starter motor retaining bolts and move the motor towards the front of the car.
11 Disconnect the back-up lamp switch wires and the seat belt sensing switch wires if fitted.
12 Remove the speedometer cable retaining screw and pull the cable out of the extension housing.
13 Support the rear of the engine with a block of wood placed on top of a jack and remove the rear engine mounting crossmember.
14 Remove the two bolts that retain the transmission extension crossmember and remove the crossmember.
15 Gradually lower the engine by means of the jack until there is sufficient clearance to remove the four bolts retaining the transmission assembly to the clutch housing.
16 Support the weight of the transmission and undo and remove the four bolts.
17 Carefully withdraw the transmission away from the clutch housing and lower it to the ground.
18 When refitting the transmission, ensure that the clutch release lever and bearing are correctly located in the clutch housing.
19 Apply a smear of light grease on the transmission input shaft splines and then install the transmission using the reverse procedure to removal. **Note:** *It may be necessary to rotate the engine to align the clutch disc and input shaft splines.*

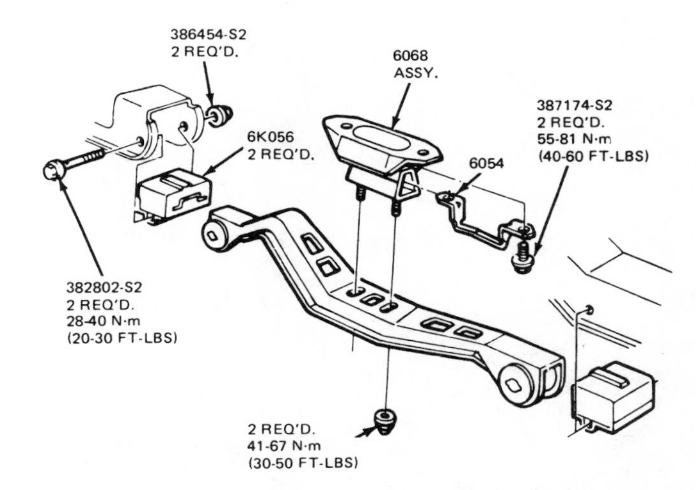

Fig. 7.4 Rear crossmember and transmission mount (Sec 2)

3 Transmission (SROD type) – disassembly

1 Place the transmission on a firm bench or in a holding fixture. In addition to the normal range of wrenches, tools, etc., you will need the following:

a) Good quality snap-ring pliers, 1 expanding and 1 contracting.
b) Copper-headed hammer, at least 2 lb.
c) Selection of steel and brass drifts.
d) Small containers for parts.
e) Vise mounted on a firm bench.
f) Selection of steel tubing for use as dummy shafts.

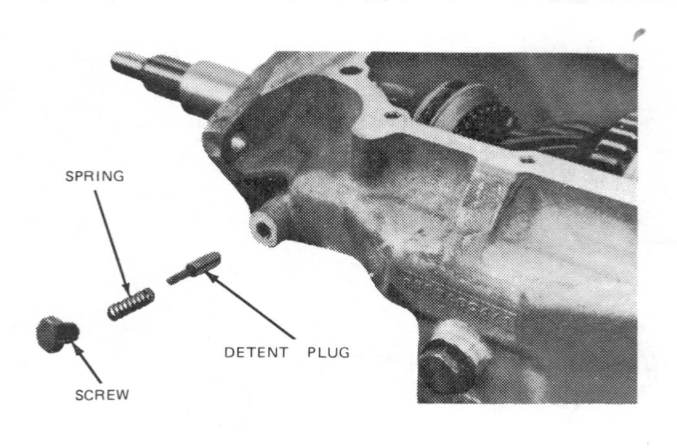

Fig. 7.5 Detent removal or installation (Sec 3)

Fig. 7.6 Removing shifter shaft roll pin (Sec 3)

Fig. 7.7 Backup lamp switch installation or removal (Sec 3)

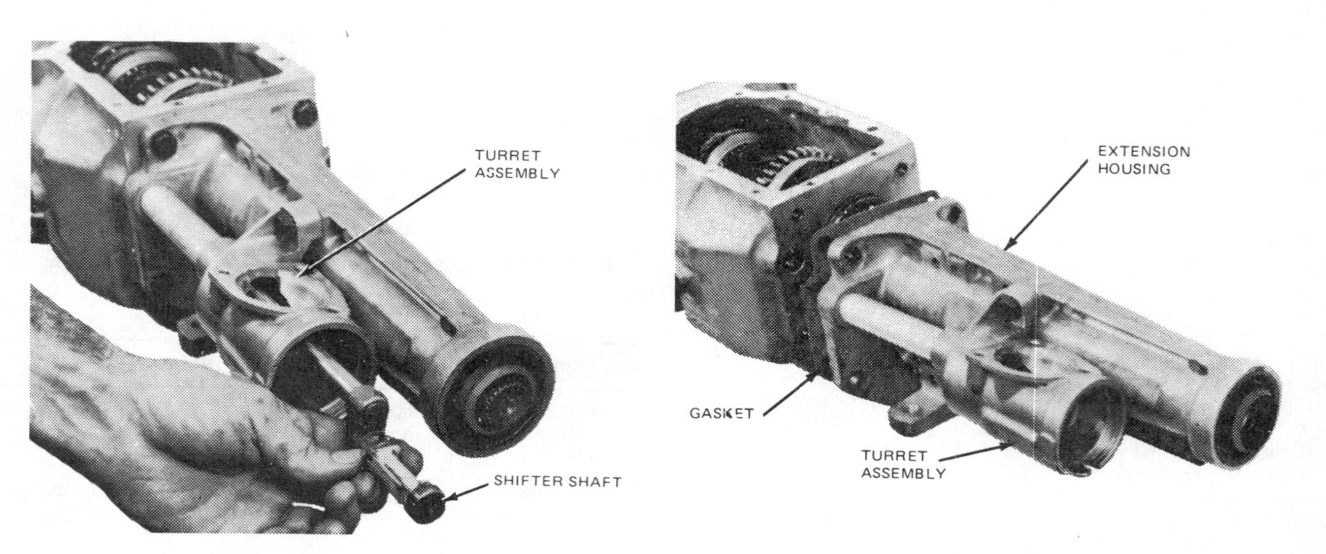

Fig. 7.8 Shifter shaft removal (Sec 3)

Fig. 7.9 Extension housing removal (Sec 3)

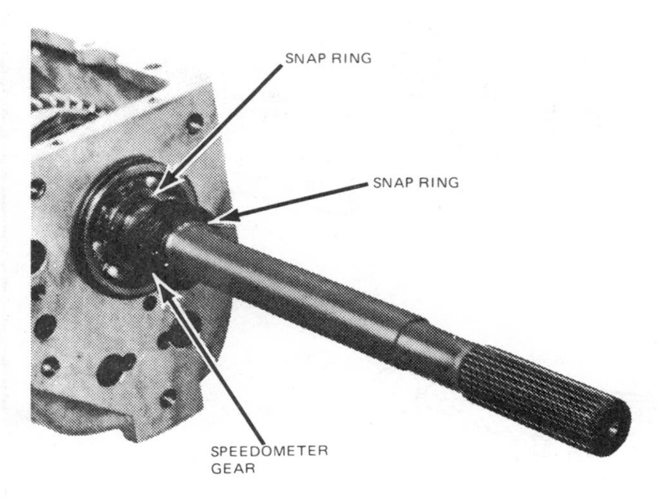

Fig. 7.10 Speedometer gear removal (Sec 3)

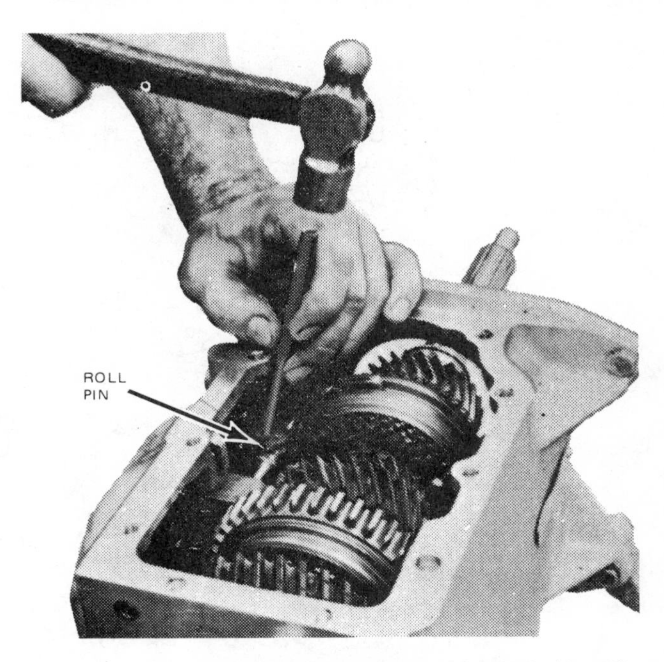

Fig. 7.13 Removing 3rd/overdrive shift fork roll pin (Sec 3)

Fig. 7.11 Removing output shaft bearing (Sec 3)

Fig. 7.14 Removing 3rd/overdrive shift rail (Sec 3)

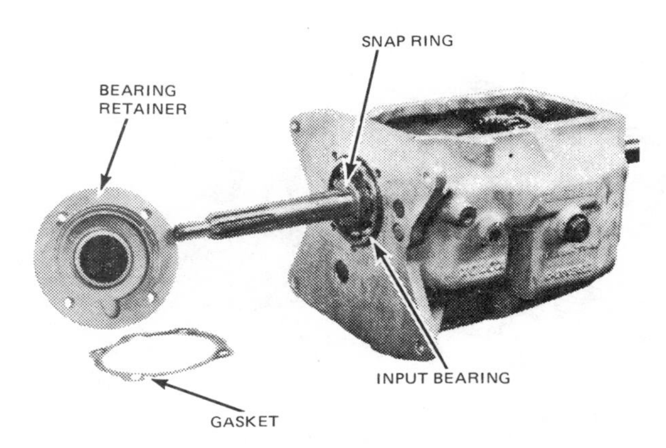

Fig. 7.12 Input shaft bearing and retainer (Sec 3)

2 Attempting to disassemble a transmission without the foregoing is not impossible, but will certainly be a much more difficult process.
3 Read this entire Section through before starting work.
4 Unbolt and remove the transmission top cover and discard the gasket.
5 Remove the screw, detent spring and detent plug from the transmission case (Fig. 7.5). It may be necessary to use a magnet to extract these parts from the transmission case.
6 Using a suitable drift, drive the shifter shaft roll pin from the case (Fig. 7.6).
7 From the rear of the extension housing, remove the backup lamp switch assembly, snap-ring and dust cover (Fig. 7.7).
8 Withdraw the shifter shaft from the turret assembly (Fig. 7.8).

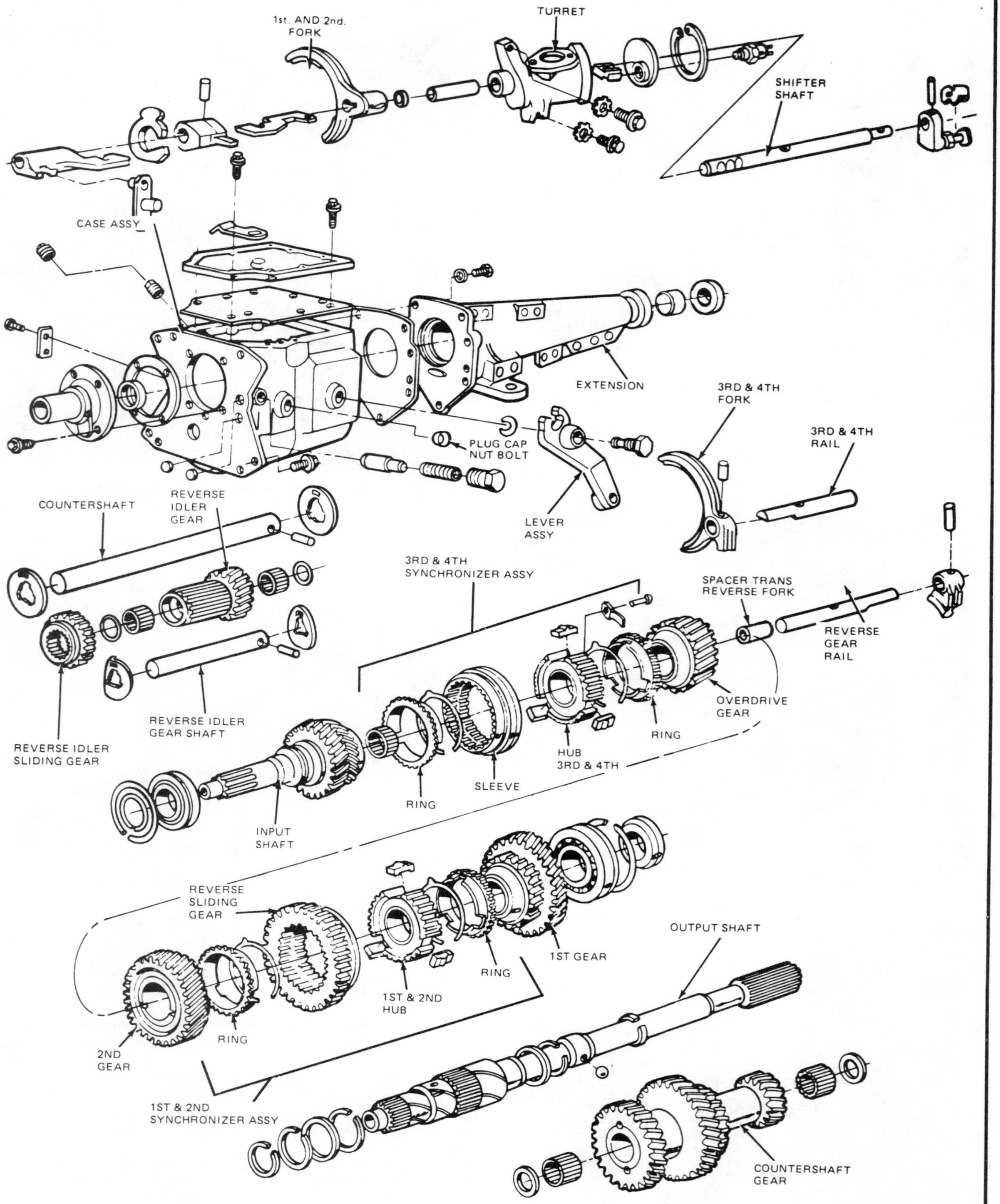

TURRET
1st. AND 2nd. FORK
SHIFTER SHAFT
CASE ASSY
EXTENSION
3RD & 4TH FORK
3RD & 4TH RAIL
PLUG CAP NUT BOLT
LEVER ASSY
COUNTERSHAFT
REVERSE IDLER GEAR
3RD & 4TH SYNCHRONIZER ASSY
SPACER TRANS REVERSE FORK
REVERSE GEAR RAIL
REVERSE IDLER GEAR SHAFT
REVERSE IDLER SLIDING GEAR
OVERDRIVE GEAR
RING
HUB 3RD & 4TH
SLEEVE
RING
INPUT SHAFT
REVERSE SLIDING GEAR
1ST GEAR
RING
1ST & 2ND HUB
OUTPUT SHAFT
RING
2ND GEAR
1ST & 2ND SYNCHRONIZER ASSY
COUNTERSHAFT GEAR

Fig. 7.15 Exploded view of SROD transmission

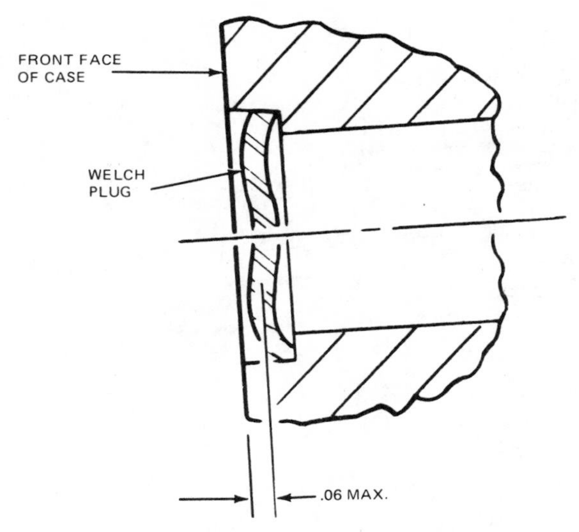

Fig. 7.16 Welch plug installation (Sec 3)

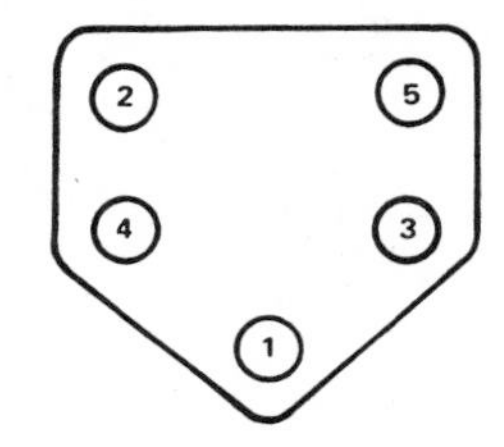

EXTENSION HOUSING (REAR VIEW)

Fig. 7.17 Extension housing bolt tightening sequence (Sec 3)

9 Unbolt and remove the extension housing from the transmission case, discarding the gasket (Fig. 7.9).
10 Remove the snap-ring which secures the speedometer drive gear to the output shaft. Slide the gear off the shaft and remove the speedometer gear drive ball (Fig. 7.10).
11 Remove the snap-ring securing the output shaft bearing to the shaft and slide the output bearing off (Fig. 7.11).
12 From the front of the transmission case, push the countershaft out through the rear of the case, using a similar size dummy shaft. Lower the countershaft into the bottom of the transmission case.
13 Remove the input shaft bearing retainer bolts and slide the retainer and gasket off the shaft (Fig. 7.12).
14 Remove the snap-ring securing the input shaft bearing to the shaft (Fig. 7.12) and slide the bearing off.
15 Remove the input shaft, blocking ring and roller bearing from the case.
16 Remove the overdrive shift pawl, gear selector and interlock plate.
17 Remove the 1-2 gearshift selector arm plate.
18 With a suitable drift, drive the roll pin from the 3rd/overdrive shift fork (Fig. 7.13).
19 Working from the rear of the case, drive the 3rd/overdrive shift rail and expansion plug out (Fig. 7.14). Remove the mainshaft assembly.
20 Remove the 1st and 2nd speed shift forks, followed by the 3rd/overdrive shift fork.
21 Lift out the countershaft gear and thrustwashers, being careful not to drop them into the case.
22 Remove the snap-ring from the front of the output shaft and slide the 3rd gear, overdrive synchronizer, blocking ring and gear off the shaft.
23 Remove the securing snap-ring and thrustwashers and remove 2nd gear.
24 Remove the next snap-ring on the shaft and remove the 1-2 synchronizer assembly.
25 From the rear of the shaft, remove the first gear and blocking ring.
26 Remove the reverse gear roll pin and withdraw the reverse shifter rail from the rear of the case. Remove the gearshift fork and reverse fork spacer.
27 Working from the front of the case, drive the reverse gear shaft out of the rear of the transmission.
28 Remove the reverse idler gear and, being careful not to drop them into the case, the thrustwashers and roller bearings.
29 Remove the retaining clip, the reverse gearshift relay lever and reverse selector fork pivot pin.
30 Remove the overdrive shift control link assembly.
31 From the rear of the case, remove the shift shaft seal.
32 Through the shift shaft rail hole, remove the expansion plug from the front of the case.
33 The transmission is now completely disassembled and must be thoroughly cleaned. Any metal flakes or chips in the case are a good sign that the transmission is worn.

4 Transmission (SROD type) – inspection and overhaul

1 Carefully clean and inspect all component parts for wear, distortion, looseness of fit and damage to machined faces and threads.
2 Inspect the gears for excessive wear and chipping of the teeth. Replace with new gears as necessary.
3 Inspect the countershafts for signs of wear on the roller bearing surfaces. If a small ridge can be felt on either end of the shafts, it will be necessary to replace the shafts with new ones.
4 If the synchro-rings are badly worn it is a good idea to replace them. New rings will improve the smoothness and speed of gear shifting considerably.
5 The roller bearings located between the nose of the output shaft and the rear of the input shaft are likely to wear and should be replaced.
6 Check the endplay of the countershaft, 1st, 2nd and overdrive gears after assembly on the output shaft with a suitable gauge. If the endplay exceeds the limits in the Specifications section they must be replaced with new parts.
7 If the synchro-hubs are worn, they must be replaced as complete assemblies.
8 The nylon inserts on the selector forks should be replaced even if they appear to be in good condition. If any of the inserts have broken up, allowing any wear on the fork assembly itself, the complete fork should be replaced unless wear is minimal.
9 If the bush bearing in the extension is badly worn it should be replaced unless wear is minimal.
10 The transmission case welch plug should be replaced with a new one if there is any sign of leaking (Fig. 7.16).

5 Transmission (SROD type) – reassembly

1 Reassembly is a reversal of the disassembly procedure with the exception of the following details:
2 The transmission mainshaft bearing rollers, extension housing bushing, reverse idler, bearing rollers and the countershaft gear bearing rollers must be lubricated with 0.5 ounces of Ford ESW-M1C109-A lubricant at assembly. Lubricate the 1st, 2nd and overdrive gear bearing journals with Ford ESP-M2C83-C transmission oil or equivalent. Thoroughly flush the rest of the transmission components with 1/2 US pint of this oil also.
3 The transmission shifter shaft and gearshift damper bushing should also be lubricated with Ford ESA-M1C175-A lubricant or equivalent prior to installation.
4 Seal the transmission gearshift shaft sleeve at both ends as well as the turret cover assembly with 0.05 ounces of Ford ESE-M4G132-A sealant or equivalent. This will prevent contamination of the shifter mechanism by road dust and dirt.
5 When installing the intermediate and high rail welch plug, it must be seated firmly. It must not protrude above or below the front face of the transmission case more than 0.06 in (1.5 mm) (Fig. 7.16).
6 The gearshift selector arm must be firmly seated in the 1st/2nd shift fork plate slot. The shifter shaft must pass freely through the 1st/2nd shift fork bore without binding.
7 The extension housing must be tightened to torque specifications in the sequence shown in Fig. 7.17.

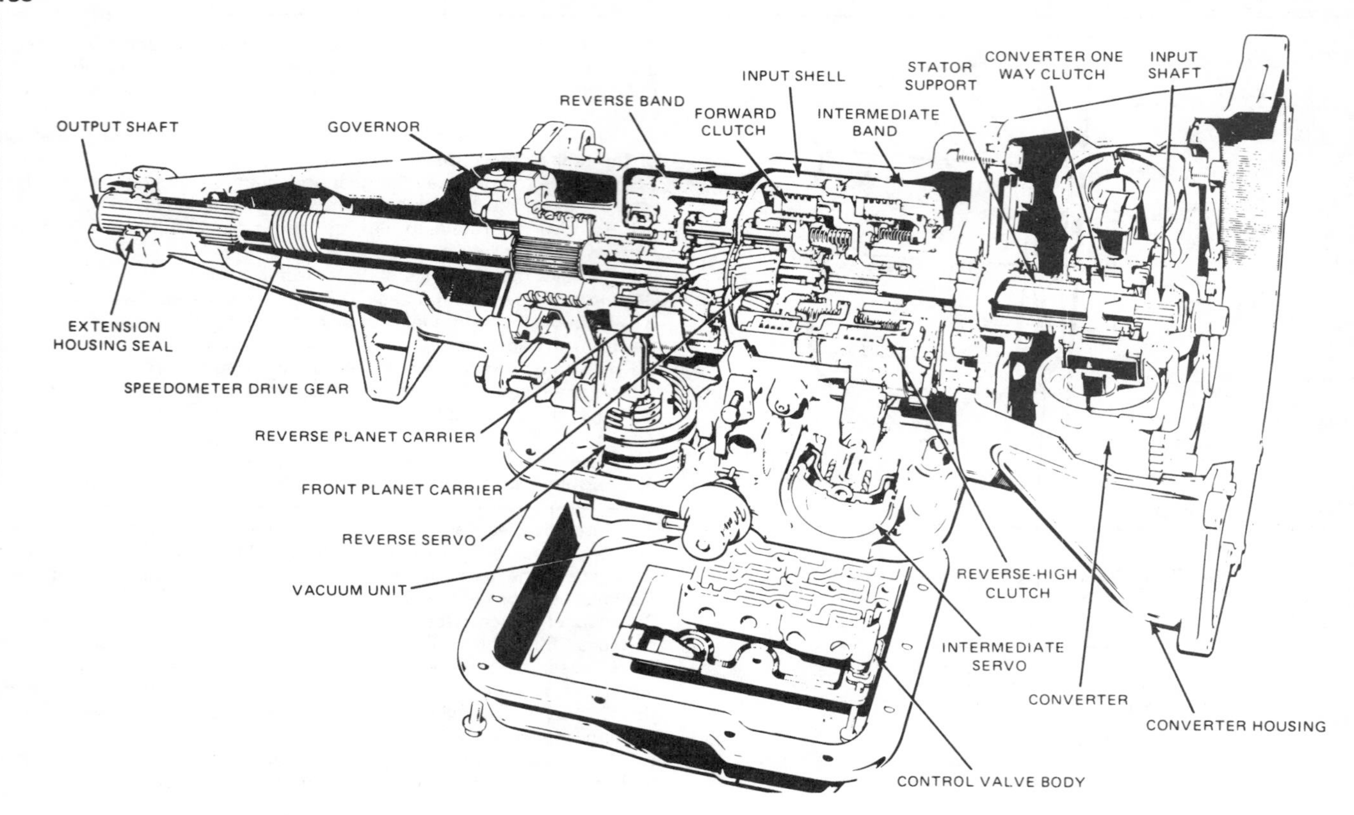

Fig. 7.18 Cutaway view of C3-type automatic transmission (Sec 6)

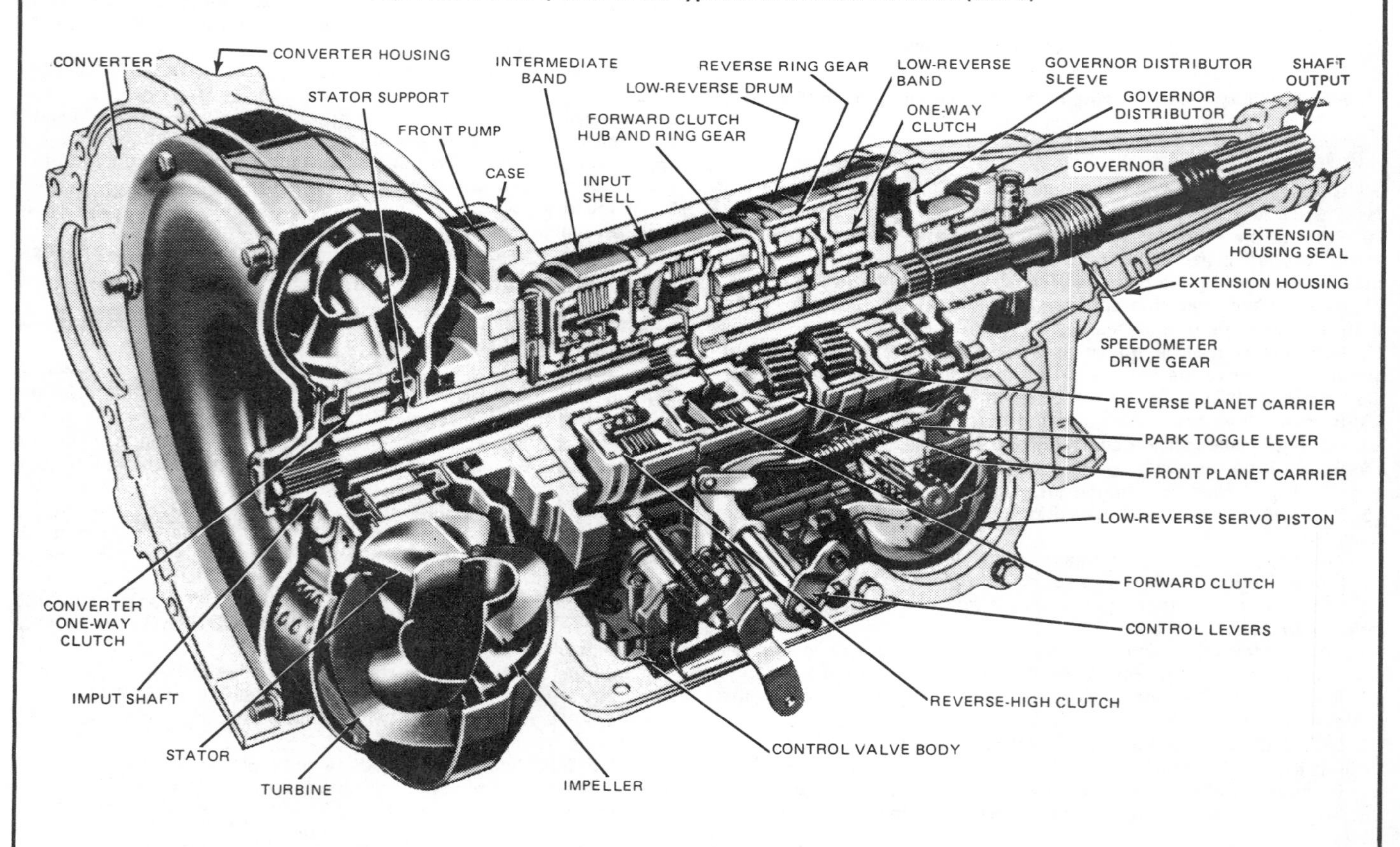

Fig. 7.19 Cutaway view of C4-type automatic transmission (Sec 6)

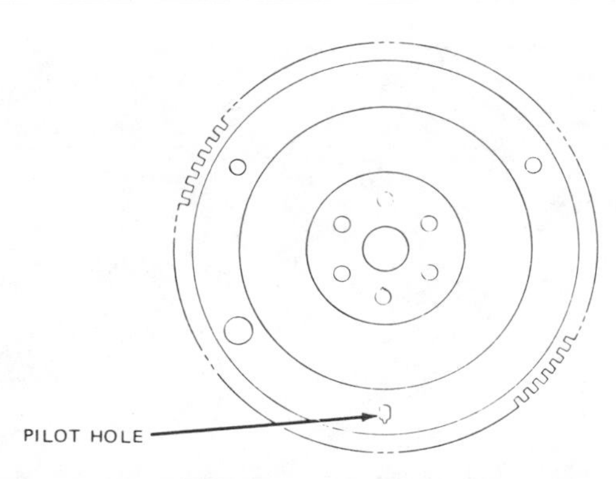

Fig. 7.20 Flywheel pilot hole which must be at six o'clock when installing bolts (Sec 9)

6 Automatic transmission – general information

The automatic transmission takes the place of the conventional clutch and gearbox, and comprises the following two main assemblies:

a) *A three element hydrokinetic torque converter coupling, capable of torque multiplication at an infinitely variable ratio.*
b) *A torque/speed responsive and hydraulically operated epicyclic gearbox comprising a planetary gearset providing three forward ratios and one reverse ratio.*

Due to the complexity of the automatic transmission unit, if performance is not up to standard, or overhaul is necessary, it is imperative that this be left to the local dealer or transmission shop who will have the special equipment for fault diagnosis and rectification. The content of the following Section is therefore confined to supplying general information and any service information and instruction that can be used by the owner.

The automatic transmission fitted is manufactured by Ford and is either the C3 or C4 type depending on the year of manufacture. Both types of transmission are very similar, but where there are major differences these are described under a separate Section heading. A transmission oil cooler is fitted as standard and ensures cooler operation of the transmission under trailer towing conditions. A vacuum connection to the inlet manifold provides smoother and more consistent downshifts under load than is the case with units not incorporating this facility.

7 Automatic transmission – fluid level checking

1 Before attempting to check the fluid level, the fluid must be at its normal operating temperature (approximately 65°C/150°F). This is best accomplished by driving the car for about 5 miles (8 km) under normal running conditions.

2 Park the car on level ground, apply the handbrake and depress the brake pedal.

3 Allow the engine to idle, then move the selector through all the positions three times.

4 Select 'P' and wait for 1 to 2 minutes with the engine still idling.

5 Now withdraw the dipstick (engine still idling), wipe it clean with a lint-free cloth, replace it and withdraw it again. Note the fluid level and, if necessary, top-up to maintain between the 'MAX' and 'MIN' dipstick markings. Only fluid meeting the stated specification should be used; this is applied through the dipstick tube.

8 Automatic transmission fluid – drain and refill

1 Raise the car and support with jack stands.
2 Place a drain pan under the transmission pan.
3 Loosen the bolts securing the transmission pan to the transmission body. As the bolts are removed allow the fluid to drain into the pan.
4 Remove the pan and gasket.
5 Clean the pan with solvent and allow to dry.
6 After allowing the transmission to drain, remove the bolts securing the transmission filter to the transmission (photo).
7 Remove the filter and discard.
8 Clean all mating surfaces with a clean, dry, lint-free cloth.
9 Fit a new transmission filter and reinstall the mounting bolts.
10 Install a new gasket on the pan.
11 Position the pan and gasket on the transmission and install the bolts.
12 Tighten the bolts in a criss-cross pattern to avoid warping the transmission pan.
13 Refill the transmission with approximately 16 pints of automatic transmission fluid (Ford type).
14 Start the engine, check for leaks.
15 Drive the car for a few minutes to allow the transmission to rise to operating temperature. Recheck the transmission level and fill as required. Check for leaks.

9 Automatic transmission: removal and installation (C3)

1 If possible, raise the car on a hoist or place it over an inspection pit. Alternatively, it will be necessary to jack-up the car to obtain the maximum possible amount of working room underneath.

2 Place a large drain pan beneath the transmission sump (oil pan) then, working from the rear, loosen the attaching bolts and allow the fluid to drain. Remove all the bolts except the two front ones to drain as much fluid as possible, then temporarily refit two bolts at the rear to hold it in place.

3 Remove the torque converter drain plug access cover and adapter plate bolts from the lower end of the converter housings.

4 Remove the three flywheel-to-converter attaching bolts, cranking the engine as necessary to gain access by means of a wrench on the crankshaft pulley attaching bolt. **Caution: Do not rotate the engine backwards.**

5 Rotate the engine until the converter drain plug is accessible, then

8.6 The metal-encased automatic transmission filter is accessible after removal of the transmission oil pan

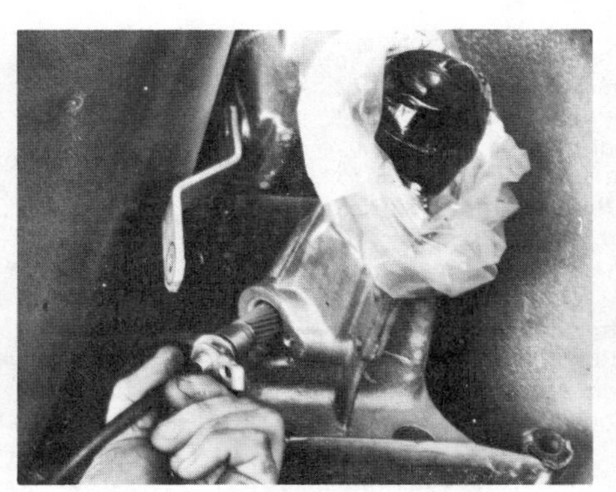

9.7 Removing the speedometer cable. Note the plastic bag plugging the end of the transmission extension housing

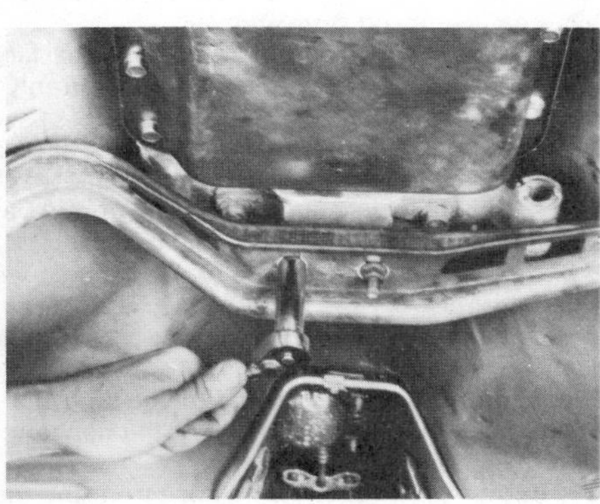

9.13 Removing the engine support nuts at the crossmember

remove the plug, catching the fluid in the drain pan. Fit and tighten the drain plug afterwards.
6 Remove the propeller shaft, referring to Chapter 8, as necessary. Place a polythene bag over the end of the transmission to prevent dirt from entering.
7 Detach the speedometer cable from the extension housing (photo).
8 Disconnect the shift rod at the transmission manual lever, and the downshift rod at the transmission downshift lever.
9 Remove the starter motor retaining bolts and position the motor out of the way.
10 Disconnect the starter inhibitor (neutral start) switch leads.
11 Disconnect the vacuum lines from the vacuum unit.
12 Position a trolley jack beneath the transmission and raise it to *just* take the transmission weight.
13 Remove the engine rear support to crossmember nut and the transmission extension housing crossmember (photo).
14 Remove the filler tube brace from the filler tube and rear engine support. Disconnect the exhaust pipe at the manifold and support it to one side.
15 Lower the trolley jack slightly, then place another jack to the front end of the engine. Raise the engine to gain access to the upper converter housing-to-engine attaching bolts.
16 Disconnect the oil cooler lines at the transmission and plug them to prevent dirt from entering.
17 Remove the lower converter housing-to-engine bolts, and the transmission filler tube.
18 Ensure that the transmission is securely mounted on the trolley jack, then remove the two upper converter housing-to-engine bolts.
19 Carefully move the transmission rearwards and downwards, and away from the car.
20 Replacing the transmission is essentially the reverse of the removal procedure, but the following points should be noted:

- a) *Rotate the converter to align the bolt drive lugs and drain plug with their holes in the flywheel.*
- b) *Do not allow the transmission to take a 'nose-down' attitude as the converter will move forward and disengage from the pump gear.*
- c) *When installing the three flywheel-to-converter bolts position the flywheel so that the pilot hole is in the six o'clock position (see Fig. 7.20). First install one bolt hrough the pilot hole and torque tighten it, followed by the two remaining bolts. Do not attempt to install it in any other way.*
- d) *Adjust the downshift cable and selector linkage as necessary (see Sections 7 and 8).*
- e) *When the car has been lowered to the ground, add sufficient fluid to bring the level up to the 'MAX' mark on the dipstick with the engine not running. Having done this, check and top-up the fluid level, as described in the previous Section.*

10 Automatic transmission – removal and installation (C4)

Any suspected fault must be referred to the local Ford dealer or specialist before unit removal, as with this type of transmission the fault must be confirmed, using specialist equipment, before the unit has been removed from the car.
1 For safety reasons, disconnect the battery ground terminal.
2 Jack up the engine and support on firmly based stands if a lift or pit is not available.
3 Refer to Chapter 8 and remove the propeller shaft.
4 Wrap a polythene bag over the end of the transmission unit to prevent oil seeping out. Alternatively, drain out the unit. If the car has just been driven the oil will be very hot.
5 Undo and remove the two upper converter housing-to-engine securing nuts.
6 Undo and remove the bolt that secures the transmission fluid filler tube to the cylinder block. Lift away the filler tube.
7 Undo and remove the bolts securing the converter cover. This is located at the lower front side of the converter housing. Lift away the cover.
8 Remove the vacuum line hose from the transmission vacuum unit. Detach this vacuum line from the retaining clip.
9 Remove the speedometer cable from the extension housing.
10 Wipe the area around the oil cooler pipe unions on the side of the transmission unit and then detach the pipes. Plug the open ends to stop loss of fluid or dirt ingress.

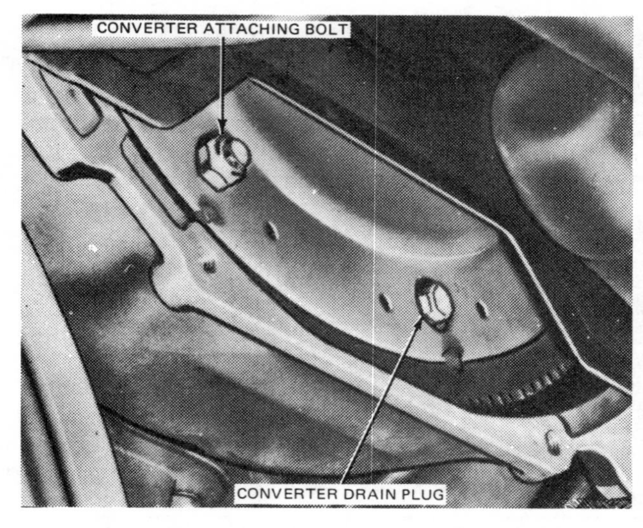

Fig. 7.21 Converter drain plug and bolts (Sec 10)

11 Disconnect the transmission shift rod at the manual selector lever.
12 Disconnect the downshift rod and spring at the transmission downshift lever.
13 Make a note of and then disconnect the neutral start and back-up switch wires from the connectors and retaining clamps.
14 Undo and remove the four nuts securing the torque converter to the flywheel. For this the engine will have to be rotated and the nuts removed working through the aperture left by removal of the converter cover (paragraph 7) (Fig. 7.21). **Caution: do not rotate the engine backwards as this could cause a belt-driven cam to jump teeth.**
15 Support the weight of the transmission unit using a jack. It will also be necessary to have an assistant to hold the transmission unit.
16 Using an overhead hoist, crane or jack, support the weight of the engine.
17 Undo and remove the bolts securing the transmission unit crossmember to the body.
18 Undo and remove the bolts securing the rear engine support crossmember.
19 Remove the front exhaust pipe section between the manifold and the resonator box (or converter).
20 Undo and remove the bolts securing the starter motor to the torque converter housing and withdraw the starter motor from its location.
21 Undo and remove the remaining bolts securing the torque converter housing to the rear of the engine.
22 Carefully draw the unit rearwards (take care because it is very heavy) and lower to the ground. Support on wooden blocks so that the selector lever is not damaged or bent.
23 To separate the converter housing from the transmission case, first lift off the converter from the transmission unit, taking suitable precautions to catch the fluid upon separation.
24 Undo and remove the bolts and spring washers which secure the converter housing to the transmission case. Lift away the converter housing.
25 Refitting the automatic transmission unit is the reverse sequence to removal, but there are several additional points which will assist you in the completion of this task:

- a) *If the torque converter has been removed, before refitting it will be necessary to align the front pump drive tangs with the slots in the inner gear and then carefully replace the torque converter. Take care not to damage the oil seal.*
- b) *Before mounting the transmission on the engine remove the two dowel pins from the converter housing flange and push them in the engine block. This is only applicable when dowels are fitted.*
- c) *Adjust the manual selector linkage, the throttle downshift cable and the inhibitor switch. Full details of these adjustments will be found in subsequent Sections.*

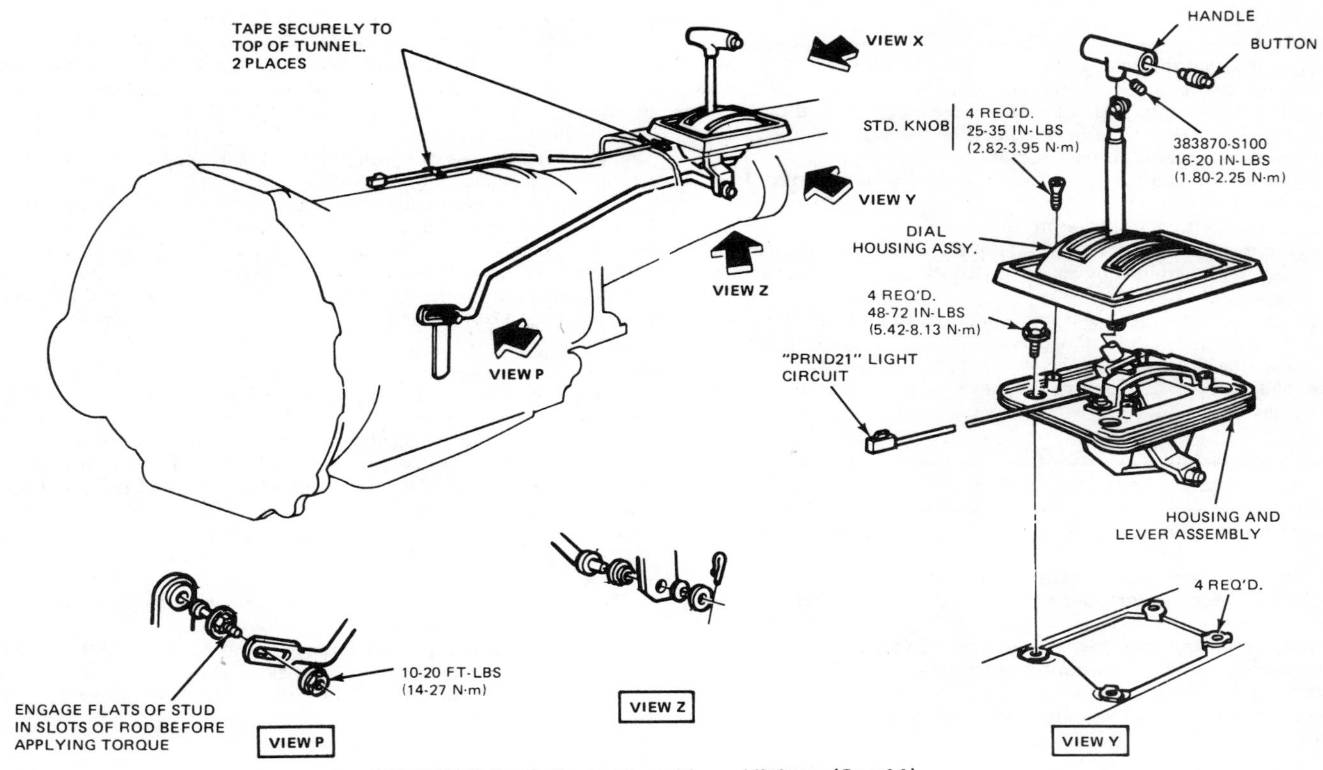

Fig. 7.22 Selector lever assembly and linkage (Sec 11)

11 Selector lever assembly – removal and replacement

1 Chock the front wheels, jack up the rear of the car and support on firmly based axle stands.
2 Working under the car, undo and remove the manual lever control rod securing nut. Detach the rod from the stud.
3 Working inside the car, remove the selector lever handle by pulling it abruptly upward with the shifter in neutral.
4 Undo and remove the screws securing the dial housing to the selector lever assembly. Lift away the dial housing.
5 Undo and remove the two screws securing the pointer back-up shield to the selector lever assembly. Lift away the shield.
6 Undo and remove the two screws that secure the dial indicator light bulb retainer to the selector lever. Remove the retainer and bulb.
7 Undo and remove the selector housing and lever assembly securing bolts. Lift away the selector lever and housing.
8 If it is necessary to detach the selector lever from the housing undo and remove the one securing nut and detach the lever from the housing.
9 To reassemble first refit the selector lever to the housing and secure with the nut.
10 Fit the handle to the selector lever.
11 Check the clearance between the detent pawl and plate. The detent pawl when correctly adjusted should clear the highest point on the detent plate.
12 To adjust the pawl height, hold the adjustment screw stationary and turn the lock nut until the correct clearance is obtained.
13 Remove the handle from the selector lever again.
14 Reassembly and refitting is now the reverse sequence to removal, and dismantling. It may be necessary to adjust the manual control linkage.

12 Neutral start switch – removal and replacement

1 Chock the front wheels, jack up the rear of the car and support on firmly based axle stands.
2 Working under the car, disconnect the downshift linkage rod from the transmission downshift lever.

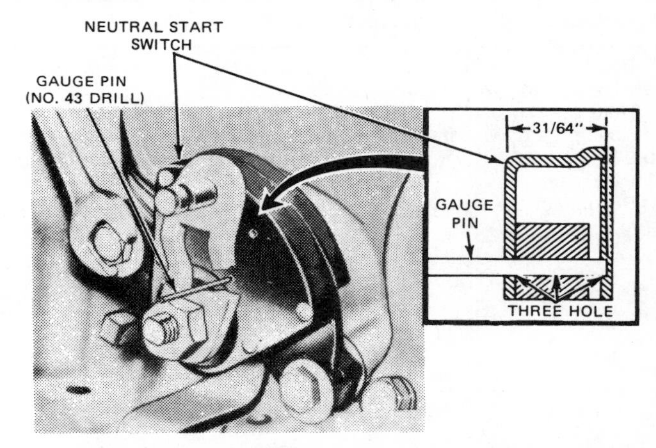

Fig. 7.23 Adjusting neutral start switch (Sec 12)

3 Apply a little penetrating oil to the downshift lever shaft and nut and allow to soak for a few minutes.
4 Undo and remove the transmission downshift outer lever retaining nut. Lift away the lever.
5 Undo and remove the two neutral start switch securing bolts.
6 Disconnect the multi-wire connector from the neutral switch and lift away the switch.
7 To refit the switch, place on the transmission unit and lightly secure with the two bolts.
8 Move the selector lever to the 'N' (neutral) position. Rotate the switch and fit a No. 43 drill into the gauge pin hole. It must be inserted a full 0.48 in (12.30 mm) into the three holes of the switch. Tighten the switch securing bolts fully and remove the drill.
9 Refitting is now the reverse sequence to removal. Check that the engine only starts with the selector lever in the 'N' and 'P' positions.
Note: *The neutral start switch on the C3 transmission is non-adjustable and any fault will be due to a malfunctioning switch, wear on the internal actuating cam or faulty wiring. If the switch is suspect, replace it with a new one. Always use a new O-ring seal and tighten to the specified torque.*

13 Selector linkage – adjustment (C3)

1 First check that the selector lever is correctly adjusted. To do this, use feeler gauges to check the end-clearance between the lever pawl and the quadrant notch. This should be between 0.005 and 0.010 in (0.13 and 0.25 mm). If necessary, adjust the cable lock nut which is accessible after removal of the selector lever housing plug.
2 Disconnect the shift lever at the base of the hand control lever (adjustable end of rod).
3 Place the hand control lever in 'D'.
4 Place the selector lever on the side of the transmission housing in 'D'. This can be determined by counting two 'clicks' back from the fully forward position.
5 Now attempt to reconnect the shift rod to the selector hand control lever by pushing in the clevis pin. The pin should slide in without any side stress at all. If this is not the case, release the lock nut on the shift rod and adjust its effective length by screwing the adjusting link in, or out.

14 Selector linkage – adjustment (C4)

1 Chock the front wheels, jack up the rear of the car and support on firmly based axle stands.
2 Move the transmission selector lever to the 'D' position.
3 Working under the car loosen the manual lever shift rod retaining nut.
4 Move the manual lever to the 'D' position. This is the fourth detent position from the rear of the transmission unit.
5 With transmission selector lever and manual lever in the 'D' positions tighten the retaining nut to a torque wrench setting of 10 – 12 ft-lb (13 – 16 Nm).

15 Kick-down rod – adjustment

1 Disconnect the downshift rod return spring and hold the throttle shaft lever in the wide open position.
2 Hold the downshift rod against the through detent stop.
3 Adjust the downshift screw so as to provide a clearance of 0.050 – 0.070 in (1.27 – 1.78 mm) between the screw tip and the throttle shaft lever tab.
4 Reconnect the downshift lever spring.

16 Intermediate band (C3 and C4) – adjustment

1 The intermediate or front band is used to hold the sun gear stationary so as to give the second gear ratio. If it is not correctly adjusted there will be noticeable slip during first to second gearchange or from third to second gearchange. The first symptoms of these conditions will be very sluggish gearchange instead of the usual crisp action.
2 To adjust the intermediate band, undo and remove the adjustment screw lock nut located on the left-hand side of the transmission case. Tighten the adjusting screw using a torque wrench set to 10 ft-lbs (13.5 Nm) and then slacken off the adjustment screw 1½ turns. A new lock nut should be fitted and tightened to a torque wrench setting of 35 – 45 ft-lb (47 – 61 Nm).

17 Low and reverse band (C4 only) – adjustment

1 The low and reverse band or rear band is in action when 'L' or 'R' position of the selector lever is obtained to hold the low and reverse pinion carrier stationary. If it is not correctly adjusted there will be a noticeable malfunction of the automatic transmission unit, whereby there will be no drive with the selector lever in the 'R' position, also associated with no engine braking on first gear when the selector lever is in the 'L' position.
2 To adjust the rear band undo and remove the adjusting screw lock nut located on the left-hand side of the transmission case. Tighten the adjusting screw using a torque wrench set to 10 ft-lb (13.5 Nm) and then slacken off the adjustment screw exactly 3 turns. A new lock nut should be fitted and tightened to a torque wrench setting of 35 – 45 ft-lb (47 – 61 Nm).

18 Fault diagnosis – automatic transmission

As has been mentioned elsewhere in this Chapter, no service repair work should be considered by anyone without the specialist knowledge and equipment required to undertake this work. This is also relevant to fault diagnosis. If a fault is evident carry out the various adjustments previously described and if the fault still exists consult the local garage or specialist.

Chapter 8 Driveshaft, rear axle and differential

Contents

Specifications

Driveshaft

Type	One-piece, Cardan-type universal joints at each end

Rear axle-differential unit

Type	Integral carrier
Ring and pinion gear ratios, by I.D. tag number	
WGX-S	2.73 : 1
WGX-R	3.08 : 1
WGS-T	3.45 : 1
WGX-U	2.26 : 1
Ring gear diameter	7.5 in (191 mm)
Rear axle oil capacity	3.50 U.S. pts.
Oil type	ESW-M2C-154-A

Torque specifications

	ft-lb	Nm
Flange bolts	8 to 15	11 to 20
Bearing cap bolts	70 to 85	95 to 115
Ring gear mounting bolts	70 to 85	95 to 115
Rear cover screws	25 to 35	34 to 47
Oil filler plug	25 to 50	34 to 67
Nuts, rear axle shaft retaining bolts	20 to 40	28 to 54
Pinion preload		
With new oil seal and original bearings	8 to 14 in-lb	0.91 to 1.5
With new oil seal and new bearings	17 to 27 in-lb	2.0 to 3.0

1 Driveshaft – general description

The driveshaft is a one-piece, tubular unit with a Cardan-type universal joint fitted to each end. The forward end of the front universal joint is splined and fits into the output shaft at the end of all transmissions. The rear universal joint connects to the differential through matching machined flanges which are bolted together. The universal joints are replaceable components.

2 Driveshaft – removal and installation

1 Position the car on a level work area.
2 Shift the transmission into PARK (if automatic) or into any forward gear (if manual) and set the parking brake.
3 Block the front end of the car and raise the rear.
4 Support the rear of the car on jack stands.
5 Mark the flange located between the rear universal joint and the differential housing with chalk or crayon. Since the driveshaft is balanced as an assembly at the factory, it must be mounted in the same position when installing (Fig. 8.2).
6 Loosen and remove the four bolts securing the driveshaft to the pinion flange. Support the driveshaft so that it does not fall.
7 Carefully lower the rear end of the driveshaft while pulling the assembly towards the rear of the car. Be careful not to disturb the seal in the tailpiece of the transmission.
8 Place a tray or pan under the end of the transmission to catch any fluid that may leak.
9 Replacing the driveshaft is done by reversing the steps as shown above with the following words of caution.
10 Be sure that the front yoke is free of dirt and grit.
11 Inspect the transmission tailpiece seal for cracks. Replace as needed.
12 Be sure to align the marks made in step 5 before bolting the assembly together.
13 After completion, check the transmission fluid level.

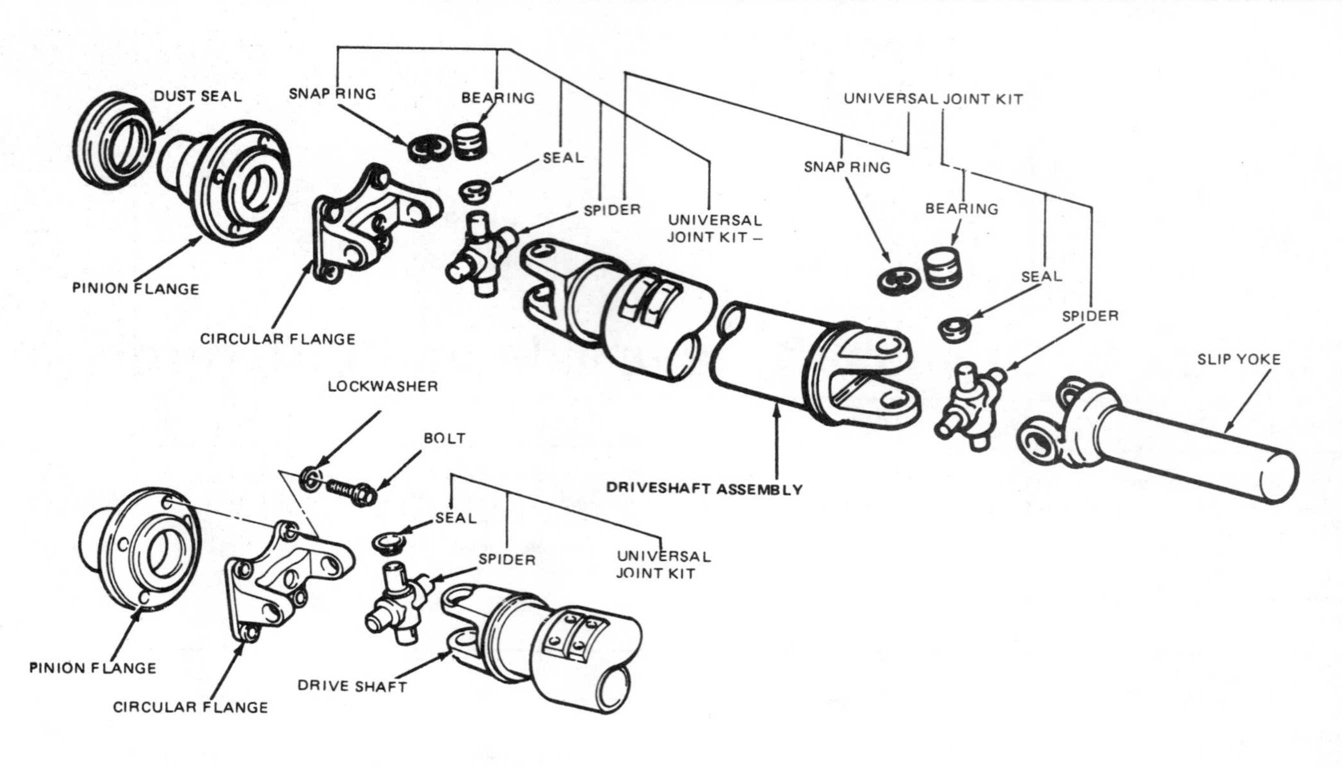

Fig. 8.1 Driveshaft and universal joint components (Secs 1 and 4)

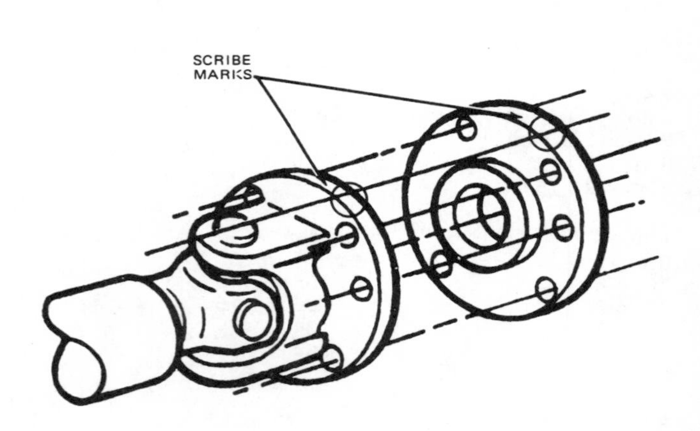

Fig. 8.2 Always mark the driveshaft-to-universal joint connection when removing to avoid disturbing balance (Sec 2)

4.3 The universal joint snap-rings can be removed with small pliers

3 Universal joints – inspection

1 Wear in the universal joints is characterized by vibration in the drive-line, "clunks" on starting from a standstill, metallic squeaking, and ultimately grating and shrieking. Many drive-line bearing problems can be identified by a harmonic "rumbling" at a constant speed.
2 To make a simple check of the drive-line bearings, place the car on a level surface and block the wheels. Place the car in gear (or PARK) with the emergency brake on.
3 Hold the axle pinion flange with one hand while moving the driveshaft with the other. If there is any noticeable slack in the universal joint area, the U-joints may be worn.
4 Repeat the check for the front of the driveshaft to check the condition of the front universal joints.
5 If the driveshaft has been removed, examine the splines (transmission end) for cracks and rounded or missing teeth on the transmission output shaft.

4 Front universal joint – removal, service and/or replacement

1 Remove the driveshaft from the vehicle.
2 Clean away any dirt and foreign matter from the universal joint area of the driveshaft.
3 Remove the snap-rings from the U-joint end cap (photo).
4 Remove the bearing cups from the U-joint yoke. Refer to Fig. 8.1. If a press is unavailable the cups may be removed as follows:
5 A vise, a selection of sockets and a quantity of bearing grease are needed. Open the vise wide enough to provide room for the U-joint and two sockets.

4.6A Using a vise and different sized sockets to press out the bearing cups

4.6B The bearing cup can be extracted with locking pliers

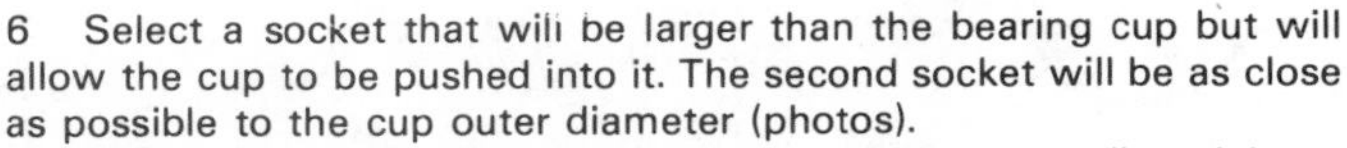

6 Select a socket that will be larger than the bearing cup but will allow the cup to be pushed into it. The second socket will be as close as possible to the cup outer diameter (photos).
7 Refer to the illustrations. When the U-joints, small and large sockets and vise are used, the bearing cups are easily and safely removed.
8 The alternative method of cup removal is that which uses a hammer and socket; this can be effective but there is a danger of the yoke being damaged.
9 Clean the yokes with an approved solvent.
10 If the bearings are to be reinstalled, clean and re-grease them, filling the cups approximately one third full with grease.
11 Replace the cups using new parts (seals) as necessary.
12 Install the bearing snap-rings.
13 Check the U-joint for free movement in all directions.
14 Replace the driveshaft to the vehicle.

5 Rear universal joint – removal, service and/or replacement

1 The rear universal joint service procedure is identical to that of the front. However, there are fewer parts to be concerned with. Follow all steps and precautions as necessary.

6 Driveshaft – balance

1 If the previous steps have been performed and vibration or clunking persists, the driveshaft may be bent or out of balance.
2 This is most easily corrected not by a home mechanic, but by the services of a local dealer or drive-line specialist.

7 Rear axle and differential – description

1 The rear axle is an integral type housing of hypoid gear design. The center-line of the pinion is set below the center-line of the ring gear.
2 The hypoid gear set comprises a ring gear and an overhung drive pinion supported at either end by two roller bearings. Pinion bearing preload is maintained by a crush-type spacer on the pinion shaft and is adjusted by tightening the pinion nut.
3 The housing assembly consists of a cast center section with attachment points for rear suspension. Axle tubes are slug welded to either side to house the axle assemblies. The semi-floating axleshafts are retained in the housing by bearing retainers at the outermost ends of the axle housing.
4 A cover on the rear of the center casting is removable to allow for access to the differential for inspection and adjustment.
5 Due to the complexity of the differential unit and the need for special tools, it is recommended that any major work be entrusted to the local authorized dealership or qualified repair shop.

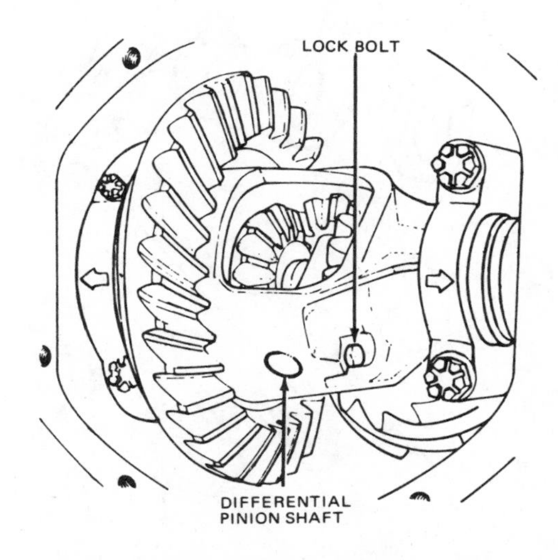

Fig. 8.3 Differential pinion shaft and lock bolt (Sec 8)

8 Axleshaft – removal and replacement

1 Park the car on level ground, block the front wheels, loosen the lug nuts on the side of the car to be worked on, jack up the car. Place the car securely on jack stands and remove the wheel(s) on the side(s) requiring work.
2 Release the handbrake.
3 Remove the brake drum. Retain the speed nuts.
4 Carefully clean the differential cover of dirt and grease. Use a wire brush, solvent and clean, lint free cloths as cleanliness is very important.
5 Remove the rear cover and allow all of the oil to drain from the differential into a suitable container.
6 Remove the differential pinion shaft lock screw and pinion shaft (Fig. 8.4).
7 Push the flanged (outer) end of the axle inward toward the center of the car and remove the C-locks from the groove in the inner end of the axleshaft (Fig. 8.5).
8 Withdraw the axleshaft from the housing, making sure that it does'nt damage the oil seal

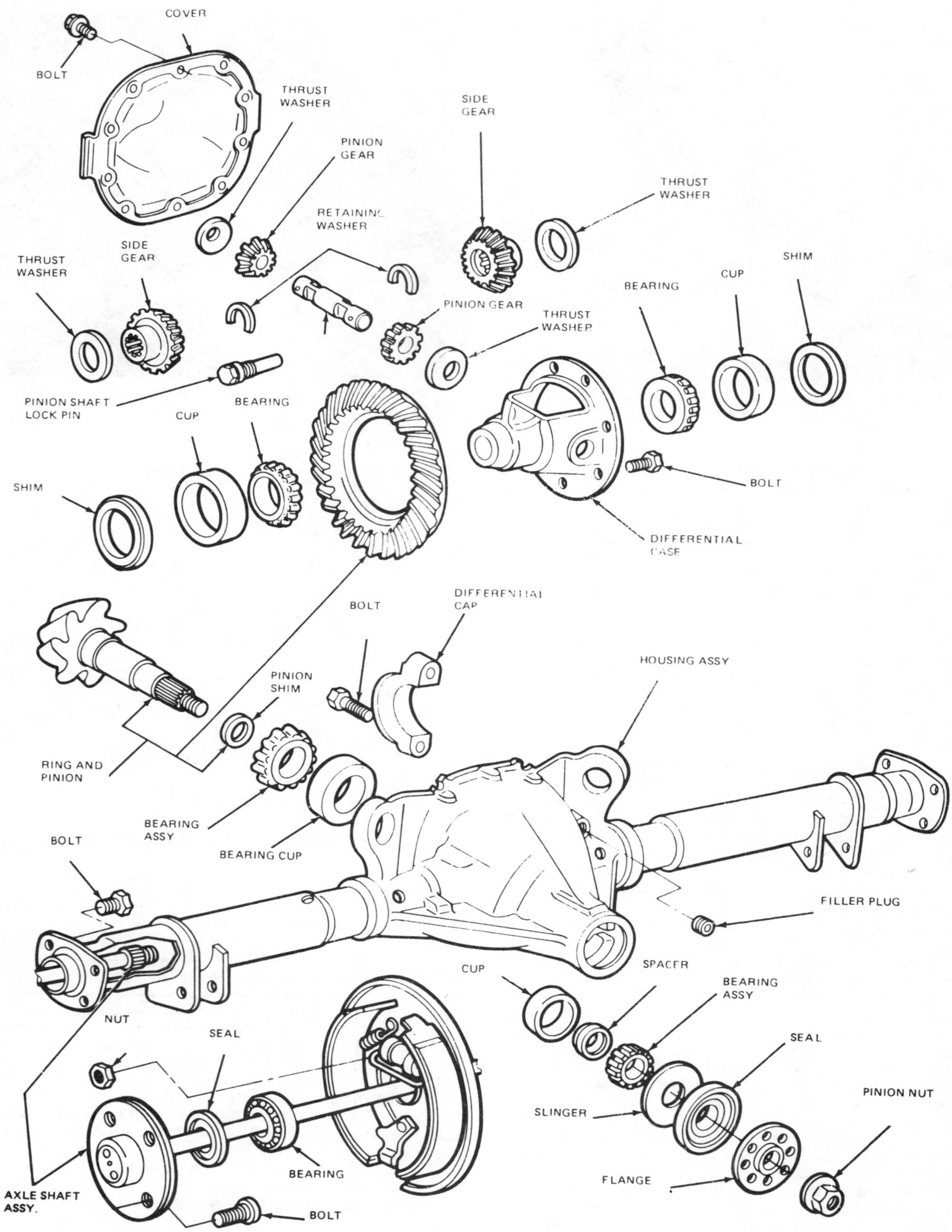

Fig. 8.4 Rear axle and differential components (Secs 7 and 8)

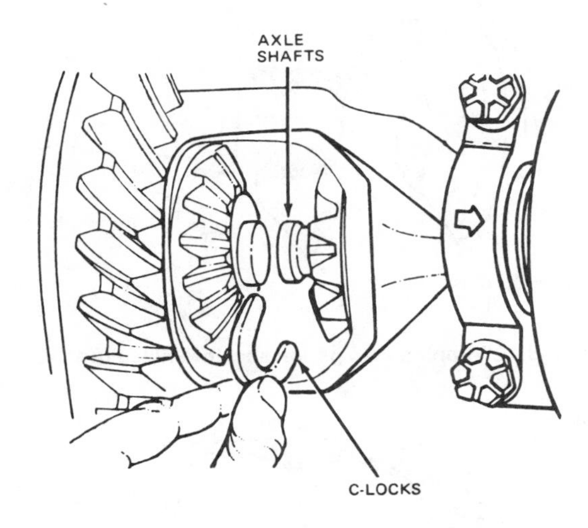

Fig. 8.5 Removing C-lock from axleshaft (Sec 8)

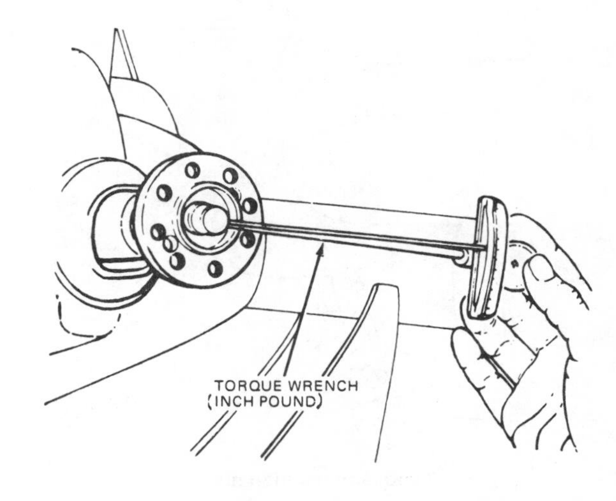

Fig. 8.8 Checking axle pinion preload with torque wrench (Sec 9)

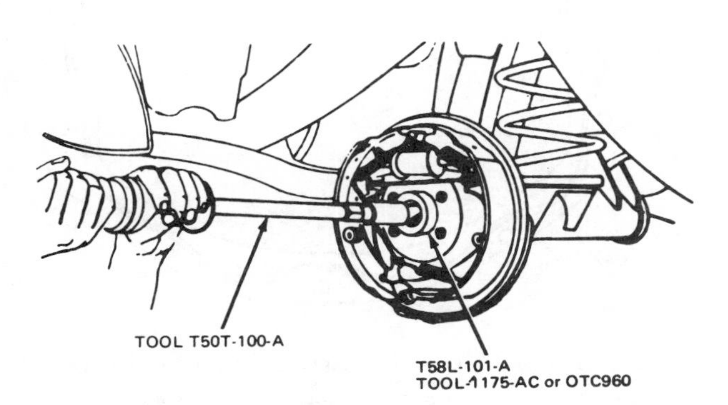

Fig. 8.6 Removing axle bearing and seal (Sec 8)

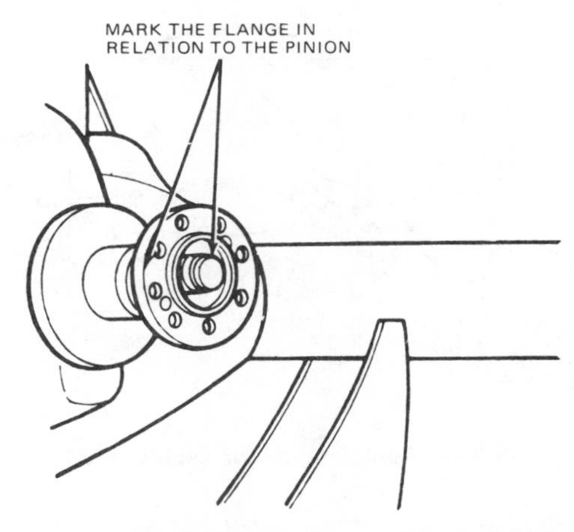

Fig. 8.9 Marking pinion shaft flange and shaft (Sec 9)

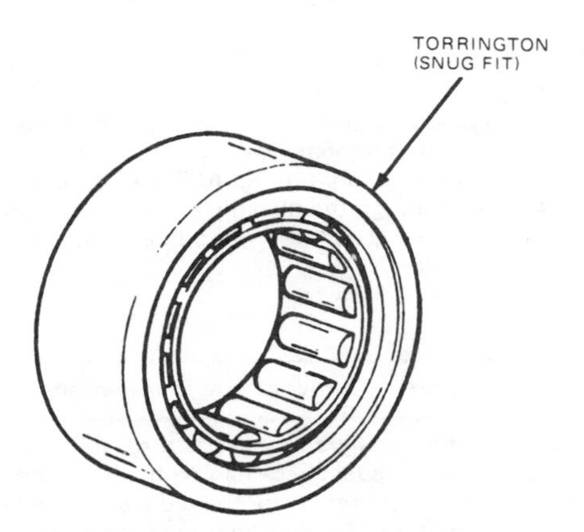

Fig. 8.7 Axle bearing (Sec 8)

9 Inspect the axle for nicks and rough spots. If there is any sign of blueing, consult a qualified repair shop. Replace any worn or damaged parts.
10 The bearing and seal are removed as a unit from the axle housing, using a slide hammer tool (Fig. 8.6).
11 The new bearing should be lubricated with rear axle oil and installed squarely in the axle housing bore.
12 Install the new seal taking care that it is not cocked in the bore. Tap the seal into place until it is seated squarely in the bore. If the seal or the bearing are not installed straight in the bore early failure or leakage could occur.
13 Slide the axle shaft carefully into the axle housing so that the bearing and seal assembly are not damaged. Align the splines with the side gear and push firmly until the end of the axle can be seen in the differential case.
14 Slide the C-lock onto the bottom end of the axle shaft splines. Push the shaft outward until the shaft splines engage and the C-lock becomes seated in the counterbore of the differential side gear.
15 Insert the differential pinion shaft through the case and pinion gears, lining up the hole in the shaft with the lock screw hole. Install the differential pinion shaft lock bolt and tighten to specifications.
16 Install the rear cover as described in Section 11.
17 Install the brake drum assembly and wheel cover.
18 Remove the jack stands and wheel chocks. If oil loss is suspected, check the rear axle oil level.

9 Pinion oil seal – removal and installation

1 Raise the rear of the car and install jack stands.
2 Remove the rear wheels and brake drums.
3 Mark the driveshaft and axle pinion flange to allow for proper realignment when assembling. Unbolt the driveshaft and remove. Place a pan underneath the transmission to catch any leakage.

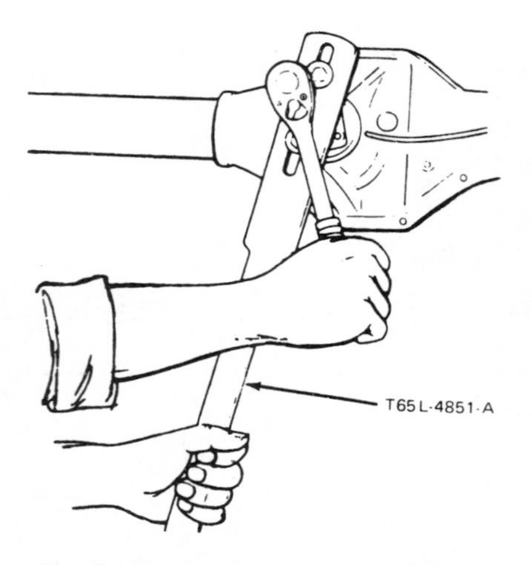

Fig. 8.10 Loosening pinion nut (Sec 9)

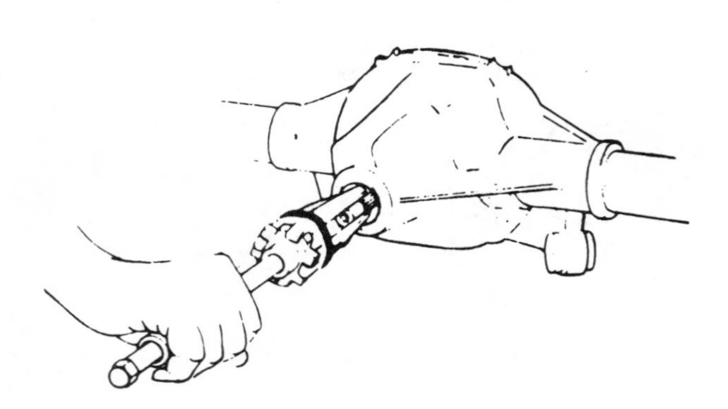

Fig. 8.11 Removing pinion seal (Sec 9)

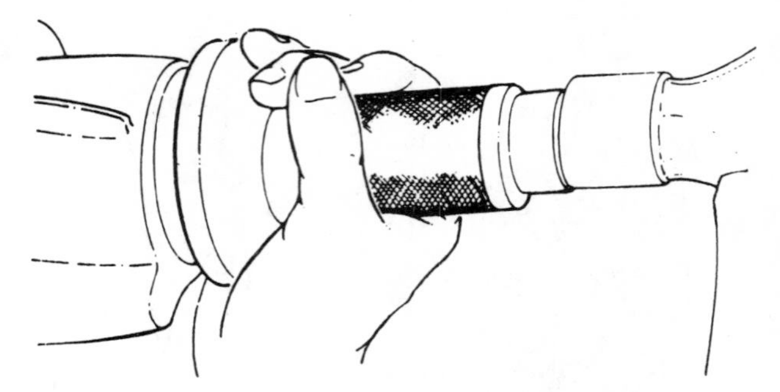

Fig. 8.12 Tapping new pinion seal into place (Sec 9)

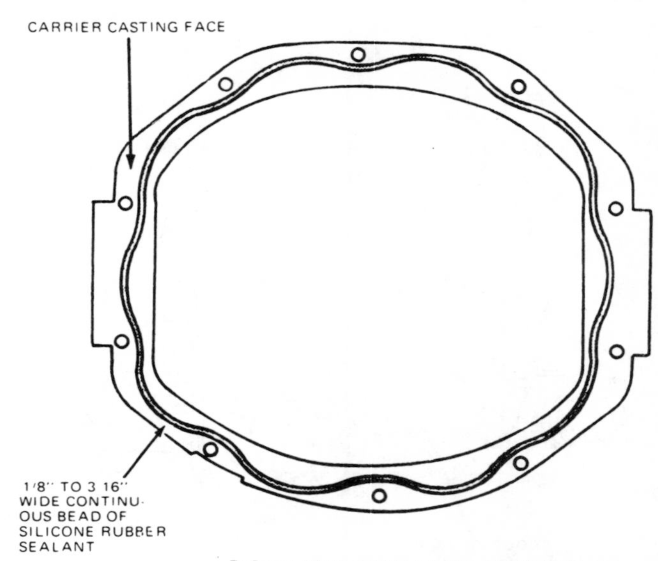

Fig. 8.13 Installation of silicone sealant gasket bead to axle casting face (Sec 11)

4 Install a torque wrench to the pinion nut and record the torque through several revolutions (Fig. 8.8). Mark the position of the flange to the pinion shaft (Fig 8.9).
5 While holding the flange against turning, loosen the pinion nut. Remove the differential flange (Fig. 8.10).
6 Pry out the old seal. This can be done with a small slide hammer and reversed jaws (Fig. 8.11).
7 Clean the oil seal mounting surface.
8 Tap the new seal into place. Do not allow it to be misaligned or scratched (Fig. 8.12).
9 Check the splines on the pinion shaft for burrs or chips. They may be removed with crocus cloth working in a circular motion. Wipe the splines clean.
10 Replace the differential flange to its proper position as marked during removal.
11 Tighten the pinion nut while allowing the assembly to turn and reseat.
12 Take frequent pinion bearing load readings until the original readings are attained.
13 Install the driveshaft.
14 Replace the brake drums and wheels.
15 Check oil level in the differential. Fill as needed.
16 Remove the jack stands.
17 After driving, check for leaks.

10 Rear axle oil – draining and filling

1 Place the vehicle on a flat surface.
2 Locate a drain pan underneath the rear axle drain plug.
3 Loosen the plug and allow the oil to drain. Because the oil is thick, allow 15 minutes for complete drainage.
4 Reinstall the drain plug, tighten to 25-45 ft-lb (34-67 Nm).
5 Refill the axle through the fill plug located on the upper side of the casting. Use 2.5 pints U.S. (2.08 pints Imperial).
6 Refit the fill plug.
7 Check for leaks.

11 Differential cover – removal and installation

1 Should the differential be suspect as the reason for noise or driveline vibration, a quick visual check can be made by the removal of the differential cover. Once removed the housing can be checked for cracks, missing teeth on the ring gear, and metal in the oil.
2 Drain the oil as done in the preceding step.
3 Remove the bolts securing the differential cover to the axle housing.
4 When any visual checks are complete, clean the mating surface of the two parts.
5 Apply a thin line of silicone to the cover as shown (Fig. 8.13).
6 Locate the cover to the housing and secure with bolts.
7 Tighten in a criss-cross pattern to 25-35 ft-lb (34-67 Nm).
8 Refill with oil.
9 After a short drive, check for leaks.

Chapter 9 Braking system

Refer to Chapter 13 for specifications related to 1981 thru 1987 models

Contents

Specifications

Type of system	Disc at front, drum at rear
Footbrake	Hydraulic on all four wheels
Parking brake	Mechanical to rear wheels only
Front brake layout	Trailing calipers
Hydraulic system	Dual line, tandem master cylinder and servo assisted

Front disc brakes

Type	Single cylinder, sliding caliper
Disc diameter	9.3 in (236.22 mm)
Thickness:	
Std	0.870 in
Reground	0.810 in

Lining size

Inner	5.12 x 1.42 in (130 x 36 mm)
Outer	6.02 x 1.42 in (153 x 36 mm)

Rear drum brakes

Drum diameter	
Std	9.000 in (228.6 mm)
Reground	9.060 in (230.124 mm)
Maximum ovality	0.007 in (0.1778 mm)
Linings:	
Primary	1.75 x 6.12 in (44 x 156 mm)
Secondary	1.75 x 8.63 in (44 x 219 mm)
Wheel cylinder bore	0.875 in (22 mm)

Master cylinder

Type	Tandem
Bore	0.938 in (23.813 mm)

Brake pedal

	Max.
Free height (power brakes)	7.0 in (177 mm)
Free height (standard brakes)	8.8 in (223 mm)
Pedal travel (power brakes)	2.0 in (50 mm)
Pedal travel (standard brakes)	3.0 in (76 mm)

Torque specifications

	ft-lb	**Nm**
Bleed valves (screws)	2.5 to 5.5	3.4 to 7.4
Hydraulic lines	12 to 20	9 to 15
Hoses	12 to 20	9 to 15
Metal lines	10 to 15	7 to 11

	ft-lb	Nm
Caliper bolts	30 to 40	40 to 54
Parking brake assembly bolts	13 to 25	10 to 18
Master cylinder bolts	13 to 25	10 to 18
Wheel cylinder bolts	5 to 7	4 to 5
Pressure differential bolts	7 to 11	5 to 8
Front backplate bolts	9 to 14	7 to 10
Rear backplate bolts	20 to 40	15 to 30
Servo unit to firewall	13 to 25	10 to 18
Parking brake securing bolts	10 to 25	15 to 18
All fasteners not listed, use the following torque wrench settings:		
Metric thread sizes		
M-6	6 to 9	9 to 12
M-8	14 to 21	19 to 28
M-10	28 to 40	38 to 54
M-12	50 to 71	68 to 96
M-14	80 to 140	109 to 154
Pipe thread sizes		
$\frac{1}{8}$	5 to 8	7 to 10
$\frac{1}{4}$	12 to 18	17 to 24
$\frac{3}{8}$	22 to 33	30 to 44
$\frac{1}{2}$	25 to 35	34 to 47
U.S. thread sizes		
$\frac{1}{4}$ – 20	6 to 9	9 to 12
$\frac{5}{16}$ – 18	12 to 18	17 to 24
$\frac{5}{16}$ – 24	14 to 20	19 to 27
$\frac{3}{8}$ – 16	22 to 32	30 to 43
$\frac{3}{8}$ – 24	27 to 38	37 to 51
$\frac{7}{16}$ – 14	40 to 55	55 to 74
$\frac{7}{16}$ – 20	40 to 60	55 to 81
$\frac{1}{2}$ – 13	55 to 80	75 to 108

1 General description

The standard braking system comprises disc brakes on the front wheels and self-adjusting drum brakes on the rear. Rear disc brakes are available on some models as an option. A vacuum brake booster provides servo assistance.

The rear drum brake system is of the single anchor, internal expanding and self-adjusting assembly type. To expand the shoes a dual piston single cylinder is used.

The self-adjusting mechanism comprises a cable, cable guide, adjusting lever adjusting screw assembly and an adjuster spring. The cable is hooked over the anchor pin at the top and is connected to the lever at the bottom and is passed along the web of the secondary brake shoe by means of the cable guide. The adjuster spring is hooked onto the primary brake shoe and also to the lever.

The automatic adjuster operates when the brakes are applied and the car is backing up, or when the secondary brake shoe is able to move towards the drum beyond a certain limit.

The self-centering pressure differential valve assembly body has a stepped bore to accommodate a sleeve and seal which is fitted over the piston and into the large valve body in the front brake system area.

The brake light warning switch is located at the center of the valve body and the spring loaded switch plunger fits into a tapered shoulder groove in the center of the piston. When in this condition the electric circuit through the switch is broken and the warning light on the instrument panel is extinguished.

The disc brake assembly comprises a ventilated disc and a caliper. The caliper is of the single piston, sliding pin design and mounted to the strut arms. The cylinder bore contains one piston with a square sectioned rubber seal located in a groove in the cylinder bore to provide sealing between the cylinder and piston.

An independent parking brake system is provided, and is operated by a lever mounted in the tunnel between the front seats. The parking brake operates the rear wheel brakes only, through a system of cables. The equalizer rod is connected directly to the parking brake lever and an equalizer. The brake cables are routed from the equalizer to brackets mounted on the tunnel and then pass rearwards through clips welded to the floor panel, then through the rear brake backing plates. Finally they are connected to the parking brake levers on the rear brake secondary shoes.

2 Bleeding the hydraulic system

1 Removal of all the air from the hydraulic fluid in the braking system is essential to the correct working of the braking system. Before undertaking this task, examine the fluid reservoir cap to ensure that the vent hole is clear, also check the level of fluid in the reservoir and top-up if necessary.

2 Check all brake line unions and connections for possible leakage, and at the same time check the condition of the rubber hoses which may be cracked or worn.

3 If the condition of a caliper or wheel cylinder is in doubt, check for signs of fluid leakage.

4 If there is any possibility that incorrect fluid has been used in the system, drain all the fluid out and flush through with methylated spirits. Replace all piston seals and cups as they will be affected and could possibly fail under pressure.

5 Gather together a clean jar, a 12 inch (304 mm) length of rubber tubing which fits tightly over the bleed valves and a container of the correct grade of brake fluid.

6 The primary (front) and secondary (rear) hydraulic brake systems are individual systems and are therefore bled separately. Always bleed the longest line first.

7 To bleed the secondary system (rear) clean the area around the bleed valves and start at the rear right-hand wheel cylinder by first removing the rubber cap over the end of the bleed valve.

8 Place the end of the tube in the clean jar which should contain sufficient fluid to keep the end of the tube submerged during the operation.

9 Open the bleed valve approximately $\frac{3}{4}$ turn with a wrench and depress the brake pedal slowly through its full travel.

10 Close the bleed valve and allow the pedal to return to the released position.

11 Continue this sequence until no more air bubbles issue from the bleed tube. Give the brake pedal two more strikes to ensure that the line is completely free of air, and then re-tighten the bleed valve, ensuring that the bleed tube remains submerged until the valve is closed.

12 At regular intervals during the bleeding sequence, make sure that the reservoir is kept topped-up, otherwise air will enter again at this point. Do not re-use fluid bled from the system.

13 Repeat the whole procedure on the rear left-hand brake line.
14 To bleed the primary system (front), start with the front right-hand side and finish with the front left-hand side cylinder. The procedure is identical to that previously described (photo).
Note: *Some models have a bleed valve incorporated in the master cylinder. Where this is the case, the master cylinder should be bled before the brake lines. The bleeding procedure is identical to that already described. Do not use the secondary piston stop screw which is located on the bottom of some master cylinders for bleeding. This could damage the secondary piston on the stop screw.*
15 Top-up the master cylinder to within 0.25 inch of the top of the reservoirs, check that the diaphragm type gasket is correctly located in the cover and then refit the cover.

3 Pressure differential valve – centralization

1 After any repair or bleed operations it is possible that the dual brake warning light will come on due to the pressure differential valve remaining in an off-center position.
2 To centralize the valve, first turn the ignition switch to the ON or ACC position.
3 Depress the brake pedal several times and the piston will center itself again causing the warning light to go out.
4 Turn the ignition off.

4 Flexible hoses – inspection, removal and replacement

1 Inspect the condition of the flexible hydraulic hoses leading to each of the front disc brake calipers and the one at the front of the rear axle. If they are swollen, damaged or chafed, they must be replaced.
2 Wipe the top of the brake master cylinder reservoir and unscrew the cap. Place a piece of polythene sheet over the top of the reservoir and refit the cap. This is to stop hydraulic fluid siphoning out during subsequent operations.
3 To remove a flexible hose wipe the union and any supports free from dust and undo the union nuts from the metal pipe ends.
4 Undo and remove the lock nuts and washers securing each flexible hose end to the support and lift away the flexible hose.
5 Refitting is the reverse sequence to removal. It will be necessary to bleed the brake hydraulic system as described in Section 2. If one hose has been removed it is only necessary to bleed either the front or rear brake hydraulic system.

2.14 Front disc brake bleeding, note the rubber tube leading from the bleed screw to container

5 Front disc pads – removal, inspection and replacement

1 Raise the vehicle and support with jack stands.
2 Remove the wheel assembly.
3 Remove the master cylinder cap and remove approximately one-half of the fluid in the reservoir. Discard.
4 Loosen the caliper locating bolt/pins.
5 Support the caliper with a piece of wire and remove the locating bolt/pins. This will allow the caliper to move freely without putting any strain on the hydraulic brake hose (photos).
6 Lift the caliper from its mounting position.
7 The brake pads can be unsnapped from their position in the caliper (photos).
8 Discard the locating bolt/pin insulators. They are not designed to be re-used.
9 Inspect the brake pads for cracks and missing material.
10 Replace the pads (as an axle set) if there is less than $\frac{1}{8}$ inch (0.125 in) of friction material left on any pad, measured from the metal backing plate.

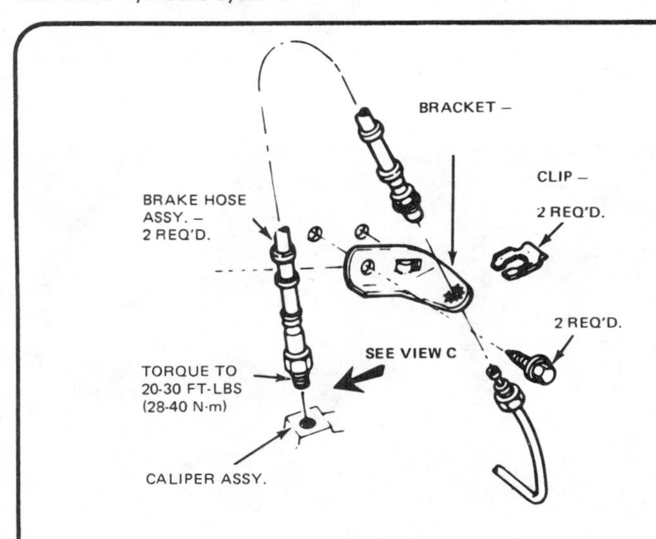

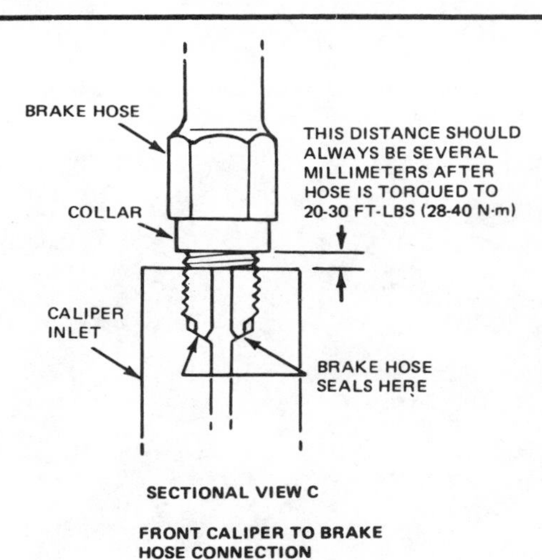

Fig. 9.1 Brake hose installation (Sec 4)

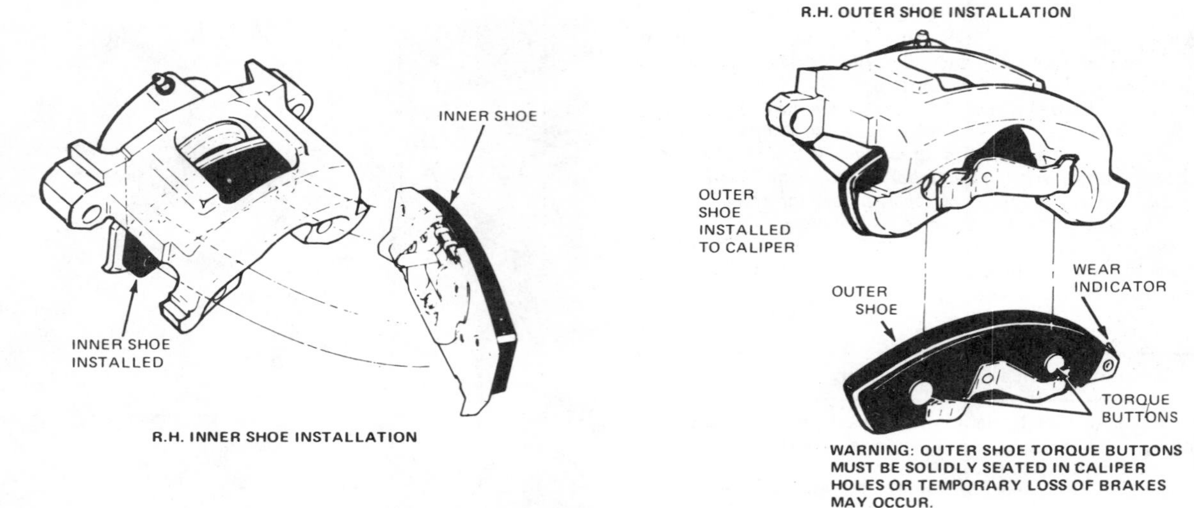

Fig. 9.2 Brake pad installation (Sec 5)

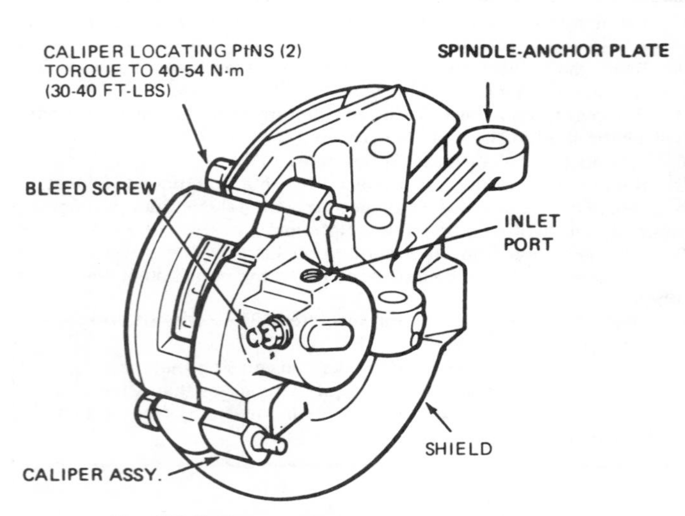

Fig. 9.3 Caliper assembly components (Sec 5)

5.5A Removing the caliper bolt slider pin. These are not to be re-used and should be replaced with new ones

5.5B Pull the caliper outward to compress the piston and then rearward to remove the caliper

5.5C To avoid damage to the brake line, hang the caliper out of the way with a piece of wire

5.7A Slide the inner pad forward and then outward to remove it

5.7B Remove the outer pad by releasing the clips and sliding the pad forward

5.13 The round torque buttons on the back of the outer pad must be securely seated in the holes in the caliper

11 Insert new insulator sleeves into the mounting holes.
12 Depress the piston. Use a block of wood and a C-clamp if necessary to drive the piston back into the caliper casting.
13 Reinstall the brake pads. Make sure the two round torque buttons on the outer pad are solidly seated in the caliper (photo).
14 Position the caliper on the mounting ears.
15 Insert the locating bolt/pins.
16 Tighten the locating bolt/pins.
17 Reinstall the wheel assembly.
18 Remove the jack stands. Pump the brake pedal a few times and check the hydraulic fluid level; fill as needed. Test for a solid brake pedal before and during a test drive.

6 Front disc brake disc and hub – removal and replacement

1 Refer to Section 5, and remove the caliper and anchor plate assembly. To save extra work and time, if the caliper and anchor plate are not requiring attention, it is not necessary to disconnect the flexible brake hose from the caliper. Suspend the assembly with string or wire from the upper suspension arm.
2 Carefully remove the grease cap from the wheel spindle (photo).
3 Withdraw the cotter pin and nut lock from the wheel bearing adjusting nut.
4 Undo and remove the wheel bearing adjusting nut from the spindle.
5 Grip the hub and disc assembly and pull it outwards far enough to loosen the washer and outer wheel bearing.
6 Push the hub and disc back onto the spindle and remove the washer and outer wheel bearing from the spindle (photo).
7 Grip the hub and disc assembly and pull it from the wheel spindle.
8 Carefully pry out the grease seal and lift away the inner tapered bearing from the back of the hub assembly (photos).
9 Clean out the hub and wash the bearings with solvent making sure that no grease or oil is allowed to get onto the brake disc. Clean any grease from the rotor with denatured alcohol or an approved brake cleaner.

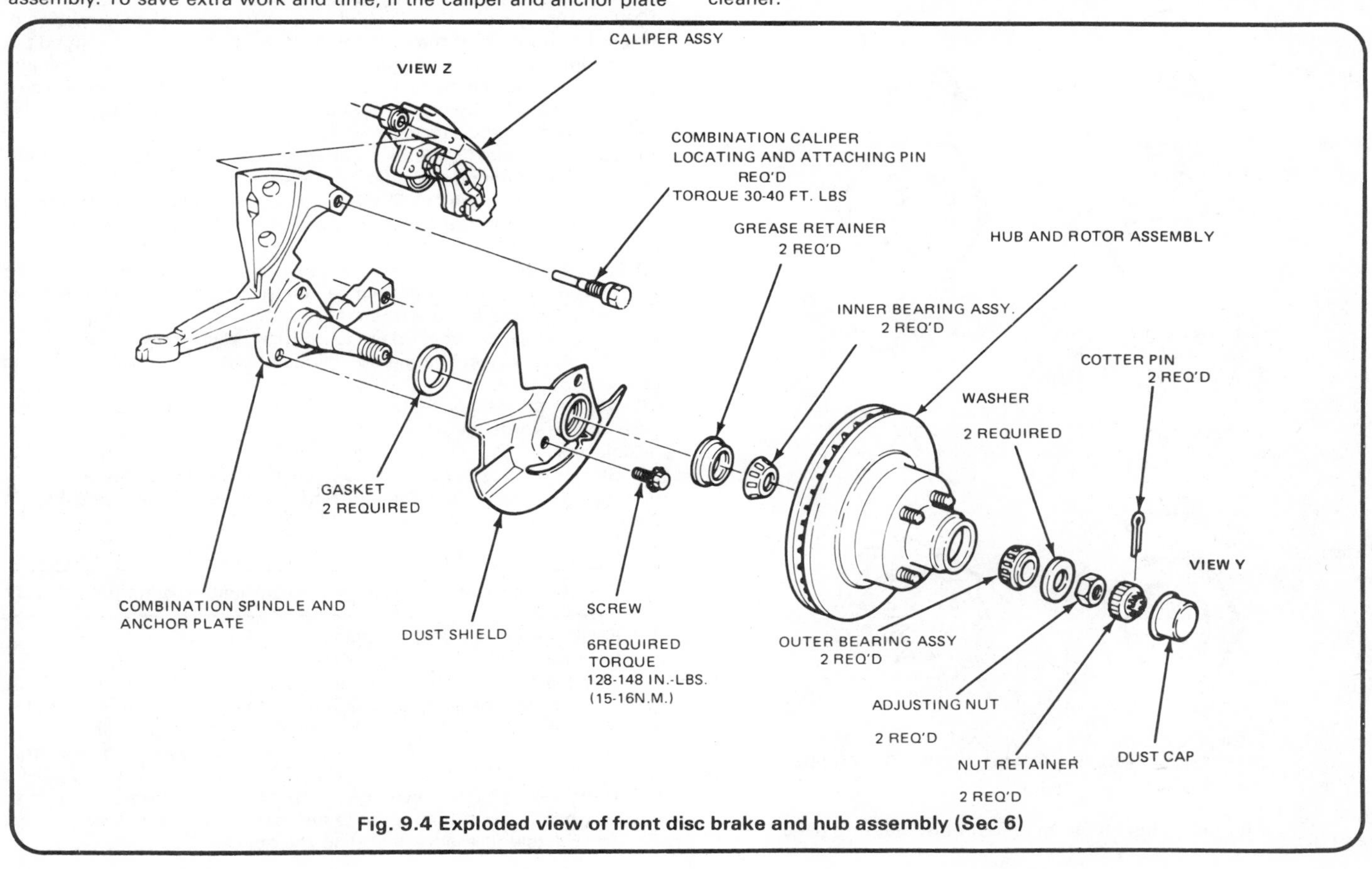

Fig. 9.4 Exploded view of front disc brake and hub assembly (Sec 6)

6.2 Channel lock type pliers are excellent for removing the grease cap without damage

6.6 The wheel bearing and washer are easily removed after they have been dislodged by pulling the hub outward

6.8A Carefully pry out the inner grease seal

6.8B Removing the inner wheel bearing

6.11 Work the grease up into the roller bearing from the back of the bearing cage

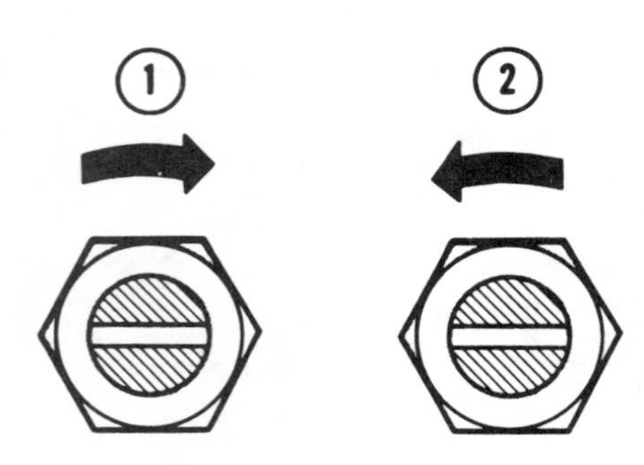

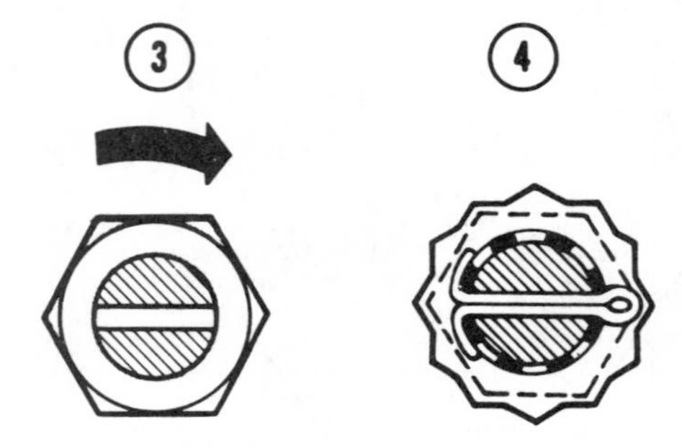

Fig. 9.5 Front wheel bearing adjustment diagram (Sec 6)

10 Thoroughly clean the disc and inspect for signs of deep scoring or excessive corrosion. If these are evident the disc may be reground but the minimum thickness of the disc must not be less than the figure given in the Specifications. It is desirable however, to fit a new disc if at all possible. A new disc should be cleaned to remove its protective coating, using carburetor cleaner.

11 To reassemble, first work a suitable grease well into the bearings; fully pack the bearing cages and rollers (photo).

12 To reassemble the hub fit the inner bearing and then gently tap the grease seal back into the hub. A new seal should always be fitted. The lip must face inward to the hub.

13 Replace the hub and disc assembly onto the spindle keeping the assembly centered on the spindle to prevent damage to the inner grease seal or the spindle threads.

14 Place the outer wheel bearing and flat washer on the spindle.

15 Screw the wheel bearing adjusting nut onto the spindle according to Fig. 9.5.

16 Detach the caliper from the upper suspension arm and guide the assembly towards the disc. Be careful not to stretch or twist the brake flexible hose.

17 Start by sliding the caliper assembly onto the disc at the lower part of the caliper and continue refitting the assembly as described in Section 5.

7 Disc brake rotor splash shield – removal, inspection and refit

1 Raise the vehicle and support with jack stands.

2 Remove the wheel assembly and caliper.

3 Remove the rotor assembly, refer to Section 6. Inspect the spindle bearing surfaces for scoring or signs that the race is spinning (photo).

4 Remove the bolts securing the splash shield to the spindle.

5 Lift the shield away from the spindle and remove the gasket from the spindle mount.

6 The splash shield should be replaced if it is broken, cracked or severely bent. The mounting bolts and gasket should not be re-used.

7 To reinstall, fit a new gasket to the spindle.

7.3 Inspect the spindle for scoring or pitting

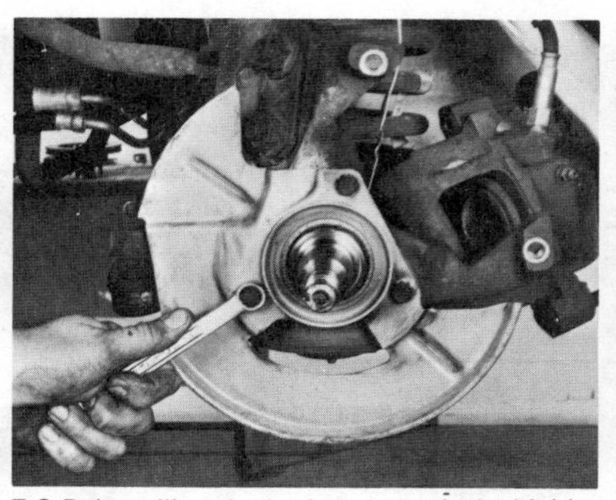
7.8 Reinstalling the brake rotor splash shield

8.2 Plugging the brake line with a piece of hose with a bolt threaded into it

8.3 Removing the piston and boot by striking the caliper on a block of wood

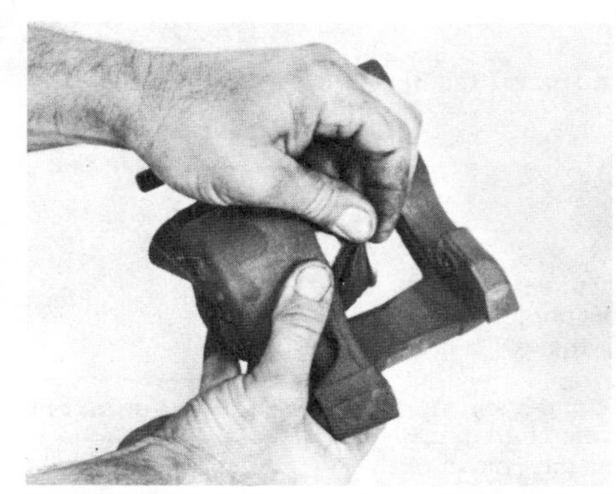
8.5 Removing the rubber piston seal from the caliper bore

8.10 Insert the piston into the bore until it bottoms out

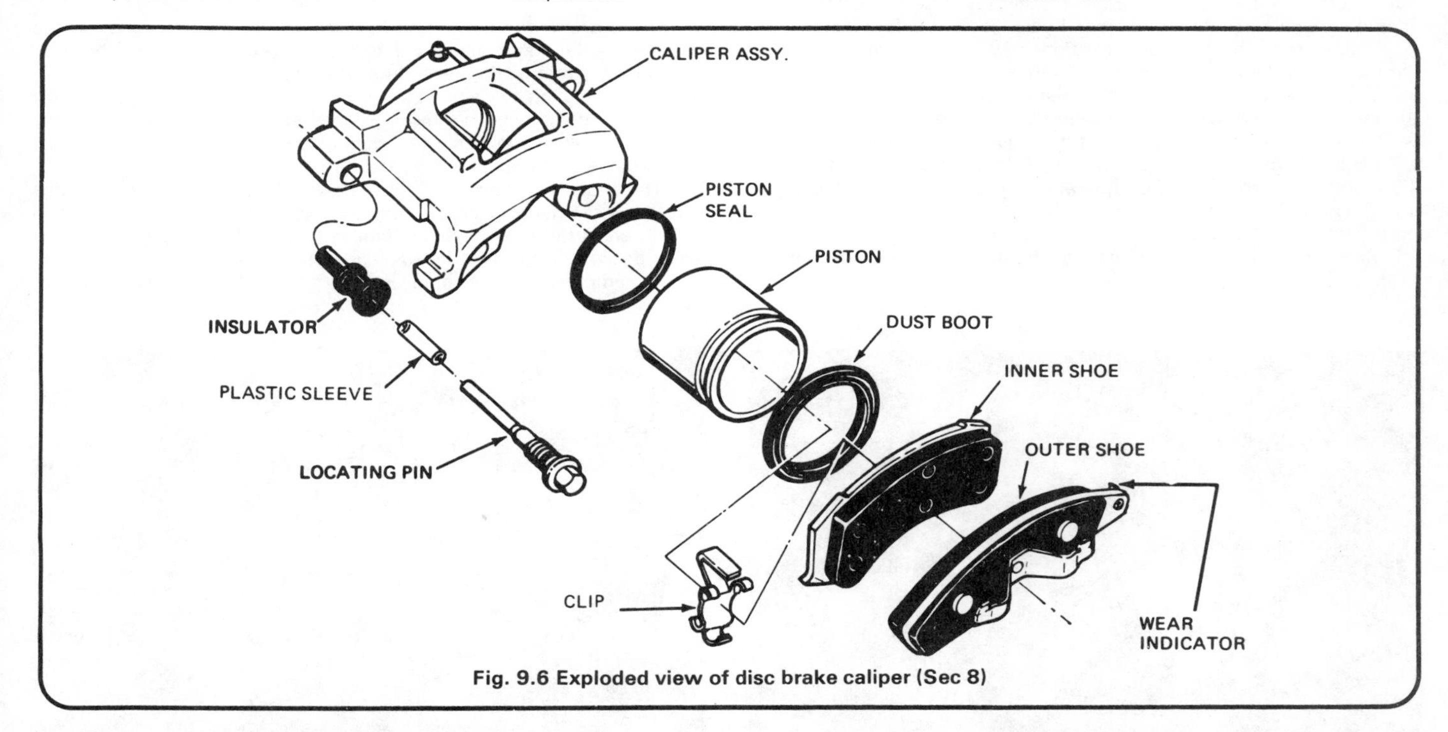

Fig. 9.6 Exploded view of disc brake caliper (Sec 8)

8 Position the splash shield to the spindle. Secure with new bolt (photo).
9 Tighten the bolts to 9-14 ft-lb (7 to 11 Nm).
10 Refit the rotor assembly, caliper assembly, and wheel.
11 Check for solid brake 'feel'.
12 Check hydraulic fluid level.
13 Test drive.

8 Disc brake caliper – inspection and overhaul

1 If hydraulic fluid is leaking from the caliper seal it will be necessary to replace the seals. Should brake fluid be found running down the side of the wheel or if the master cylinder fluid level drops excessively, it is also indicative of seal failure.

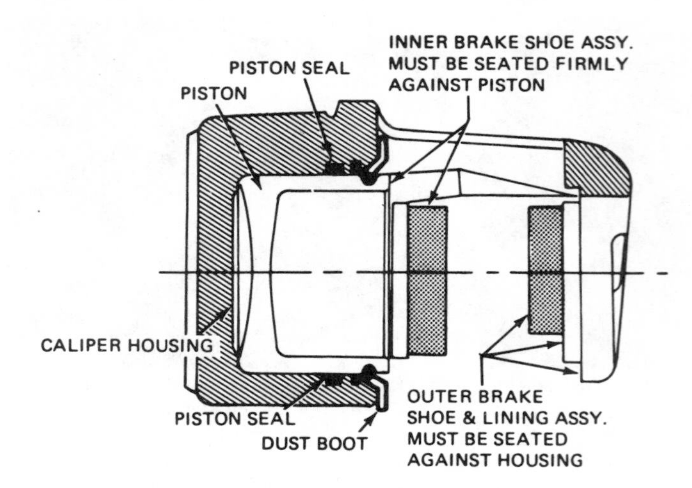

Fig. 9.7 Sectional view of typical caliper and pads (Sec 8)

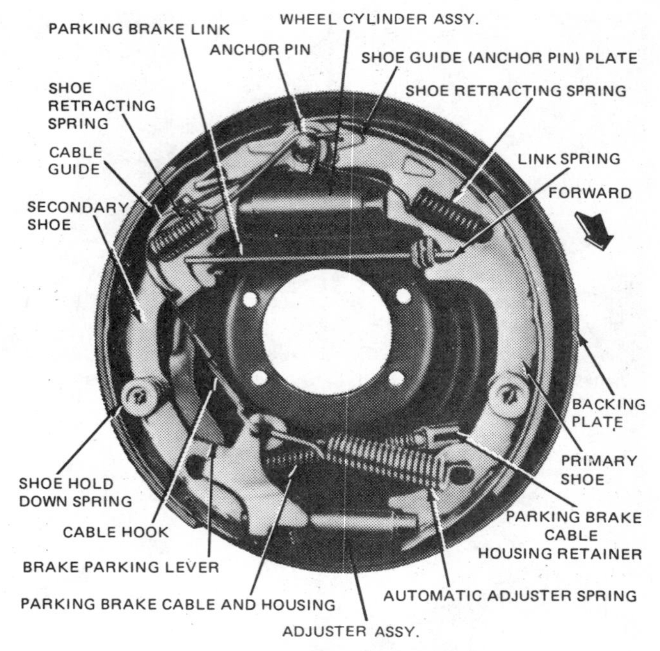

Fig. 9.8 Rear drum brake layout (Sec 9)

2 Remove the caliper and disconnect the hydraulic line at the caliper. Plug the brake line to avoid fluid leakage (photo).
3 Remove the rubber dust boot by striking the caliper sharply against a block of wood (photo).
4 Fit a rag or shop cloth next to the piston bore and again strike the caliper on the block to dislodge the piston, with the cloth catching it. Several attempts may be necessary before the piston comes out.
5 Remove the rubber piston seal from the cylinder bore (photo).
6 Thoroughly wash all parts in the proper solvent or clean hydraulic fluid. During reassembly new rubber seals must be fitted and these should be well lubricated with clean hydraulic fluid before installation.
7 Inspect the piston and bore for signs of wear, score marks or other damage. If evident a new caliper assembly will be necessary.
8 To reassemble, insert the new piston seal in the inner groove of the cylinder bore after lubricating with brake fluid.
9 Install the dust boot by setting it in the outer groove of the bore. Lock it in the groove with your finger while seating the boot.
10 Carefully insert the piston squarely in the boot and slide the piston into the bore. Push the piston in until it bottoms against the end of the bore (photo).
11 Reassembly is now complete and the unit is ready for installation in the vehicle.

9 Rear drum brake shoes – inspection, removal and replacement

1 Chock the front wheels, jack up the rear of the car and support on firmly based axle stands. Remove the roadwheel.
2 Remove the three Tinnerman nuts and remove the brake drum (photos).
3 If the drum will not come off, remove the rubber cover from the brake backplate and insert a narrow screwdriver through the slot. Disengage the adjusting lever from the adjusting screw.
4 While holding the adjusting lever away from the screw, back off the adjusting screw with either a second screwdriver or shaped piece of metal as shown in Fig. 9.9. Take care not to burr, chip or damage the notches in the adjusting screw.
5 The brake linings should be replaced if they are worn to within 0.03 in of the rivets or will be before the next routine check. If bonded linings are fitted they must be replaced when the lining material has worn down to 0.06 in at its thinnest part.
6 To remove the brake shoes detach and remove the secondary shoe

9.2A Removing the brake drum retaining clips

9.2B Withdrawing the brake drum

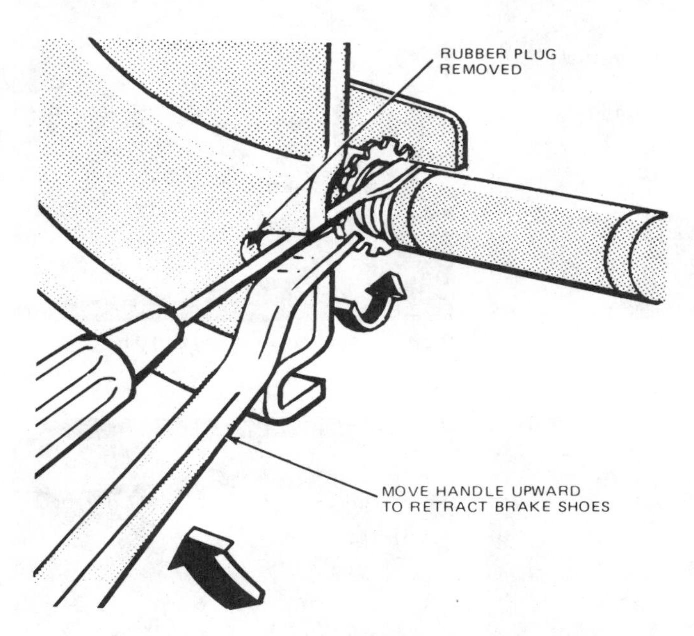

Fig. 9.9 Backing off the rear brake adjuster (Sec 9)

9.7 Releasing the shoe return springs from the anchor pin

to anchor spring and lift away the spring.

7 Detach the primary shoe to anchor spring and lift away the spring (photo).

8 Unhook the adjusting cable eye from the anchor pin (photo).

9 Remove the shoe hold-down springs followed by the shoes, adjusting screw, pivot nut, socket and automatic adjustment parts (photos).

10 Remove the parking brake link and spring. Disconnect the parking brake cable from the parking brake lever (photo).

11 After the secondary shoe has been removed, the parking brake lever should be detached from the shoe (photo).

12 It is recommended that only one brake assembly be overhauled at a time unless the parts are kept well apart. This is because the brake shoe adjusting screw assemblies are not interchangeable and, if interchanged, would in fact operate in reverse, thereby increasing the drum to lining clearance every time the car is backed up.

13 To prevent any mix-up the socket end of the adjusting screw is stamped with an 'R' or 'L'. The adjusting pivot nuts can be identified by the number of grooves machined around the body of the nut. Two grooves on the nut indicate a right-hand thread and one groove indicates a left-hand thread.

14 If the shoes are to be left off for a while, place a warning on the steering wheel as accidental depression of the brake pedal will eject the pistons from the wheel cylinder.

15 Thoroughly clean all traces of dust from the shoes, backplate and brake drums using a stiff brush. Excessive amounts of brake dust can cause judder or squeal and it is therefore important to remove all traces. It is recommended that compressed air is *not* used for this operation as this increases the possibility of the dust being inhaled.

16 Check that the pistons are free in the cylinder, that the rubber dust covers are undamaged and in position, and that there are no hydraulic fluid leaks.

17 Prior to reassembly smear a trace of brake grease on the shoe support pads, brake shoe pivots and on the ratchet wheel face and threads (photos).

18 To reassemble just fit the parking brake lever to the secondary shoe and secure with the spring washer and retaining clip.

19 Place the brake shoes on the backplate and retain with the hold-down springs (photo).

20 Fit the parking brake link and spring. Slacken off the parking brake adjustment and connect the cable to the parking brake lever.

21 Fit the shoe guide (anchor pin) plate on the anchor pin (when fitted) (photo).

22 Place the cable eye over the anchor pin with the crimped side towards the backplate.

23 Replace the primary shoe to anchor spring (photo).

24 Fit the cable guide into the secondary shoe web with the flanged hole fitted into the hole in the secondary shoe web. Thread the cable around the cable guide groove. It is very important that the cable is positioned in this groove and not between the guide and the shoe web.

25 Fit the secondary shoe to anchor spring.

26 Check that the cable eye is not twisted or binding on the anchor pin when fitted. All parts must be flat on the anchor pin.

27 Apply some brake grease to the threads and socket end of the adjusting screw. Turn the adjusting screw into the adjusting pivot nut fully and then back off by $\frac{1}{2}$ turn.

28 Place the adjusting socket on the screw and fit this assembly between the shoe ends with the adjusting screw toothed wheel nearest to the secondary shoe.

29 Hook the cable hook into the hole in the adjusting lever. The adjusting levers are stamped with an 'R' or 'L' to show their correct fitment to the left or right brake assembly.

30 Position the hooked end of the adjuster spring completely into the large hole in the primary shoe web. The last coil of the spring must be at the edge of the hole.

31 Connect the loop end of the spring to the adjuster lever holes.

32 Pull the adjuster lever, cable and automatic adjuster spring down and towards the rear to engage the pivot hook in the large hole in the secondary shoe web (photo).

33 After reassembly check the action of the adjuster by pulling the section of the cable between the cable guide and the anchor pin towards the secondary shoe web far enough to lift the lever past a tooth on the adjusting screw wheel.

34 The lever should snap into position behind the next tooth and releasing the cable should cause the adjuster spring to return the lever to its original position. This return motion of the lever will turn the adjusting screw one tooth.

35 If pulling the cable does not produce the desired action, or if the lever action is sluggish instead of positive and sharp, check the position of the lever on the adjusting screw toothed wheel. With the brake unit in a vertical position (the anchor pin at the top), the lever should contact the adjusting wheel 0.1875 in $\pm$ 0.0313 in above the center-line of the screw.

36 Should the contact point be below this center-line the lever will not lock on the teeth in the adjusting screw wheel, and the screw will not be turned as the lever is actuated by the cable.

37 Incorrect action should be checked as follows:

- *a) Inspect the cable and fittings. They should completely fill or extend slightly beyond the crimped section of the fittings. If this is not so, the cable assembly should be replaced.*
- *b) Check the cable length. The cable should measure 8.4063 in from the end of the cable anchor to the end of the cable hook.*
- *c) Inspect the cable guide for damage. The cable groove should be parallel to the shoe web, and the body of the guide should lie flat against the web. Replace the guide if it is damaged.*
- *d) Inspect the pivot hook on the lever. The hook surfaces should be square to the body of the lever for correct pivoting action.*

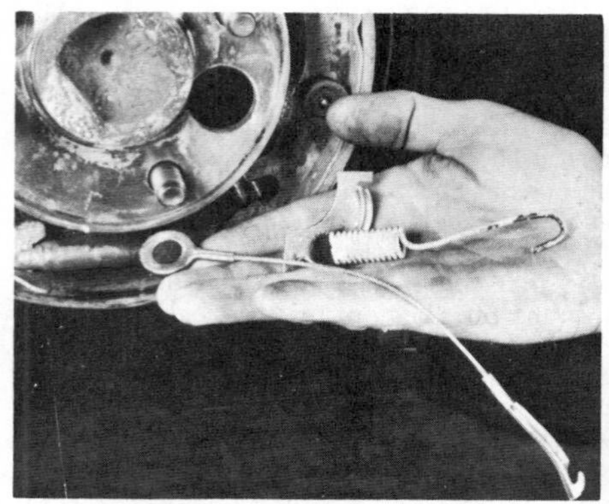

9.8 The automatic adjustment cable, spring and adjustment lever

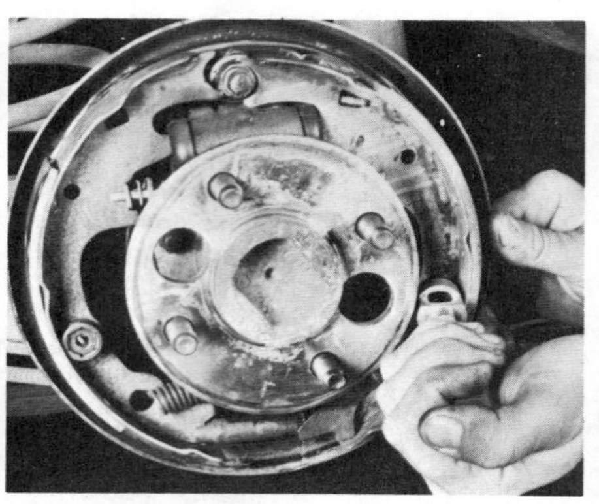

9.9A Releasing the shoe hold-down spring

9.9B The hold-down spring and pin

9.9C The automatic adjustment pivot nut and socket assembly

9.10 Removing the parking brake link and spring

9.11 Detaching the parking brake lever from the secondary shoe

9.17A Smearing brake grease on the shoe support pads

9.17B Applying grease to the anchor pivot

9.17C Lubricating the adjuster ratchet wheel face

9.19 Installing the hold-down springs to retain the brake shoes

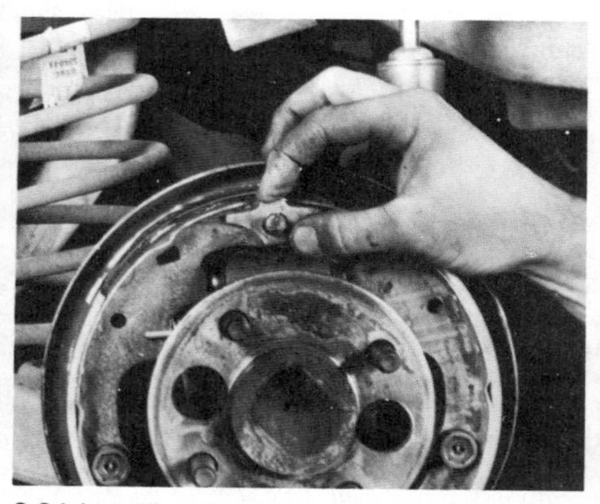

9.21 Installing the shoe guide over the anchor pin

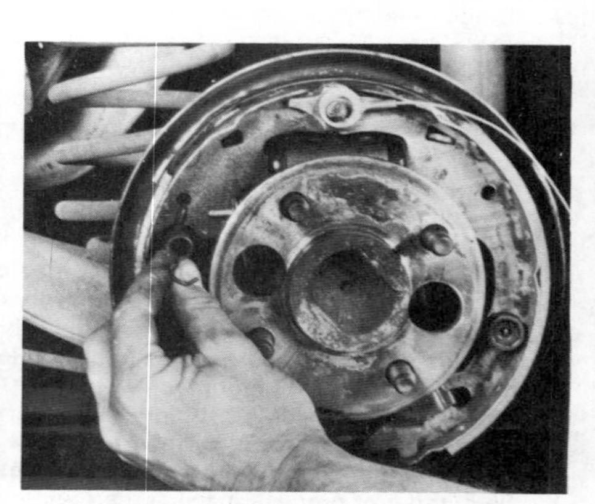

9.23 Installing the primary shoe return spring

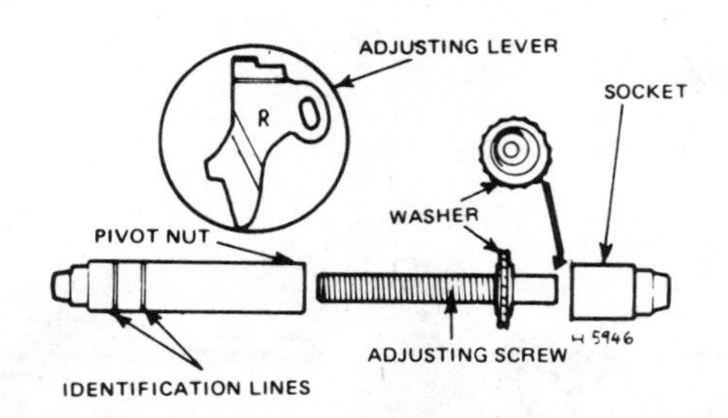

Fig. 9.10 Brake adjuster component parts (Sec 9)

Replace the lever if the hook shows signs of damage.

e) Check that the adjustment screw socket is correctly seated in the notch in the shoe web.

38 Refit the brake drum and roadwheel, lower the car to the ground and take it for a short test run to check the operation of the parking brake and footbrake.

9.32 Installing the adjuster to the secondary shoe

10 Rear drum brake wheel cylinder – removal and replacement

1 Refer to Section 9, and remove the brake shoes as described in paragraphs 1 to 11 inclusive.
2 Unscrew the brake pipe union from the rear of the wheel cylinder. Do not pull the metal tube from the cylinder as it will bend, making refitting difficult (photo).
3 Undo and remove the two bolts securing the wheel cylinder to the brake backplate assembly (photo).
4 Lift away the rear wheel cylinder assembly.
5 Plug the end of the hydraulic pipe to stop loss of too much hydraulic fluid.
6 Refitting the wheel cylinder is the reverse sequence to removal. It will be necessary to bleed the brake hydraulic system as described in Section 2.

10.2 Removing the brake line from the back of the wheel cylinder

11 Rear drum brake wheel cylinder – inspection and overhaul

1 Remove the wheel cylinder as described in the previous Section.
2 To dismantle the wheel cylinder, first remove the rubber boot from each end of the cylinder and push out the two pistons, cup seals and return spring (see Fig. 9.11).
3 Inspect the pistons for signs of scoring or scuff marks; if these are present the pistons should be replaced.
4 Examine the inside of the cylinder bore for score marks or corrosion. If these conditions are present the cylinder can be taken to a machine shop for boring (maximum oversize 0.003 in). However the best policy is to replace it.
5 If the cylinder is sound, thoroughly clean it out with fresh hydraulic fluid (photo).
6 Remove the bleed screw and check that the hole is clean (photo).
7 The old rubber cups will probably be swollen and visibly worn. Smear the new rubber cups and insert one into the bore followed by one piston.
8 Place the return spring in the bore and push up until it contacts the rear of the first seal.
9 Refit the second seal and piston into the cylinder bore (photo).
10 Replace the two rubber boots (photo).
11 The wheel cylinder is now ready for refitting to the brake backplate.

12 Rear drum brake backplate – removal and replacement

1 Refer to Section 10, and remove the brake shoes and wheel cylinder from the backplate.
2 Disconnect the parking brake lever from the cable.
3 Refer to Chapter 8 and remove the axle shaft.
4 Disconnect the parking brake cable retainer from the backplate.
5 The backplate and gasket may now be lifted away from the end of the axle housing.

10.3 Unbolting the wheel cylinder from the backing plate

BOOT
CYLINDER
CUP
BOOT
CUP
PISTON
BLEEDER SCREW
RETURN SPRING AND CUP EXPANDER ASSY
PISTON

Fig. 9.11 Exploded view of wheel cylinder (Sec 11)

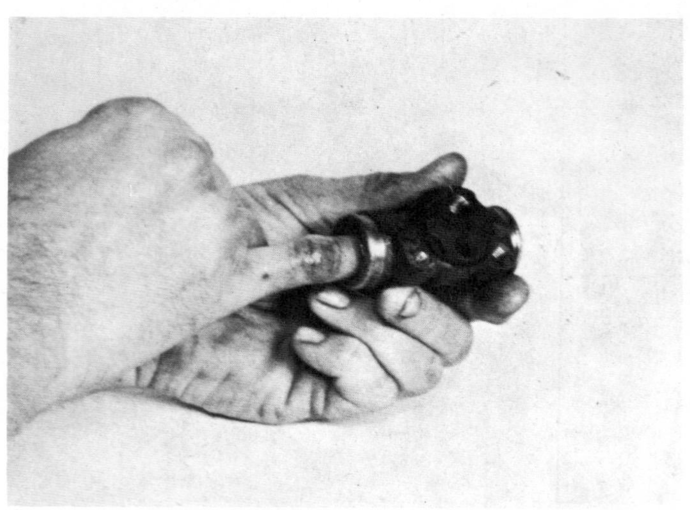

11.5 After inspecting the wheel cylinder, clean it thoroughly with fresh brake fluid

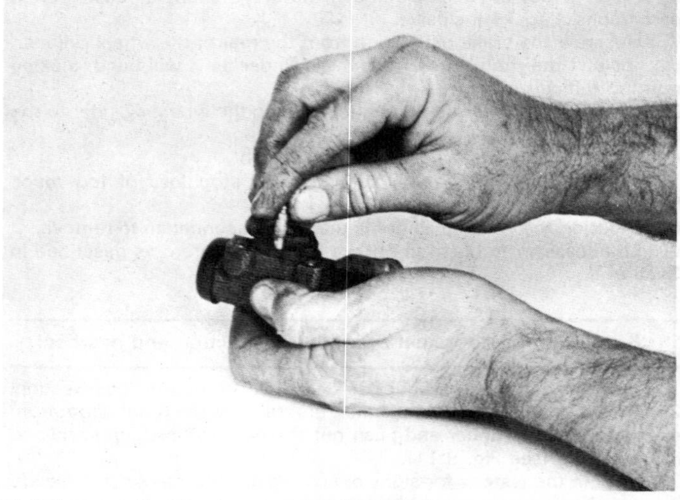

11.6 Remove the bleed screw and check the hole for obstructions

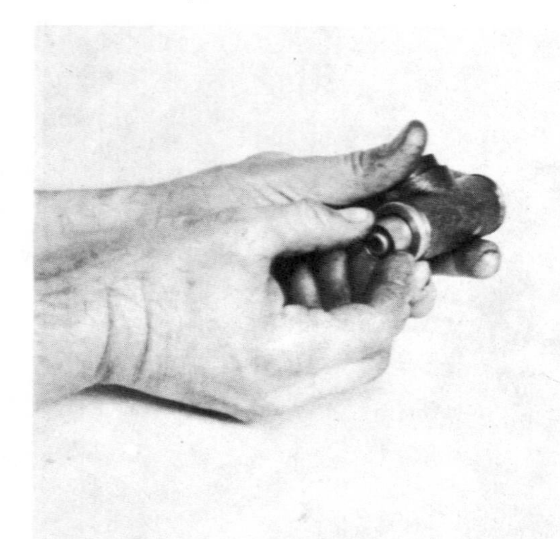

11.9 Insert the seal and piston into the wheel cylinder bore

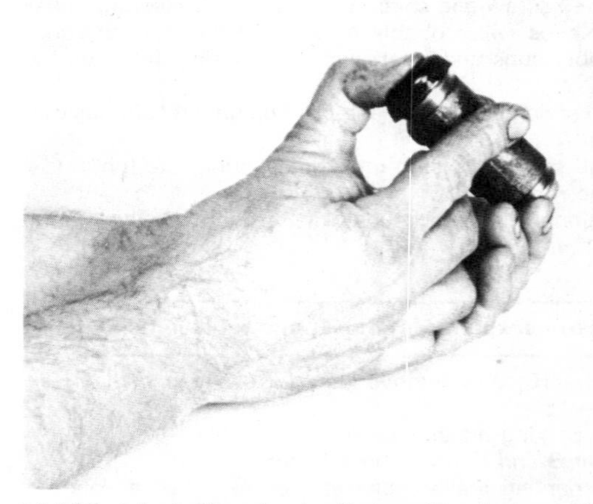

11.10 Lubricate the wheel cylinder rubber boots with brake fluid to ease installation

6 Refitting the brake backplate is the reverse sequence to removal. It will be necessary to bleed the brake hydraulic system as described in Section 2. Do not forget to top-up the rear axle oil level if necessary.

13 Rear drum brake shoes – adjustment

Automatic adjusters are fitted to the rear drum brakes and these operate when the car is backed-up and stopped. Should car use be such that it is not backed-up very often and the pedal movement has increased then it will be necessary to adjust the brakes as follows:

1 Drive the car rearwards and apply the brake pedal firmly. Now drive it forwards, and again, apply the brake pedal firmly.

2 Repeat the cycle until a desirable pedal movement is obtained. Should this not happen, however, it will be necessary to remove the drum and hub assemblies and inspect the adjuster mechanism as described in Section 9, paragraphs 33 to 37 inclusive.

14 Brake master cylinder – removal and replacement

1 Unscrew the brake pipes from the primary and secondary outlet parts of the master cylinder. Plug the ends of the pipes to prevent contamination. Take suitable precautions to catch the hydraulic fluid as the unions are detached from the master cylinder body (photo).

2 Undo and remove the two screws securing the master cylinder to the dashpanel (or servo unit) (photo).

3 Pull the master cylinder forward and lift it upward from the car. Do not allow brake fluid to contact any paintwork as it acts as a solvent (photo).

4 Refit the master cylinder using the reverse procedure to removal. It will be necessary to bleed the hydraulic system as described in Section 2.

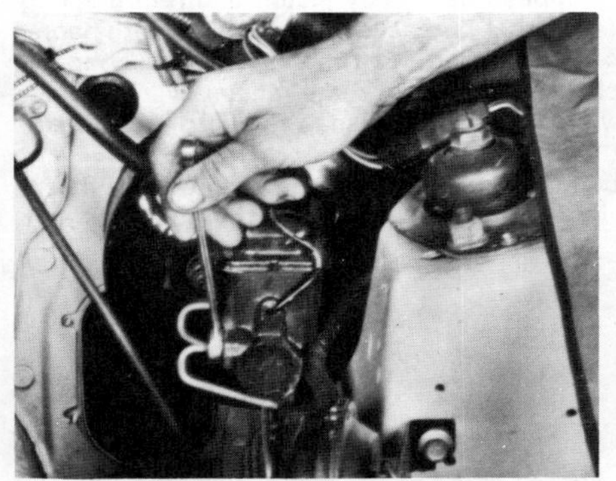
14.1 Disconnecting the fluid lines at the master cylinder, being careful not to bend them

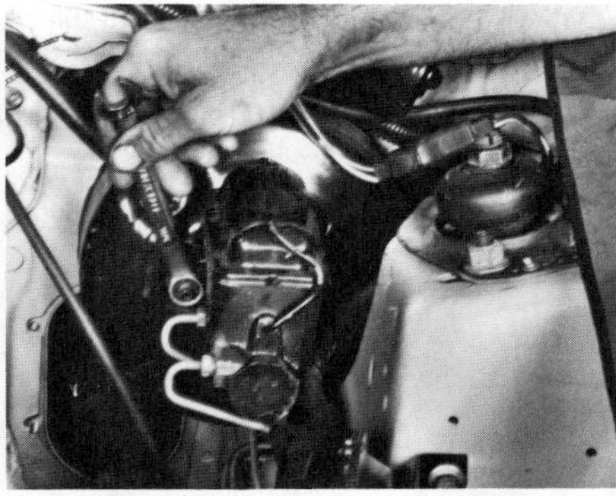
14.2 Unbolting the master cylinder from the brake booster

14.3 Lifting the master cylinder from the engine compartment. Note the newspaper to catch dripping brake fluid which could damage paint

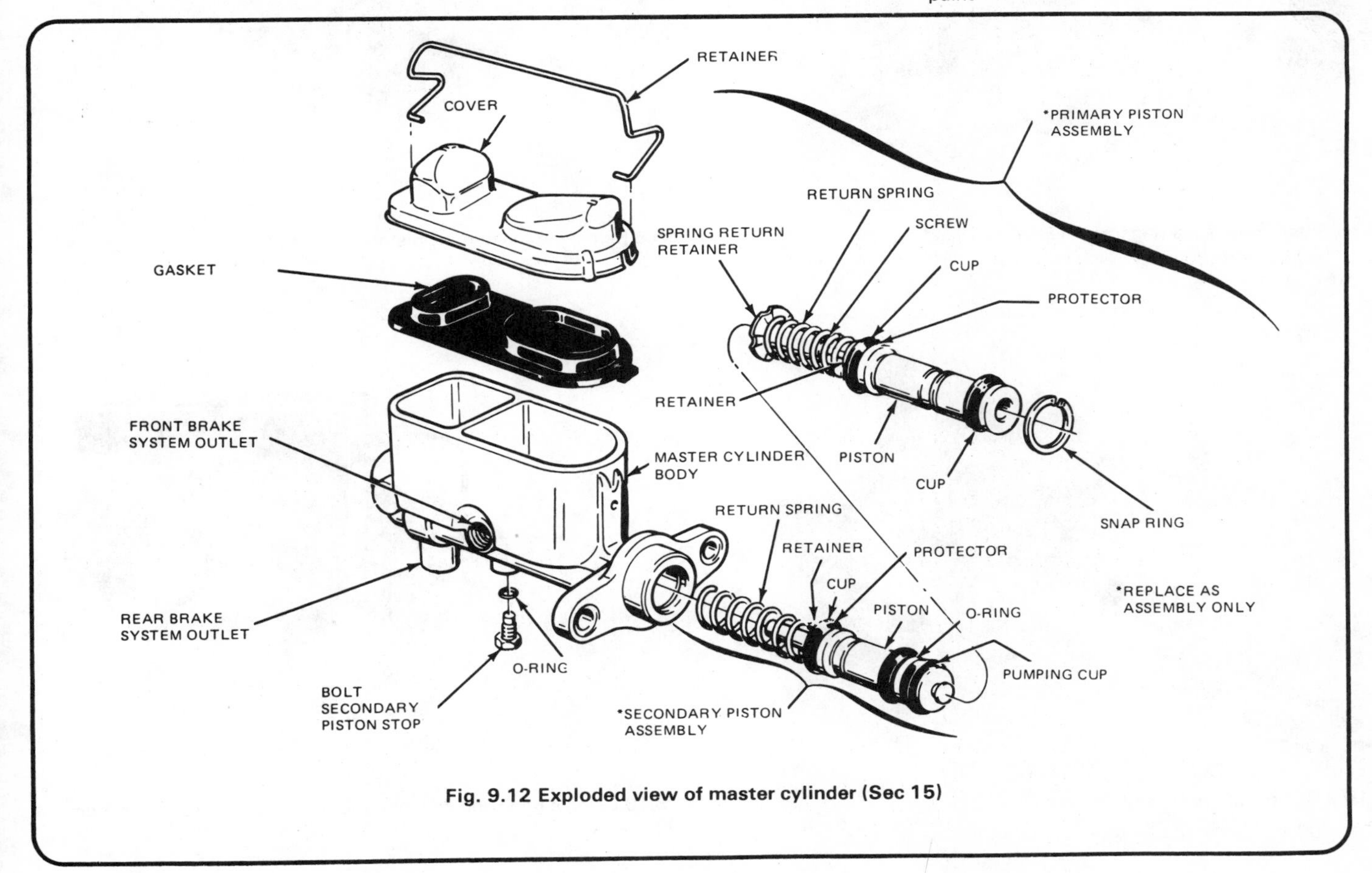

Fig. 9.12 Exploded view of master cylinder (Sec 15)

15 Brake master cylinder – dismantling, examination and reassembly

If a replacement master cylinder is to be fitted, it will be necessary to lubricate the seals before fitting to the car as they have a protective coating when originally assembled. Remove the blanking plugs from the hydraulic pipe union seatings. Inject some clean hydraulic fluid into the master cylinder and operate the pushrod several times so that the fluid spreads over all the internal working surfaces.

If the master cylinder is to be dismantled after removal proceed as follows:

1 Clean the exterior of the master cylinder and wipe dry with a lint-free rag.

2 Remove the filler cover and diaphragm (sometimes called gasket) from the top of the reservoir and pour out any remaining hydraulic fluid.

3 Undo and remove the secondary piston stop bolt from the bottom of the master cylinder body.

4 Undo and remove the bleed screw.

5 Depress the primary piston and remove the snap-ring from the groove at the rear of the master cylinder bore (photo).

6 Remove the pushrod and the primary piston assembly (photo).

7 **Do not** remove the screw that retains the primary return spring retainer, return spring, primary cup and protector on the primary piston. This is factory set and must not be disturbed.

8 Remove the secondary piston assembly (photo).

9 **Do not** remove the outlet pipe seats, outlet check valves and outlet check valve springs from the master cylinder body.

10 Examine the bore of the cylinder carefully for any signs of scores or ridges. If this is found to be smooth all over new seals can be fitted. If, however, there is any doubt of the condition of the bore then a new master cylinder must be fitted. Minor scratches or scoring in the bore can be removed using a honing tool (photo).

11 If the seals are swollen, or very loose on the pistons, suspect oil contamination in the system. Oil will swell these rubber seals and if one is found to be swollen it is reasonable to assume that all seals in the braking system will need attention.

12 Thoroughly clean all parts in clean hydraulic fluid or methylated spirits. Ensure that the ports are clear.

13 All components should be assembled wet after dipping in fresh brake fluid.

14 Carefully insert the complete secondary piston and return spring assembly into the master cylinder bore, easing the seals into the bore, taking care that they do not roll over. Push the assembly fully home.

15 Insert the primary piston assembly into the master cylinder bore.

16 Depress the primary piston and fit the snap-ring into the cylinder bore groove.

17 Refit the pushrod, boot and retainer onto the pushrod and fit the assembly into the end of the primary piston. Check that the retainer is

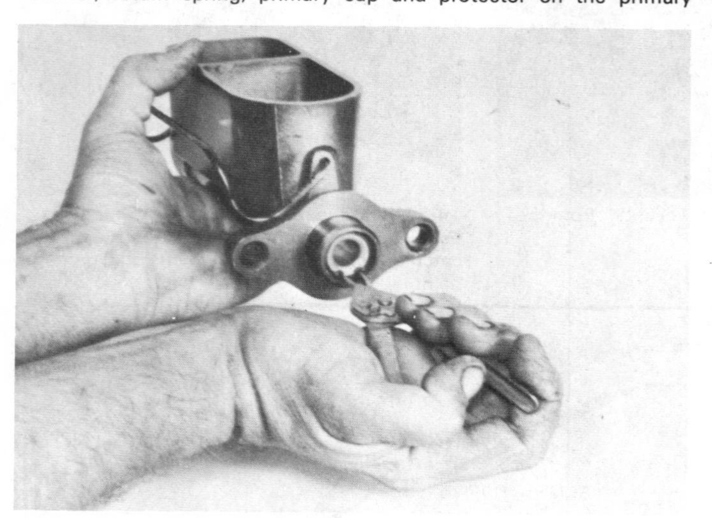

15.5 Removing snap ring from the master cylinder piston

15.6 Removing the primary piston

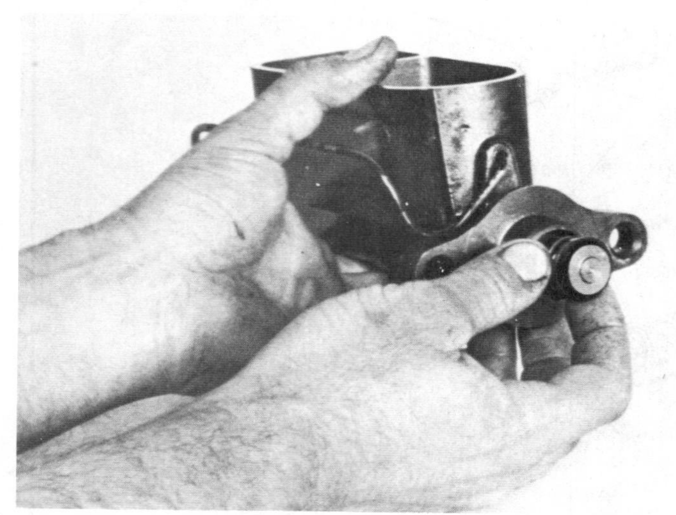

15.8 Removing the secondary piston

15.10 Using a hone and drill motor to remove minor scratches from the bore

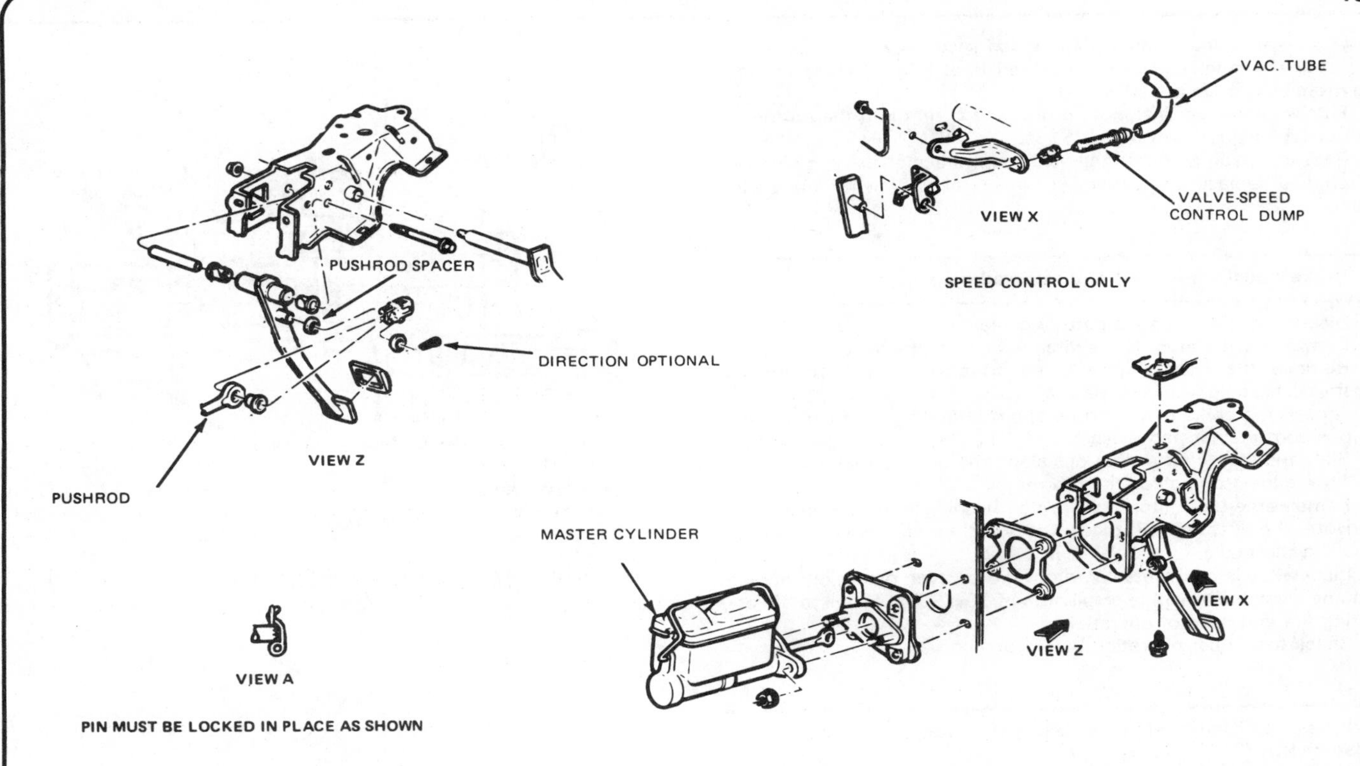

Fig. 9.13 Brake pedal and master cylinder installation (Sec 16)

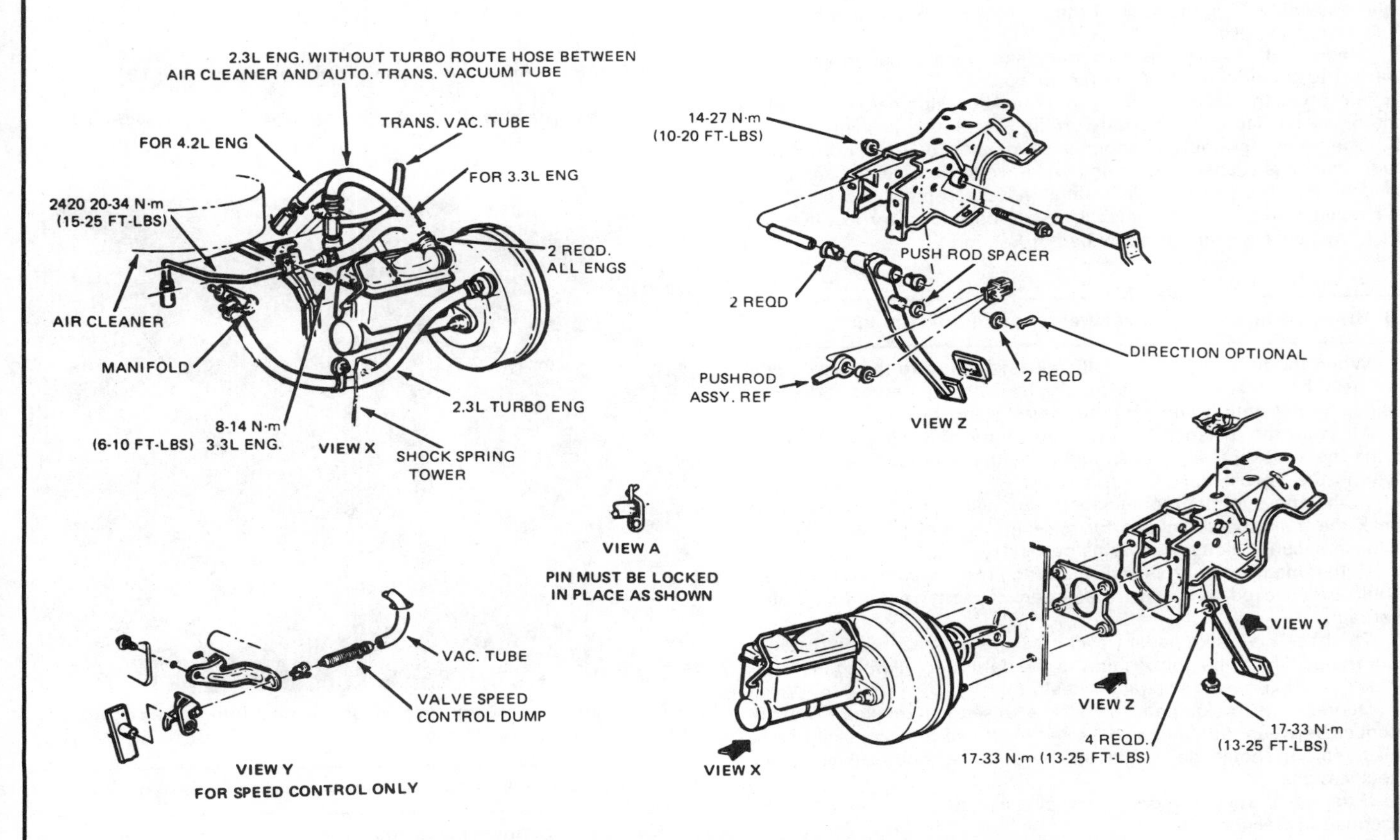

Fig. 9.14 Servo unit and brake pedal installation (Secs 16 and 23)

correctly seated and holding the pushrod securely.
18 Place the inner end of the pushrod boot in the master cylinder body retaining groove.
19 Fit the secondary piston stop bolt and O-ring into the bottom of the master cylinder body.
20 Refit the diaphragm into the filler cover making sure it is correctly seated and replace the cover. Secure in position with the spring retainer.

16 Brake pedal – removal and reinstallation

1 Disconnect the negative battery cable.
2 Disconnect the stop light switch wire from the switch.
3 Remove the clutch cable clevis from the pedal on manual transmission equipped vehicles.
4 Loosen the brake booster nuts approximately $\frac{1}{4}$ inch and remove the pushrod retainer and washer.
5 Slide the stop light switch out along the brake pedal to clear the pin. Lower the stop light switch to remove.
6 Remove the black stop light switch bushing from the push rod.
7 Note the location of the pivot location and washers before removing the pedal.
8 Installation is the reverse of removal. However, during installation, coat any pivot points with a small drop of 10W30 motor oil to prolong bearing life and ease of operation.
9 Check for proper operation before driving.

17 Pressure differential valve assembly – removal and replacement

1 Disconnect the brake warning light connector from the warning light switch.
2 Disconnect the front inlet and rear outlet pipe unions from the valve assembly. Plug the ends of the pipes to prevent loss of hydraulic fluid or dirt ingress.
3 Undo and remove the two nuts and bolts securing the valve bracket to the underside of the fender apron.
4 Lift away the valve assembly and bracket taking care not to allow any brake fluid to contact paintwork as it acts as a solvent.
5 The valve assembly cannot be overhauled or repaired, so if its performance is suspect a new unit will have to be obtained and fitted.
6 Refitting the pressure differential valve assembly and bracket is the reverse sequence to removal. It will be necessary to bleed the brake hydraulic system as described in Section 2.

18 Brake pedal travel – measurement and adjustment

1 When the parking brake is fully released measure the brake pedal free height by first inserting a needle through the carpet and sound deadening felt until it contacts the metal dashpanel.
2 Measure the distance from the top center of the brake pedal pad to the metal dashpanel. This should be within the pedal height limits given in the Specifications.
3 If the measurement obtained is not within the specified limit, check the brake pedal linkage for missing, worn or damaged bushes or loose securing bolts. Rectify as necessary.
4 If the measurement is still incorrect then the master cylinder should be checked to see if it has been correctly reassembled after overhaul.
5 To check the brake pedal travel measure and record the distance from the pedal free height position to the datum point which is the six o'clock position on the steering wheel rim.
6 Depress the brake pedal and take a second reading. The differences between the brake pedal free height and the depressed pedal measurement should be within the pedal travel figure given in the Specifications.
7 If the pedal travel is more than that specified, adjust the brakes as described in Section 13.
8 Should this still not produce the desired results the drums will have to be removed to check that the linings are not badly worn and the automatic adjusters are operating correctly. Rectify any faults found.

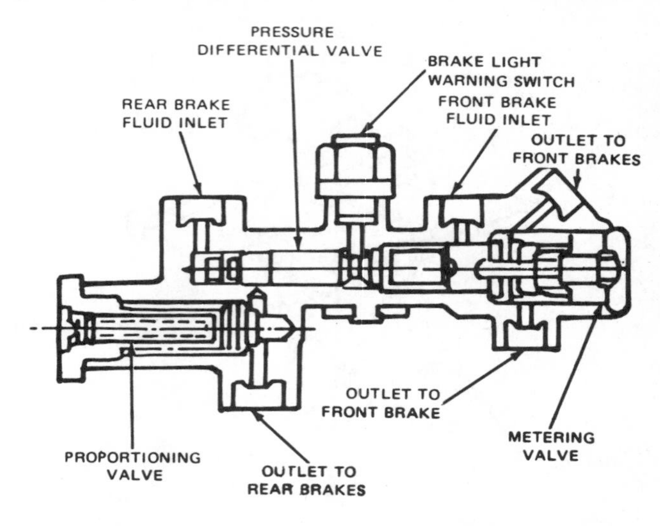

Fig. 9.15 Sectional view of brake differential valve (Sec 17)

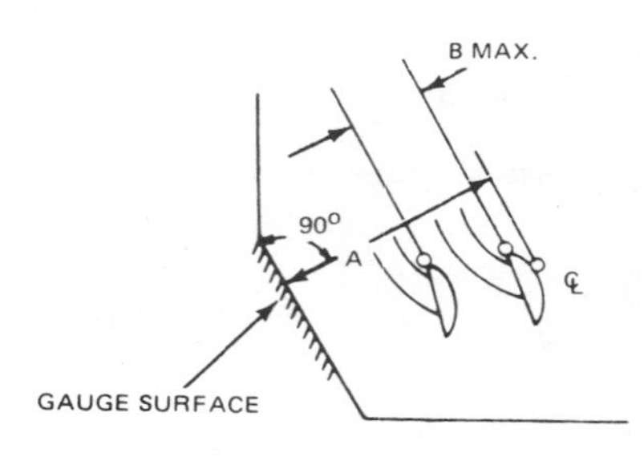

Fig. 9.16 Brake pedal travel measurement (Sec 18)

A. Pedal free height *B. Pedal free travel (max.)*

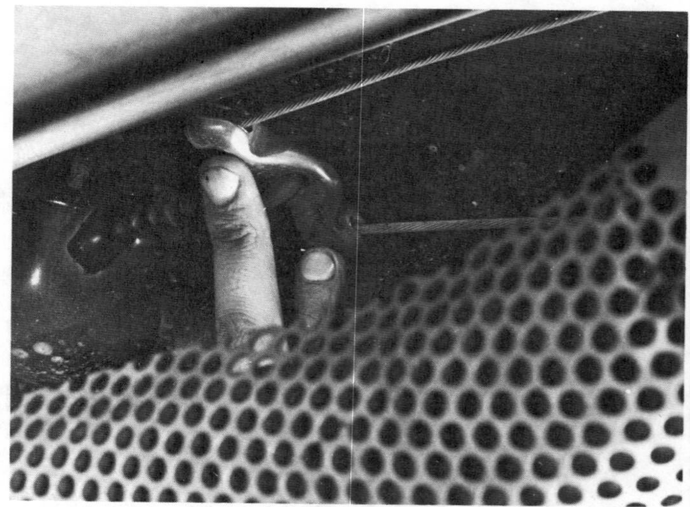

19.1 The parking brake equalizer is located underneath the car, directly below the parking brake handle

19 Parking brake assembly – removal and replacement

1 Undo and remove the adjustment nut from the equalizer rod (photo).
2 Undo and remove the screws that secure the parking brake assembly to the floor tunnel and lift away the assembly.
3 Refitting the parking brake assembly is the reverse sequence to

removal. The following additional points should be noted:

a) *Tighten the securing screws to the specified torque wrench setting.*
b) *Lubricate all moving parts with a little grease.*
c) *Adjust the linkage as described in Section 20.*

20 Parking brake – adjustment

1 Refer to Section 13, and adjust the brakes.
2 Chock the front wheels, jack-up the rear of the car and support on firmly based stands.
3 Release the parking brake fully and move the shift to the neutral position.
4 Slowly tighten the adjustment nut on the equalizer rod at the parking brake lever assembly until the rear brakes are just applied (photo).
5 Back-off the adjusting nut until the rear brakes are just fully released.
6 Lower the car and check parking brake lever free-movement.

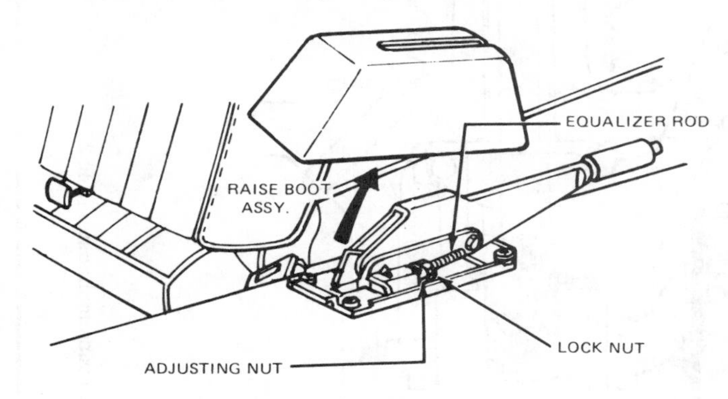

Fig. 9.17 Parking brake boot removal (Sec 20)

21 Parking brake cable – removal and replacement

1 Chock the front wheels, jack-up the rear of the car and support on firmly based axle stands. Remove the wheels.
2 Refer to Section 9, and remove the brake drums.
3 Release the parking brake and back off the adjusting nut.
4 Remove the cable from the equalizer.
5 Compress the retainer prongs and pull the cable rearwards through the cable brackets by a sufficient amount to release the cable.
6 Remove the clips retaining each cable to the top of the rear springs.
7 Remove the self-adjuster springs and remove the cable retainers from the backplate.

20.4 The parking brake equalizer adjustment nuts

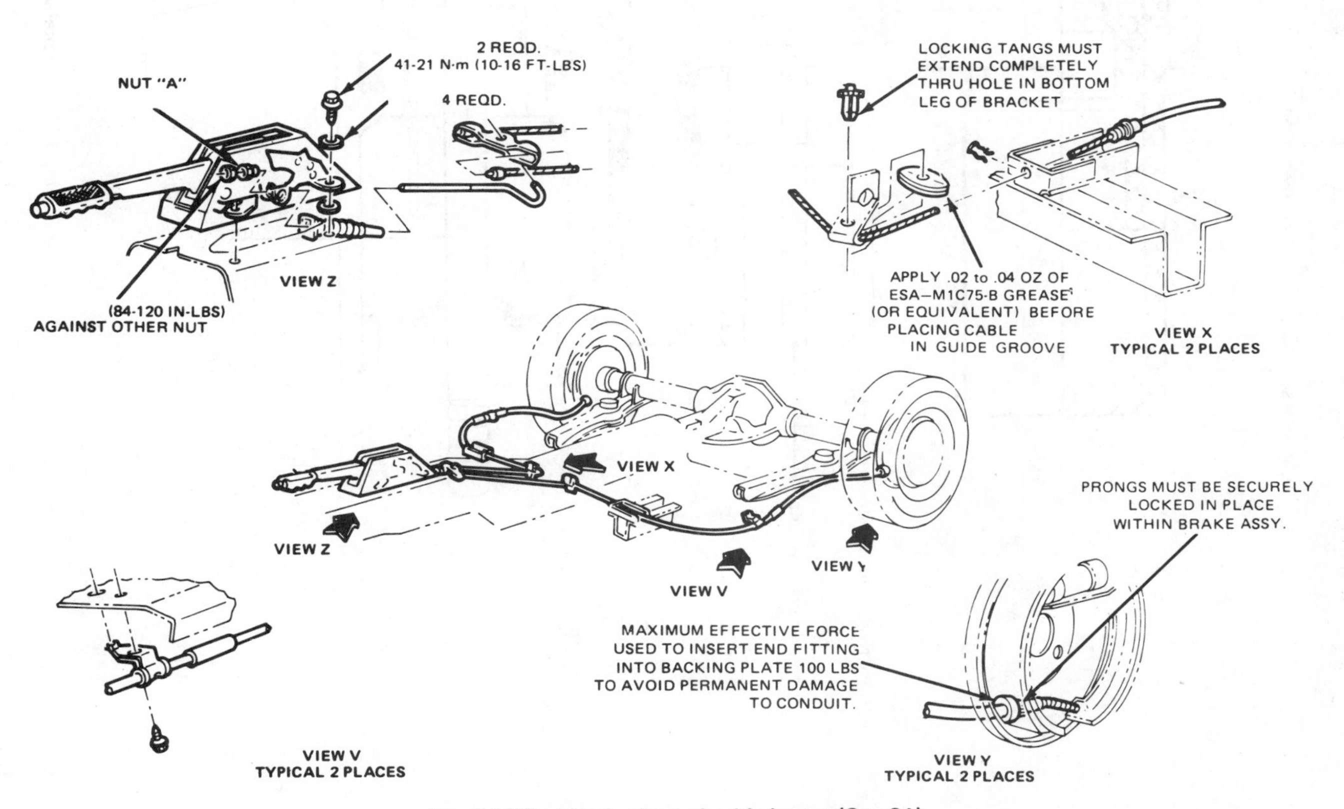

Fig. 9.18 Parking brake and cable layout (Sec 21)

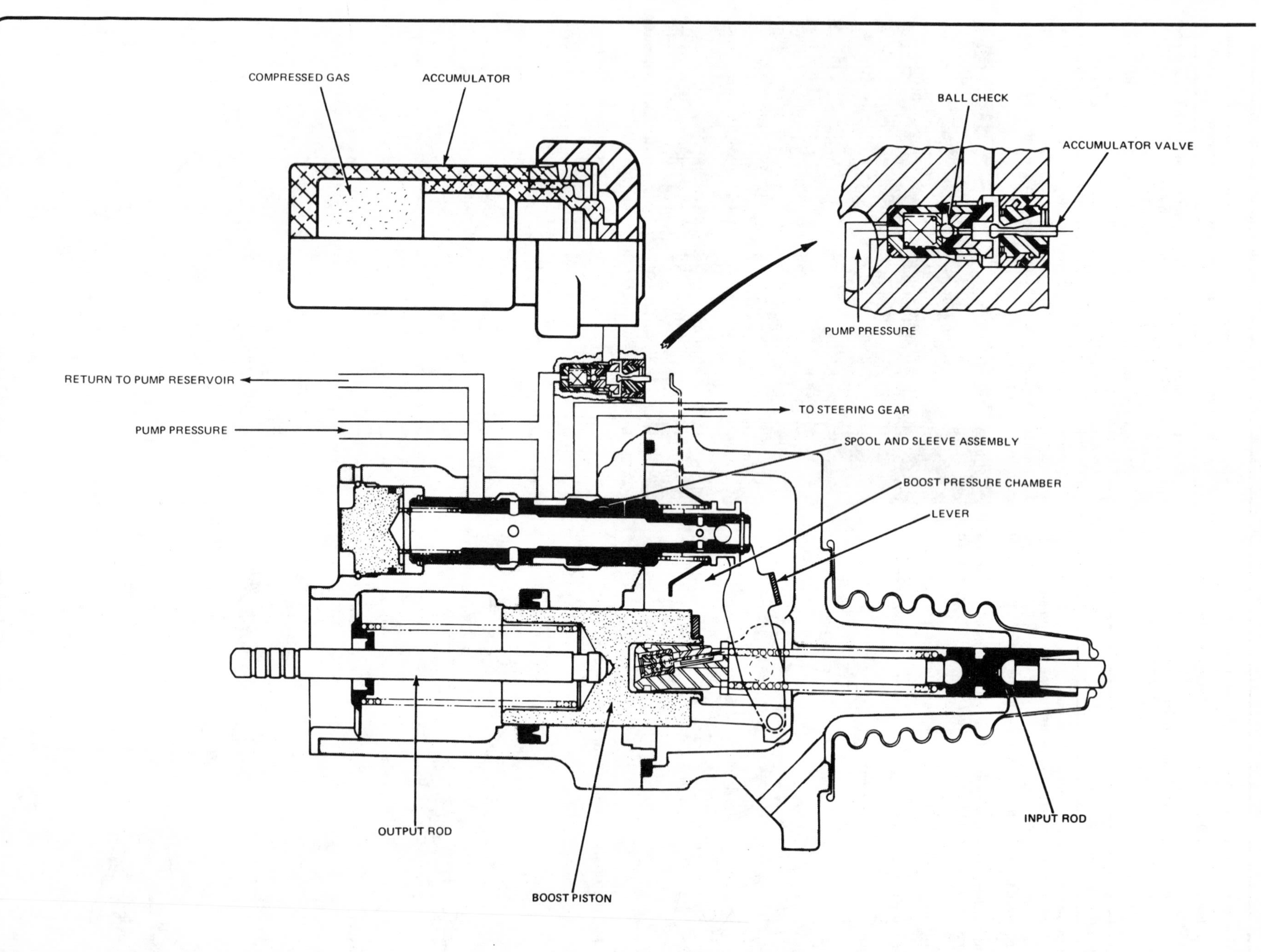

Fig. 9.19 Sectional view of vacuum booster (Sec 22)

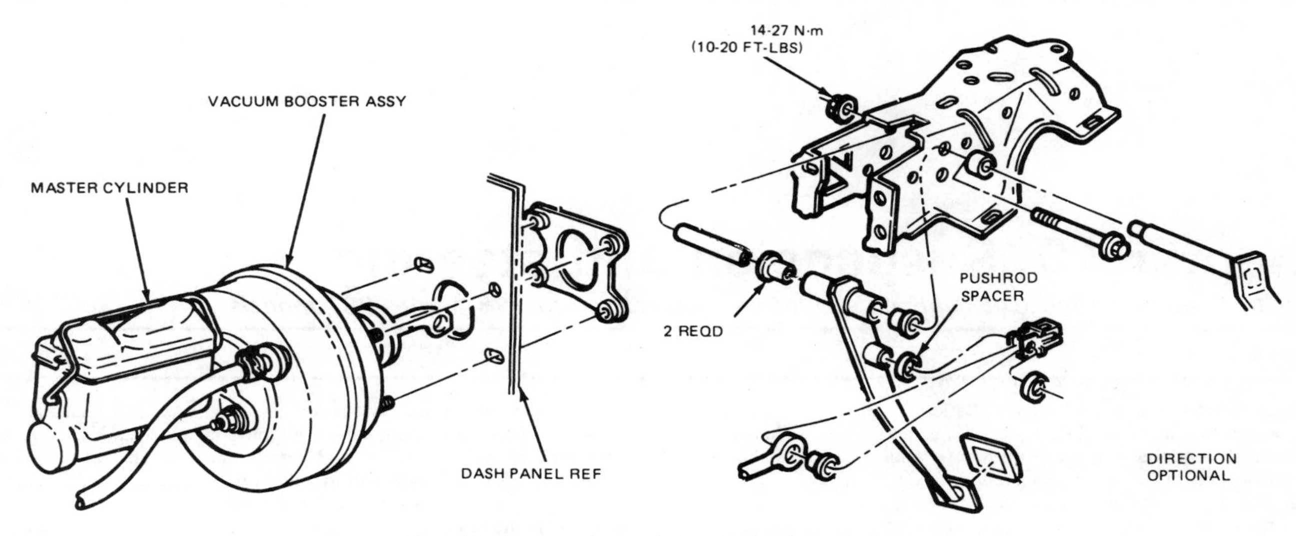

Fig. 9.20 Vacuum booster installation (Sec 23)

8 Disconnect the ends of the cables from the parking brake levers on the secondary brake shoes.
9 Compress the cable retainer prongs and pull the cable ends from the backplates.
10 Undo and remove the nuts and bolts from the cable retainers on the rear springs. Lift away the cable from the retainers and remove from under the car.
11 Refitting the parking brake cable is the reverse sequence to removal. It will be necessary to adjust the parking brake as described in Section 20.

22 Vacuum servo unit – description

1 A vacuum servo unit is fitted into the brake hydraulic circuit in series with the master cylinder, to provide assistance to the driver when the brake pedal is depressed. This reduces the effort required by the driver to operate the brakes under all braking conditions.
2 The unit operates by vacuum obtained from the induction manifold and comprises basically a booster diaphragm and check valve. The servo unit and hydraulic master cylinder are connected together so that the servo unit piston rod acts as the master cylinder pushrod. The driver's braking effort is transmitted through another pushrod to the servo unit piston and its built-in control system. The servo unit piston does not fit tightly into the cylinder, but has a strong diaphragm to keep its edges in constant contact with the cylinder wall, so ensuring an air tight seal between the two parts. The forward chamber is held under the vacuum conditions created in the inlet manifold of the engine, and during periods when the brake pedal is not in use, the controls open a passage to the rear chamber, so placing it under vacuum conditions as well. When the brake pedal is depressed, the vacuum passage to the rear chamber is cut off and the chamber opened to atmospheric pressure. The consequent rush of air pushes the servo piston forward in the vacuum chamber and operates the main pushrod to the master cylinder.
3 The controls are designed so that assistance is given under all conditions and, when the brakes are not required, vacuum in the rear chamber is established when the brake pedal is released. All air from the atmosphere entering the rear chamber is passed through a small air filter.
4 Under normal operating conditions the vacuum servo unit will give trouble-free service for a very long time. If, however, it is suspected that the unit is faulty, ie, increase in foot pressure is required to apply the brakes, it must be exchanged for a new unit. No attempt should be made to repair the old unit as it is not a serviceable item.

23 Vacuum servo unit – removal and replacement

1 Remove the stop light switch and actuating rod from the brake pedal as described in Section 16.
2 Working under the hood, remove the air cleaner from the carburetor and the vacuum hose from the servo unit.
3 On four cylinder engines only (2.3 liter), it will be necessary to remove the two screws securing the throttle cable bracket to the engine and move the bracket in toward the engine. Remove the water inlet hose from the automatic choke house and move it out of the way. Also detach the vacuum hose from the EGR reservoir if necessary.
4 Refer to Section 14 and remove the master cylinder.
5 From inside the car, remove the nuts securing the servo unit to the dashpanel.
6 Working inside the engine compartment, move the servo unit forward until the actuating rod is clear of the dashpanel, rotate it through 90° and lift the unit upward until clear of the engine compartment.
7 Refitting a new servo unit is the reverse sequence to removal. It will be necessary to bleed the brake hydraulic system as described in Section 2.

Chapter 10 Suspension and steering

Refer to Chapter 13 for specifications and information related to 1981 thru 1987 models

Contents

Specifications

Front suspension

Type	Modified MacPherson strut
Toe-in	$\frac{3}{16}$ to $\frac{5}{16}$ in
Caster	$\frac{1}{4}$° to $1\frac{3}{4}$° positive **
Camber	$\frac{1}{4}$° positive

** Caster is set at the factory and is not adjustable

Toe-out on turns	
Inner	20 degrees
Outer	19.74 degrees

Rear suspension

Type	Four link design with coil springs and hydraulic telescopic shock absorbers

Steering

Type	Rack and pinion
Gear ratio	24.9 straight ahead 21.7 at full turn
Oil capacity	5 oz (approx. 0.31 pints U.S.)

Tires

Size	Refer to the tire information decal located on the front of the L.H. door pillar
Pressure	As above

Torque specifications

	ft-lb	Nm
Front suspension		
Lower arm to crossmember	200 to 220	271 to 298
Sway bar mounting clamp	14 to 26	19 to 39
Sway bar to lower arm	9 to 12	12 to 16
Spindle to shock strut	150 to 180	203 to 244
Sway bar mounting bracket to underbody	35 to 50	47 to 68
Balljoint to spindle	80 to 120	108 to 163
Shock upper mount (3 nuts)	60 to 75	81 to 102
Steering gear to crossmember	90 to 100	122 to 136
Tie-rod end to spindle	35 to 47	47 to 64
Rear suspension		
Shock absorber to upper mount	14 to 26	19 to 35
Brake backing plate	20 to 40	28 to 54
Shock lower mount	40 to 45	54 to 74
Wheel lug nut	70 to 115	90 to 156

All fasteners not listed, use the following torque wrench settings:

Metric thread sizes	ft-lb	Nm
M-6	6 to 9	9 to 12
M-8	14 to 21	19 to 28
M-10	28 to 40	38 to 54
M-12	50 to 71	68 to 96
M-14	80 to 140	109 to 154
Pipe thread sizes		
$\frac{1}{8}$	5 to 8	7 to 10
$\frac{1}{4}$	12 to 18	17 to 24
$\frac{3}{8}$	22 to 33	30 to 44
$\frac{1}{2}$	25 to 35	34 to 47
US thread sizes		
$\frac{1}{4}$ to 20	6 to 9	9 to 12
$\frac{5}{16}$ to 18	12 to 18	17 to 24
$\frac{5}{16}$ to 24	14 to 20	19 to 27
$\frac{3}{8}$ to 16	22 to 32	30 to 43
$\frac{3}{8}$ to 24	27 to 38	37 to 51
$\frac{7}{16}$ to 14	40 to 55	55 to 74
$\frac{7}{16}$ to 20	40 to 60	55 to 81
$\frac{1}{2}$ to 13	55 to 80	75 to 108

1 General description

The front suspension fitted to all models is modified MacPherson strut comprising a shock absorber/strut assembly, coil spring, and lower A-arm.

Each front wheel rotates on a spindle, the upper end mounted to the lower strut and the lower end to the A-arm. The lower spindle is attached with a balljoint.

The upper end of the strut is attached to the body structure through an insulator bushing.

The coil spring mounts between the front frame crossmember and the lower A-arm. To control body roll in corners a front stabilizer bar is fitted.

Each rear wheel, hub and brake drum assembly is bolted to the rear axle shaft flange and the wheel and axle shaft rotates in the rear axle housing.

The rear axle housing rests on a spring assembly suspended from hangers integral with the body. Location of the axle assembly is controlled by four pressed steel arms. Two of the arms connect the bodywork to the axle housing center, two others connect the housing at the outer ends of the axle. Rubber insulated shock absorbers are fitted at each side.

The steering gear is rack and pinion type with power assistance as optional. The steering wheel is connected to the gear through a collapsible shaft and flexible couplings.

A tie-rod is attached to each end of the rack joint which allows the tie-rod to move with any deflection in the front suspension unit. The

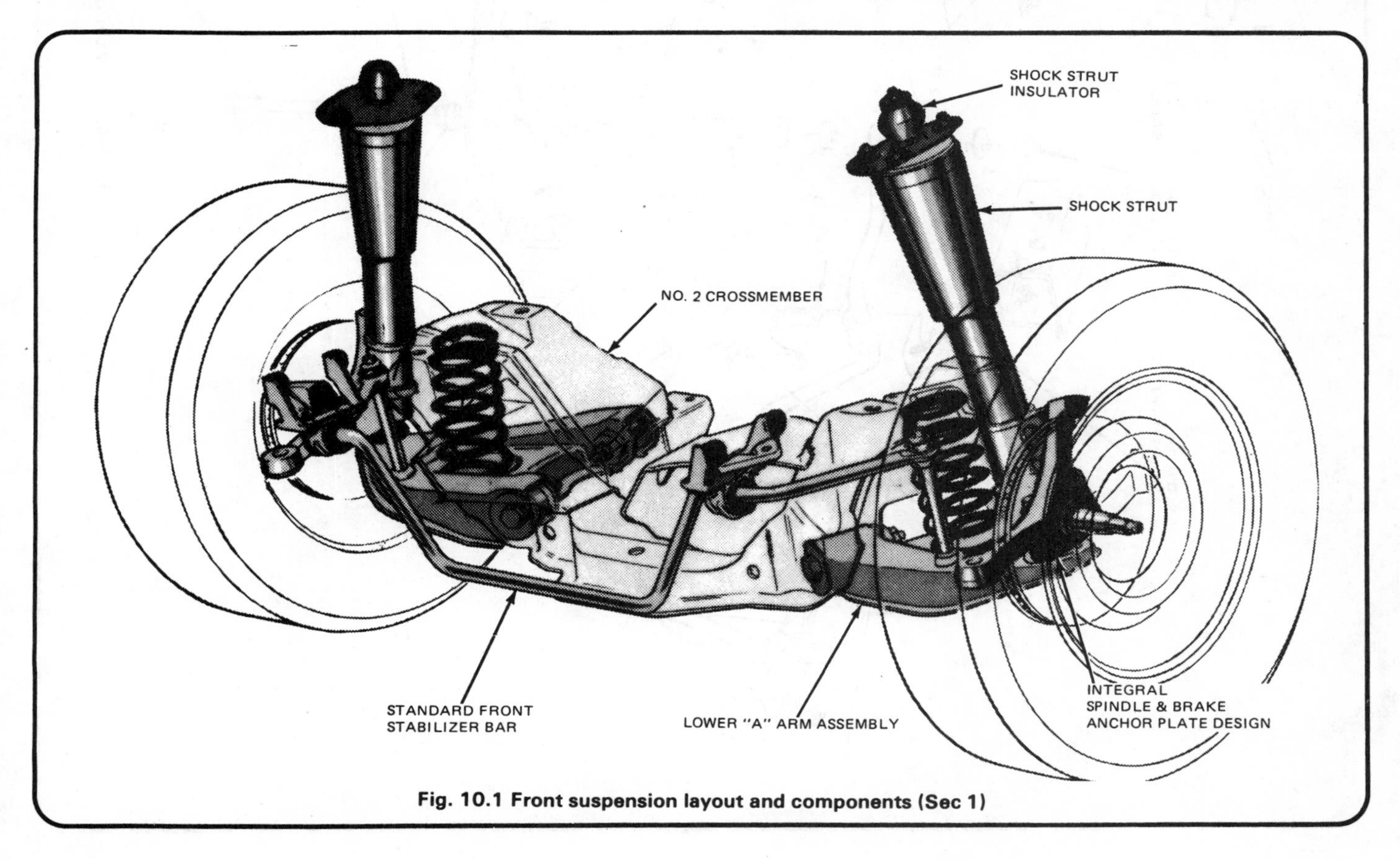

Fig. 10.1 Front suspension layout and components (Sec 1)

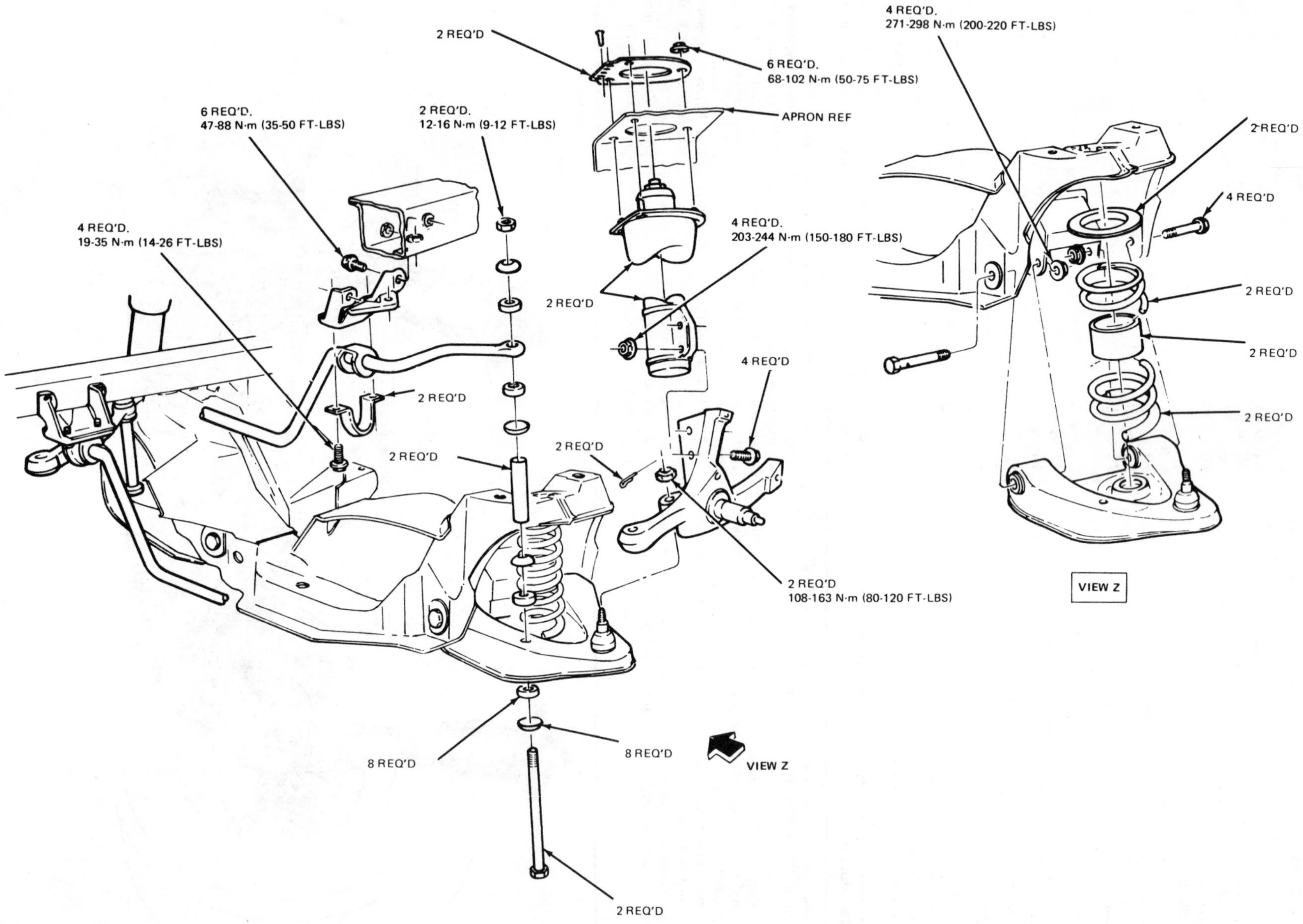

Fig. 10.2 Exploded view of front suspension (Secs 1, 4, 5, 6, 7 and 8)

rack and pinion assembly ends are sealed by rubber bellows.

Couplings attached to the tie-rods are retained on the rack and pinned with roll pins. The rack, housing, valve assembly and rack piston are rebuildable.

The steering column is of the safety type. A locking mechanism is actuated by depressing the button located on the steering column. This prevents inadvertent locking of the steering wheel by blocking the actuator out of the lock position.

The outer column tube terminates just below the attachment to the brake support bracket. Energy absorption is accomplished by the lower column mounting bracket. There is no shift tube in this assembly.

The steering shaft has a machined bar with grooves in the lower half designed to accept two anti-rattle clips. The lower shaft comprises an upper section that is a formed tube to fit into the upper shaft.

The column is secured to the brake support brackets bolted to the flanges on the brake support. The lower column attaching collar contains a sintered iron ring with internal protrusions. These protrusions act as a guide which deforms the outer tube as the column collapses.

2 Front wheel bearings – removal and replacement

1 Chock the rear wheels, apply the parking brake, loosen the front wheel nuts, jack up the front of the car and support on firmly based axle stands. Remove the roadwheel.
2 Refer to Chapter 9 and detach the disc brake caliper.
3 Carefully remove the grease cap from the hub.
4 Withdraw the cotter pin and lift away the nut lock, adjusting nut and plain washers from the spindle.
5 Lift away the outer bearing cone and roller assembly.
6 Remove the disc from the wheel spindle.
7 Using a screwdriver or tapered drift remove the grease seal. This must not be used again but always replaced.
8 Remove the inner bearing cone and roller assembly from the hub.
9 Remove grease from the inner and outer bearing cups and inspect for signs of wear, scratching or pitting. Damage of this kind means that the bearings must be replaced, using a tapered drift. The outer bearing cups can be removed.
10 Clean the inner and outer bearing cone and roller assemblies and wipe dry with a clean lint-free rag.
11 Carefully inspect the cone and roller assemblies for signs of wear or damage which, if evident, mean that complete race assemblies must be obtained. Do not use a new cone and roller assembly in an old cup,
12 Clean the spindle and lubricate with fresh grease.
13 If the inner and/or outer bearing cups were removed the new cups should be fitted using a suitable diameter drift. Make sure they are replaced the correct way round and also correctly seated (Fig. 10.4).
14 Pack the inside of the hub with fresh grease until it is flush with the inside diameter of both bearing cups.
15 With each bearing cone and roller assembly clean off old grease, pack with fresh grease taking care to work the grease well in between the rollers.
16 Place the inner bearing cone and roller assembly in the inner cup.
17 Apply a smear of grease to the lip of the grease seal and replace using a suitable diameter drift. Ensure the seal is correctly seated.
18 Refit the disc onto the wheel spindle taking care to keep the hub in a central position so that the grease retainer is not damaged (photo).
19 Replace the outer bearing cone and roller assembly. Follow this with the plain washer and adjustment nut.
20 Adjust the wheel bearing as described in Section 3.
21 Fit a new cotter pin and bend the ends around the castellations of the nut lock to prevent interference with the radio static collector in the grease cap (if equipped).
22 Replace the grease cap, tapping in position with a soft faced hammer.
23 Refer to Chapter 9 and replace the caliper.
24 Refit the wheel and secure. Lower the car to the ground. Before driving the vehicle, pump the brake pedal to restore normal brake pedal travel.

3 Front wheel bearings – adjustment

1 Front wheel bearings should be adjusted if the wheel is loose on the spindle or if the wheel does not rotate freely.
2 Chock the rear wheels and apply the parking brake. Jack up the front of the car and support on firmly based stands.

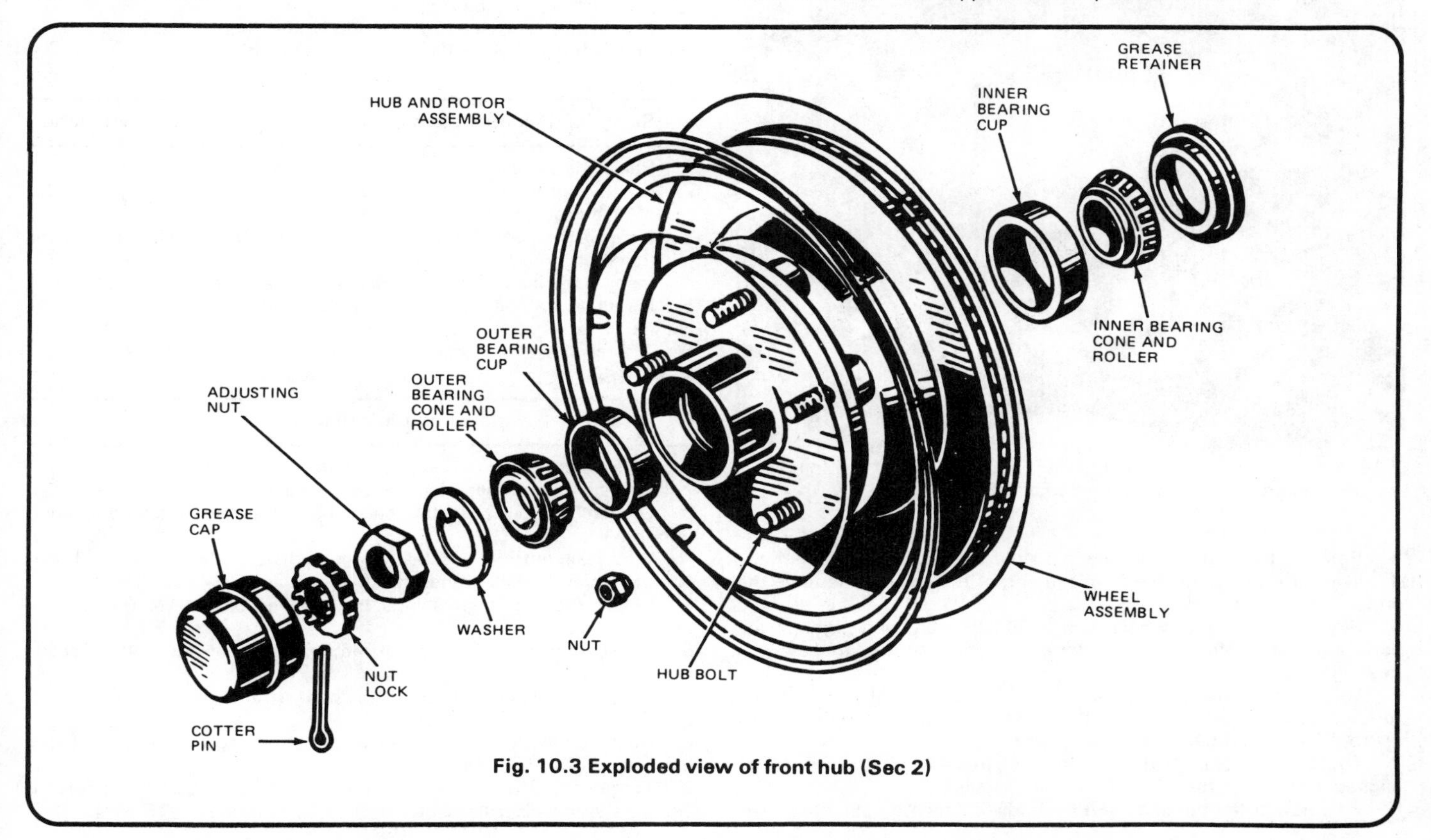

Fig. 10.3 Exploded view of front hub (Sec 2)

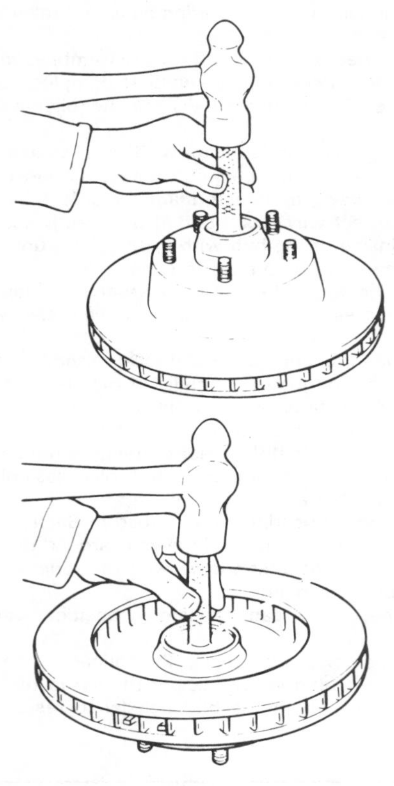

Fig. 10.4 Installing wheel bearing cups (Sec 2)

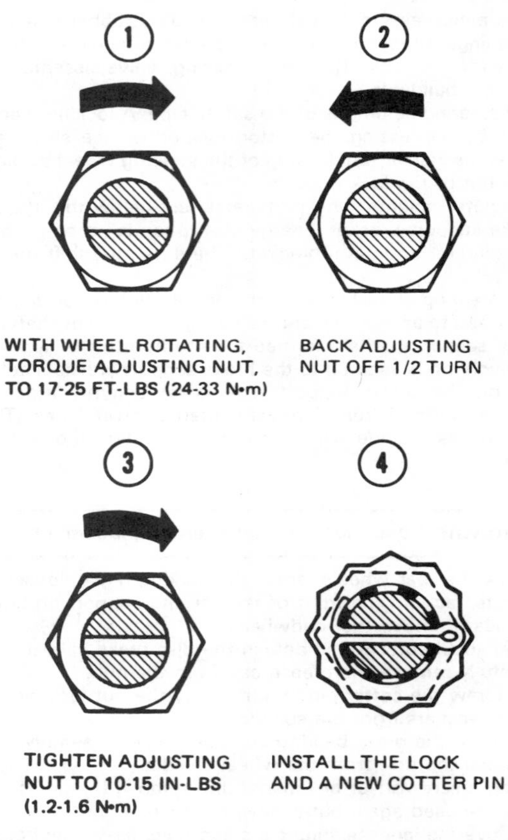

Fig. 10.5 Wheel bearing nut adjustment sequence (Sec 3)

2.18 The hub should be centered as it is installed so that the spindle threads and grease retainer aren't damaged

3 Remove the hub cap and ease off the grease cap from the hub.
4 Wipe the excess grease from the end of the spindle. Remove the cotter pin and nut lock.
5 Slowly rotate the wheel and hub assembly and tighten the adjusting nut to the specified torque wrench setting to seat the bearings.
6 Using a box wrench back off the adjustment nut by one half of a turn and then retighten the adjusting nut to a torque wrench setting of 10 to 15 lb-in or finger-tight (Fig. 10.5).
7 The castellations on the nut lock on the adjusting nut must be aligned with the cotter pin hole in the spindle.
8 Fit a new cotter pin and bend the ends of the cotter pin around the castellated flange of the nut.
9 Check that the wheel rotates freely and then replace the grease cap and hub cap. Lower the car to the ground.

4 Sway bar link insulators – removal, inspection and installation

1 Raise the vehicle and support with jack stands.
2 Remove the nut, washer and insulator from the top of the stabilizer bar bolt.
3 Remove the bolt, washers and spacers. Note their location for reinstallation.
4 Inspect the insulators for cracks or breakage, replace as necessary.
5 Install the stabilizer bar insulators by reversing the above procedure.
6 Tighten the attaching nut to 9 to 12 ft-lb (12 to 16 Nm).

5 Sway bar – removal and installation

1 Raise the vehicle and support with jack stands.
2 Loosen the bolt securing the sway bar to the sway bar link.
3 Loosen the bolts at the sway bar insulator attaching clamps (photo).
4 When all tension has been removed from the sway bar bolts, complete their removal and lift out the sway bar.
5 Check the plastic bushings for grooves or cracks. Replace as necessary.
6 Installation is the reverse of removal with the following precautions:
7 Coat any rubber/metal junction with a rubber lubricant to avoid galling.
8 Replace any bolt used either at the attaching clamp or the sway bar link.
9 Torque the attaching brackets to 14 to 26 ft-lb (19 to 35 Nm). Torque the stabilizer link bolts to 9 to 12 ft-lb (12 to 16 Nm).

5.3 Sway bar attachment clamp bolts loosened to permit bar removal

6.5A Loosen the tie-rod nut a few turns so that the threads will be protected during removal

6.5B Using a small bearing puller to disconnect the tie-rod

6 Front coil spring – removal and installation

1 Raise the vehicle and support with jack stands.
2 Remove the wheel and tire assembly.
3 Disconnect the stabilizer link from the lower A-arm.
4 Disconnect the steering coupler bolts.
5 Disconnect the tie-rod from the steering spindle, using a 'pickle fork' (small-bone wedge) or bearing puller (photos).
6 Using a spring compressor, available from most tool rental shops, insert as shown and compress the spring. When installing the compressor, turn the end piece to hold as much of the spring as possible (photo).
7 Tighten the spring compressor until the spring is loose in the seat.
8 With an assistant, support the inboard end of the arm and remove the two bolts securing it to the front crossmember. A hydraulic jack is the safest way of providing the support.
9 Carefully lower the jack to remove the spring.
10 Carefully remove the compressor to relieve spring tension.
11 Installation is the reverse of removal, with the following precautions:
12 Check that the spring is fully seated onto the spring perch before releasing the compressor.
13 Retorque the lower A-arm bolts to 120 to 180 ft-lb (203 to 244 Nm).
14 Torque the tie-rod nut to 35 to 47 ft-lb (47-64 Nm).
15 Check for binds and loose bolts before driving the car.

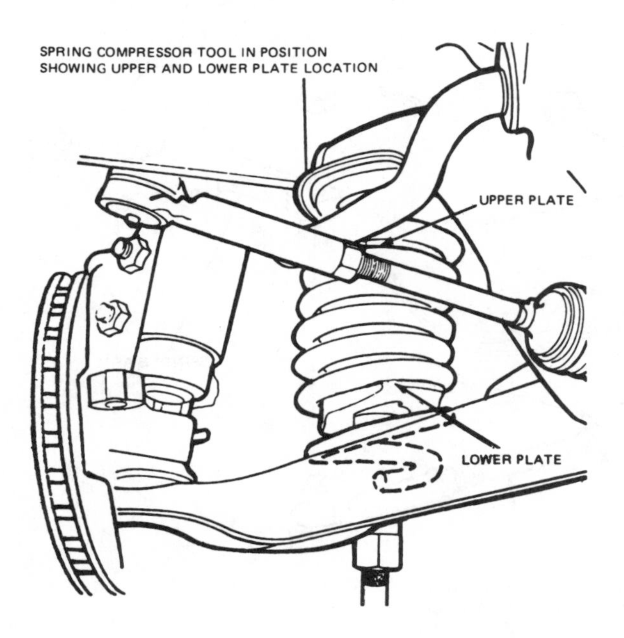

Fig. 10.6 Spring compressor tool in position (Sec 6)

7 Strut – replacement

1 Raise the front of the vehicle by the lower control arms and position safety stands under the frame jacking pads. **Caution:** *The following procedure should be done with the full weight of the vehicle on the lower control arms, and not the safety stands. Be sure the vehicle is supported firmly before proceeding.*
2 Turn to ignition key to the unlock position to allow free movement of the front wheels.
3 Inside the engine compartment on top of the inner fender, loosen the strut mount nut. Using a screwdriver in the slot will keep the rod stationary.
4 Remove the wheel, rotor, and dust shield. The brake caliper can be supported with a wire (see Chapter 9).
5 Remove the two lower nuts and bolts holding the strut to the spindle. Remove the upper strut nut.
6 The struts are not rebuildable; should there be any evidence of leakage, rust on the shaft, or cracks, the must be replaced.
7 Installation is the reverse of removal.
8 Be sure to torque all the strut mounting bolts to specification.

8 Spindle – removal and installation

1 Raise the vehicle and support with jack stands.
2 Remove the wheel assembly, rotor, brake caliper, and dust shield.
3 Remove the tie-rod end.
4 Remove the cotter pin from the balljoint nut.
5 Loosen the nut two or three turns, but do not remove the nut at this time.

6.6 Make sure that the spring compressor plates are fully seated before applying pressure

6 Strike the side of the A-arm to relieve the stud pressure.
7 Position a floor jack under the A-arm and compress the coil spring until working clearance is obtained.
8 Remove the two nuts and bolts securing the spindle to the strut and the loosened balljoint nut. Remove the spindle.
9 Installation is the reverse of the removal instruction sequence.
10 Place the spindle on the balljoint stud and install the nut finger-tight.
11 Position the strut to the spindle and install the two bolts and nuts. Tighten to 150 to 180 ft-lb (203 to 244 Nm).
12 Tighten the balljoint nut to 80 to 120 ft-lb (108 to 163 Nm).
13 Remove the floor jack.
14 Install the stabilizer link and torque the nut to 9 to 12 ft-lb (12 to 16 Nm).
15 Attach the tie-rod and torque the nut to 35 to 47 ft-lb (47 to 64 Nm). Install the cotter pin.
16 Install the brake caliper, dust shield, rotor and wheel assembly.
17 Remove jack stands.

9 Steering rack and pinion – removal and installation

1 Raise the vehicle and support with jack stands. Disconnect the battery negative cable.
2 Disconnect the flexible coupling at the input shaft.
3 Remove both tie-rod ends, referring to Section 6.
4 Mark the position of the steering coupler halves. Remove the bolts.
5 Loosen the bolts securing the steering rack to the front crossmember.
6 Disconnect the two steering pressure lines. Plug the open ends to prevent contamination.
7 Remove the nuts from the mounting bolts (loosened in step 5) and lower the rack.
8 The steering rack assembly is a rebuildable unit; however, due to its complexity and need for special factory tools, any repair is best left to a qualified technician.
9 To install, position the rack unit on the front crossmember and install the mounting nuts and bolts. Do not tighten.
10 Reconnect the tie-rod ends and tighten to 35 to 47 ft-lb (47 to 64 Nm).
11 Position the wheels in a straight-ahead position.
12 Center the steering wheel and reconnect the steering coupler. The indexing flat on the input shaft should be pointing down when inserted into the flexible coupling. Check for alignment of the marks made during disassembly. Install the bolts and tighten to 20 to 37 ft-lb (28 to 50 Nm).
13 Torque the rack mounting bolts to 80 to 100 ft-lb (109 to 135 Nm).
14 Connect the steering hydraulic lines. The manufacturer recommends their replacement if they are disconnected. New lines are available from your local dealer or parts store. Tighten all connections firmly.
15 Remove the vehicle from the jack stands. Turn the ignition to the OFF position and re-connect the negative battery cable.
16 Start the car operating the steering in both directions. Check for leakage from the hydraulic lines. Fill the fluid reservoir to the recommended level.
17 Because the alignment is critical for tire wear and economy, recheck the alignment. Refer to a dealer or alignment shop for this service.

10 Rear suspension coil spring – removal and installation

Note: *Springs must always be replaced in pairs.*
1 Raise the vehicle and support it securely on jack stands under the frame so that the rear suspension is fully extended. Remove the rear wheels.
2 Remove the rear stabilizer bar, if equipped.
3 Support the axle under the differential so that the shock absorbers are compressed about one inch.
4 With a jack under the lower suspension arm pivot bolt, remove the bolt and nut.
5 Slowly lower the jack to relieve the spring pressure. Remove the spring and insulator (if equipped) (photos).
6 To install, place the upper and lower spring insulators (if equipped) in position. Tape in place if necessary. Position the spring on the lower suspension arm spring seat so that the pigtail on the lower arm is at the rear and pointing toward the left side of the vehicle (Fig. 10.10).
7 Raise the jack slowly until the spring is compressed and the pivot bolt holes are in alignment.
8 Install the pivot bolt and nut with the nut facing outwards. The manufacturer recommends using new bolts and nuts. Do not tighten

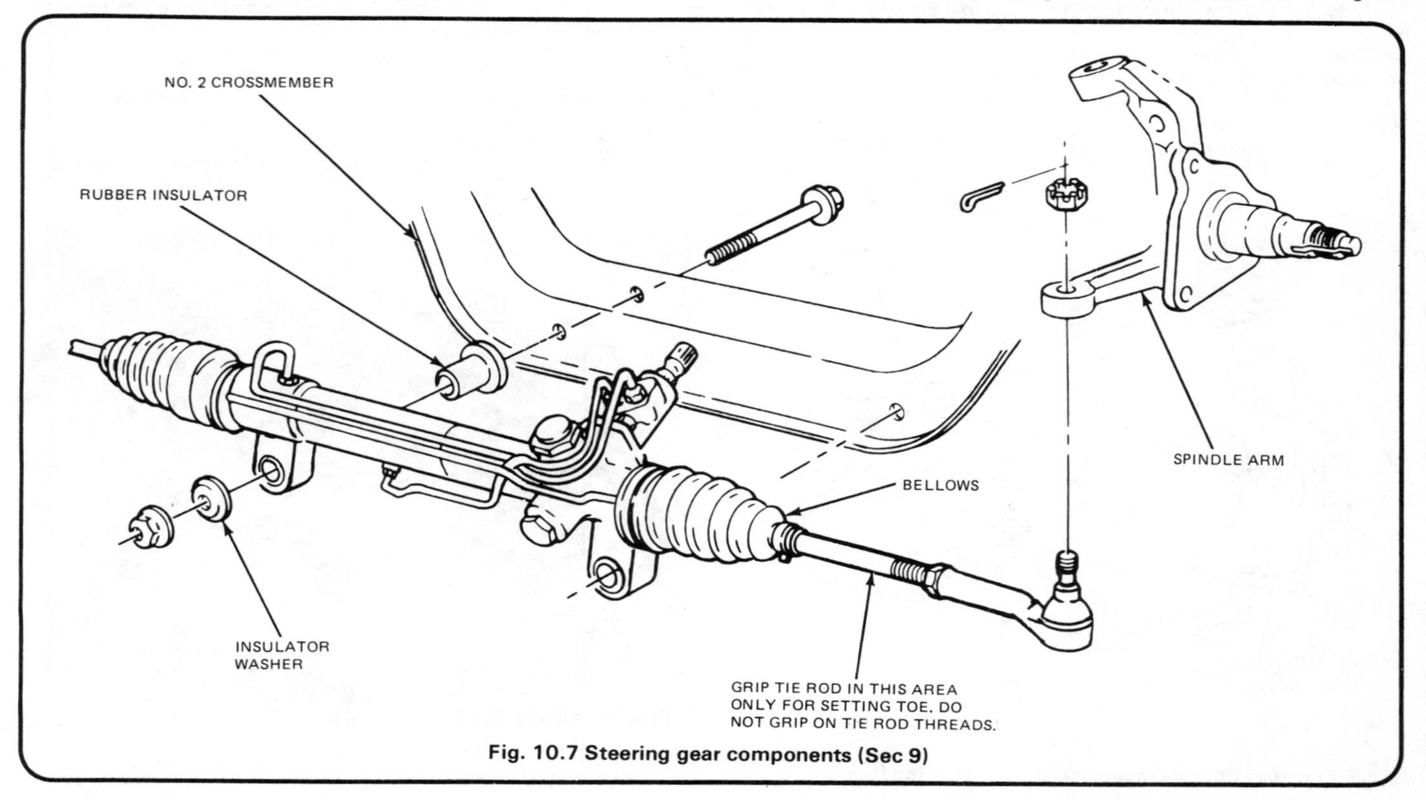

Fig. 10.7 Steering gear components (Sec 9)

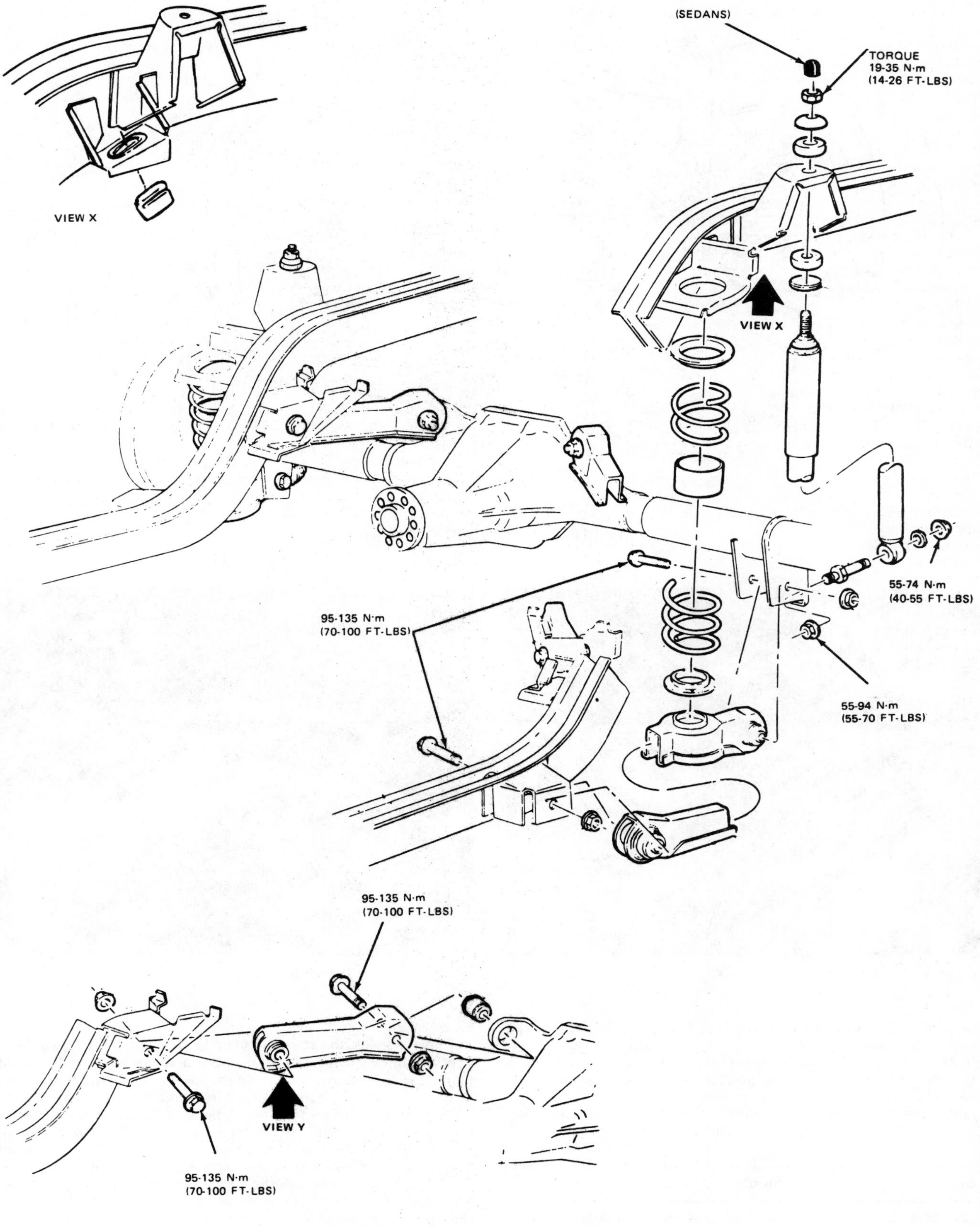

(SEDANS)

TORQUE
19-35 N·m
(14-26 FT-LBS)

VIEW X

VIEW X

95-135 N·m
(70-100 FT-LBS)

55-74 N·m
(40-55 FT-LBS)

55-94 N·m
(55-70 FT-LBS)

95-135 N·m
(70-100 FT-LBS)

VIEW Y

95-135 N·m
(70-100 FT-LBS)

Fig. 10.8 Rear suspension components (Secs 10 and 12)

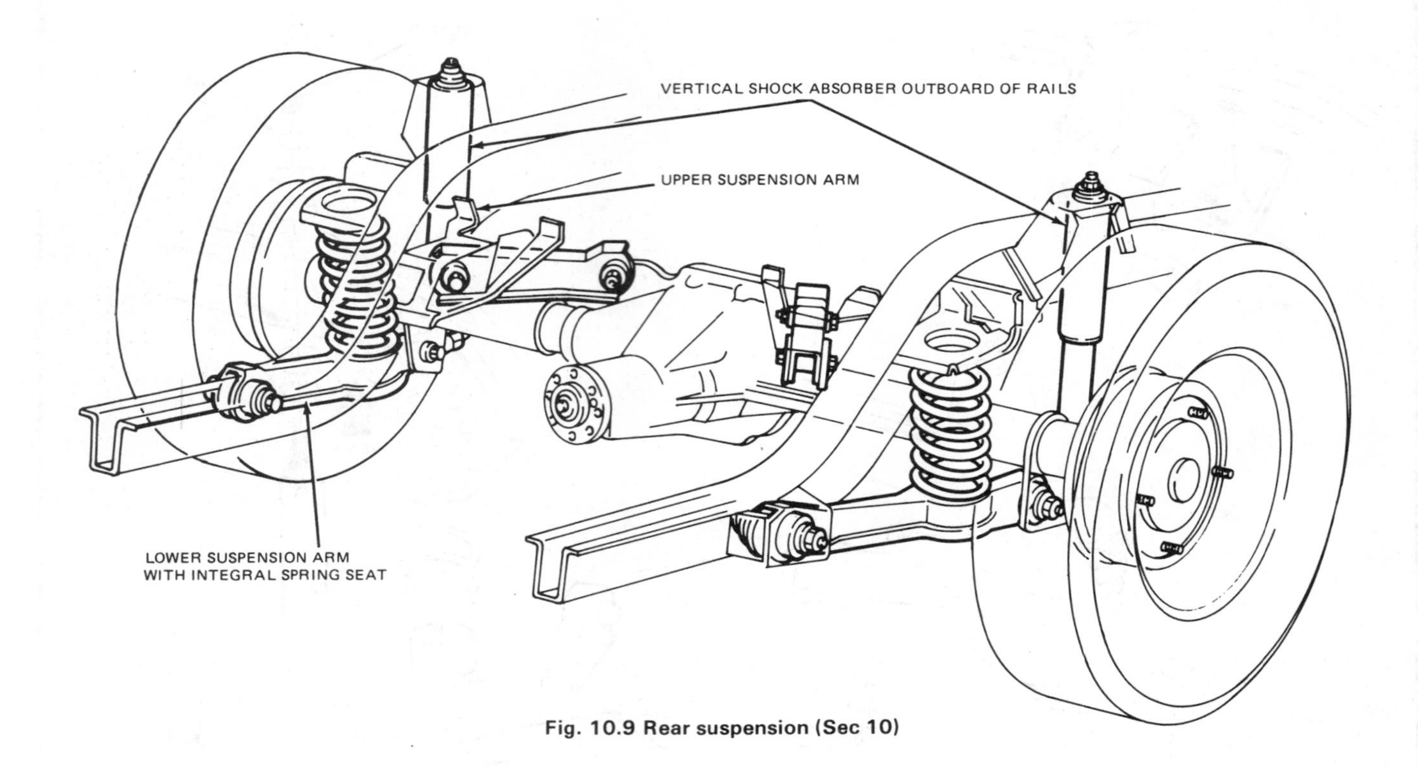

Fig. 10.9 Rear suspension (Sec 10)

10.5A Lower the jack to release the spring

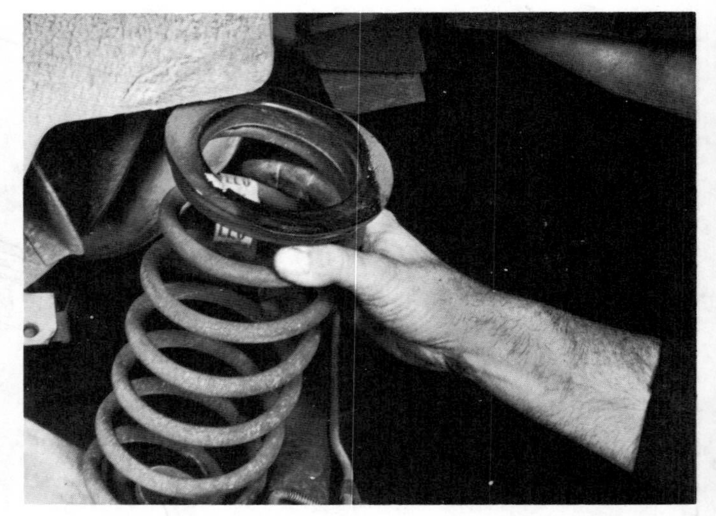

10.5B Removing the spring

the nuts to torque specifications until the vehicle weight is lowered onto the suspension.

9 Install the rear sway bar, if equipped.

10 Remove the support from the pivot point and axle and install the rear wheels.

11 Lower the vehicle so that its weight is resting on the suspension and torque tighten lower suspension arm pivot bolts.

11 Shock absorbers – inspection

1 The most common test of the shock absorber's damping is simply to bounce the rear corners of the vehicle several times and observe whether or not the car stops bouncing once the action is stopped by you. A slight rebound and settling indicates good damping, but if the vehicle continues to bounce several times, the shock absorbers must be replaced.

2 If your shock absorbers stand up to the bounce test, crawl beneath your car and visually inspect the shock body for signs of fluid leakage, punctures or deep dents in the metal of the body, and that the shock absorber is straight from several angles. If the piston rod is bent, you will not be able to see that it is. A bend in the shock body or signs of the upper portion of the shock body rubbing on the lower section will let you know. Replace any shock absorber which is leaking or damaged, in spite of proper damping indicated in the bounce test.

3 When you have removed a shock absorber, pull the piston rod out and push it back in several times to check for smooth operation throughout the travel of the piston rod. Replace the shock absorber if it gives any signs of hard or soft spots in the piston travel.

4 When you install a new shock absorber, pump the piston rod fully in and out several times to lubricate the seals and fill the hydraulic sections of the unit.

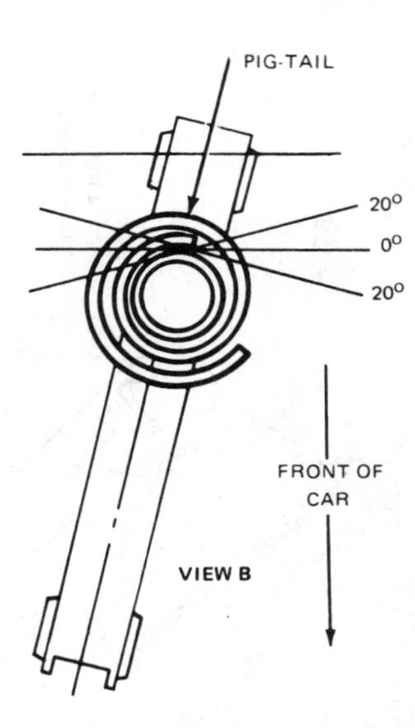

Fig. 10.10 Rear spring installation diagram. Lower pigtail must point to the left of the vehicle (Sec 10)

12 Rear shock absorber – removal and installation

Note: *Shock absorbers should always be replaced in pairs.*

1 The upper shock absorber bolt is accessible inside the trunk on 2-door models or after the removal of interior trim panels on 3-door models. Remove the rubber cap (2-door) and remove the shock absorber nut, washer and insulator.

2 Chock the front wheels, raise the car, support it securely and remove the rear wheels.

3 From underneath the car, reach up and compress the shock absorber by pulling it down from the upper shock tower hole.

4 Remove the lower shock absorber nut and washer (photo).

5 Remove the shock absorber and inspect it (Section 11).

6 To install, compress the shock absorber, place the lower mounting eye on the mounting stud and install the washer and nut. Do not tighten.

12.4 Removing the lower shock absorber nut and washer after compressing the shock absorber

7 Install the inner washer and insulator on the upper attaching stud and extend the shock absorber upward into position in the upper mounting hole.

8 Tighten the lower mounting nut to 40-55 ft-lb (55-74 Nm).

9 Lower the vehicle and install the insulator, washer and nut. Tighten to 14-26 ft-lb (19-35 Nm).

10 Replace the rubber cap (2-door) or trim panels (3-door).

13 Power steering – general description

1 The power steering systems available on these cars have a pulley-driven Ford Model CII type pump. This pump delivers fuel to a servo assisted rack and pinion gear assembly.

2 Servo assistance is obtained through a piston mounted on the rack and running in the rack tube. The degree of assistance is controlled by a spool valve mounted concentrically with the input and pinion shaft.

3 The power steering pump incorporates an integral fluid reservoir.

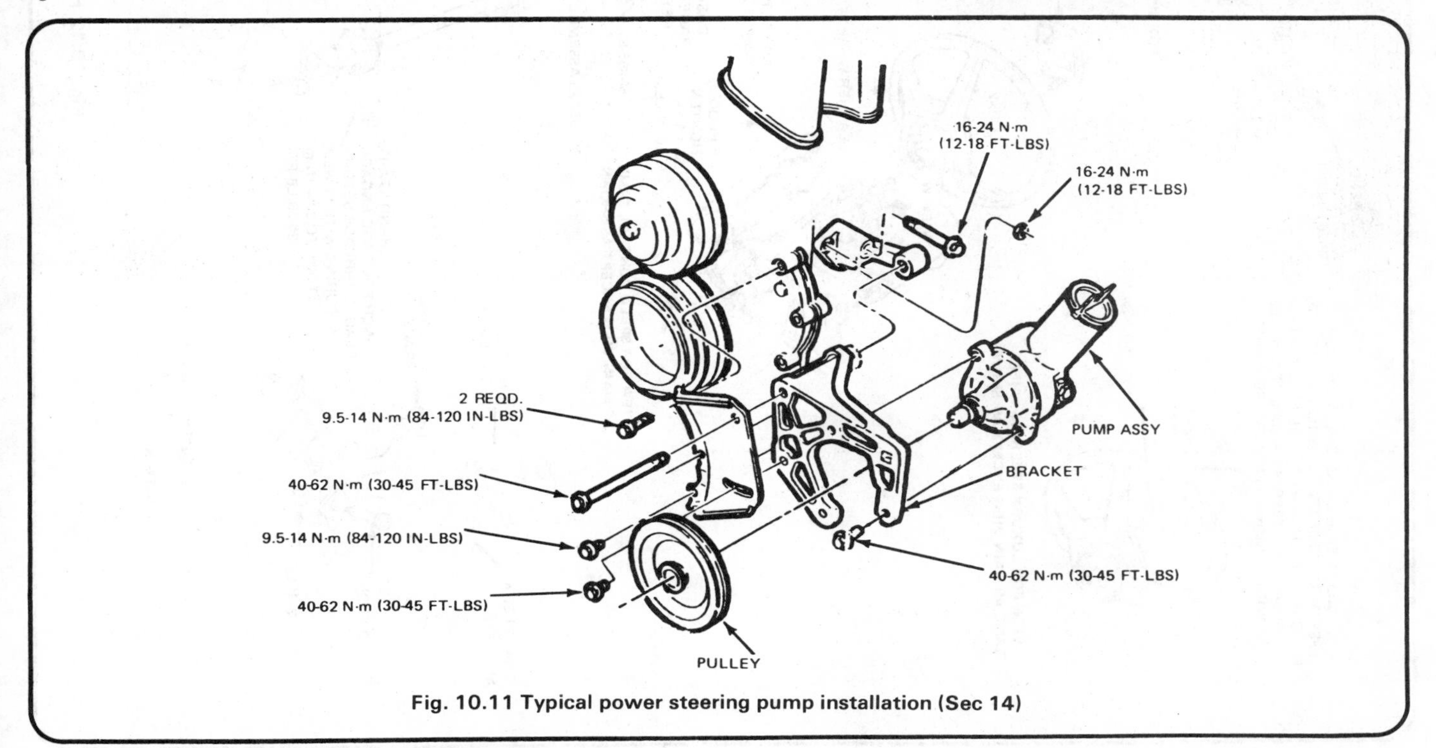

Fig. 10.11 Typical power steering pump installation (Sec 14)

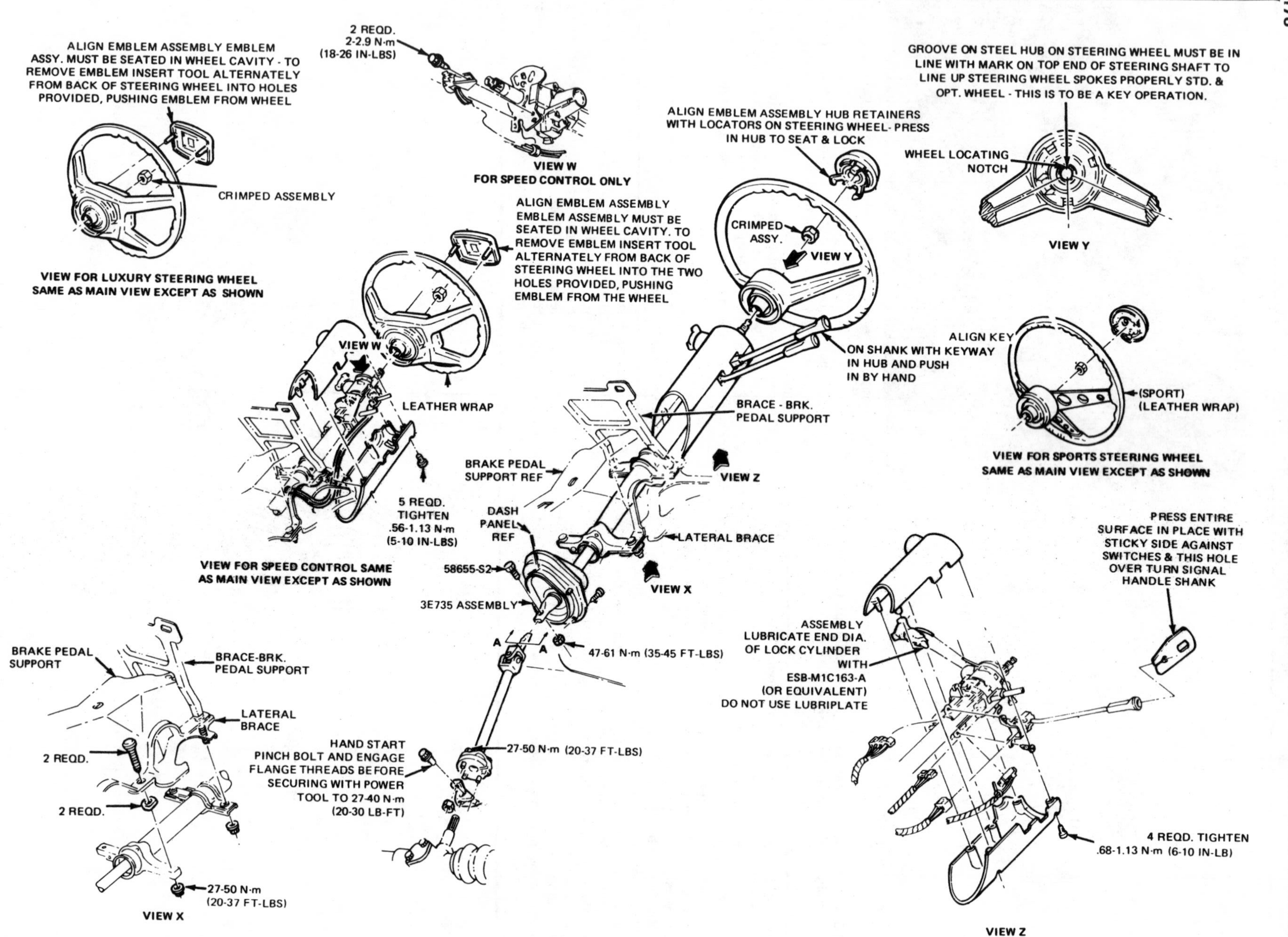

Fig. 10.12 Fixed steering column components (Sec 17)

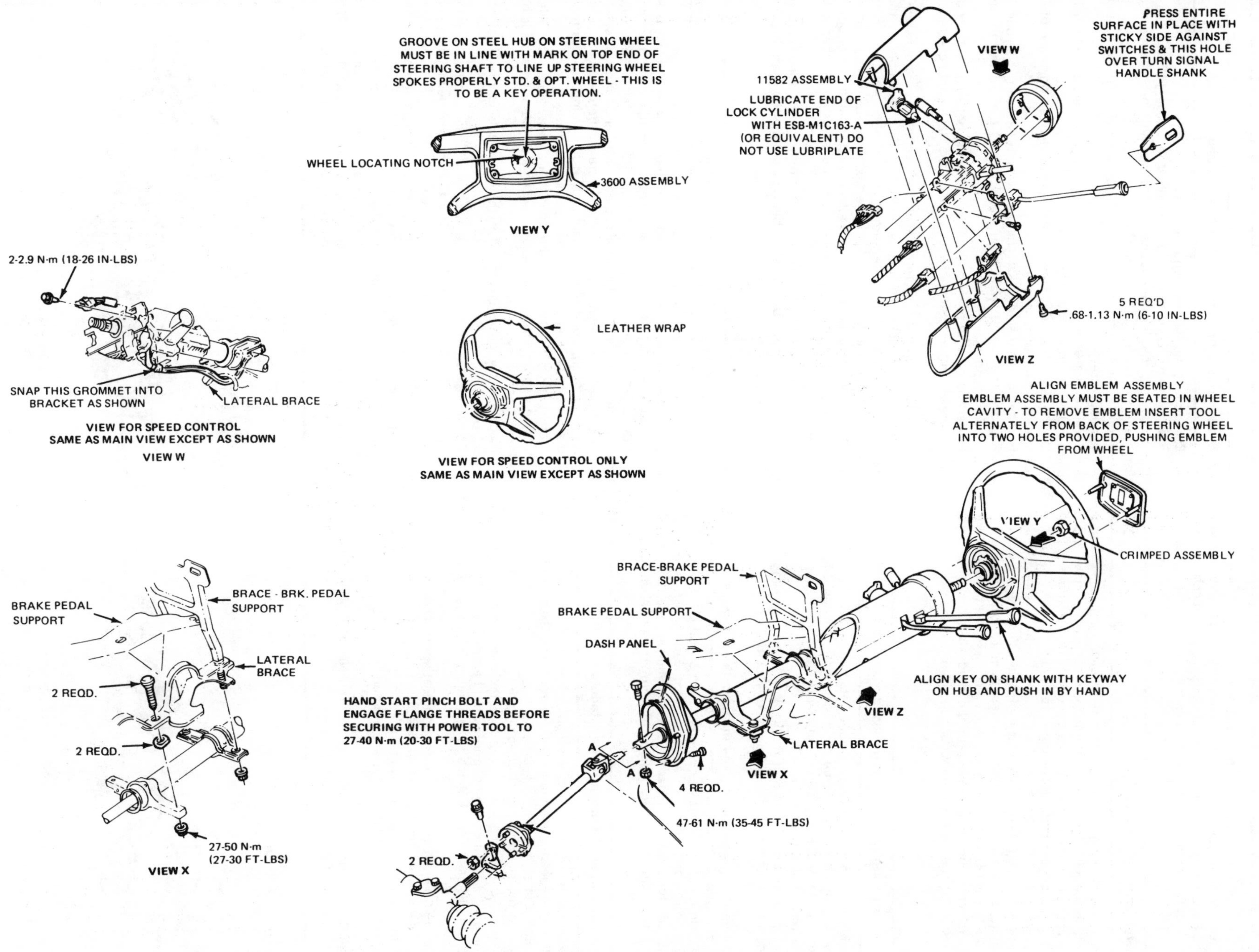

GROOVE ON STEEL HUB ON STEERING WHEEL MUST BE IN LINE WITH MARK ON TOP END OF STEERING SHAFT TO LINE UP STEERING WHEEL SPOKES PROPERLY STD. & OPT. WHEEL - THIS IS TO BE A KEY OPERATION.

WHEEL LOCATING NOTCH

3600 ASSEMBLY

VIEW Y

11582 ASSEMBLY

LUBRICATE END OF LOCK CYLINDER WITH ESB-M1C163-A (OR EQUIVALENT) DO NOT USE LUBRIPLATE

VIEW W

PRESS ENTIRE SURFACE IN PLACE WITH STICKY SIDE AGAINST SWITCHES & THIS HOLE OVER TURN SIGNAL HANDLE SHANK

5 REQ'D .68-1.13 N·m (6-10 IN-LBS)

VIEW Z

2-2.9 N·m (18-26 IN-LBS)

SNAP THIS GROMMET INTO BRACKET AS SHOWN

LATERAL BRACE

VIEW FOR SPEED CONTROL SAME AS MAIN VIEW EXCEPT AS SHOWN

VIEW W

LEATHER WRAP

VIEW FOR SPEED CONTROL ONLY SAME AS MAIN VIEW EXCEPT AS SHOWN

ALIGN EMBLEM ASSEMBLY EMBLEM ASSEMBLY MUST BE SEATED IN WHEEL CAVITY - TO REMOVE EMBLEM INSERT TOOL ALTERNATELY FROM BACK OF STEERING WHEEL INTO TWO HOLES PROVIDED, PUSHING EMBLEM FROM WHEEL

VIEW Y

CRIMPED ASSEMBLY

BRAKE PEDAL SUPPORT

BRACE - BRK. PEDAL SUPPORT

LATERAL BRACE

2 REQD.

2 REQD.

27-50 N·m (27-30 FT-LBS)

VIEW X

BRACE-BRAKE PEDAL SUPPORT

BRAKE PEDAL SUPPORT

DASH PANEL

ALIGN KEY ON SHANK WITH KEYWAY ON HUB AND PUSH IN BY HAND

VIEW Z

LATERAL BRACE

VIEW X

HAND START PINCH BOLT AND ENGAGE FLANGE THREADS BEFORE SECURING WITH POWER TOOL TO 27-40 N·m (20-30 FT-LBS)

A

A

4 REQD.

47-61 N·m (35-45 FT-LBS)

2 REQD.

Fig. 10.13 Tilt steering column components (Sec 17)

4 Because of the complexity of the power steering system it is recommended that servicing etc, is limited to that given in the following Sections. In the event of a fault occurring it is recommended that repair or overhaul be entrusted to a specialist in this type of work.

14 Power steering – bleeding

1 The power steering system will only need bleeding in the event of air being introduced into the system, ie, where pipes have been disconnected or where a leakage has occurred. To bleed the system proceed as described in the following paragraphs.
2 Open the hood and check the fluid level in the fluid reservoir. Top up if necessary using the specified type of fluid.
3 If fluid is added, allow two minutes then run the engine at approximately 1500 rpm. Slowly turn the steering wheel from lock-to-lock, whilst checking and topping-up the fluid level until the level remains steady, and no more bubbles appear in the reservoir.
4 Clean and refit the reservoir cap, and close the hood.

15 Power steering pump – removal and installation

1 Loosen the pump adjusting bolt and retaining bolts.
2 Push the pump in toward the engine, and remove the drivebelt.
3 Disconnect the power system fluid lines from the pump and drain the fluid into a suitable container.
4 Plug, or tape over, the end of the lines to prevent dirt ingress.
5 If necessary, remove the alternator drivebelt(s) as described in Chapter 2.
6 Remove the bolts attaching the pump to the engine bracket and remove the pump. **Note**: *On some engine installations it may be necessary to remove the pump complete with bracket.*
7 Replacing is a direct reversal of the removal procedure. Ensure that the fluid lines are tightened to the specified torque, top-up the system with an approved fluid, adjust the alternator drivebelt tension.

16 Steering wheel – removal and installation

1 Disconnect the battery negative cable.
2 Pull out on the steering wheel hub cover (2- and 3-spoke) or push the emblem out from behind (4-spoke).
3 Remove the steering wheel attaching nut.
4 Remove the steering wheel with a suitable wheel puller. Do not strike the end of the steering column with a hammer or use a knock-off type of puller as this will damage the collapsible steering column bearing.
5 When reinstalling align the marks on the steering shaft with those on the wheel. Make sure that the wheels are pointed straight ahead in relation to the steering wheel position.
6 Install the steering wheel nut and tighten to 30-40 ft-lb (41-54 Nm).
7 Align the hub cover pins or springs with their holes or slots in the steering wheel and push into place.

17 Steering column – removal and replacement

1 Disconnect the battery negative cable.
2 Remove the steering wheel as described in Section 16.
3 Disconnect the flexible coupling at the steering input flange and disengage the safety strap assembly.
4 Remove the column trim shrouds which are held in place by five self-tapping screws
5 Remove the steering column cover and hood release which is located directly under the column.
6 Disconnect all of the steering column switches and mark their positions for ease of reassembly.
7 Remove the four screws attaching the dust boot to the dash panel.
8 Remove the four attaching nuts which hold the column to the brake pedal support.
9 Lower the column to clear the four mounting bolts and pull it out so that the U-joint assembly passes through the dash panel clearance hole.
10 Refer to Chapter 11 for removal of the ignition lock and switch.
11 When reinstallating the safety strap and bolt assembly to the steering gear input shaft, make sure that the strap is positioned to prevent metal-to-metal contact. Also, the flexible coupling must not be distorted when the bolts are tightened. By prying the shaft up or down with a suitable pry bar the insulator can be adjusted so that it is installed flat.
12 The rest of reinstallation is a reversal of removal. Be sure to install the dust boot over the steering shaft before inserting the shaft through the dash panel.

18 Steering angles and front wheel alignment

1 Accurate front wheel alignment is essential for good steering and tire wear. Before considering the steering angle, check that the tires are correctly inflated, that the front wheels are not bent, the hub bearings are not worn, or incorrectly adjusted and that the steering linkage is in good order, without slackness or wear at the joints.
2 Toe-in is the amount by which the distance between the front inside edges of the roadwheels (measured at hub height) is less than the distance measured between the rear inside edges.
3 Front wheel alignment (toe-in) checks are best carried out with modern setting equipment but a reasonably accurate alternative is by means of the following procedure.
4 Place the car on level ground with the wheels in the 'straight-ahead' position.
5 Obtain or make a toe-in gauge. One may easily be made from a length of rod or tubing, cranked to clear the sump or bellhousing and having a setscrew and lock nut at one end.
6 With the gauge, measure the distance between the two inner wheel rims at hub height at the front of the wheel.
7 Rotate the roadwheel through 180° (half a turn) by pushing or pulling the car and then measure the distance again at hub height between the inner wheel rims at the rear of the roadwheel. This measurement should either be the same as the one just taken or

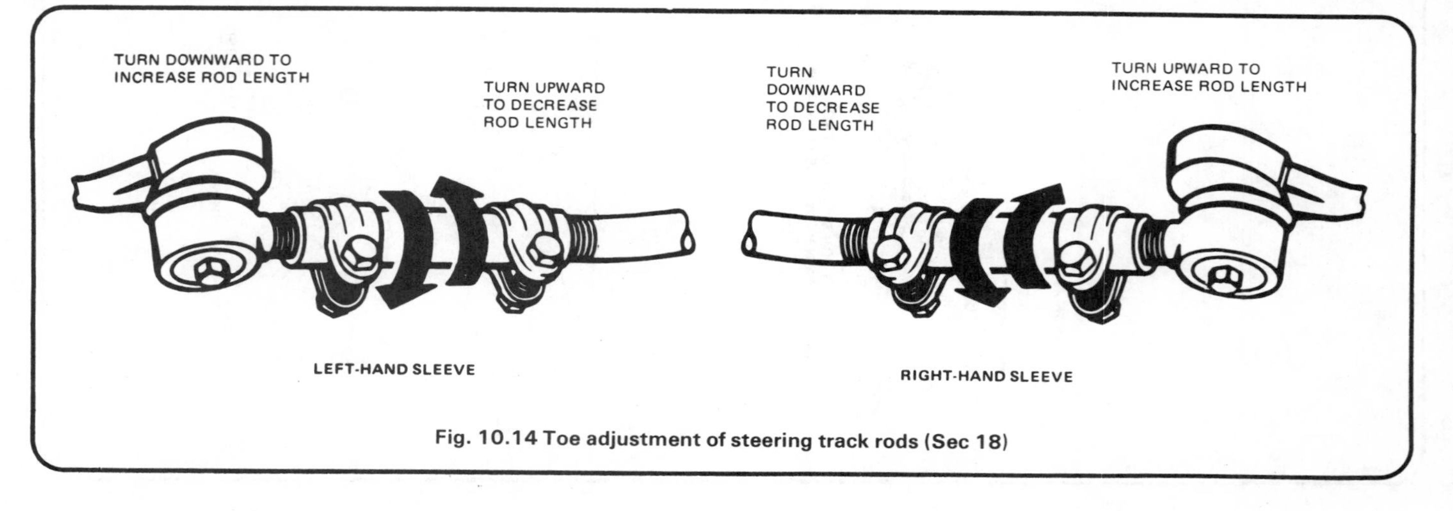

Fig. 10.14 Toe adjustment of steering track rods (Sec 18)

greater by not more than 0.28 in (7 mm).

8 Where the toe-in is found to be incorrect slacken the lock nuts on each trackrod, also the flexible bellows clips and rotate each trackrod by an equal amount until the correct toe-in is obtained. Tighten the trackrod-end lock nuts while the balljoints are held in the center of their arcs of travel. It is imperative that the lengths of the trackrods are always equal otherwise the wheel angles on turns will be incorrect. If new components have been fitted, set the roadwheels in the 'straight-ahead' position and also centralize the steering wheel. Now adjust the lengths of the trackrods by turning them so that the tie-rod-end balljoint studs will drop easily into the eyes of the steering arms. Measure the distances between the centers of the balljoints and the grooves on the inner ends of the trackrods and adjust, if necessary, so that they are equal. This is an initial setting only and precise adjustment must be carried out as described in earlier paragraphs of this Section.

19 Wheels and tires

1 Check the tire pressures weekly (when they are cold).

2 Frequently inspect the tire walls and treads for damage and pick out any large stones which have become trapped in the tread pattern.

3 If the wheels and tires have been balanced on the car then they should not be moved to a different axle position. If they have been balanced off the car then, in the interests of extending tread life, they can be moved between the front and rear on the same side of the car and the spare incorporated in the rotational pattern.

4 Never mix tires of different construction or very dissimilar tread patterns.

5 Always keep the roadwheels tightened to the specified torque and if the bolt holes become elongated or flattened, replace the wheel.

6 Occasionally, clean the inner faces of the roadwheels and if there is any sign of rust or corrosion, paint them with metal preservative paint. **Note**: *Corrosion on aluminum alloy wheels may be evidence of a more serious problem which could lead to wheel failure. If corrosion is evident, consult your local authorized dealer for advice.*

7 Before removing a roadwheel which has been balanced on the car, always mark one wheel stud and bolt hole so that the roadwheel may be refitted in the same relative position to maintain the balance.

Chapter 11 Electrical system

Refer to Chapter 13 for specifications and information related to 1981 thru 1987 models

Contents

Specifications

Battery

Rating	Check battery identification stickers for rating.

Alternator

Type	rear terminal
Manufacturer	Ford
Color codes	orange, black, green
Amp rating at 15 volts	
orange	40 amp
black	65 amp
green	60 amp
Watt rating at 15 volts	
orange	600 watts
black	975 watts
green	900 watts
Slip ring turning (all)	
new	1.22 in, minimum diameter
runout	0.0005 in, maximum
Brush length	
new	0.5 in
wear limit	0.1875 in
Type	side terminal
Manufacturer	Ford
Color code	black
Amp rating at 15 volts	70 amp
Watt rating at 15 volts	1050 watts

Slip ring turning	
new	1.22 in, minimum diameter
runout	0.0005 in, maximum
Brush length	
new	0.5 in
wear limit	0.3125 in

Bulb specifications

	Number
Air conditioning and heater control	161
Clock illumination	194
Instrument cluster illumination	194
Console ashtray illumination	194
Dome light	906
Dual brake warning indicator	194
Engine compartment light	89
Glove box	1816
Heated rear window warning indicator	2162
High beam indicator	194
Luggage compartment light	89
Automatic transmission (PRNDL) indicator light	1893
Turn indicator	194
Back-up light	1156
Front side marker	194
Headlight high beam	H-4651
Headlight low beam	H-4656
Seat belt warning indicator	194

Torque specifications

	ft-lb	Nm
Pulley nut, rear terminal alternator	60 to 100	82 to 135
Pulley nut, side terminal alternator	80 to 100	109 to 135

For belt tensions, see Specifications, Chapter 2.

All fasteners not listed, use the following torque wrench settings:

	ft-lb	Nm
Metric thread size		
M-6	6 to 9	9 to 12
M-8	14 to 21	19 to 28
M-10	28 to 40	38 to 54
M-12	50 to 71	68 to 96
M-14	80 to 140	109 to 154
Pipe thread size		
1/8	5 to 8	7 to 10
1/4	12 to 18	17 to 24
3/8	22 to 33	30 to 44
1/2	25 to 35	34 to 47
U.S. thread size		
1/4 – 20	6 to 9	9 to 12
5/16 – 18	12 to 18	17 to 24
5/16 – 24	14 to 20	19 to 27
3/8 – 16	22 to 32	30 to 43
3/8 – 24	27 to 38	37 to 51
7/16 – 14	40 to 55	55 to 74
7/16 – 20	40 to 60	55 to 81
1/2 – 13	55 to 80	75 to 108

1 General description

The major components of the 12 volt negative ground system comprise a 12 volt battery, an alternator (driven from the crankshaft pulley), and a starter motor.

The battery supplies a steady amount of current for the ignition, lighting and other electrical circuits and provides a reserve of electricity when the current consumed by the electrical equipment exceeds that being produced by the alternator.

The alternator has its own integral regulator which ensures a high output if the battery is in a low state of charge and the demand from the electrical equipment is high, and a low output if the battery is fully charged and there is little demand for the electrical equipment.

When fitting electrical accessories to cars with a negative ground system it is important, if they contain silicone diodes or transistors that they are connected correctly, otherwise serious damage may result to the components concerned. Items such as radios, tape recorders, electronic ignition system, electrical tachometer, automatic dipping etc, should all be checked for correct polarity.

It is important that the battery positive lead is always disconnected if the battery is to be boost charged, also if body repairs are to be carried out using electronic welding equipment – the alternator must be disconnected, otherwise serious damage can be caused. Whenever the battery has to be disconnected it must always be reconnected with the negative terminal grounded

2 Battery – removal and replacement

1 The battery is on a carrier fitted to the right-hand fender apron of the engine compartment. It should be removed once every three months for cleaning and testing. Disconnect the positive and then the negative leads from the battery terminals by undoing and removing the plated nuts and bolts.

2 Unscrew and remove the nut and plain washer that secures the clamp plate to the bodywork, remove the two nuts securing the battery clamp. Lift away the clamp plate. Carefully lift the battery from its carrier holding it vertically to ensure that none of the electrolyte is spilled.

3 Replacement is a direct reversal of this procedure **Note:** *Replace the negative lead before the positive lead and smear the terminals with petroleum jelly to prevent corrosion. Never use ordinary grease.*

3 Battery – maintenance and inspection

1 Normal weekly battery maintenance consists of checking the electrolyte level of each cell to ensure that the separators are covered by $\frac{1}{4}$ inch of electrolyte. If the level has fallen, top up the battery using distilled water only. Do not overfill. If a battery is overfilled or any electrolyte spilled, immediately wipe away and neutralize, as electrolyte attacks and corrodes any metal it comes into contact with very rapidly.

2 If the battery has the 'Auto-fil' device fitted, a special topping up sequence is required. The white balls in the 'Auto-fil' battery are part of the automatic topping-up device which ensures correct electrolyte level. The vent chamber should remain in position at all times except when topping-up or taking specific gravity readings. If the electrolyte level in any of the cells is below the bottom of the filling tube, top-up as follows:

a) Lift off the vent chamber cover (photo).
b) With the battery level, pour distilled water into the trough until all the filling tubes and trough are full.
c) Immediately replace the cover to allow the water in the trough and tubes to flow into the cells. Each cell will automatically receive the correct amount of water.

3 As well as keeping the terminals clean and covered with petroleum jelly, the top of the battery, and especially the top of the cells, should be kept clean and dry. This helps prevent corrosion and ensures that the battery does not become partially discharged by leakage through dampness and dirt.

4 Once every three months remove the battery and inspect the battery securing bolts, the battery clamp plate, tray, and battery leads for corrosion (white fluffy deposits on the metal which are brittle to the touch). If any corrosion is found, clean off the deposits with ammonia and paint over the clean metal with an anti-rust anti-acid paint.

5 At the same time inspect the battery case for cracks. If a crack is found, clean and plug it with one of the proprietary compounds marketed for this purpose. If leakage through the crack has been excessive then it will be necessary to replace the battery. Cracks are frequently caused to the top of the battery case by pouring in distilled water in the middle of winter after instead of before a run. This gives the water no chance to mix with the electrolyte and so the former freezes and splits the battery case.

6 If topping-up the battery becomes excessive and the case has been inspected for cracks that could cause leakage, but none are found, the battery is being overcharged and the voltage regulator will have to be checked and reset.

7 With the battery on the bench at the three monthly interval check, measure its specific gravity with a hydrometer to determine the state of charge and condition of the electrolyte. There should be very little variation between the different cells and if a variation in excess of 0.025 is present it will be due to either:

a) Loss of electrolyte from the battery at some time caused by spillage or a leak resulting in a drop in the specific gravity of the electrolyte, when the deficiency was replaced with distilled water instead of fresh electrolyte.
b) An internal short circuit caused by buckling of the plates or a similar malady pointing to the likelihood of a total battery failure in the near future.

3.2 Removing the vent cover to check battery electrolyte level

8 The specific gravity of the electrolyte for fully charged conditions at the electrolyte temperature indicated, is listed in Table A. The specific gravity of a fully discharged battery at different temperatures of the electrolyte is given in Table B.

Table A
Specific gravity – Battery fully charged
1.268 at 100°F or 38°C electrolyte temperature
1.272 at 90°F or 32°C electrolyte temperature
1.276 at 80°F or 27°C electrolyte temperature
1.280 at 70°F or 21°C electrolyte temperature
1.284 at 60°F or 16°C electrolyte temperature
1.288 at 50°F or 10°C electrolyte temperature
1.292 at 40°F or 4°C electrolyte temperature
1.296 at 30°F or -1.5°C electrolyte temperature

Table B
Specific gravity – Battery fully discharged
1.098 at 100°F or 38°C electrolyte temperature
1.102 at 90°F or 32°C electrolyte temperature
1.106 at 80°F or 27°C electrolyte temperature
1.110 at 70°F or 21°C electrolyte temperature
1.114 at 60°F or 16°C electrolyte temperature
1.118 at 50°F or 10°C electrolyte temperature
1.122 at 40°F or 4°C electrolyte temperature
1.126 at 30°F or -1.5°C electrolyte temperature

4 Battery – electrolyte replenishment

1 If the battery is in a fully charged state and one of the cells maintains a specific gravity reading which is 0.025 or more lower than the others, and a check of each cell has been made with a voltmeter to check for short circuits (a four to seven second test should give a steady reading of between 1.2 to 1.8 volts) then it is likely that electrolyte has been lost from the cell with the low reading.

2 Top-up the cell with a solution of 1 part sulphuric acid to 2.5 parts of water. If the cell is already fully topped up, draw some electrolyte out of it with a pipette.

3 When mixing the sulphuric acid and water **never add water to sulphuric acid** – always pour the acid slowly onto the water in a glass container. **If water is added to sulphuric acid it will explode.**

4 Continue to top-up the cell with the freshly made electrolyte and then recharge the battery and check the hydrometer readings.

5 Battery – charging

1 In winter time when heavy demand is placed upon the battery, such as when starting from cold, and much electrical equipment is continually in use, it is a good idea occasionally to have the battery fully charged from an external source at the rate of 3.5 to 4 amps.

2 Continue to charge the battery at this rate until no further rise in specific gravity is noted over a four hour period.

3 Alternatively, a trickle charger charging at the rate of 1.5 amps can be safely used overnight.

4 Specially rapid 'boost' charges which are claimed to restore the power of the battery in 1 or 2 hours are to be avoided as they can cause serious damage to the battery plates through overheating.

5 While charging the battery, note that the temperature of the electrolyte should never exceed 100°F (37.8°C).

6 Alternator – general description

1 The main advantage of the alternator lies in its ability to provide a

high charge at low revolutions. Driving slowly in heavy traffic with a generator invariably means no charge is reaching the battery. In similar conditions even with the wiper, heater, lights and perhaps radio switched on the alternator will ensure a charge reaches the battery.

2 The alternator is of rotating field, ventilated design. It comprises 3-phase output winding; a twelve pole rotor carrying the field windings – each end of the rotor shaft runs in ball race bearings which are lubricated for lift; natural finish aluminum die case end brackets, incorporating the mounting lugs; a rectifier pack for converting AC output of the machine to DC for battery charging, and an output control regulator.

3 The rotor is belt driven from the engine through a pulley keyed to the rotor shaft. A pressed steel fan adjacent to the pulley draws cooling air through the unit. This fan forms an integral part of the alternator specification. It has been designed to provide adequate air flow with minimum noise, and to withstand the high stesses associated with maximum speed. Rotation is clockwise viewed on the drive end. Maximum continuous rotor speed is 12 500 rpm.

4 Rectification of the alternator output is achieved by six silicone diodes housed in a rectifier pack and connected as a 3-phase full wave bridge. The rectifier pack is attached to the outer face of the slip ring end bracket and contains also three 'field' diodes. At normal operating speeds, rectified current from the stator output windings flows through these diodes to provide the self excitation of the rotor field, via brushes bearing on face type slip rings.

5 The slip rings are carried on a small diameter molded form attached to the rotor shaft outboard of the slip ring end bearing. The inner ring is centered on the rotor shaft axle, while the outer ring has a mean diameter of $\frac{3}{4}$ inch approximately. By keeping the mean diameter of the slip rings to a minimum, relative speeds between brushes and rings, and hence wear, are also minimal. The slip rings are connected to the rotor field windings by wires carried in grooves in the rotor shaft.

6 The brush gear is housed in a molding fitted to the inside of the rear casing. This molding thus encloses the slip ring and brush gear assembly, and together with the shield bearing, protects the assembly against the entry of dust and moisture.

7 The regulator is set during manufacture and is located on the right-hand inner fender panel. It requires no further attention but should its operation be faulty it must be replaced as a complete unit.

7 Alternator – maintenance

1 The equipment has been designed for the minimum amount of maintenance in service, the only items subject to wear being the brushes and bearings.

2 Brushes should be examined after about 75,000 miles (120,000 km) and replaced with new ones if necessary. The bearings are pre-packed with grease for life, and should not require further attention.

3 Check the fan belt at the specified service intervals for correct adjustment which should be 0.5 inch (13 mm) total movement at the center of the run between the alternator and water pump pulleys.

8 Alternator – special procedures

Note: *Whenever the electrical system of the car is being attended to, and external means of starting the engine is used, there are certain precautions that must be taken, otherwise serious and expensive damage to the alternator can result.*

1 Always made sure that the negative terminal of the battery is grounded. If the terminal connections are accidentally reversed or if the battery has been reverse charged the alternator diodes will be damaged.

2 The output terminal on the alternator marked 'BAT' or 'B+' must never be grounded but should always be connected directly to the positive terminal of the battery.

3 Whenever the alternator is to be removed or when disconnecting the terminals of the alternator circuit, always disconnect the battery ground terminal first.

4 The alternator must never be operated without the battery to alternator cable connected.

5 If the battery is to be charged by external means always disconnect both the battery cables before the external charger is connected.

6 Should it be necessary to use a booster charger or booster battery to start the engine always double check that the negative cable is connected to negative terminal and the positive cable to positive terminal.

9 Alternator – removal and installation

1 The alternator is located to the right side of the engine compartment underneath the air conditioning compressor (if fitted), next to the battery.

2 Loosen the alternator adjusting bolt.

3 Loosen the alternator pivot bolt.

4 Remove the electrical connection plugs.

5 Ease the wiring away from the alternator and remove the cable guide.

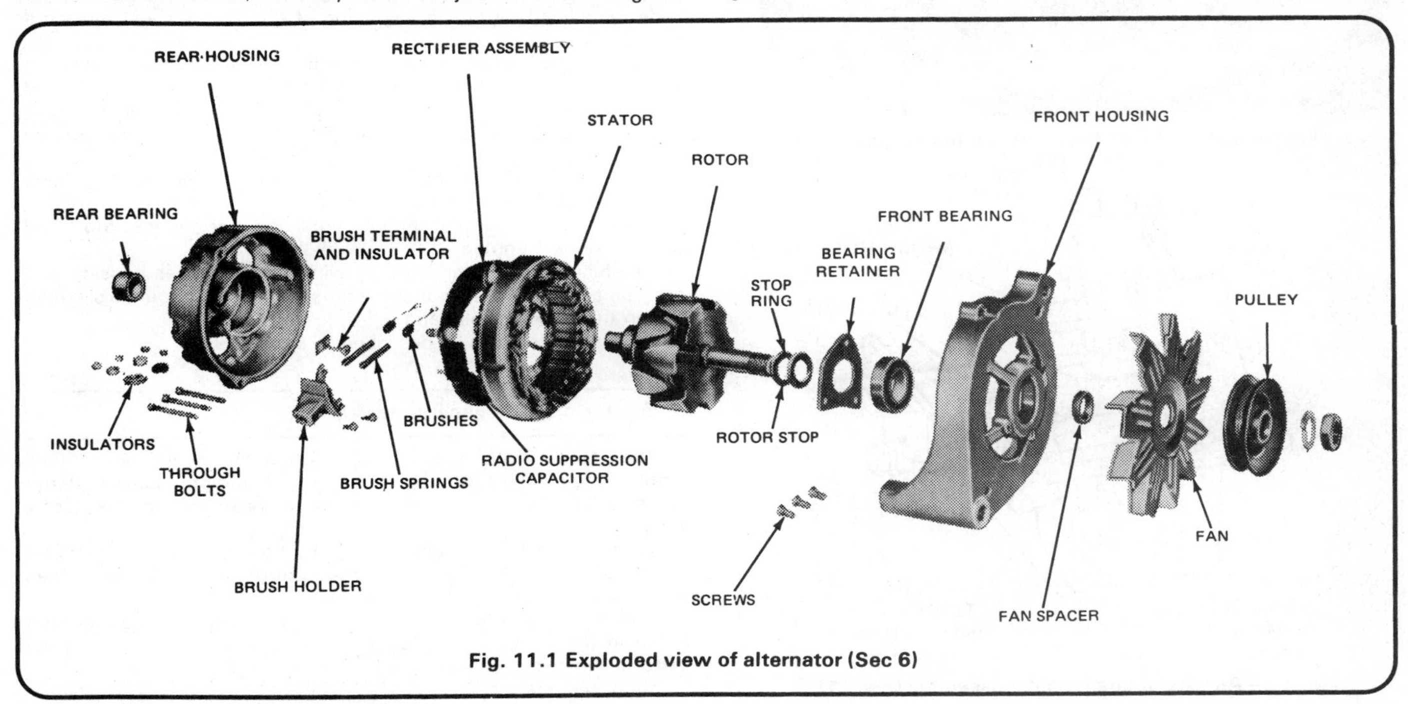

Fig. 11.1 Exploded view of alternator (Sec 6)

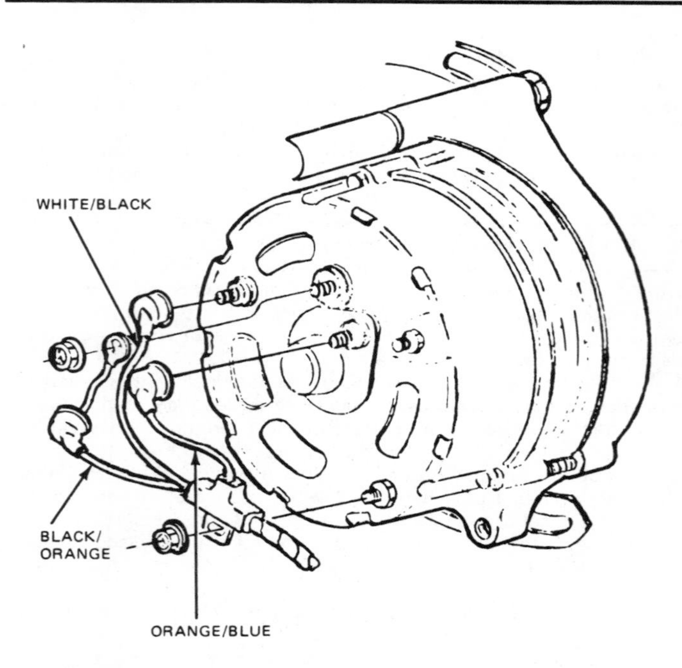

Fig. 11.2 Typical alternator and wiring harness (Sec 10)

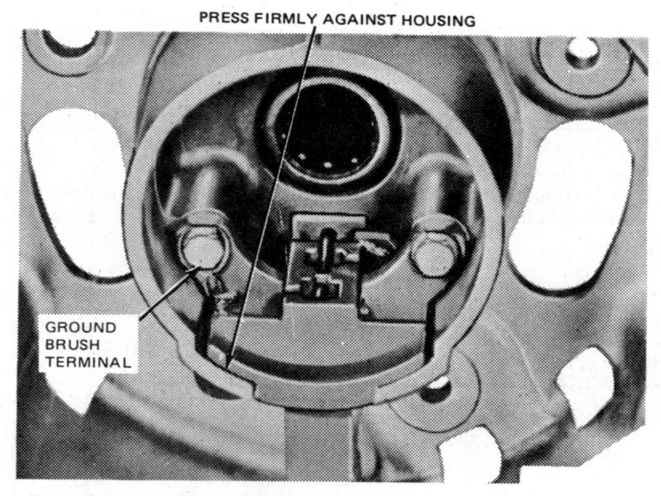

Fig. 11.3 Location of brush holder in rear housing assembly (Sec 11)

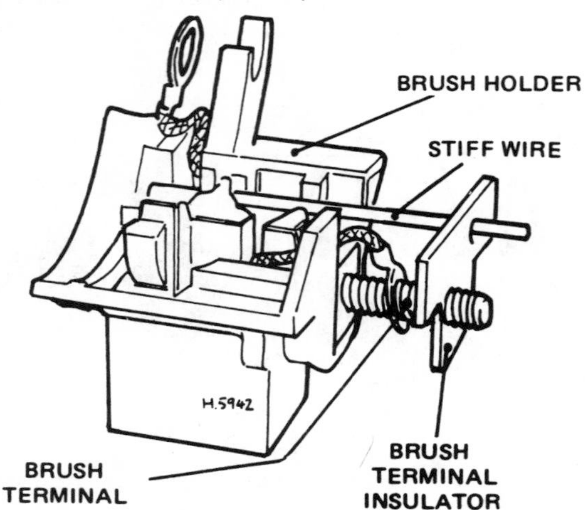

Fig. 11.4 Alternator brush holder assembly (Sec 11)

6 While supporting the alternator, remove the drive belt adjusting and pivot bolts.
7 Lift the alternator away from the vehicle.
8 Installation is the reverse of removal. Tighten the bolts to 35-50 ft-lb.
9 Check for $\frac{1}{2}$ in free play in belt. Adjust as necessary.

10 Alternator-fault diagnosis and repair

1 Due to the specialist knowledge and equipment required to test or service an alternator it is recommended that if the performance is suspect the car be taken to an automobile electrician who will have the facilities for such work. Because of this recommendation information is limited to the inspection and replacement of the brushes.
2 The ammeter (ALT) gauge on the instrument panels indicates the charge (C) or discharge (D) current passing into, or out of the battery. With the electrical equipment switched on and the engine idling the gauge needle may show a discharge condition. However, at fast idle or normal driving speeds the needle should stay on the 'C' side of the gauge; just how far over will depend on the charged state of the battery.
3 If the gauge does not show a charge under these conditions there is a fault in the system and the following points should be checked before inspecting the brushes or, if necessary, replacement of the alternator:

a) Check the fan belt tension, as described in Section 7.
b) Check the battery, as described in Section 3.
c) Check all electrical cable connections for cleanliness and security (Fig. 11.2).

11 Alternator brushes – removal, inspection and replacement

1 Firstly remove the alternator as described in Section 9.
2 Scratch a line across the length of the alternator housing to ensure correct reassembly.
3 Remove the three housing through-bolts, and the nuts and insulators from the rear housing. Make a careful note of all insulator positions.
4 Withdraw the rear housing section from the stator, rotor and front housing assembly (Fig. 11.3).
5 Remove the brushes and springs from the brush holder assembly which is located inside the rear housing.
6 Check the length of the brushes against the wear dimension given in the Specifications at the beginning of this Chapter and replace if necessary.
7 Refit the springs and brushes into the holder assembly and retain them in place by inserting a piece of wire through the rear housing and brush terminal insulator as shown in Fig. 11.4. Make sure enough wire protrudes through the rear of the housing so that it may be withdrawn at a later stage.
8 Refit to the stator the rear housing, rotor and front housing assembly, making sure that the scribed marks line up.
9 Refit the three housing through-bolts and rear end insulators and nuts, but do not tighten.
10 Carefully extract the piece of wire from the rear housing and ascertain as far as possible that the brushes are seated on the slip ring. Tighten the through-bolts and rear housing nuts.
11 Refit the alternator as described in Section 9.

12 Starter motor – general description

1 The starter motor system comprises a motor with an integral positive engagement drive, the battery, a remote control starter switch, a neutral start switch, the starter relay and the necessary wiring.
2 When the ignition switch is turned to the start position the starter relay is energized through the starter control circuit. The relay then connects the battery to the starter motor.
3 Cars fitted with an automatic transmission have a neutral start switch in the starter control circuit which prevents operation of the starter if the selector lever is not in the 'N' or 'P' positions.
4 With the starter in its rest position one of the field coils is

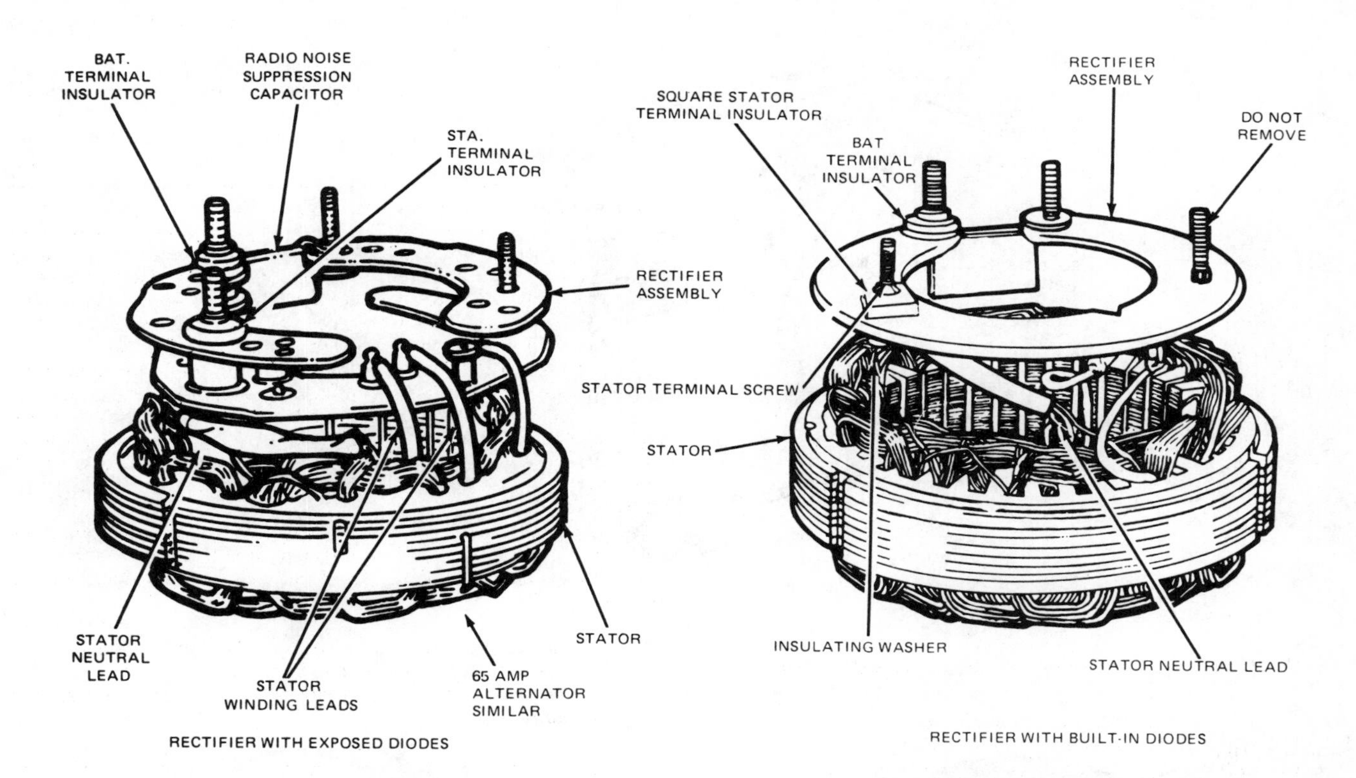

Fig. 11.5 The two types of alternator stator and rectifier assemblies (Sec 11)

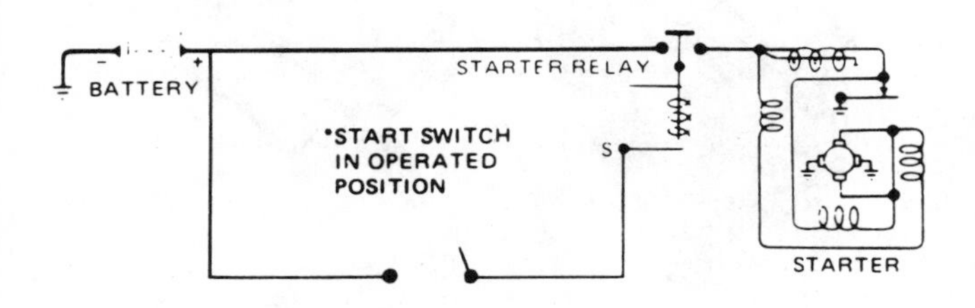

Fig. 11.6 Starting circuit diagram (Sec 12)

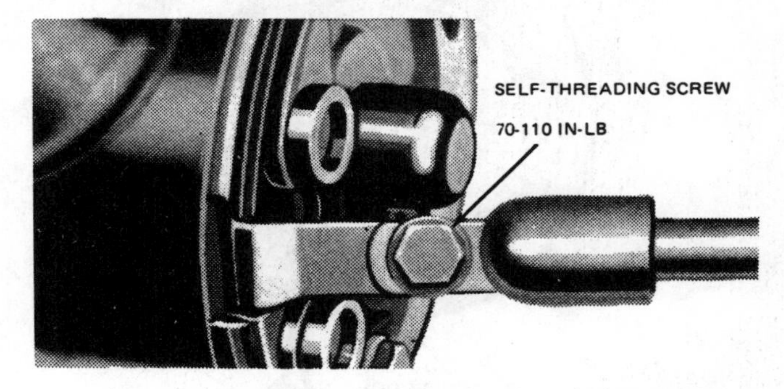

Fig. 11.7 Connector at rear of starter motor (Sec 14)

connected directly to ground through a set of contacts. When the starter is first connected to the battery, a large current flows through the grounded field coil and operates a movable pole shoe. The pole-shoe is attached to the starter drive plunger lever and so the drive is engaged with the ring gear on the flywheel.
5 When the movable pole shoe is fully seated, it opens the field coil grounding contacts and the starter is in a normal operational condition.
6 A special holding coil is used to maintain the movable pole shoe in the fully seated position whilst the starter is turning the engine.

13 Starter motor – testing on engine

1 If the starter motor fails to operate, then check the condition of the battery by turning on the headlights. If they glow brightly for several seconds and then gradually dim, the battery is in a discharged condition.
2 If the headlights continue to glow brightly and it is obvious that the battery is in good condition, check the tightness of the battery leads and all cables relative to the starting system. If possible, check the wiring with a voltmeter or test light for breaks or short circuits.
3 Check that there is current at the relay when the ignition switch is operated. If there is, then the relay should be suspect.
4 If there is no current at the relay, then suspect the ignition switch. On models with automatic transmission check the neutral start switch.
5 Should the above checks prove negative then the starter motor brushes probably need replacement or at the worst there is an internal fault in the motor.

14 Starter motor – removal and replacement

1 Chock the rear wheels, apply the parking brake, jack-up the front of the car and support on firmly based stands.
2 Disconnect the two battery terminals.
3 From beneath the car, remove the four bolts retaining the crossmember beneath the clutch housing, lower the crossmember to the ground.
4 Remove the flexible coupling from the steering gearbox, and remove the three bolts that secure the steering gearbox to the chassis crossmember (refer to Chapter 10).
5 Disengage the steering gearbox from the flexible coupling and pull it downward to provide access to the starter motor.
6 Disconnect the starter motor cable from the starter motor.
7 Undo and remove the three starter motor securing bolts and lift out the motor.
8 Refit the motor using the reverse procedure to removal. When replacing the steering gear assembly refer to Chapter 10.

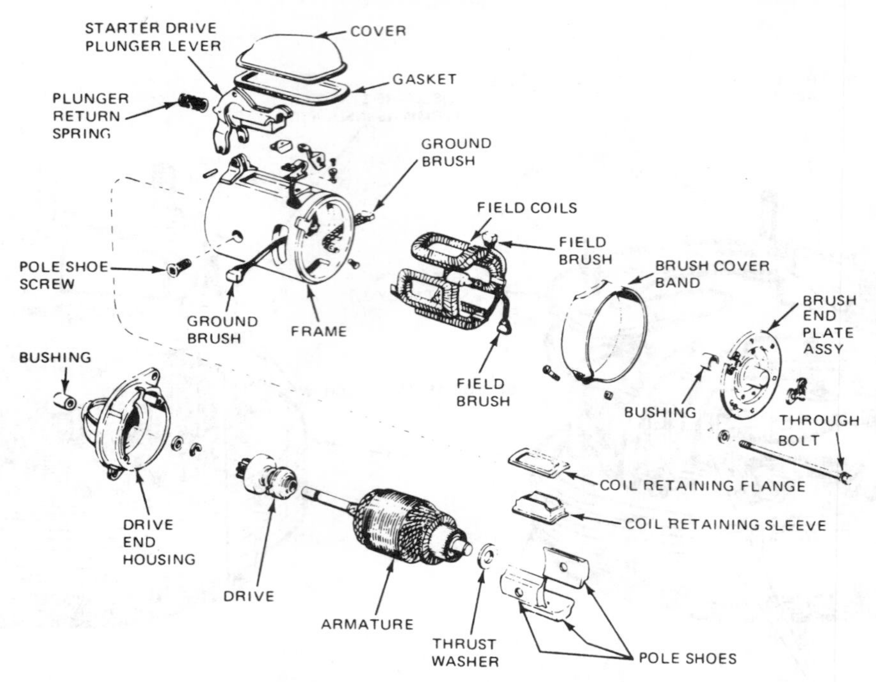

Fig. 11.8 Starter components (Sec 15)

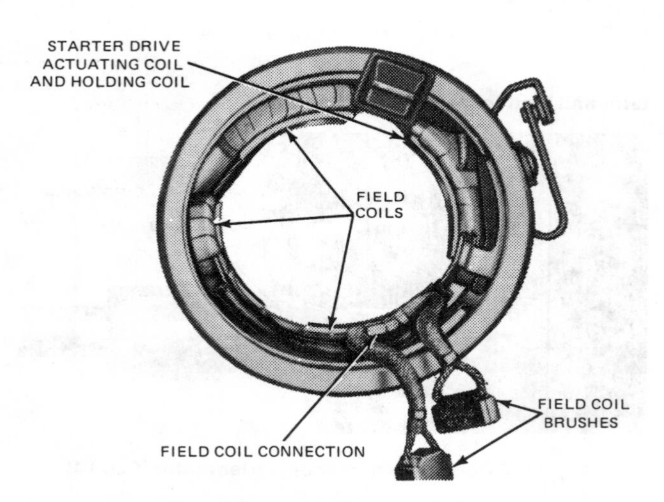

Fig. 11.9 Starter motor brushes and field coils (Sec 15)

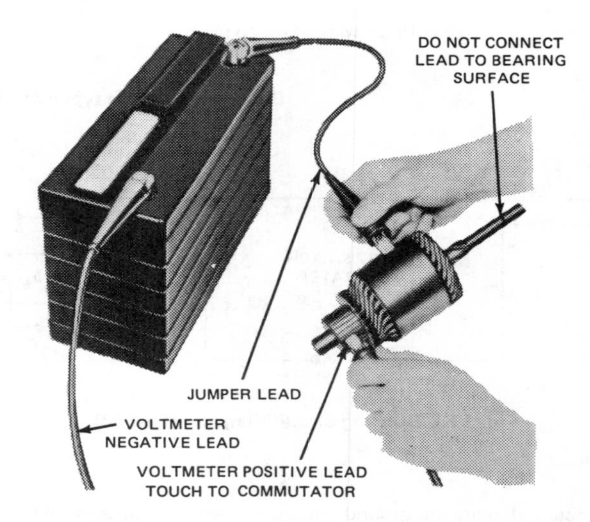

Fig. 11.10 Commutator-grounded test using voltmeter and battery (Sec 15)

15 Starter motor – dismantling, overhaul and reassembly

1 Loosen the brush cover band retaining screw and remove the brush cover band and starter drive plunger lever cover.
2 Note the positions of the leads to ensure correct reassembly and then remove the commutator brushes from the brush holder.
3 Undo and remove the long through-bolts and lift off the drive end housing.
4 Remove the starter drive plunger lever return spring.
5 Remove the pivot pin that retains the starter gear plunger lever, using a suitable diameter pin punch.
6 Lift away the lever and withdraw the armature.
7 Remove the stop ring retainer followed by the stop ring that retains the starter drive gear onto the end of the armature shaft. The stop ring must be discarded and a new one obtained ready for reassembly.
8 Slide the starter drive assembly from the end of the armature.
9 Remove the brush endplate.
10 Unscrew the two screws that secure the ground brushes to the frame.
11 Dismantling should now be considered to be complete as removal of the field coils requires special equipment.
12 Clean the field coils, armature, commutator, armature shaft, brush endplate and drive end housing using a lint-free cloth and brush. Other parts may be washed in a suitable solvent.
13 Carefully inspect the armature windings for broken or burned insulation and unsoldered connections.
14 Test the four field coils for an open circuit. Connect a 12 volt battery and 12 volt bulb to one of the leads between the field terminal post and the tapping point of the field coils to which the brushes are connected. An open circuit is proved by the bulb not lighting.
15 If the bulb lights it does not necessarily mean that the field coils are in order, as there is a possibility that one of the coils will be grounded to the starter yoke or pole shoes. To check this remove the lead from the brush connector and place it against a clean portion of the starter yoke. If the bulb lights, the field coils are grounding.
16 Replacement of the field coils calls for the use of a wheel operated screwdriver, a soldering iron, caulking and riveting operations, and is beyond the scope of the majority of owners. The starter yoke should be taken to a reputable automotive electrical shop for new field coils to be fitted. Alternatively purchase an exchange starter motor.

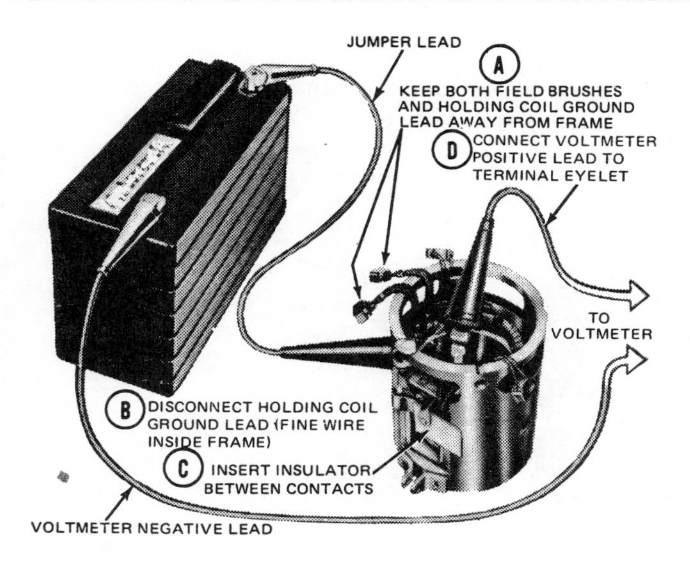

Fig. 11.11 Field coil grounded test (Sec 15)

17 If the armature is damaged this will be evident on inspection. Look for signs of burning, discoloration and for conductors that have lifted away from the commutator.
18 If a bearing is worn so allowing excessive side play of the armature shaft, the bearing bush must be replaced with a new one. Drift out the old bush with a piece of suitable diameter rod, preferably with a shoulder on it to stop the the bush collapsing.
19 Soak a new bush in engine oil for 24 hours or, if time does not permit, heat in an oil bath at 100°C (212°F) for two hours prior to fitting.
20 As a new bush must not be reamed after fitting, it must be pressed into position using a small mandrel of the same internal diameter as the bush and with a shoulder on it. Place the bush on the mandrel and press into position using a bench vise.
21 If the brushes are replaced, their flexible connectors must be unsoldered and the connectors of new brushes soldered in their place. Check that the new brushes move freely in their holders as detailed above. If cleaning the commutator with gasoline fails to remove all the burnt areas and spots, then wrap a piece of glass paper around the commutator and rotate the armature.
22 If the commutator is very badly worn, remove the drive gear. Then mount the armature in a lathe and, with the lathe turning at high speed, take a very fine cut out off the commutator. Do not undercut the mica insulators between the commutator segments.
23 Make sure that the drive moves freely on the armature shaft splines without binding or sticking.
24 To reassemble the starter motor is the reverse sequence to dismantling. The following additional points should be noted:

a) Fill the drive end housing approximately ¼ full with grease.
b) Always use a new stop ring.
c) Lightly lubricate the armature shaft splines with a Lubriplate 777 or thin oil.

16 Starter relay – removal and replacement

1 For safety reasons, disconnect the battery.
2 Make a note of and then disconnect the battery cables, ignition switch and coil wire from the relay.
3 Undo and remove the two screws that secure the relay to the fender apron and lift away the relay.
4 Refitting the starter relay is the reverse sequence to removal.

17 Headlight unit – removal and replacement

1 Remove the screws that secure the chrome headlight door to the front fender. Remove the door (photo).
2 Remove the four screws that secure the sealed beam unit to the adjusting frame.
3 Lift the frame from the bulb unit (photo).
4 Support the bulb while unplugging the multi-pin connector (photo).
5 Connect the connector to the new bulb and complete installation in reverse of above steps.

18 Headlight – alignment

1 It is always advisable to have the headlights aligned on proper optical beam setting equipment but if this is not available the following procedure may be used:
2 Position the car on level ground 10 ft (3.048 meters) in front of a dark wall or board. The wall or board must be at right-angles to the center-line of the car.
3 Draw a vertical line on the board or wall in line with the center-line of the car.
4 Bounce the car on its suspension to ensure correct settlement and then measure the height between the ground and the center of the headlights.
5 Draw a horizontal line across the board or wall at this measured height. On this horizontal line mark a cross on either side of the vertical center-line, the distance between the center of the light unit and the center of the car.
6 Remove the headlight rims and switch the headlights onto full beam.
7 By careful adjusting of the horizontal and vertical adjusting screws on each light, align the centers of each beam onto the crosses which were previously marked on the horizontal line.
8 Bounce the car on its suspension again and check that the beams return to the correct position. At the same time check the operation of the dipswitch. Replace the headlight rims.

17.1 Removing the headlight bezel

17.3 When removing the headlight frame, be careful not to disturb the headlight adjusting screws

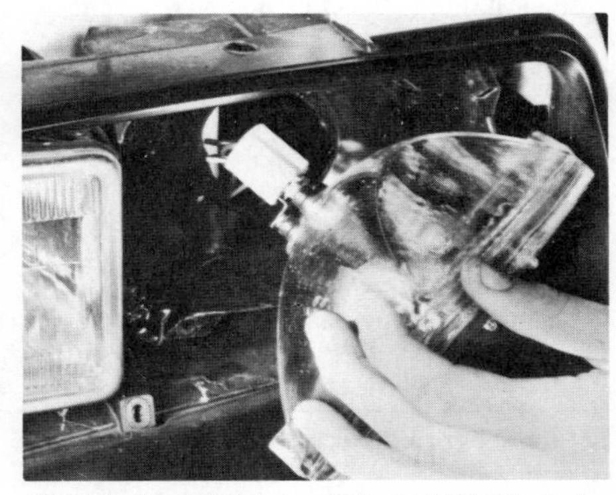

17.4 The headlight should be held firmly and the connector removed from it

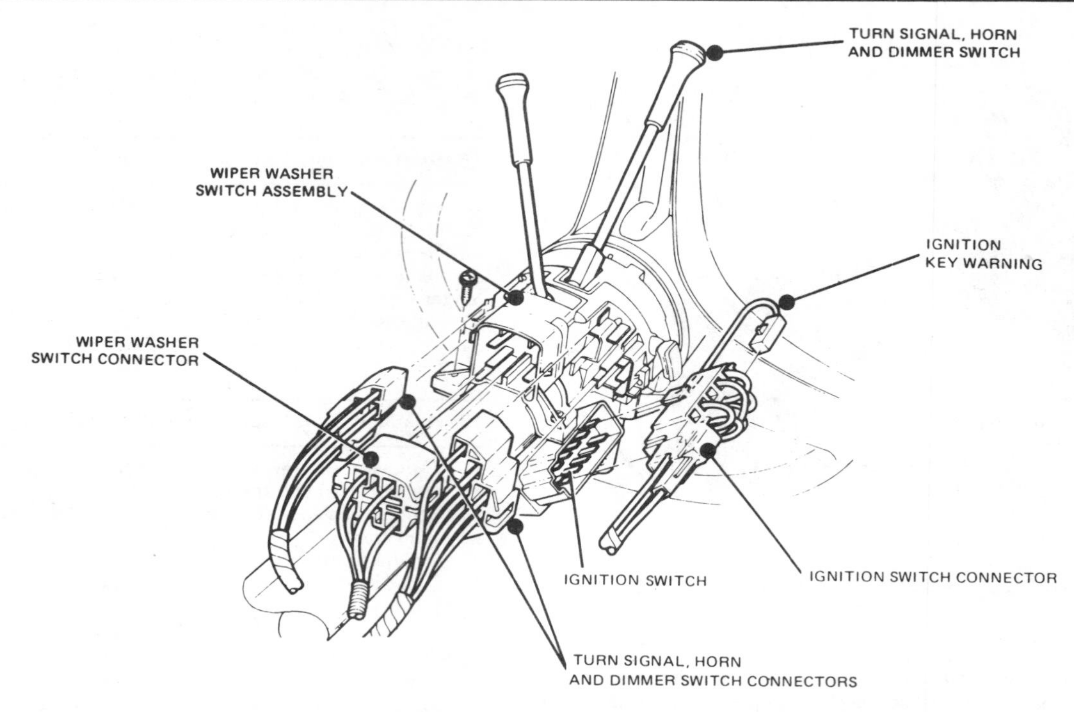

Fig. 11.12 Headlight dimmer and turn signal switches (Secs 19, 20 and 34)

19 Headlight dimmer switch – removal and replacement

1 Disconnect the negative battery cable.
2 Remove the plastic covers on the steering column.
3 Disconnect the wiring connector on the bottom of the steering column.
4 Loosen the retaining screws of the combination horn, turn signal, and dimmer switch.
5 Lift the assembly from the column.
6 Installation is the reverse of removal.

20 Turn signal switch – removal and replacement

1 The turn signal switch is an integral part of the dimmer switch as removed in Section 19. Should replacement be necessary, follow the same steps and precaution.

21 Parking and side clearance lights – removal and replacement

Bulb replacement

1 Unclip the bulb holder and bulb from the backside of the light body assembly (photo).
2 Push the bulb against the tension spring and turn counter-clockwise.
3 Installation is the reverse of removal.

Parking light – body removal

4 Remove the bulb and holder.
5 Remove the four bolts securing the front bumper and brace to the vehicle.
6 Remove the two screws securing the light body to the brace.
7 Installation is the reverse of removal.

22 Rear light cluster – bulb replacement

1 Open the rear deck or trunk lid.
2 Grasp the light bulb holder assembly and turn to release from the housing.

21.1 The front parking lamp bulb can be replaced by reaching up from underneath the car

3 Remove the bulb by depressing and turning counter-clockwise.

23 License plate light – bulb replacement

1 Open the rear deck or trunk lid.
2 Remove the two screws holding the trim plate to the lens.
3 Remove the lens for access to the bulb.
4 Turn and depress the bulb to remove.

24 Stop light switch – removal and replacement

1 Disconnect the negative battery cable.
2 Above the brake pedal near the pivot, remove the electrical wires from the switch.
3 Unclip the pushrod retainer and slide the switch, nylon washers

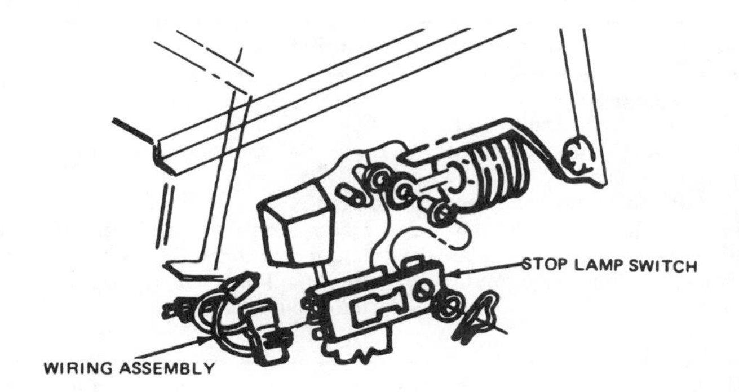

Fig. 11.13 Typical stoplamp switch installation (Sec 24)

and pushrod away from the pedal.

4 Slide the switch off the bracket.

5 Refit the stop light switch in reverse order of removal.

25 Instrument cluster – removal and replacement

Note: *U.S. Federal law requires that the odometer in any replacement speedometer must register the same mileage as that registered in the removed speedometer.*

1 Disconnect the negative battery cable.

2 Remove the three screws retaining the trim to the upper trim cover. Carefully remove the trim (photo).

3 Remove the two upper and two lower retaining screws securing the cluster to the instrument panel.

4 Pull the cluster about 2 inches and support while reaching behind to disconnect the speedometer cable. Press gently on the flat surface of the cable connector to release the cable.

5 Still supporting the cluster, lift the cluster out far enough to gain access to the two electrical connectors attached to the printed circuit receptacles.

6 Disconnect the connectors and lift the cluster away.

7 Installation is the reverse of removal.

25.2 With the trim panel off, the instrument panel is ready for removal

26 Speedometer – removal and replacement

1 Remove the instrument cluster.

2 Remove the seven screws that retain the cluster lens and mask assembly.

3 Remove the two retaining screws on the back of the speedometer head.

4 Remove the speedometer.

5 To replace, position the speedometer head to the cluster housing and secure with 2 screws.

6 Install the cluster lens and mask assembly.

7 Apply a $\frac{3}{16}$ inch ball of silicon damping grease into the drive hole of the speedometer head.

8 Install the instrument cluster

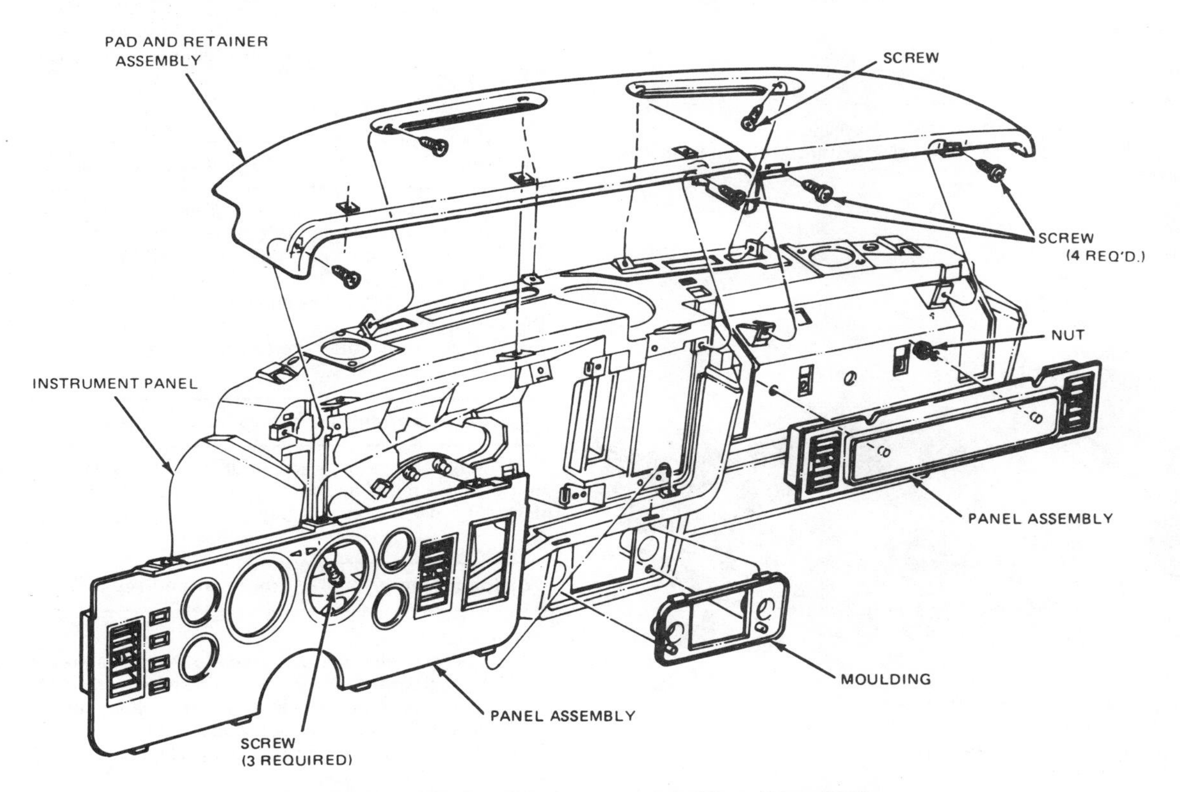

Fig. 11.14 Instrument panel pad components (Secs 25 and 26)

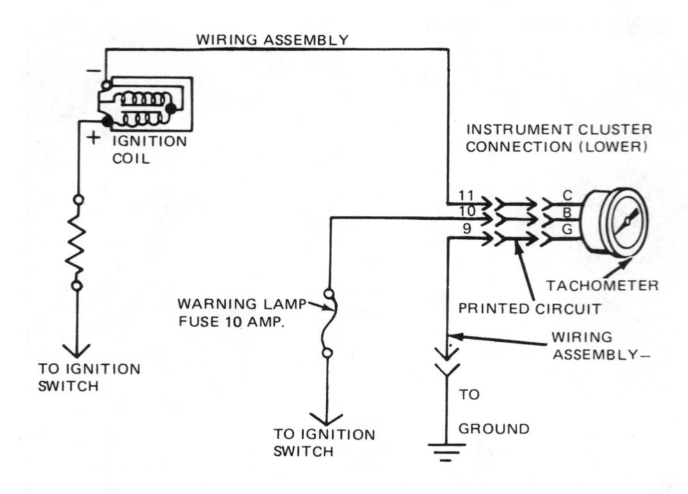

Fig. 11.15 Tachometer wiring diagram (Sec 27)

29.1A Instrument cluster after removal. The printed circuit is on the reverse side

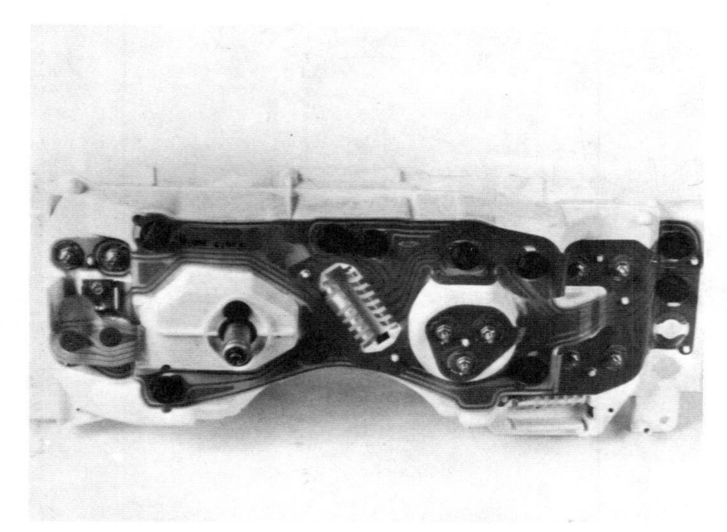

29.1B Instrument cluster printed circuit

27 Tachometer – removal and installation

1 Remove the instrument cluster.
2 Remove the mask and lens assembly.
3 Remove the three nuts securing the tachometer head to the cluster housing.
4 Lift the tachometer from the cluster.
5 The tachometer is fully electric and is not repairable. Should the tachometer require replacement, be sure that the 4/6/8 cylinder mode screw is adjusted to match the correct number of cylinders of the engine. Once set it requires no further adjustment

28 Oil, fuel, amp and temperature gauges – removal and installation

1 Remove the instrument cluster.
2 Remove the two retaining screws for the instrument to be removed.
3 Lift the instrument from the cluster.
4 Installation is the reverse of removal.

29 Instrument cluster printed circuit – service precautions

1 The printed circuit that comprises the 'wiring' of the instrument panel should be handled as little as possible to avoid damage to the circuit sheet (photos).
2 Should the printed circuit sheet require removal, proceed as follows:
3 Loosen the special nuts securing the circuit sheet to the instrument cluster back. Lift out the instrument lights.
4 Carefully lift the sheet from around the mounting studs with a dull-tipped tool. Do not allow the removal tool to scratch the surface of the circuit sheet.
5 Lift the sheet a little at a time across the entire cluster back in order that the sheet is not pulled or creased.
6 For refitting, place the circuit sheet to the back of the cluster. Push the sheet gently onto the mounting studs.
7 Use a small socket to push the circuit sheet to bottom on the stud against the cluster housing. Install the smaller printed circuit sheet first.
8 Snug the special lock nuts, do not overtighten and stress the circuit sheet.

30 Turn signal flasher unit – removal and replacement

1 The turn signal flasher unit is fitted on the main fuse panel which is located in the lower left of the instrument panel behind a trim panel.
2 The flasher unit simply plugs into the fuse panel and is retained by a spring clip.
3 To remove, grip firmly and pull straight out, taking care not to bend the connector tabs.
4 Replace using the reverse procedure.

31 Hazard warning lights flasher unit – removal and replacement

1 The hazard warning flasher unit is fitted adjacent to the turn signal unit and the removal and replacement procedure is the same as that described in the previous Section.

32 Speedometer cable – removal and replacement

Inner Cable

1 Working behind the instrument panel disconnect the speedometer cable from the rear of the speedometer head.
2 Carefully pull the speedometer inner cable out from the upper end of the speedometer cable outer casing.
3 If the inner cable is broken, raise the car and working underneath undo and remove the bolt that secures the speedometer cable mounting clip to the transmission.

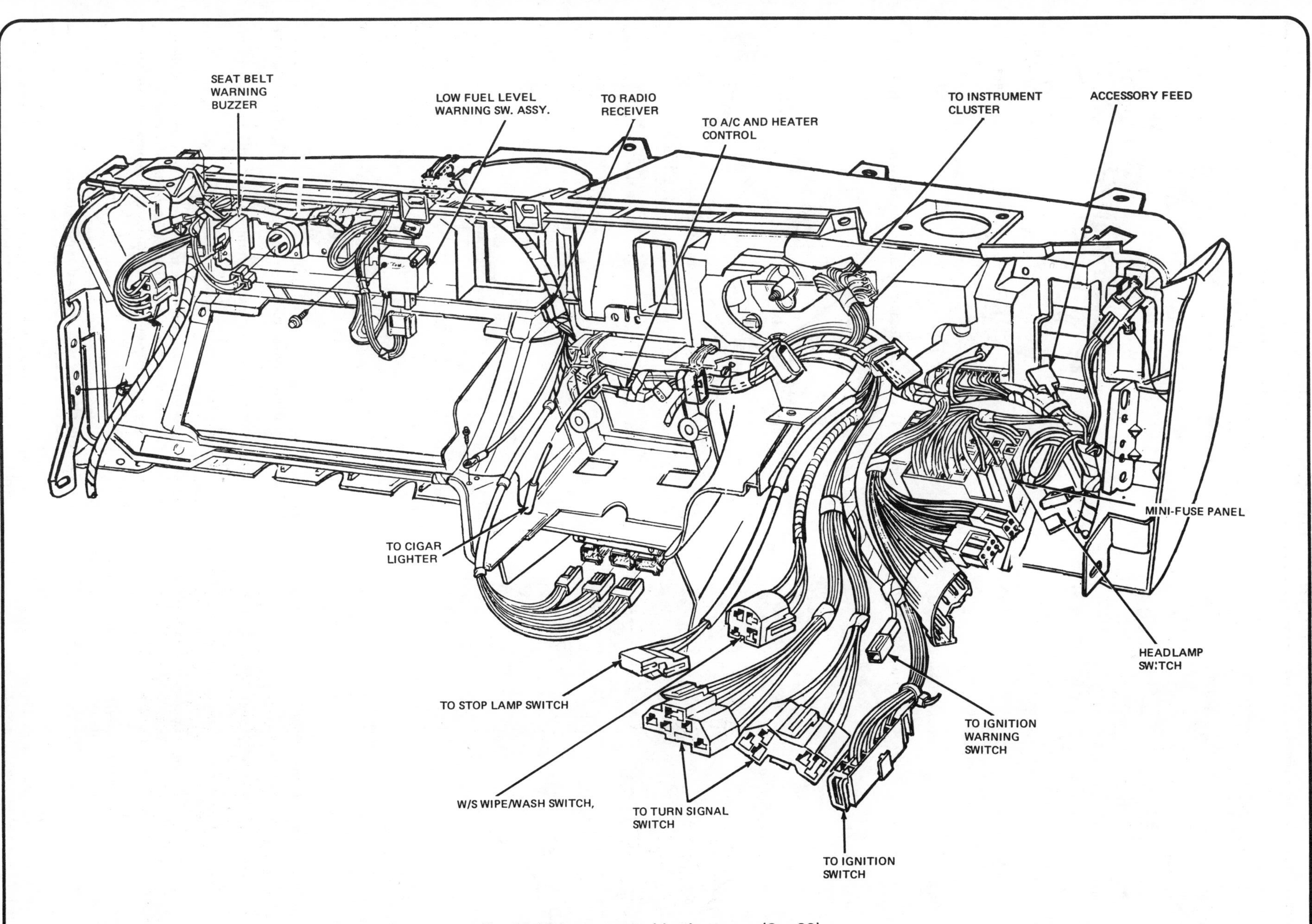

Fig. 11.16 Instrument wiring harnesses (Sec 29)

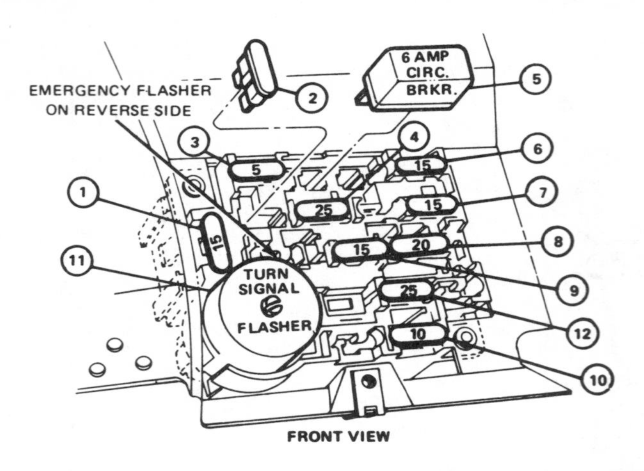

Fig. 11.17 Fuse panel and circuit breaker (Secs 30 and 37)

1 *Turn signal back-up lamps 15 amp. fuse*
2 *Heater (std.) 15 amp. fuse air conditioning 30 amp. fuse*
3 *Instrument panel lamps 5 amp. fuse*
4 *Accessory- A/C clutch 25 amp. fuse*
5 *Windshield wiper/washer 6 amp. circuit breaker*
6 *Stop lamps – emergency warning 15 amp. fuse*
7 *Courtesy lamps 15 amp. fuse*
8 *Cigar lighter - horn 20 amp fuse*
9 *Radio 15 amp. fuse*
10 *Warning lamps 10 amp. fuse*
11 *Turn signal flasher*
12 *Electric choke 25 amp. fuse*

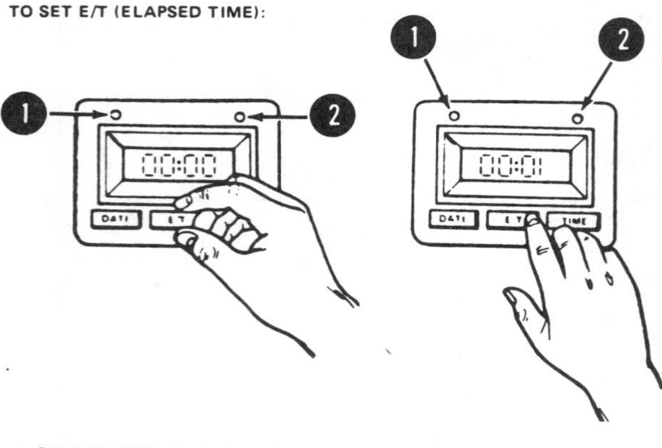

Fig. 11.19 Digital clock Elapsed Time (E/T) setting procedure (Sec 33)

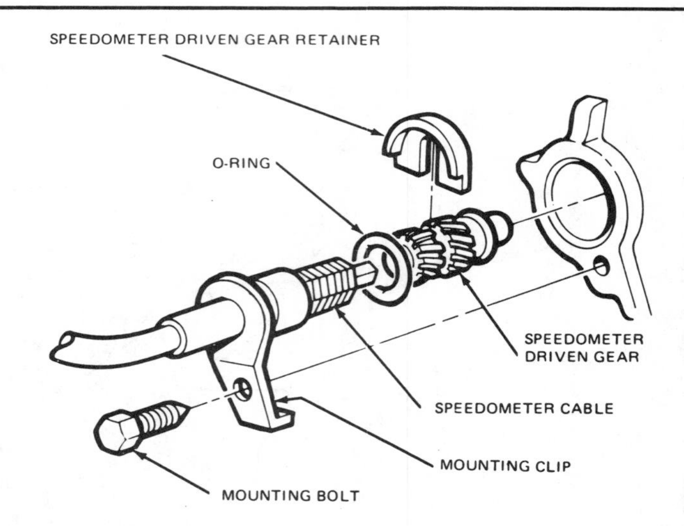

Fig. 11.18 Speedometer connection at transmission (Sec 32)

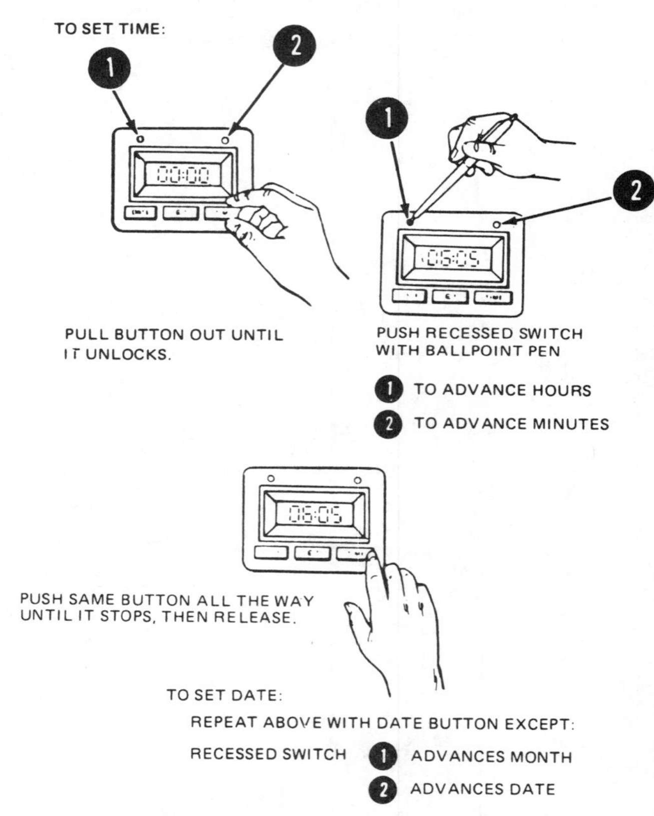

Fig. 11.20 Digital clock time and date setting procedure (Sec 33)

4 Remove the speedometer cable shaft and driven gear from the transmission.
5 Remove the driven gear retainer and the driven gear and shaft from the cable.
6 Remove the lower part of the broken inner cable from the end of the outer casing.
7 Refitting the new speedometer inner cable is the reverse sequence to removal.
8 Lightly lubricate the inner cable and insert into the outer casing. When the cable has nearly all been inserted turn the end to ensure that the squared end is engaged with the speedometer driven gear.

Outer cable

9 Working behind the instrument panel disconnect the speedometer cable from the rear of the speedometer head.
10 Push the outer cable and grommet through the opening in the dashboard panel.
11 Raise the car and working underneath detach the cable from all its retaining clips.
12 Disconnect the cable from the transmission as described earlier in this Section and withdraw from under the car (Fig. 11.18).
13 Refit the speedometer cable using the reverse procedure to removal.

33 Electric clock – removal and replacement

1 Disconnect the battery ground terminal.
2 Remove the screws securing the top of the instrument panel trim, unsnap the lower trim fingers from the panel and remove the trim.

3 Undo and remove the screws that secure the clock to the instrument panel.
4 Lift out the clock and disconnect the feed wire and bulb socket.
5 Replace the clock using the reverse procedure to removal.

Clock adjustment

6 Adjustment of the clock is automatic. Should the clock run too fast or too slow it is only necessary to reset the clock to the correct time. This action will automatically reset the adjuster.

34 Ignition switch – removal and replacement

1 The ignition switch is located on the upper side of the steering wheel under the shroud and is operated by a rod connected to the key-actuated lock cylinder.
2 Remove the steering column shroud.
3 Disconnect the battery ground cable.
4 Pull apart the ignition switch electrical connector.
5 Using a $\frac{1}{8}$ inch drill, drill out the two 'break off head' bolts which connect the switch to the lock cylinder.
6 Remove the bolts using an 'easy out' tool.
7 Remove the pin that connects the switch plunger to the actuating rod and lift away the switch.
8 To adjust the switch during installation, slide the carrier to the LOCK position. Insert a .050 inch drill bit through the switch housing into the carrier so that the carrier can't move.
9 To hold the mechanical parts of the column in the LOCK position, move the selector lever to PARK (automatic transmission) or to the reverse position (manual transmission). Turn the key to the LOCK position and remove the key.
10 New replacement switches are supplied pinned in the LOCK position by a plastic pin inserted in the end of the switch.
11 Position the hole in the end of the switch up to the hole in the actuator and install the connecting pins.
12 Install new 'break off head' bolts and tighten them until the heads break off.
13 Adjust the pin to release the drill bit used for adjustment.
14 Remove the plastic locking pin re-connect the electrical connector, steering column shroud and battery negative cable.
15 Check for proper operation.

35 Ignition switch lock cylinder – removal and replacement

1 For safety reasons, disconnect the battery ground terminal.
2 Remove the horn pad and steering wheel as described in Chapter 10.
3 Insert a wire pin in the hole located inside the column halfway down the lock cylinder housing.
4 Move the selector lever to the PARK position (automatic transmission) or the reverse position (manual gearbox) and turn the lock cylinder with the ignition key inserted to the RUN position.
5 To remove the lock cylinder press the wire pin while pulling up on the lock cylinder.
6 To fit the lock cylinder insert it into its housing in the flange casing. Turn the key to the OFF position. This action will extend the cylinder retaining pin into the cylinder housing.
7 Turn the key to ensure correct operation in all positions.
8 Refit the steering wheel and horn pad.

36 Seat belt and ignition warning buzzers – removal and replacement

1 Disconnect the negative battery terminal.
2 The seat belt warning buzzer, and key-in-the-ignition warning buzzer are located behind the right-hand side of the instrument panel.
3 Remove the three screws retaining the top of the right-hand side trim panel, unclip the lower fingers, and lift off the panel.
4 Remove the buzzer retaining clips and lift out the buzzer. Disconnect the wiring connectors.
5 Refit the buzzer using the reverse procedure.

37 Fuses

1 The fuse panel is located behind a removable cover in the left side of the instrument panel.
2 Most of the electrical circuits are protected by fuses and fuse identification is given in the caption to Fig. 11.17. If a fuse blows always trace the cause and rectify before replacing the fuse.

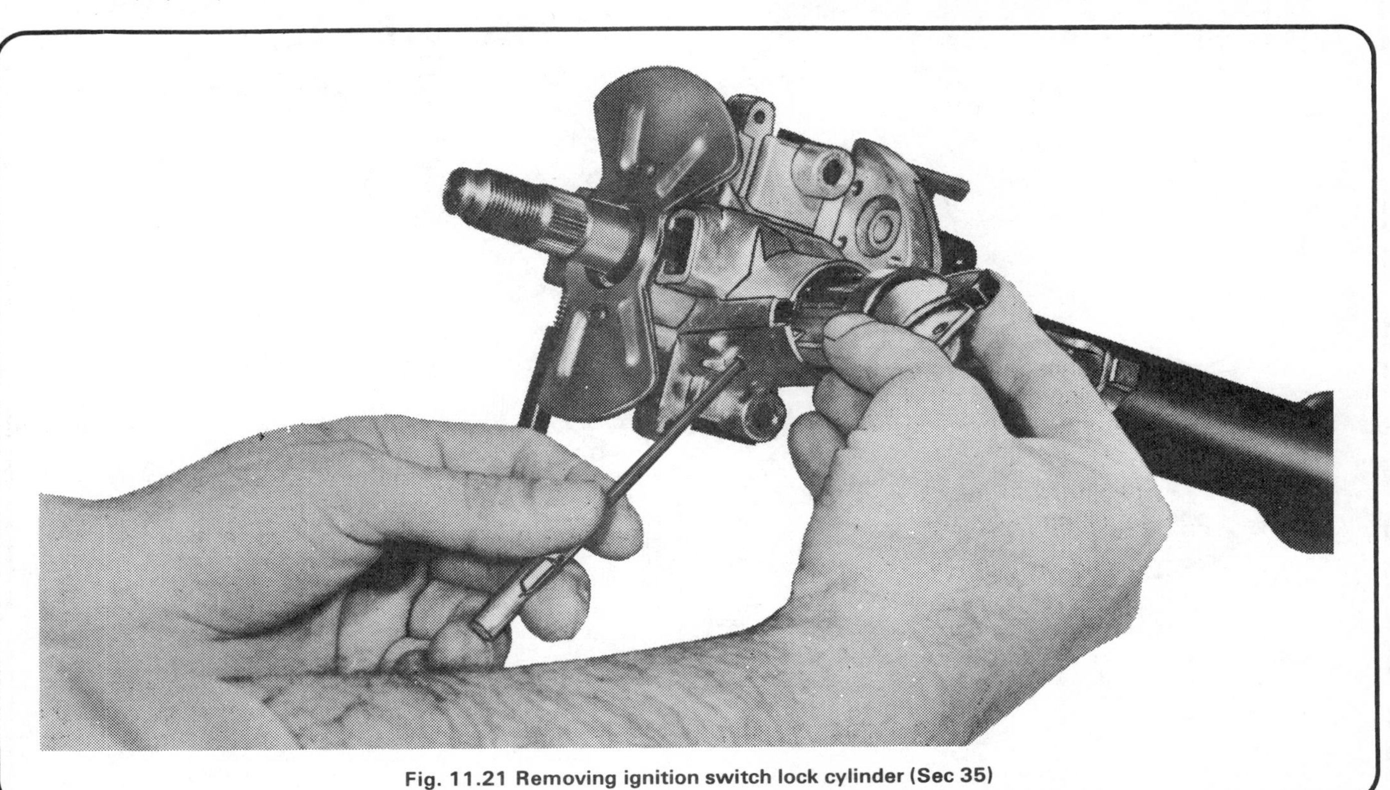

Fig. 11.21 Removing ignition switch lock cylinder (Sec 35)

38 Windshield wiper blades – removal and replacement

The windshield wiper blades fitted can be one of two types. With the bayonet type the blade saddle slides over the end of the arm and is engaged by a locking stud. With the side saddle pin type a pin on the arm indexes into the side of the blade saddle and engages a spring loaded clip in the saddle.

Bayonet type – 'TRICO'

1 To remove a 'TRICO' blade press down on the arm to disengage the top stud.
2 Depress the tab on the saddle to release the top stud and pull the blade from the arm.

Bayonet type – 'ANCO'

3 To remove an 'ANCO' blade press inwards on the tab and pull the blade from the arm.

Saddle pin type – 'TRICO'

4 To remove a pin type 'TRICO' blade insert a screwdriver into the spring release opening of the blade saddle, depress the spring clip and pull the blade from the arm.

39 Windshield wiper arm – removal and replacement

1 Before removing a wiper arm, turn the windshield wiper switch on and off to ensure the arms are in their normal parked position parallel with the bottom of the windshield.
2 To remove the arm, swing the arm away from the windshield, depress the spring clips in the wiper arm boss and pull the arm off the spindle.
3 When replacing the arm, position it in the parked position and push the boss onto the spindle.

40 Windshield wiper mechanism – fault diagnosis and rectification

1 Should the windshield wipers fail, or work very slowly, then check the terminals on the motor for loose connections, and make sure the insulation of all the wiring is not cracked or broken, thus causing a short circuit. If this is in order then check the current the motor is taking by connecting an ammeter in the circuit and turning off the wiper switch. Consumption should be between 2.3 and 3.1 amps.
2 If no current is passing through the motor, check that the switch is operating correctly.
3 If the wiper motor takes a very high current check the wiper blades for freedom of movement. If this is satisfactory check the gearbox cover and gear assembly for damage.
4 If the motor takes a very low current ensure that the battery is fully charged. Check the brush gear and ensure the brushes are bearing on the commutator. If not, check the brushes for freedom of movement and, if necessary, renew the tension springs. If the brushes are very worn they should be replaced with new ones. Check the armature by substitution if this unit is suspect.

41 Windshield wiper motor – removal and installation

1 Remove the air vent grille, loosen the two nuts and disconnect the wiper pivot shaft and link assembly from the motor drive arm ball.
2 Undo and remove the three bolts securing the motor to the engine compartment firewall.
3 Disconnect the multi-pin connector from the main wiring harness and lift away the motor.
4 Refitting the windshield wiper motor is the reverse sequence to removal.

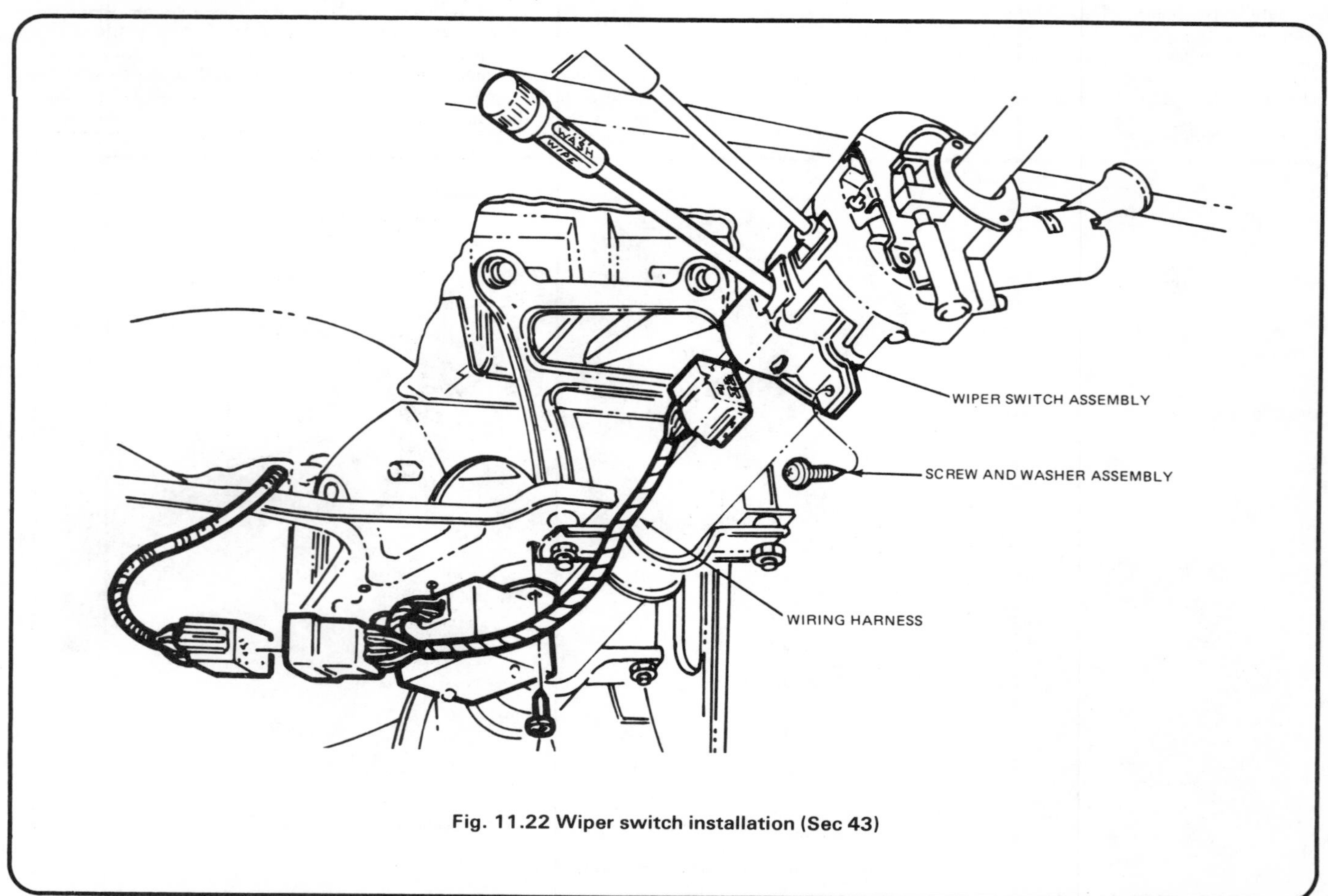

Fig. 11.22 Wiper switch installation (Sec 43)

42 Windshield wiper pivot shaft and link assembly – removal and installation

1 Disconnect the battery ground cable.
2 Remove the air vent grille (see Chapter 12).
3 Remove the linkage drive arm clip and disconnect the drive arm from the motor crank pin.
4 Remove the two bolts retaining the right pivot shaft to the cowl and the large nut, washer and spacer from the left pivot shaft.
5 Before reinstallation, make certain that the motor is in PARK. The distance between the wiper blades and windshield lower molding should be between $1\frac{1}{2}$ and $3\frac{1}{2}$ inches. The right-hand pivot shaft should be torque tightened to 60-85 in-lb (7-9 Nm) and the left-hand pivot nut should be tightened to 70-100 in-lb (8-12 Nm).
6 The remainder of reinstallation is a reversal of removal.

43 Windshield wiper switch – removal and installation

1 Disconnect the battery ground cable.
2 Remove the four screws holding the steering column shroud in place. Separate by grasping the top and bottom of the shroud and pulling apart.
3 Using a flat bladed screwdriver, push off the wiper switch connector.
4 Remove the two wiper switch attaching screws (Fig. 11.22).
5 Remove the wiper switch.
6 Installation is the reverse of removal.

44 Windshield wiper motor – dismantling, inspection and reassembly

1 Undo and remove the gear cover securing screws and lift away the ground terminal and cover (Fig. 11.23).
2 Carefully remove the idler gear and pinion retainer.
3 Lift away the idler gear and pinion and recover the thrust washer.
4 Undo and remove the two long motor through-bolts, and separate the housing, switch terminal insulator sleeve and armature.
5 Suitably mark the position of the output arm relative to the shaft to ensure correct reassembly.
6 Undo and remove the output arm retaining nut, output arm, spring washer, flat washer, output gearshaft assembly, thrust washer and parking switch lever and washer in that order.
7 Remove the brushplate and switch assembly and finally remove the switch contact to parking lever pin from the gear housing.
8 Thoroughly clean all parts and then inspect the gear housing for signs of cracks, distortion, or damage.
9 Carefully check all shafts, brushes and gears for signs of scoring or damage.
10 If the brushes are worn they should be replaced with new ones.
11 Any serious fault with the armature such as a breakdown in insulation necessitates a new motor assembly.
12 Reassembly of the windshield wiper motor is the reverse sequence to dismantling and will present no problems provided that care is taken.

45 Windshield washer reservoir and pump – removal and replacement

1 Remove the wiring connector plug and washer hose.
2 Undo and remove the retaining screws and lift the washer and motor assembly away from the left-hand side fender apron.
3 To remove the pump motor from the reservoir, pry out the retaining ring and carefully pull the motor out of the reservoir recess (see Fig. 11.24).
4 The motor and pump assembly cannot be repaired, and if faulty must be replaced with a new unit.
5 When refitting the motor into the reservoir, make sure the projection on the motor body is lined up with the slot in the reservoir.
6 Press on the motor retaining ring and refit the reservoir assembly to the car using the reverse procedure to removal.

46 Horn – fault diagnosis and rectifiation

1 If the horn works badly or fails completely, check the wiring leading to the horn plug located on the body panel next to the horn

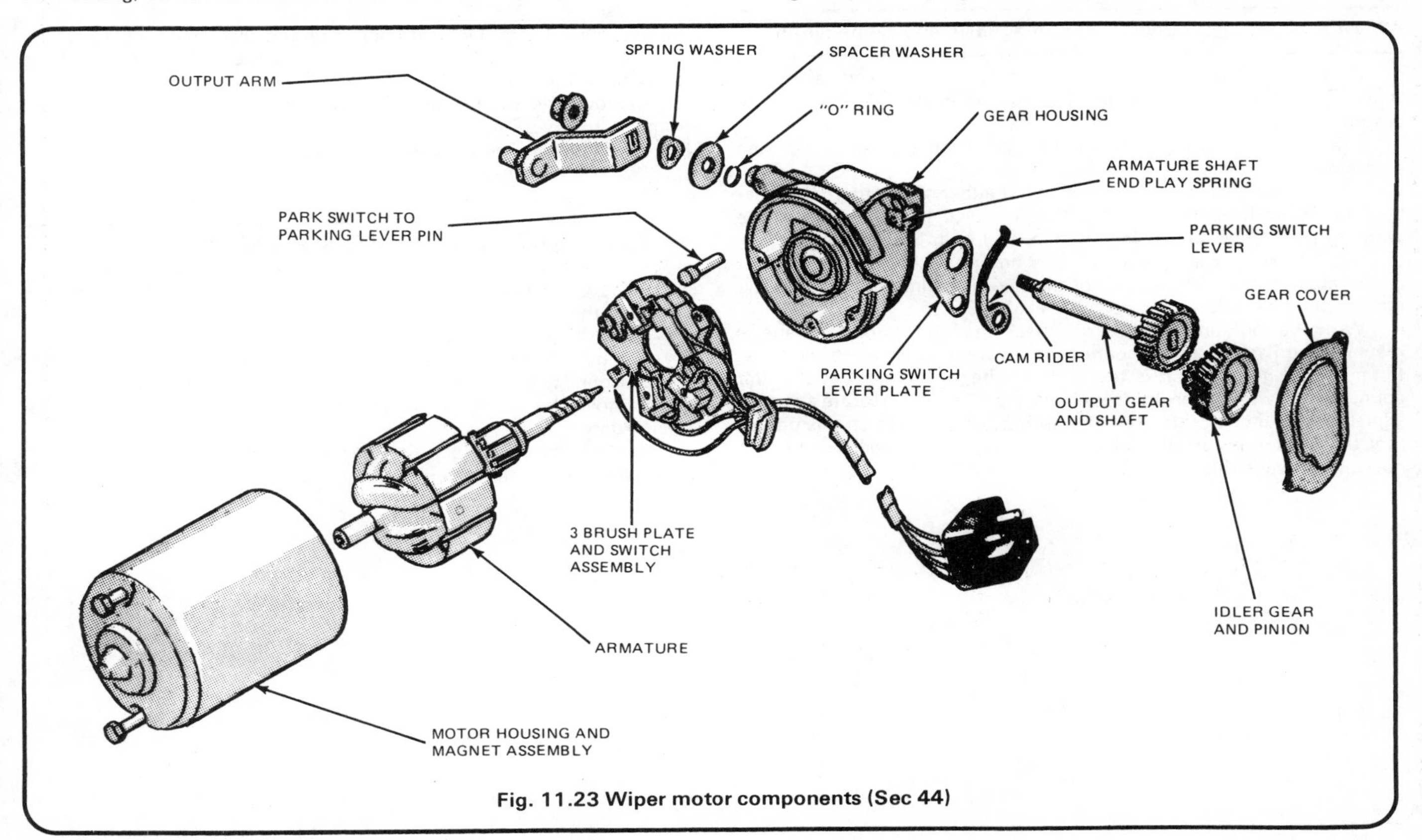

Fig. 11.23 Wiper motor components (Sec 44)

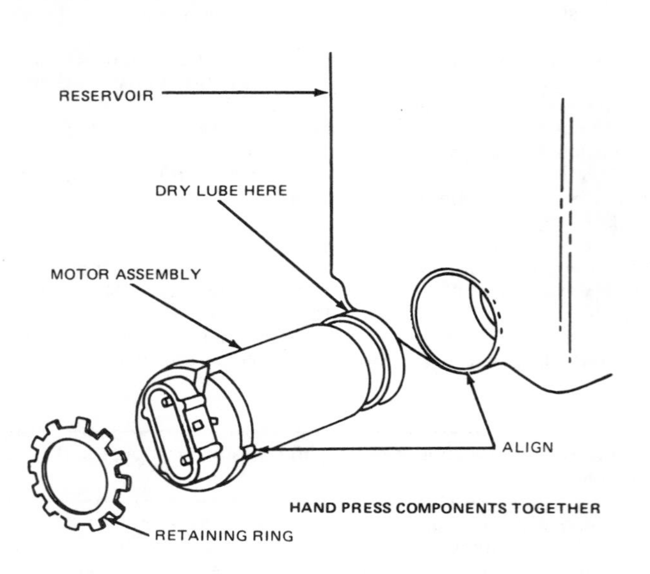

Fig. 11.24 Windshield washer reservoir and motor (Sec 45)

itself. Also check that the plug is properly pushed home and is in a clean condition free from corrosion etc.

2 Check that the horn is secure on its mounting and that there is nothing lying on the horn body.

3 If the fault is not an external one, remove the horn cover and check the leads inside the horn. If they are sound, check the contact breaker contacts. If these are burnt or dirty clean them with a fine file and wipe all traces of dirt and dust away with a solvent-moistened rag.

47 Turn signal light circuit – fault diagnosis and rectification

Should the flasher unit fail to operate, or work very slowly or rapidly, check out the turn signal circuit as detailed below, before assuming that there is a fault in the unit.

1 Examine the turn signal light bulbs, both front and rear, for broken filaments.

2 If the external flashers are working but either of the internal flasher warning lights have ceased to function, check the filaments in the warning light bulbs and replace with a new bulb if necessary.

3 If a flasher bulb is sound but does not work check all the flasher circuit connections with the aid of the relevant wiring diagram at the end of this Chapter.

4 With the ignition switched on check that the correct voltage is reaching the flasher unit by connecting a voltmeter between the 'plus' terminal and ground. If it is found that voltage is correct at the unit connect the two flasher unit terminals together and operate the turn signal switch. If one of the flasher warning lights comes on this proves that the flasher unit itself is at fault and must be replaced as it is not possible to dismantle and repair it.

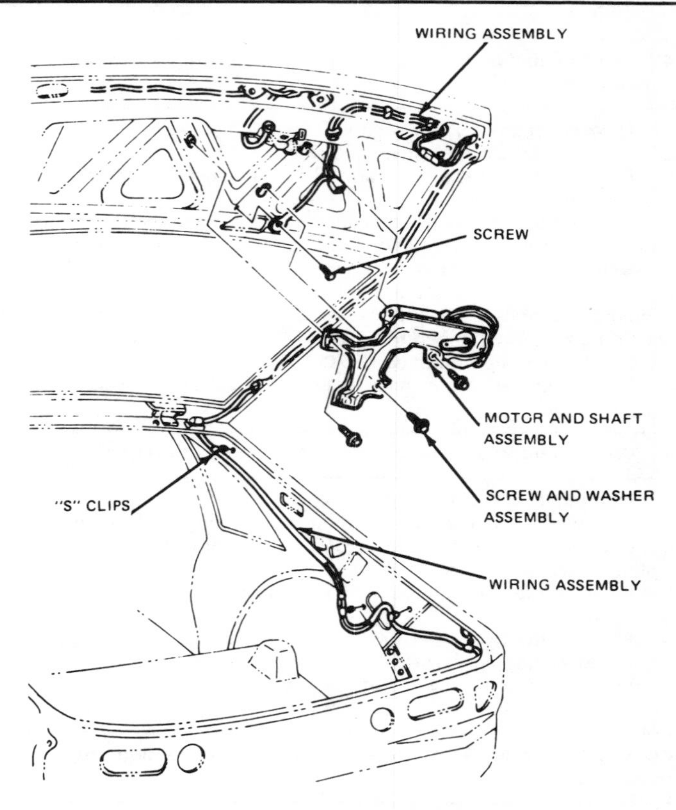

Fig. 11.25 Rear window wiper installation (Sec 49)

48 Rear window washer – removal and installation

1 Remove the screws securing the left rear trim panel and remove the panel.

2 Disconnect the electrical connector and reservoir supply hose.

3 Using a small standard screwdriver, pry the motor assembly from its mounting position.

4 Remove the washer screen and seal. Flush any foreign matter from the reservoir or motor.

5 Installation is the reverse of removal.

49 Rear wiper and motor – removal and installation

1 Raise the wiper arm off the rear window. Pull the slide latch and lift away the wiper arm.

2 Remove the pivot shaft nuts and washers.

3 Remove the liftgate trim screws and panel.

4 Disconnect the electrical plug to the wiper motor.

5 Remove the three screws securing the motor and linkage to the rear liftgate.

6 Remove the motor and linkage as an assembly.

7 Installation is the reverse of removal.

Identification of wiring diagram ground codes

Ground codes	Location
G-101	On dash behind battery
G-401	Eyelet on 14290 near L.H. headlamp
G-402	Eyelet on 14398 near R.H. headlamp
G-403	Eyelet on 15A808 near transmission indicator lamp
G-405	Eyelet on 14334 for grounding dome lamp
G-501	In 14405, on deck lid striker plate
G-502	In 14401, behind glove box
G-601	Part of heater motor assembly, located in engine compartment or R.H. side of dash panel
G-602	Part of A/C clutch, located on compressor
G-603	Under mounting bolt of solenoid valve
G-904	Eyelet on 13412, or 14A549, near license lamps
G-905	Eyelet on 4405
G-906	In 14A303, under shield near seat
G-907	Eyelet on 13B440
G-908	In 9A340, near inertia switch
G-1000	Eyelet on 18C617, mounted to instrument panel
G-1001	Eyelet on 18C620 attached to R.H. inner panel
G-1003	Eyelet on 14025 to L.H. front door inner panel
G-1004	Eyelet on 18C617
G-1005	Eyelet on 9A839 speed control
G-1100	Eyelet on 17N400 rear window wiper motor
G-1101	Eyelet on 17A413 for rear windshield washer pump motor
G-1400	Part of W/S wiper governor

Identification of wiring diagram splice codes

Splice codes	Location
S-102	In 14305, near T/O to starter relay
S-104	In 14A435, near connector to starter motor relay
S-105	In 14401, near T/O to windshield wiper switch
S-106	In 14398, near T/O alternator regulator
S-109	In 15K702, near T/O to starter motor relay
S-110	In 14401, near T/O to W/S/Wiper switch
S-111	In 14401, near T/O to windshield wiper switch
S-112	In 14401, near T/O to radio
S-115	In 14398, near T/O to starter relay
S-116	In 14398, near T/O to starter relay
S-202	In 14398, near T/O to starter motor relay
S-206	In 14401, near T/O to printed circuit
S-301	In 14401, near T/O to 14290
S-302	In 14401, near T/O to radio
S-303	In 14401, near T/O to transmission
S-304	In 14305, near T/O to electric choke
S-305	In 13A705, near T/O to diode
S-306	In 13A705, near T/O to diode
S-307	In 14290, near T/O to diode
S-401	In 14290, near T/O to L.H. parking lamp
S-404	In 14290, near T/O to ground
S-406	In 14405, near T/O to R.H. tail lamps
S-408	In 14398, near T/O to R.H. front side marker lamp
S-501	In 14398, near T/O to L.H. tail lamps
S-502	In 14405, near T/O to license lamp
S-503	In 14405, near T/O to 14401
S-504	In 14405, near T/O to L.H. tail lamps
S-505	In 14405, near T/O to R.H. rear stop and turn light
S-508	In 18C617, near heated backlite warning lamp
S-510	In 13412, or 14A549 or 198516
S-511	In 14335, near T/O to dome lamp
S-701	In 14401, near T/O to headlamp switch
S-702	In 14A200, near T/O to 14A285
S-703	In 14024, near T/O to power door lock switch
S-704	In 14024, near T/O to power door lock switch
S-802	In 14401, near T/O to printed circuit
S-803	In 14398, near T/O to R.H. headlamp
S-804	In 14401, near T/O to seat belt warning buzzer
S-805	In 14401, near T/O to back up lamp switch
S-806	Mode switch in 19049, near T/O to A/C
S-807	Blower resistor in 19049, near T/O to A/C
S-808	In 9E724, near ground eyelet
S-809	In 14290, near grommet
S-810	In 14290, near T/O to W/S wiper motor
S-904	In 14405, near T/O to L.H. license lamp
S-905	In 14303, R.H. side of I/P
S-906	In 14A303, under shield near seat
S-907	In 14290, near starter relay
S-908	In 14290, near starter relay
S-1002	In 14A318, near T/O to 14401
S-1003	In 14A318, near T/O to cigar lighter
S-1004	In 18C618, near T/O to L.H. license lamp
S-1005	In 14A318, near T/O to clock in console

Key to wiring diagrams – 1979 models (Figs. 11.26 thru 11.45)

Wiring color key Primary colors	
Black	Bk
Brown	Br
Tan	T
Red	R
Pink	Pk
Orange	O
Yellow	Y
Dark green	Dg
Light green	Lg
Dark blue	Db
Light blue	Lb
Purple	P
Gray	Gy
White	W
Hash	(H)
Dot	(D)

Stripe is understood and has no color key

Component	Diag	
Alternator		
40 Amp	2	A1
60 Amp	2	B3
70 Amp	2	B4
Ammeter	2	B12
Amplifier		
Speed control	10	C5
Armature		
Luggage comp door latch	8	E16
Backlite		
Heated	5	E16
Battery		
12 Volt	1	B3
12 Volt	2	B5
Capacitor		
Radio ignition interference	2	F3
Radio ignition interference	2	D11
Choke		
Electric	2	D2
Radio receiver suppression	3	B5
Clock	8	C15
Coil		
Ignition	2	D11
Control		
AM Radio RR speaker volume	6	D4
Distributor		
2.3 Liter breakerless	2	D6
2.8 Liter breakerless	2	F6
8 Cyl 302 breakerless	2	E6
Flasher		
Emergency warning	4	C7
Turn signal	4	B6
Gauge		
Fuel	3	B12
Water temp	3	B2
Governor		
W/S Wiper	10	C14
Heater		
Engine block	3	D16
Horn		
High pitch	4	E3
Lamp		
A/C & Heater controls illum	7	D4
Clock illumination	7	D2
Cluster illumination (2)	7	B7
Cluster illumination (5)	7	C5
Console ash tray illumination	7	B8
Dome	8	D9
Dome	8	D10

Component	Diag	
Dome/map switch	8	E5
Dome/map switch	8	D11
Dual brake warning indicator	3	B3
Engine compartment	8	C3
Glove box switch	8	C14
Heater backlite warning ind	5	E15
Heater controls illumination	7	D3
Hi beam indicator	4	F4
I/P Ash tray illumination	7	D1
L.H. Backup	5	E3
L.H. Front side marker	4	D9
L.H. Hi beam head	4	D10
L.H. License	5	D6
L.H. Lo beam head	4	D10
L.H. Front park & T/S	4	D11
L.H. Stop and park	5	D4
L.H. Stop and park	5	D5
L.H. Turn indicator	4	F5
Luggage compartment	8	E13
PRNDL Illumination (floor)	7	A8
R.H. Backup	5	E3
R.H. Front side marker	4	D16
R.H. Hi beam head	4	D15
R.H. License	5	C7
R.H. Lo beam head	4	D14
R.H. Front park & T/S	4	D13
R.H. Stop and park	5	E6
R.H. Stop and park	5	E7
R.H. Turn indicator	4	F7
Seat belts warning indicator	3	D13
Stereo indicator	6	A8
Lighter		
Cigar	8	C2
Modulator		
Breakerless ignition	2	C14
Motor		
Blower	7	E10
Blower	7	E12
Starter	2	B6
W/S Washer pump	10	E9
W/S Washer pump	10	F14
W/S Wiper	10	E10
W/S Wiper	10	F12
Panel		
Fuse	1	B3
Receiver		
AM Radio	6	B2
AM Radio	7	D5
AM with stereo rape radio	7	D8
AM/FM Monaural radio	6	B3
AM/FM Monaural radio	7	E6
AM/FM/MPX Radio	6	B4
AM/FM/MPX Radio	7	D6
Cassette AM/FM/MPX Radio	6	B7
Stereo tape/ AM/FM/MPX Radio	6	A12
Stereo tape/ AM/FM/MPX Radio	7	E7
Regulator		
Alternator	2	E1
Instrument cluster voltage	3	C5
Relay		
Back window heat control	5	B14
Starter motor	1	B4
Starter motor	2	B6
Resistor		
Blower motor	7	D9
Blower motor	7	D11
Sender		
A.T.C. Water temp ind SW	3	F2

Component	Diag	
Fuel gauge	3	D13
Water temperature indicator	3	F1
Sensor		
Exhaust gas oxygen	2	B13
Servo		
Speed control	10	F5
Solenoid		
A/C Clutch	7	E14
Carb throttle emission cont	3	F4
Carburetor float bowl vent	3	E3
Carburetor float bowl vent	3	D5
Carburetor valve control	2	E15
Speaker		
R.H. Front radio receiver	6	D8
R.H. Front radio receiver	6	C16
Radio receiver	6	E1
Radio receiver	6	D1
Radio receiver	6	D6
Radio receiver	6	C10
Radio receiver rear seat	6	F2
Radio receiver rear seat	6	F4
Radio receiver rear seat	6	F6
Radio receiver rear seat	6	F8
Radio receiver rear seat	6	E10
Radio receiver rear seat	6	E16
Switch		
A/C Mode	7	A13
Back window heater control	5	A13
Backup lamp	5	B3
Backup lamp	5	B4
Courtesy lamp	8	A6
Courtesy lamp	8	A7
Dual brake warning	3	E2
Gear shift neutral	3	E5
Gear shift neutral	5	B1
Headlamp	1	C10
Headlamp	4	C2
Headlamp	8	A4
Heater blower	7	C10
Heater mode	7	A9
Ignition	1	D5
Ignition	3	D8
Ignition key warning	8	E6
L.H. Power door lock	5	D9
Luggage comp door lock	8	A16
Oil pressure	2	E16
Park brake signal lamp	3	D15
R.H. Power door lock	5	D13
Rear window washer	10	C10
Rear hatch courtesy lamp	8	C13
Seat belt buckle	3	D14
Seat belt warning indicator	3	B14
Seat belt warning indicator	8	C6
Speed control	10	E2
Stoplamp	4	B5
Stoplamp	10	A5
Turn and emergency signal	4	C5
Turn and emergency signal	9	C5
W/S/W Washer	10	B11
W/S/W Washer	10	B14
A/C Control	7	C11
Tachometer	3	D12
Thermostat		
A/C Evaporator	7	C16
Valve		
Carburetor solenoid vacuum	7	E13

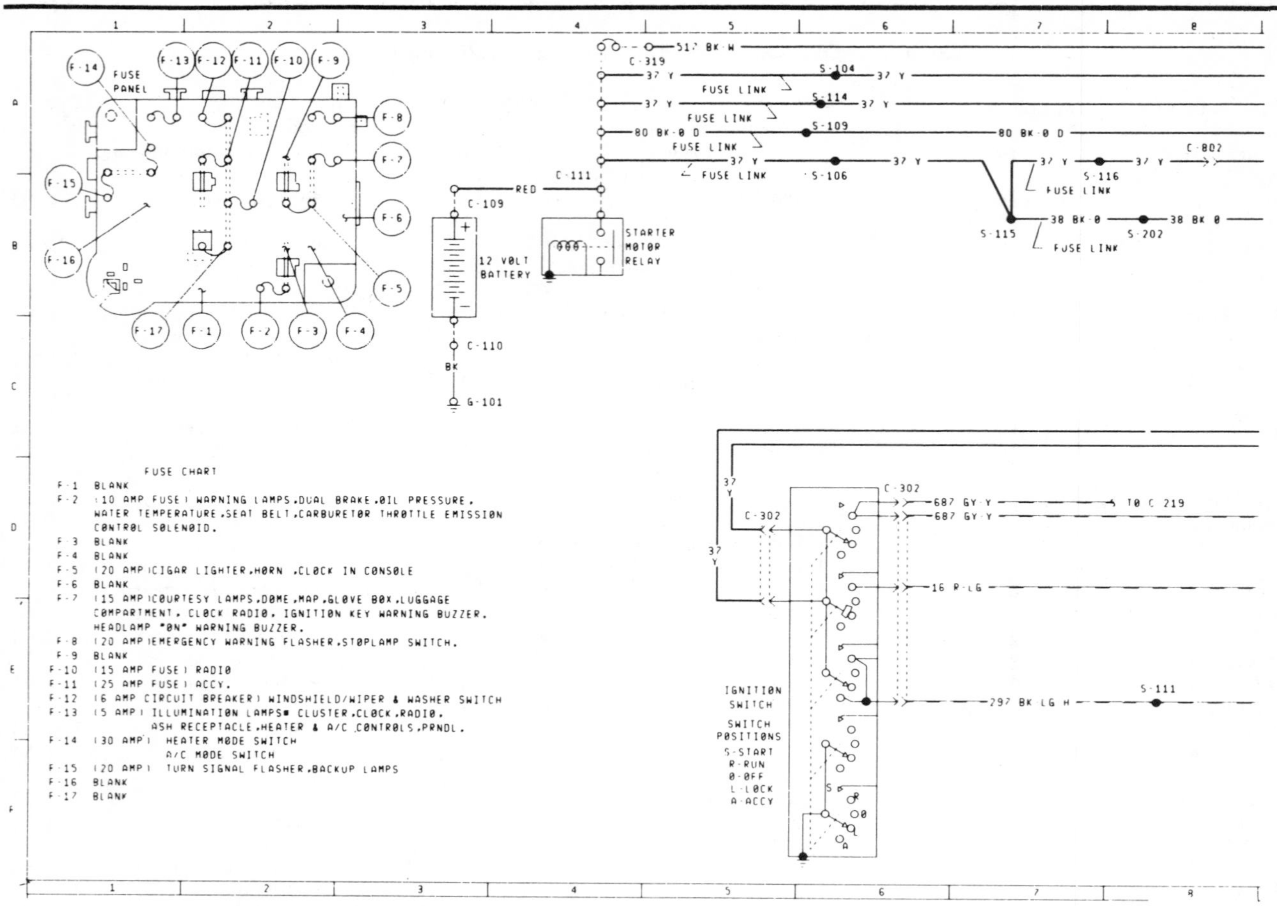
FUSE PANEL
C-319
517 BK-W
37 Y
S-104
FUSE LINK
S-114
80 BK-O D
S-109
S-106
S-116
C-802
38 BK-O
S-115
S-202
C-111
RED
C-109
12 VOLT BATTERY
STARTER MOTOR RELAY
C-110
BK
G-101
FUSE CHART
F-1 BLANK
F-2 (10 AMP FUSE) WARNING LAMPS,DUAL BRAKE,OIL PRESSURE, WATER TEMPERATURE,SEAT BELT,CARBURETOR THROTTLE EMISSION CONTROL SOLENOID.
F-3 BLANK
F-4 BLANK
F-5 (20 AMP)CIGAR LIGHTER,HORN ,CLOCK IN CONSOLE
F-6 BLANK
F-7 (15 AMP)COURTESY LAMPS,DOME,MAP,GLOVE BOX,LUGGAGE COMPARTMENT, CLOCK RADIO, IGNITION KEY WARNING BUZZER, HEADLAMP "ON" WARNING BUZZER.
F-8 (20 AMP)EMERGENCY WARNING FLASHER,STOPLAMP SWITCH.
F-9 BLANK
F-10 (15 AMP FUSE) RADIO
F-11 (25 AMP FUSE) ACCY.
F-12 (6 AMP CIRCUIT BREAKER) WINDSHIELD/WIPER & WASHER SWITCH
F-13 (5 AMP) ILLUMINATION LAMPS* CLUSTER,CLOCK,RADIO, ASH RECEPTACLE,HEATER & A/C CONTROLS,PRNDL.
F-14 (30 AMP) HEATER MODE SWITCH A/C MODE SWITCH
F-15 (20 AMP) TURN SIGNAL FLASHER,BACKUP LAMPS
F-16 BLANK
F-17 BLANK
C-302
687 GY-Y
TO C 219
16 R-LG
297 BK-LG H
S-111
IGNITION SWITCH
SWITCH POSITIONS
S-START
R-RUN
O-OFF
L-LOCK
A-ACCY

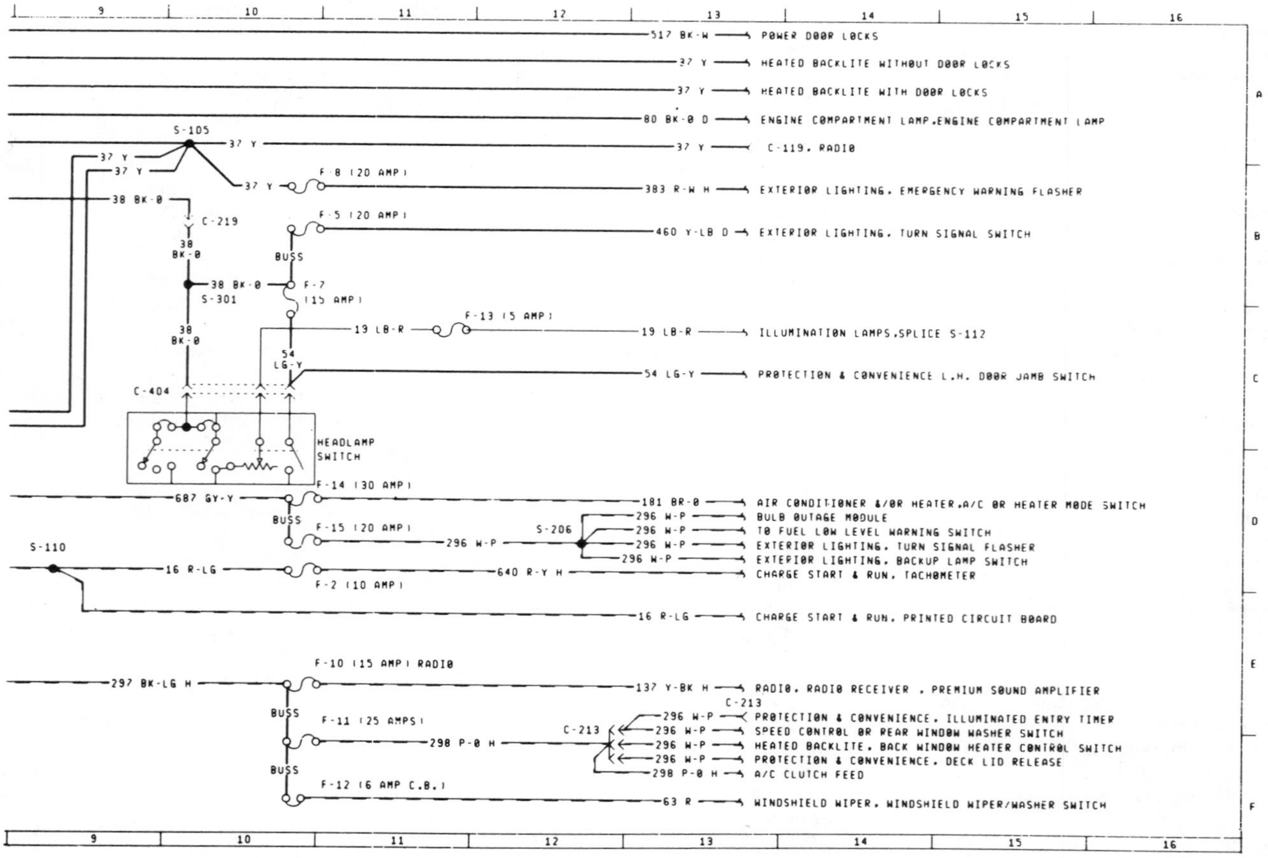
517 BK-W POWER DOOR LOCKS
37 Y HEATED BACKLITE WITHOUT DOOR LOCKS
37 Y HEATED BACKLITE WITH DOOR LOCKS
80 BK-O D ENGINE COMPARTMENT LAMP,ENGINE COMPARTMENT LAMP
S-105
37 Y C-119, RADIO
F-8 (20 AMP)
383 R-W H EXTERIOR LIGHTING, EMERGENCY WARNING FLASHER
C-219
F-5 (20 AMP)
460 Y-LB D EXTERIOR LIGHTING, TURN SIGNAL SWITCH
BUSS
S-301
F-7 (15 AMP)
F-13 (5 AMP)
19 LB-R ILLUMINATION LAMPS,SPLICE S-112
54 LG-Y PROTECTION & CONVENIENCE L.H. DOOR JAMB SWITCH
C-404
HEADLAMP SWITCH
F-14 (30 AMP)
181 BR-O AIR CONDITIONER &/OR HEATER,A/C OR HEATER MODE SWITCH
F-15 (20 AMP)
S-206
296 W-P BULB OUTAGE MODULE
296 W-P TO FUEL LOW LEVEL WARNING SWITCH
296 W-P EXTERIOR LIGHTING, TURN SIGNAL FLASHER
296 W-P EXTERIOR LIGHTING, BACKUP LAMP SWITCH
S-110
F-2 (10 AMP)
640 R-Y H CHARGE START & RUN, TACHOMETER
16 R-LG CHARGE START & RUN, PRINTED CIRCUIT BOARD
F-10 (15 AMP) RADIO
137 Y-BK H RADIO, RADIO RECEIVER , PREMIUM SOUND AMPLIFIER
F-11 (25 AMPS)
C-213
296 W-P PROTECTION & CONVENIENCE, ILLUMINATED ENTRY TIMER
296 W-P SPEED CONTROL OR REAR WINDOW WASHER SWITCH
296 W-P HEATED BACKLITE, BACK WINDOW HEATER CONTROL SWITCH
296 W-P PROTECTION & CONVENIENCE, DECK LID RELEASE
298 P-O H A/C CLUTCH FEED
F-12 (6 AMP C.B.)
63 R WINDSHIELD WIPER, WINDSHIELD WIPER/WASHER SWITCH

Figs. 11.26 and 11.27 Wiring diagram – Power distribution (1) 1979 models

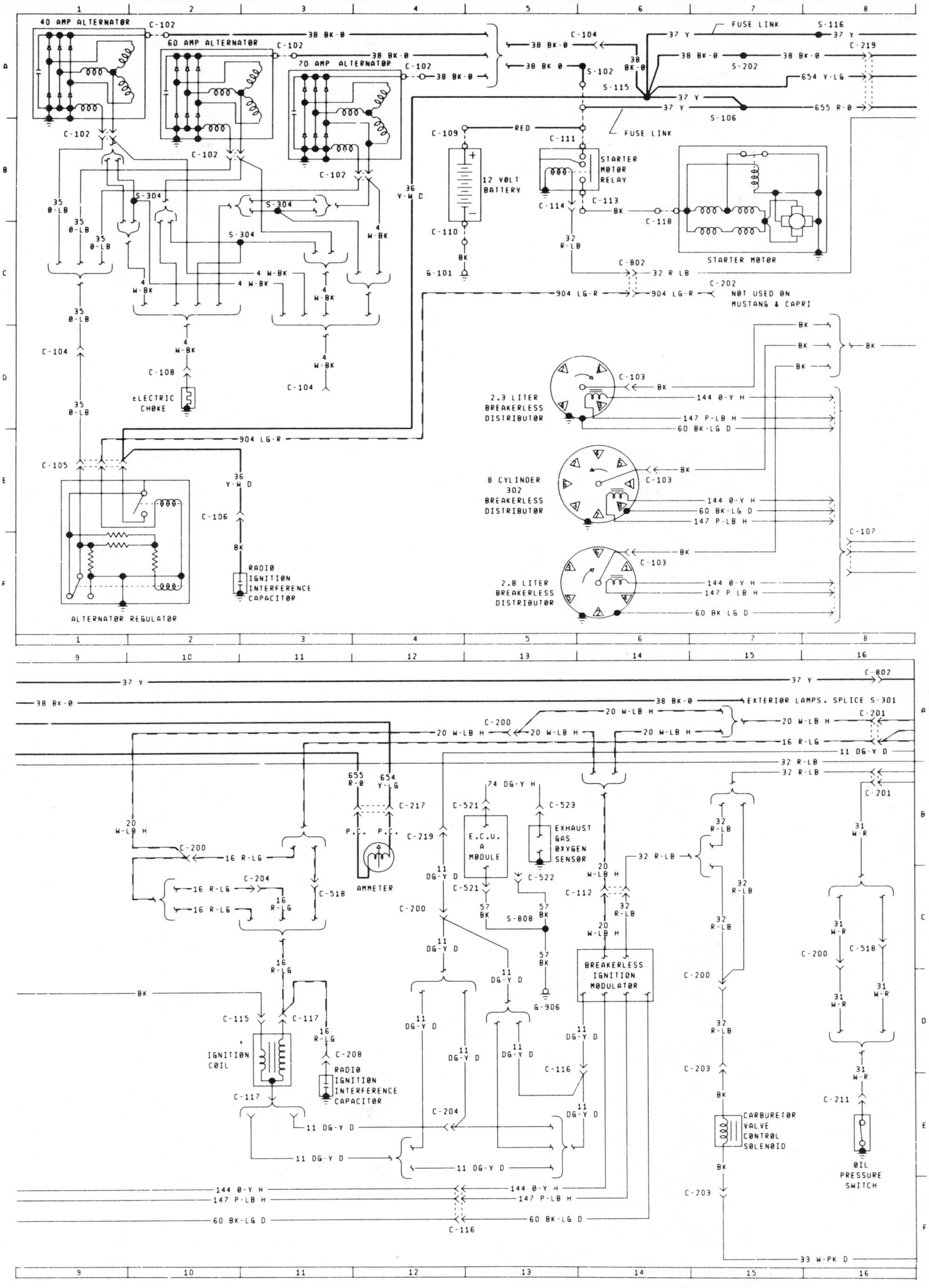

Figs. 11.28 and 11.29 Wiring diagram – Charging, starting and running circuits (2) 1979 models

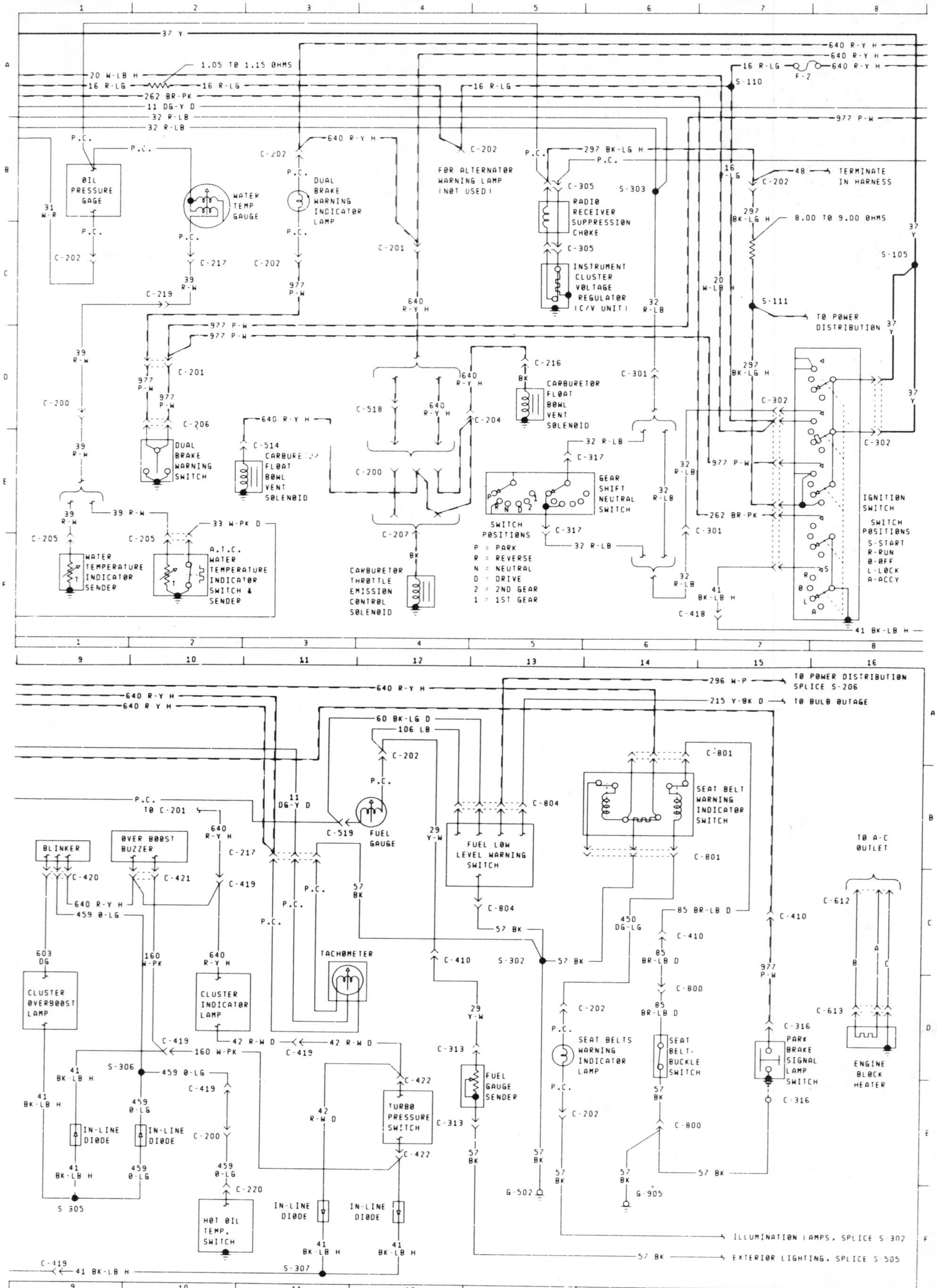

Figs. 11.30 and 11.31 Wiring diagram – Charging, starting, running, protection and convenience (3) 1979 models

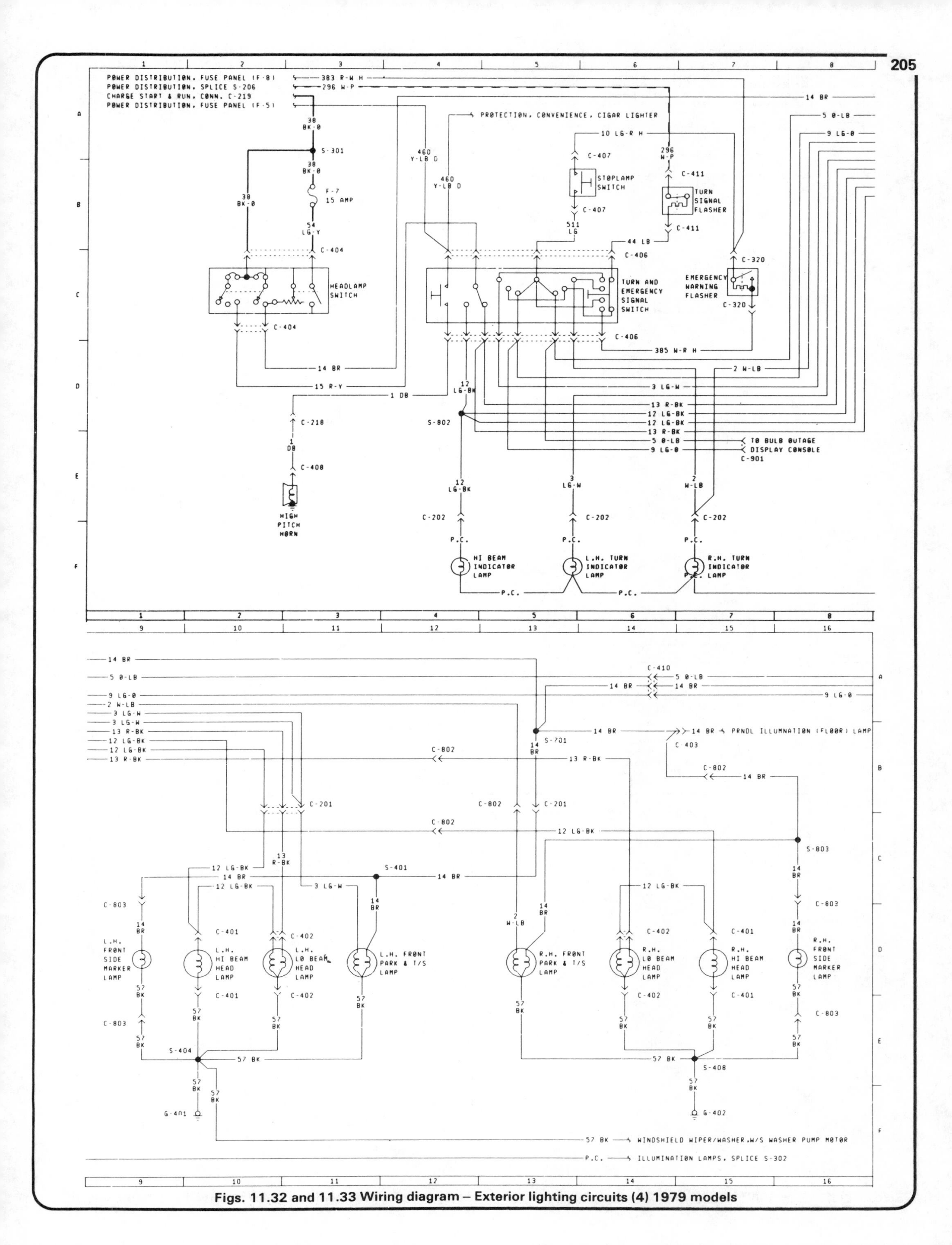

Figs. 11.32 and 11.33 Wiring diagram – Exterior lighting circuits (4) 1979 models

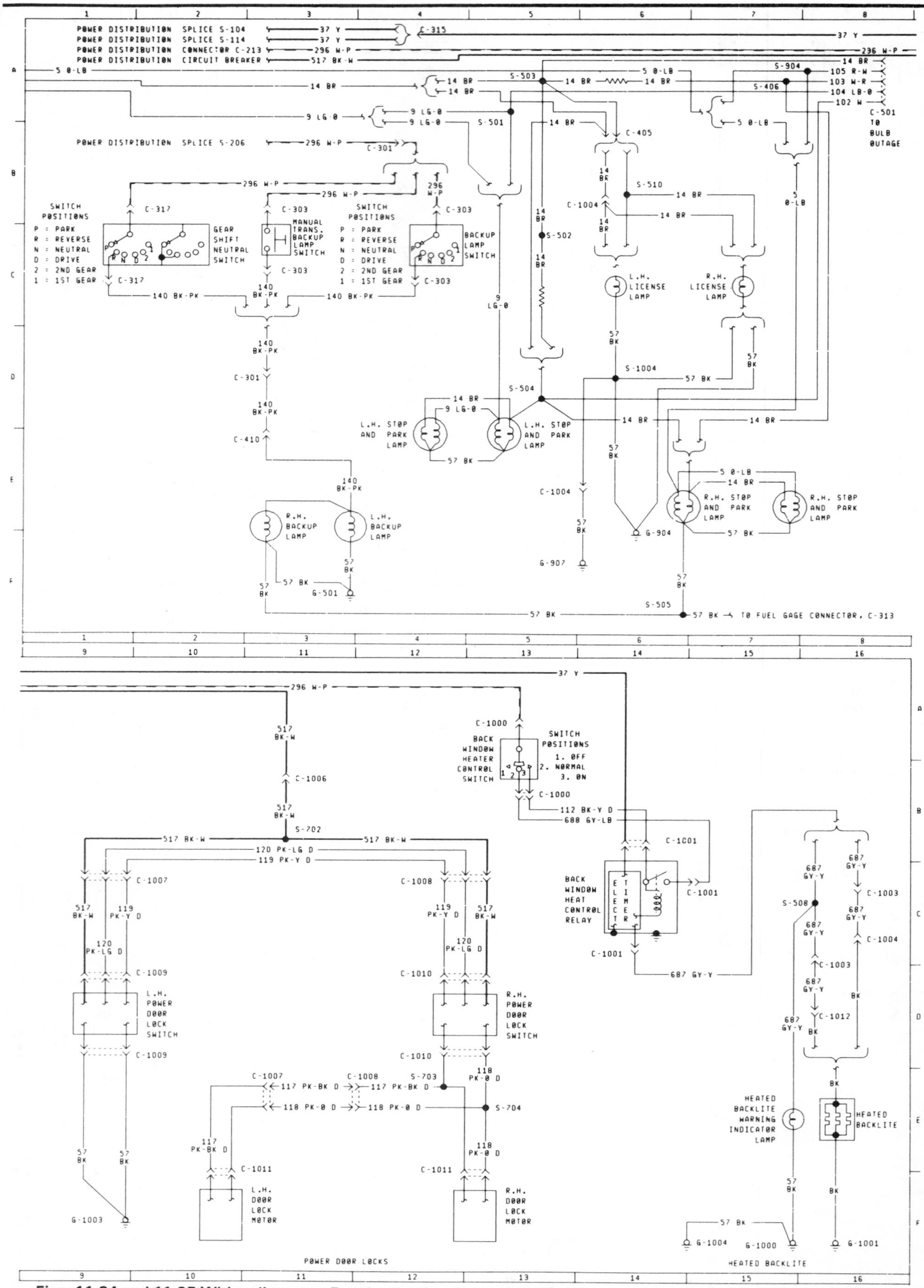

Figs. 11.34 and 11.35 Wiring diagram – Exterior lighting, heated backlite and power door lock circuits (5) 1979 models

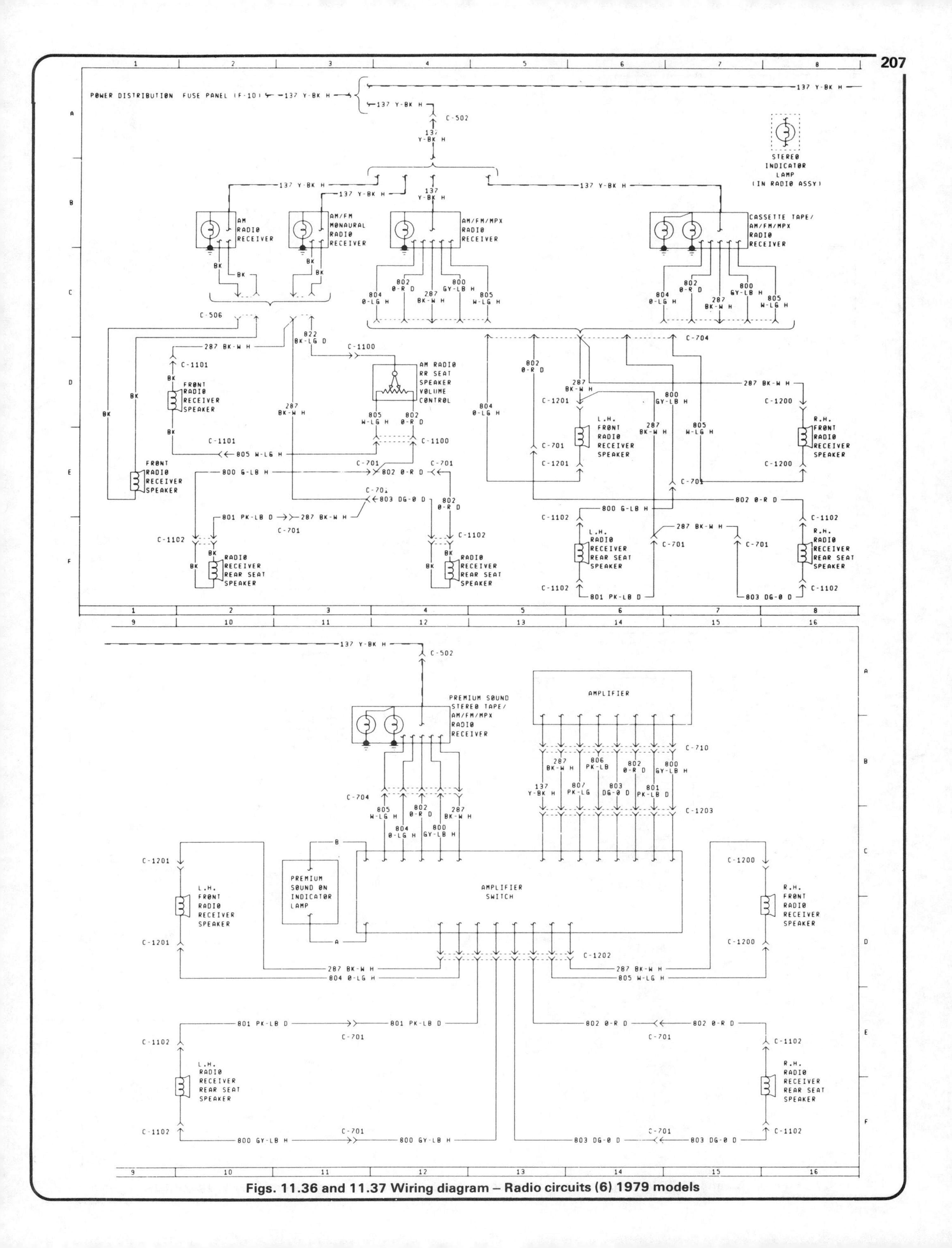

Figs. 11.36 and 11.37 Wiring diagram – Radio circuits (6) 1979 models

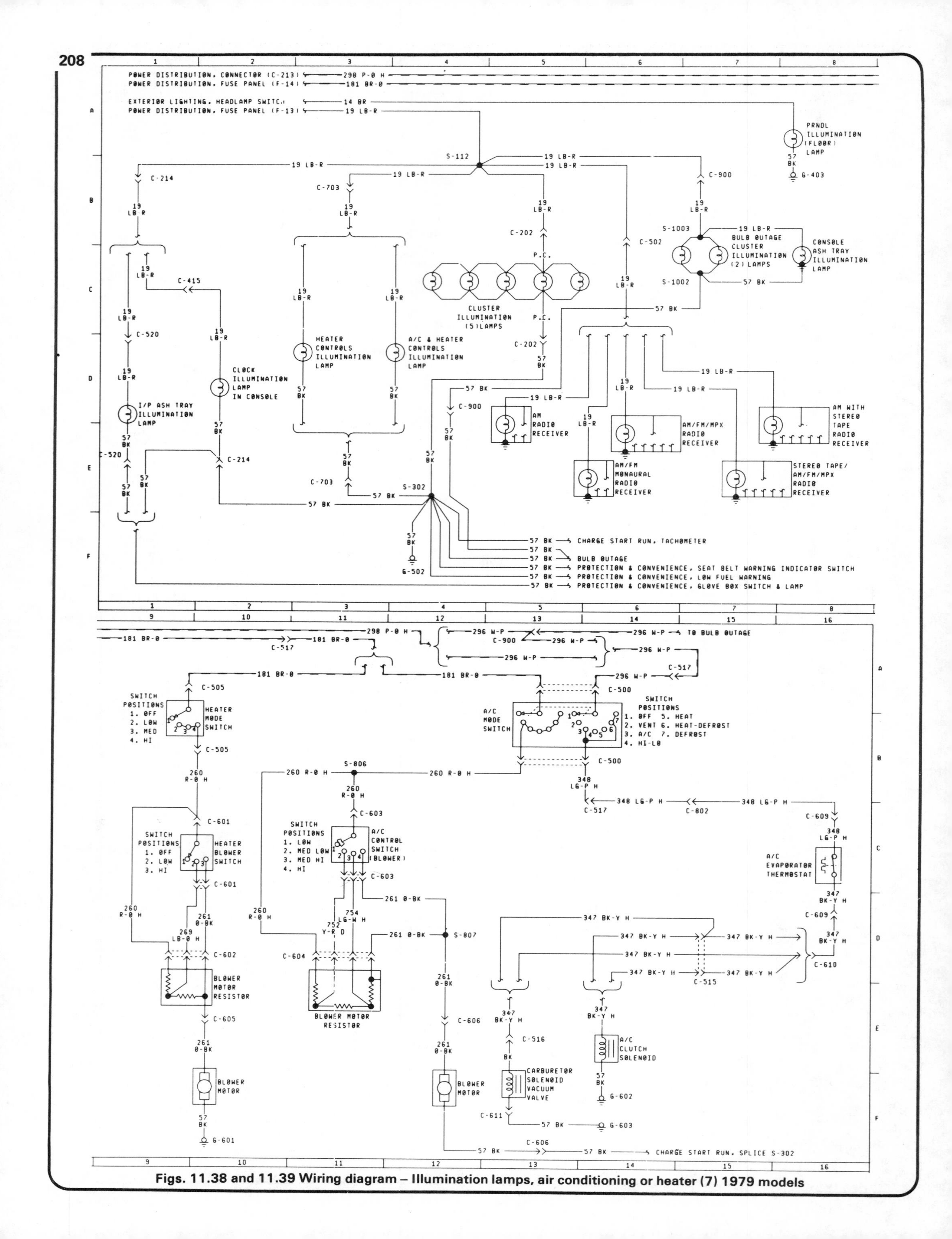

Figs. 11.38 and 11.39 Wiring diagram – Illumination lamps, air conditioning or heater (7) 1979 models

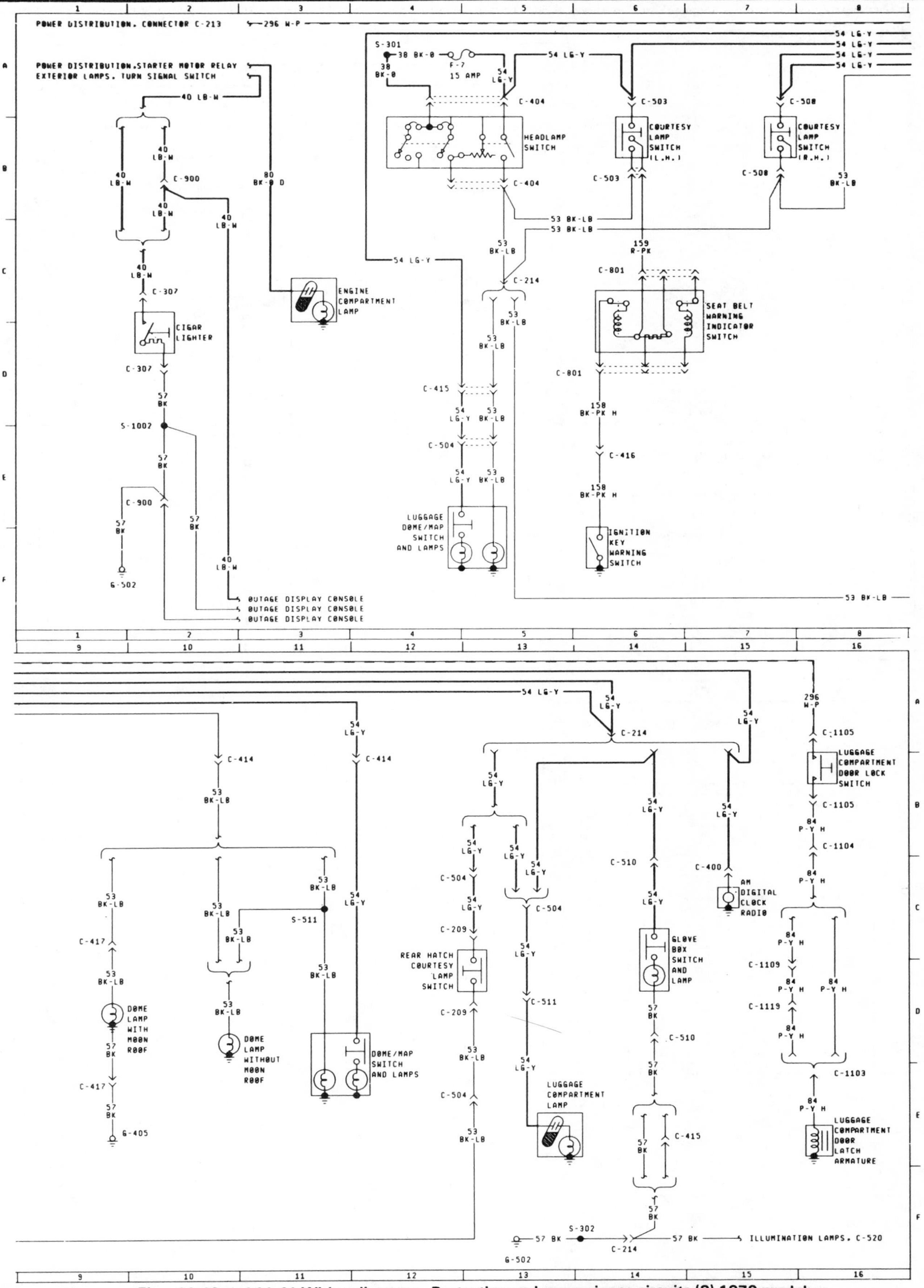

POWER DISTRIBUTION. CONNECTOR C-213

296 W-P

POWER DISTRIBUTION.STARTER MOTOR RELAY
EXTERIOR LAMPS. TURN SIGNAL SWITCH

40 LB-W

C-900

80 BK-O D

S-301

38 BK-O

F-7
15 AMP

54 LG-Y

C-404

HEADLAMP SWITCH

C-503

COURTESY LAMP SWITCH (L.H.)

C-508

COURTESY LAMP SWITCH (R.H.)

53 BK-LB

159 R-PK

C-307

CIGAR LIGHTER

ENGINE COMPARTMENT LAMP

C-214

C-801

SEAT BELT WARNING INDICATOR SWITCH

57 BK

S-1002

C-415

C-504

158 BK-PK H

C-416

LUGGAGE DOME/MAP SWITCH AND LAMPS

IGNITION KEY WARNING SWITCH

G-502

OUTAGE DISPLAY CONSOLE
OUTAGE DISPLAY CONSOLE
OUTAGE DISPLAY CONSOLE

C-414

C-417

S-511

DOME LAMP WITH MOON ROOF

DOME LAMP WITHOUT MOON ROOF

DOME/MAP SWITCH AND LAMPS

G-405

C-209

REAR HATCH COURTESY LAMP SWITCH

C-511

LUGGAGE COMPARTMENT LAMP

C-510

GLOVE BOX SWITCH AND LAMP

C-400

AM DIGITAL CLOCK RADIO

C-1105

LUGGAGE COMPARTMENT DOOR LOCK SWITCH

84 P-Y H

C-1104

C-1109

C-1119

C-1103

LUGGAGE COMPARTMENT DOOR LATCH ARMATURE

S-302

ILLUMINATION LAMPS. C-520

Figs. 11.40 and 11.41 Wiring diagram – Protection and convenience circuits (8) 1979 models

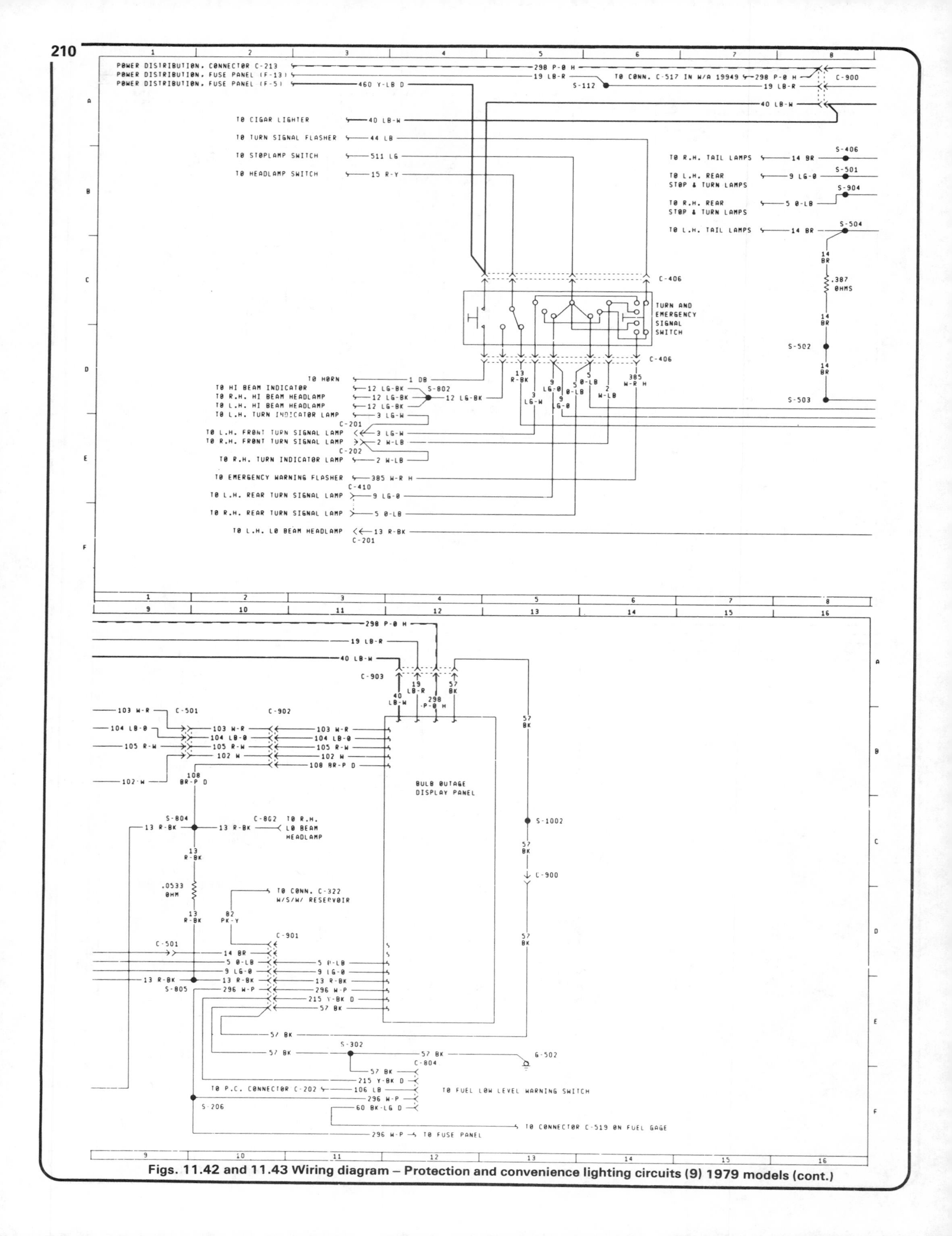

Figs. 11.42 and 11.43 Wiring diagram – Protection and convenience lighting circuits (9) 1979 models (cont.)

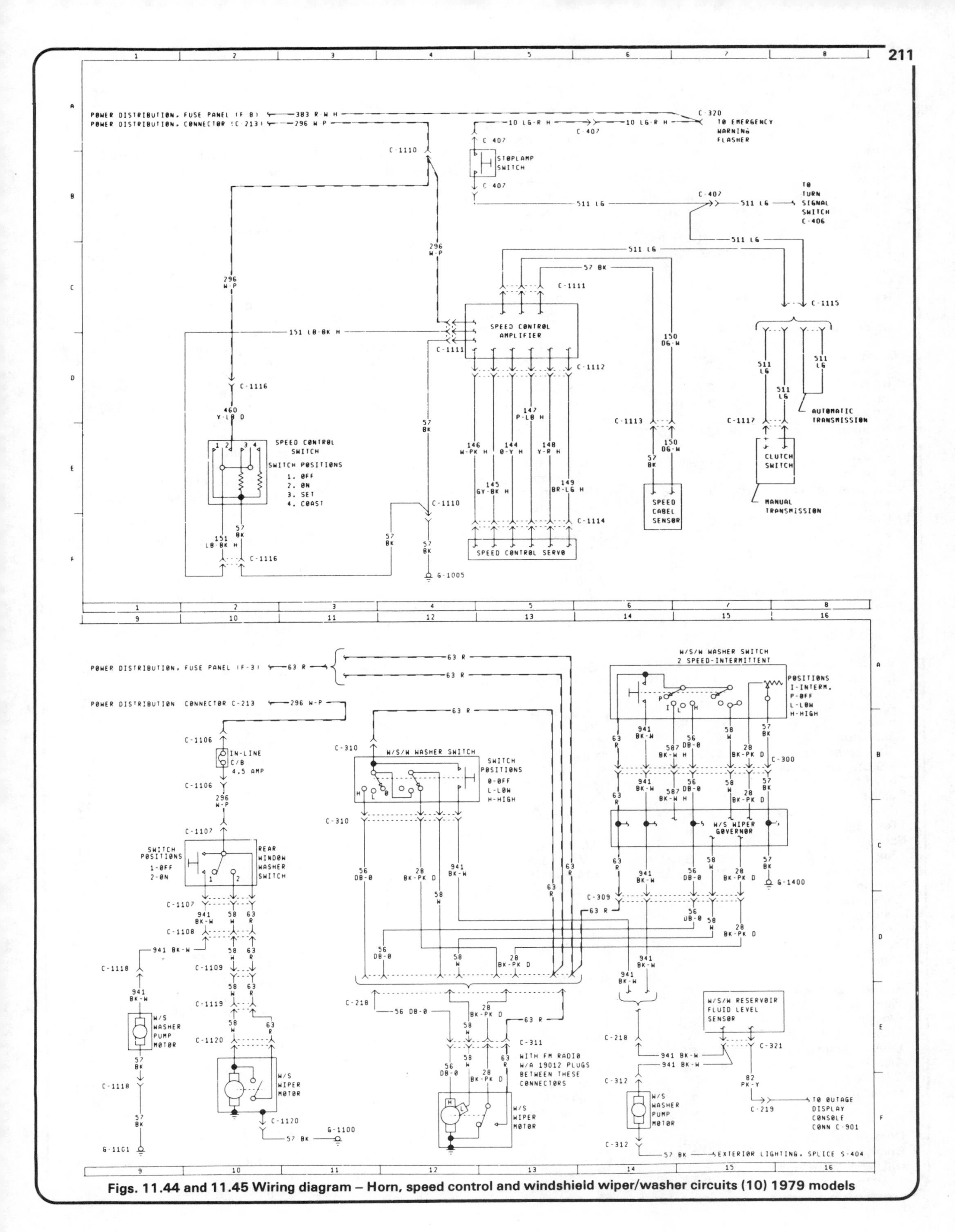

Figs. 11.44 and 11.45 Wiring diagram – Horn, speed control and windshield wiper/washer circuits (10) 1979 models

Key to wiring diagrams – 1980 models (Figs. 11.46 thru 11.67)

Wiring color key Primary colors

Black	Bk
Brown	Br
Tan	T
Red	R
Pink	Pk
Orange	O
Yellow	Y
Dark green	Dg
Light green	Lg
Dark blue	Db
Light blue	Lb
Purple	P
Gray	Gy
White	W
Hash	(H)
Dot	(D)

Stripe is understood and has no color key

Component	Diag	
Alternator		
40 Amp	2	A1
60 Amp	2	B3
70 Amp	2	84
Ammeter	2	B15
Amplifier		
Speed control	11	C5
Armature		
Luggage comp door latch	9	E16
Backlite		
Heated	6	E16
Battery		
12 Volt	1	B3
12 Volt	2	B4
Capacitor		
Radio ignition interference	2	F3
Choke		
Electric	2	D3
Radio receiver suppression	3	B5
Clock	9	C15
Coil		
Ignition	2	D8
Control		
AM Radio or speaker volume	7	D4
Distributor		
2.3 Liter breakerless	2	D5
2.8 Liter breakerless	2	F5
8 Cyl 302 breakerless	2	E5
Flasher		
Emergency warning	5	C7
Turn signal	5	B6
Gauge		
Fuel	3	B12
Water temp	3	B2
Governor		
W/S wiper	11	C14
Heater		
Engine block	10	D1
Horn		
High pitch	5	E3
Lamp		
A/C & Heater controls illum	8	C4
Clock illumination	8	B5
Cluster illumination	8	B7
Cluster illumination	8	B8
Cluster illumination (5)	8	C4
Console ash tray illumination	8	B6
Dome	9	D9
Dome	9	D10
Dome/map switch	9	E3
Dome/map switch	9	D11
Dual brake warning indicator	3	B3

Component	Diag	
Engine compartment	10	D7
Glove box switch	9	C14
Heater backlite warning ind	6	E15
Heater controls illumination	8	C4
Hi beam indicator	5	F4
I/P ash tray illumination	8	D1
L.H. Backup	6	E3
L.H. Front side marker	5	D9
L.H. Hi beam head	5	D10
L.H. License	6	C6
L.H. Lo beam head	5	D10
L.H. Front park & T/S	5	D11
L.H. Stop and park	6	E4
L.H. Stop and park	6	E5
L.H. Turn indicator	5	F5
Luggage compartment	9	E13
PRNDL illumination (floor)	8	D2
R.H. Backup	6	E2
R.H. Front side marker	5	D16
R.H. Hi beam head	5	D15
R.H. License	6	C7
R.H. Lo beam head	5	D14
R.H. Front park & T/S	5	D13
R.H. Stop and park	6	E6
R.H. Stop and park	6	F8
R.H. Turn indicator	5	F7
Seat belts warning indicator	3	D13
Stereo indicator	7	A8
Lighter		
Cigar	10	D4
Cigar	10	D5
Modulator		
Breakerless ignition	2	D15
Motor	4	D12
Blower	8	C9
Blower	8	B11
Fuel pump	4	D8
Starter	2	B6
W/S Washer pump	11	E9
W/S Washer pump	11	F14
W/S Wiper	11	E10
W/S Wiper	11	F12
Panel		
Fuse	1	B3
Receiver		
AM Radio	7	B2
AM Radio	8	D5
AM with stereo tape radio	8	D7
AM/FM Monaural radio	7	B3
AM/FM Monaural radio	8	E6
AM/FM/MPX Radio	7	B4
AM/FM/MPX Radio	8	D6
Cassette AM/FM/MPX Radio	7	B7
Stereo tape/AM/FM/MPX Radio	7	A12
Stereo tape/AM/FM/MPX Radio	8	E7
Regulator		
Alternator	2	E1
Instrument cluster voltage	3	C5
Relay		
Back window heat control	6	C14
Carburetor choke control	4	C7
Electric fuel pump	4	D12
Engine cooling fan motor	4	C15
Engine electronic control	4	E15
Exh gas recirc sol vac valve	4	B3
Light sensor	4	B15
Starter motor	1	B4
Starter motor	2	B6
Resistor		
Blower motor	8	D9

Component	Diag	
Blower motor	8	F11
Sender		
Fuel gauge	3	E13
Water temperature indicator	3	F1
Servo		
Speed control	11	F5
Solenoid		
A/C CLutch	8	F12
A/C Clutch	8	D13
A/C Clutch	8	D14
A/C Clutch	8	D16
Carb throttle emission cont	3	F4
Carb throttle emission cont	8	E12
Carburetor float bowl vent	3	F3
Exhaust gas recirc vac valve	4	E4
Speaker		
R.H. Front radio receiver	7	D8
R.H. Front radio receiver	7	C16
Radio receiver	7	E1
Radio receiver	7	D1
Radio receiver	7	D6
Radio receiver	7	C10
Radio receiver rear seat	7	F2
Radio receiver rear seat	7	F4
Radio receiver rear seat	7	F6
Radio receiver rear seat	7	F8
Radio receiver rear seat	7	E10
Radio receiver rear seat	7	E16
Switch		
A/C Mode	8	B13
Back window heater control	6	A13
Backup lamp	6	B3
Backup lamp	6	B4
Carb idle thermactor air pump	4	D2
Courtesy lamp	9	B5
Courtesy lamp	9	B7
Dual brake warning	3	E3
Fan motor	4	E10
Fan motor	4	E16
Fuel pump	4	B8
Gear shift neutral	3	E5
Gear shift neutral	6	B1
Headlamp	9	B2
Ignition	1	D5
Ignition	3	D8
Ignition key warning	9	E4
L.H. Power door lock	6	D9
Luggage comp door lock	9	A16
Oil pressure	2	E16
Oil pressure	2	E16
Oil pressure	4	E7
Park brake signal lamp	3	D15
R.H. Power door lock	6	D13
Rear window washer	11	C10
Rear water courtesy lamp	9	C13
Seat belt buckle	3	D14
Seat belt warning indicator	3	B14
Seat belt warning indicator	9	D5
Speed control	11	D2
Stoplamp	5	B5
Stoplamp	11	A5
Turn and emergency signal	5	C5
W/S/W Washer	11	B11
W/S/W Washer	11	B14
A/C Control	8	D11
Tachometer	3	D12
Thermostat		
A/C Evaporator	4	E13
Valve		
Distributor modulator	4	E3

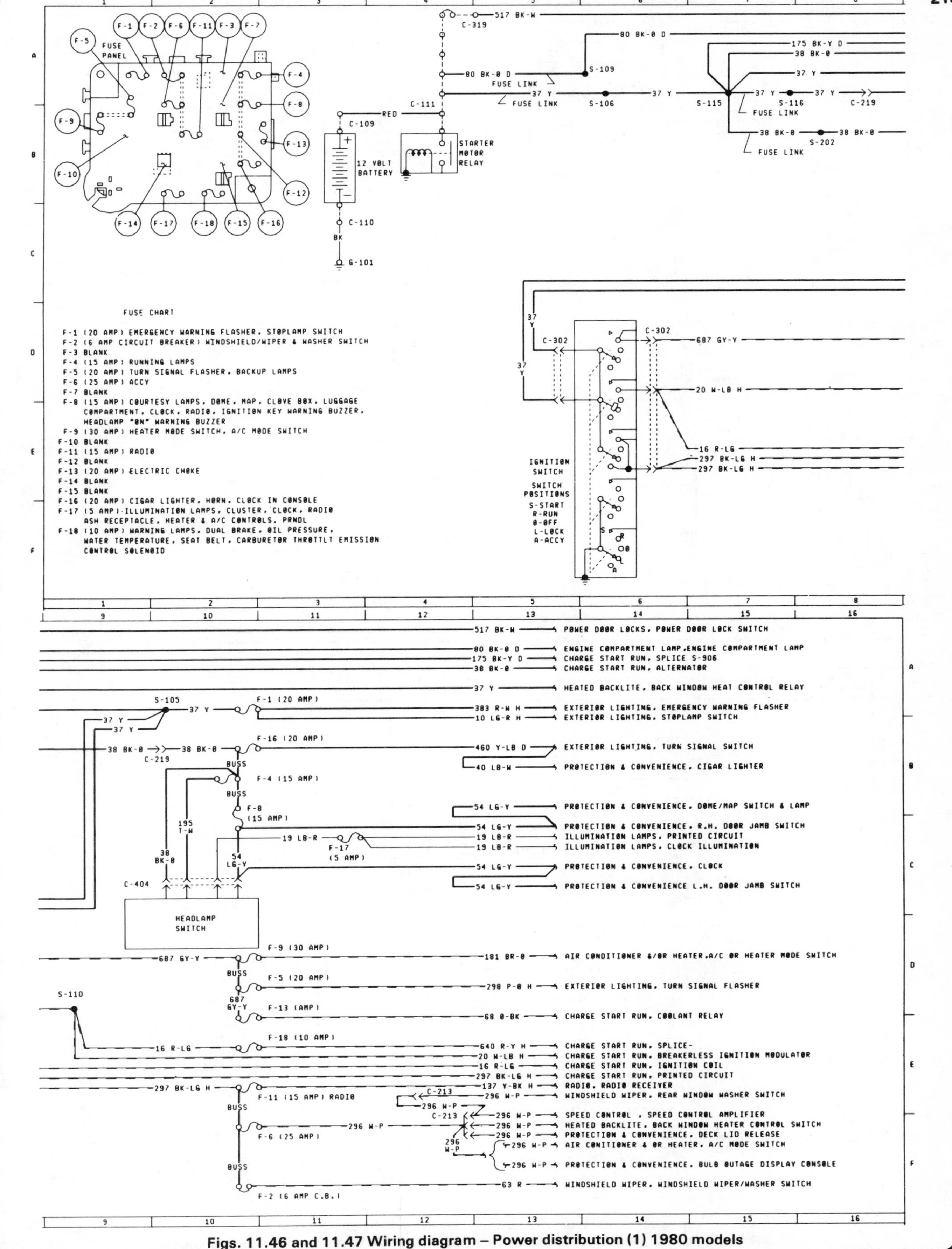

Figs. 11.46 and 11.47 Wiring diagram – Power distribution (1) 1980 models

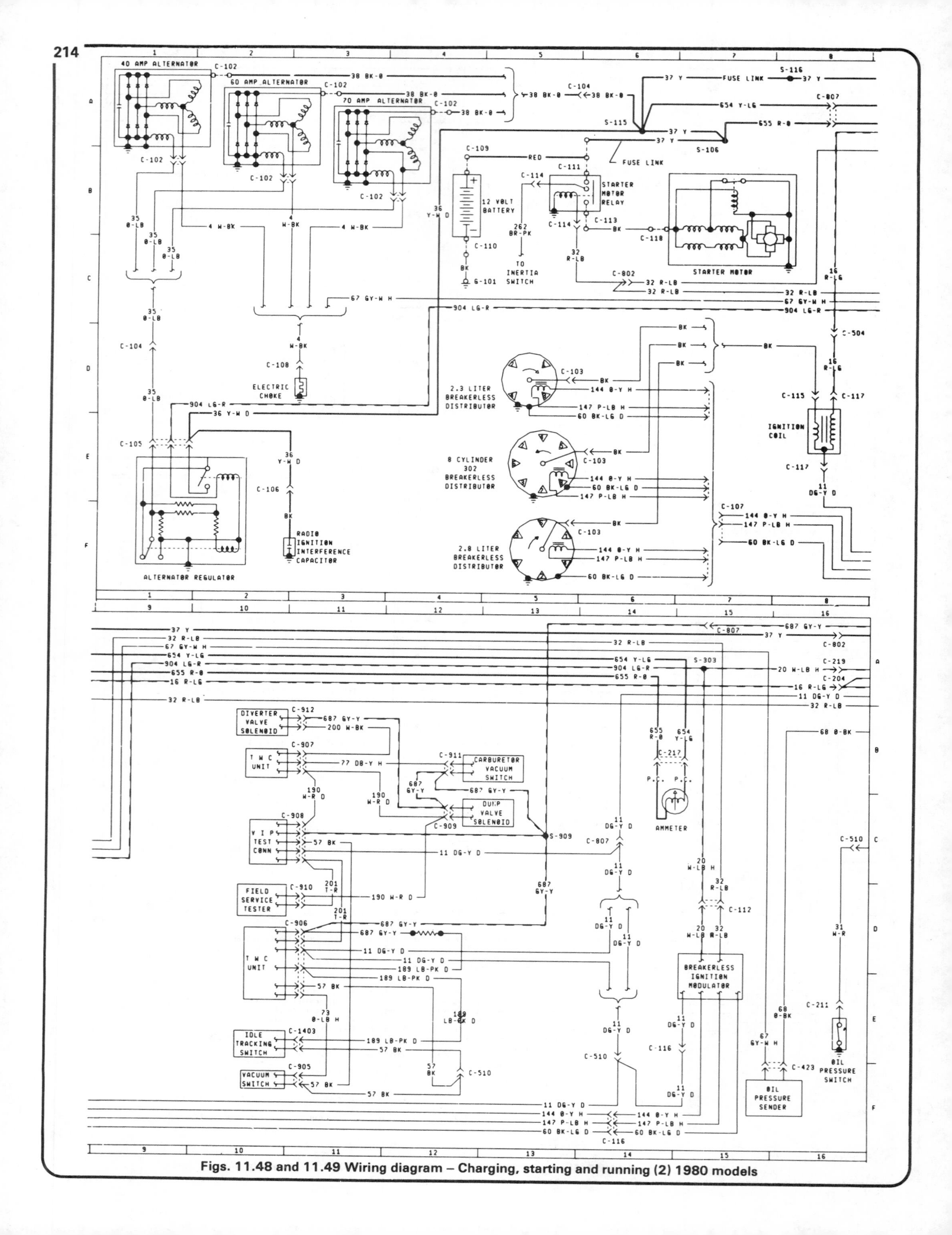

Figs. 11.48 and 11.49 Wiring diagram – Charging, starting and running (2) 1980 models

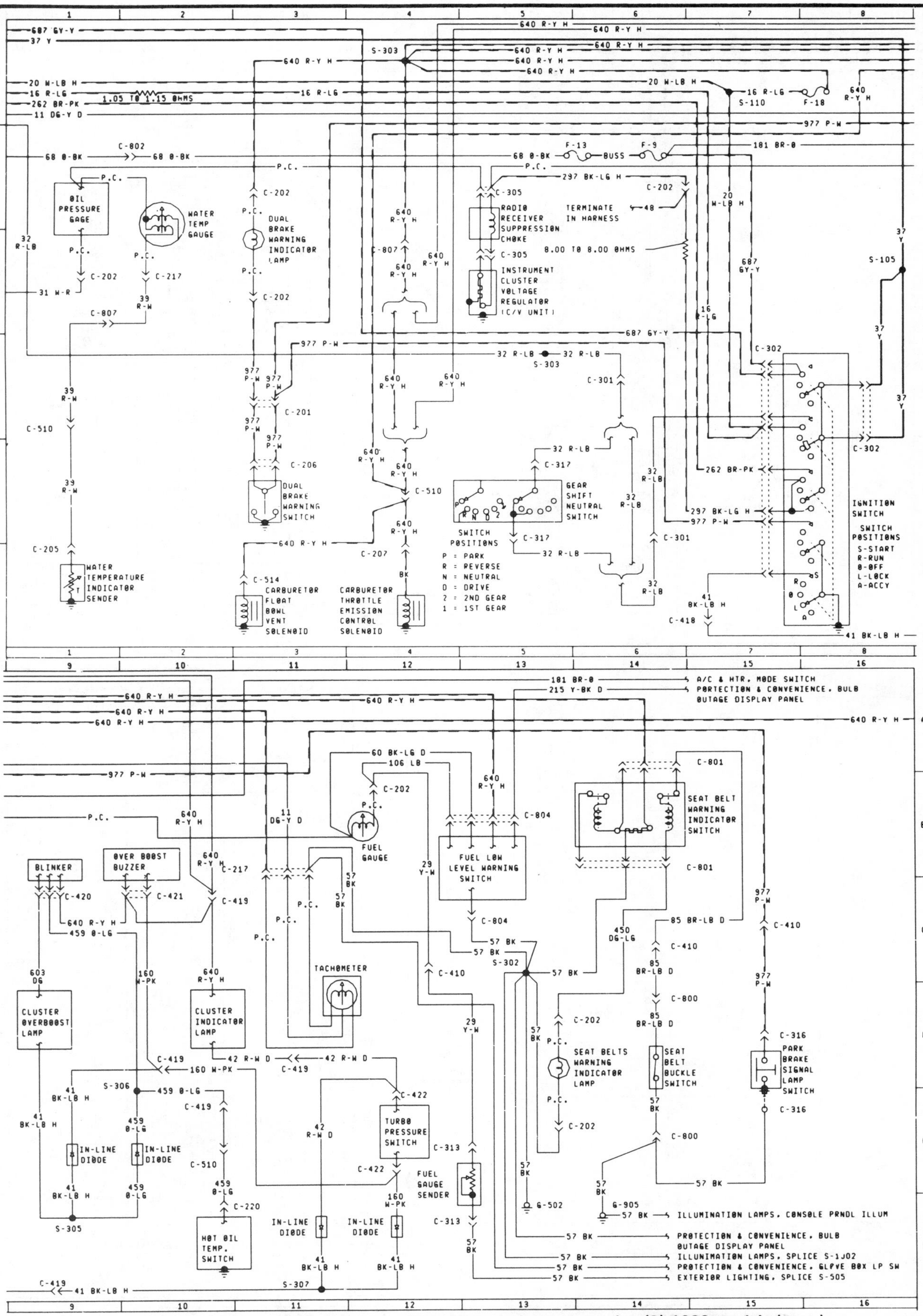

Figs. 11.50 and 11.51 Wiring diagram – Charging, starting and running (3) 1980 models (cont.)

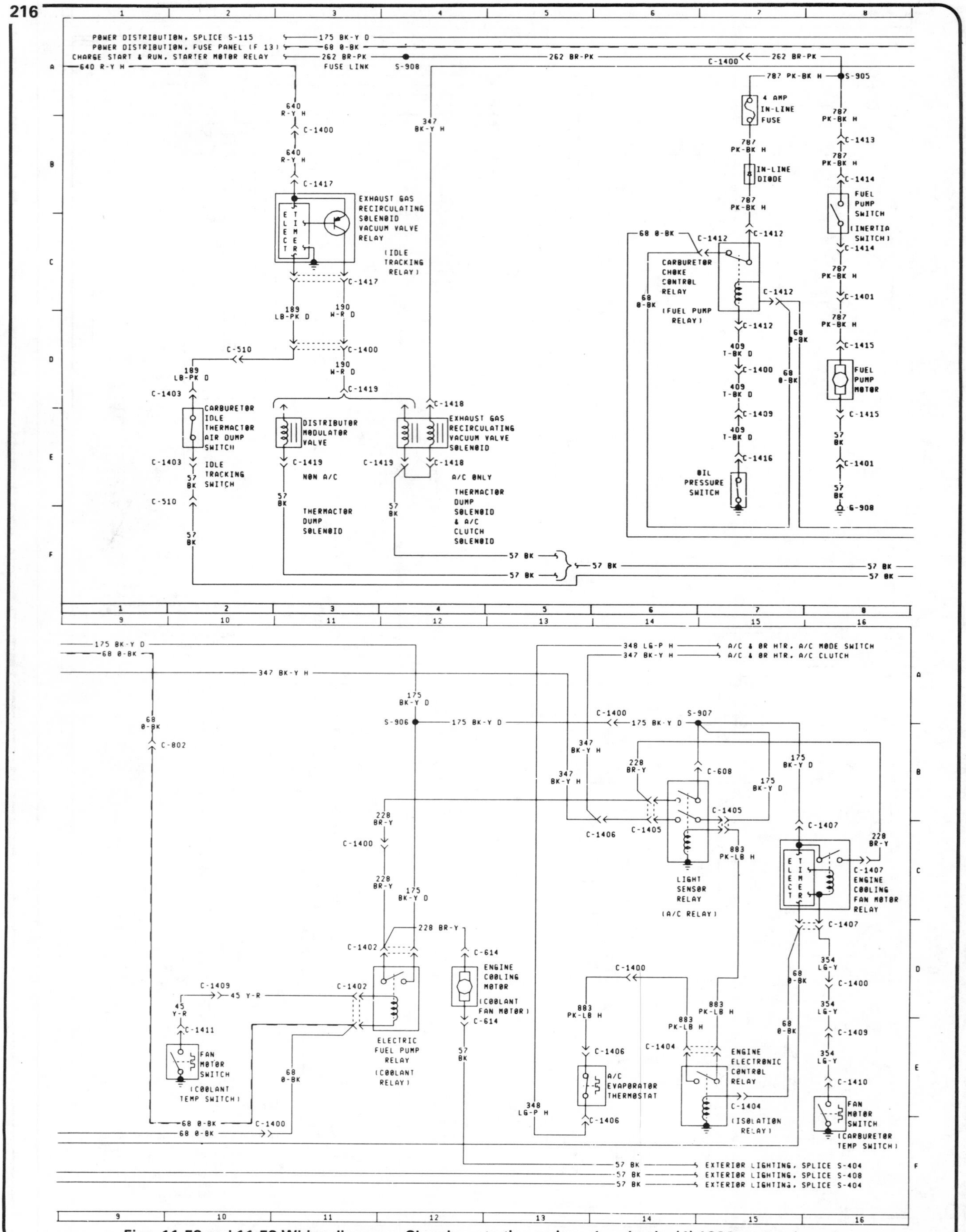

1 2 3 4 5 6 7 8

POWER DISTRIBUTION, SPLICE S-115 — 175 BK-Y D
POWER DISTRIBUTION, FUSE PANEL (F 13) — 68 O-BK
CHARGE START & RUN, STARTER MOTOR RELAY — 262 BR-PK — FUSE LINK — S-908 — 262 BR-PK — C-1400 — 262 BR-PK
640 R-Y H

640 R-Y H
C-1400
640 R-Y H
C-1417
EXHAUST GAS RECIRCULATING SOLENOID VACUUM VALVE RELAY (IDLE TRACKING RELAY)
ELECTR
C-1417
189 LB-PK D
190 W-R D
C-510
C-1400
189 LB-PK D
190 W-R D
C-1419
C-1403
CARBURETOR IDLE THERMACTOR AIR DUMP SWITCH
C-1403
IDLE TRACKING SWITCH
57 BK
C-510
57 BK
DISTRIBUTOR MODULATOR VALVE
C-1419
NON A/C
57 BK
THERMACTOR DUMP SOLENOID
347 BK-Y H
C-1418
EXHAUST GAS RECIRCULATING VACUUM VALVE SOLENOID
C-1419
C-1418
A/C ONLY
57 BK
THERMACTOR DUMP SOLENOID & A/C CLUTCH SOLENOID
57 BK
57 BK
57 BK
57 BK
57 BK

787 PK-BK H
S-905
4 AMP IN-LINE FUSE
787 PK-BK H
IN-LINE DIODE
787 PK-BK H
68 O-BK
C-1412
C-1412
CARBURETOR CHOKE CONTROL RELAY (FUEL PUMP RELAY)
68 O-BK
C-1412
C-1412
68 O-BK
409 T-BK D
C-1400
68 O-BK
409 T-BK D
C-1409
409 T-BK D
C-1416
OIL PRESSURE SWITCH
787 PK-BK H
C-1413
787 PK-BK H
C-1414
FUEL PUMP SWITCH (INERTIA SWITCH)
C-1414
787 PK-BK H
C-1401
787 PK-BK H
C-1415
FUEL PUMP MOTOR
C-1415
57 BK
C-1401
57 BK
G-908

9 10 11 12 13 14 15 16

175 BK-Y D
68 O-BK
347 BK-Y H
348 LG-P H — A/C & OR HTR, A/C MODE SWITCH
347 BK-Y H — A/C & OR HTR, A/C CLUTCH
68 O-BK
C-802
175 BK-Y D
S-906
175 BK-Y D
C-1400
175 BK-Y D
S-907
347 BK-Y H
347 BK-Y H
228 BR-Y
C-608
175 BK-Y D
175 BK-Y D
C-1405
C-1406
C-1405
228 BR-Y
C-1400
228 BR-Y
175 BK-Y D
883 PK-LB H
LIGHT SENSOR RELAY (A/C RELAY)
C-1407
228 BR-Y
ELECTR
C-1407
ENGINE COOLING FAN MOTOR RELAY
C-1407
228 BR-Y
C-1402
C-614
ENGINE COOLING MOTOR (COOLANT FAN MOTOR)
C-614
57 BK
C-1409
45 Y-R
C-1402
45 Y-R
C-1411
FAN MOTOR SWITCH (COOLANT TEMP SWITCH)
ELECTRIC FUEL PUMP RELAY (COOLANT RELAY)
68 O-BK
68 O-BK
C-1400
68 O-BK
C-1400
883 PK-LB H
883 PK-LB H
883 PK-LB H
C-1406
A/C EVAPORATOR THERMOSTAT
C-1406
348 LG-P H
C-1404
ENGINE ELECTRONIC CONTROL RELAY (ISOLATION RELAY)
C-1404
68 O-BK
68 O-BK
354 LG-Y
C-1400
354 LG-Y
C-1409
354 LG-Y
C-1410
FAN MOTOR SWITCH (CARBURETOR TEMP SWITCH)
57 BK — EXTERIOR LIGHTING, SPLICE S-404
57 BK — EXTERIOR LIGHTING, SPLICE S-408
57 BK — EXTERIOR LIGHTING, SPLICE S-404

9 10 11 12 13 14 15 16

Figs. 11.52 and 11.53 Wiring diagram – Charging, starting and running circuits (4) 1980 models (cont.)

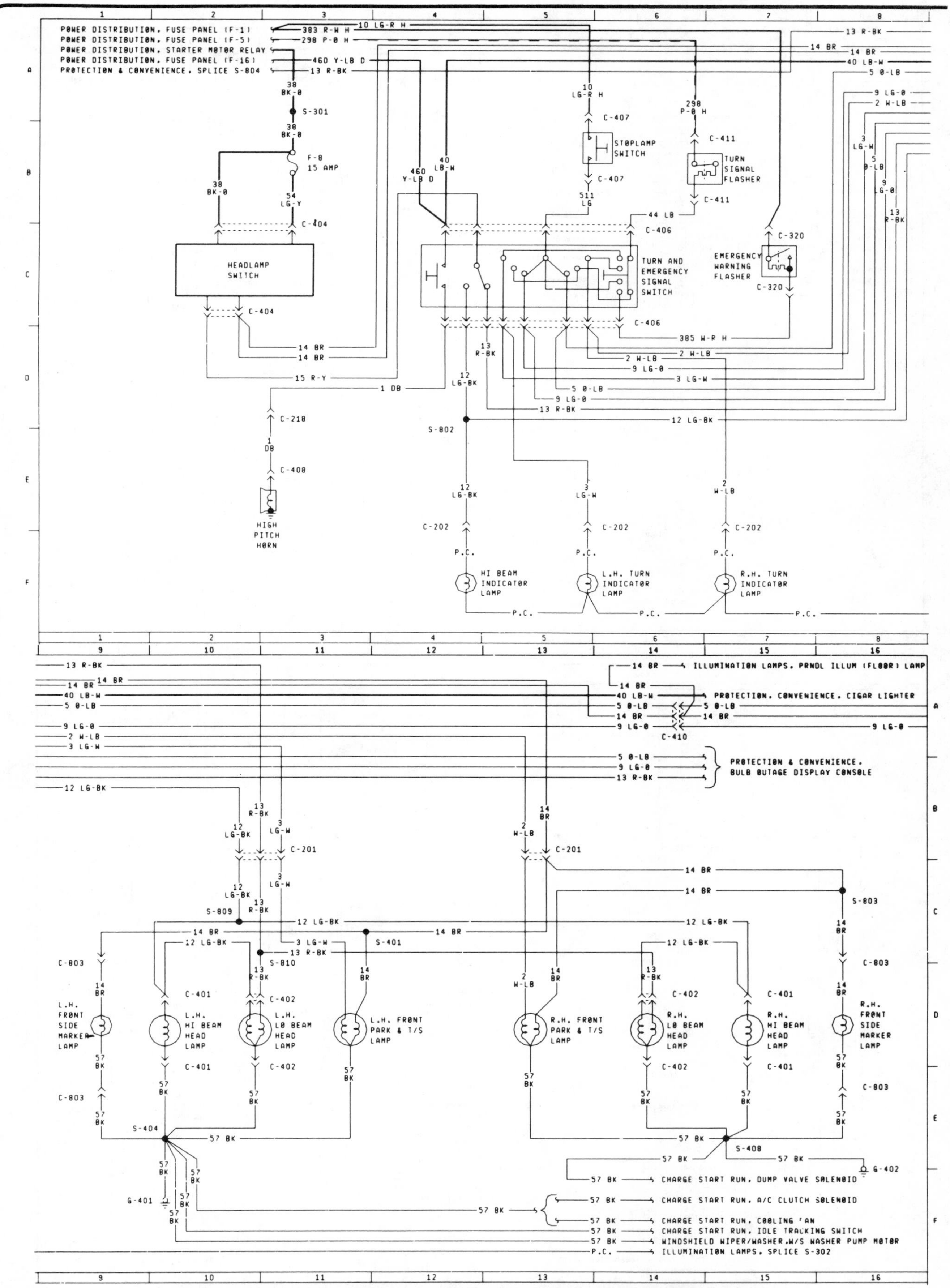

POWER DISTRIBUTION, FUSE PANEL (F-1) — 383 R-W H
POWER DISTRIBUTION, FUSE PANEL (F-5) — 298 P-O H
POWER DISTRIBUTION, STARTER MOTOR RELAY
POWER DISTRIBUTION, FUSE PANEL (F-16) — 460 Y-LB D
PROTECTION & CONVENIENCE, SPLICE S-804 — 13 R-BK

10 LG-R H
13 R-BK
14 BR
14 BR
40 LB-W
5 O-LB
9 LG-O
2 W-LB

38 BK-O
S-301
38 BK-O
F-8 15 AMP
38 BK-O
54 LG-Y
C-404
HEADLAMP SWITCH
C-404
14 BR
14 BR
15 R-Y
1 DB
C-218
1 DB
C-408
HIGH PITCH HORN

460 Y-LB D
40 LB-W
10 LG-R H
C-407
STOPLAMP SWITCH
C-407
511 LG
298 P-O H
C-411
TURN SIGNAL FLASHER
C-411
44 LB
C-406
TURN AND EMERGENCY SIGNAL SWITCH
C-406
C-320
EMERGENCY WARNING FLASHER
C-320
3 LG-W
5 O-LB
9 LG-O
13 R-BK
385 W-R H
2 W-LB
2 W-LB
9 LG-O
3 LG-W
5 O-LB
9 LG-O
13 R-BK
12 LG-BK
12 LG-BK
S-802
12 LG-BK
C-202
P.C.
HI BEAM INDICATOR LAMP
3 LG-W
C-202
P.C.
L.H. TURN INDICATOR LAMP
2 W-LB
C-202
P.C.
R.H. TURN INDICATOR LAMP
P.C.

13 R-BK
14 BR
14 BR
40 LB-W
5 O-LB
9 LG-O
2 W-LB
3 LG-W
12 LG-BK
14 BR — ILLUMINATION LAMPS, PRNDL ILLUM (FLOOR) LAMP
14 BR
40 LB-W — PROTECTION, CONVENIENCE, CIGAR LIGHTER
5 O-LB — 5 O-LB
14 BR — 14 BR
9 LG-O — 9 LG-O
C-410
5 O-LB
9 LG-O
13 R-BK
PROTECTION & CONVENIENCE, BULB OUTAGE DISPLAY CONSOLE

12 LG-BK
13 R-BK
3 LG-W
C-201
2 W-LB
14 BR
C-201
14 BR
14 BR
S-803
S-809
12 LG-BK
14 BR
12 LG-BK
3 LG-W
S-401
13 R-BK
S-810
12 LG-BK
12 LG-BK
C-803
C-401
C-402
C-402
C-401
C-803
L.H. FRONT SIDE MARKER LAMP
L.H. HI BEAM HEAD LAMP
L.H. LO BEAM HEAD LAMP
L.H. FRONT PARK & T/S LAMP
R.H. FRONT PARK & T/S LAMP
R.H. LO BEAM HEAD LAMP
R.H. HI BEAM HEAD LAMP
R.H. FRONT SIDE MARKER LAMP
C-401
C-402
C-402
C-401
C-803
C-803
57 BK
S-404
57 BK
S-408
57 BK
G-401
57 BK
G-402
57 BK — CHARGE START RUN, DUMP VALVE SOLENOID
57 BK — CHARGE START RUN, A/C CLUTCH SOLENOID
57 BK — CHARGE START RUN, COOLING FAN
57 BK — CHARGE START RUN, IDLE TRACKING SWITCH
57 BK — WINDSHIELD WIPER/WASHER, W/S WASHER PUMP MOTOR
P.C. — ILLUMINATION LAMPS, SPLICE S-302

Figs. 11.54 and 11.55 Wiring diagram – Exterior lighting circuits (5) 1980 models

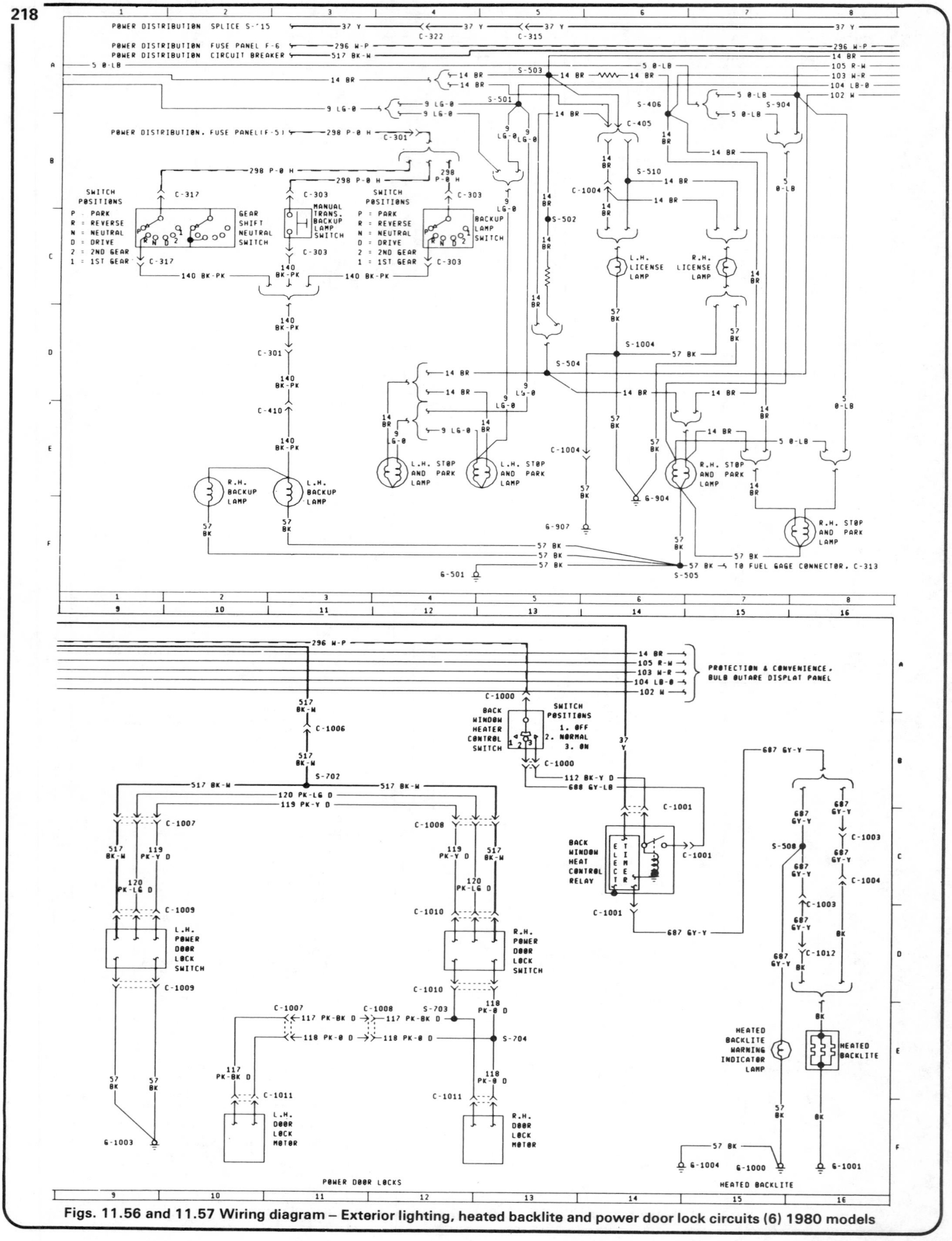

POWER DOOR LOCKS

HEATED BACKLITE

Figs. 11.56 and 11.57 Wiring diagram – Exterior lighting, heated backlite and power door lock circuits (6) 1980 models

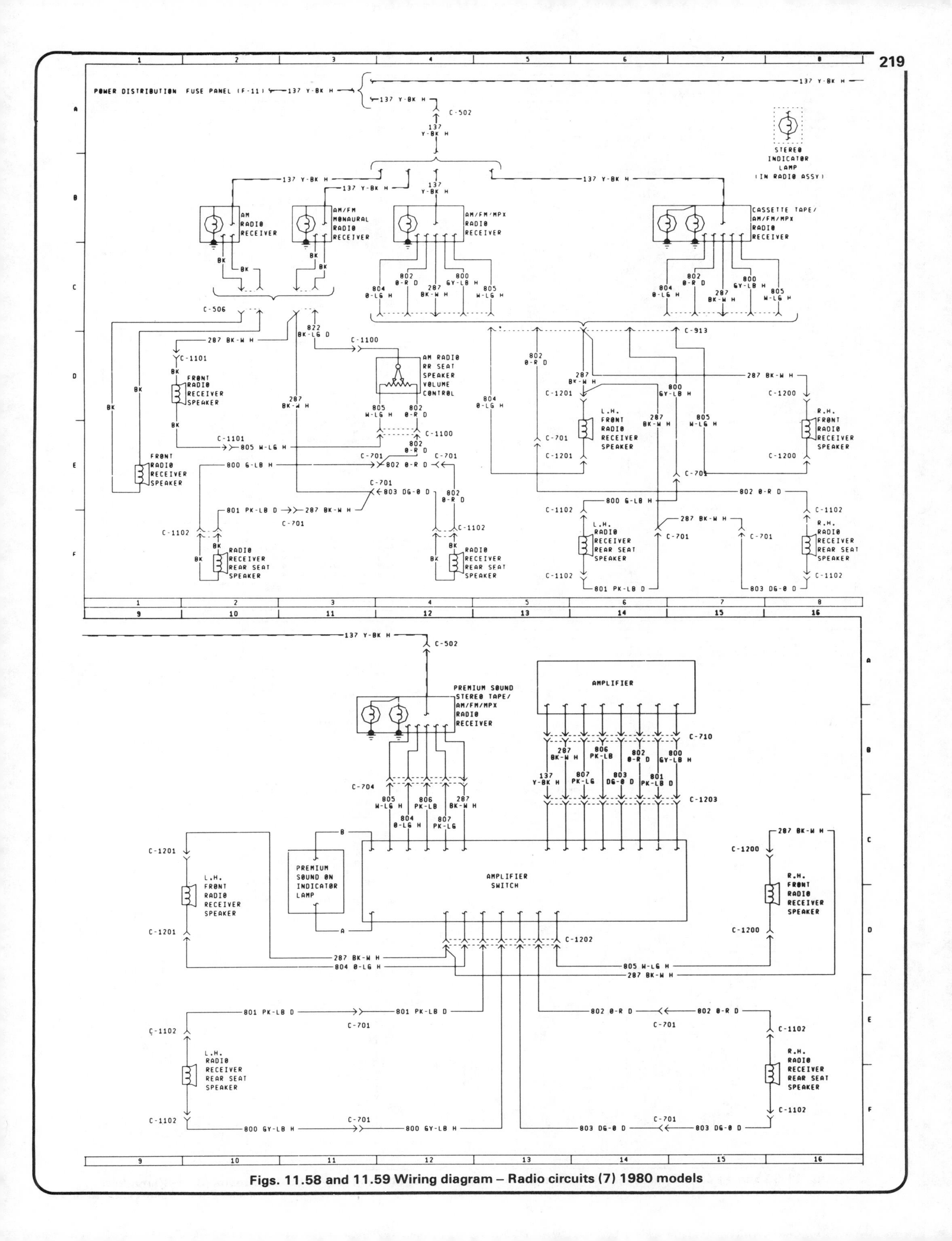

Figs. 11.58 and 11.59 Wiring diagram – Radio circuits (7) 1980 models

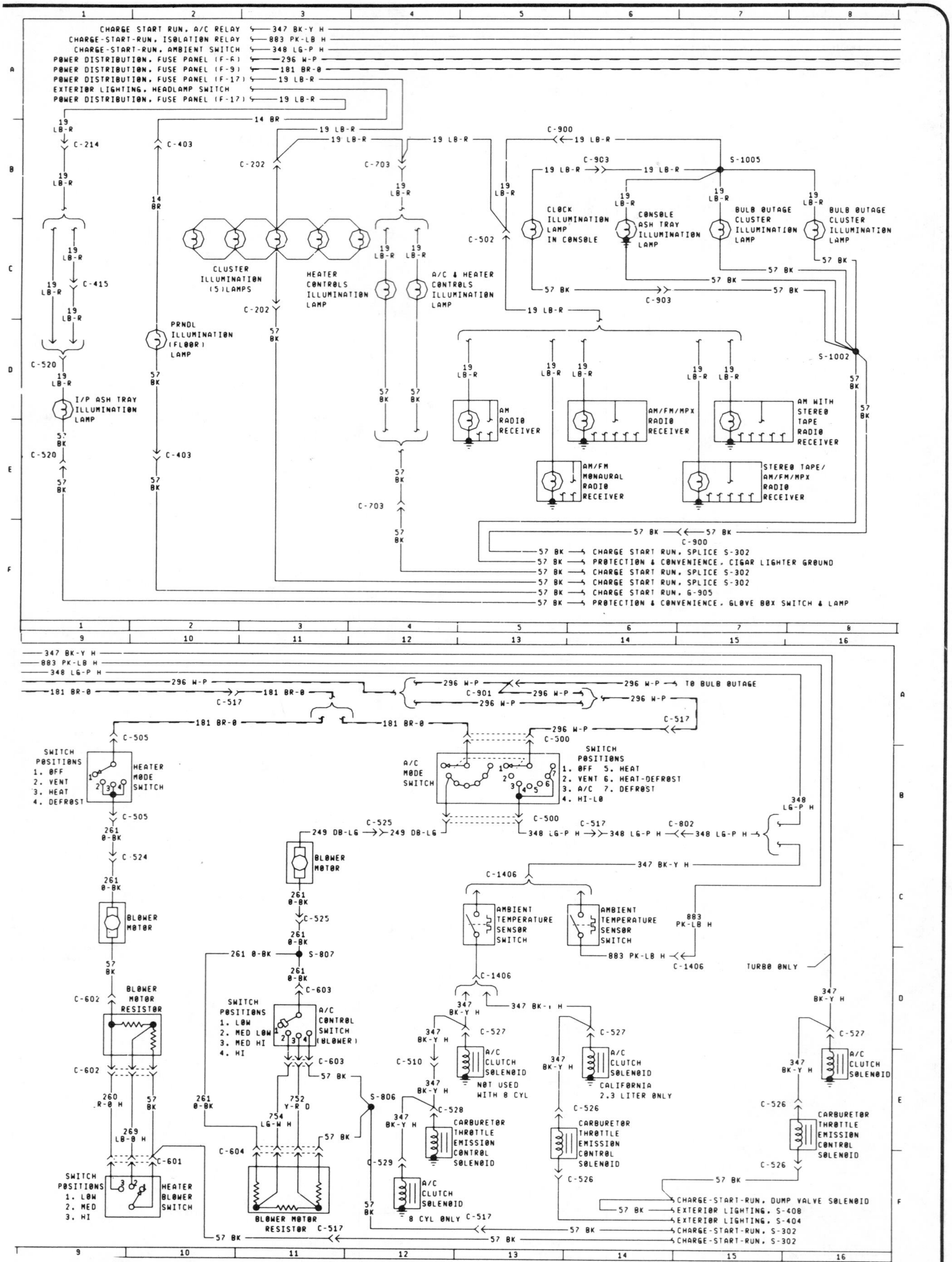

CHARGE START RUN, A/C RELAY — 347 BK-Y H
CHARGE-START-RUN, ISOLATION RELAY — 883 PK-LB H
CHARGE-START-RUN, AMBIENT SWITCH — 348 LG-P H
POWER DISTRIBUTION, FUSE PANEL (F-6) — 296 W-P
POWER DISTRIBUTION, FUSE PANEL (F-9) — 181 BR-O
POWER DISTRIBUTION, FUSE PANEL (F-17) — 19 LB-R
EXTERIOR LIGHTING, HEADLAMP SWITCH
POWER DISTRIBUTION, FUSE PANEL (F-17) — 19 LB-R

14 BR
19 LB-R
C-214
C-403
C-202
C-703
C-900
C-903
S-1005
C-415
C-520
C-502
S-1002

I/P ASH TRAY ILLUMINATION LAMP
PRNDL ILLUMINATION (FLOOR) LAMP
CLUSTER ILLUMINATION (5) LAMPS
HEATER CONTROLS ILLUMINATION LAMP
A/C & HEATER CONTROLS ILLUMINATION LAMP
CLOCK ILLUMINATION LAMP IN CONSOLE
CONSOLE ASH TRAY ILLUMINATION LAMP
BULB OUTAGE CLUSTER ILLUMINATION LAMP
BULB OUTAGE CLUSTER ILLUMINATION LAMP
AM RADIO RECEIVER
AM/FM/MPX RADIO RECEIVER
AM WITH STEREO TAPE RADIO RECEIVER
AM/FM MONAURAL RADIO RECEIVER
STEREO TAPE/AM/FM/MPX RADIO RECEIVER

57 BK
57 BK — CHARGE START RUN, SPLICE S-302
57 BK — PROTECTION & CONVENIENCE, CIGAR LIGHTER GROUND
57 BK — CHARGE START RUN, SPLICE S-302
57 BK — CHARGE START RUN, SPLICE S-302
57 BK — CHARGE START RUN, G-905
57 BK — PROTECTION & CONVENIENCE, GLOVE BOX SWITCH & LAMP

347 BK-Y H
883 PK-LB H
348 LG-P H
296 W-P
181 BR-O
C-517
C-901
296 W-P — TO BULB OUTAGE
C-505
C-500
C-525
C-524
C-802
C-1406
S-807
C-603
C-602
S-806
C-604
C-601
C-527
C-510
C-528
C-529
C-526

SWITCH POSITIONS
1. OFF
2. VENT
3. HEAT
4. DEFROST

HEATER MODE SWITCH

A/C MODE SWITCH

SWITCH POSITIONS
1. OFF 5. HEAT
2. VENT 6. HEAT-DEFROST
3. A/C 7. DEFROST
4. HI-LO

249 DB-LG
261 O-BK
BLOWER MOTOR
BLOWER MOTOR
BLOWER MOTOR RESISTOR
AMBIENT TEMPERATURE SENSOR SWITCH
AMBIENT TEMPERATURE SENSOR SWITCH
TURBO ONLY

SWITCH POSITIONS
1. LOW
2. MED LOW
3. MED HI
4. HI

A/C CONTROL SWITCH (BLOWER)

260 R-O H
269 LB-O H
754 LG-W H
752 Y-R D

SWITCH POSITIONS
1. LOW
2. MED
3. HI

HEATER BLOWER SWITCH

BLOWER MOTOR RESISTOR

A/C CLUTCH SOLENOID — NOT USED WITH 8 CYL
A/C CLUTCH SOLENOID — CALIFORNIA 2.3 LITER ONLY
A/C CLUTCH SOLENOID — 8 CYL ONLY
A/C CLUTCH SOLENOID
CARBURETOR THROTTLE EMISSION CONTROL SOLENOID
CARBURETOR THROTTLE EMISSION CONTROL SOLENOID
CARBURETOR THROTTLE EMISSION CONTROL SOLENOID

57 BK — CHARGE-START-RUN, DUMP VALVE SOLENOID
57 BK — EXTERIOR LIGHTING, S-408
EXTERIOR LIGHTING, S-404
57 BK — CHARGE-START-RUN, S-302
57 BK — CHARGE-START-RUN, S-302

Figs. 11.60 and 11.61 Wiring diagram – Illumination lamps, air conditioning and/or heater circuits (8) 1980 models

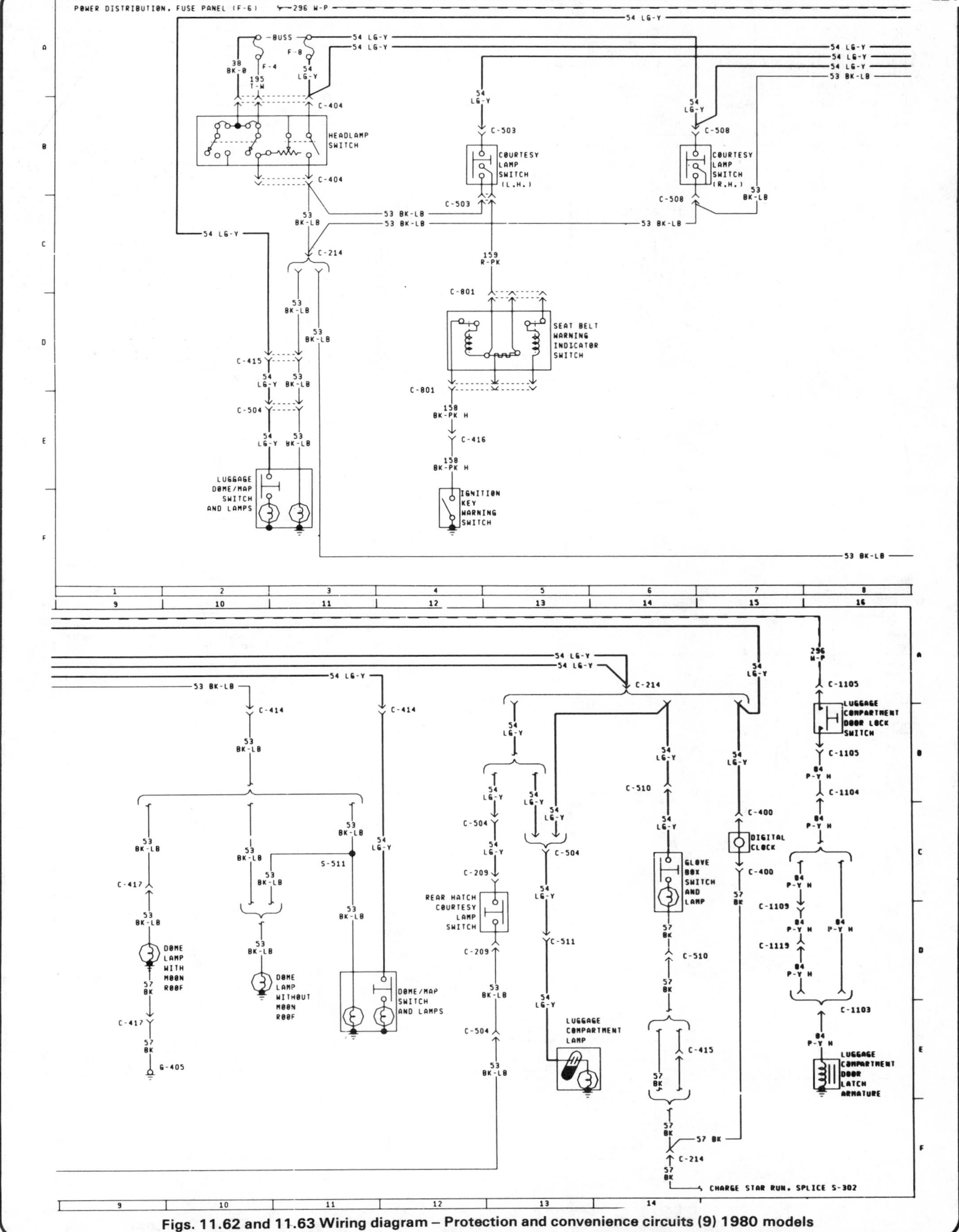

Figs. 11.62 and 11.63 Wiring diagram – Protection and convenience circuits (9) 1980 models

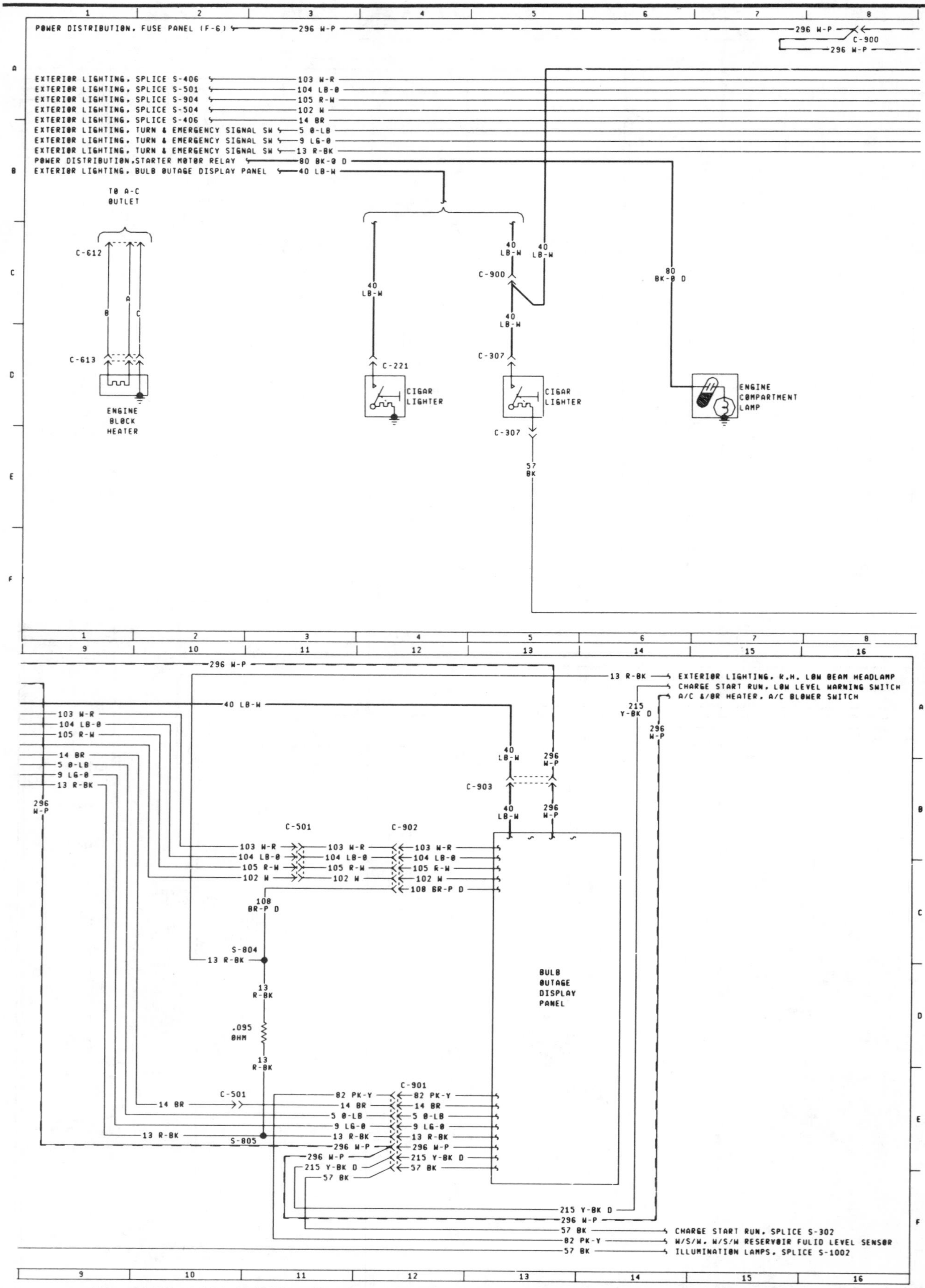

1 2 3 4 5 6 7 8

POWER DISTRIBUTION, FUSE PANEL (F-6) — 296 W-P — 296 W-P — C-900 — 296 W-P

EXTERIOR LIGHTING, SPLICE S-406 — 103 W-R
EXTERIOR LIGHTING, SPLICE S-501 — 104 LB-O
EXTERIOR LIGHTING, SPLICE S-904 — 105 R-W
EXTERIOR LIGHTING, SPLICE S-504 — 102 W
EXTERIOR LIGHTING, SPLICE S-406 — 14 BR
EXTERIOR LIGHTING, TURN & EMERGENCY SIGNAL SW — 5 O-LB
EXTERIOR LIGHTING, TURN & EMERGENCY SIGNAL SW — 9 LG-O
EXTERIOR LIGHTING, TURN & EMERGENCY SIGNAL SW — 13 R-BK
POWER DISTRIBUTION, STARTER MOTOR RELAY — 80 BK-O D
EXTERIOR LIGHTING, BULB OUTAGE DISPLAY PANEL — 40 LB-W

TO A-C OUTLET

C-612
B A C
C-613
ENGINE BLOCK HEATER

40 LB-W
C-221
CIGAR LIGHTER

40 LB-W
40 LB-W
C-900
40 LB-W
C-307
CIGAR LIGHTER
C-307
57 BK

80 BK-O D
ENGINE COMPARTMENT LAMP

9 10 11 12 13 14 15 16

296 W-P
13 R-BK — EXTERIOR LIGHTING, R.H. LOW BEAM HEADLAMP
CHARGE START RUN, LOW LEVEL WARNING SWITCH
215 Y-BK D — A/C &/OR HEATER, A/C BLOWER SWITCH
296 W-P

103 W-R
104 LB-O
105 R-W
14 BR
5 O-LB
9 LG-O
13 R-BK
296 W-P

40 LB-W
40 LB-W
296 W-P
C-903
40 LB-W
296 W-P

C-501
C-902
103 W-R — 103 W-R — 103 W-R
104 LB-O — 104 LB-O — 104 LB-O
105 R-W — 105 R-W — 105 R-W
102 W — 102 W — 102 W
108 BR-P D
108 BR-P D

S-804
13 R-BK
13 R-BK
.095 OHM
13 R-BK

BULB OUTAGE DISPLAY PANEL

C-901
C-501
82 PK-Y — 82 PK-Y
14 BR — 14 BR — 14 BR
5 O-LB — 5 O-LB
9 LG-O — 9 LG-O
13 R-BK — 13 R-BK — 13 R-BK
S-805
296 W-P — 296 W-P
296 W-P
215 Y-BK D — 215 Y-BK D
57 BK — 57 BK

215 Y-BK D
296 W-P
57 BK — CHARGE START RUN, SPLICE S-302
82 PK-Y — W/S/W, W/S/W RESERVOIR FULID LEVEL SENSOR
57 BK — ILLUMINATION LAMPS, SPLICE S-1002

9 10 11 12 13 14 15 16

Figs. 11.64 and 11.65 Wiring diagram – Protection and convenience circuits (10) 1980 models (cont.)

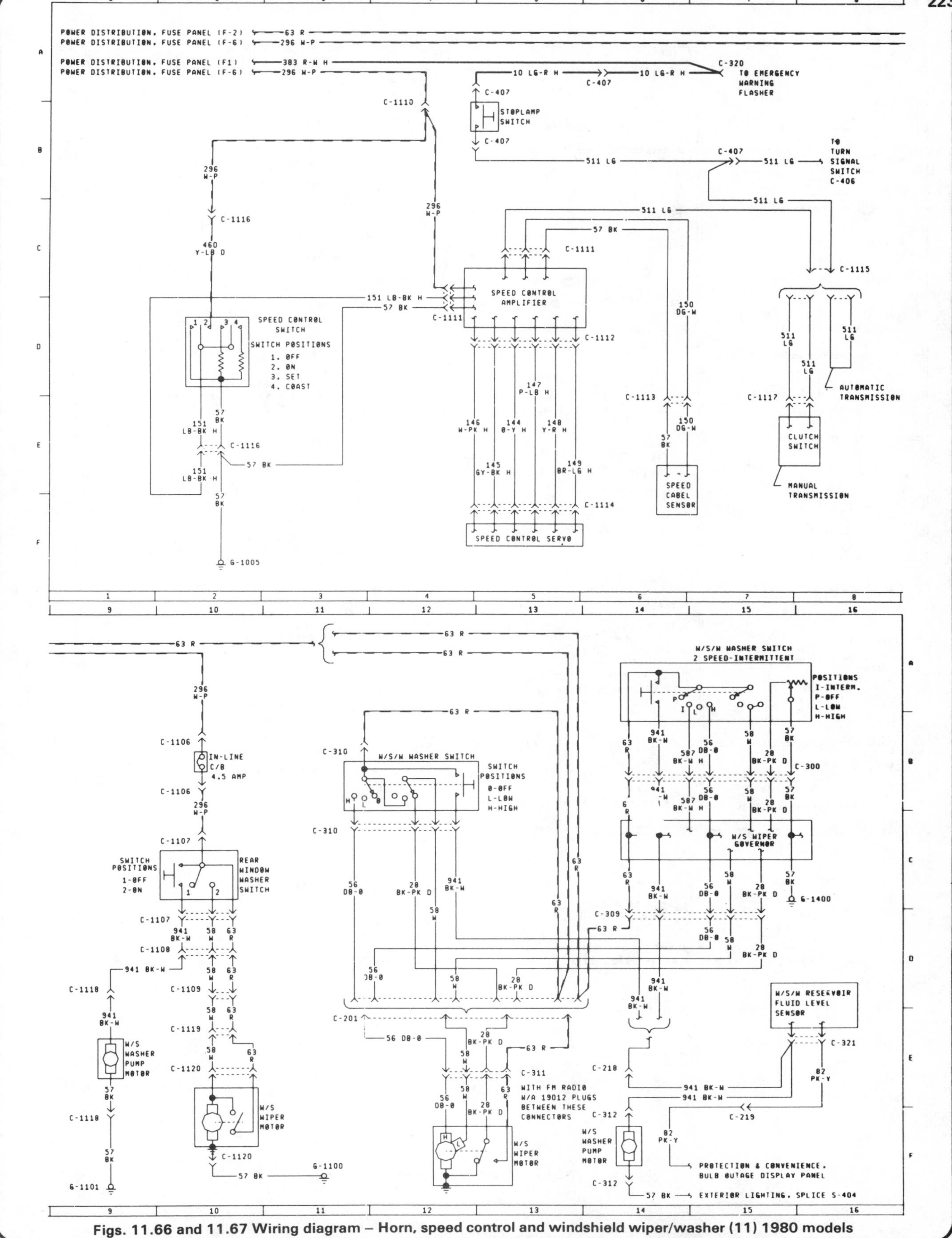

Figs. 11.66 and 11.67 Wiring diagram – Horn, speed control and windshield wiper/washer (11) 1980 models

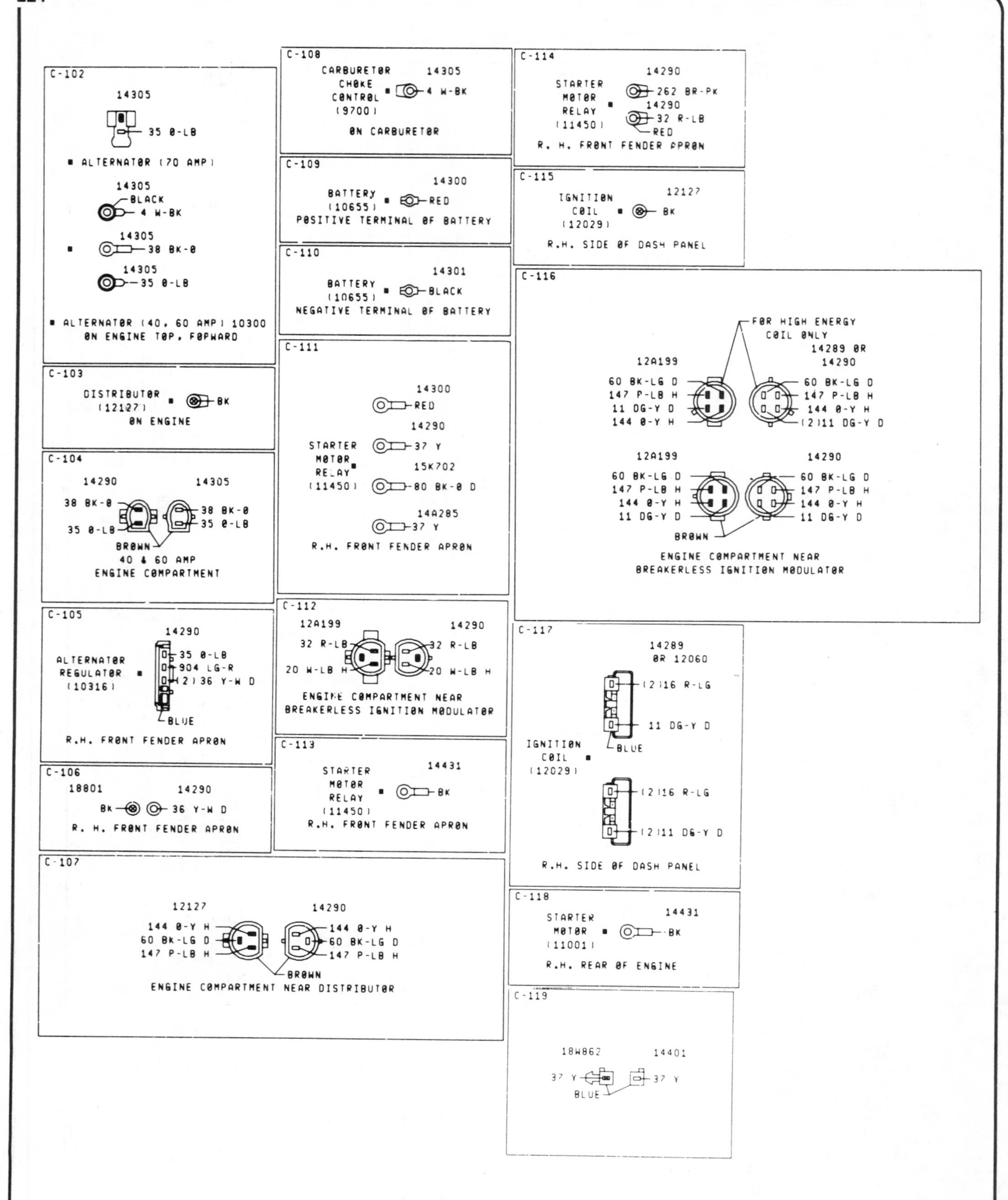

Fig. 11.68 Wiring diagram connectors – 100 series

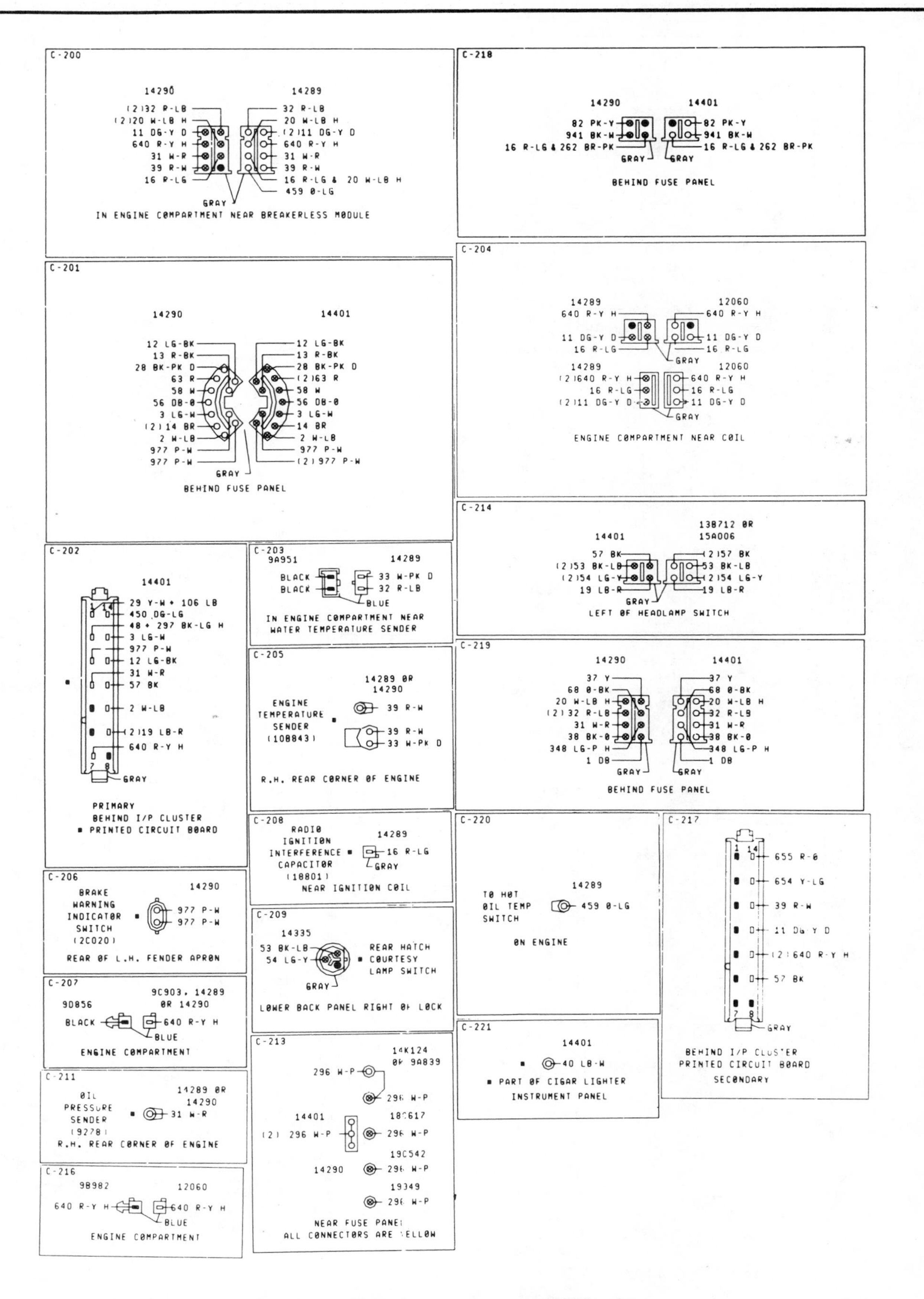

Fig. 11.69 Wiring diagram connectors – 200 series

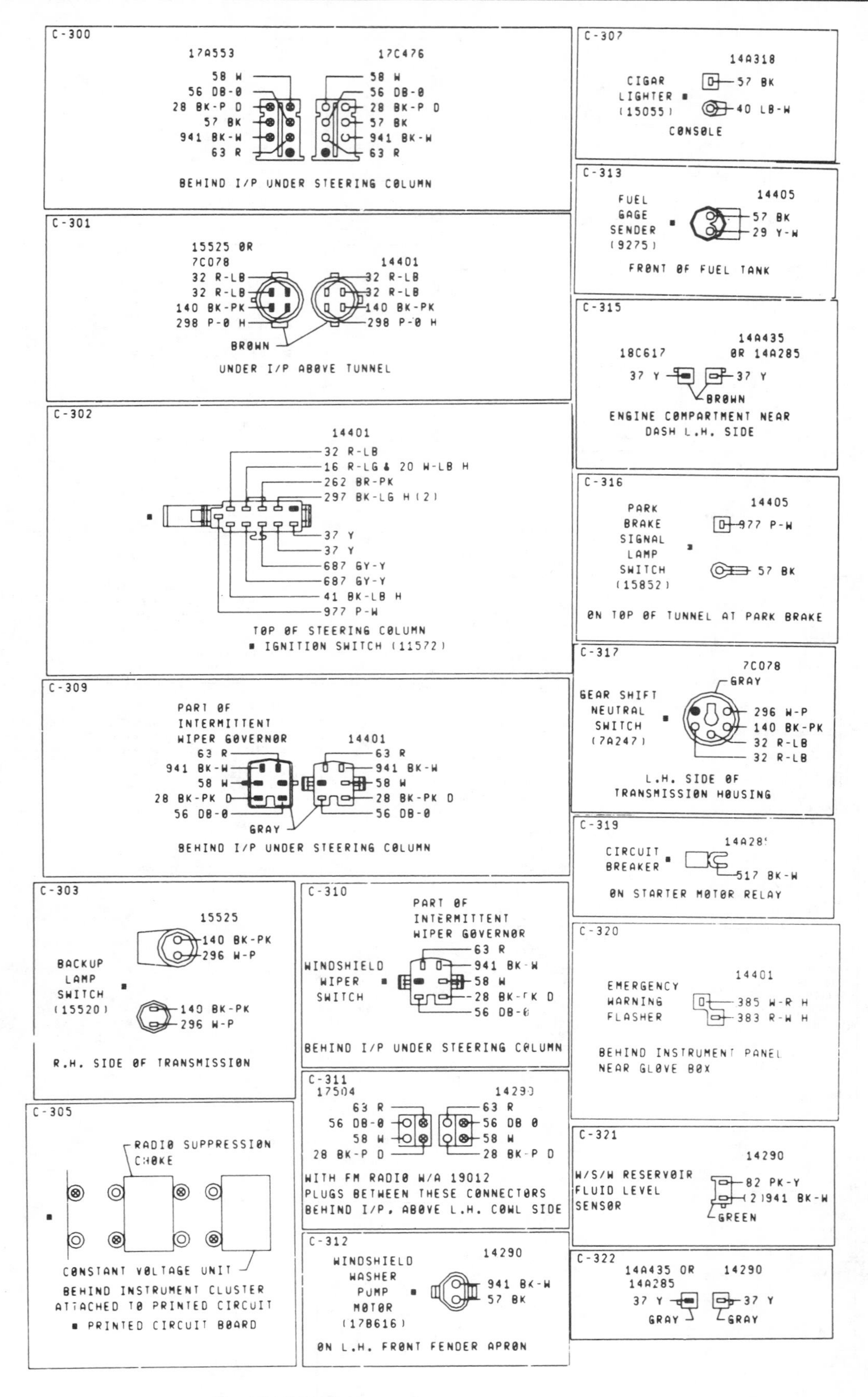

Fig. 11.70 Wiring diagram connectors – 300 series

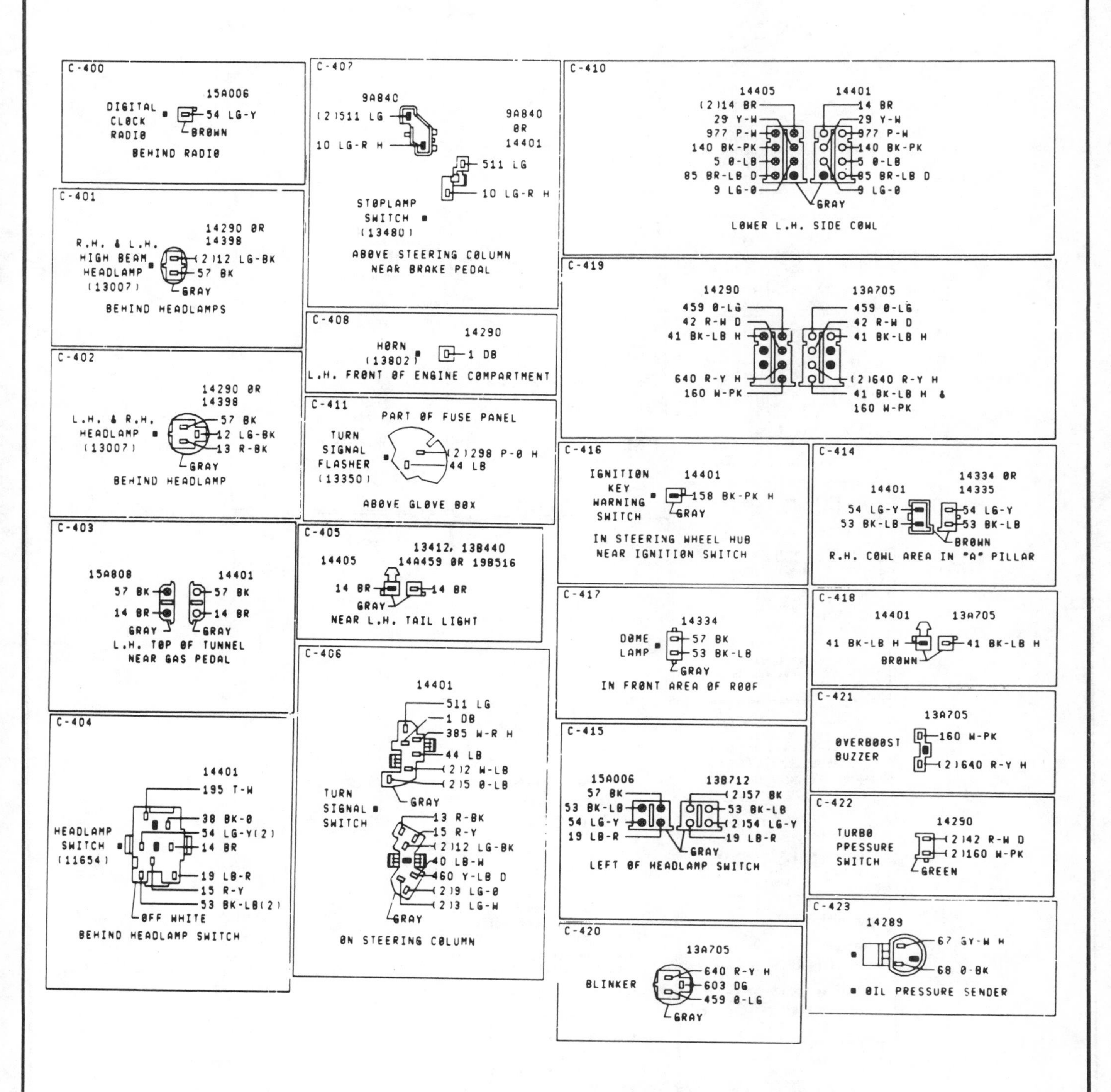

Fig. 11.71 Wiring diagram connectors – 400 series

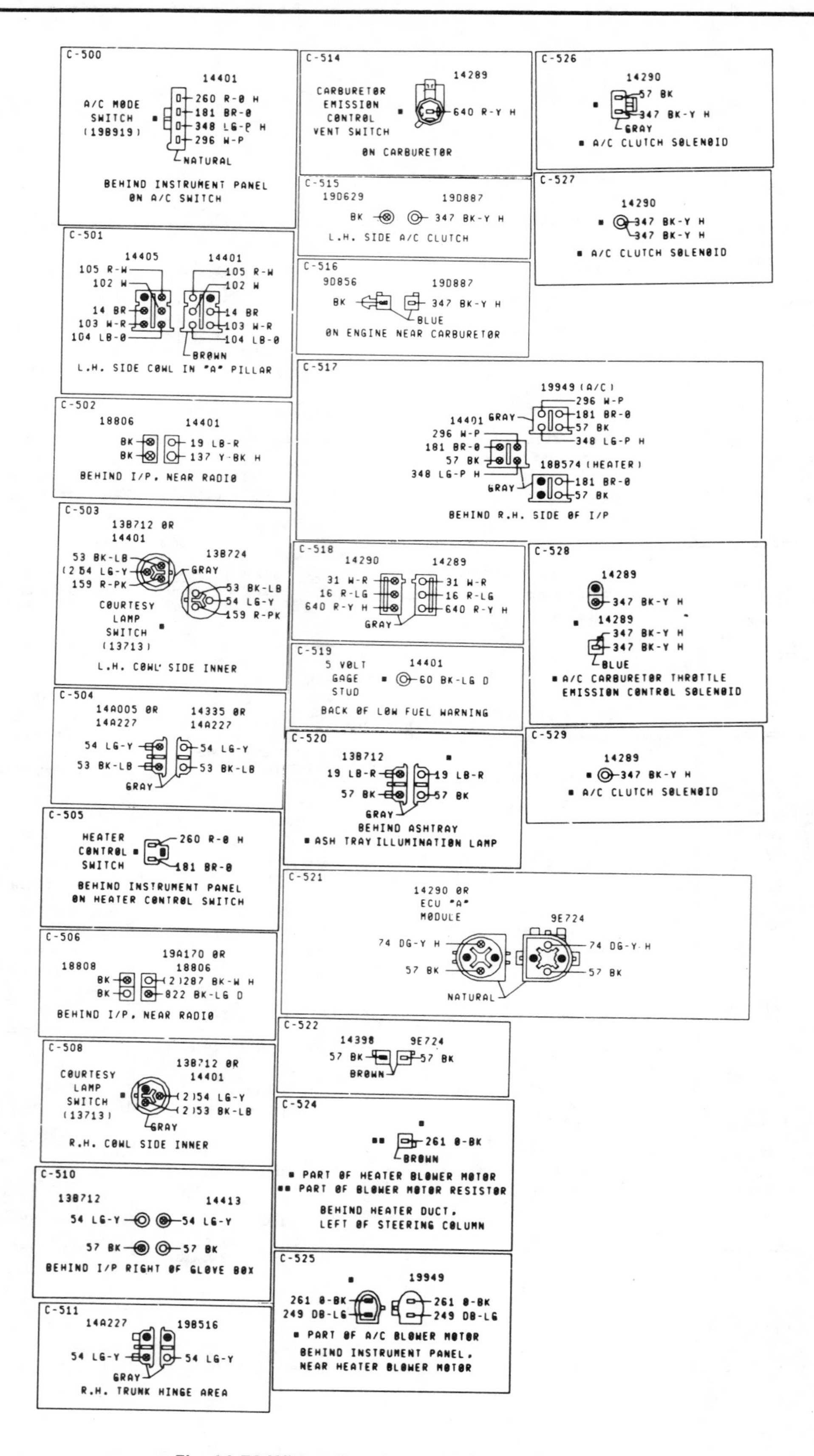

Fig. 11.72 Wiring diagram connectors – 500 series

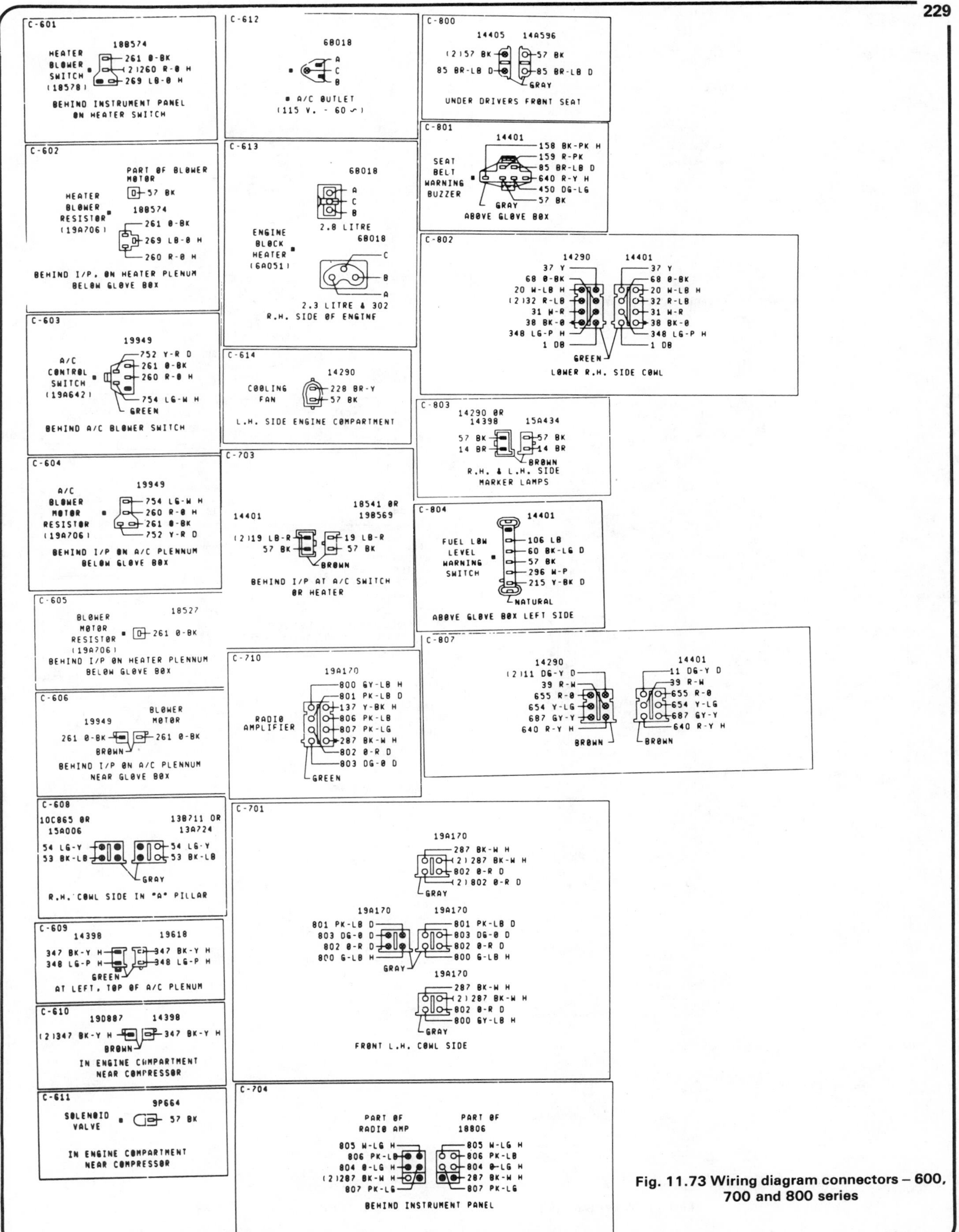

Fig. 11.73 Wiring diagram connectors – 600, 700 and 800 series

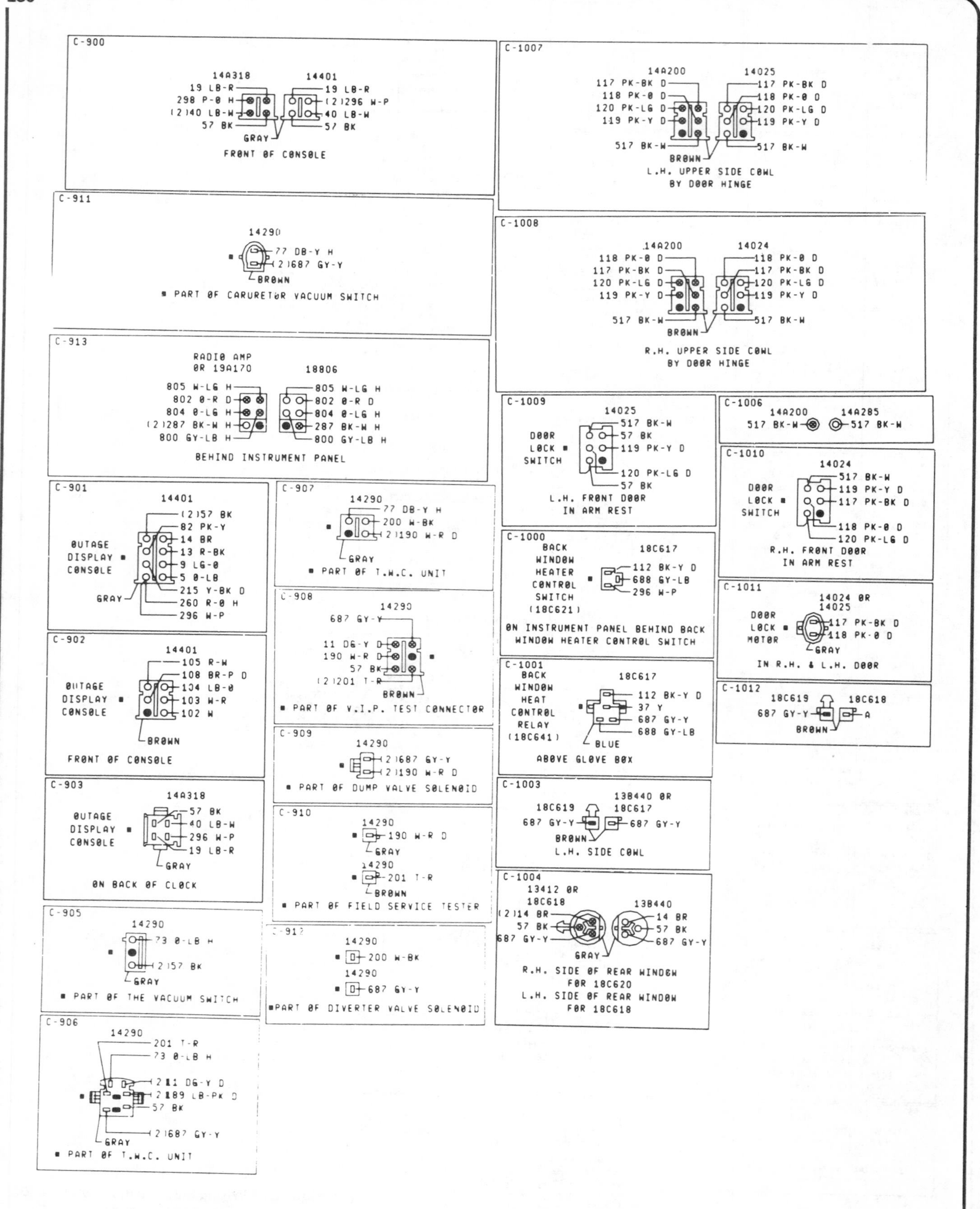

Fig. 11.74 Wiring diagram connectors – 900 and 1000 series

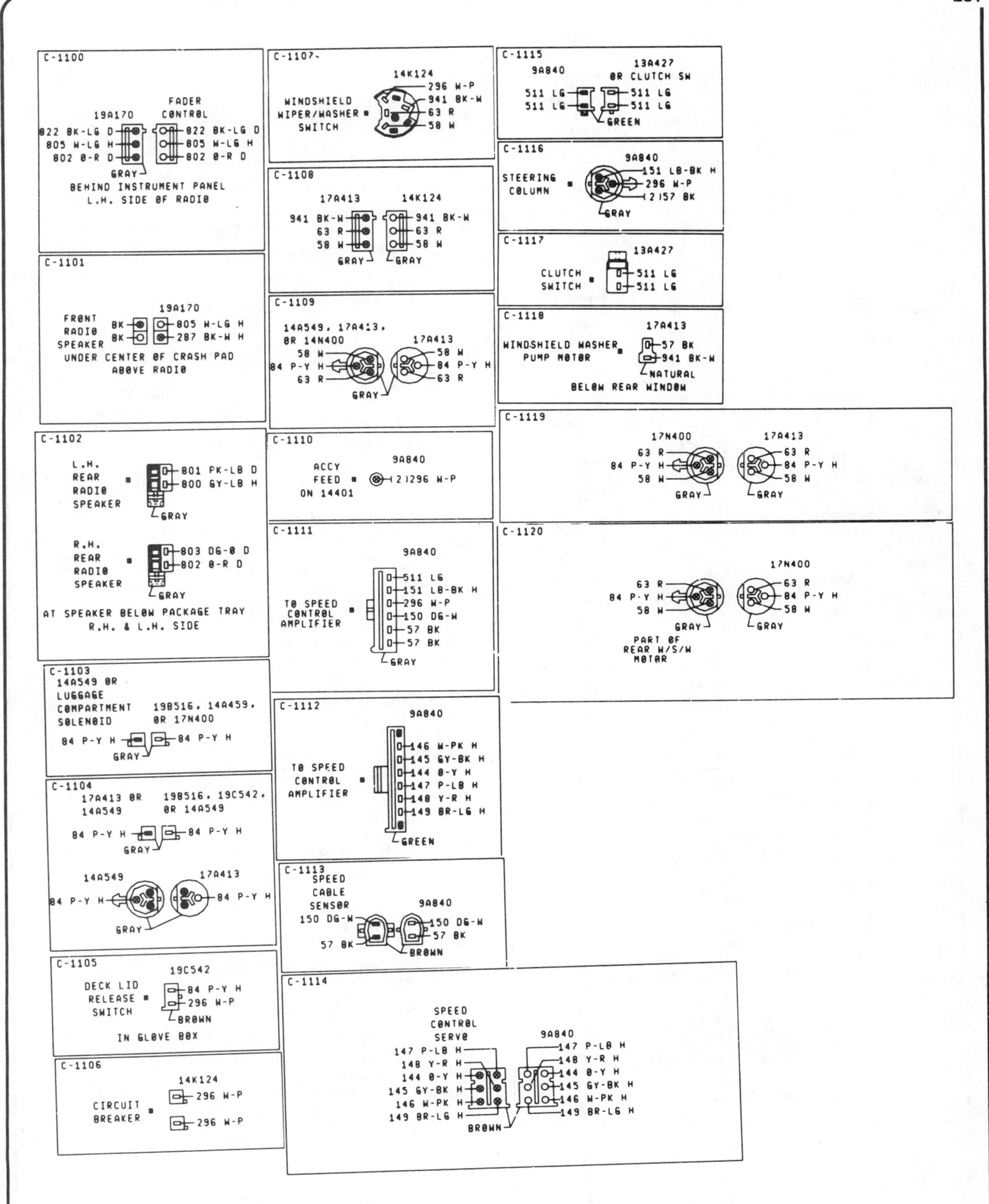

Fig. 11.75 Wiring diagram connectors – 1100 series

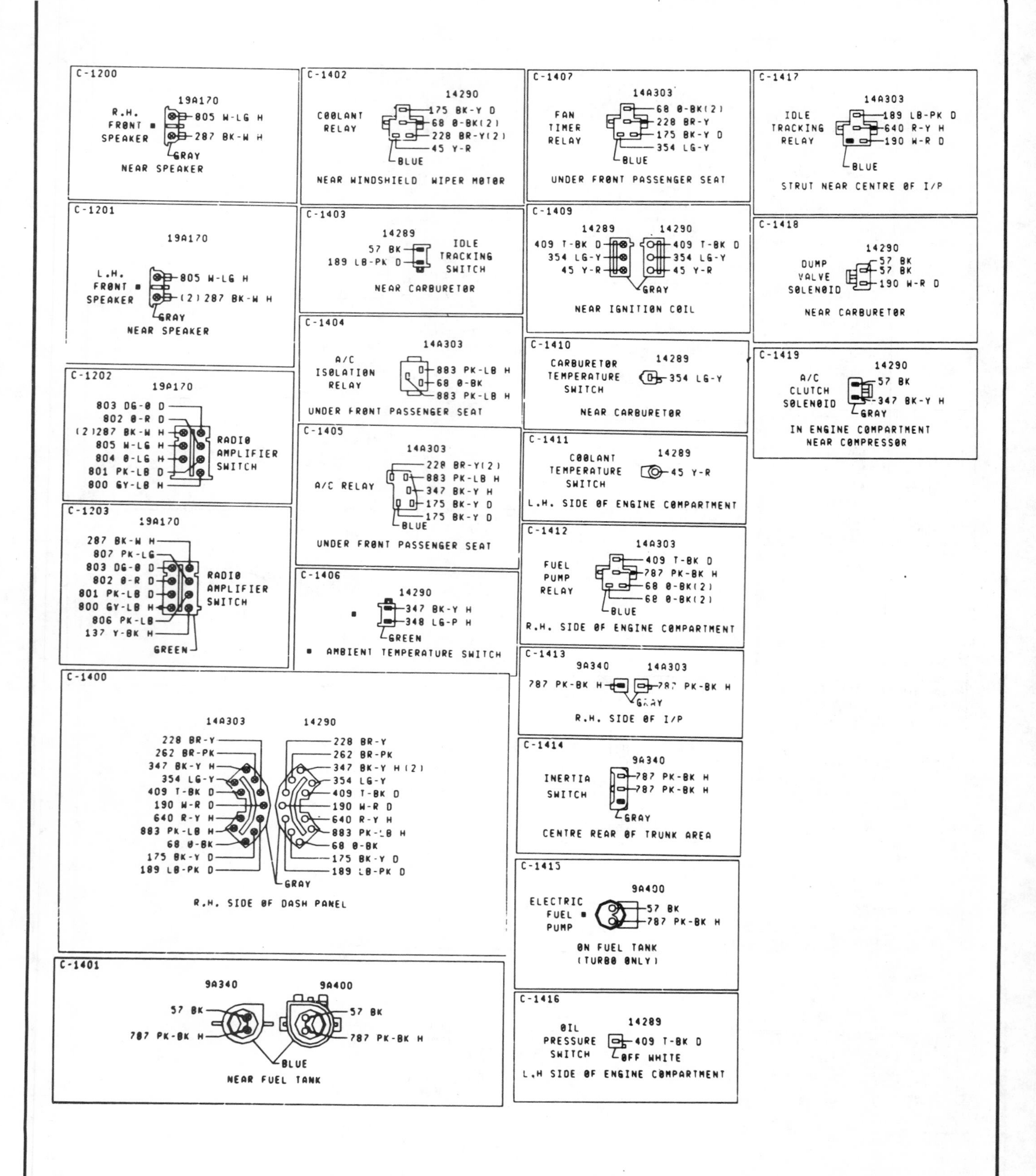

Fig. 11.76 Wiring diagram connectors – 1200 and 1400 series

Chapter 12 Bodywork

Contents

Specifications

Torque specifications	ft-lb	Nm
All fasteners use the following torque wrench settings:		
Metric thread sizes		
M-6	6 to 9	9 to 12
M-8	14 to 21	19 to 28
M-10	28 to 40	38 to 54
M-12	50 to 71	68 to 96
M-14	80 to 140	109 to 154
Pipe thread sizes		
$\frac{1}{8}$	5 to 8	7 to 10
$\frac{1}{4}$	12 to 18	17 to 24
$\frac{3}{8}$	22 to 33	30 to 44
$\frac{1}{2}$	25 to 35	34 to 37
U.S. thread sizes		
$\frac{1}{4}$ – 20	6 to 9	9 to 12
$\frac{5}{16}$ – 18	12 to 18	17 to 24
$\frac{5}{16}$ – 24	14 to 20	19 to 27
$\frac{3}{8}$ – 16	22 to 32	30 to 43
$\frac{3}{8}$ – 24	27 to 38	37 to 51
$\frac{7}{16}$ – 14	40 to 55	55 to 74
$\frac{7}{16}$ – 20	40 to 60	55 to 81
$\frac{1}{2}$ – 13	55 to 80	75 to 108

1 General description

The two-door body is of a unitized, all-welded construction which makes it a strong torsionally rigid shell which can withstand a considerable amount of stress.

The body is available in two configurations: sedan and fastback.

2 Maintenance – body exterior

1 A car's appearance is the first indication of proper care. Neglect, either from minor damage or carelessness will not only detract from the enjoyment of the car but from the resale value.

2 The basic maintenance for the exterior is washing; first loosening the dirt and grime with lots of water, followed with sponge or soft cloth and car washing solution. Check your owner's manual for specific recommendations for car wash products.

3 The wheel wells and underbody need washing in the same way to remove any accumulated mud which will retain moisture and contribute to rust. The best time to clean these areas is during wet weather as the mud will be soft from the rain and will come off easily. If you live in a coastal area, regular cleaning of the underside of the car will inhibit rust.

4 Periodically, it is a good idea to have the underside, engine compartment and wheel wells steam cleaned so that a thorough inspection can be made of the car's condition. Steam cleaning is available at many dealers, repair shops, and coin operated locations. If

none of these are available, there are a number of degreasers, cleaners, and solvents that can be sprayed on and hosed off with a garden hose.

5 After washing the exterior, remove excess water with a chamois or soft cloth. A coat of car wax or protectant will give the added protection against harmful pollutants in the air. The same applies to chrome trim. Refer to your owner's manual, dealer, or local auto parts store for the proper product for your car.

6 Windshields can be kept clear of grease and road film by cleaning them with any number of commercial products. Do not use wax or polish on glass surfaces. Refill the wiper reservoir with water mixed with commercially available wiper cleaner solution.

7 After cleaning the vehicle inside and out, check that the drain and ventilation holes are clear of foreign matter so water is not left standing inside car bodywork. Refer to the illustrations in this Chapter for their location.

3 Maintenance – body interior

1 Mats and carpets should be brushed or vacuum cleaned regularly to keep them free from dirt and grit. Seats and interior panels can be cleaned with a damp cloth using either water or mild cleaning solution. Because of the wide variety of interior options and upholstery, refer to the owner's manual for the proper solution or cleaner/protectant for your car. Don't forget the headliner.

2 When cleaning carpets or upholstery, do not allow water to be soaked into the material. This will avoid offensive odors or rot. Should this happen, do not use heaters or lamps as they could overly dry the material or cause a fire. Allow the moisture to dry by leaving the doors and windows open to allow fresh air to circulate.

4 Minor body damage – repair

See also the photo sequence on pages 238 and 239

Repair of minor scratches in the bodywork

1 If the scratch is very superficial, and does not penetrate to the metal of the bodywork, repair is very simple. Lightly rub the area of the scratch with a rubbing compound, or a very fine cutting paste, to remove loose paint from the scratch and to clear the surrounding bodywork of wax polish. Rinse the area with clean water.

2 Apply touch-up paint to the scratch using a thin paint brush; continue to apply thin layers of paint until the surface of the paint in the scratch is level with the surrounding paintwork. Allow the new paint at least two weeks to harden: then blend it into the surrounding paintwork by rubbing the paintwork, in the scratch area, with a rubbing compound or a very fine cutting paste. Finally, apply wax polish.

3 If the car is painted with a two-coat metallic finish an entirely different technique is required. The materials may be obtained from an authorized dealer. Two types of repair are possible, the 80°C drying method and the Air-drying method. A 'wet-on-wet' procedure for the topcoat and clear lacquer is used. The repair can be done satisfactorily only if the specified top coat and lacquer are used with the specially developed synthetic thinner. After filling with Filler L145 if required sand down with the 400-500 'wet and dry' paper. Apply the first top coat using synthetic resin metallic paint LKL or spraying viscosity 15-17 seconds (DIN cup 4 mm). Let the paint flash off for 25 minutes, then apply the second layer of Air-drying L100 clear varnish with hardener L101 mixed in proportion 8:1. This becomes unusable after six hours. The repair is dust dry after 30 minutes but requires up to 8 days for complete drying. As can be seen it is a complicated process and you are advised to go to your dealer for advice if you have not done the job before. If you have other than a metallic finish then proceed as follows.

4 Where a scratch has penetrated right through to the metal of the bodywork causing the metal to rust, a different repair technique is required. Remove any loose rust from the bottom of the scratch with a penknife, then apply rust inhibiting paint to prevent the formation of rust in the future. Using a rubber or nylon applicator fill the scratch with scratch filler paste. If required, this paste can be mixed with thinners to provide a very thin paste which is ideal for filling narrow scratches. Before the paste in the scratch hardens, wrap a piece of smooth cotton rag around the tip of a finger. Dip the finger in a compatible paint thinner and then quickly sweep it across the surface of the paste in the scratch; this will ensure that the surface of the paste is slightly hollowed. The scratch can now be painted over as described earlier in this Section.

Repair of dents in the bodywork

5 When deep denting of the car's bodywork has taken place, the first task is to pull the dent out, until the affected bodywork almost attains its original shape. There is little point in trying to restore the original shape completely, unless you are an experienced bodywork specialist, as the metal in the damaged area will have stretched on impact and cannot be reshaped fully to its original contour. It is better to bring the level of the dent up to a point which is about $\frac{1}{8}$ in (3 mm) below the level of the surrounding bodywork. In cases where the dent is very shallow anyway, it is not worth trying to pull it out at all.

6 If the underside of the dent is accessible, it can be hammered out gently from behind, using a mallet with a wooden or plastic head. Whilst doing this, hold a suitable block of wood firmly against the outside of the panel to absorb the impact from the hammer blows and thus prevent a large area of the bodywork from being 'belled-out'.

7 Should the dent be in a section of the bodywork which has double skin or some other factor making it inaccessible from behind, a different technique is called for. Drill several small holes through the metal inside the area – particularly in the deeper sections. Then screw long self-tapping screws into the holes just sufficiently for them to gain a good purchase in the metal. Now the dent can be pulled out by pulling on the protruding heads of the screws with a pair of pliers.

8 The next stage of the repair is the removal of the paint from the damaged area, and from an inch or so of the surrounding 'sound' bodywork. This is accomplished most easily by using a wire brush or abrasive pad on a power drill, although it can be done just as effectively by hand using sheets of abrasive paper. To complete the preparation for filling, score the surface of the bare metal with a screwdriver or the tang of a file, or alternatively, drill small holes in the affected areas. This will provide a really good 'key' for the filler paste.

9 To complete the repair see the Section on filling and re-spraying.

Repair of rust holes or gashes in the bodywork

10 Remove all paint from the affected area and from an inch or so of the surrounding 'sound' bodywork, using an abrasive pad or a wire brush on a power drill. If these are not available a few sheets of abrasive paper will do the job just as effectively. With the paint removed you will be able to gauge the severity of the corrosion and therefore decide whether to renew the whole panel (if this is possible) or to repair the affected area. Replacement body panels are not as expensive as most people think and it is often quicker and more satisfactory to fit a new panel than to attempt to repair large areas of corrosion.

11 Remove all fittings from the affected area except those which will act as a guide to the original shape of the damaged bodywork (eg headlamp shells etc). Then, using tin snips or a hacksaw blade, remove all loose metal and any other metal badly affected by corrosion. Hammer the edges of the hole inwards in order to create a slight depression for the filler paste.

12 Wire brush the affected area to remove the powdery rust from the surface of the remaining metal. Paint the affected area with rust inhibiting paint; if the back of the rusted area is accessible treat this also.

13 Before filling can take place it will be necessary to block the hole in some way. This can be achieved by the use of one of the following materials: Zinc gauze, Aluminum tape or Polyurethane foam.

14 Zinc gauze is probably the best material to use for a large hole. Cut a piece to the approximate size and shape of the hole to be filled, then position it in the hole so that its edges are below the level of the surrounding bodywork. It can be retained in position by several blobs of filler paste around its periphery.

15 Aluminum tape should be used for small or very narrow holes. Pull a piece off the roll and trim it to the approximate size and shape required, then pull off the backing paper (if used) and stick the tape over the hole; it can be overlapped if the thickness of one piece is insufficient. Burnish down the edges of the tape with the handle of a screwdriver or similar to ensure that the tape is securely attached to the metal underneath.

16 Polyurethane foam is best used where the hole is situated in a section of bodywork of complex shape, backed by a small box section (eg where the sill panel meets the rear wheel arch – most cars). The usual mixing procedure for this foam is as follows. Put equal amounts

of fluid from each of the two cans provided into one container. Stir until the mixture begins to thicken, then quickly pour this mixture into the hole, and hold a piece of cardboard over the larger apertures. Almost immediately the polyurethane will begin to expand, squirting out of any holes left unblocked. When the foam hardens it can be cut back to just below the level of the surrounding bodywork with a hacksaw blade.

Bodywork repairs – filling and painting

17 Before using this Section, see the Sections on dent, deep scratch, rust hole and gash repairs.

18 Many types of bodyfiller are available, but generally speaking those proprietary kits which contain a tin of filler paste and a tube of resin hardener are best for this type of repair. A wide, flexible plastic or nylon applicator will be found invaluable for imparting a smooth and well contoured finish to the surface of the filler.

19 Mix up a little filler on a clean piece of card or board – use the hardener sparingly (follow the maker's instructions on the packet) otherwise the filler will set very rapidly. Check the packages for warnings before mixing these agents on paper. Some catalyzing agents produce enough heat to ignite paper when mixed.

20 Using the applicator apply the filler paste to the prepared area; draw the applicator across the surface of the filler to achieve the correct contour and to level the filler surface. As soon as a contour that approximates the correct one is achieved, stop working the paste – if you carry on too long the paste will become sticky and begin to 'pick up' on the applicator. Continue to add thin layers of filler paste at twenty-minute intervals until the level of the filler is just above the surrounding bodywork.

21 Once the filler has hardened, excess can be removed using a Surform plane or file. From then on, progressively finer grades of abrasive paper should be used, starting with a 40 grade production paper and finishing with 400 grade 'wet-and-dry' paper. Always wrap the abrasive paper around a flat rubber, cork, or wooden block – otherwise the surface of the filler will not be completely flat. During the smoothing of the filler surface the 'wet-and-dry' paper should be periodically rinsed in water. This will ensure that a very smooth finish is imparted to the filler at the final stage.

22 At this stage the dent should be surrounded by a ring of bare metal, which in turn should be encircled by the finely 'feathered' edge of the good paintwork. Rinse the repair area with clean water, until all of the dust produced by the rubbing-down operation is gone.

23 Spray the whole repair area with a light coat of primer – this will show up any imperfections in the surface of the filler. Repair these imperfections with fresh filler paste or scratch filler, and once more smooth the surface with abrasive paper. If scratch filler is used, it can be mixed with compatible paint thinners to form a really thin paste which is ideal for filling small holes. Repeat this spray and repair procedure until you are satisfied that the surface of the filler, and the feathered edge of the paintwork are perfect. Clean the repair area with clean water and allow to dry fully.

24 The repair area is now ready for final spraying. Paint spraying must be carried out in a warm, dry, windless and dust-free atmosphere. This condition can be created artificially if you have access to a large indoor working area, but if you are forced to work in the open, you will have to pick your day very carefully. If you are working indoors, dousing the floor in the work area with water will 'lay' the dust which would otherwise be in the atmosphere. If the repair area is confined to one body panel, mask off the surrounding panels; this will help to minimize the effects of a slight mis-match in colors. Bodywork fittings (eg chrome strips, door handles etc) will also need to be masked off. Use genuine masking tape and several thicknesses of newspaper for the masking operations.

25 Before commencing to spray, agitate the aerosol can thoroughly, then spray a test area (an old tin, or similar) until the technique is mastered. Cover the repair area with a thick coat of primer; the thickness should be built up using several thin layers of paint rather than one thick one. Using 400 grade 'wet-and-dry' paper, rub down the surface of the primer until it is really smooth. While doing this, the work area should be thoroughly doused with water, and the 'wet-and-dry' paper periodically rinsed in water. Allow to dry before spraying on more paint.

26 Spray on the top coat, again building up the thickness by using several thin layers of paint. Start spraying in the center of the repair area and then, using a circular motion, work outwards until the whole repair area and about 2 inches of the surrounding original paintwork is covered. Remove all masking material 10 to 15 minutes after spraying on the final coat of paint.

27 Allow the new paint at least two weeks to harden, then, using a rubbing compound or a very fine cutting paste, blend the edges of the paint into the existing paintwork. Finally, apply wax polish.

5 Major body damage – repair

In the event of serious damage where large areas of the bodywork need replacement, it is recommended that a professional be consulted. If the damage is due to impact the vehicle will have to be inspected for chassis alignment and hidden damage. As the construction of the new cars is that of a unibody, a specialist's services are necessary.

6 Hood – removal and installation

1 Before starting, mark the bolts and the brackets so that the hood may be replaced in its original position.

2 Place a blanket or newspaper under the corners of the hood to protect the paint of both the hood and body.

3 Loosen the bolts securing the hood to the hinges. This may require assistance as the hood is difficult to support.

4 When the bolts are removed, lift the hood away from the body. Check to see that the hood support rod is not interfering (photo).

5 Install the hood in reverse order of removal being careful not to damage the painted surfaces.

6 Install the hood mounting bolts. Align the bolt heads to the marks made during removal. For final alignment, move the hood on the hinges in order to line up the hood, cowl and fenders.

7 Tighten hood mounting bolts. Check for proper fit.

7 Hood latch – adjustment

1 The hood latch can be moved from side-to-side to align it with the latch hook and up-and-down to obtain a flush fit with the front fenders. The hood must be properly aligned before adjusting the hood latch.

2 If the latch location was marked prior to its removal, start by aligning it with the existing marks. If not, start by installing the latch assembly leaving the bolts loose (photo).

3 Position the latch in alignment with the hood latch lock.

4 Adjust the hood latch up or down to obtain the correct, flush fit between the fenders and the hood.

5 Raise the two hood bumpers to remove any looseness when the hood is closed. Tighten the hood bumper lock nuts.

8 Auxiliary hood catch – adjustment

1 To check the engagement of the auxiliary hood catch, release the hood latch to the open position and pull upwards on the hood. The catch should prevent the hood from opening.

9 Hood latch control cable – removal and replacement

1 Remove the hood latch cable retainer plate screw at the hood latch assembly.

2 Remove the three cable clips which locate the cable along the side of the engine compartment.

3 Remove the clip from the end of the hood latch cable and unhook the cable from the latch assembly.

4 From inside the vehicle, on the driver's side kick panel, remove the screws holding the hood release handle bracket to the interior panel.

5 Lower the handle assembly 2 or 3 inches and carefully pull the cable assembly through the firewall. Be careful to loosen the grommet before the latch end of the cable is pulled through.

6 To reinstall, position the cable through the firewall seating the grommet securely.

7 Install the handle bracket to the kick panel.

8 Route the cable through the engine compartment and secure with cable retaining clips.

9 Install the end of the cable to the hood latch assembly and secure

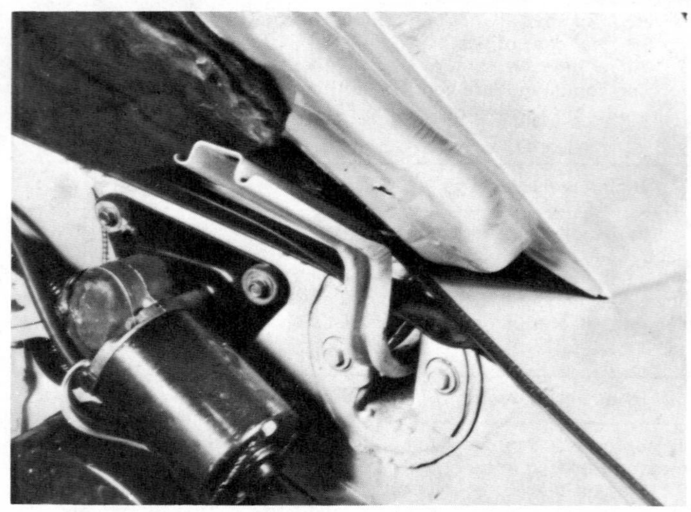

6.4 Lifting hood from vehicle. Note padding protecting windshield

7.2 Scribing around the hood latch to minimise adjustment when reinstalling

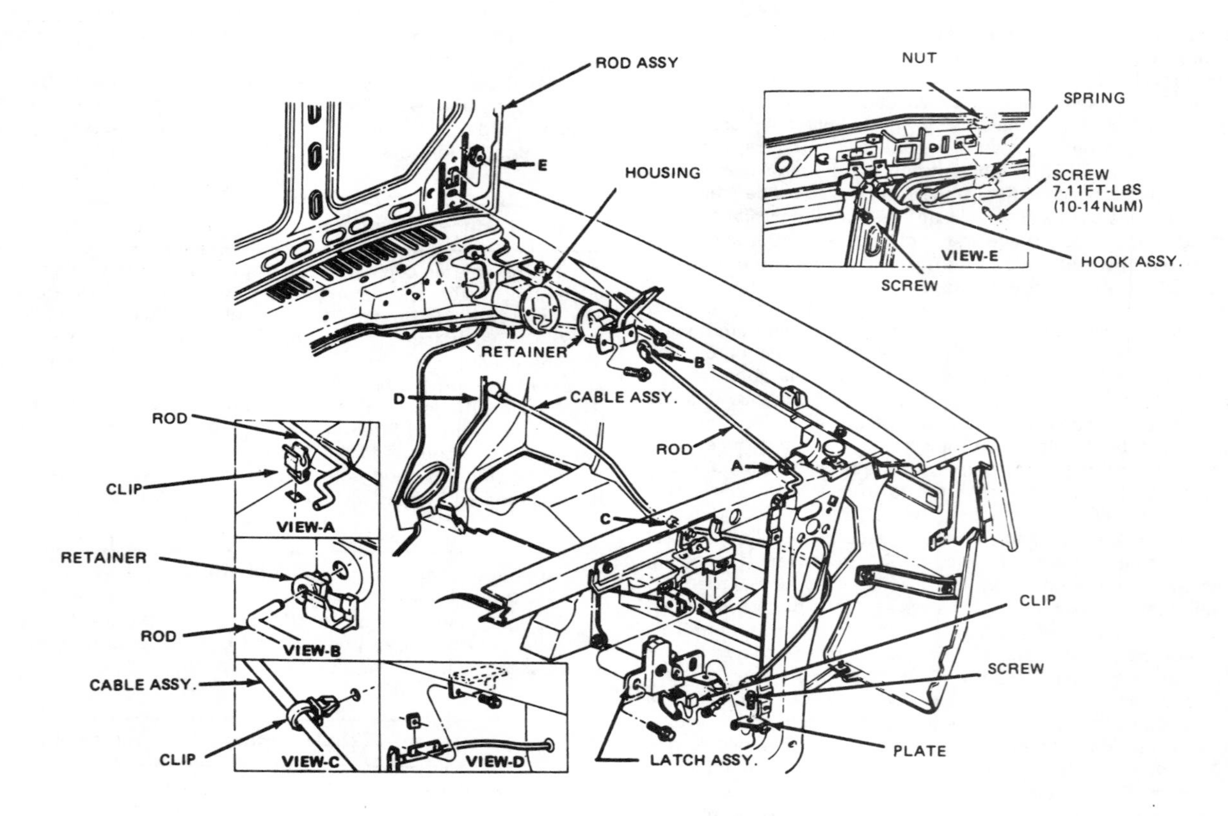

Fig. 12.1 Hood latch components (Secs 7, 8 and 9)

with cable clip.
10 Check for proper operation.

10 Trunk lid torsion bar – adjustment

1 Check the trunk lid for pop-up of at least 3 inches when the latch is released. If the lid does not provide this clearance, the torsion bar tension will have to be increased.
2 Use a piece of tubing approximately 6 inches long and place over the end of the torsion spring.
3 Raise or lower as required to allow the trunk lid to give the proper finger clearance.

11 Hatchback – adjustment

1 Remove the center, interior garnish molding screws and panel.
2 Loosen the hinge to roof panel attaching bolts and adjust hinges left-to-right or up-and-down as required.
3 Check for proper fit.
4 Tighten the mounting bolts and replace the garnish molding.

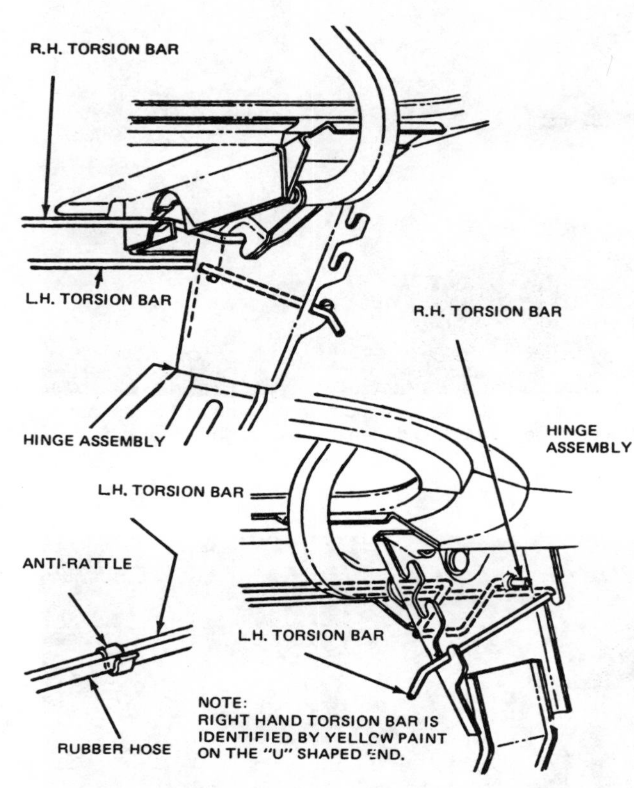

Fig. 12.2 Trunk lid torsion bar components (Sec 10)

12 Hatchback lift assembly – inspection and replacement

1 The hatchback is raised by two gas-filled lift assemblies resembling long, thin shock absorbers. If the hatchback does not raise itself upon release of the latch, one or both of the gas springs may be defective.

2 One at a time, remove the securing spring from one end of the gas spring.

3 Check to see that the gas spring extends fully. If it does not extend, it is defective and needs to be replaced.

13 Doors – removal and installation

1 The doors of the Mustang/Capri are of a weld-on-door/bolt-on-body design. That is, there is no adjustment on the doors as on other cars. Any adjustment should be referred to a local dealer or body shop.

2 To remove the doors, remove the six large screws located at the hinge area. Be sure to support the door when the screws are removed as the door assembly is heavy.

14 Door trim – removal and installation

1 Remove the door lock pushbutton knob by unscrewing it from the control rod.

2 Remove the window regulator handle screw and withdraw handle (photo).

3 Pull the interior door handle release and remove the single screw found just underneath.

4 Unclip the door release rod from the latch and remove the handle assembly.

5 Remove the screw on the front of the door armrest.

6 Pry with a gasket scraper or putty knife the back of the armrest to release the snap connectors. Remove the armrest.

7 Remove the side view mirror trim cover screw and cover.

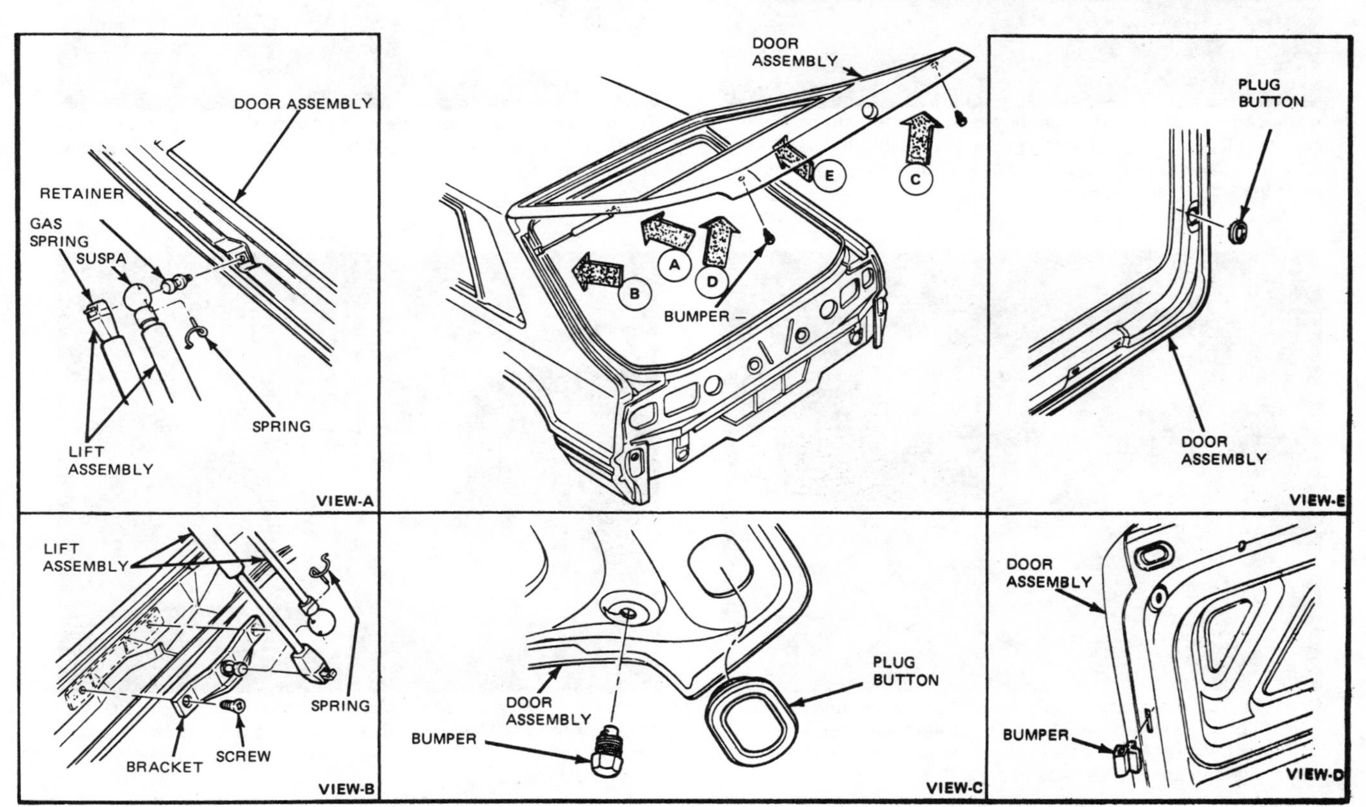

Fig. 12.3 Hatchback components (Sec 11)

This photo sequence illustrates the repair of a dent and damaged paintwork. The procedure for the repair of a hole is similar. Refer to the text for more complete instructions

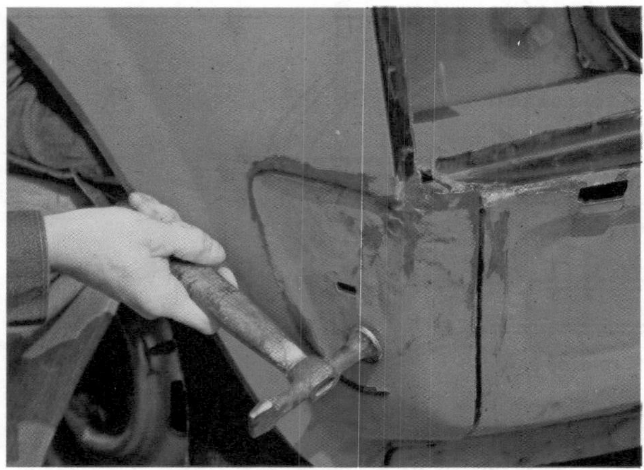
After removing any adjacent body trim, hammer the dent out. The damaged area should then be made slightly concave

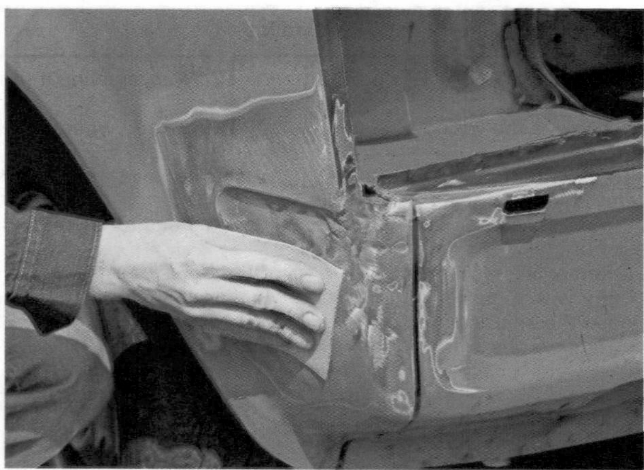
Use coarse sandpaper or a sanding disc on a drill motor to remove all paint from the damaged area. Feather the sanded area into the edges of the surrounding paint, using progressively finer grades of sandpaper

The damaged area should be treated with rust remover prior to application of the body filler. In the case of a rust hole, all rusted sheet metal should be cut away

Carefully follow manufacturer's instructions when mixing the body filler so as to have the longest possible working time during application. Rust holes should be covered with fiberglass screen held in place with dabs of body filler prior to repair

Apply the filler with a flexible applicator in thin layers at 20 minute intervals. Use an applicator such as a wood spatula for confined areas. The filler should protrude slightly above the surrounding area

Shape the filler with a surform-type plane. Then, use water and progressively finer grades of sandpaper and a sanding block to wet-sand the area until it is smooth. Feather the edges of the repair area into the surrounding paint.

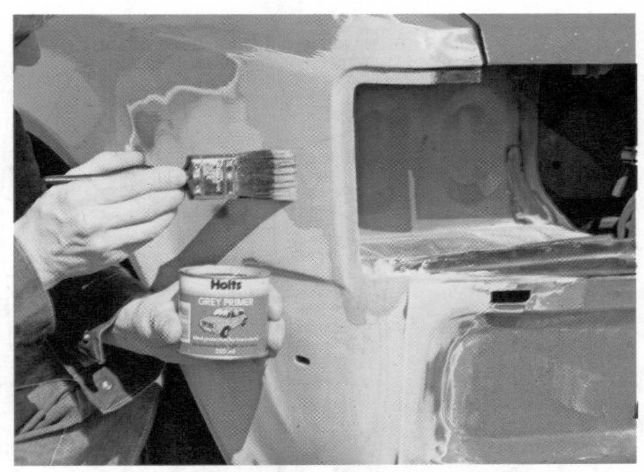

Use spray or brush applied primer to cover the entire repair area so that slight imperfections in the surface will be filled in. Prime at least one inch into the area surrounding the repair. Be careful of over-spray when using spray-type primer

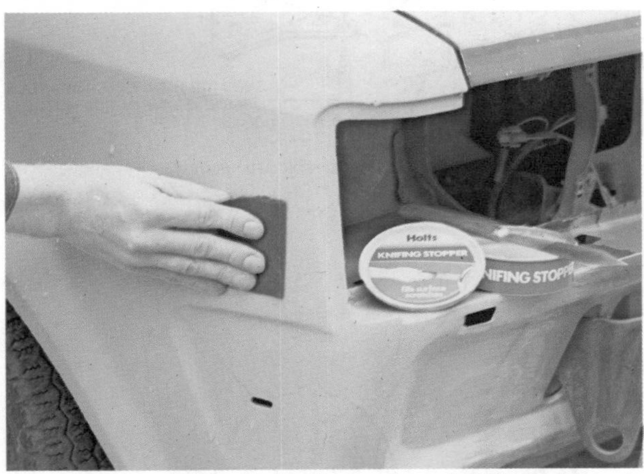

Wet-sand the primer with fine (approximately 400 grade) sandpaper until the area is smooth to the touch and blended into the surrounding paint. Use filler paste on minor imperfections

After the filler paste has dried, use rubbing compound to ensure that the surface of the primer is smooth. Prior to painting, the surface should be wiped down with a tack rag or lint-free cloth soaked in lacquer thinner

Choose a dry, warm, breeze-free area in which to paint and make sure that adjacent areas are protected from over-spray. Shake the spray paint can thoroughly and apply the top coat to the repair area, building it up by applying several coats, working from the center

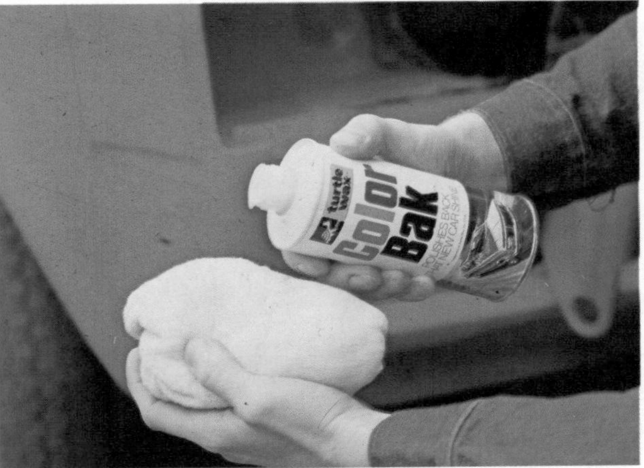

After allowing at least two weeks for the paint to harden, use fine rubbing compound to blend the area into the original paint. Wax can now be applied

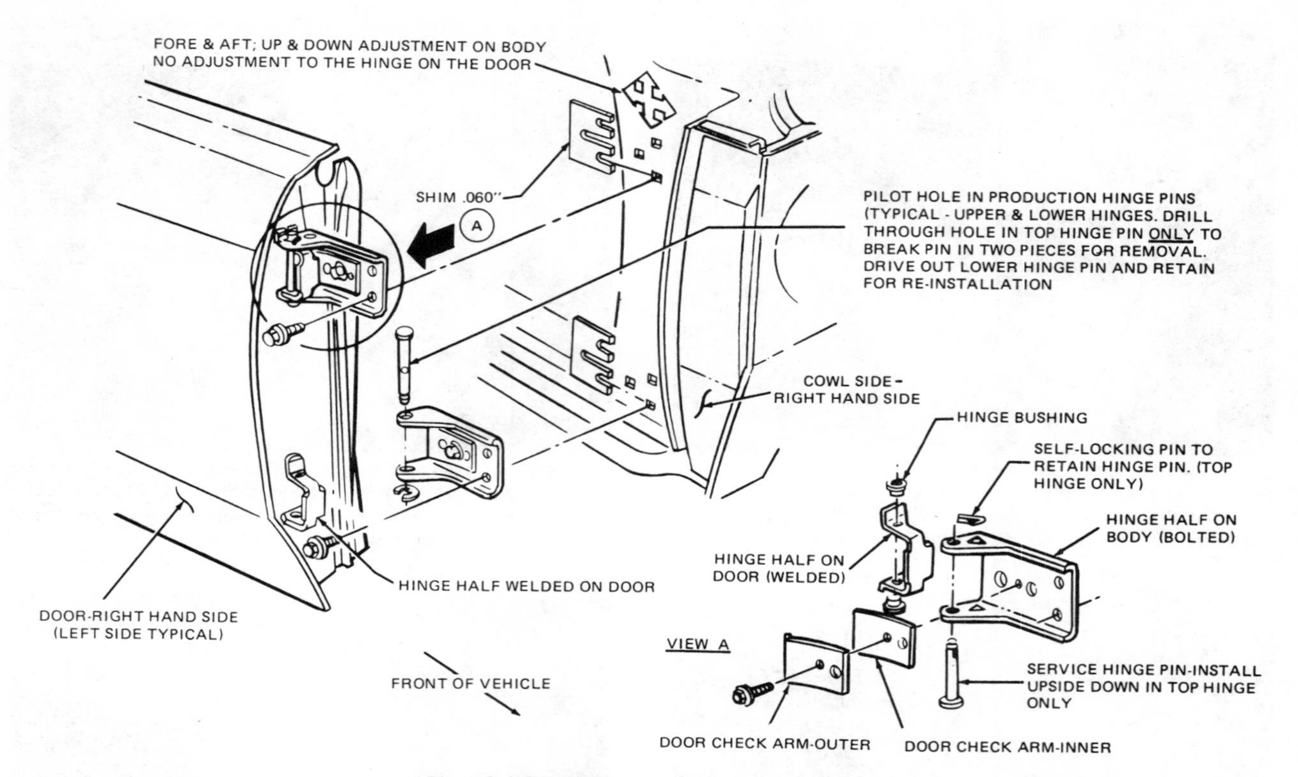

Fig. 12.4 Door hinge components (Sec 13)

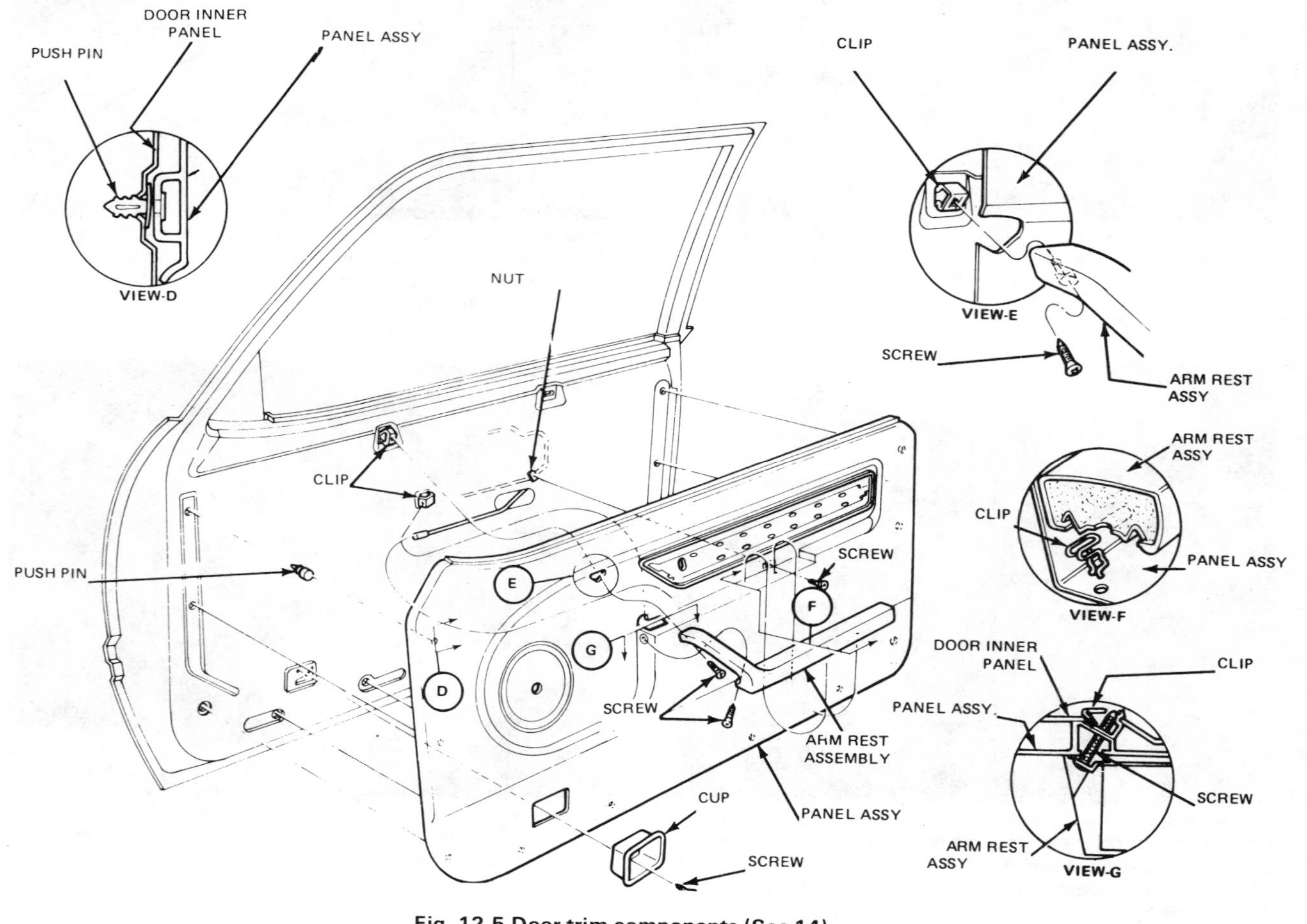

Fig. 12.5 Door trim components (Sec 14)

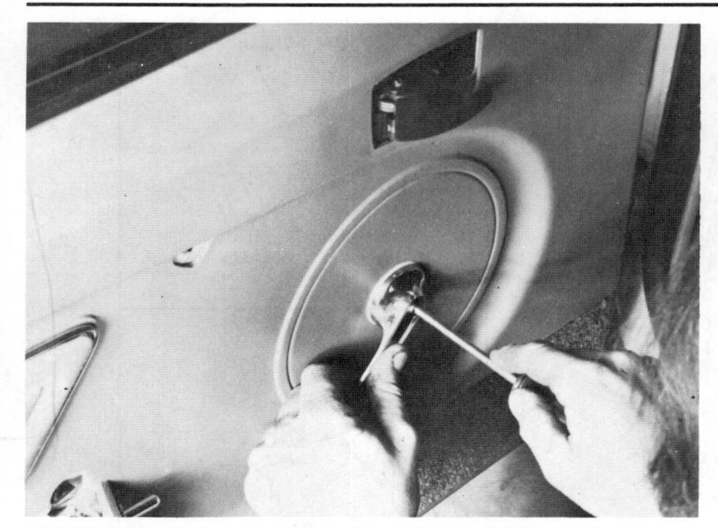
14.2 Hold the window regulator with one hand while removing the screw

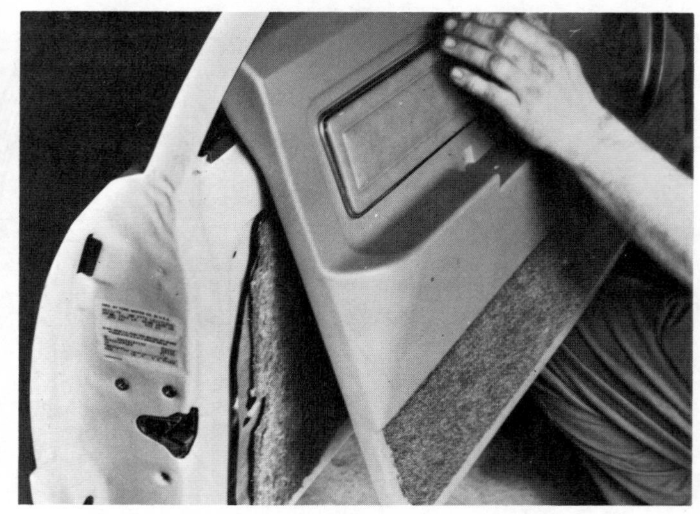
14.9 The door panel should be lifted upward and away when removing

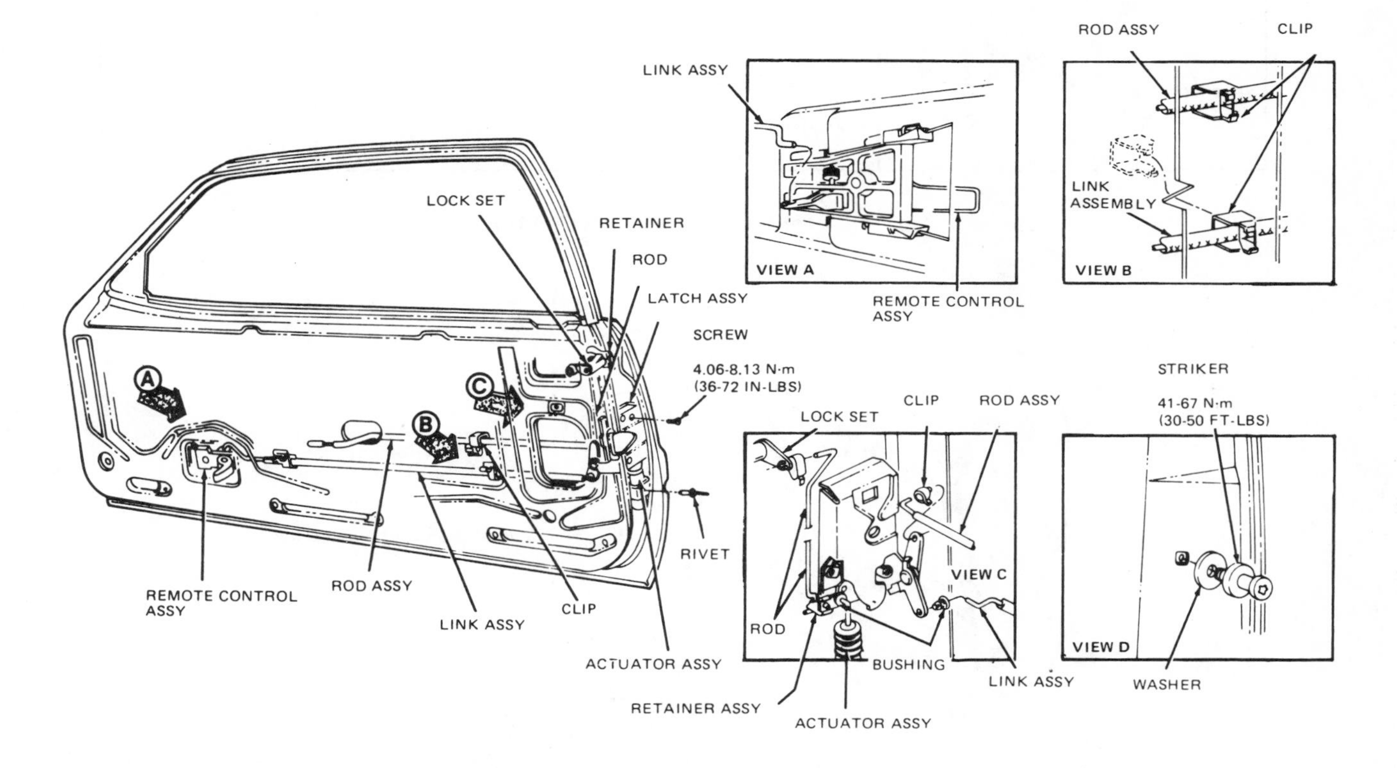

Fig. 12.6 Door lock mechanism (Sec 15)

8 Pry the perimeter of the door panel sides and bottom only. When the panel is loose, lift up the window glass interior strip and remove.
9 Lift the door panel up and away from the door assembly (photo).
10 Installation is the reverse of removal. However, take your time for a proper fit to eliminate any rattles.

15 Door lock mechanism – removal and installation

1 Remove the door trim panel and inner pad.
2 Check all actuating rod locations and operation against the illustrations in Fig. 12.6.
3 Disconnect the rods from the latch assembly.
4 Remove the screws holding the latch to the door.
5 Depress the lock cylinder retaining clip and remove.
6 Remove the lock cylinder.
7 Remove the latch cylinder from the door.
8 Installation is the reverse of disassembly. Be sure to compare the latch and rod of the car to those in the illustrations.

16 Door glass and regulator

1 The door glass and mechanism is held in with special rivets and connectors. For service or replacement, refer to your local dealer or repair shop.

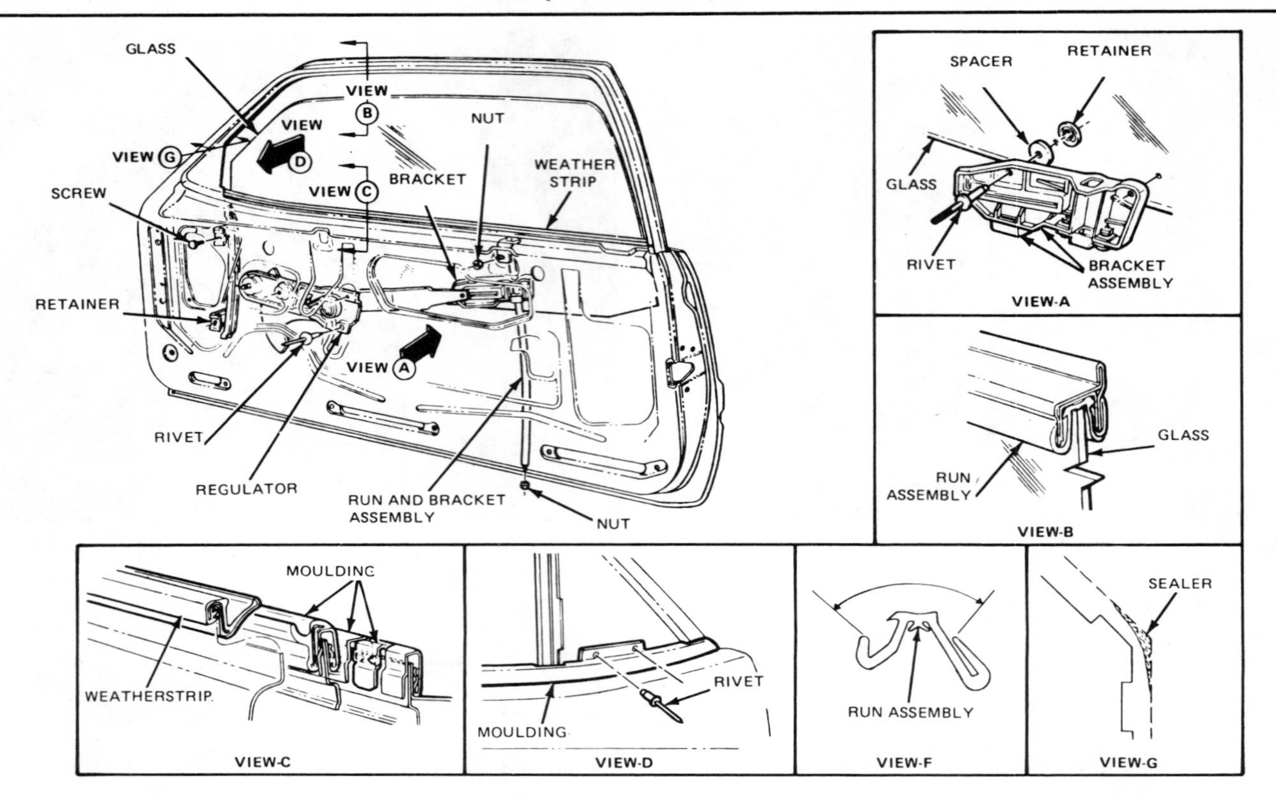

Fig. 12.7 Door glass and regulator (Sec 16)

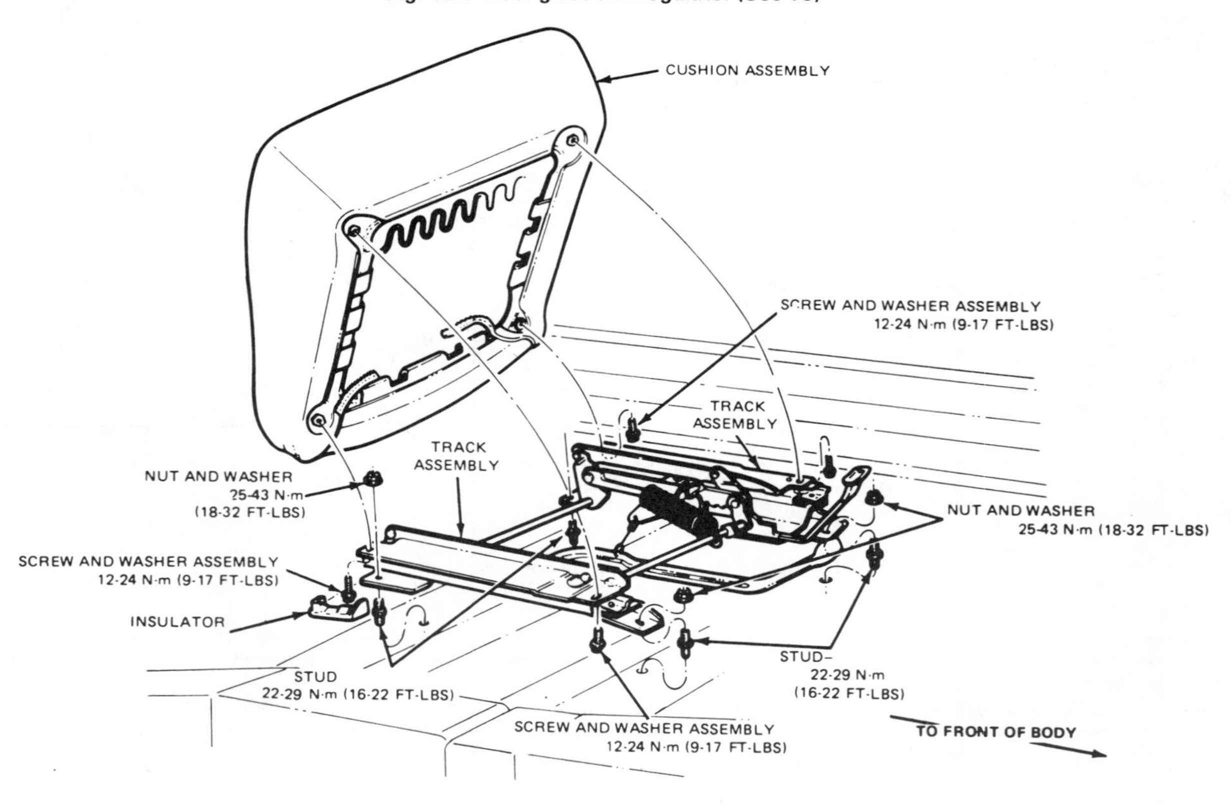

Fig. 12.8 Bucket seat and track installation (Sec 17)

17 Seats – removal and installation

1 Pry off the plastic trim pieces covering the seat hold-down nuts.

2 Unscrew the nuts and lift the seat up.

3 When installing the seats, check for carpet or other foreign matter slipping under the seat mount pads so that the seat is bolted down securely.

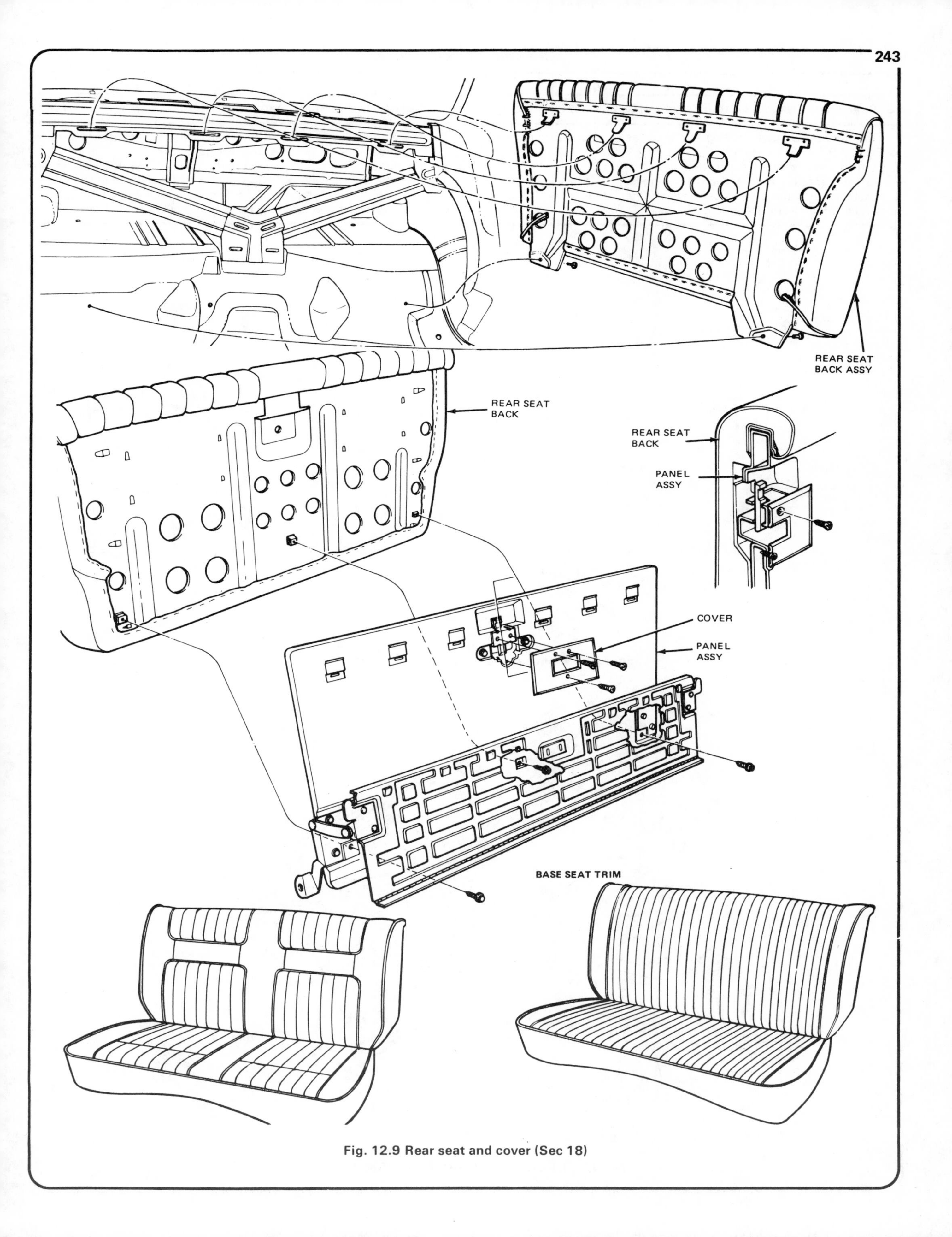

Fig. 12.9 Rear seat and cover (Sec 18)

18 Rear seat – removal and installation

1 Remove the screws holding the seat base to the floor pan. Refer to Fig. 12.9 for their location.
2 Lift the seat bottom away.
3 Lift the seat back up and out to remove.
4 Installation is the reverse of removal. Check that the seat belts do not catch underneath the seat cushions.

19 Seat belts – removal and installation

1 The seat belts are secured to the floor pan and chassis by special "star" bolts requiring the use of a special socket.
2 To remove the inboard seat belt, unsnap the trim cover and unscrew the special bolt holding the belt to the floor pan.
3 The outer belt is held inside a side panel along with an inertia reel. When the door is open the belt is free to move in order to adjust to the

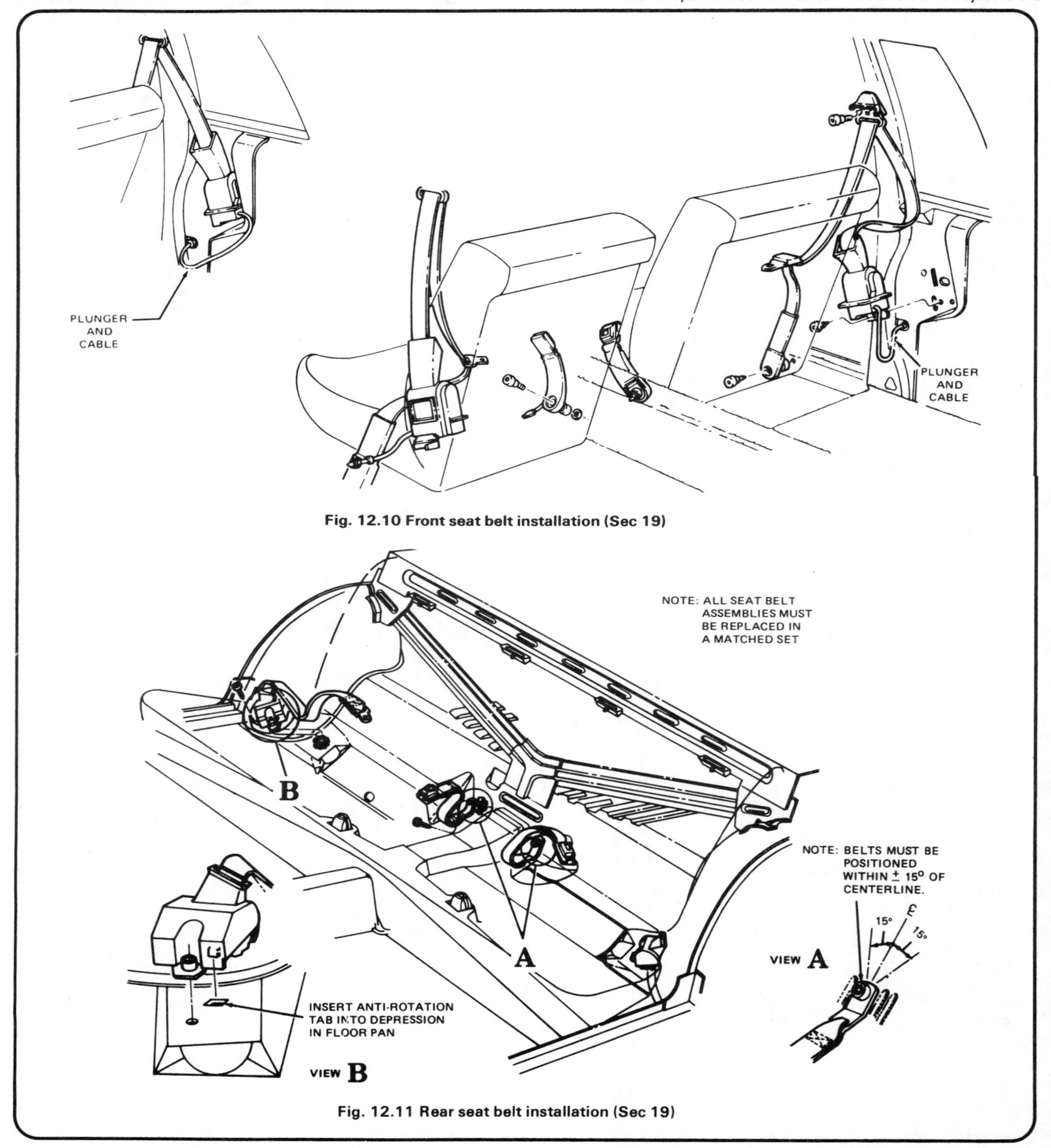

Fig. 12.10 Front seat belt installation (Sec 19)

Fig. 12.11 Rear seat belt installation (Sec 19)

size of the occupant.
4 Unscrew the bolts securing the rear seat base and remove.
5 Lift the trim for the coat hook and remove the seat belt pivot screw.
6 Unscrew the rear side trim panel. Pry the panel away from the body to remove.
7 Unscrew and remove the trim panel surrounding the rear side window.
8 Lift away all trim panels, unscrew the seat belt reel assembly.
9 In the door opening, turn and unclip the seat belt positioning latch actuator. Remove the actuator assembly.
10 Lift out the entire seat belt assembly.
11 Installation is the reverse of removal.

20 Windshield and rear glass

1 Both of these glass pieces should be repaired as necessary by a local repair or auto glass shop.

21 Console – removal and installation

1 Pry the rear of the shifter trim plate and remove (photo).
2 Lift out the ashtray and remove the two screws underneath (photo).
3 Remove the screws toward the bottom rear of the console.

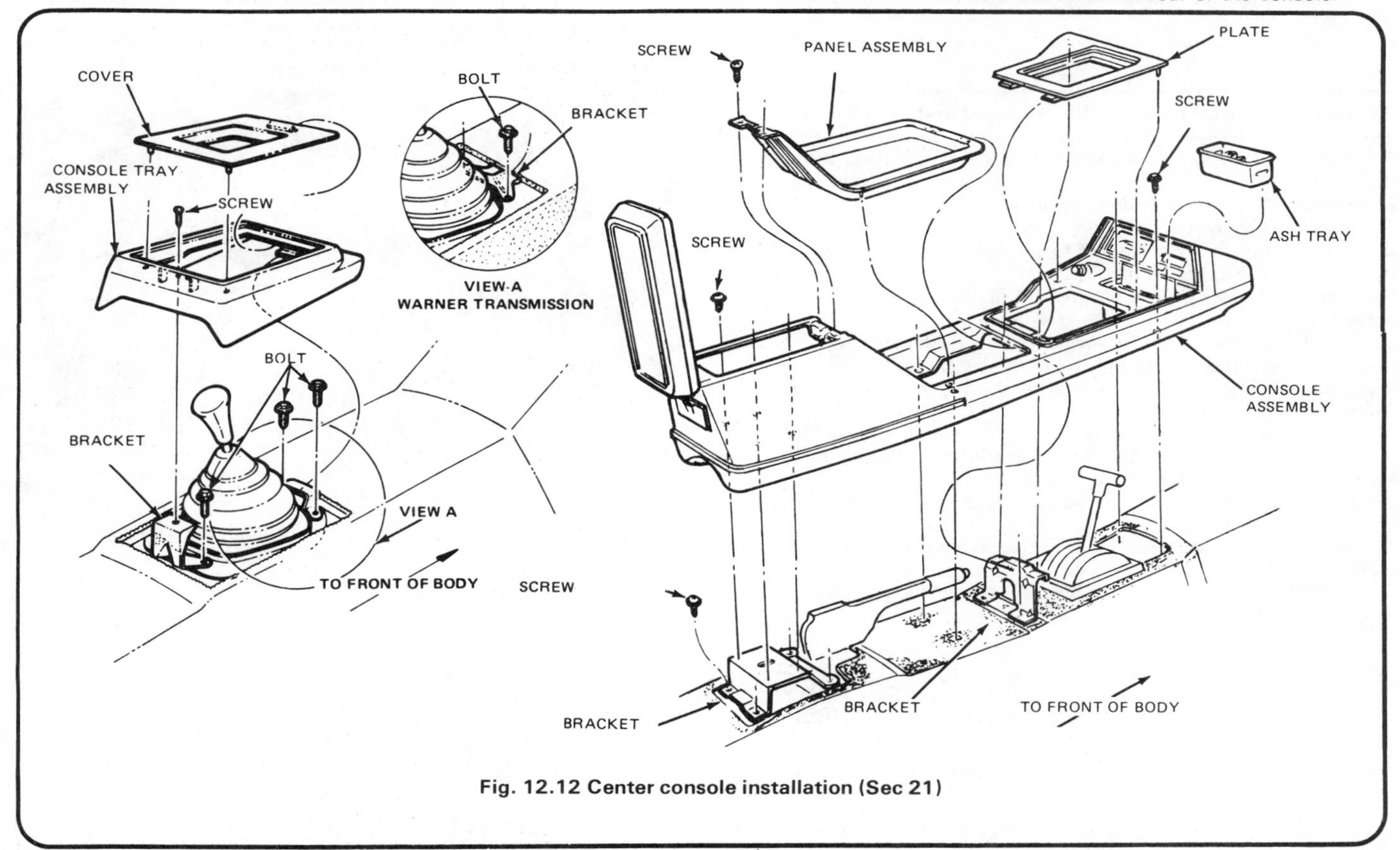

Fig. 12.12 Center console installation (Sec 21)

21.1 Remove the shift plate by prying it loose and lifting it over the shift lever

21.2 After lifting out the ashtray, remove the 2 screws holding the console to the floor

4 Lift the console approximately four inches and disconnect the electrical connectors.
5 Lifting from the rear, remove the console from the interior. Be careful not to damage surrounding trim.
6 Installation is the reverse of removal.

22 Glove compartment door – removal and installation

1 Remove the two screws holding the door to the hinge and remove the door.
2 To install, fit the door to the hinge with the screws. Do not tighten.
3 Position the glove compartment door as needed to fit the surrounding trim.
4 Tighten the screws.

23 Dashboard and instruments – removal and installation

1 Before starting any work around electrical connections, disconnect the battery.
2 Remove the three instrument panel screws.
3 Remove the screws holding the instrument front panel.
4 Remove the screws adjacent to the defroster opening grilles. Lift the instrument pad to remove.
5 Remove the four screws holding the instrument cluster to the dash assembly.
6 Pull the instrument cluster away from the dash panel approximately 4 inches and disconnect the speedometer cable. Place the instrument cluster on the steering column and disconnect the gauge light wiring (photo).
7 Remove the instrument cluster.
8 Remove the screws securing the trim panel underneath the steering column. Remove the trim and place aside.
9 Reach underneath the left bottom of the dash and unplug the headlight harness plug.
10 Remove the sheet metal screws fitted to the dash assembly. Refer to Fig. 12.13.
11 Loosen the bolts on the dash support brackets on both the right and left sides of the assembly.
12 When all the screws and bolts are removed check to see that all wiring looms and connectors are free to hang down without tangling in the dash assembly. If the dash does not pull easily from the front, recheck for connections and other hardware that may be caught.
13 Loosen the four bolts securing the steering column and lower the assembly to rest on the floor or seat. Disconnect the wiring from the column.
14 Lift the dash assembly up to clear the upper dash metal work and pull towards the rear of the car.
15 Note the position of wiring, connectors and supplementary brackets under the dash.
16 Installation is the reverse of removal. It is best to take the time to

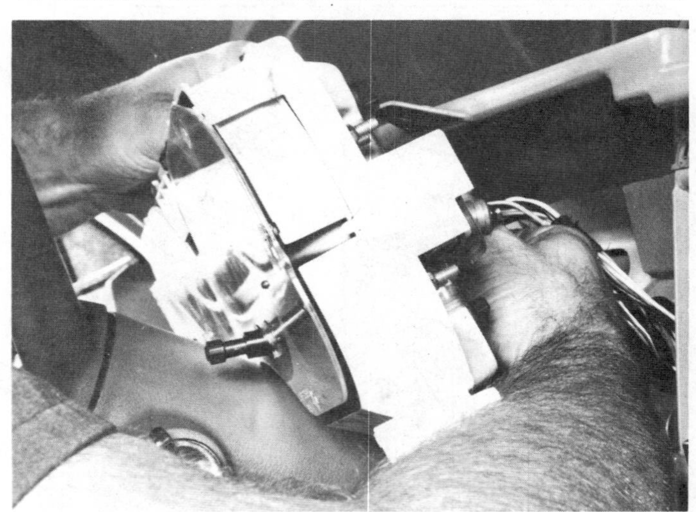

23.6 Rest the the instrument cluster on the steering column during removal of speedometer cable and wiring connectors

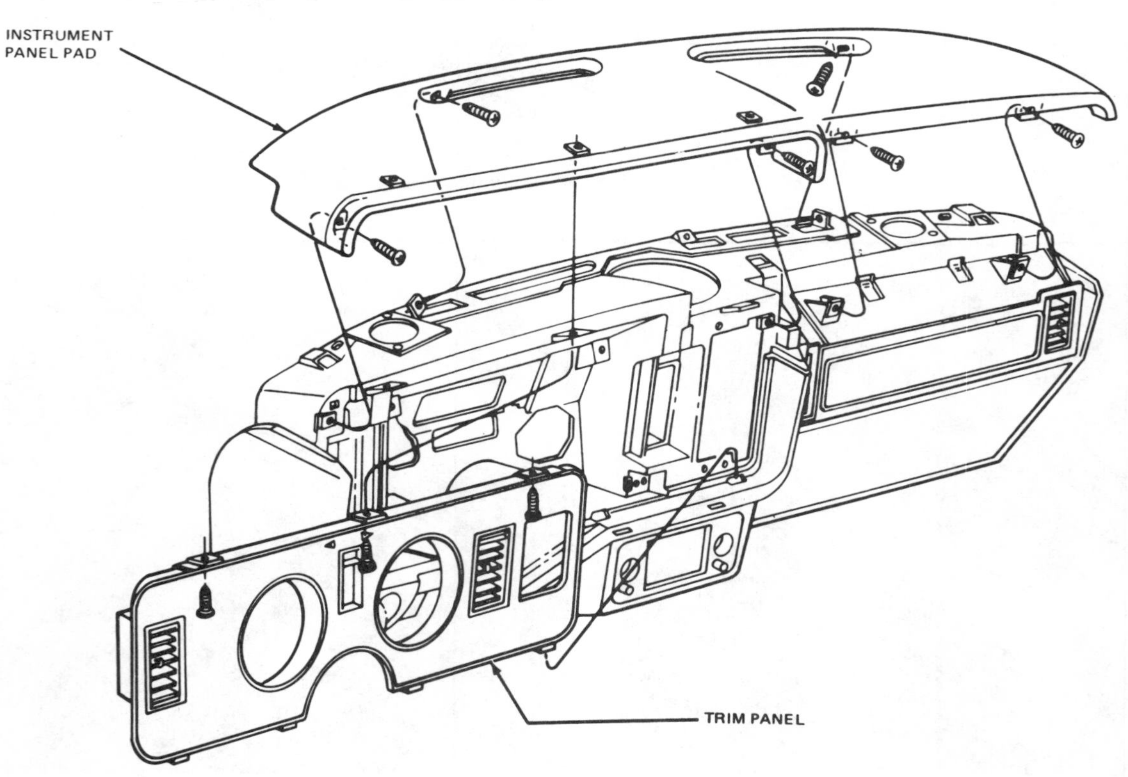

Fig. 12.13 Instrument panel and pad assembly (Sec 23)

check and recheck the wiring and connectors as many of them will be out of reach when the dash assembly is refitted.
17 When the dash is complete, re-connect the battery to the electrical system and check all the functions and instruments of the vehicle.

24 Handbrake – removal and reinstallation

1 Remove the center console (Section 21).
2 Loosen the handbrake cable adjusters.
3 Tie or restrict the cable from dropping into the cable tunnel.
4 Remove the cable adjuster nuts (photo).
5 Disconnect the single wire from the emergency brake ON switch (photo).
6 Remove the two bolts securing the handbrake assembly to the floor. Lift the assembly up to remove.
7 Installation is the reverse of removal. Adjust the handbrake cables to engage a maximum of 6 clicks when the lever is moved to engage the brake.

25 Fuse block – removal and reinstallation

1 Disconnect the battery leads.
2 Remove the screw securing the lower edge of the fuse panel.
3 Pull the assembly forward and down.
4 Remove connectors as needed.
5 Installation is the reverse of removal.
6 Check the operation of all electrical components' connections before driving.

24.4 Use two wrenches to remove the handbrake adjustment nuts

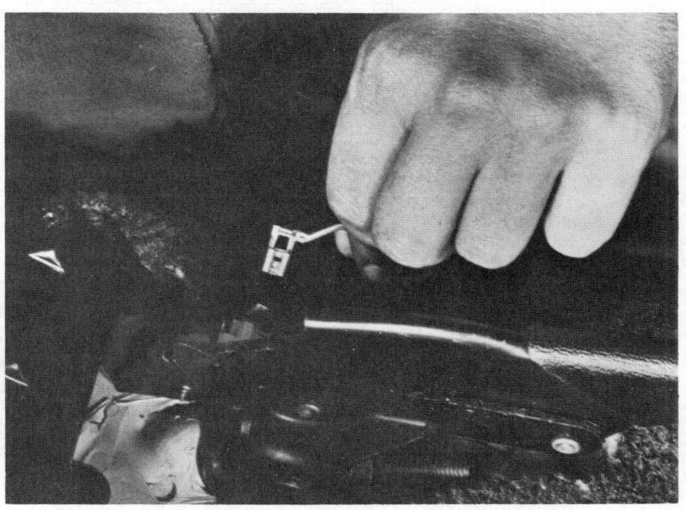

24.5 The handbrake connector is located next to the driver's seat

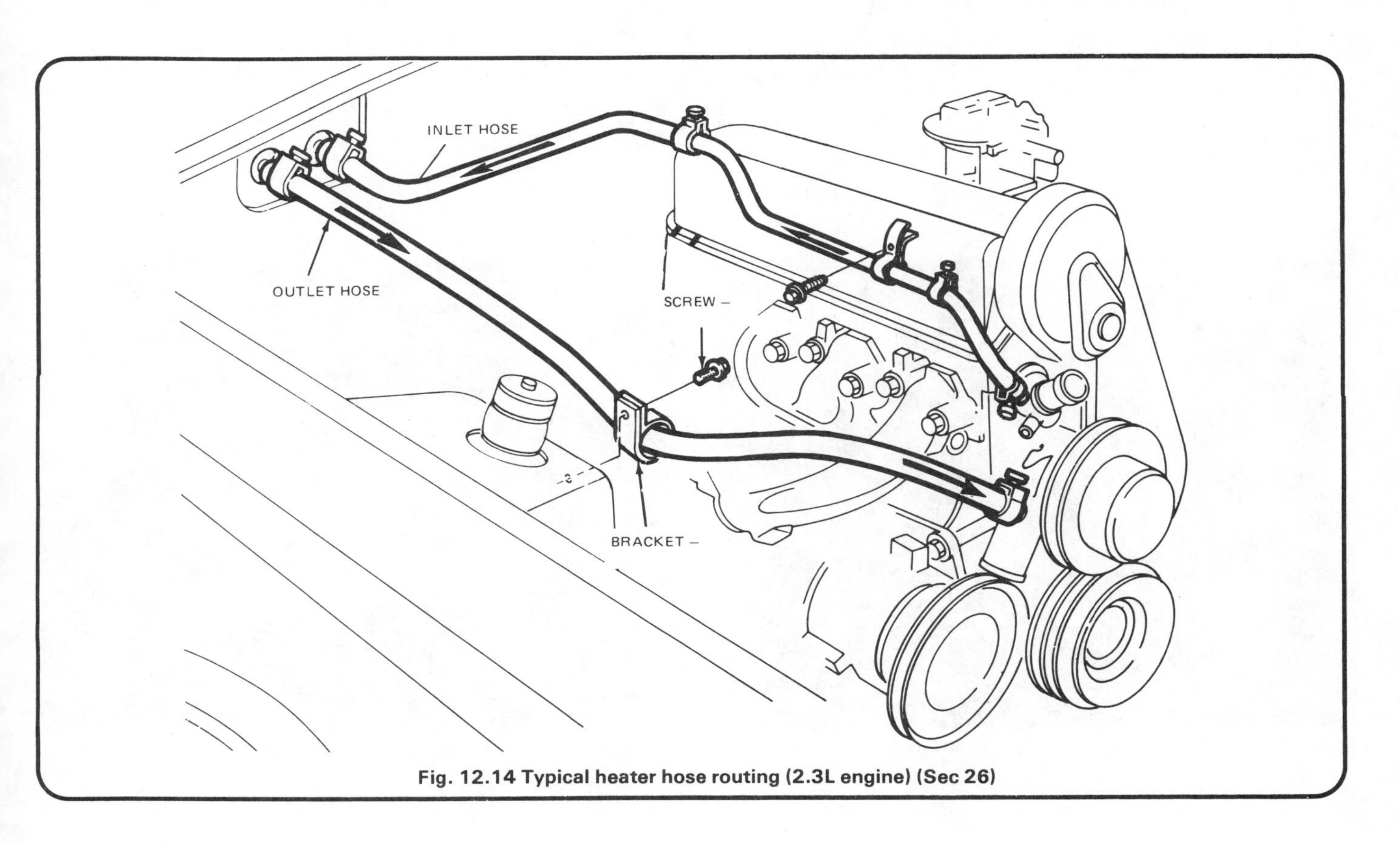

Fig. 12.14 Typical heater hose routing (2.3L engine) (Sec 26)

26 Heater – removal and reinstallation

1 Disconnect the battery from the electrical system.
2 Remove the dash and instrument assemblies.
3 Evacuate the air conditioning system. Refer this to your local dealer or air conditioning repair shop.
4 Drain the radiator and cooling system.
5 In the engine compartment, disconnect the high and low pressure hoses from the combination valve. Use a wrench to support the valve body while loosening.
6 Cap the hoses and valve to prevent contaminating the air conditioning system.
7 Remove the screws attaching the air inlet ducts to the cowling.
8 Remove the support brace.
9 Disconnect the vacuum lines from the heater control panel (photos).
10 Disconnect the blower motor wiring.
11 From the engine compartment, remove the two nuts holding the evaporator case to the dash panel.
12 Inside the car, remove the screw attaching the evaporator case support bracket to the top of the dash panel.
14 Remove the screw at the bottom of the heater assembly where it meets the dash panel. Carefully lift the heater assembly from the car.
15 Installation is the reverse of removal. However, be advised to check all wiring, connections, and cables to the illustration. Refill the

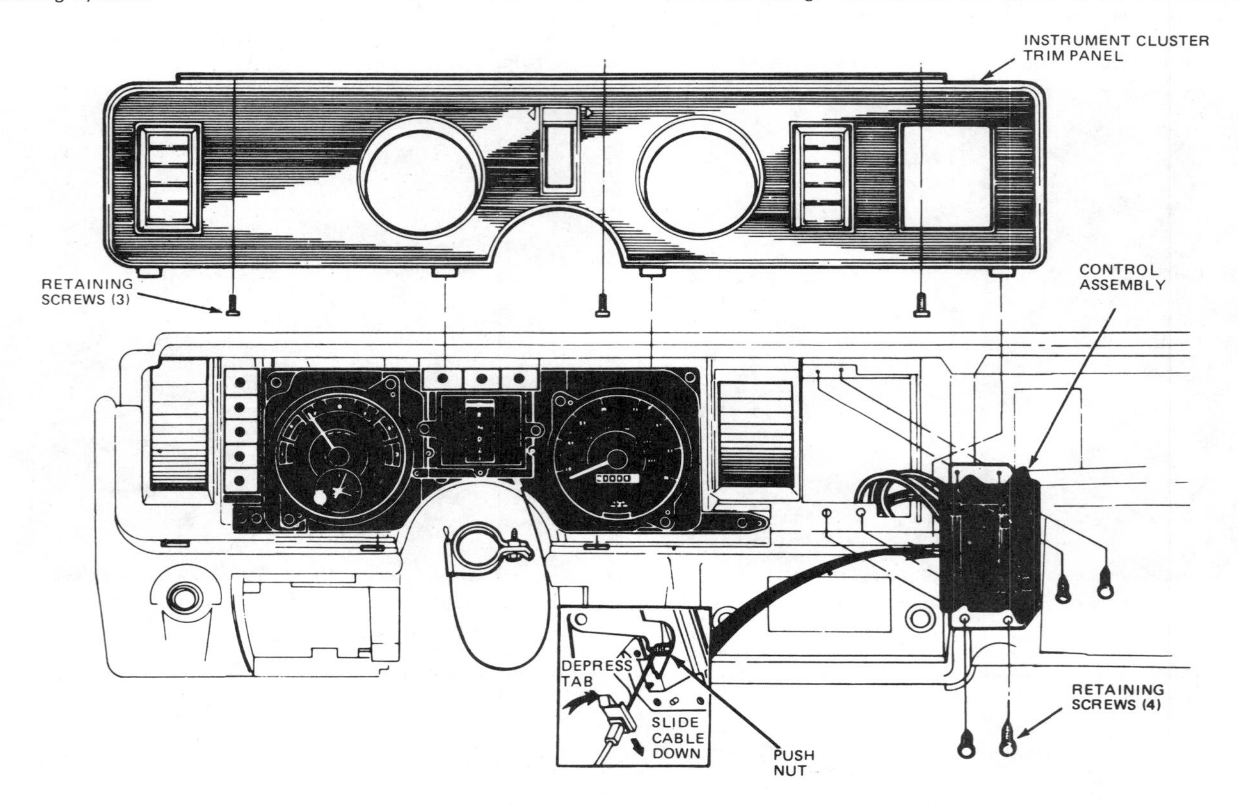

Fig. 12.15 Heater control removal (Sec 26)

26.9A Withdrawing the heater control from the dash

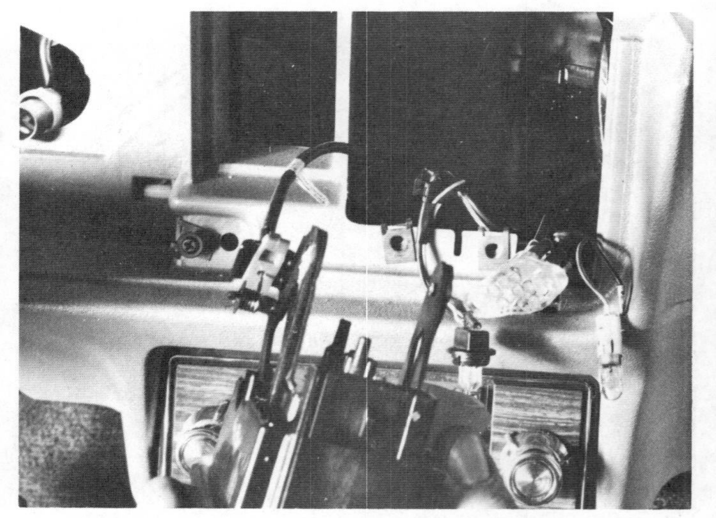

26.9B Removing the control connections and vacuum lines

cooling system to the proper level and recharge the air conditioning system as soon as the repairs are complete.
16 Check for proper operation.
17 Connect the battery and check for system operation.

27 Evaporator core – removal and reinstallation

1 Remove the heater/evaporator assembly from the vehicle.
2 Remove the five screws attaching the heater core access cover to the case. Remove the cover.
3 Remove the heater blower assembly nut and remove the heater assembly.
4 Remove the two nuts securing the heater door to the actuating arm. Remove the door.
5 Remove the nine screw and snap clips securing the two halves of the evaporator case together. Split the cases after checking for screws and spring clips.
6 Remove the combination valve from the evaporator core.
7 Remove the seal and combination with the core.
8 Installation is the reverse of removal. Check that the drain tube is not pinched and that the vacuum lines run without restriction.

28 Blower motor and wheel assembly – removal and reinstallation

1 Remove the dash assembly from the car.
2 Remove the heater/evaporator assembly.
3 Loosen the screws securing the blower assembly to the blower housing.
4 Lift the blower motor assembly clear.
5 Installation is the reverse of removal. Check for proper run of the heater motor wire away from clamps or screws.

29 Front bumper/nosepiece

1 The nosepiece is of a vacuum formed plastic derivative and steel. It is held to the car through a number of special rivets and bolts. Should the nosepiece require repair or replacement, refer this work to your local dealer or repair shop.

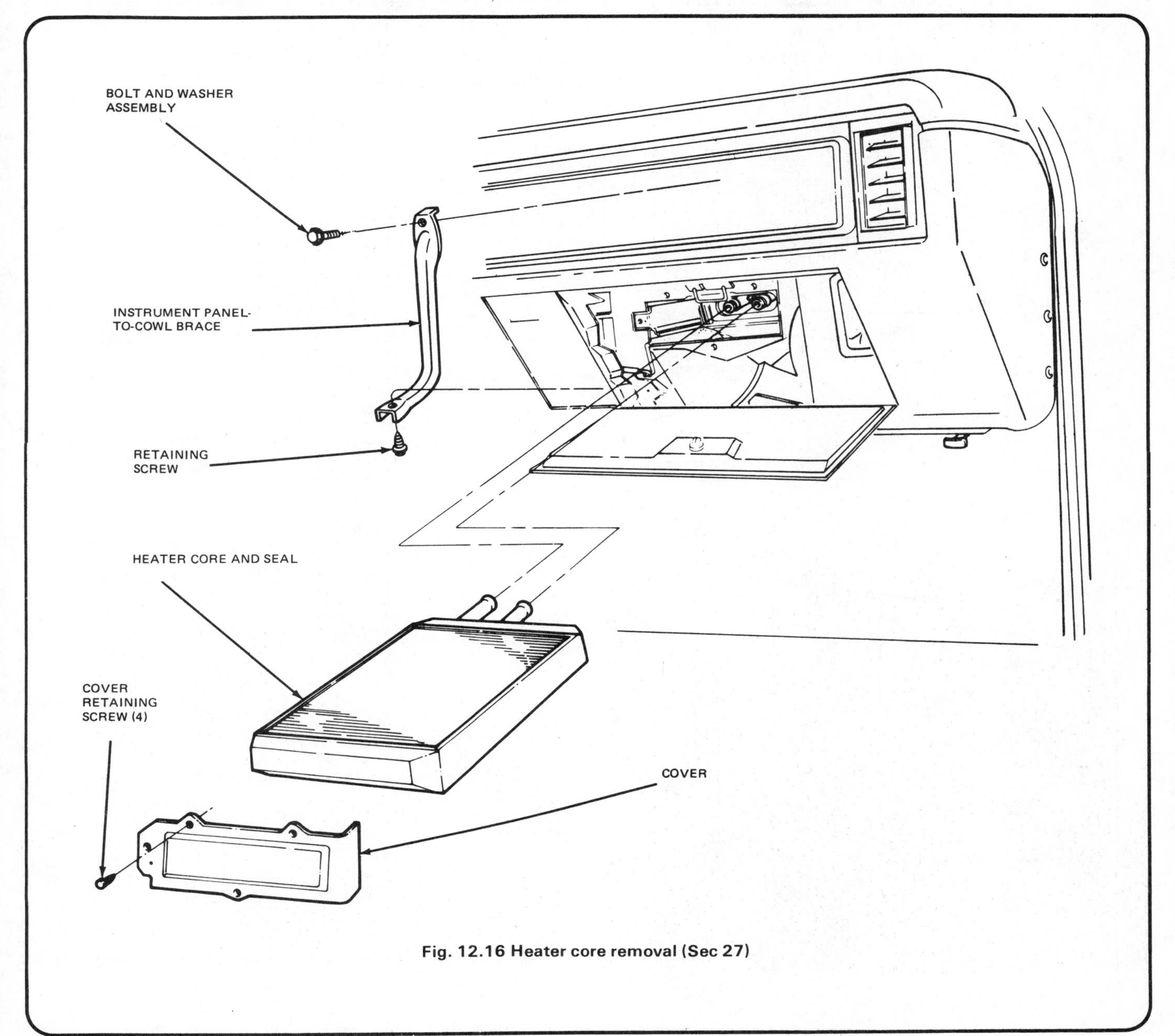

Fig. 12.16 Heater core removal (Sec 27)

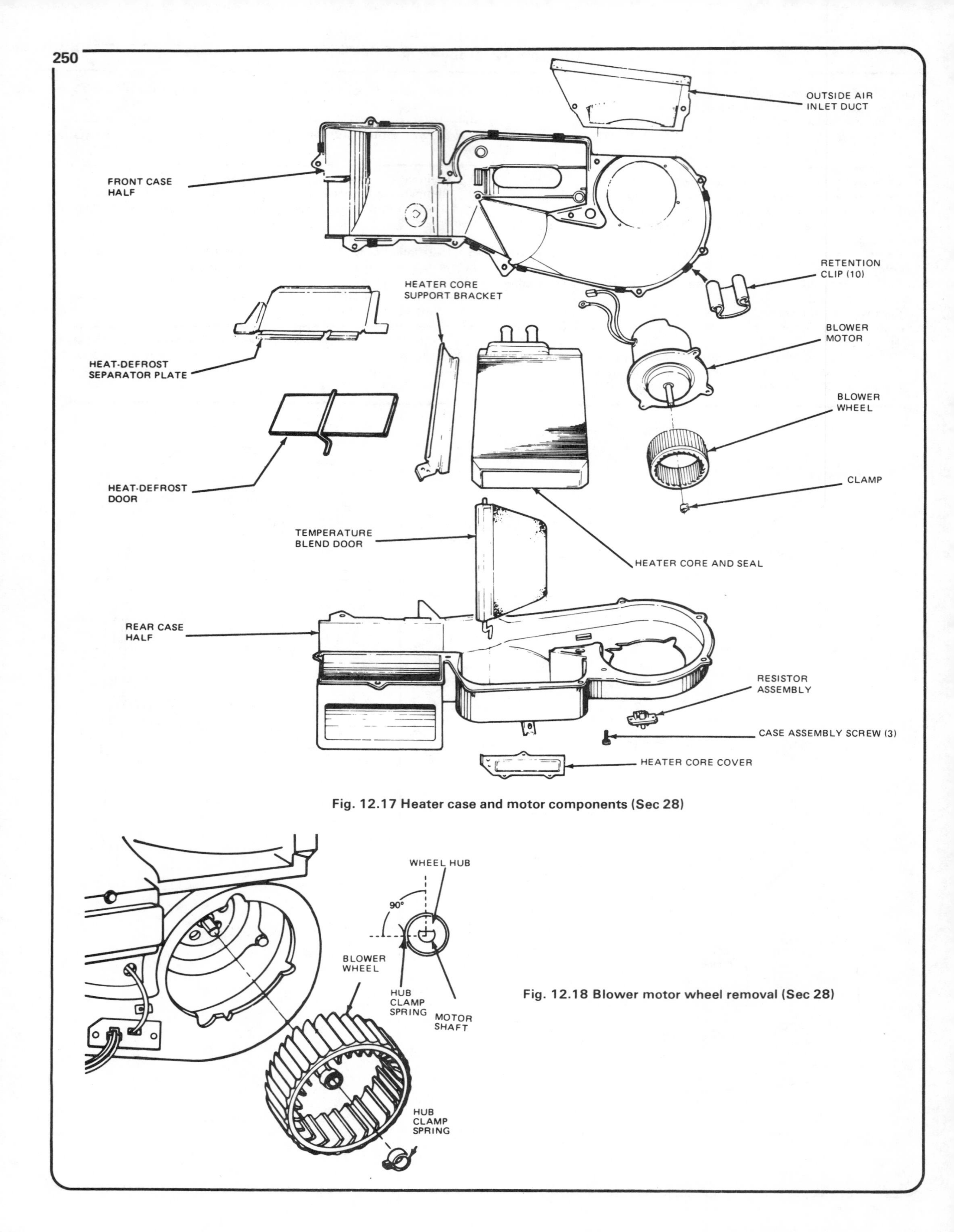

Fig. 12.17 Heater case and motor components (Sec 28)

Fig. 12.18 Blower motor wheel removal (Sec 28)

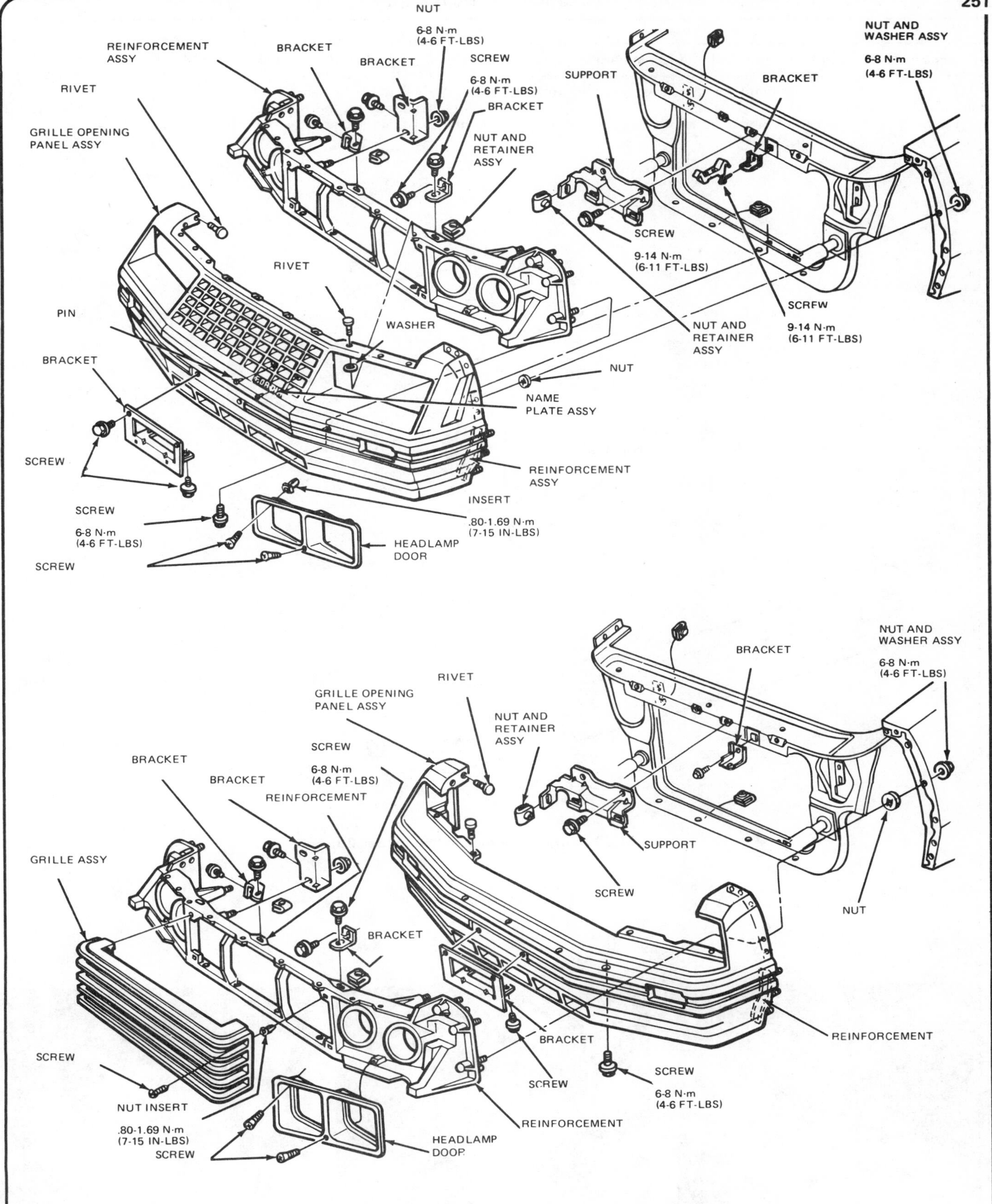

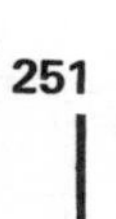

Fig. 12.19 Body front nosepiece and components (Sec 29)

30 Rear bumper assembly – removal and reinstallation

1 Remove the screws securing the bumper cover assembly. Refer to (Fig. 12.21) for their location.
2 Lift the bumper cover assembly up and off.
3 While supporting the bumper from falling, remove the six bolts holding the bumper to the isolator assembly (photos).
4 When the bolts are removed the bumper can be lifted away.
5 Installation is the reverse of removal.
6 After installing the metal bumper, check for 15$\frac{3}{8}$ inches (39.05 cm) from the bottom of the bumper to the ground.

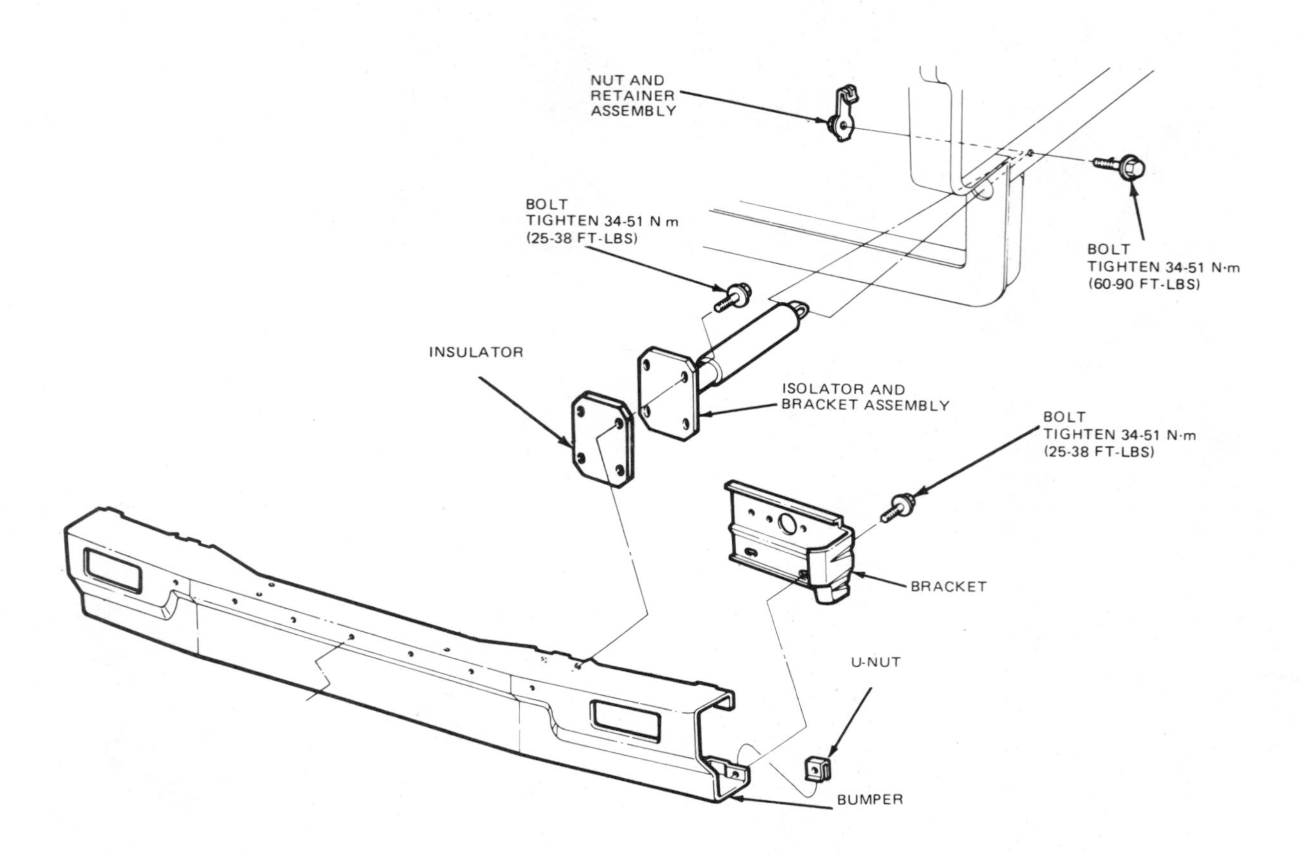

Fig. 12.20 Front bumper installation (Sec 29)

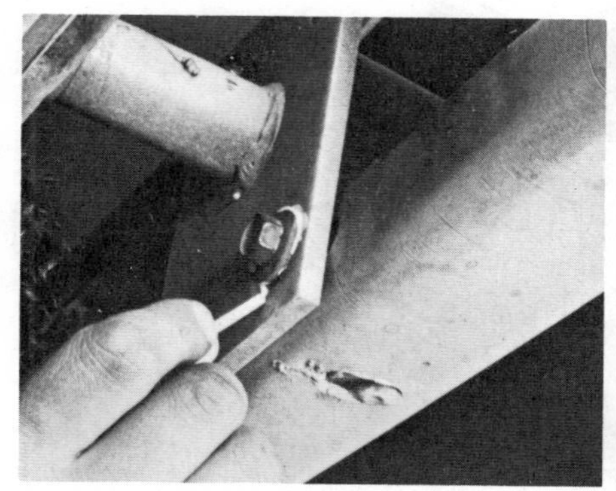

30.3A Mark the bumper bolt locations with paint for ease of reinstallation

30.3B While removing the bolts, have someone help hold the bumper

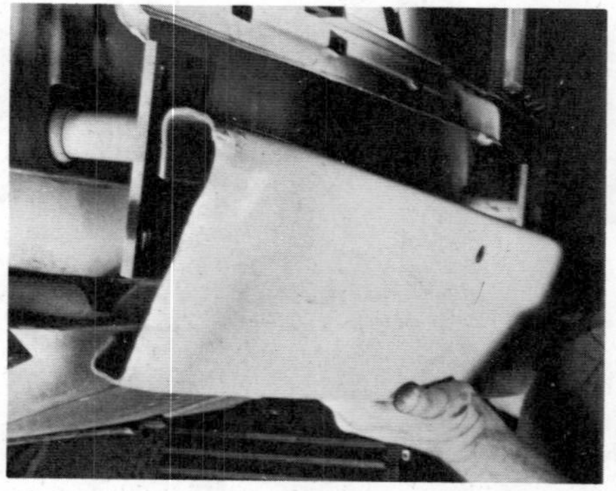

30.3C Lift the bumper away from the vehicle

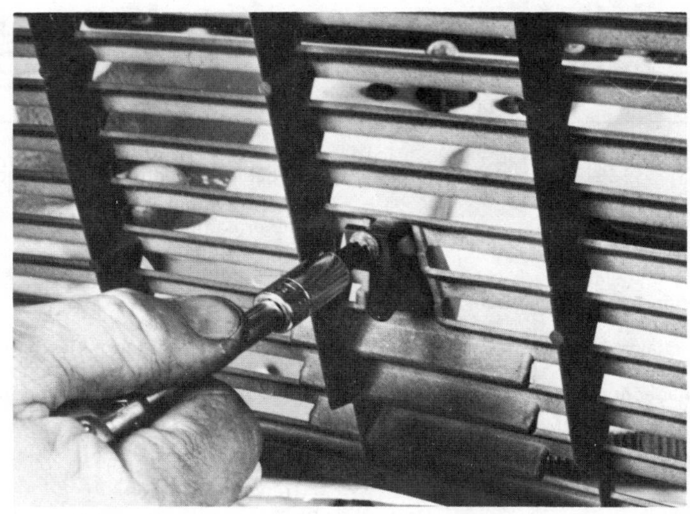
31.4 Lift the air vent grille up about 3 inches and remove the windshield washer nozzle

31 Air vent grille – removal and reinstallation

1 Unclip the rear hood air seal.
2 Remove the passenger side wiper arm assembly.
3 Remove the three sheet metal screws securing the air grille.
4 Lift the grille about 3 inches and disconnect the windshield washer nozzle hose (photo).
5 Remove the air vent grille.
6 Installation is the reverse of removal.

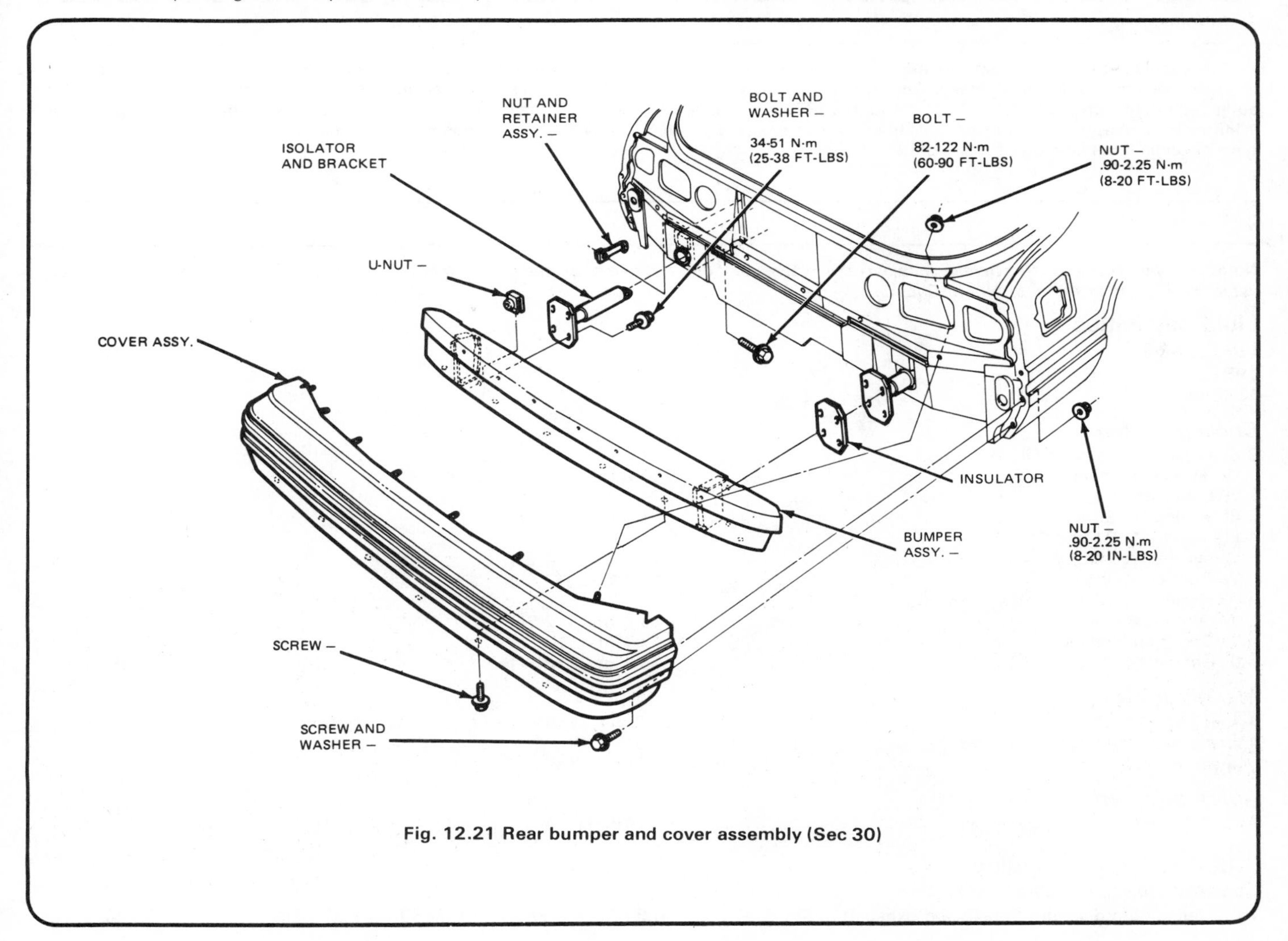

Fig. 12.21 Rear bumper and cover assembly (Sec 30)

Chapter 13 Supplement: Revisions and information on later models

Contents

1 Introduction

This supplement contains specifications and service procedure changes that apply to all Ford Mustang/Mercury Capri V6 and V8 engine equipped models produced from 1981 through 1987. Also included is information related to previous models that was not available at the time of original publication of this manual.

Where no differences — or very minor differences — exist between 1980 models and later models, no information is given. In those instances, the original material included in Chapters 1 through 12, pertaining to 1980 models, should be used.

2 Specifications

Note: *The specifications listed here include only those items that differ from those listed in Chapters 1 through 12. For information not specifically listed here, refer to the appropriate Chapter.*

Fluid capacities

Fuel tank

1981	12.5 gal.
1982 on	15.4 gal.

Cooling system

3.8L engine (1981 thru 1984)	
W/ air conditioning	10.8 qts. (10.2L)
W/O air conditioning	10.7 qts. (10.1L)
3.8L engine (1985 on)	11.5 qts. (10.9L)
4.2L engine (1981 and 1982)	
W/ air conditioning	15.0 qts. (14.2L)
W/O air conditioning	14.7 qts. (13.9L)
5.0L engine (1982 thru 1984)	
W/ air conditioning	13.4 qts. (12.7L)
W/O air conditioning	13.1 qts. (12.3L)
5.0L engine (1985 on)	14.1 qts. (13.3L)

Manual transmission

4-speed	2.8 pts. (1.3L)
4-speed overdrive (1981 and 1982)	4.5 pts. (2.1L)
5-speed overdrive (1983 on)	3.7 pts. (2.6L)

Automatic transmission

Automatic overdrive	12 qts. (11.4L)

3.8L (232 cu in) engine

Cylinder head and valve train

Valve guide bore diameter (intake and exhaust)	0.3443 to 0.3433 in (8.745 to 8.720 mm)

Valve seats	
Width (intake and exhaust)	0.060 to 0.080 in
Angle	44.5 degrees
Runout	0.003 in
Valve stem-to-guide clearance	
Intake	0.001 to 0.0028 in
Exhaust	0.0015 to 0.0033 in
Valve face runout limit	0.002 in
Valve face angle	45.8 degrees
Valve stem diameter	
Intake	0.3423 to 0.3415 in
Exhaust	0.3418 to 0.3410 in
First oversize	
Intake	0.3573 to 0.3565 in
Exhaust	0.3568 to 0.3560 in
Second oversize	
Intake	0.3723 to 0.3715 in
Exhaust	0.3718 to 0.3710 in
Valve spring installed height	
Thru 1985	1.70 to 1.78 in
1986 on	2.02 in
Valve lifter	
Diameter	0.874 to 0.8745 in
Clearance to bore	0.0007 to 0.0027 in
Service limit	0.005 in
Collapsed tappet gap (nominal)	
Intake	0.088 to 0.189 in
Exhaust	0.088 to 0.189 in

Camshaft

Lobe lift	
Intake	0.240 in
Exhaust	0.241 in
Bore inside diameter	
No. 1	2.192 to 2.191 in
No. 2	2.177 to 2.176 in
No. 3	2.177 to 2.176 in
No. 4	2.192 to 2.191 in
Journal to bearing clearance	0.001 to 0.003 in
Journal diameter (all)	2.0515 to 2.0505 in
Timing chain deflection	1/2 in

Cylinder block

Head gasket surface flatness	0.003 inch in any 6 inches or 0.006 inch overall
Cylinder bore	
Diameter	3.810 in
Out of round limit	0.002 in
Taper limit	0.002 in
Main bearing bore diameter	2.713 to 2.712 in

Crankshaft and flywheel

Main bearing journal	
Out of round limit	0.0003 in
Taper limit	0.0003 in per inch
Journal runout limit	0.002 in
Thrust bearing journal length	1.1703 to 1.1722 in
Connecting rod journal	
Diameter	2.3103 to 2.3111 in
Out of round limit	0.0003 in
Taper limit	0.0003 in per inch
Main bearing thrust face runout limit	0.001 in
Flywheel ring gear lateral runout (automatic only)	0.070 in
Crankshaft endplay	0.004 to 0.008 in
Connecting rod bearing oil clearance	
Desired	0.001 to 0.0014 in
Allowable	0.00086 to 0.0027 in
Main bearing oil clearance	
Desired	0.001 to 0.0014 in
Allowable	0.0005 to 0.0023 in

Connecting rod, piston and rings

Piston pin bore diameter	0.9096 to 0.9112 in
Crankshaft journal bore	
Diameter	2.4266 to 2.4274 in
Out of round limit	0.0003 in
Taper limit	0.013 in per inch
Connecting rod length (center to center)	5.912 to 5.915 in

Connecting rod alignment (bore to bore — max)	
Twist	0.003 in per inch
Bend	0.0016 in per inch
Side clearance (assembled to crankshaft)	
Standard	0.0047 to 0.0114 in
Service limit	0.014 in

Piston

Diameter	
Coded red	3.8095 to 3.8101 in
Coded blue	3.8107 to 3.8113 in
Coded yellow	3.8119 to 3.8125 in
Piston to bore clearance	0.0014 to 0.0032 in
Pin bore diameter	0.9122 to 0.9128 in
Ring groove width	
Top compression	0.080 to 0.0809 in
Bottom compression	0.080 to 0.0809 in
Oil	0.1587 to 0.1596 in
Piston pin	
Length	3.012 to 3.039 in
Diameter	0.9119 to 0.9124 in
Pin to piston clearance	0.0002 to 0.0005 in
Pin to rod clearance	Interference fit

Piston rings

Ring gap	
Top compression	0.010 to 0.020 in
Bottom compression	0.010 to 0.020 in
Oil	0.015 to 0.0583 in
Side clearance	
Top compression	0.0016 to 0.0037 in
Bottom compression	0.0016 to 0.0037 in

Lubrication system

Oil pump relief valve spring tension	17.1 to 15.2 lbs. at 1.20 in
Driveshaft to housing clearance	0.0030 to 0.0015 in
Relief valve to bore clearance	0.0029 to 0.0017 in
Oil pump gear backlash	0.008 to 0.012 in
Oil pump gear radial clearance	0.0055 to 0.002 in
Oil pump gear end height	0.0055 to 0.0005 in
Idler shaft to idler gear clearance	0.0017 to 0.0005 in

5.0L engine

Valve train

Rocker arm ratio	1.59:1
Hydraulic tappet clearance (collapsed)	
Desired	
5.0L	0.096 to 0.146 in
5.0L HO	0.123 to 0.146 in
Allowable	
5.0L	0.071 to 0.171 in
5.0L HO	0.098 to 0.198 in

Crankshaft

Connecting rod journal diameter	2.1228 to 2.1236 in
Main bearing oil clearance	
Desired	No. 1, 0.0004 to 0.0025 in — all others, 0.0004 to 0.0015 in
Allowable	No. 1, 0.0001 to 0.0030 in — all others, 0.0004 to 0.0021 in
Connecting rod piston pin bore diameter	0.9112 to 0.9096 in
Piston	
Diameter	Measured at piston pin bore center line, at 90° to the pin
Coded red	3.9984 to 3.9990 in
Coded blue	3.9996 to 4.0002 in
Pin bore diameter	0.9124 to 0.9127 in

Cooling system

Thermostat operating temperature (3.8L)	193 to 200°F, fully open at 221°F
Coolant type (3.8L)	ESE-M97B43-A, ESE-M97B44-A or Prestone II
Pressure cap rating (1985 on)	16 psi

Fuel system

Static pressure

Tested at	Normal operating temperature at curb idle, transmission in Neutral
3.8L V6	6.0 to 8.0 psi
5.0L HO	7.0 to 9.0 psi
5.0L EFI	39 psi

Minimum volume flow

Tested at	Same conditions as above with smallest passage 0.220 in diameter
3.8L and 5.0L HO	1 pt. in 20 sec.

Carburetor

1981 thru 1983 V6 and V8 engines	
49-states	2150-2V
California	7200VV-2V
1984 3.8L V6	
All	Central Fuel Injection (CFI)
1984 and 1985 5.0L V8	
5.0L HO	4180-C (4V)
5.0L	Central Fuel Injection (CFI)
1986 and 1987 5.0L V8	
All	Sequential Electronic Fuel Injection (SEFI)

Torque specifications	**Ft-lbs**	**Nm**
Fuel pump-to-block (3.8L V6)	15 to 22	20 to 30
Central Fuel Injection (CFI)		
CFI Carburetor to intake manifold	120*	14
Injector retainer	30 to 60*	4.7
Fuel pressure regulator retaining screws	27 to 40*	3 to 4.5
Throttle body retaining screws	10 to 15*	1 to 2
Sequential Electronic Fuel Injection (SEFI) (5.0L engine)		
Lower intake manifold to head	23 to 25	32 to 33
Air supply tube clamps	15 to 23*	2 to 3
Upper intake manifold to lower intake manifold bolts	15 to 22	20 to 30
Throttle body to EGR spacer and upper intake manifold	12 to 18	17 to 24
Air bypass valve to throttle body	71 to 102*	8 to 11
Throttle position sensor to throttle body	14 to 16*	1.6 to 1.8
Fuel pressure regulator to fuel rail assembly	27 to 40*	3 to 4.5
Fuel rail assembly to intake manifold	70 to 105*	8 to 11
Throttle cable bracket to manifold	8 to 10	11 to 13

* In-lbs

Ignition system

Duraspark II and III distributors

Type	Solid state, breakerless
Automatic advance	Vacuum and centrifugal
Direction of rotation	Counterclockwise
Static advance	Refer to emission control decal

EEC IV distributor

Type	Solid state, breakerless
Automatic advance	Electronic
Direction of rotation	Counterclockwise
Static advance	Refer to emission control decal
Spark plug type and gap	Refer to emission control decal

Torque specifications	**Ft-lbs**	**Nm**
Spark plugs		
14mm taperseat	7 to 15	9 to 20
14mm gasket seat	15 to 22	20 to 30
18mm taperseat	15 to 20	20 to 27
Distributor clamp bolt		
3.8L V6	17 to 22	23 to 30
All V8's	17 to 25	23 to 34

Transmission

Manual transmission, ET type

Number of gears	4 forward, 1 reverse
Type of gears	Helical, constant mesh
Synchromesh	All forward gears
Lubricant type	ESP-M2C83-C
Lubricant capacity	2.8 US pts
Countershaft gear endplay	0.006 to 0.018 in

Manual transmission (T5/T50D), 5-speed overdrive (1981 thru 1987)

Number of gears	5 forward, 1 reverse
Type of gears	Helical, constant mesh
Synchromesh	All forward gears
Lubricant type	ESP-M2C83-C
Lubricant capacity	3.7 US pts

Component endplay	
Countershaft gear	0.001 to 0.005 in
Output shaft endplay	0.001 to 0.005 in

Automatic transmission, type C-5

Type	Fluid drive with hydrodynamic torque converter, 3 forward speeds and 1 reverse
Lubricant type	Motorcraft type H
Lubricant capacity	11 qts

Automatic transmission, type AOD

Type	Fluid drive with hydrodynamic torque converter, 3 forward speeds and 1 reverse
Lubricant type	Dextron II
Lubricant capacity	12 qts

Torque specifications	**Ft-lbs**	**Nm**
Manual transmission (1981 and 1982) 5-speed		
Transmission front bearing retainer	7 to 10	9 to 14
Output shaft rear bearing retainer	8 to 10	11 to 14
Extension housing retaining bolts	40 to 60	54 to 81
Detent plunger plug	12 to 14	16 to 19
Transmission case cover	8 to 10	11 to 14
Transmission retaining bolts	35 to 45	47 to 61
Speedometer cable clamp retaining bolts	36 to 54*	4.1 to 6.1
Shifter retaining bolts	17 to 24	22 to 33
Crossmember bolts	28 to 40	38 to 54
Extension housing to crossmember bolts	50 to 70	68 to 95
Fan shroud retaining bolts	24 to 48*	3 to 5
Manual transmission (1983 thru 1987) 5-speed		
Transmission front bearing retainer	7 to 10	9 to 14
Extension housing retaining bolts	20 to 45	27 to 61
Shift cover	8 to 10	11 to 14
Transmission to flywheel housing	35 to 55	61 to 88
Speedometer cable clamp retaining bolts	3 to 5	4 to 6
Shift lever to transmission	23 to 32	31 to 43
Crossmember bolts	36 to 50	48 to 68
Extension housing to crossmember bolts	50 to 70	68 to 95
Shift tower to extension housing	23 to 32	31 to 43
Turret cover	11 to 15	15 to 20
Automatic transmission, type AOD		
Valve body to case	80 to 100*	9 to 11
Filter to valve body	80 to 100*	9 to 11
Oil pan to case	12 to 16	16 to 22
Converter to flywheel	20 to 34	27 to 46
Converter housing cover	12 to 16	16 to 22
Inner manual lever to shaft	30 to 40	41 to 54
Outer throttle lever to shaft	12 to 16	16 to 22
Converter plug	8 to 28	11 to 38
Neutral start switch	7 to 8	9 to 11
Pressure plug	6 to 12	8 to 16
Transmission to engine	40 to 50	55 to 68
Automatic transmission, type C-5		
Filter to valve body	25 to 40*	2.8 to 4.5
Oil pan to case	12 to 16	16 to 22
Converter housing to case	28 to 40	38 to 55
Converter to flywheel	20 to 34	27 to 46
Converter housing cover	12 to 16	16 to 22
Inner manual lever to shaft	30 to 40	41 to 54
Outer throttle lever to shaft	12 to 16	16 to 22
Converter plug	15 to 18	20 to 24
Neutral start switch	55 to 75*	6.2to 8.4
Pressure plug	6 to 12	8 to 16
Transmission to engine (3.8L)	28 to 38	38 to 51
Engine rear cover plate to transmission	12 to 16	17 to 21
Band adjusting screws to case	10	13
Intermediate band adjusting screw locknut	35 to 45	47 to 61
Reverse band adjusting screw locknut	35 to 45	47 to 61
Speedometer clamp bolt	36 to 54*	4 to 6

* in-lbs

Brakes

1981

Master cylinder bore diameter	0.875 in
Rear wheel cylinder bore diameter	0.750 in

1982 thru 1987

Front disc brakes

Disc diameter	10.08 in
Minimum disc thickness	
5.0L	0.972 in
All others	0.810 in

Rear drum brakes

Wheel cylider bore	0.750 in
Master cylinder bore (1982 and 1983)	0.875 in
Master cylinder bore (1984)	0.872 in
Master cylinder bore (1985 on)	0.900 in

Front suspension

1982

Caster	1-1/8 to 1-7/8 positive *
Toe-out on turns	
Inner	20°
Outer	19.84°

1983 and 1984

Caster	1-1/4 to 2 positive *
Camber	0°
Toe-out on turns	
Inner	20°
Outer	19.84°

1985 and 1986

Caster	1/4 to 1-3/4 positive
Camber	negative 3/4 to positive 3/4
Toe-out on turns	
Inner	20°
Outer	19.84°

1987

5.0L models	
Caster	1/2 to 2.0 positive
Camber	negative 5/8 to positive 29/32
All others	
Caster	3/32 to 1-9/16 positive
Camber	negative 1/2 to positive 1.0

* Caster is preset at the factory and is not adjustable.

Rear suspension

Torque specifications	**Ft-lbs**	**Nm**
1981 and 1982		
Shock absorber to frame (upper attachment)	24 to 26	32 to 35
Upper arm to frame	100 to 110	135 to 150
Upper arm to axle	90 to 100	122 to 135
Shock absorber to axle (lower attachment)	60 to 70	88 to 95
Lower arm to frame — bolt	100 to 110	135 to 150
Lower arm to axle — nut	90 to 100	122 to 135
Stabilizer bar to lower arm	18 to 20	24 to 27
1983 thru 1986		
Shock absorber to frame (upper attachment)	17 to 27	23 to 37
Upper arm to frame	100 to 105	135 to 142
Upper arm to axle	90 to 100	122 to 135
Shock absorber to axle (lower attachment)	60 to 70	88 to 95
Lower arm to frame — bolt	100 to 105	135 to 142
Lower arm to axle — bolt	90 to 100	122 to 135
Stabilizer bar to lower arm	45 to 50	60 to 70
Traction bar U-bolt nuts	85 to 105	116 to 142
Axle damper attaching nuts	50 to 60	61 to 81
1987		
Shock absorber upper attachment	19 to 27	26 to 37
Upper arm to frame	80 to 105	108 to 142
Upper arm to axle	70 to 100	95 to 135
Shock absorber lower attachment	55 to 70	75 to 95
Lower arm to frame	80 to 105	108 to 142
Lower arm to axle	70 to 100	95 to 135
Stabilizer bar to lower arm	32 to 52	45 to 70
Shock absorber to clevis bracket bolt	45 to 60	61 to 81
Clevis bracket to axle nut	55 to 70	75 to 95

Electrical system

Bulb specifications (1985 thru 1987 models)

	Number
Rear tail/stop/turn signal	1157
License plate	168
Backup light	1156
Rear side marker	194
Rear turn signal only	1156
Turn signal indicator	194
Gauge illumination (all)	194
Dome lamp (standard)	906
Engine compartment	89
Luggage compartment	168
Automatic transmission indicator (floor type)	1893

3 Engine

General information

1 The 232 cu in V6 is similar to the V8s in construction and components used. However, important differences do exist. In the following paragraphs similarities and differences between the V6 and V8 will be noted.

2 The crankshaft is supported by four main bearings, with the number three bearing designated as the thrust bearing. The crankpins are positioned to provide a power impulse every 120 degrees of crankshaft rotation. This spacing, along with the necessary changes to camshaft lobe and distributor timing, provides smoothness of operation and quietness comparable to a V8.

3 The camshaft is also supported by four bearings. Thrust loads and endplay are limited by a thrust button and spring installed in the front of the camshaft. The spring-loaded button bears against the inside surface of the front cover with lubrication supplied by oil splash from the timing chain. Immediately behind the thrust button bore are the distributor drivegear and the fuel pump actuating eccentric. These are not separate components installed on the cam, but, like the lobes, are part of the camshaft casting.

4 The configuration of the valve train is identical to that employed in the V8 and the service procedures are the same.

5 The rotary gear type oil pump, which develops the oil pressure necessary to force-feed the lubrication system, is located in the front cover assembly. The pump driven gear is rotated by the distributor shaft through an intermediate shaft.

6 Many of the component mating surfaces which are seated with a gasket in V8 engines are sealed in the V6 with silicone rubber. The surfaces sealed in this manner in the V6 include the oil pan sides and front where they mate to the cylinder block and front cover; the thermostat housing-to-the intake manifold; the rocker arm covers-to-the cylinder head; both ends of the intake manifold-to-the-cylinder block; along the rear main bearing cap and cylinder block parting line; and the thermactor air injection secondary cover-to-the-intake manifold. When applying this sealant always use the bead size specified and join the components within 15 minutes of application. After that time the sealant begins to 'set-up' and its sealing effectiveness may be reduced.

7 Because this engine is equipped with aluminum cylinder heads a special corrosion inhibited coolant formulation is required to avoid radiator damage (see Section 2)

8 Accessories mounted on the front of the engine are driven by a single, serpentine drivebelt. It is routed over each accessory pulley and is driven by a pulley bolted to the crankshaft damper. The belt is held tight against the drive pulleys by a spring-loaded tensioner mounted on the upper right corner of the engine (see Chapter 2 for service procedures).

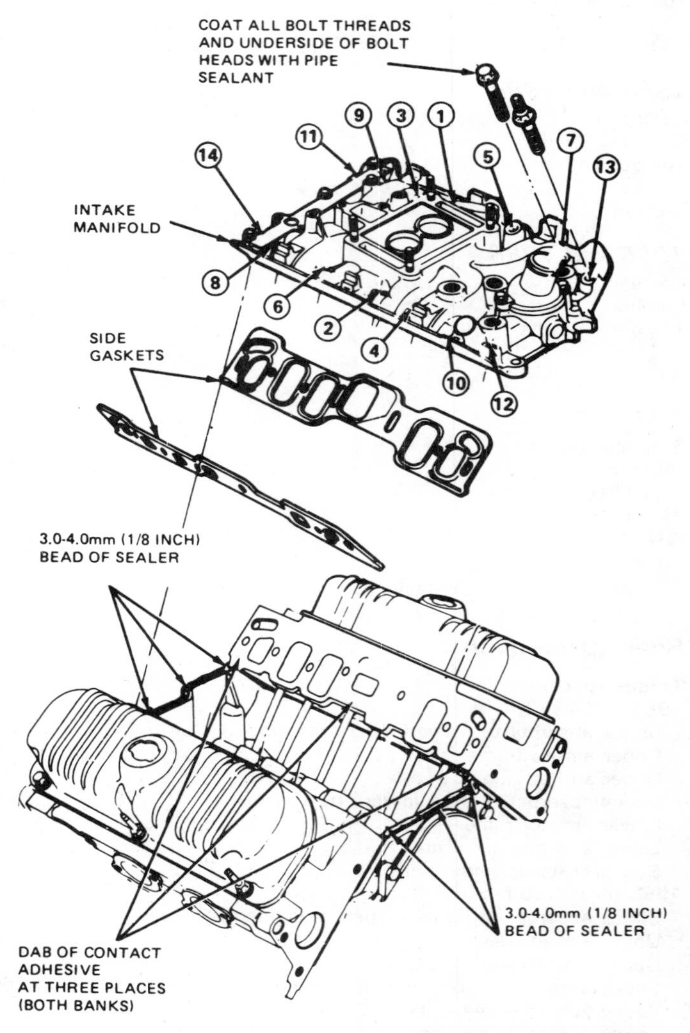

Fig. 13.1 Details of intake manifold installation procedure for the 232 V6 engine (Sec 3)

Manifolds — removal and installation

Intake manifold

9 Drain the cooling system and disconnect the cable from the negative battery terminal.

10 Remove the air cleaner assembly including the air intake duct and heat tube. Fuel is supplied from the vehicle's fuel tank by a high pressure electric fuel pump mounted in the tank. The fuel is filtered and sent to a throttle body by a second electric fuel pump mounted on the right chassis rail just forward of the fuel tank. The throttle body is mounted on an aluminum manifold which is bolted to the aluminum alloy cylinder heads. Service procedures for the heads and intake manifold are similar to those for the V8. However, a spark plug thread service procedure is provided in the event damage should occur to these threads (see Steps 107-118).

11 Disconnect the accelerator cable at the carburetor.

12 If so equipped, disconnect the transmission linkage at the carburetor.

13 Remove the attaching bolts from the accelerator cable mounting

bracket and position the cable so it will not interfere with manifold removal.
14 If equipped with a speed control, disconnect the chain at the carburetor and remove the servo bracket assembly attaching nuts. Position the assembly so it will not interfere with manifold removal.
15 Disconnect the carburetor bowl vent hose at the carburetor.
16 Disconnect the thermactor air supply hose at the check valve located at the back of the intake manifold.
17 Disconnect the upper radiator hose at the thermostat housing.
18 Disconnect the fuel inlet line at the carburetor.
19 Disconnect the coolant bypass hose at the manifold.
20 Disconnect the heater tube at the intake manifold and remove the tube support bracket attaching nut.
21 Label and disconnect the vacuum lines at the carburetor and intake manifold.
22 Disconnect the necessary electrical connectors.
23 If equipped with air conditioning, remove the air compressor support bracket attached to the left front intake manifold attaching bolt.
24 Remove the EGR tube.
25 Disconnect the PCV line at the carburetor.
26 Unbolt and remove the carburetor and gasket.
27 Remove the three EGR spacer attaching screws from the manifold.
28 With the EGR adapter and valve attached, work the EGR spacer loose from the manifold and remove the spacer and gasket.
29 Remove the PCV line.
30 Remove the intake manifold attaching bolts in the reverse order shown in Fig. 13.2.
31 Remove the intake manifold. **Note:** *The manifold is sealed at each end with RTV-type sealer. To break the seal, it may be necessary to pry on the front of the manifold with a screwdriver blade. If so, use care to prevent damage to the machined surfaces.*
32 Remove the manifold side gaskets.
33 If the manifold is to be disassembled, remove the thermostat housing and thermostat, water temperature sending unit, thermactor check valve and all vacuum fittings.
34 The heater outlet and water bypass tubes are pressed in and are not serviceable. If they are damaged, replace the manifold with a new one.
35 If the intake manifold was disassembled, apply a coat of pipe sealant to the temperature sending unit, all vacuum fittings, the spark knock sensor/adapter (if so equipped) and install them in the manifold.
36 Install the thermostat in the manifold with the outlet side up.
37 Apply a 1/16 in bead of RTV-type sealer to the thermostat housing and tighten it to the specified torque.
38 Position and install the thermactor check valve and a new gasket in the manifold, tightening the attaching bolts to the specified torque.
39 Apply a bead of contact adhesive to each cylinder head mating surface as shown in Fig. 13.2 and press new intake manifold gaskets into place, using the locating pins.
40 Apply a 1/8 in bead of RTV-type sealer at each corner where the cylinder head joins the cylinder block and a 3/8-in bead of the same sealer at each end of the cylinder block where the manifold seats against the block.
41 Carefully lower the manifold into position on the cylinder block and cylinder heads. Use the locating pins to prevent smearing the sealant and causing gasket voids.
42 Apply a thin coat of pipe sealant to the manifold attaching bolt threads and to the underside of the bolt heads.
43 Install the 12 bolts and two stud bolts and tighten them in the numerical sequence shown in Fig. 13.2. The bolts should be tightened in three steps (5, 10 and 18 ft-lbs).
44 Install the remaining components in the reverse order of removal.
45 Fill the cooling system with the specified coolant (see Section 2).
46 Start and run the engine and allow it to reach operating temperature, checking carefully for leaks.
47 Shut the engine off and retighten the manifold bolts while the engine is still warm.

Exhaust manifold — left
48 Remove the oil level dipstick tube support bracket.
49 If equipped with a speed control, reposition the air cleaner assembly and disconnect the servo chain at the carburetor.
50 Remove the servo bracket attaching bolts and nuts and position the servo/bracket assembly out of the way.
51 If so equipped, disconnect the EGO sensor at the wiring connector.
52 Disconnect the spark plug wires.
53 Raise the front of the vehicle and place it securely on jackstands.
54 Remove the manifold-to-exhaust pipe attaching nuts.
55 Remove the jackstands and lower the vehicle.
56 Remove the exhaust manifold attaching bolts and the manifold.
57 Installation is the reverse of removal. **Note:** *When installing the attaching bolts, install the pilot bolt (lower front bolt on No. 5 cylinder first.*
58 A slight warpage in the exhaust manifold may cause a misalignment between the bolt holes in the head and manifold. If so, elongate the holes in the exhaust manifold as necessary to correct the misalignment, but do not elongate the pilot hole.

Exhaust manifold — right
59 Remove the air cleaner assembly and heat tube.
60 Disconnect the thermactor hose from the downstream air tube check valve.
61 Remove the downstream air tube bracket attaching bolt at the rear of the right cylinder head.
62 Disconnect the coil secondary wire from the coil and the wires from the spark plugs.
63 Remove the spark plugs and the outer head shroud.
64 Raise the front of the vehicle and place it securely on jackstands.
65 Remove the transmission dipstick tube, if so equipped.
66 Remove the manifold-to-exhaust pipe attaching nuts.
67 Remove the jackstands and lower the vehicle.
68 Remove the exhaust manifold attaching bolts, then remove the manifold, inner heat shroud and EGR tube as an assembly.
69 Installation is the reverse of removal. If bolt holes are misaligned, see Step 58, but do not elongate the pilot hole (lower rear bolt hole on No. 2 cylinder).

Rocker arm covers — removal and installation
70 Disconnect the spark plug wires.
71 Remove the spark plug wire routing clips from the rocker arm cover attaching studs.
72 If the left rocker arm cover is being removed, remove the oil filler cap. If equipped with a speed control, reposition the air cleaner assembly and disconnect the servo chain at the carburetor. Remove the servo bracket attaching bolts and nuts and set the servo/bracket assembly aside.
73 If the right rocker arm cover is being removed, reposition the air cleaner assembly and heat tube, remove the PCV valve, then disconnect and remove the thermactor diverter valve and hose assembly at the bypass valve downstram air tube and the engine-mounted check valve.
74 Remove the valve cover attaching screws.
75 Loosen the silicone rubber gasketing material by inserting a putty knife under the cover flange. Work the cover loose and remove it. **Note:** *Pry carefully, as the plastic valve covers will break if excessive force is applied.*
76 Installation is the reverse of removal. Apply a 1/8 to 3/16-in bead of RTV-type sealer to the rocker arm cover before placing it on the head. Make sure the sealer fills the channel in the cover flange and make the installation within 15 minutes of the sealer application.

Cylinder heads — removal, inspection and installation
77 Drain the coolant into a suitable container.
78 Disconnect the cable from the negative battery terminal.
79 Remove the air cleaner assembly, including the air intake duct and heat tube.
80 Loosen the accessory drivebelt idler, then remove the drivebelt (see Chapter 2 if necessary).
81 If the left cylinder head is being removed, refer to Steps 82 through 85 and Steps 93 through 106.
82 If equipped with power steering, remove the pump mounting bracket attaching bolts.
83 Leaving the hoses connected, place the pump/bracket assembly aside, making sure that it is in a position to prevent the fluid from leaking out.
84 If equipped with air conditioning, remove the mounting bracket attaching bolts.
85 Leaving the hoses connected, position the compressor aside. **Note:** *Under no circumstances should the air conditioning hoses be disconnected except by an authorized air conditioning service technician, as personal injury and equipment damage may result.*
86 If the right cylinder head is being removed, refer to Steps 87 through 106.

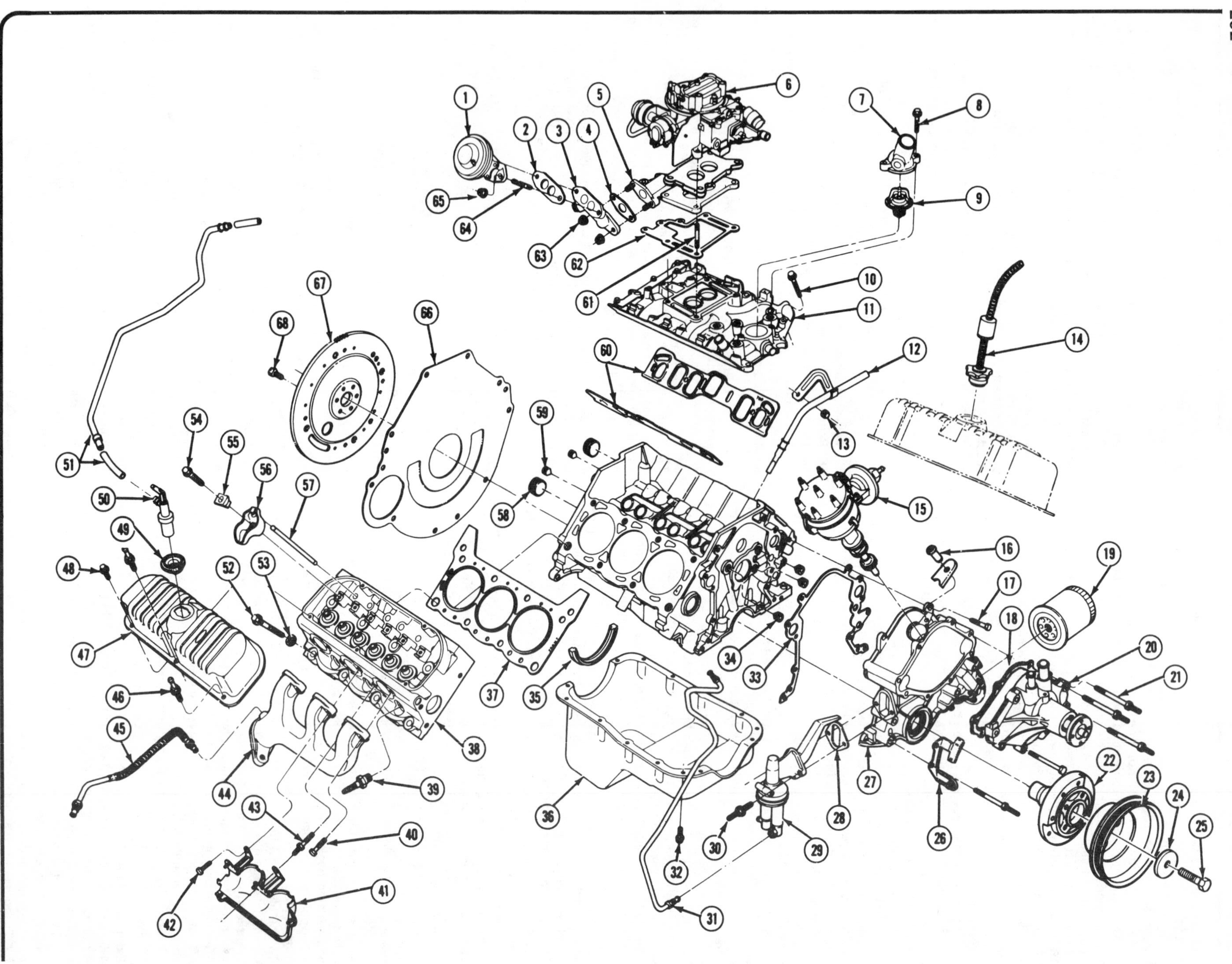
1
2
3
4
5
6
7
8
9
10
11
12
13
14
15
16
17
18
19
20
21
22
23
24
25
26
27
28
29
30
31
32
33
34
35
36
37
38
39
40
41
42
43
44
45
46
47
48
49
50
51
52
53
54
55
56
57
58
59
60
61
62
63
64
65
66
67
68

Fig. 13.2 External components of the 232 V6 engine — exploded view (Sec 3)

1 EGR valve
2 EGR valve adapter gasket
3 EGR valve adapter
4 EGR valve adapter-to-carburetor spacer gasket
5 Carburetor spacer
6 Carburetor
7 Thermostat housing
8 Thermostat housing attaching bolt
9 Thermostat
10 Manifold attaching bolt
11 Intake manifold
12 Oil level dipstick tube
13 Tube attaching nut
14 Oil filler cap, tube and filter assembly
15 Distributor
16 Distributor hold down clamp and bolt
17 Front cover attaching bolt
18 Water pump gasket
19 Oil filter
20 Water pump
21 Water pump attaching bolts
22 Crankshaft damper
23 Crankshaft pulley
24 Damper bolt washer
25 Damper attaching bolt
26 Ignition timing indicator
27 Engine front cover
28 Fuel pump gasket
29 Fuel pump
30 Fuel pump attaching stud
31 Fuel pump-to-carburetor fuel line
32 Oil pan attaching bolt
33 Front cover gasket
34 Oil gallery plug
35 Oil pan rear seal
36 Oil pan
37 Cylinder head gasket
38 Cylinder head
39 Spark plug
40 Exhaust manifold attaching bolt
41 Hot air intake shroud
42 Shroud and manifold attaching bolt
43 Shroud and manifold attaching stud
44 Exhaust manifold
45 EGR tube
46 Valve cover attaching stud
47 Valve cover
48 Valve cover attaching bolt
49 PCV valve grommet
50 PCV valve
51 PCV valve hose and tube
52 Cylinder head attaching bolt
53 Cylinder head bolt washer
54 Rocker arm fulcrum attaching bolt
55 Rocker arm fulcrum
56 Rocker arm
57 Pushrod
58 Water jacket plug
59 Rear oil gallery plug
60 Intake manifold gasket
61 Carburetor attaching stud
62 Carburetor gasket
63 Carburetor adapter attaching nut
64 EGR valve attaching stud
65 EGR valve attaching nut
66 Rear engine plate
67 Driveplate/flywheel
68 Driveplate/flywheel attaching bolt

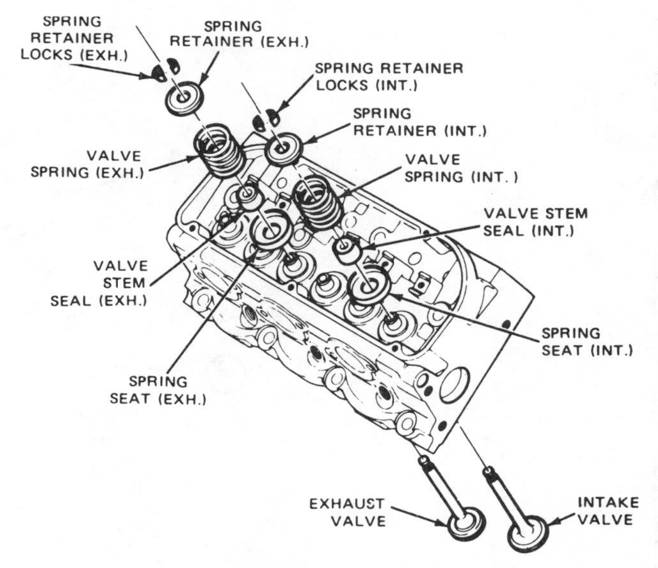

Fig. 13.3 Details of the 232 V6 cylinder head components (Sec 3)

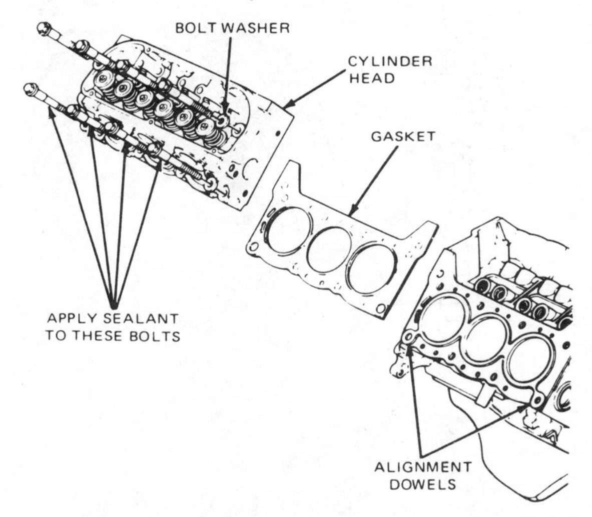

Fig. 13.4 Installing a V6 cylinder head (Sec 3)

87 Disconnect the thermactor diverter valve and hose assembly at the bypass valve and downstream air tube, then remove the assembly.
88 Remove the accessory drive idler.
89 Remove the alternator.
90 Remove the thermactor pump pulley and pump.
91 Remove the alternator bracket.
92 Remove the PCV valve.
93 Remove the intake manifold.
94 Remove the rocket arm cover(s).
95 Remove the exhaust manifold(s).
96 Remove the pushrods, making sure to note the position of each rod to facilitate installation.
97 Remove the cylinder head attaching bolts, then remove the cylinder head(s).
98 Remove and discard the old cylinder head gasket(s) and discard the cylinder head bolts.
99 Refer to Chapter 1 for cylinder head disassembly and inspection procedures.
100 Position new head gasket(s) on the cylinder block using the dowels for alignment.
101 Position the heads on the block (refer to Fig. 13.4).
102 Apply a thin coat of pipe sealant to the threads of the short cylinder head bolts (nearest to the exhaust manifold). Do not apply sealant to the long bolts.

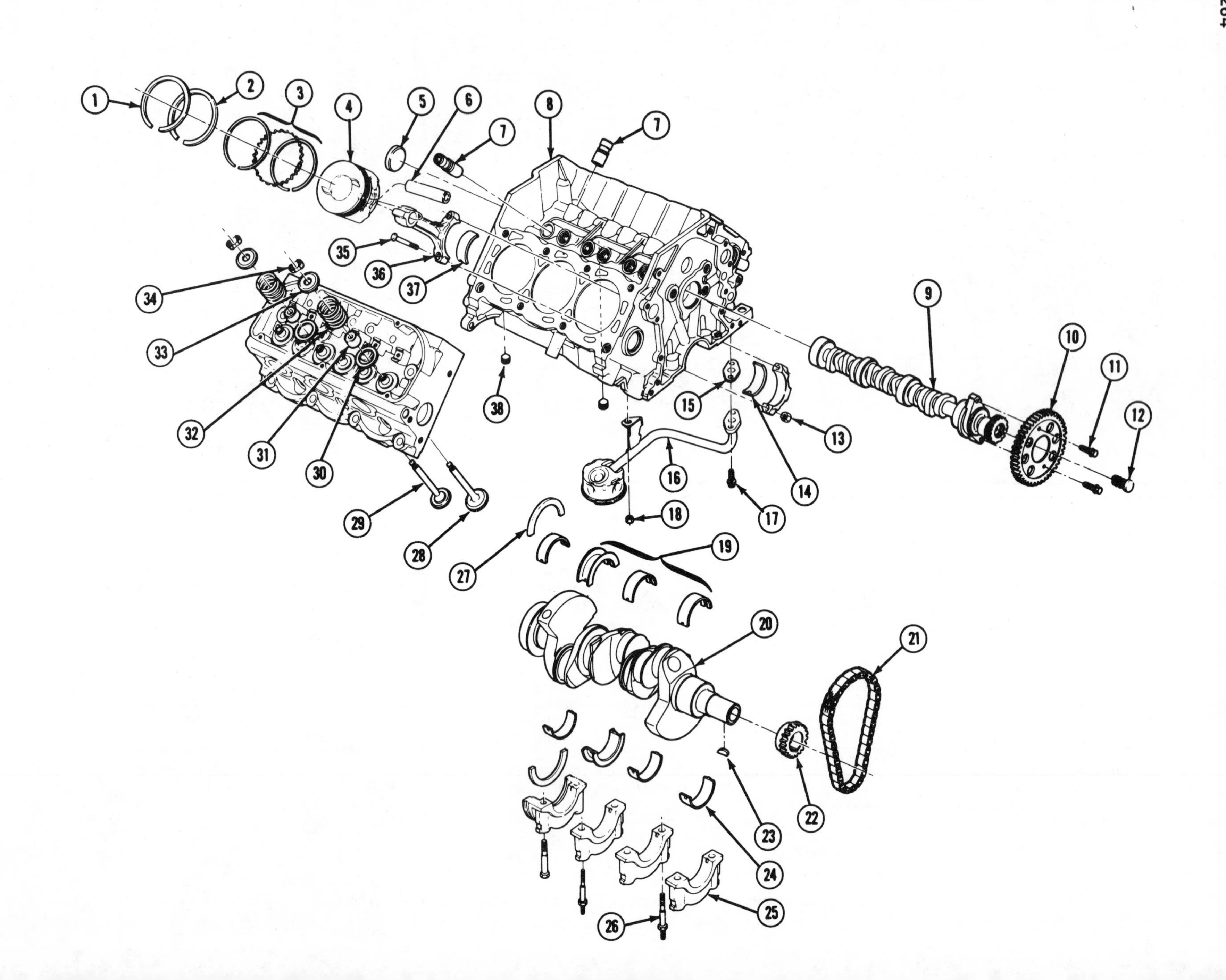
1
2
3
4
5
6
7
8
7
9
10
11
12
13
14
15
16
17
18
19
20
21
22
23
24
25
26
27
28
29
30
31
32
33
34
35
36
37
38

Fig. 13.5 Internal components of the 232 V6 engine — exploded view (Sec 3)

1 Top piston compression ring
2 Bottom piston compression ring
3 Piston oil ring
4 Piston
5 Camshaft bore plug
6 Piston pin
7 Hydraulic lifter
8 Engine block
9 Camshaft
10 Camshaft sprocket
11 Camshaft sprocket attaching bolt
12 Camshaft thrust button and spring
13 Connecting rod cap attaching nut
14 Connecting rod bearing (lower)
15 Oil pickup tube and screen assembly gasket
16 Oil pickup tube and screen assembly
17 Oil pickup tube attaching bolt
18 Oil pickup tube bracket attaching bolt
19 Main bearing (upper)
20 Crankshaft
21 Timing chain
22 Crankshaft sprocket
23 Crankshaft Woodruff key
24 Main bearing (lower)
25 Main bearing cap
26 Main bearing cap attaching bolt
27 Crankshaft rear seal
28 Intake valve
29 Exhaust valve
30 Valve spring washer
31 Valve stem oil seal
32 Valve spring
33 Valve spring retainer
34 Valve spring retainer keys
35 Connecting rod attaching bolt
36 Connecting rod
37 Connecting rod bearing (upper)
38 Engine coolant drain plug

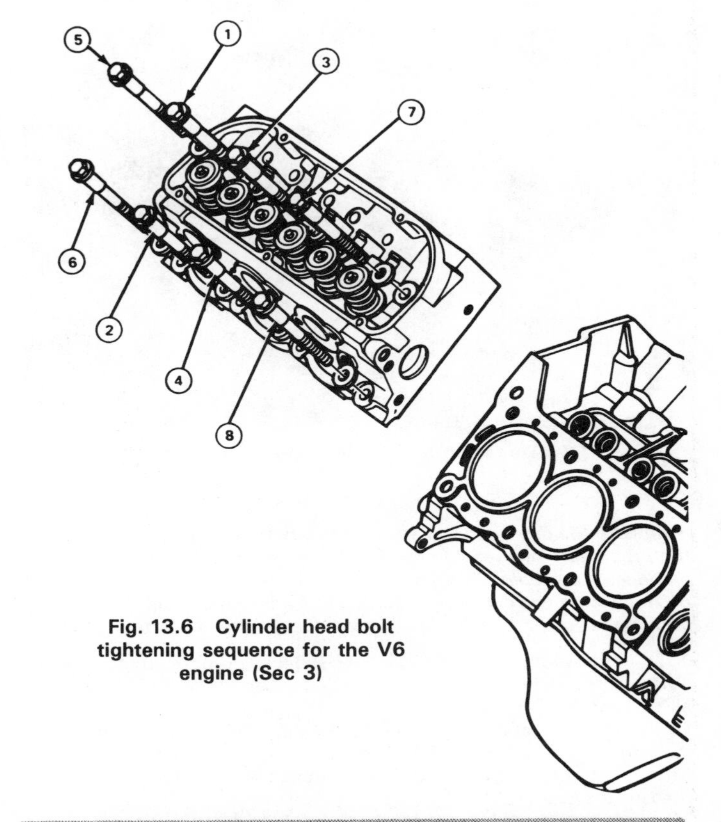

Fig. 13.6 Cylinder head bolt tightening sequence for the V6 engine (Sec 3)

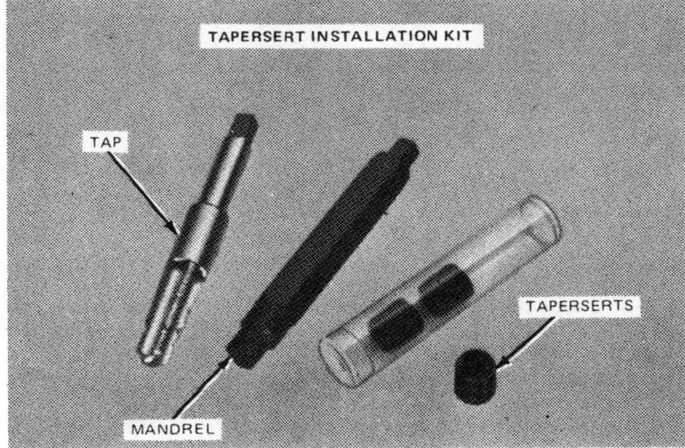

Fig. 13.7 Components of the Tapersert installation kit for damaged threads in the V6 aluminum cylinder heads (Sec 3)

103 Lightly oil the cylinder head bolt flat washers and install the flat washers and cylinder head bolts. **Note:** *Always use new cylinder head bolts.*

104 Tighten the attaching bolts in the sequence shown in Fig. 13.6 and in the torque steps listed in the Specifications.

105 When the cylinder head bolts have been tightened in the specified steps, it is not necessary to retighten the head bolts after extended engine operation. However, the bolts may be checked for tightness if desired.

106 The remaining installation steps are the reverse of those for removal. Make sure to use the proper coolant (see Section 2) when refilling the cooling system.

Spark plug thread service

Note: *This procedure is used to repair damaged threads in the V6 aluminum heads. A special kit, the Ford Tapersert Installation Kit 08-0001, or its equivalent, is required for this procedure. The cylinder*

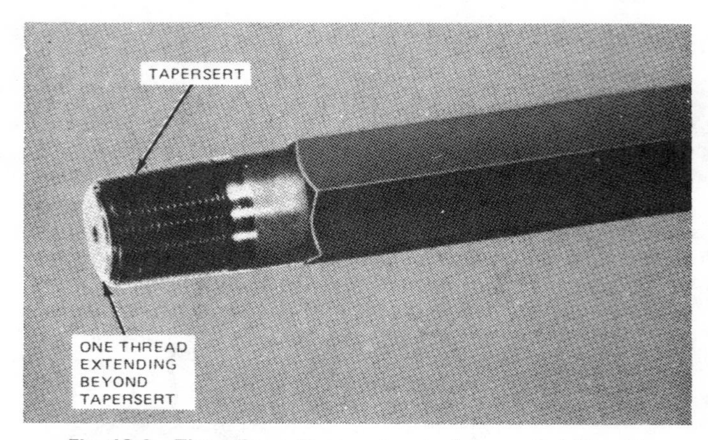

Fig. 13.8 Threading a Tapersert onto the mandrel (Sec 3)

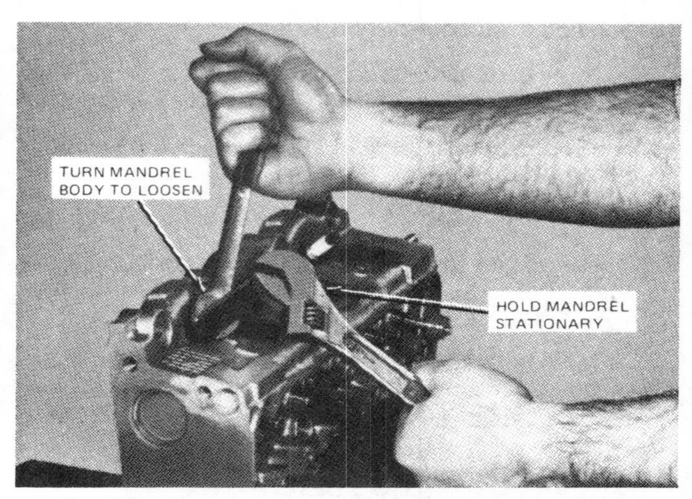

Fig. 13.9 Removing the mandrel after the Tapersert has been installed (Sec 3)

head with the damaged threads must be removed from the engine, as the procedure involves the cutting of new threads, a process which produces metal chips. Performing this procedure with the cylinder head on the engine will cause metal chips to fall into the cylinder, resulting in damage to the cylinder wall when the engine is started.

107 Remove the damaged cylinder head (see Steps 77 through 106).
108 Thoroughly clean the spark plug counterbore, seat and threads of all dirt and foreign matter.
109 Start the tap from the tapersert kit into the spark plug hole, being careful to keep it properly aligned.
110 As the tap begins to cut new threads, apply aluminum cutting fluid to the tap.
111 Continue cutting threads and applying oil until the stop ring on the tap bottoms against the spark plug seat.
112 Remove the tap.
113 Remove all metal chips from the cylinder head, using compressed air if it is available
114 Take the mandrel from the kit and coat the mandrel threads with cutting oil.
115 Taking one of the taperserts from the kit, thread the tapersert into the mandrel until one thread of the mandrel extends beyond the tapersert (see Fig. 12.8).
116 Thread the tapersert into the tapped spark plug hole using a torque wrench. Continue tightening the mandrel until the torque wrench indicates 45 ft-lbs.
117 To loosen the mandrel for removal hold the mandrel stationary and turn the mandrel body approximately 1/2 turn, then remove the mandrel (see Fig. 13.9).
118 Install the cylinder head (see Steps 97 through 106).

Front cover assembly and timing chain — removal and installation

Removal

119 Disconnect the cable from the negative battery terminal.
120 Drain the cooling system.
121 Remove the air cleaner assembly and air intake duct.
122 Remove the fan shroud attaching screws.
123 Remove the fan/clutch assembly attaching bolts.
124 Remove the fan/clutch assembly and shroud.
125 Loosen the accessory drivebelt idler (see Chapter 2 if necessary).
126 Remove the drivebelt.
127 Unbolt and remove the water pump pulley.
128 If equipped with power steering, remove the pump mounting bracket attaching bolts.
129 Leaving the hoses connected, place the pump bracket assembly aside, making sure that it is in a position that prevents the fluid from leaking out.
130 If equipped with air conditioning, remove the compressor front support bracket, leaving the compressor in place. **Caution:** *Do not attempt to disconnect the air conditioning hoses, as personal injury and/or equipment damage may result.*
131 Disconnect the engine coolant bypass hose at the water pump.
132 Disconnect the heater hose at the water pump.

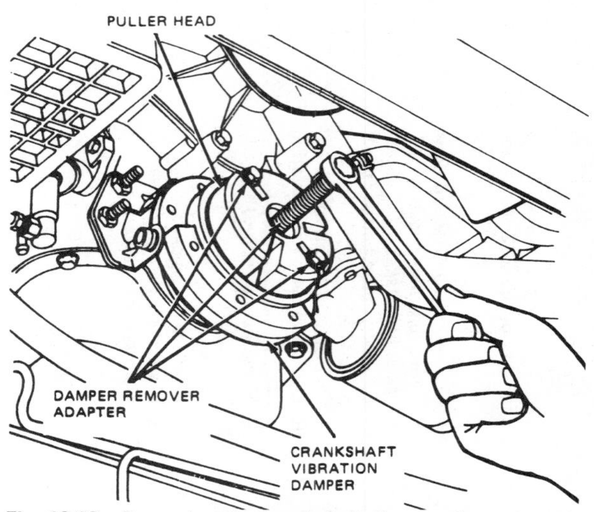

Fig. 13.10 Removing the crankshaft damper from the V6 engine (Sec 3)

133 Disconnect the radiator upper hose at the thermostat housing.
134 Disconnect the coil wire from the distributor cap, then remove the cap with the spark plug wires attached.
135 Remove the distributor hold-down clamp and lift the distributor out of the front cover.
136 Raise the vehicle and place it securely on jackstands.
137 Remove the crankshaft damper using a suitable puller.
138 Remove the fuel pump crash shield, if so equipped.
139 Disconnect the fuel pump-to-carburetor fuel line at the fuel pump.
140 Remove the fuel pump attaching bolts, pull the pump out of the front cover and lay the pump aside with the flexible line attached.
141 Remove the oil filter.
142 Disconnect the radiator lower hose at the water pump.
143 Remove the oil pan (refer to Steps 202 through 224). **Note:** *The front cover cannot be removed without lowering the oil pan.*
144 Remove the jackstands and lower the vehicle.
145 Remove the front cover attaching bolts (see Fig. 13.11 for bolt locations). It is not necessary to remove the water pump. **Note:** *Do not overlook the cover attaching bolt located behind the oil filter adapter. The front cover will break if pried upon before attaching bolts have been removed.*
146 Remove the ignition timing indicator from the front cover.
147 Remove the front cover and water pump as an assembly.
148 Remove the camshaft thrust button and spring from the end of the camshaft.
149 Remove the camshaft sprocket attaching bolts.

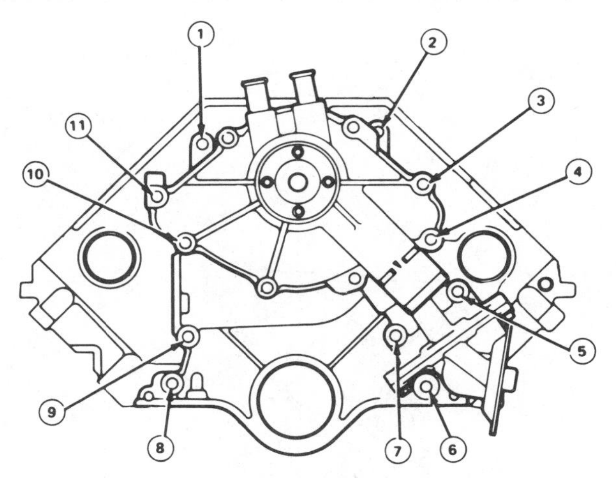

Fig. 13.11 Correct bolt tightening sequence for the front engine cover on the V6 engine (Sec 3)

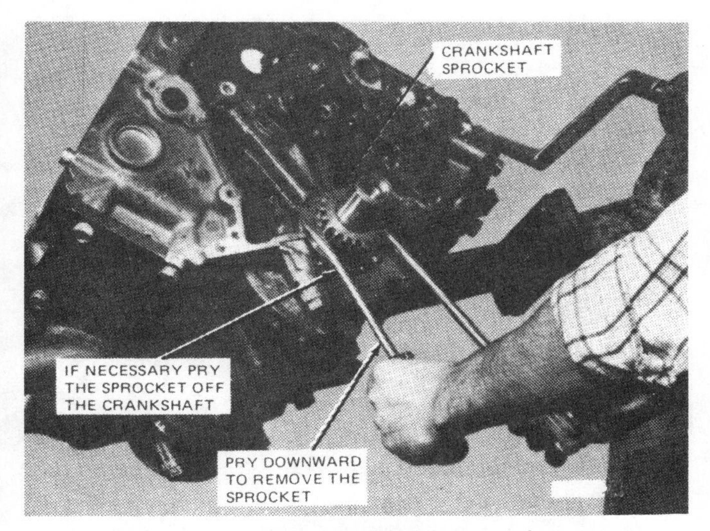

Fig. 13.13 A pair of screwdrivers can be used to remove the crankshaft sprocket (Sec 3)

150 Remove the camshaft sprocket, crankshaft sprocket and timing chain. If the crankshaft sprocket is difficult to remove, pry the sprocket off the shaft using a pair of large screwdrivers positioned on the sides of the sprocket.
151 The front cover contains the oil pump and oil pump intermediate shaft. If a new front cover is being installed, remove the water pump, oil pump, oil filter adapter and the oil pump intermediate shaft from the old cover. Refer to Steps 181 through 201 for procedures involving the oil pump assembly. Refer to Section 4 for procedures involving the water pump.

Installation

152 Lightly oil all bolt and stud threads before installation, except those specified for special sealant.
153 If reusing the front cover, replace the crankshaft front oil seal (refer to Steps 245 through 265).
154 If a new front cover is being used, install the oil pump, oil filter adapter, oil pump intermediate shaft and the water pump.
155 Rotate the crankshaft as necessary to position piston No. 1 at TDC and the crankshaft keyway at the 12 o'clock position.
156 Lubricate the timing chain with clean engine oil.
157 Install the camshaft sprocket, crankshaft sprocket and timing chain, making sure the timing marks are exactly opposite each other.
158 Install the camshaft sprocket attaching bolts and tighten them to the specified torque.
159 Lubricate the camshaft thrust button with polyethylene grease and install the thrust button and spring in the front of the camshaft. **Note:** *The thrust button and spring must be bottomed in the camshaft seat. Make sure that the thrust button and spring do not fall out during the installation of the front cover.*

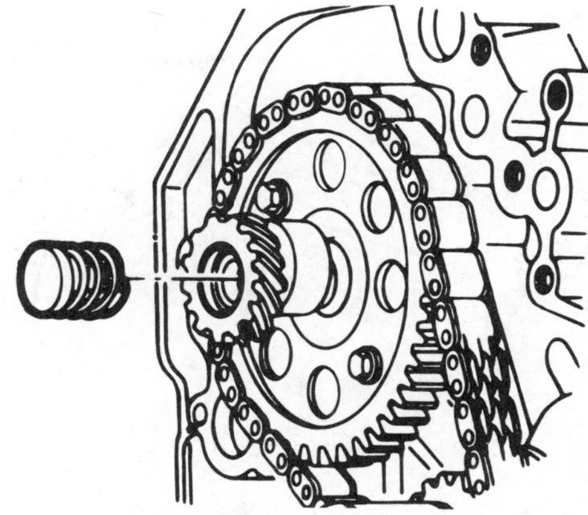

Fig. 13.12 Removing the camshaft thrust button and spring from the end of the camshaft (Sec 3)

160 Lubricate the crankshaft front oil seal with clean engine oil.
161 Position a new cover gasket on the cylinder block and install the front cover/water pump assembly, using the dowels for proper alignment. Contact adhesive may be used to hold the gasket in position while the front cover is installed.
162 Attach the ignition timing indicator to the front cover.
163 Coat the front cover attaching bolts with pipe sealant and install the front cover, tightening the bolts to the specified torque.
164 Raise the vehicle and position it securely on jackstands.
165 Install the oil pan (refer to Steps 215 through 224).
166 Connect the lower radiator hose and tighten the clamp securely.
167 Install the oil filter.
168 Turn the crankshaft clockwise 180° to position the fuel pump eccentric away from the fuel pump actuating arm. **Note:** *Failure to turn the crankshaft can result in the threads being stripped out of the front cover when the fuel pump attaching bolts are installed.*
169 Position a new gasket on the fuel pump and install the pump.
170 Connect the fuel line to the fuel pump.
171 Coat the crankshaft damper sealing surface with clean engine oil.
172 Position the crankshaft pulley key in the crankshaft keyway.
173 Using a suitable seal/damper tool (Ford tool T82L-6316-A or equivalent), install the crankshaft damper.
174 Install the damper washer and attaching bolt and tighten to the specified torque. **Note:** *This bolt may be used to push the damper onto the crankshaft if the proper installation tool in unavailable.*
175 Install the crankshaft pulley and tighten the attaching bolts to the specified torque.
176 Turn the crankshaft 180° counterclockwise to bring No. 1 back to TDC.
177 Remove the jackstands and lower the vehicle.
178 The remaining installation procedures are the reverse of those for removal. When installing tthe distributor, make sure the rotor is pointing at the No. 1 distributor cap tower (refer to Section 6).
179 Start the engine and check for coolant, oil or fuel leaks.
180 Check the ignition timing and idle speed and adjust as required (refer to Sections 5 and 6 respectively).

Oil pump assembly — removal, inspection and installation

181 Remove the front cover assembly (refer to Steps 119 through 151).
182 Remove the oil pump cover attaching bolts, then remove the cover.
183 Lift the pump gears out of the pocket in the front cover.
184 Refer to Chapter 1B Section 36 for the oil pump inspection procedures.
185 To assemble the oil pump, lightly pack the gear pocket with petroleum jelly or heavy oil. **Note:** *Do not use chassis lubricant.*
186 Install the gears in the cover pocket, making sure that the petroleum jelly fills all the voids between the gears and the pocket. **Note:** *Failure to properly coat the oil pump gears may result in failure of the pump to prime when the engine is started, leading to severe engine damage.*

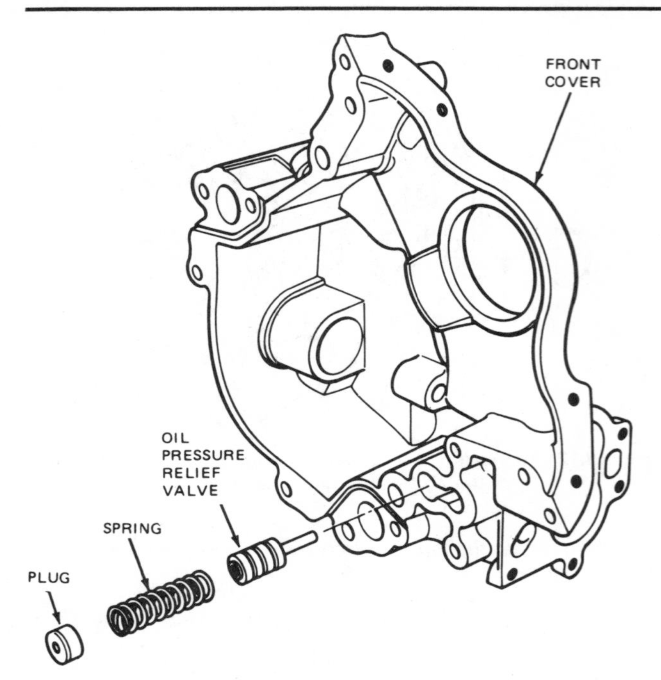

Fig. 13.14 Removing the spring and oil pressure relief valve from the bore of the V6 front engine cover (Sec 3)

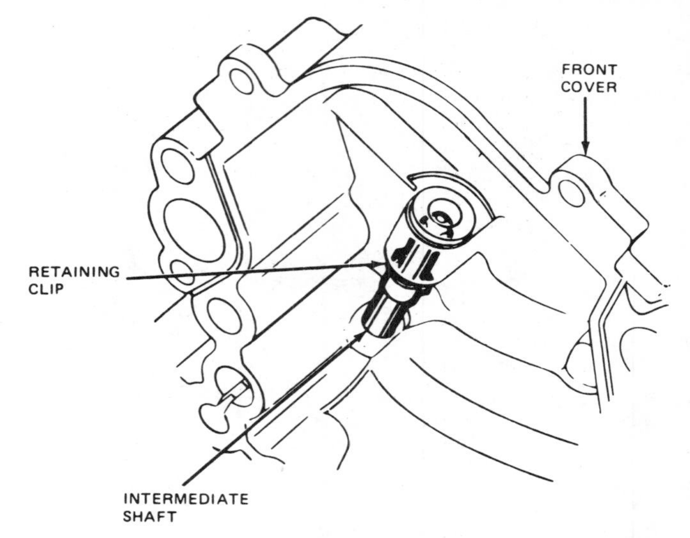

Fig. 13.15 Removing the oil pump drive intermediate shaft from the V6 front engine cover (Sec 3)

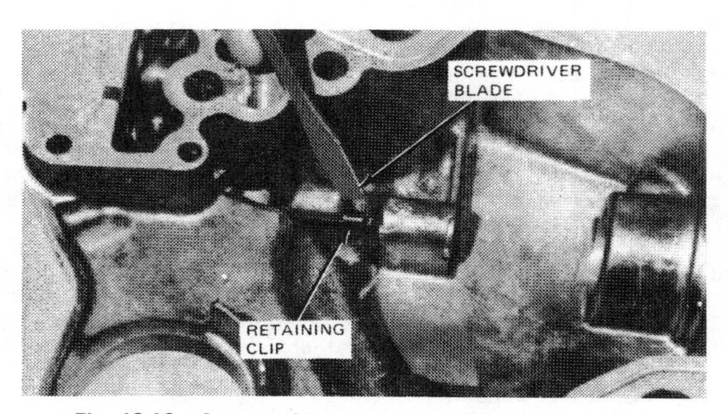

Fig. 13.16 A screwdriver can be used to remove the intermediate shaft retaining clip (Sec 3)

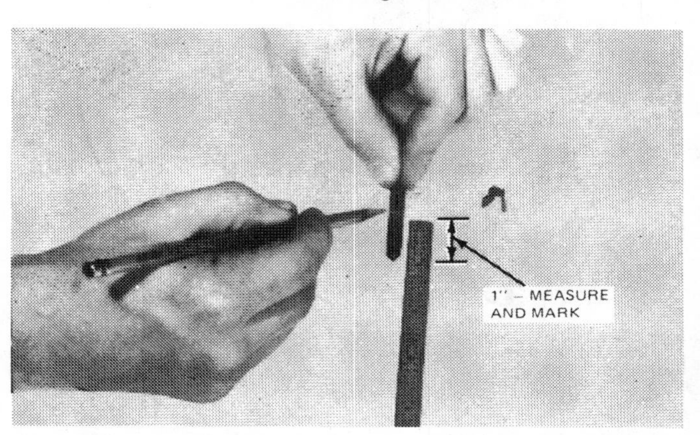

Fig. 13.17 Before installation mark the shaft one inch from the end (Sec 3)

187 Position the cover gasket and install the pump cover.
188 Tighten the pump cover attaching bolts to the specified torque.
189 Using an electric drill, drill a small hole through the center of the relief valve plug.
190 Remove the plug with a sheet metal screw and slide hammer or by prying it out with an ice pick or similar tool.
191 Remove the spring and valve from the bore.
192 Thoroughly clean the valve bore and valve to remove any metal chips which may have entered the bore as a result of drilling the plug.
193 Refer to Chapter 28 Section 36 for further relief valve inspection procedures.
194 Lubricate the relief valve with engine oil and install it in its bore.
195 Position the spring in the bore.
196 Tap a new plug into the bore using a soft-faced hammer. Make sure the plug is flush with the machined surface.
197 Remove the clip from the intermediate shaft and slide the shaft out of the cover (refer to Fig. 13.16.
198 Before installing the shaft, measure and mark the shaft one inch from the end (refer to Fig. 13.17).
199 Position the shaft in the cover, making sure that it is seated in the oil pump drive gear.
200 Install the clip on the shaft so the top of the clip is just below the mark made in Step 198. Use a screwdriver blade to snap the clip onto the shaft.
201 Install the front cover assembly (refer to Steps 152 through 180).

Oil pan — removal, inspection and installation

Note: *This procedure is intended for removal of the oil pan with the engine in the vehicle. If the engine has been removed from the vehicle, perform only Steps 214 through 215 and 218 through 222.*

202 Disconnect the cable from the negative battery terminal.
203 Remove the air cleaner assembly.
204 Remove the bolts attaching the fan shroud to the radiator and position the shroud over the fan.
205 Remove the engine oil dipstick.
206 Raise the vehicle and place it securely on jackstands.
207 Remove the oil filter.
208 Disconnect the muffler inlet pipes from the exhaust manifolds.
209 Remove the clamp attaching the inlet pipe to the converter pipe and remove the inlet pipe from the vehicle.
210 Disconnect the transmission shift linkage at the transmission (see Chapter 7, if necessary).
211 If so equipped, disconnect the transmission cooler lines at the radiator.
212 Remove the nuts attaching the engine supports to the chassis brackets (see Chapter 1B if necessary).
213 Using a jack with a block of wood placed on top of the lifting pad, lift the engine and place wood blocks between the engine supports and the chassis brackets, then remove the jack.
214 Remove the oil pan attaching bolts and drop the oil pan. Unbolt the oil pickup and tube assembly and then lay them in the pan, then remove the pan from the vehicle. Remove the old gaskets and rear pan seal.
215 Clean the oil pan and sealing surfaces. Inspect the gasket sealing

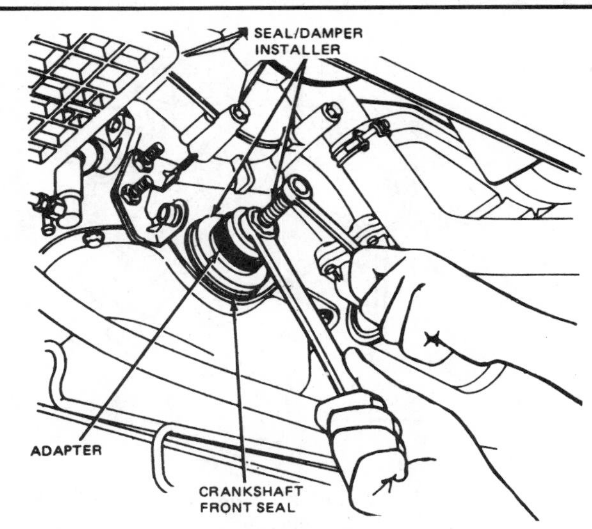

Fig. 13.18 Installing the crankshaft front seal on the V6 engine (Sec 3)

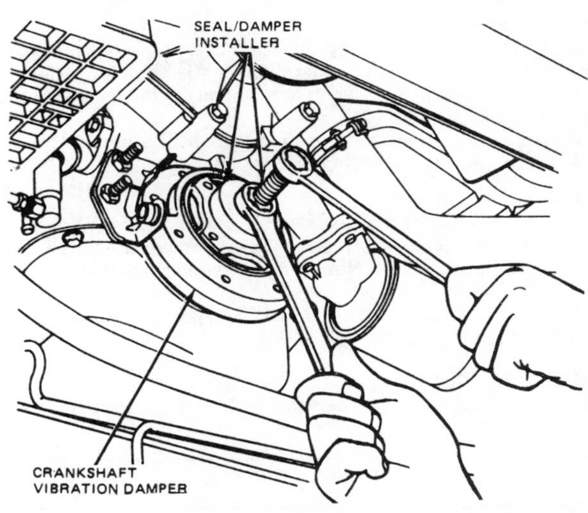

Fig. 13.19 Installing the crankshaft damper on the V6 engine (Sec 3)

surfaces for damage and distortion due to overtightening of the bolts. Repair and straighten as required.
216 Trial fit the pan to the cylinder block. Make sure enough clearance exists to allow the pan to be installed without the sealant scraping off when the pan is positioned for final installation.
217 Lower the oil pan and let it rest on the frame crossmember.
218 Using a new gasket, install the oil pickup and tube assembly. Make sure that the support bracket engages the stud on the No. 2 main bearing cap attaching bolt.
219 Tighten the pickup and tube assembly attaching nuts and bolts to the specified torque.
220 Install a new rear pan seal in the seal groove in the rear main cap.
221 Apply a 1/8-in bead of RTV-type sealant to the seam where the front cover and cylinder block join, to each end of the rear seal where the rear main cap and cylinder block join, and along the oil pan rails on the cylinder block. Where the bead crosses the front cover, increase the bead width to 1/4-in.
222 Position the oil pan on the bottom of the engine and attach it with the retaining bolts. Tighten the bolts to the specified torque.
223 Raise the engine and remove the wood blocks.
224 The remaining installation procedures are the reverse of those for removal.

Camshaft and lifters — removal, inspection and installation

Removal

Note: *If the engine is in the vehicle and it is equipped with air conditioning, the condenser must be removed. This requires discharging of the air conditioning system by an authorized air conditioning system technician. Under no circumstances should the home mechanic attempt to discharge the system or disconnect any of the air conditoning system lines while they are still pressurized, as this can cause serious personal injury as well as damage to the air conditioning system.*

225 Disconnect the cable from the negative battery terminal.
226 Drain the coolant into a suitable container.
227 Remove the radiator if the engine is in the vehicle (refer to Chapter 2).
228 If equipped with air conditioning, see note at the beginning of this Section.
229 Remove the grille if the engine is in the vehicle (see Chapter 12).
230 Remove the intake manifold (refer to Steps 9 through 47).
231 Remove the rocker arm covers (refer to Steps 70 through 76).
232 Loosen the rocker arm nuts and rotate the rocker arms to the side.
233 Mark the pushrods if they re to be reused and remove them from the engine.
234 Remove the valve lifters from the engine using a special tool designed for this purpose. Sometimes they can be removed with a magnet if there is no varnish build-up or wear on them. If they are stuck in their bores, you will have to obtain a special tool designed for grasping lifters internally and work them out.
235 Remove the timing cover, chain and gears (refer to Steps 119 through 151).
236 Remove the oil pan (refer to Steps 202 through 224).
237 Remove the camshaft from the front of the engine by slowly withdrawing it, being careful not to damage the bearings with the cam lobes.

Inspection

238 Visually inspect the hydraulic valve lifters for cupping on the camshaft mating face and for signs of excessive wear, galling, or cracking.
239 The hydraulic valve lifters must be tested using special equipment. This procedure must be handled by a suitably equipped automotive machine shop.
240 If you suspect that a lifter is defective, replace it with a new one. It is not necessary to test a new lifter before installation.
241 Check the camshaft lobe lift on a special V-block cradle with a dial indicator. Again, this is a procedure which should be handled by a suitably equipped automotive machine shop.
242 Visually check the camshaft bearing surfaces for any signs of galling or excessive wear. If any of these conditions are present, or if there is a question about the camshaft (and you have no access to testing or measuring equipment), replace it with a new one.

Installation

243 Lubricate the cam lobes and bearing surfaces with heavy duty engine oil.
244 The remaining installation procedures are the reverse of those for removal.

Crankshaft oil seals — replacement

Front seal

245 Disconnect the cable from the negative battery terminal.
246 Remove the fan shroud attaching screws.
247 Remove the fan/clutch assembly attaching bolts.
248 Remove the fan/clutch assembly and shroud.
249 Loosen the accessory drivebelt idler.
250 Raise the vehicle and place it securely on jackstands.
251 Disengage the accessory drivebelt and remove the crankshaft pulley.
252 Using a suitable puller, remove the crankshaft damper.
253 Remove the seal from the front cover using a suitably sized screwdriver. Be careful not to damage the front cover and crankshaft.
254 Inspect the front cover and crankshaft damper for nicks, burrs or other roughness which my cause the seal to fail. If defects are found, replace the damaged components with new ones.
255 Lubricate the new seal lip with engine oil and install the seal using a suitable seal/damper installation tool.
256 Lubricate the damper seal nose with engine oil and install the damper using a suitable seal/damper installation tool.
257 Install the damper attaching bolt and tighten it to the specified torque.
258 Position the crankshaft pulley and tighten the attaching bolts to

the specified torque.

259 Position the accessory drivebelt over the crankshaft pulley.

260 Remove the jackstands and lower the vehicle.

261 The remaining installation procedures are the reverse of those for removal.

262 Adjust the drivebelt tension (refer to Chapter 2).

263 Start the engine and check for oil leaks.

Rear Seal

264 The crankshaft rear seal can be replaced with the engine in the vehicle. To gain access to the rear seal, remove the oil pan (refer to Steps 202 through 224). **Note:** *The oil pump does not have to be removed on this engine.*

265 Refer to Chapter 1B Section 21 and perform Steps 3 through 8 to complete the procedure.

Engine overhaul

For all overhaul procedures refer to Chapter 1 Part B.

4 Cooling system

Water pump — removal and installation (3.8L engine)

1 Refer to Chapter 2 (section 11) for the removal and installation procedures, with the following notes:

a) 3.8L engines are equipped with an electro-drive cooling fan. Refer to Steps 2 through 8 for the removal procedure.
b) If equipped with power steering, remove the pump mounting bracket attaching bolts. Leaving the hoses connected, place the pump/bracket assembly aside in a position to prevent fluid from leaking.
c) If equipped with air conditioning, remove the compressor front support bracket, leaving the compressor in place.
d) If equipped with a tripminder, remove the fuel flow sensor support bracket (the fuel lines will support the flow meter).
e) On reinstallation lightly oil the bolt threads before installation except the No. 1 water pump attaching bolt, which should be coated with a pipe sealant (see illustration).
f) Tighten all water pump attaching bolts to 15-22 ft-lbs.

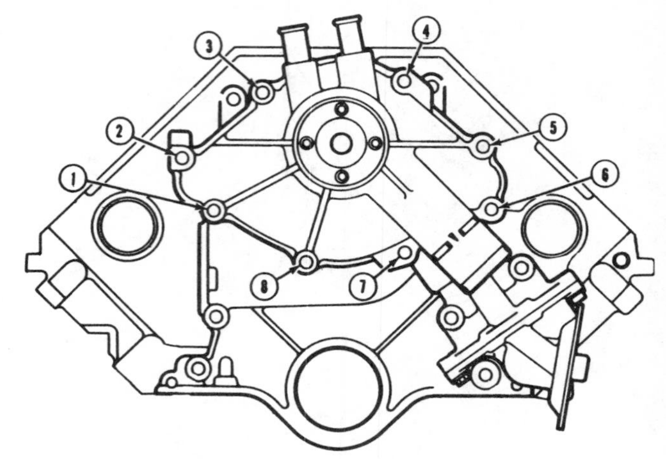

Fig. 13.20 Location of the water pump bolts on the V6 engine (Sec 4)

Electric cooling fan — removal and installation

2 Disconnect the negative battery terminal.

3 Remove the fan wiring harness from the routing clip.

4 Disconnect the wiring harness from the fan motor connector (push down on the two locking fingers to separate the connector).

5 Remove the four mounting bracket attaching screws and remove the fan assembly from the vehicle.

6 Remove the retaining clip from the end of the motor shaft and remove the fan. Remove the the nuts attaching the motor to the bracket.

7 Installation is the reverse of removal.

8 Tighten the fan motor-to-bracket attaching nuts to 70-95 in-lb.

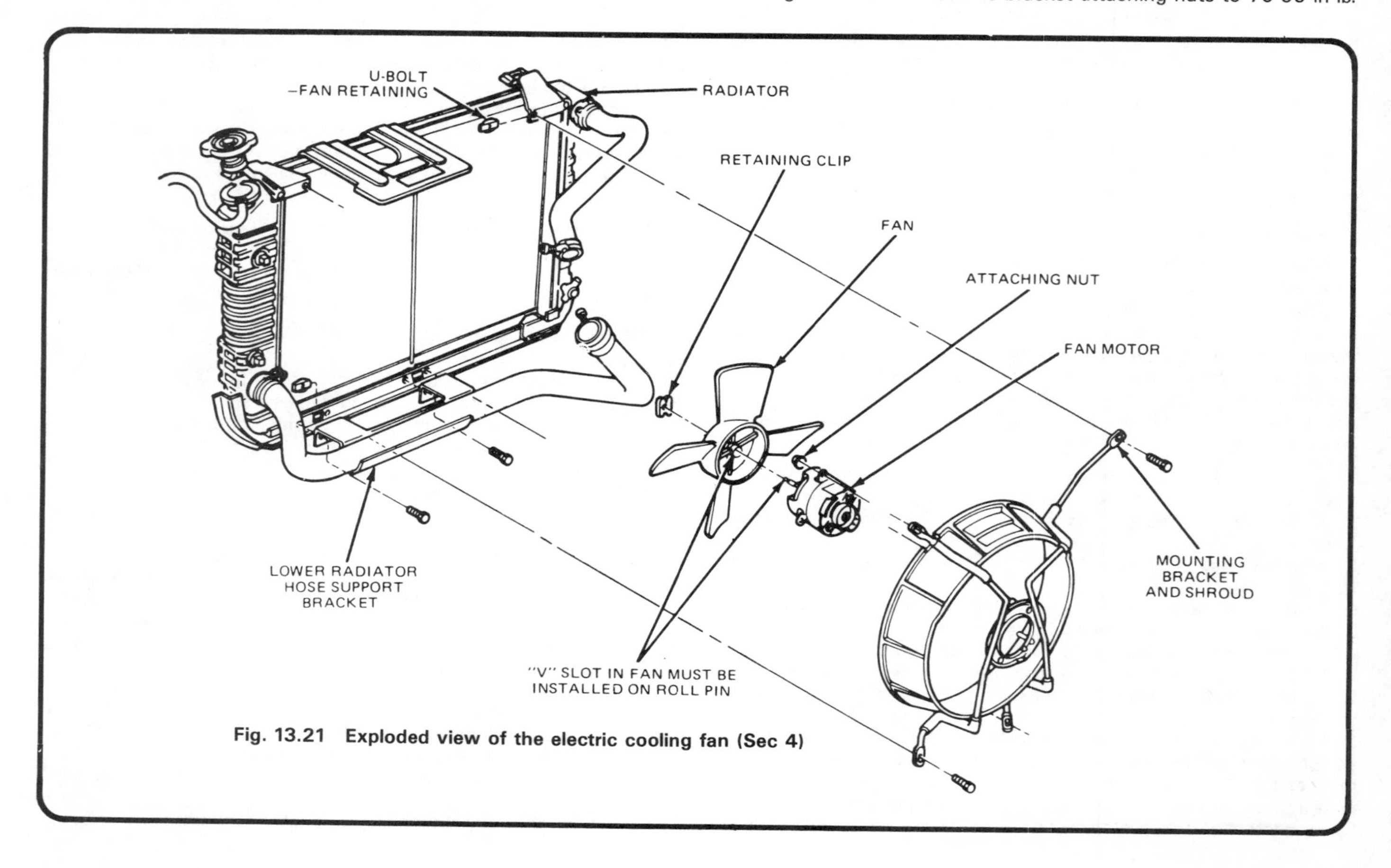

Fig. 13.21 Exploded view of the electric cooling fan (Sec 4)

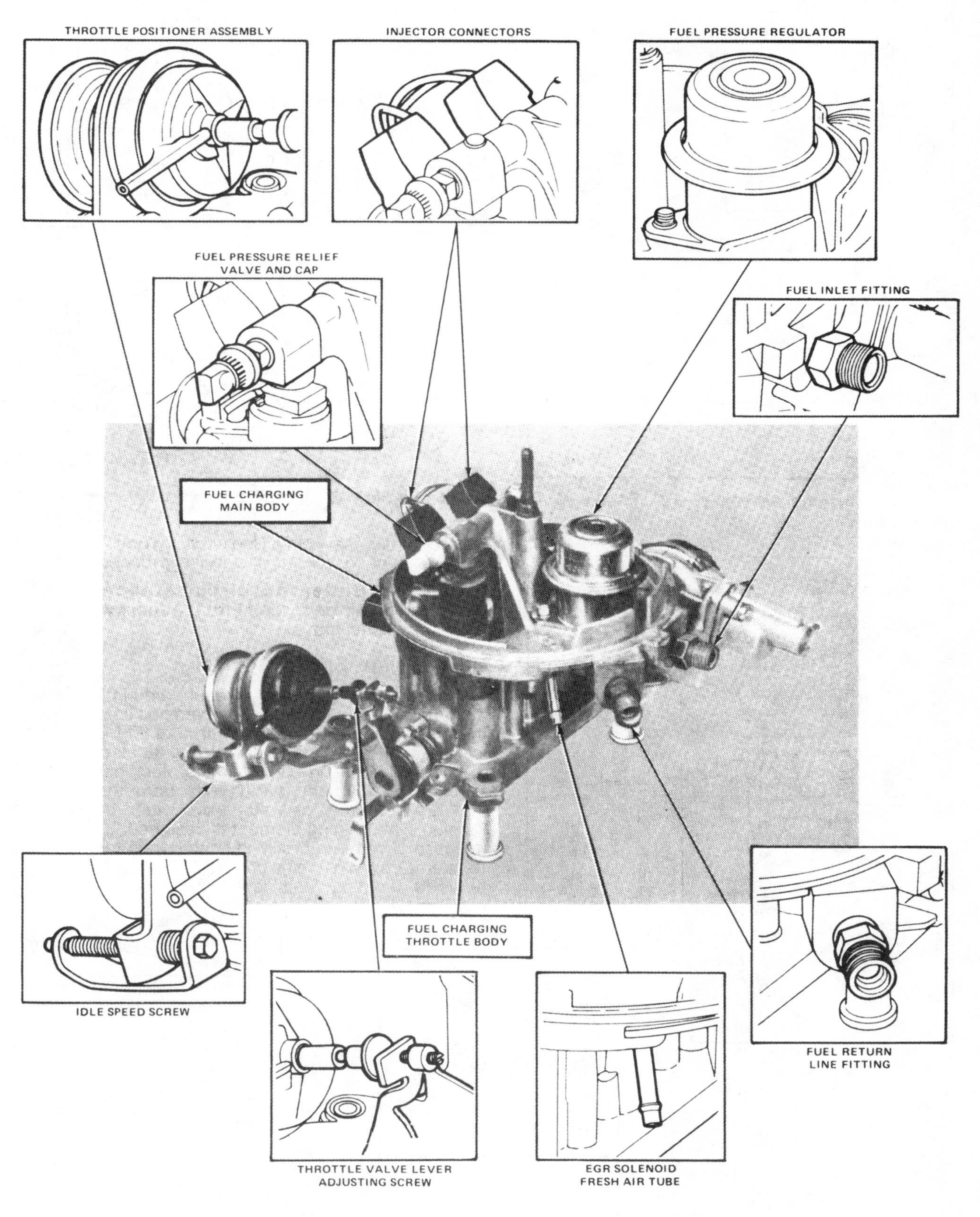

Fig. 13.22 Central fuel injection components — right front view (Sec 5)

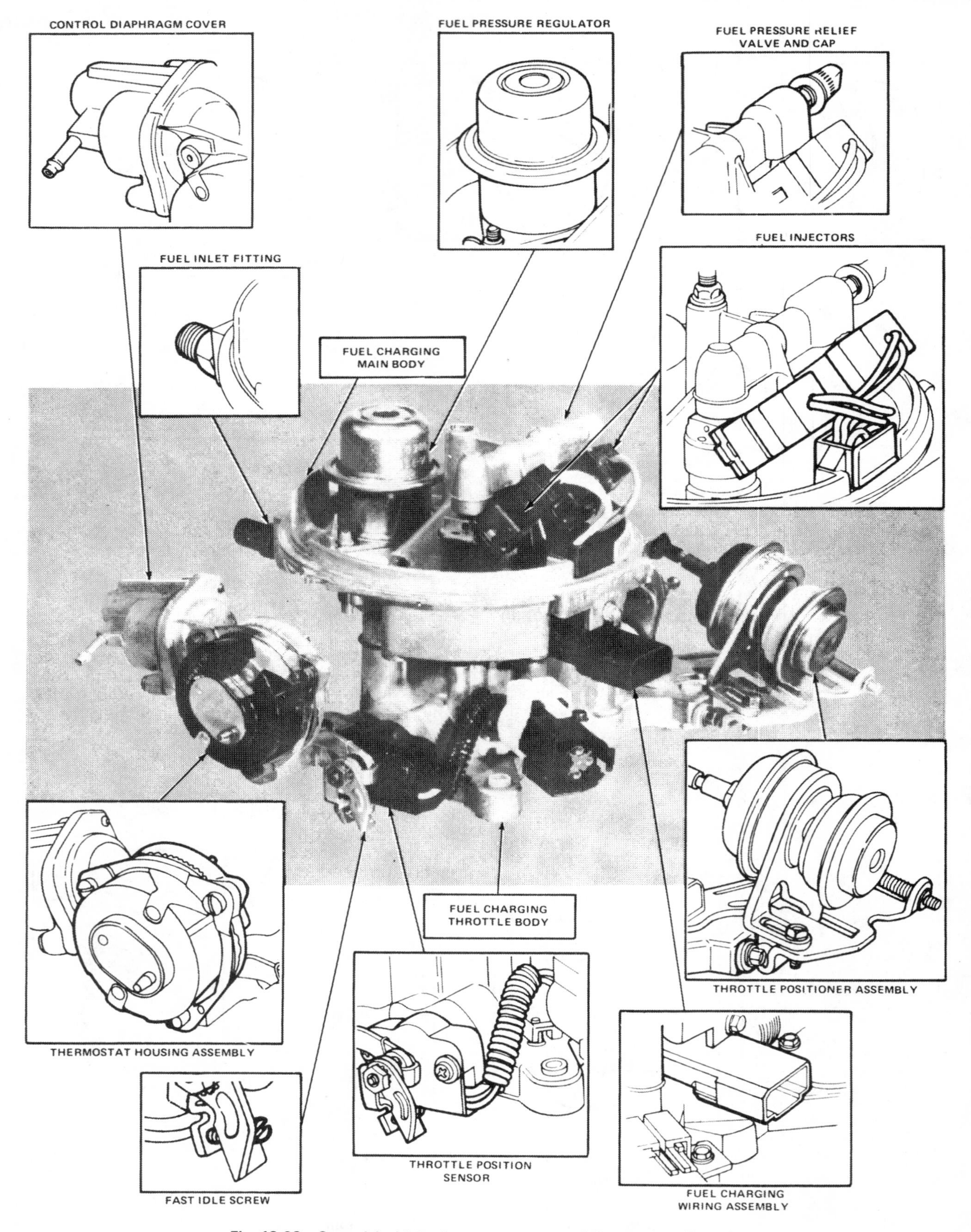

Fig. 13.23 Central fuel injection components — left rear view (Sec 5)

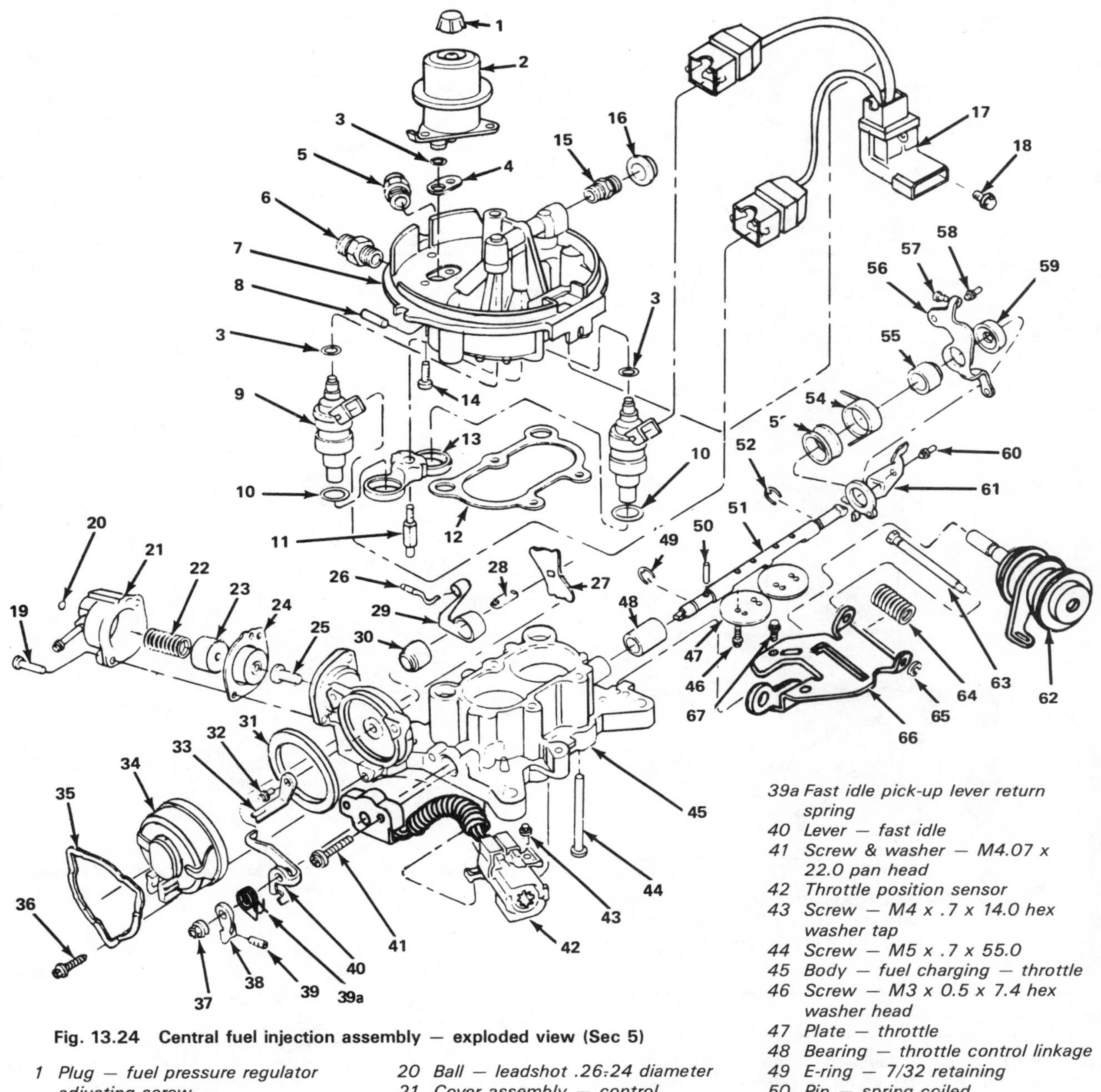

Fig. 13.24 Central fuel injection assembly — exploded view (Sec 5)

1 Plug — fuel pressure regulator adjusting screw
2 Regulator assembly — fuel pressure
3 Seal — 5/16 x .070 O-ring
4 Gasket — fuel pressure regulator
5 Connector — 1/4 pipe to 1/2-20
6 Connector — 1/8 pipe to 9/16-16
7 Body — fuel charging main
8 Plug — 1/16 x 27 headless hex
9 Injector assembly — fuel
10 Seal — 5/8 x .103 O-ring
11 Screw — fuel injector retaining
12 Gasket — fuel charging body
13 Retainer — fuel injector
14 Screw — M5.0 x 20.0 pan head
15 Valve assembly — diagnostic valve
16 Cap — fuel pressure relief valve
17 Wiring assembly — fuel charging
18 Screw — M3.5 x 1.27 x1.27 pan head
19 Screw and washer — M4 x 7.0 x 20.00
20 Ball — leadshot .26-.24 diameter
21 Cover assembly — control diaphragm
22 Spring — control modulator
23 Retainer — pulldown diaphragm
24 Diaphragm — pulldown control
25 Adjuster — pulldown control
26 Rod — fast idle control
27 Cam — fast idle
28 Shaft — choke housing
29 Positioner — fast idle control rod
30 Bushing — choke housing
31 Gasket — thermostat housing
32 Screw & washer — M3.5 x 0.6 x 6 pan head
33 Lever — choke thermostat
34 Housing assembly — thermostat
35 Retainer — housing assembly
36 Screw
37 Nut & washer assembly
38 Lever — fast idle cam adjuster
39 Screw — No. 10-32 x .50 set slotted head
39a Fast idle pick-up lever return spring
40 Lever — fast idle
41 Screw & washer — M4.07 x 22.0 pan head
42 Throttle position sensor
43 Screw — M4 x .7 x 14.0 hex washer tap
44 Screw — M5 x .7 x 55.0
45 Body — fuel charging — throttle
46 Screw — M3 x 0.5 x 7.4 hex washer head
47 Plate — throttle
48 Bearing — throttle control linkage
49 E-ring — 7/32 retaining
50 Pin — spring coiled
51 Shaft — throttle
52 C-ring — throttle shaft bushing
53 Bearing — throttle control linkage
54 Spring — throttle return
55 Bushing — accelerator pump over travel spring
56 Lever — transmission linkage
57 Screw — M4 x 0.7 x 7.6
58 Pin — transmission linkage lever
59 Spacer — throttle shaft
60 Ball — throttle lever
61 Lever — throttle
62 Positioner assembly — throttle
63 Screw — 1/4-28 x 2.53 hex head adjusting
64 Spring — throttle positioner retaining
65 E-ring — retaining
66 Bracket — throttle positioner
67 Screw — M5 x 8 x 14.0 hex washer tap

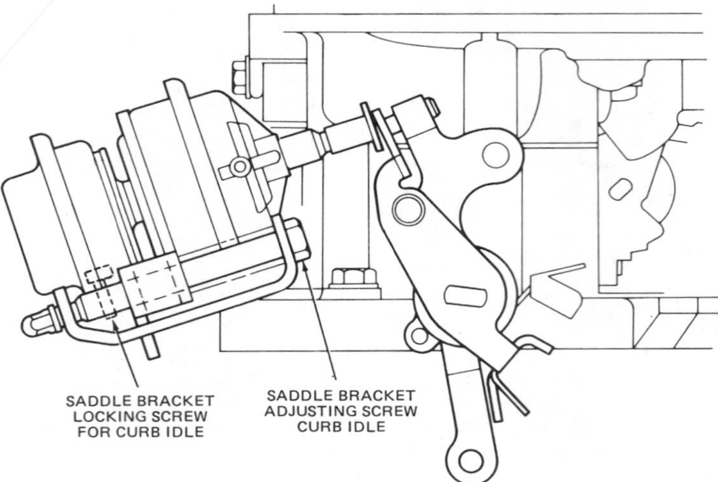

Fig. 13.25 Curb idle adjusting screw — 5.0L with central fuel injection (Sec 5)

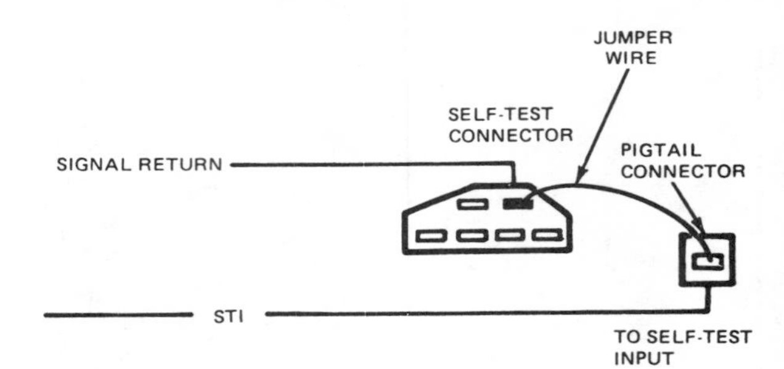

Fig. 13.26 A small wire can be used to jump the test terminal when checking the idle speed on 3.8L engine with central fuel injection (Sec 5)

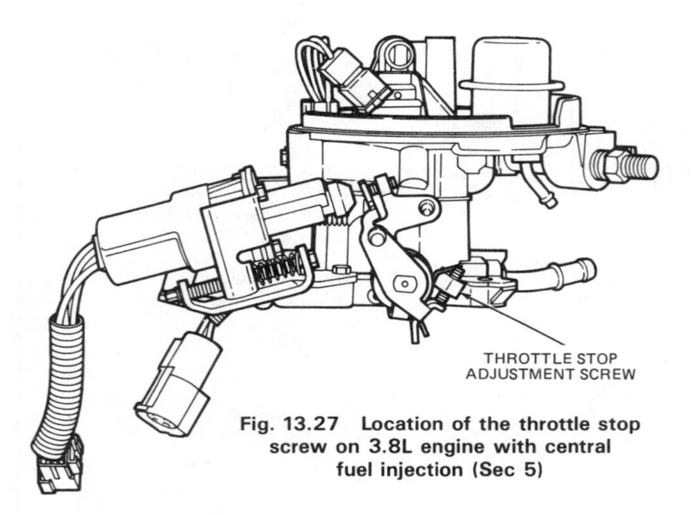

Fig. 13.27 Location of the throttle stop screw on 3.8L engine with central fuel injection (Sec 5)

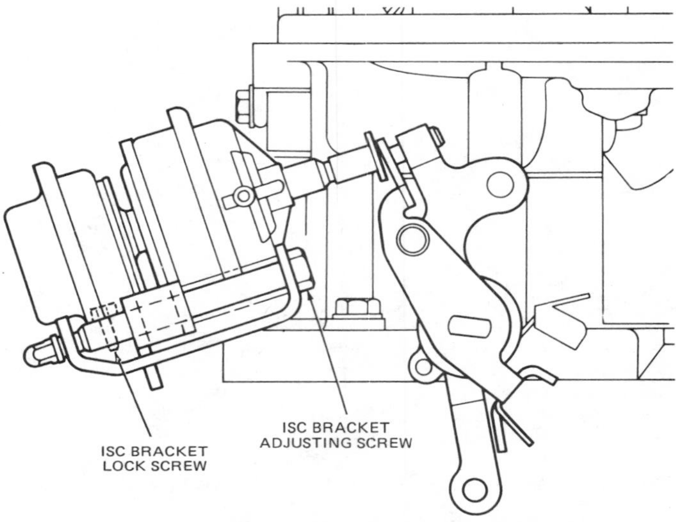

Fig. 13.28 Location of lock screw and ISC bracket adjusting screw (Sec 5)

5 Fuel and exhaust systems

There are three notable additions to the late model Mustang/Capri. One is the use of a Holley carburetor (model 4180C-4V) on the 5.0L high output engine. Central fuel injection was also added as standard equipment on all 3.8L models and 5.0L models with an automatic transmission. Beginning in 1987, a multi-point Sequential Electronic Fuel Injection system (SEFI) was offered on the 5.0L engine.

Central Fuel Injection

General information

1 The central fuel injection system incorporates two injectors mounted to a throttle body similar to that of a conventional carburetor. This produces greatly improved fuel metering in all running conditions and, since most of the control mechanism is electronic, reduces maintenance and minor repair problems. If the problem happens to be in this electronic control module however, the only assistance the owner can provide (unless equipped with lots of highly specialized equipment) is a phone call to a specialist with the proper diagnostic facilities.

2 The electronic engine control (EEC) module automatically adjusts the air/fuel mixture according to engine load and performance. A fuel pressure regulator mounted to the fuel charging assembly regulates the electric pump-generated fuel pressure at a constant 39 psi. The injectors consist essentially of a solenoid-actuated pintel valve and a small in-line fuel filter, and are energized by time-modulated electronic pulses from the EEC. **Warning:** *Prior to any operation in which a fuel line will be disconnected the high pressure in the system must first be relieved as described in Step 32. Disconnect the negative battery cable to prevent sources of ignition when fuel vapors are present.*

5.0 L — idle speed adjustment

3 Place the transmission in Neutral or Park and firmly set the parking brake. Turn the air conditioning selector to the Off position.

4 Start the engine and let it run until it reaches normal operating temperature.

5 Without restarting the engine run it at 2000 rpm for more than 10 seconds. If the vehicle is not equipped with a tachometer, attach an external one to the engine according to the manufacturer's instructions. Return the speed to idle and allow the engine to stabilize for 10 seconds. Again bring the engine speed to 2000 rpm and let it stabilize for approximately 10 seconds.

6 If adjustment is necessary, loosen the saddle bracket locking screw, then turn the adjusting screw clockwise to increase the idle speed or counterclockwise to decrease the speed until the specified rpm is obtained (see the emissions control label for proper idle speed).

7 Tighten the saddle bracket locking screw and repeat the idle stabilization procedure in Step 5 to verify the final setting.

3.8L — curb idle speed check and throttle stop fast idle adjustments

Note: *Idle speed on 3.8L CFI-equipped engines is not owner-adjustable and must be serviced by a Ford Service Department.*

8 Set parking brake and block wheels. If equipped with automatic parking brake release, always place in reverse when checking curb idle. Make all adjustments at normal operating temperature and with accessories off.

9 After engaging transmission in Drive (or Reverse) and idling for 60 seconds, idle rpm should be within specification (refer to emissions

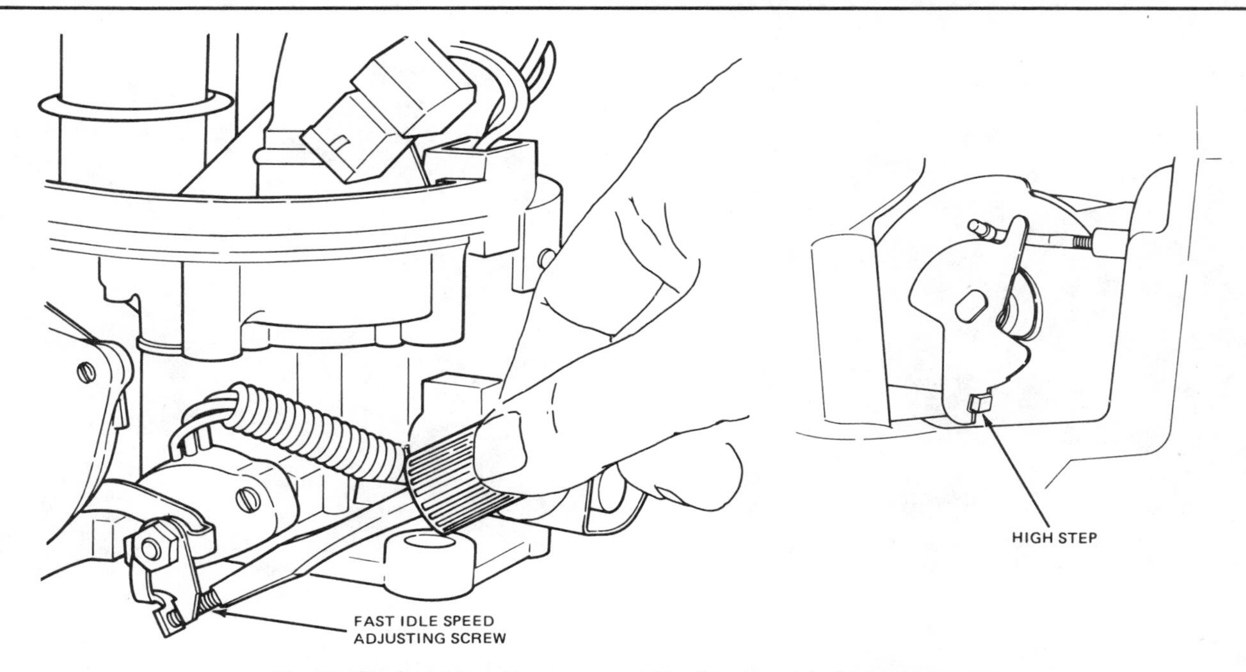

Fig. 13.29 Fast idle adjustment — 5.0L with central fuel injection (Sec 5)

decal for speeds).

10 If engine curb idle is above specification and it is observed that the throttle lever is not in contact with the ISC motor, but held open by the throttle stop adjustment screw (TSAS), the ISC plunger must be retracted by performing the following procedure in the exact sequence described below:

11 Shut engine off and remove the air cleaner. In the engine compartment, locate the self-test connector and self-test input (STI) connector. These two connectors are located next to each other.

12 Connect a jumper wire between the STI connector and the signal return pin on the self-test connector (Fig 13.26).

13 Turn the ignition to the run position. *Do not start engine.*

14 The ISC plunger will retract. Wait until the plunger is fully retracted (about ten seconds). **Note:** *If the plunger does not retract it will have to be serviced by a qualified professional.*

15 Shut off the key.

16 Remove the jumper wire.

17 Using pliers, grasp the TSAS screw threads and turn the screw until it is removed from the CFI assembly. Install a new screw.

18 With the throttle plate closed, turn the new screw inward until there is a .005 inch gap between the screw tip and the throttle lever surface.

19 Perform the fast idle adjustment by first removing the rubber dust cover from the ISC motor tip.

20 Push the tip back toward the motor to remove any lash, but without engaging the idle tracking switch.

21 Using a 9/32-inch drill bit as a gauge, attempt to pass it between the ISC motor tip and and the throttle lever. **Note:** *Be sure not to push the idle tracking switch back with the gauge. It must pass through while making light contact with both surfaces.*

22 If the clearance between the ISC motor tip and the throttle lever is incorrect, loosen the ISC bracket lock screw and turn the ISC bracket adjusting screw until proper clearance is obtained (see accompanying illustration).

23 Retighten the lock screw and replace the rubber dust cover.

24 Reinstall the air cleaner.

5.0L — fast idle RPM adjustment

25 Place transmission in Park or Neutral.

26 Bring engine to normal operating temperature.

27 Disconnect the vacuum hose at the EGR valve and plug it.

28 Disconnect and plug the vacuum hose at the fast idle pulldown motor.

29 Set the fast idle lever on the high step of the fast idle cam.

30 Check and adjust the fast idle RPM (no time limit).

31 Remove the plug from the EGR hose and reconnect it. Remove the plug from the fast idle pulldown motor vacuum hose and reconnect it.

Fuel pressure diagnostic valve — pressure relief

32 A Schrader-type diagnostic pressure valve is located on top of the fuel charging assembly. This valve is for monitoring fuel pressure, pressure relief prior to servicing and for bleeding the fuel system of any air after servicing. A special Ford tool (No. T80L-9974-A or equivalant) is connected to this valve to relieve the pressure in the lines prior to any service.

Central fuel injection — removal and installation

33 It is necessary to remove the CFI before cleaning the injector filter screens. It may also be financially advantageous to remove the CFI unit before taking it in for professional servicing or to exchange it for a rebuilt unit.

34 Disconnect the negative lead from the battery.

35 Remove the air cleaner.

36 Carefully release the fuel line pressure at the diagnostic valve on the fuel charging assembly (Step 32). Use absorbent material to prevent the pressurized fuel from spraying.

37 Disconnect the throttle cable and transmission throttle valve lever.

38 Disconnect all fuel, vacuum and electrical connections at the CFI body.

39 Remove the body-to-manifold retaining nuts, then remove the fuel charging assembly/CFI body from the vehicle. Remove the mounting gaskets from the intake manifold and spacer plate, making sure all gasket mating surfaces are clean.

40 To install, place new gaskets on either side of the spacer plate, then place the gasket/spacer assembly over the studs on the intake manifold.

41 Position the CFI body over the four mounting studs and secure it with the attaching nuts. Tighten the nuts finger tight, then in three steps to 120 in-lbs.

42 Reconnect the fuel line, electrical connectors, throttle cable and all emission system lines. Start the engine and check for leaks. Adjust the idle speed if necessary (see steps 3 through 7).

Injector filter screen cleaning

43 A dirty or clogged injector filter screen will normally first appear as decreased engine performance at high rpm and under heavy load. Bear in mind that fuel-injected models incorporate two additional fuel filters; one in-line near the intake manifold and one mounted to the electric fuel pump inside the fuel tank. These filters are also suspect. If all filters are clean, check the fuel pump(s) according to the procedure in this Chapter.

44 Remove the CFI unit from the intake manifold (refer to Steps 33 through 42).

45 Remove the center air cleaner mounting stud from the top of the

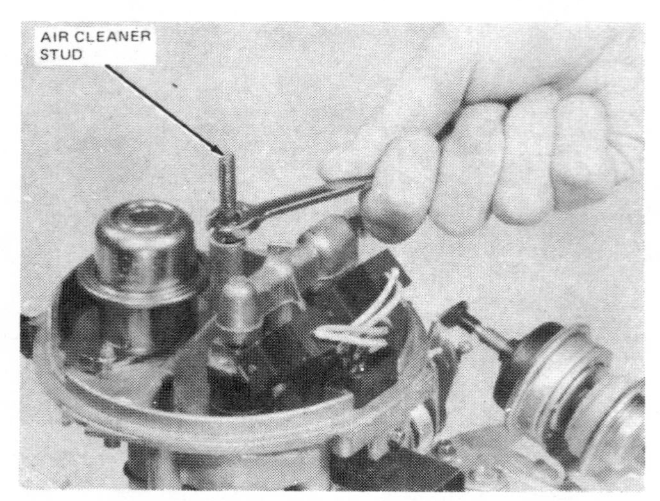

Fig. 13.30 Removing the air cleaner mounting stud from the CFI fuel charging body (Sec 5)

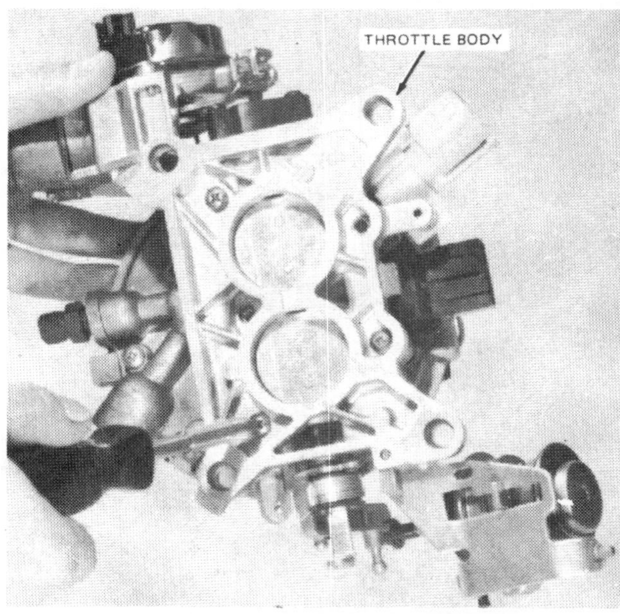

Fig. 13.31 The throttle body to main body retaining screws can be accessed through the bottom of the CFI assembly (Sec 5)

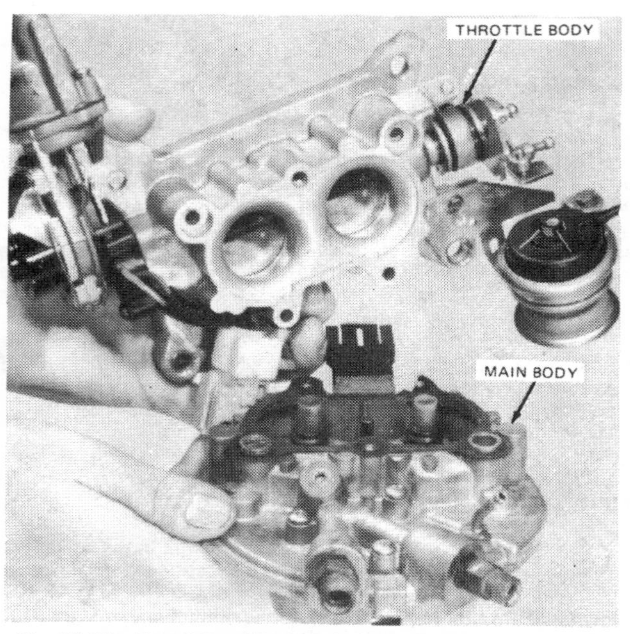

Fig. 13.32 Removing the throttle body from the main body (Sec 5)

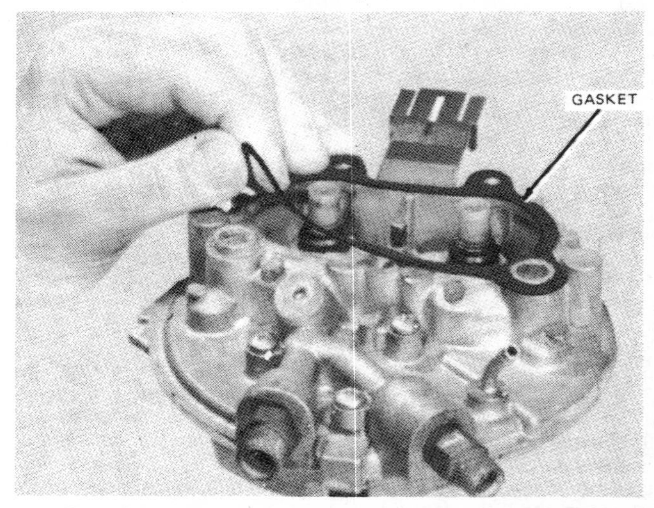

Fig. 13.33 Removing the CFI fuel charging assembly gasket. Replace it with a new one upon reassembly (Sec 5)

main fuel charging body (Fig. 13.30).

46 Invert the CFI assembly and remove the four retaining screws. Separate the throttle body from the main body.

47 Carefully remove and discard the gasket. Do not damage the gasket surfaces.

48 Remove the three pressure regulator retaining screws and the pressure regulator.

49 Disconnect the electrical connectors from the two injectors by pulling them directly outward. Mark the connectors so they return to the same injectors when reassembled.

50 Remove the injector retainer screw and the injector retainer.

51 Carefully remove each injector, noting by the mark on the injector body whether it inserts at the 'choke' or 'throttle' side.

52 Carefully remove the filter screens and replace them with new ones.

53 Reassembly of the injector unit is basically the reverse of disassembly. Note that the injector retainer, pressure regulator, throttle body and CFI unit-to-manifold retaining bolts and screws must be correctly torqued and all affected gaskets must be replaced with new ones.

Electric fuel pump

General information

54 The electric fuel pump system used on Mustang/Capri uses a low pressure in-tank mounted pump and an externally mounted high pressure in-line pump. The fuel tank has an internal sump cavity in which the low pressure fuel pump inlet rests. This design provides for satisfactory pump operation during extreme vehicle maneuvers and steep vehicle attitudes with low tank fill levels.

55 The low pressure electic fuel pump is to provide pressurized fuel to the inlet of the high pressure pump. The inlet of the low pressure fuel pump has a nylon filter on it to prevent dirt and other particulate matter from entering the system. The low pressure pump has an external resistor in the electrical circuit to reduce the operating voltage to 11 volts.

56 The externally mounted fuel pump is a high pressure unit with a working pressure of 39 psi. The pump has an internal relief valve to provide overpressure protection in the event the fuel flow becomes restricted (clogged filter, damaged fuel lines, etc.). The system pressure is controlled by a pressure regulator on the engine. The electrical system

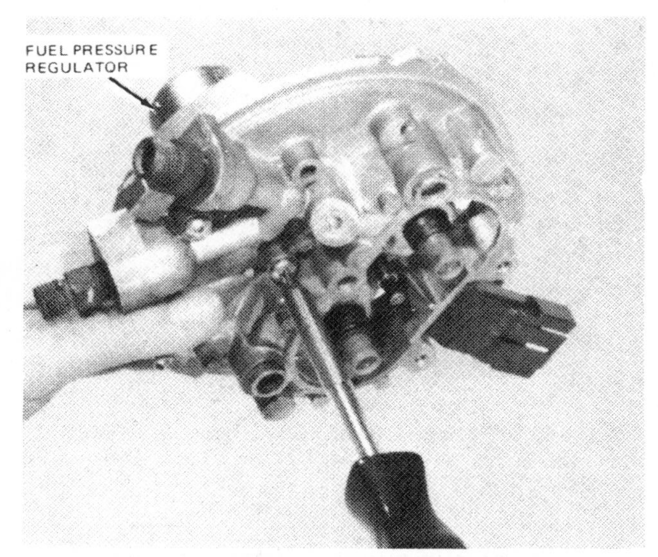

Fig. 13.34 Removing the CFI pressure regulator retaining screws (Sec 5)

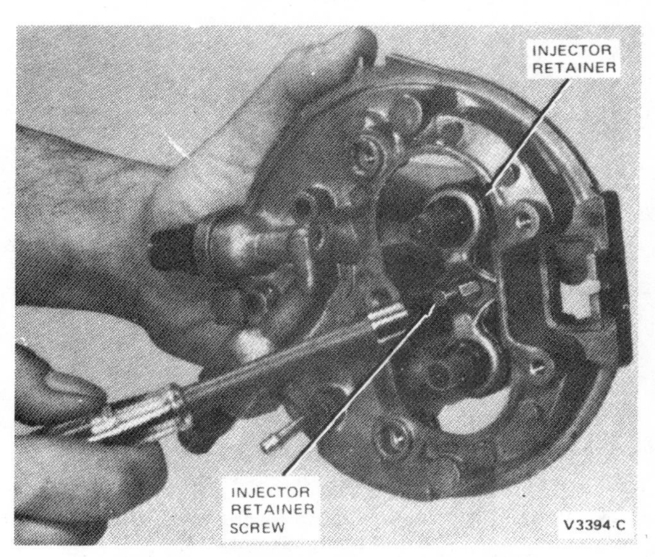

Fig. 13.35 Removing the CFI injector retainer (Sec 5)

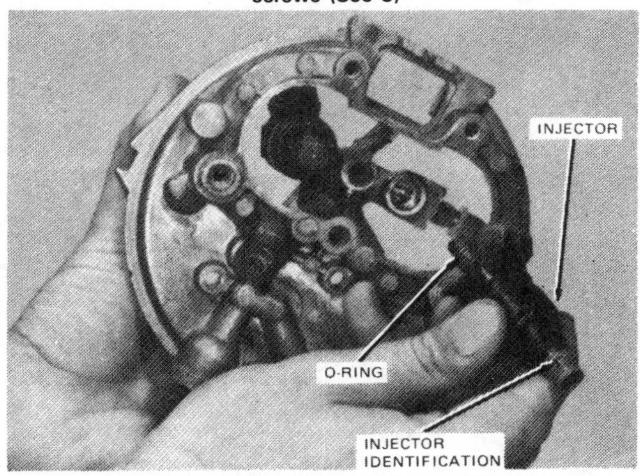

Fig. 13.36 Identify the injectors as shown during removal to avoid confusion during reassembly (Sec 5)

has a fuel pump control relay controlled by the electronic engine control (EEC) module, which provides power to the fuel pump under various operating conditions.

Diagnosis

57 Almost any electric fuel pump malfunction that can occur will result in a loss or reduction of fuel flow and/or pressure. This diagnosis procedure will concentrate on determining if the electric fuel pump is operating properly.
58 Check the fuel tank for adequate fuel supply. **Note:** *Tank must be at least half full for the following procedures.*
59 Check for fuel leakage at all fittings and lines.
60 Check for electrical continuity to the fuel pump by disconnecting the electrical connector at the high pressure pump.
61 Connect a voltmeter to the body wiring harness connector.
62 Turn the key to On while watching the voltmeter.
63 The voltage should rise to battery voltage, then return to zero after approximately one second.
64 If the voltage is not as specified check the inertia switch and electrical system.
65 Connect a continuity tester (ohmmeter) to the pump wiring harness connector; if no continuity is present check continuity directly at pump terminals.
66 If there is no continuity at the pump terminals, replace the pump. If continuity is present here but not in Step 65, service or replace the wiring harness.
67 Connect the continuity tester (ohmmeter) across the body wiring harness connector. If continuity is present (about 5 ohms), low pressure pump circuit is electrically OK.
68 If no continuity is present in Step 67 it will be necessary to remove the fuel tank (refer to Chapter 3 section 29) and check for continuity at the fuel pump/pump sender flange terminals. If no continuity at pump flange terminals is present, replace the assembly. If continuity is present at the pump but not in Step 67, service or replace the wiring harness to the low pressure pump.
69 To check electric fuel pump operation, disconnect the return line at the fuel rail. Use care to avoid fuel spillage.
70 Connect a hose from the fuel rail fitting to a calibrated container of at least one quart.
71 Connect pressure gauge T80L-9974-A or equivalent to fuel diagnostic valve on fuel rail.
72 Disconnect the electrical connector to the electric fuel pump located just forward of the pump outlet if not already disconnected from Step 60.
73 Connect an auxiliary wiring harness to the electical connector to the fuel pump.
74 Energize the fuel pump for 10 seconds by connecting the auxiliary wiring harness to a fully charged 12 volt battery; observe pressure while energized. If there is no pressure, check polarity of wiring harness and also check terminal connectors at the fuel pump.
75 Allow fuel to drain from the hose into the container and observe volume.
76 The fuel pump is operating properly if:

- a) The fuel pressure reaches 35-40 psi.
- b) Fuel flow is a minimum of 9.5 oz in 10 seconds.
- c) Fuel pressure remains at a minimum of 30 psi immediately after de-energization.

77 If all three conditions are met the fuel pump is operating normally.
78 If pressure condition is met but flow is not, check for a blocked filter(s) and fuel supply lines. After correcting any blockages recheck per above procedure. If flow conditions are still not met replace the fuel pump.
79 If both pressure and flow conditions are met but pressure will not maintain after de-energization, check for a leaking regulator or injectors. If both check OK then replace the fuel pump.
80 If no flow or pressure is seen the fuel system should be checked as in Step 78. If no trouble is found replace the fuel pump and drop the fuel tank and replace the fuel filter on the low pressure pump.
81 Check the low pressure in-tank pump as follows:
82 Remove inlet push connect fitting and line from high pressure pump assembly. **Caution:** *Raise end of fitting above level of fluid in tank to prevent siphon action.*
83 Connect a hose from the fuel tank to a calibrated container of at least one quart capacity.

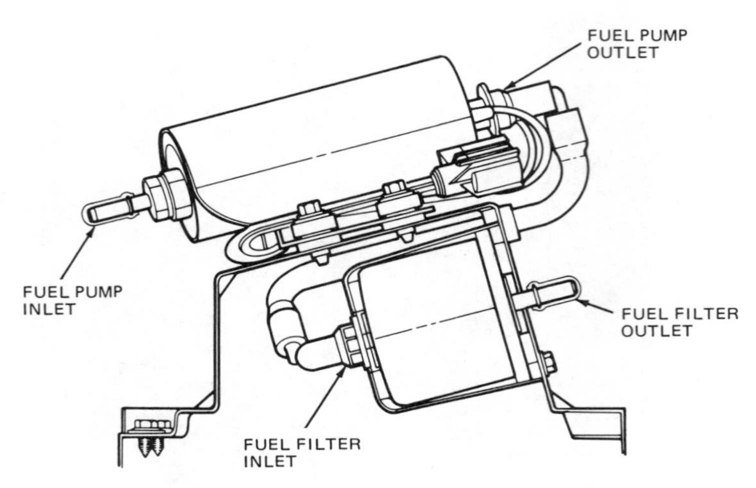

Fig. 13.37 High pressure in-line electric fuel pump and filter assembly (Sec 5)

84 Place the ignition switch in the Run position until the fuel pump times out (about 1 second).
85 Check the container for presence of some fuel (if necessary, lift container to prevent siphon action). The amount of fuel should be a minimum of 1.5 oz for one second of operation.
86 If no fuel is present, repeat Steps 85 and 86 two or three times (recycle key).
87 If no fuel is present, check for pinched line between fuel tank and fitting and then proceed to drop fuel tank (refer to Chapter 3 section 29).
88 Connect a voltmeter to the chassis electrical connector from the fuel pump and turn the key to the On position. Voltage should rise to about battery voltage for one second and then return to zero volts.
89 If voltage is as specified and the electrical connector is OK at the pump, replace the fuel pump assembly and repeat low pressure pump test.
90 If no voltage is present service the electrical circuit in vehicle.

High pressure in-line pump assembly — removal and installation

Note: *Refer to Fig. 13.37.*

91 Depressurize fuel system (refer to Step 32).
92 Raise vehicle and support it on jackstands.
93 Disconnect the electical connector from the body harness. Remove inlet and outlet lines from the fuel pump.
94 The fuel pump may now be removed from the assembly by bending tab out and sliding the pump out of the ring.
95 The electical wiring harness may be removed from the assembly by inserting a screwdriver or knife between the connector and retaining clip and sliding the connector towards pump inlet.
96 Installation is basically the reverse of removal with the following points:
97 Make sure the fittings on the pump have gaskets in place, are properly positioned and that fittings have been tightened properly, inlet 19-22 lb-ft, outlet 8-12 lb-ft. Check the wiring harness boots to make sure they are pushed onto the pump terminals far enough to seal and that the wire terminals are pushed onto pump terminals fully.
98 After wrapping the isolator around the fuel pump, locate the slot in the isolator so it faces the bracket base and push the pump and isolator assembly into the bracket. Make sure the tab of the isolator contacts tab of the bracket and that the bracket tabs do not contact the pump case. After the pump is fully inserted into the bracket and the wiring harness comes out the bottom of the ring, bend the rear tab to keep the pump from sliding out.
99 Start vehicle and check for proper operation of pump and for leaks.

Low pressure in-tank pump assembly — removal and installation

100 The low pressure fuel pump is located in the top of the fuel tank and requires removal of the fuel tank for servicing (refer to Chapter 3 Section 29 for fuel tank removal). The low pressure pump is removed in the same manner as the fuel sender; i.e., remove hoses from fittings, remove locking ring and remove assembly from tank.

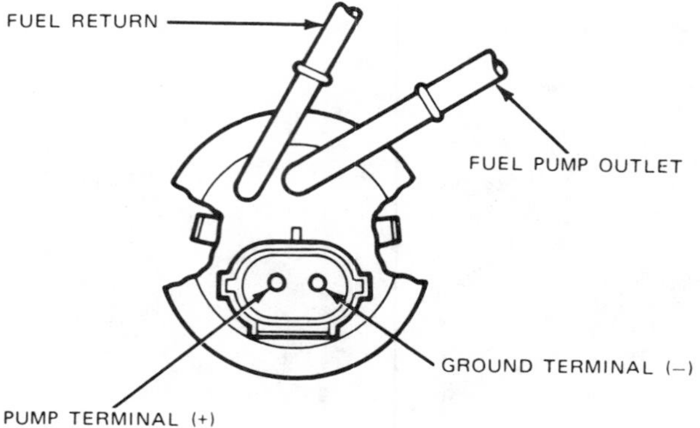

Fig. 13.38 Flange view of the in-tank pump assembly (Sec 5)

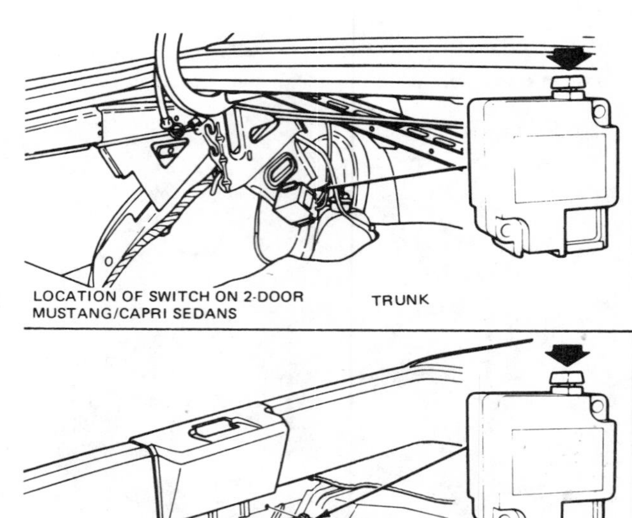

Fig. 13.39 Inertia switch location (Sec 5)

Installation

101 Clean the fuel pump mounting flange and the fuel tank mounting surface and seal ring groove.
102 Put a light coating of heavy duty grease on a new seal ring to hold it in place during assembly and install in the fuel ring groove.
103 Install the fuel pump and bracket assembly carefully to insure that the filter is not damaged. Be sure that the locating keys are in the keyways and the seal ring remains in the groove.
104 Hold the pump assembly in place and install the locking ring finger tight, being sure that all the locking tabs are under the tank lock ring tabs.
105 Secure the fuel pump unit with the locking ring by rotating clockwise with the tool until the ring stops against stops.
106 Install electrical connector.
107 Install fuel line fitting.
108 Install tank.
109 Turn the ignition key to the On position for 3 seconds. Turn the ignition key Off and On for 3 seconds repeatedly (5 to 10 times) to pressurize the system. Check for leaks at the fittings.
110 Start the engine and recheck for leaks.

Inertia switch

111 In the event of a collision, the contacts in the inertia switch open and the fuel pump shuts off. The fuel pump will shut off even if the

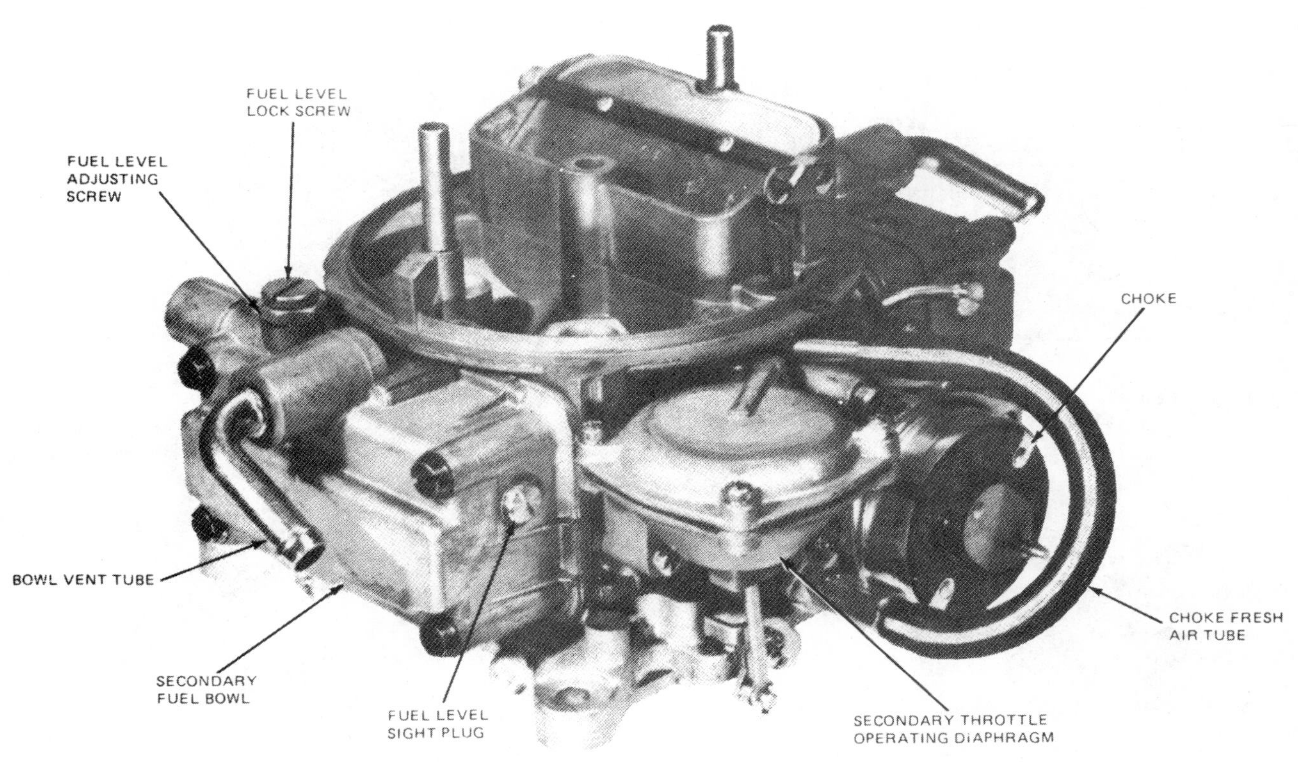

Fig. 13.40 Holley (4180-C) — front view (Sec 5)

Fig. 13.41 Holley (4180-C) — rear view (Sec 5)

engine does not stop running. Once the contacts have opened the engine will not restart until the inertia switch is manually reset. The inertia switch is located in the trunk on the left hinge support on 2-door models, and near the left hand corner of the spare tire well on the rear body panel on 3-door models. **Caution:** *Do not reset the inertia switch until the complete fuel system has been inspected.*

112 To reset the inertia switch, simply press the button on top of the switch.

Carburetor (4180C-4V)

General description

113 The Holley 4180C-4V carburetor is a downdraft, two-stage carburetor. It can be considered as two carburetors; one supplying a fuel-air mixture throughout the entire range of engine operation (primary stage), and the other functioning only when a greater quantity of fuel-air mixture is required (secondary stage).

114 The primary stage (front section) of the carburetor contains a fuel

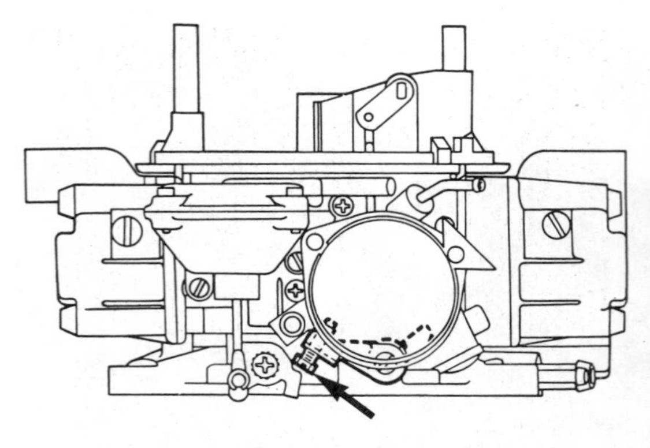
Fig. 13.42 Fast idle speed adjusting screw location (4180-C) (Sec 5)

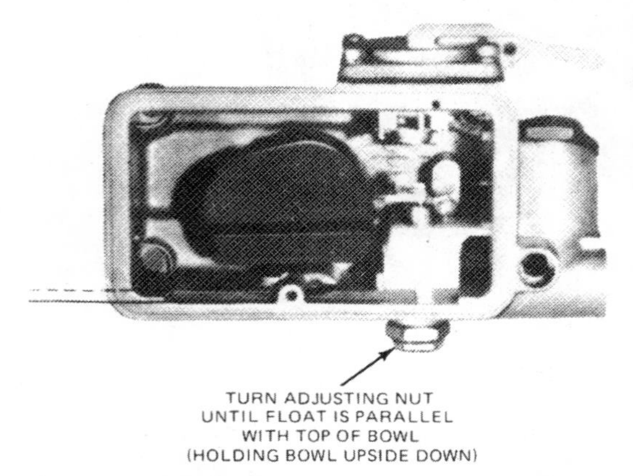

Fig. 13.44 Dry float adjustment (Sec 5)

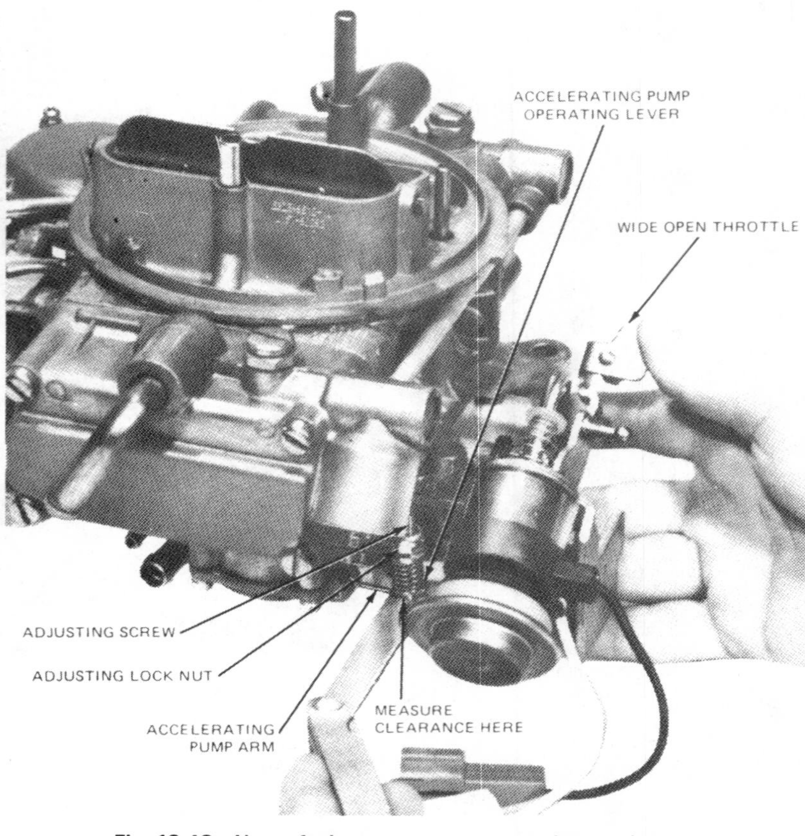

Fig. 13.43 Use a feeler gauge to measure the accelerator pump lever clearance (Sec 5)

bowl, metering block and an accelerating pump assembly. The primary barrels each contain a primary and booster venturi, main fuel discharge nozzle, throttle plate, and idle fuel passage.

115 The secondary stage (rear section), of the carburetor contains a fuel bowl, metering body, and secondary throttle operating diaphragm assembly. Each secondary barrel contains a primary and booster venturi, idle fuel passages, main secondary fuel discharge nozzle, throttle plate, and a transfer system fuel passage from the primary fuel bowl.

116 A fuel inlet system for both the primary and the secondary stages of the carburetor provides the fuel metering system with a constant supply of fuel.

117 The model 4180C-4V uses an electric choke.

5.0L engine (4180C-4V) – fast idle adjustment

Note: *Refer to Fig.13.42 for location of adjusting screw.*

118 Place the transmission in Neutral or Park.

119 Bring engine to normal operating temperature.

120 Disconnect the vacuum hose at the EGR valve and plug.

121 Place the fast idle adjustment on the specified step of the fast idle cam and check/adjust fast idle rpm to specification (refer to the emissions decal for specified step and RPM).

122 Rev engine momentarily, place fast idle adjustment on the specified step and recheck fast idle rpm.

123 Remove plug from EGR vacuum hose and reconnect.

5.0L engine (4180C-4V) – curb idle adjustment

Note: *No A/C kicker speed set required.*

124 Place the transmission in Neutral or Park.

125 Bring the engine to normal operating temperature.

126 Place A/C-Heat selector to the Off position.

127 Disconnect and plug the vacuum hose at the throttle kicker.

128 Place the transmission in specified position.

129 Check/adjust curb idle rpm if adjustment is required (refer to the emissions decal for RPM).

130 Adjust the curb idle speed screw.

131 Place the transmission in Neutral or Park, rev the engine momentarily.

132 Place the transmission in specified position and recheck curb idle rpm. Readjust only if required.

133 Remove the plug from the throttle kicker vacuum hose and reconnect.

134 Whenever it is required to adjust engine idle speed by more than 50 rpm, the adjustment screw on the AOD linkage lever at the carburetor should also be readjusted, (refer to Section 8).

Accelerator pump lever – adjustment

135 Using a feeler gauge and with the throttle plates (primary throttle plates) in the wide open position, there should be the specified clearance between the accelerating pump operating lever adjustment screw head and the pump arm when the pump arm is depressed manually (Fig. 13.43).

136 If adjustment is required, loosen and then hold the lock screw and turn the adjusting nut in to increase the clearance and out to decrease the clearance. One half turn of the adjusting nut is equal to approximately 0.015 in (0.381 mm). When the proper adjustment has been obtained hold the adjustment in position with a wrench and tighten the nut.

Fuel level float adjustment – dry

137 The dry float adjustment is a preliminary fuel level adjustment only. The final adjustment (fuel level float adjustment – wet) must be performed after the carburetor is installed on the engine.

138 With the fuel bowls and float assemblies removed, adjust the floats so that the floats are parallel to the fuel bowls, with the top of the fuel bowls inverted.

Fuel level adjustment – wet

139 The fuel pump must be in good condition prior to performing the following adjustments. Refer to Chapter 3 Section 8 for fuel pump

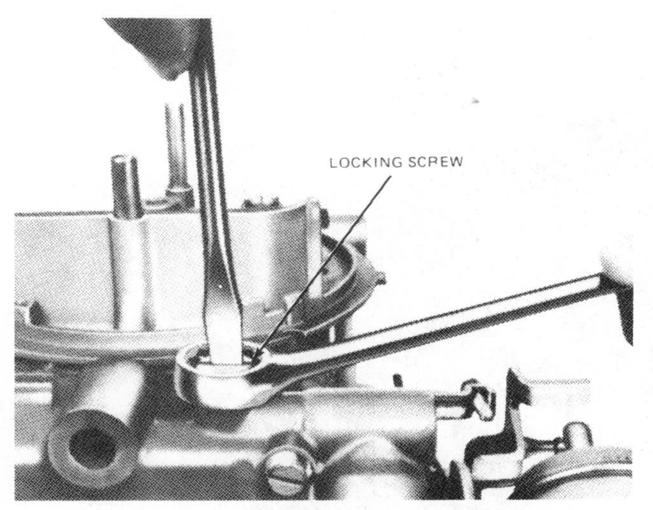

Fig. 13.45 Wet float adjustment (Sec 5)

Fig. 13.46 Adjusting screw for the secondary throttle plate adjustment (Sec 5)

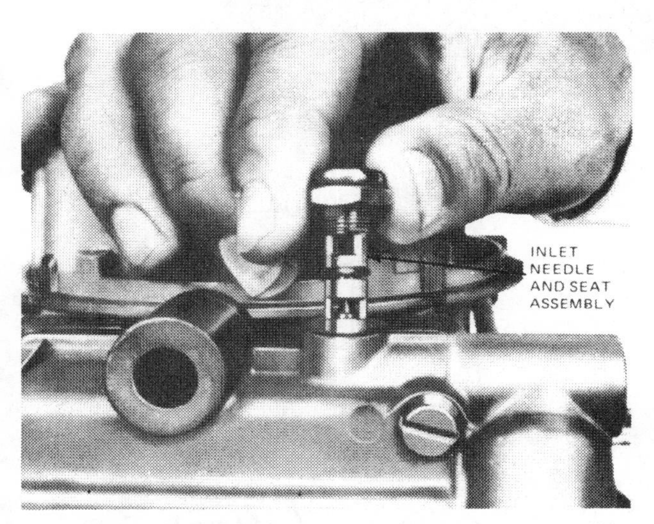

Fig. 13.47 Carefully remove the needle and seat assembly (Sec 5)

testing procedure.

140 Operate the engine to normalize engine temperatures and place the vehicle on a flat surface, as near level as possible. Remove the air cleaner if it was not previously removed.

141 Run engine at 1000 rpm for about 30 seconds to stabilize the fuel level.

142 Stop engine and remove sight plug on side of primary carburetor bowl.

143 Check fuel level. It should be at the bottom of the sight plug hole. If fuel spills out when the sight plug is removed, lower the fuel level. If fuel level is below sight plug hole, raise the fuel level. **Caution:** *Do not loosen the lock screw or nut or attempt to adjust fuel level with the sight plug removed or engine running because fuel may spray out, creating a fire hazard.*

144 Adjust the front level as necessary by loosening the lock screw and turning the adjusting nut clockwise to lower fuel level or counterclockwise to raise fuel level. (1/6 turn of the adjusting nut will change fuel level approximately 1/32 in). Tighten the lock screw and install sight plug, using the old gasket. Start engine and run at 1000 rpm for about 30 seconds to stabilize fuel level.

145 Stop the engine, remove sight plug and check fuel level. Repeat Step 144 until fuel level is at bottom of sight plug hole. When fuel level is at bottom of sight plug hole, install the sight plug using a new plug gasket.

146 Repeat Steps 139 through 145 for secondary fuel bowl. **Note:** *The secondary throttle must be used to stabilize the fuel level in the secondary fuel bowl.*

Secondary throttle plate — adjustment

Note: *Refer to Fig 13.46.*

147 With carburetor off the engine, hold the secondary throttle plates closed.

148 Turn the secondary throttle shaft lever adjusting screw (stop screw) out (counterclockwise) until the secondary throttle plates seat in the throttle bores.

149 Turn the screw in clockwise until the screw *just contacts the secondary lever, then turn screw in (clockwise) 1/4 turn.*

Fuel inlet needle and seat — removal and installation

Note: *The fuel inlet needle and seat assembly can be replaced without removing the fuel bowl.*

150 Remove the air cleaner.

151 Remove the fuel level adjustment lock screw and gasket. Turn the adjusting nut out and remove the adjusting nut and gasket. Remove the fuel inlet needle and seat assembly. **Note:** *Do not disassemble the fuel inlet needle and seat assembly. They are matched parts and are serviced as an assembly.*

152 Position the fuel inlet needle and seat assembly in the fuel bowl.

153 Position the adjusting nut gasket and nut on the fuel inlet needle and seat assembly. Align the flat on the ID of the nut with the flat on the OD of the fuel inlet needle and seat assembly.

154 Install the fuel level adjustment lock screw and gasket.

155 Adjust the fuel level (refer to Steps 139 through 145).

Choke thermostatic spring housing — removal and installation

156 Remove the carburetor from vehicle (refer to Chapter 3 Section 16).

157 Using a hacksaw carefully cut a slot in the head of the breakaway screw (Fig.13.48). Using a proper size straight blade screw driver, remove the breakaway screw.

158 Repeat Step 157 for the remaining breakaway screw.

159 Remove the standard screw. Remove the retaining ring, choke cap and gasket. **Note:** *Before removal of the choke cap, note the position of the index mark for reinstallation.*

160 Install the choke cap gasket. Install the choke cap by engaging the bimetal loop on the choke thermostatic lever.

161 Install the retaining ring. Loosely install two new breakaway screws and one standard screw.

162 Align the choke cap to the proper index mark.

163 Tighten the breakaway screws until the heads break off. Tighten the standard screw to 16-18 in-lb.

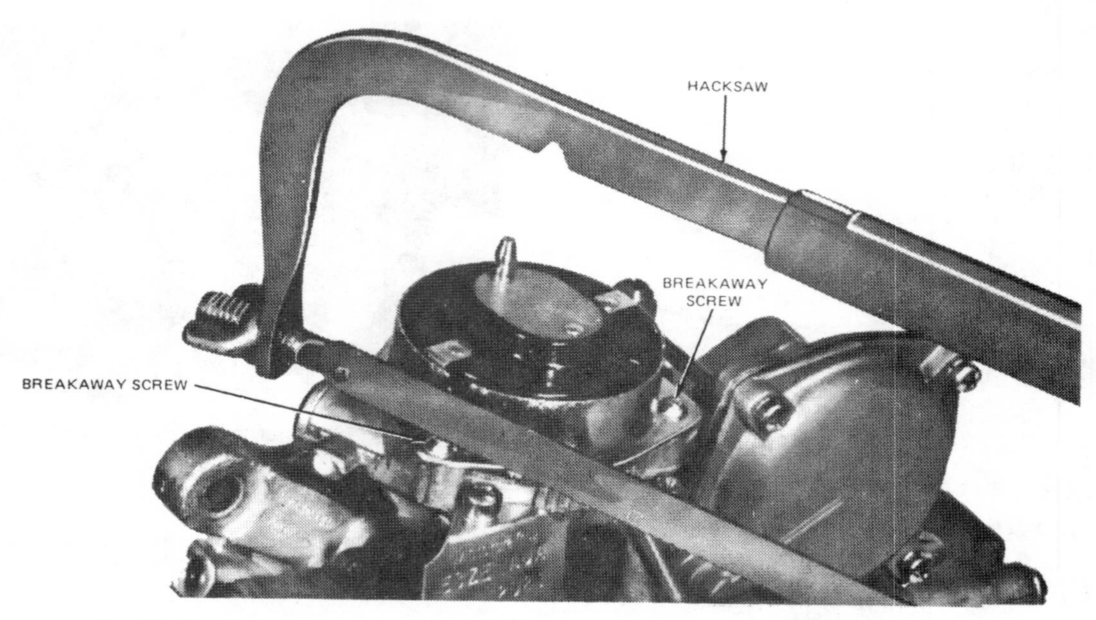

Fig. 13.48 Use a hacksaw to remove the breakaway screws on the choke housing (Sec 5)

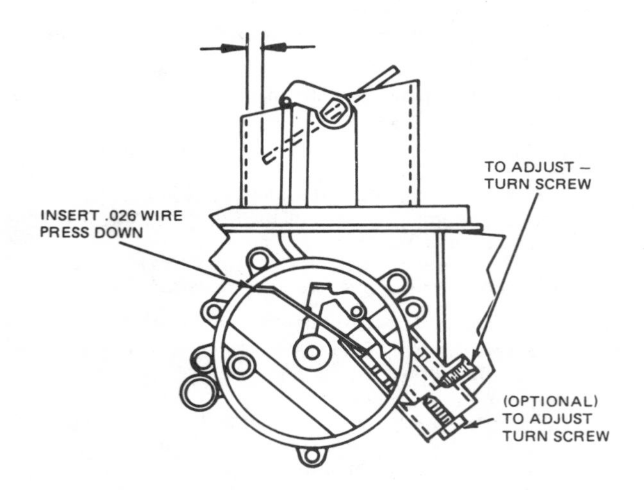

Fig. 13.49 Use a small piece of wire to adjust the choke pull down (Sec 5)

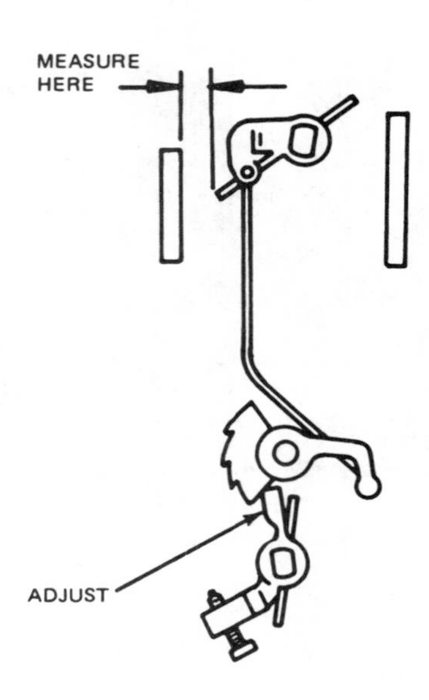

Fig. 13.50 Measure the gap between the choke plate and the air horn as illustrated (Sec 5)

Choke pulldown adjustment

164 Remove choke thermostat housing, gasket and retainer. Refer to steps 156 through 163 for instructions on removal of choke cap retainer.

165 Insert a piece of wire into the choke piston bore to move the piston down against the stop screw. Maintain light closing pressure on the choke plate and measure the gap between the lower edge of the choke plate and the air horn wall. It should be .195 to .215 in.

166 To adjust, remove the putty covering the adjustment screw and turn the screw clockwise to decrease or counterclockwise to increase the gap setting. Take care to close the choke plate during screw adjustment. Screw may be turned into side of piston, resulting in damage to piston. (Some models may have an adjusting screw in the bottom of the piston housing).

167 Reinstall the choke thermostatic housing, gasket and retainer.

De-choke adjustment

168 Hold the throttle in the wide open position.

169 Apply light closing pressure on the choke plate and measure the gap between the lower edge of the choke plate and the air horn wall. It should be 0.30 in.

170 To adjust, bend the pawl on the fast idle lever.

Carburetor (4180C-4V) – disassembly

Note: *The carburetor disassembled view is shown in Fig.13.51.*

171 To facilitate working on the carburetor and to prevent damage to the throttle plates, install bolts about 2-1/4-in long of the correct diameter through the carburetor retaining bolt holes with a nut above and below the flange (or install carburetor legs).

172 Use a separate container for the component parts of the various assemblies to facilitate cleaning, inspection and assembly.

Primary fuel bowl and metering block

173 Remove the fuel bowl and gasket and the metering block and gasket.

174 Remove the pump transfer tube from the metering block.

175 Remove the fuel line tube.

176 Remove the main jets.

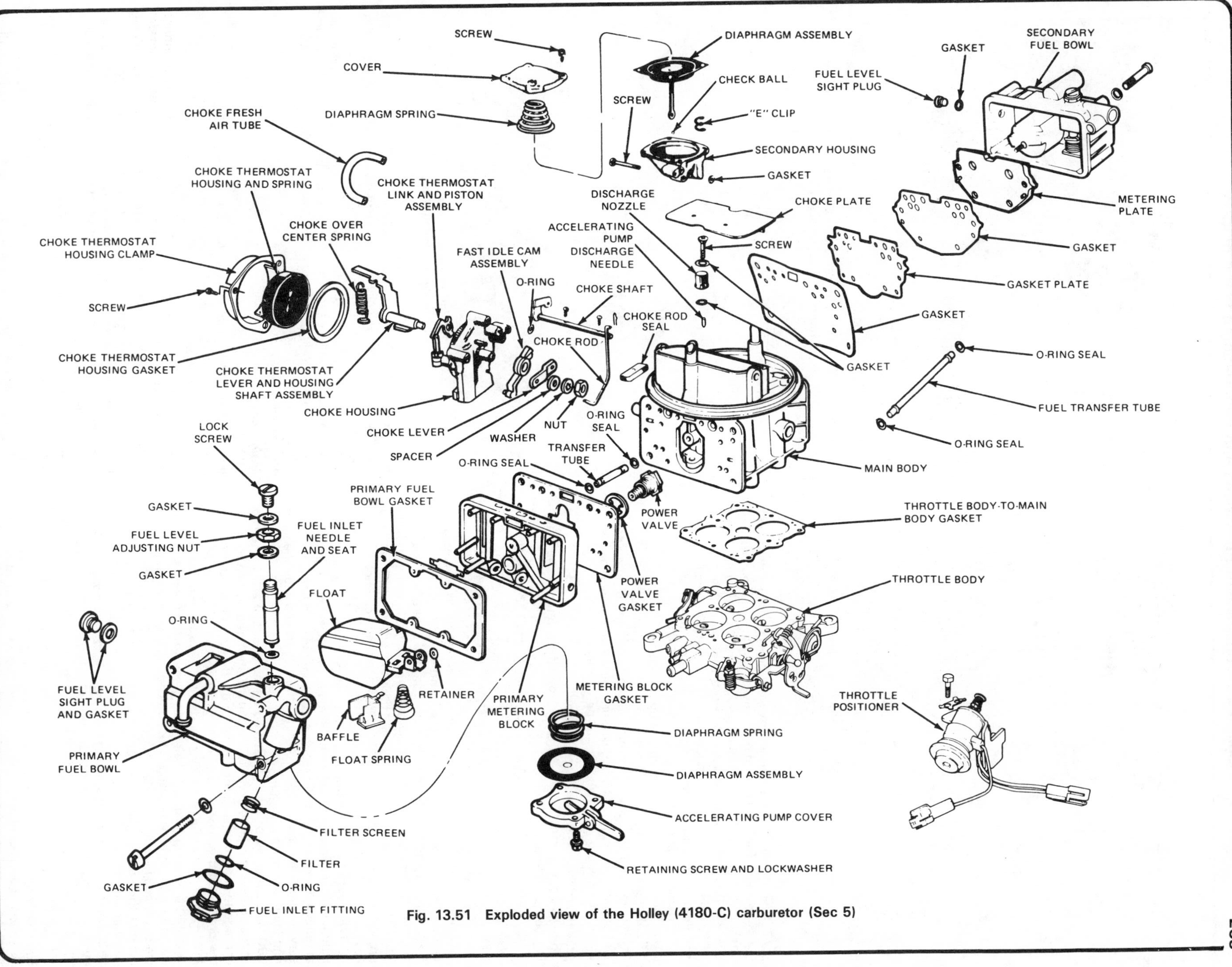

Fig. 13.51 Exploded view of the Holley (4180-C) carburetor (Sec 5)

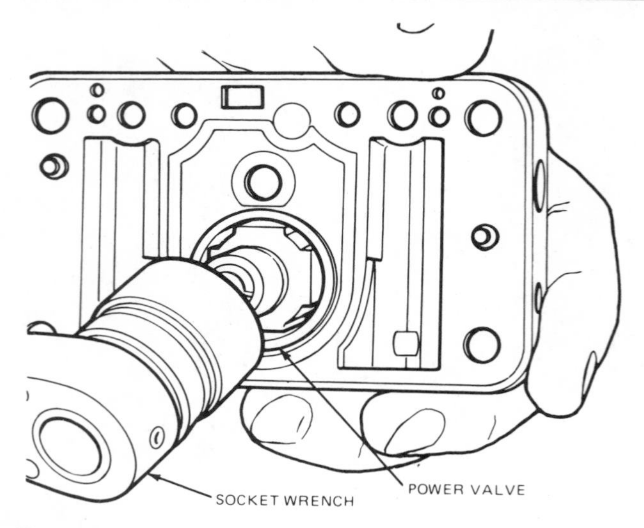

Fig. 13.52 Use a socket to remove the power valve (Sec 5)

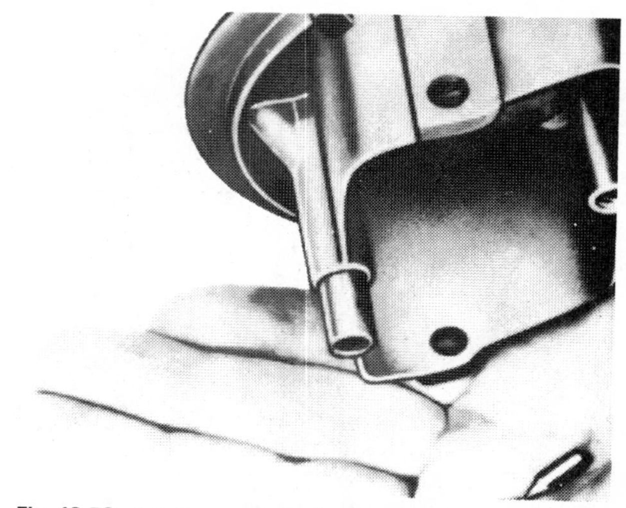

Fig. 13.53 Let the pump discharge needle fall into your hand during removal (Sec 5)

177 Using a socket wrench, remove the power valve and gasket.
178 Remove the fuel level adjustment lock screw and gasket. Turn the adjusting nut counterclockwise and remove the adjusting nut and gasket. Remove the fuel inlet needle and seat assembly.
179 Using needle-nose pliers, remove the float shaft retainer clip. Slide the float off the shaft. Remove the spring from the float.
180 Remove the baffle plate from the fuel bowl.
181 Remove the fuel level sight plug and gasket.
182 Remove the fuel inlet fitting, gaskets and filter.
183 Invert the fuel bowl and remove the accelerating pump cover, diaphragm and spring. The accelerating pump inlet check ball is not serviced separately and should not be removed.

Secondary fuel bowl and metering body

184 Remove the fuel bowl. Using a screwdriver, remove the metering body, plate and gaskets.
185 Disassemble the fuel bowl by following Steps 173 through 181.

Main body

186 Remove the air cleaner anchor stud and remove the secondary diaphragm link E-clip.
187 Invert the carburetor and remove the throttle body retaining screws and lockwashers. Lift off the throttle body.
188 Remove the choke rod cotter pin from the choke housing shaft and lever assembly. Remove the thermostatic spring housing and gasket. Refer to choke thermostatic spring housing removal and installation procedure (Steps 156 through 163). Remove the choke housing and gaskets from the main body.
189 Remove the choke housing shaft nut, star washer and spacer. Remove the shaft and fast idle cam. Remove the choke piston and lever assembly. Remove the choke rod and seal from the main body. If necessary, remove the choke plate from the choke shaft and slide the shaft and lever out of the air horn.
190 The retaining screws are staked to the choke shaft. If the tips of the screws are flared excessively, file off the flared portion to avoid damage to the threads in the choke shaft. Be careful not to damage the choke shaft or venturi while filing the screws.
191 Remove the three screws and then remove the secondary diaphragm housing from the main body. Remove the O-ring from the secondary diaphragm housing. The housing must be removed before the cover can be removed. Remove the diaphragm housing cover, then remove the spring, diaphragm and the vacuum check ball from the housing.
192 Remove the staked accelerator pump discharge nozzle screw, then lift the pump discharge nozzle and gaskets out of the main body. Invert the main body and let the accelerating pump discharge needle fall into your hand.

Throttle body

193 Do not disassemble the throttle body. Parts are matched to meet emission control standards and must be serviced as an assembly.

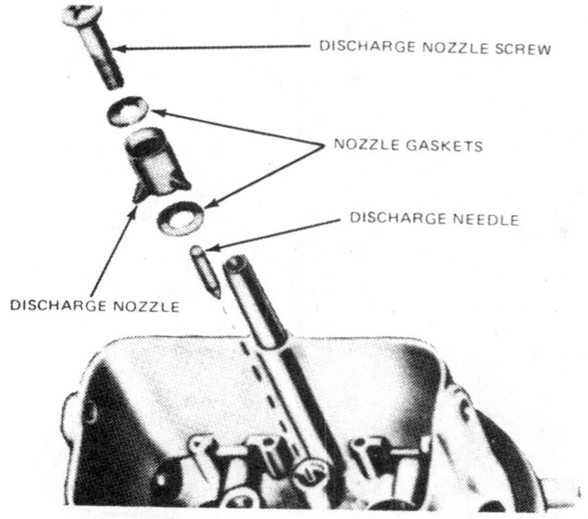

Fig. 13.54 Exploded view of the accelerator pump discharge assembly (Sec 5)

Carburetor (4180C-4V) – reassembly

194 Reassembly is basically the reverse of dissassembly with attention paid to the following:
195 Make sure all holes in the new gaskets have been properly punched and that no foreign material has adhered to the gaskets. Make sure the accelerating pump and secondary operating diaphragms are not cut or torn.
196 Clean all gasket mating surfaces.

Main Body

197 After dropping the accelerator pump discharge needle into its well (Fig. 13.54), lightly seat the needle with a brass drift and hammer. **Note:** *Pump discharge gaskets, nozzle and screw must be installed before any other parts are installed to the main body.*
198 Using a flat punch, stake the nozzle screw in position. **Caution:** *Do not use excessive force when staking nozzle screws. Make certain that any chips broken from the nozzle screw during staking are cleaned from carburetor throttle openings before continuing assembly.*
199 The secondary diaphragm housing must be installed before the choke housing. The diaphragm housing must be removed from the main body to install the cover.
200 Be sure the projection on the choke rod is placed under the fast idle cam so that the cam will be lifted when the choke plate is closed.

Primary fuel bowl and metering block

201 When placing the accelerating pump diaphragm spring and diaphragm in the accelerating pump chamber, the diaphragm must be posi-

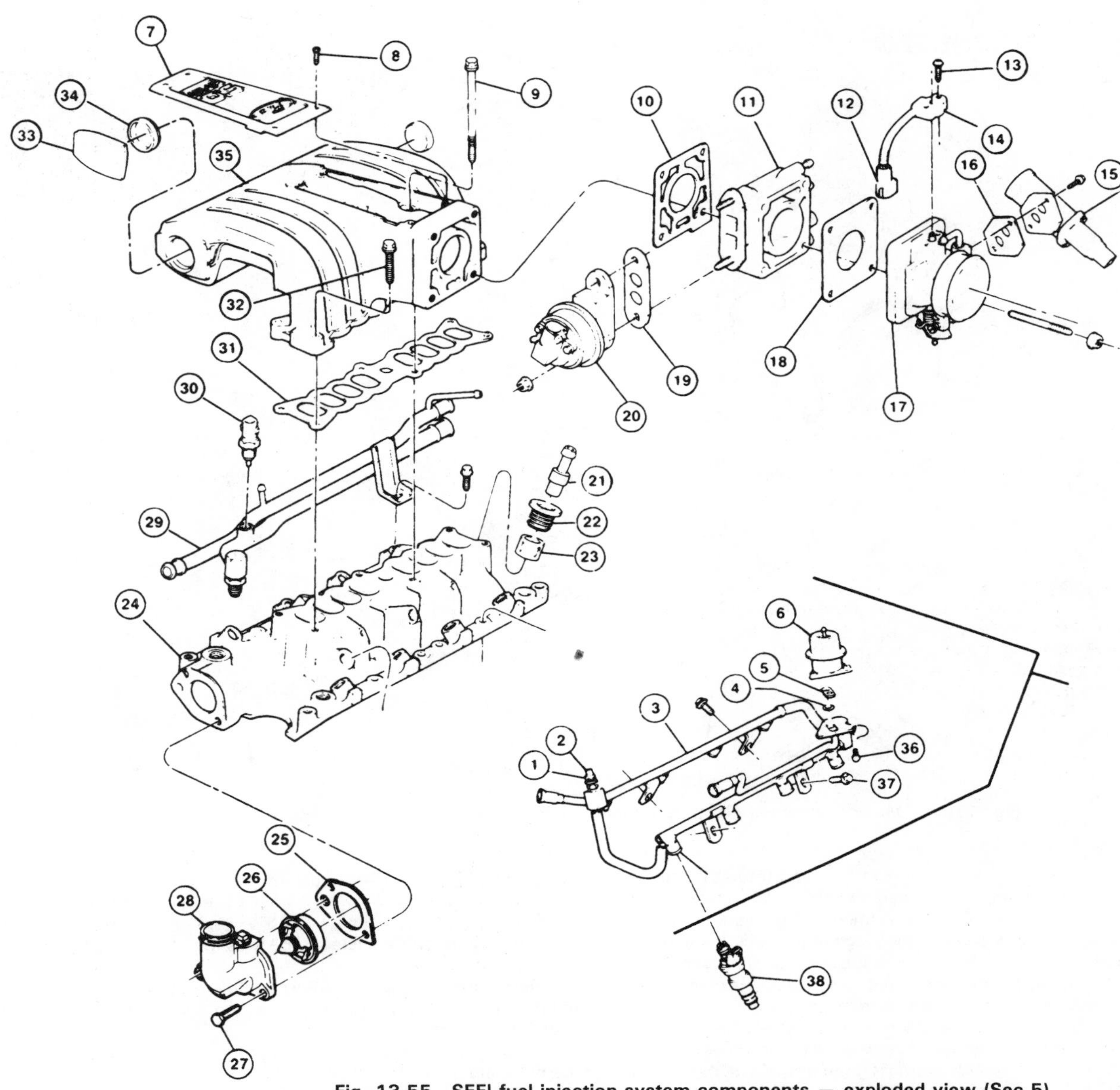

Fig. 13.55 SEFI fuel injection system components — exploded view (Sec 5)

1 Schrader valve
2 Schrader valve cap
3 Fuel rail assembly
4 O-ring seal
5 Gasket
6 Fuel pressure regulator
7 Upper manifold cover
8 Screw
9 Bolt
10 Gasket
11 EGR spacer
12 TP sensor connector
13 Screw
14 Throttle position sensor
15 Throttle air bypass valve
16 Gasket
17 Throttle body assembly
18 Gasket
19 Gasket
20 EGR valve assembly
21 PCV valve assembly
22 PCV grommet
23 Crankcase vent element
24 Lower intake manifold
25 Thermostat housing gasket
26 Thermostat
27 Bolt
28 Engine coolant outlet connector assembly
29 Heater water supply and return tube
30 EEC coolant temperature sensor
31 Gasket
32 Bolt
33 Decorative end cover
34 Plug cap
35 Upper intake manifold
36 Allen-head screw
37 Bolt
38 Fuel injector

tioned so that the large end of the rivet will be against the operating lever. Make sure the diaphragm is centered, then tighten the cover screws to 10-14 in-lb.
202 After installing the float spring on the float and sliding the float onto the shaft, be sure the float spring is between the ridges of the boss on the floor of the fuel bowl.
203 Use petroleum jelly on a new O-ring seal before sliding it on the fuel inlet needle and seat assembly.
204 As a preliminary float adjustment on both floats, refer to the float adjustment — dry procedure (Steps 137 and 138).
205 After applying petroleum jelly to the fuel line tube O-ring seal, position it into the secondary fuel bowl recess. Position the fuel bowl on the main body, guiding the fuel line tube with O-ring into the recess in the primary fuel bowl. Install the retaining screws with a new compression gasket. **Note:** *Inspect O-rings to ensure they are not pinched.*
206 Refer to Adjustments and perform the accelerating pump lever, accelerating pump stroke and automatic choke adjustments.

Sequential Electronic Fuel Injection (SEFI)

General Information

The Sequential Electronic Fuel Injection System (SEFI) is a multi-point injection system which, unlike the Central Fuel Injection system,

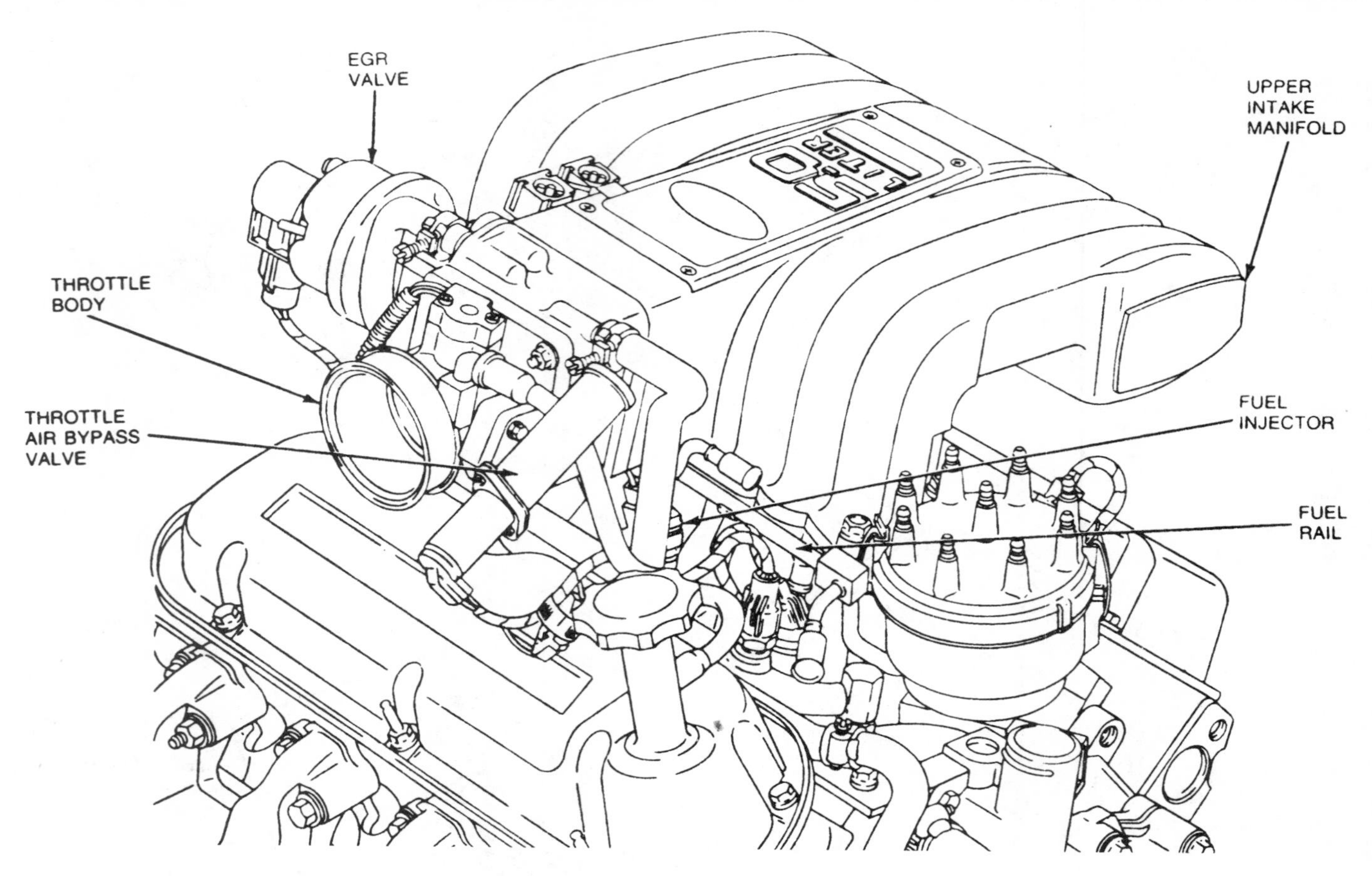

Fig. 13.56 Major Sequential Electronic Fuel Injection (SEFI) system components (Sec 5)

delivers fuel directly to each intake port rather than through a single intake manifold. The system is controlled by Ford's EEC-IV electronic engine control computer. The EEC-IV accepts data from various engine sensors and compensates for altitude, load, age of the vehicle and other factors necessary to maintain a prescribed fuel/air ratio throughout the entire engine operational range. A constant fuel pressure is maintained by a pressure regulator positioned downstream from the fuel injectors. Excess fuel not required by the engine is returned to the fuel tank via the regulator. **Warning:** *The fuel pressure must be relieved before any SEFI lines or components are removed! Refer to Step 32 above. If the Ford special tool isn't available, locate the inertia switch mounted near the left-hand tail light in the luggage compartment. Detach the switch, with the wires still in place, and hit the luggage compartment floor with it. This should open the switch. Start the engine and let it run until it dies, which means the fuel system pressure has been relieved. When you're done working on the fuel system, push the reset button on the inertia switch, reinstall it and start the engine. Check carefully for fuel leaks.*

SEFI fuel charging assembly — removal and installation

207 Disconnect the battery ground cable and secure it out of the way.
208 Remove the fuel cap from the fuel tank.
209 Release the pressure from the fuel system as described later in this Section. The pressure relief (Schrader) valve is located on the fuel rail assembly.
210 Unplug the electrical connectors at the air bypass valve, the throttle position sensor and the EGR position sensor.
211 Disconnect the throttle linkage at the throttle ball and the transmission linkage from the throttle body.
212 Remove the two bolts securing the bracket to the intake manifold and position the bracket with the cables out of the way.
213 Disconnect the upper intake manifold vacuum fitting connections by disconnecting all vacuum lines from the vacuum tree, the EGR valve and the single line to the fuel pressure regulator. Mark all lines and fittings with tape to ensure correct reinstallation.
214 Disconnect the PCV hose from the fitting on the rear of the upper manifold.
215 Remove the two canister purge lines from the fittings on the throttle body.
216 Remove the six upper intake manifold retaining bolts and detach the upper intake manifold and throttle body as an assembly from the lower intake manifold.
217 Clean and inspect the mounting faces of the lower and upper intake manifolds.
218 Position a new gasket on the lower intake manifold and attach the upper intake manifold and throttle body assembly to the lower manifold. Alignment studs may be helpful in holding the gasket in place.
219 Install the six upper manifold retaining bolts and tighten them to the specified torque.
220 Attach the canister purge lines to the fittings on the throttle body.
221 Connect the PCV hose to the rear of the upper manifold and connect the other vacuum lines to the vacuum tree, the EGR valve and to the fuel pressure regulator.
222 Attach the throttle linkage bracket with the cables to the upper intake manifold. Install the two bolts and tighten them securely.
223 Connect the throttle cable and AOD transmission cable to the throttle body.
224 Reconnect the electrical leads to the TP sensor, EGR position sensor and bypass valve. **Note:** *If the lower intake manifold was removed, refill the cooling system as outlined in Chapter 2.*

Throttle body — removal and installation

225 Disconnect the throttle position sensor and throttle air bypass valve connectors.
226 Remove the PCV vent closure hose at the throttle body
227 Remove the four throttle body mounting nuts.
228 Carefully separate the throttle body from the EGR spacer and intake manifold.
229 Clean the gasket mating surfaces, being careful not to damage

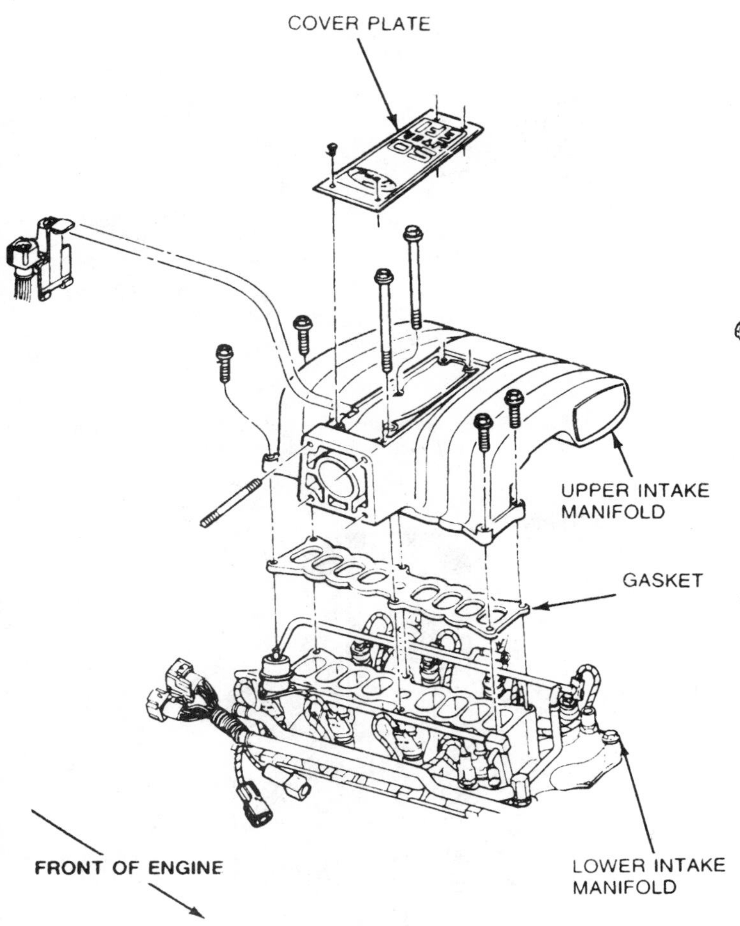

Fig. 13.57 SEFI fuel charging assembly — exploded view (Sec 5)

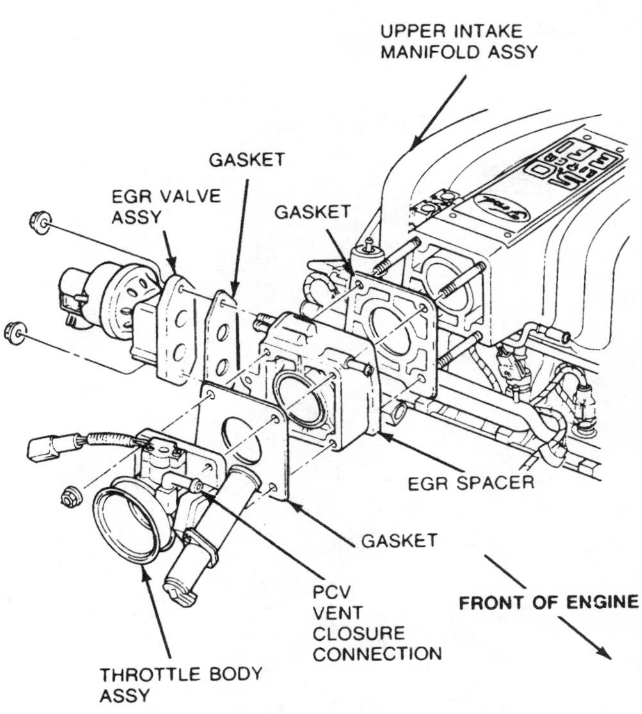

Fig. 13.58 Air intake throttle body assembly and related components — exploded view (Sec 5)

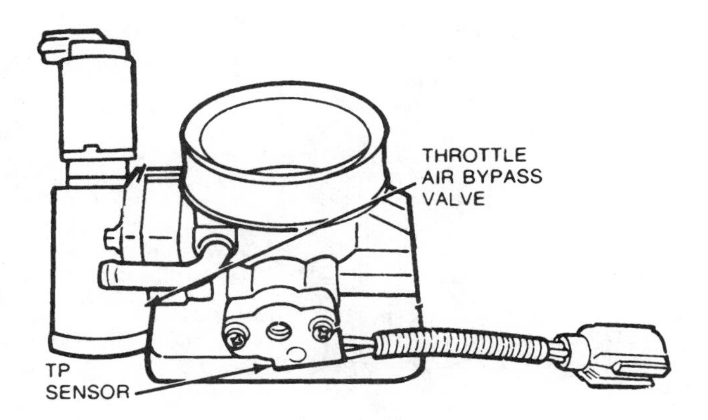

Fig. 13.59 Throttle Position (TP) sensor location (Sec 5)

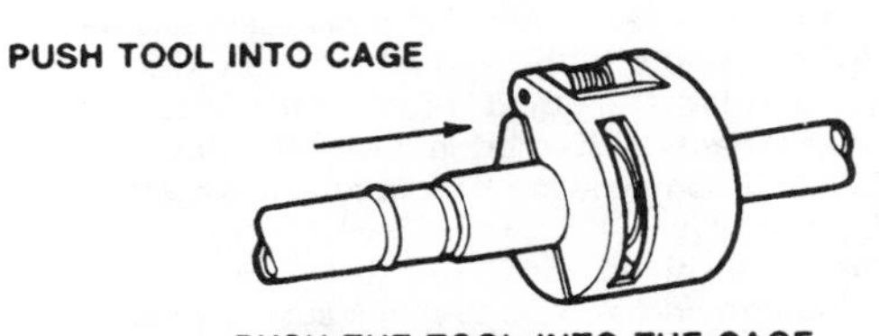

Fig. 13.60 Disconnecting the crossover fuel hose from the fuel rail assembly using the Ford special tool (Sec 5)

them or to allow material to fall into the manifold.

230 To install the throttle body, place a new gasket on the four studs of the EGR spacer and tighten the mounting nuts to the specified torque.

Throttle position (TP) sensor — removal and installation

231 Disconnect the throttle position sensor from the wiring harness.

232 Scribe a reference mark across one edge of the sensor and throttle body to ensure correct alignment during installation.

233 Remove the two TP sensor retaining screws and detach the sensor.

234 Installation is the reverse of removal. Tighten the retaining screws securely.

Air bypass valve assembly — removal and installation

235 Disconnect the air bypass valve connector from the wiring harness.

236 Remove the two air bypass valve retaining bolts and detach the valve.

237 Clean the gasket mating surface, being careful not to damage the surface or drop material into the throttle body.

238 Installation is the reverse of removal. Tighten the retaining bolts securely.

Fuel rail assembly — removal and installation

239 Remove the Fuel charging assembly as outlined earlier in this Section.

240 Remove the upper manifold as well.

241 Using the special Ford tool (no. T81P-19623-G), disconnect the crossover fuel hose from the fuel rail assembly.

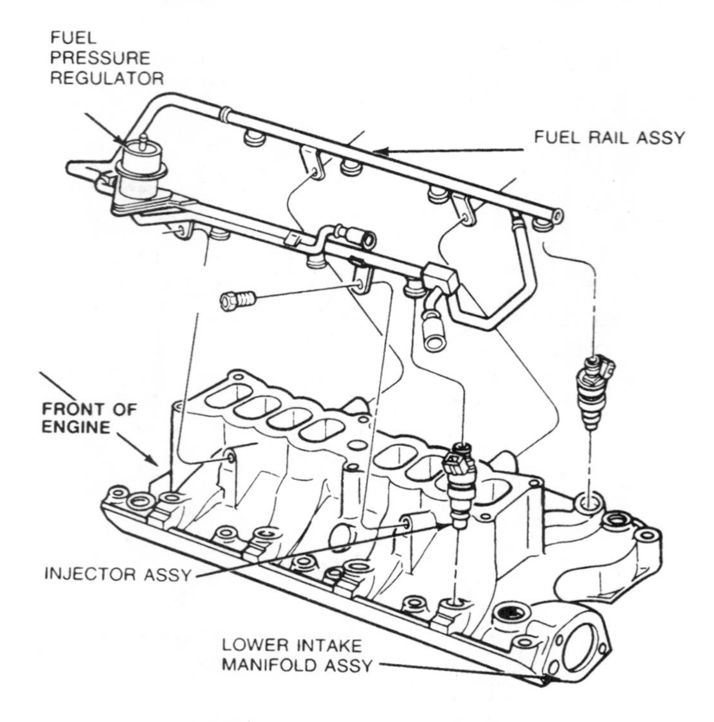

Fig. 13.61 SEFI fuel rail assembly and injectors — exploded view (Sec 5)

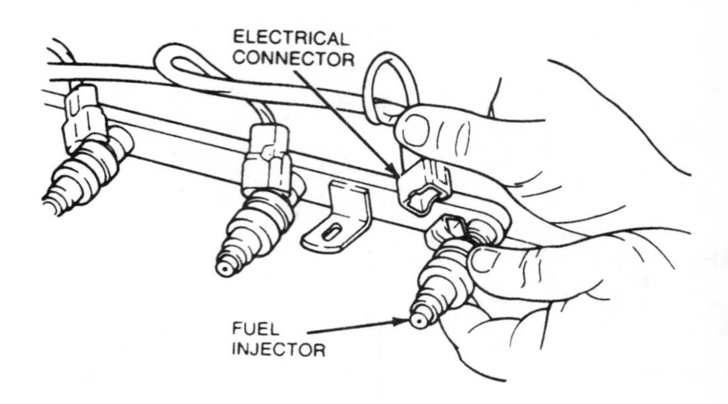

Fig. 13.62 Removing the SEFI fuel injector from the electrical harness (Sec 5)

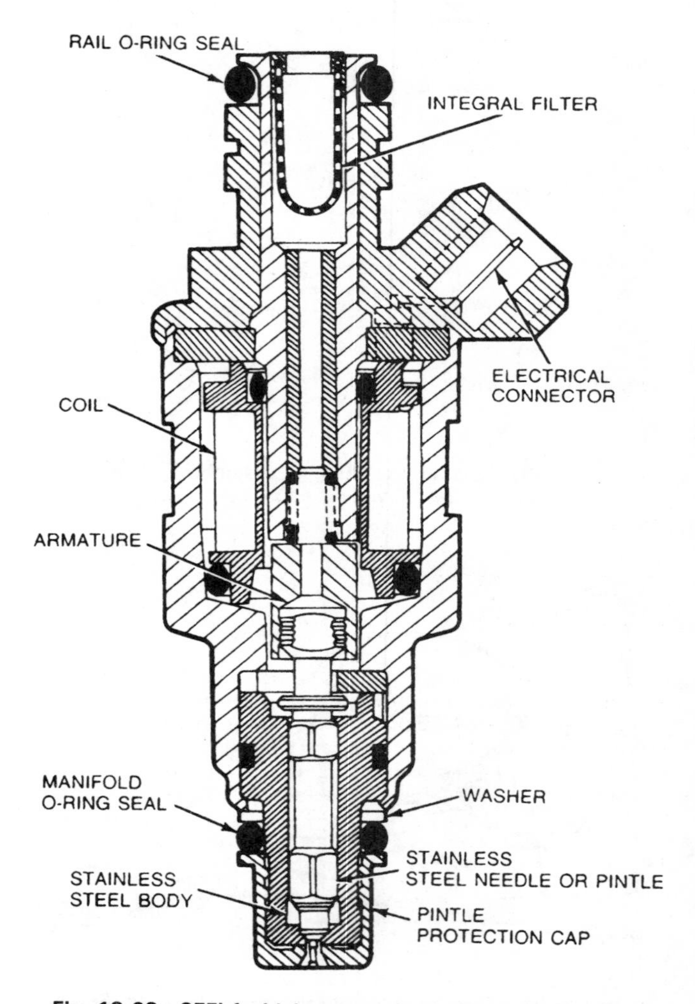

Fig. 13.63 SEFI fuel injector — check the rubber O-rings carefully for wear and deterioration and replace them with new ones if necessary (Sec 5)

242 Remove the four fuel rail assembly retaining bolts.
243 Carefully disengage the fuel rail from the fuel injectors and remove the fuel rail. It may be easier to remove the injectors with the fuel rail as an assembly. In this case, use a rocking, side-to-side motion while lifting up to remove the injectors from the fuel rail.
244 To install the fuel rail assembly, first make sure the injector caps are clean and free of contamination. Place the rail assembly over the injectors and seat the injectors in the fuel rail. Be sure the injectors are completely seated. Another method is to seat the injectors in the fuel rail before seating the entire assembly in the lower intake manifold.
245 Secure the fuel rail assembly with the four retaining bolts. Tighten them to the specified torque.
246 Reconnect the fuel inlet and outlet lines to the fuel rail assembly and use a push-pull action on the lines to make sure they are locked to the fuel rail connectors.

Fuel pressure regulator — removal and installation

247 Remove the fuel charging assembly as outlined earlier in this Section.
248 Remove the vacuum line at the pressure regulator.
249 Remove the three Allen-head screws from the regulator housing.
250 Detach the pressure regulator assembly, gasket and O-ring. Discard the gasket and inspect the O-ring for signs of cracks and deterioration.
251 To install the fuel pressure regulator, lubricate the O-ring with engine oil. DO NOT use silicone grease or silicone spray. Ensure that the gasket surfaces of the regulator and fuel rail assembly are clean.
252 Install the O-ring and a new gasket on the regulator.
253 Install the fuel pressure regulator on the fuel rail assembly and tighten the three retaining screws to the specified torque.
254 Install the fuel charging assembly as outlined earlier in this Section.

Fuel injectors — removal and installation

255 Remove the fuel charging assembly as outlined earlier in this Section.
256 Remove the upper intake manifold.
257 Remove the fuel supply manifold.
258 Carefully detach the electrical harness connectors from the individual injectors. Grasping the injector body, pull up while gently rocking the injector from side-to-side.
259 Inspect the injector O-rings (two per injector) for signs of deterioration and replace them with new ones if necessary.
260 Inspect the injector ''plastic hat'' covering the injector pintle and the washer for signs of deterioriation. If the ''hat'' is missing, look for it in the intake manifold.
261 To install the injectors, lubricate new O-rings with engine oil and install two on each injector. DO NOT use silicone grease or spray.

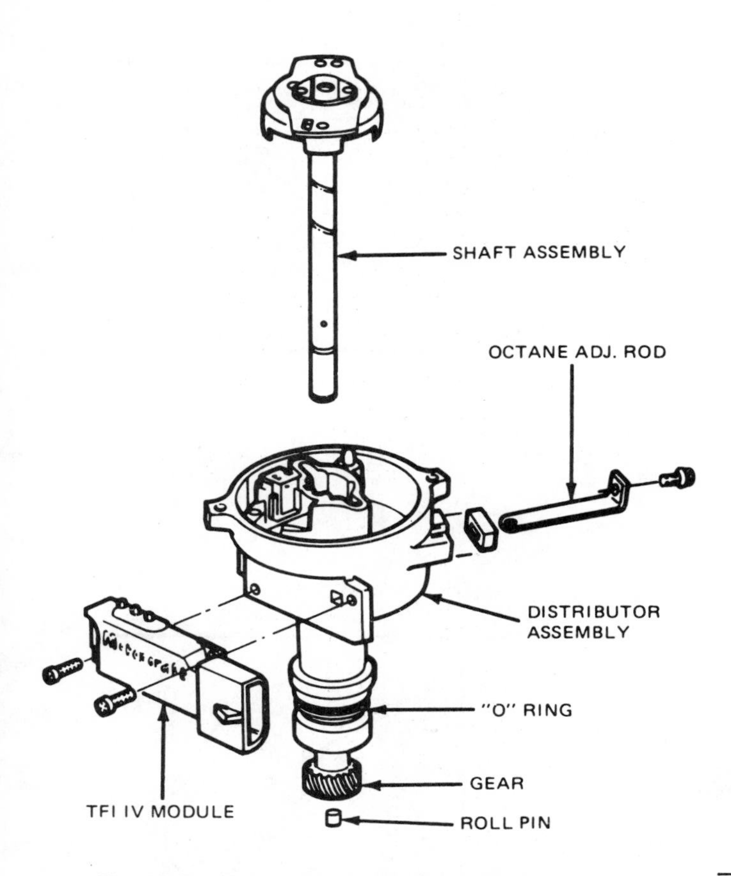

Fig. 13.64 Exploded view of the TFI distributor (Sec 6)

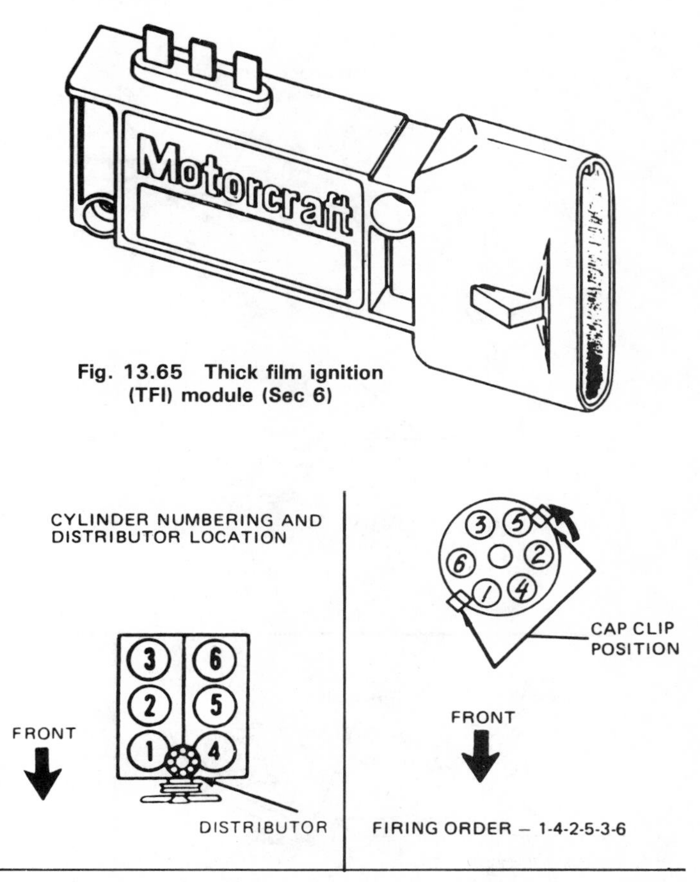

Fig. 13.65 Thick film ignition (TFI) module (Sec 6)

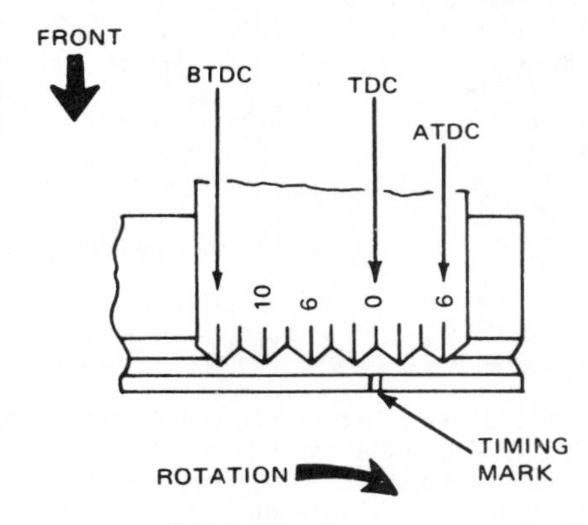

Fig. 13.66 Ignition timing marks, firing order and distributor location (Sec 6)

262 Use a light pushing-twisting motion to install the injectors and install the fuel rail assembly as outlined earlier in this Section.
263 Reattach the electrical harness connectors to the injectors.
264 Install the upper intake manifold and fuel charging assembly.

6 Ignition system

General information

1 With the use of fuel injection and stricter emission standards very accurate ignition timing is necessary. On vehicles with fuel injection a Thick Film Integrated Ignition System is used as part of the EEC-IV (Electronic Engine Control — system IV).

2 The ignition system uses a universal distributor which has no centrifugal or vacuum advance. The distributor has a die-cast base which incorporates an integrally mounted TFI-IV ignition module, a 'Hall-Effect' vane switch stator assembly and a rod for octane adjustment. No distributor calibration is required and initial timing is not a normal adjustment.

3 The TFI-IV module features a 'push start' mode. This allows 'push starting' of the vehicle should it be necessary (manual transmission only).

4 Due to the complexity of the EEC-IV system, accurate diagnosis requires specialized test equipment and should be left to a professional. Procedures for setting initial timing and TFI-IV module replacement are included in this section.

TFI-IV ignition module — removal and installation

5 Remove the distributor (refer to Chapter 5, section 7).

6 With the distributor on a work bench, remove the two TFI attaching screws.

7 Using a back and forth rocking motion carefully disengage the module terminals from the connector in the base of the distributor.

8 With the terminals completly disengaged, slide the module down, pulling gently away from the distributor. **Caution:** *Do not attempt to remove the module from the distributor until the connector pins are fully disengaged to avoid breaking the pins at the distributor/module connector.*

9 Installation is the reverse of removal.

10 Before installing the TFI module coat the metal base with silicone compound approximately 1/32-inch thick. Use a silicone dielectric compound or an equivalent grease.

Engine initial timing — setting

1981 and 1982 models, except 5.0L engines with MCU ignition
1983 models, except 5.0L engines with MCU ignition
1984 models, 5.0L high output engines only

11 Place the transmission in Park or Neutral, A/C in the Off position.

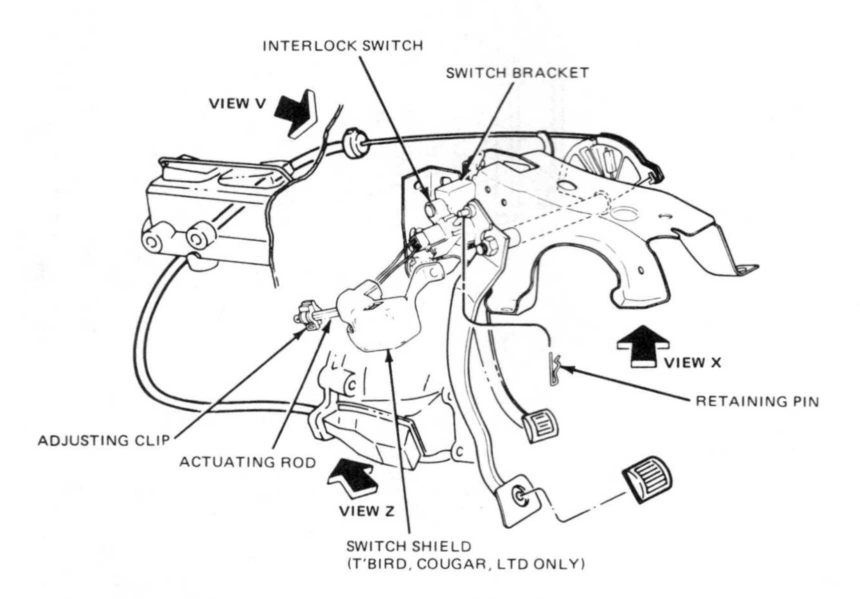

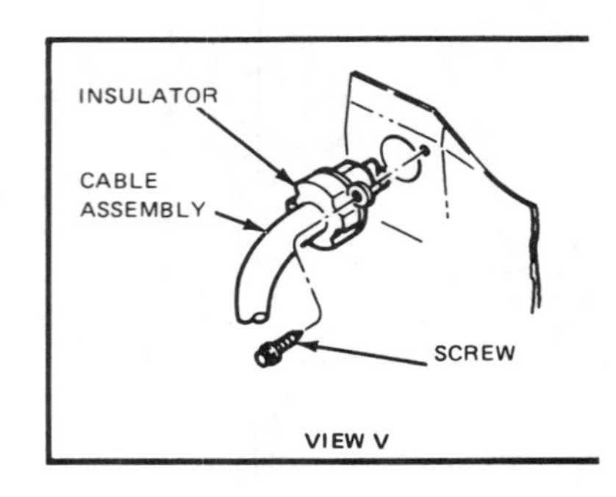

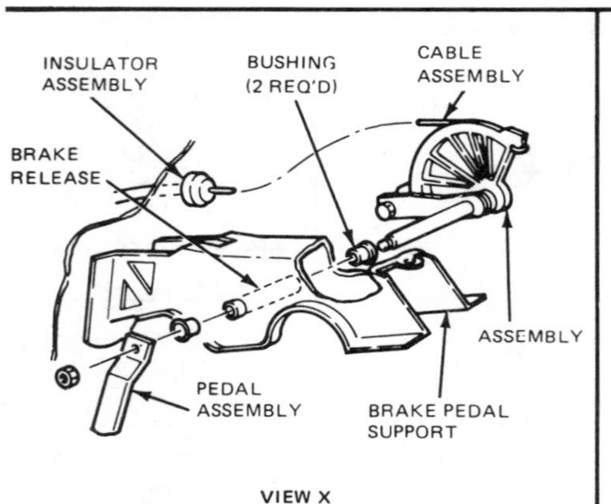

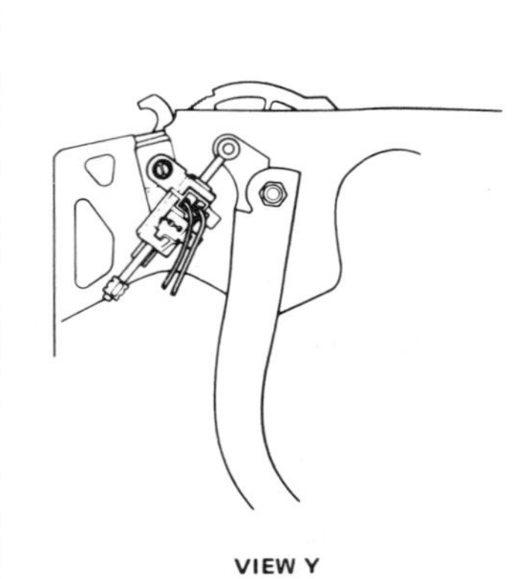

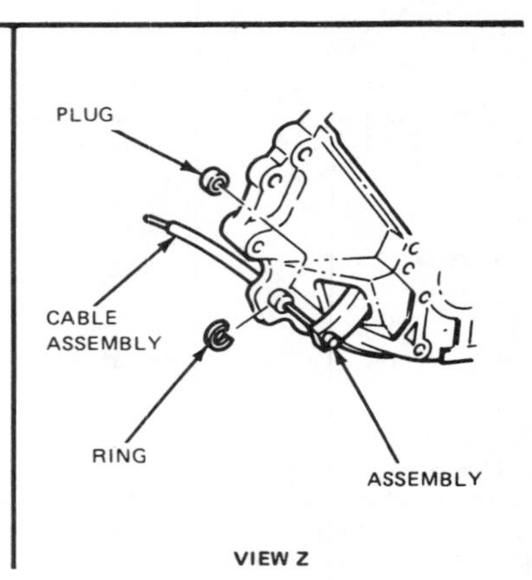

Fig. 13.67 Typical self adjusting clutch mechanism (Sec 7)

12 Remove and plug the vacuum hoses at the distributor vacuum advance canister.
13 Connect an inductive timing light and a hand held tachometer according to the manufacturer's instructions.
14 If the vehicle is equipped with a barometric pressure sensor, disconnect it from the ignition module and place a jumper between the pins on the ignition module connector (yellow and black wires).
15 Start the engine and let it reach operating temperature.
16 With the engine at timing RPM, check and adjust the ignition timing to specification (refer to the emissions decal).
17 Unplug and reconnect the vacuum hoses.
18 Remove the jumper wire from the ignition module and reinstall the connections.

1981 through 1983 5.0L engine with MCU ignition
19 Place the transmission in Park or Neutral, A/C in the Off position.
20 Remove and plug the vacuum hoses at the distributor vacuum advance canister.
21 Connect an inductive timing light and a hand-held tachometer according to the manufacturer's instructions.
22 If the vehicle is equipped for high altitude operation, disconnect the wire from the MCU electrical harness to ignition module and place a jumper wire across the pins at the ignition module.
23 Start the engine and let it reach operating temperature.
24 With the engine at timing RPM, check and adjust the ignition timing to specification (refer to the emissions decal).
25 Unplug and reconnect the vacuum hoses.
26 Remove the jumper wire from the ignition module and reinstall the connections.

3.8L engine and 5.0L engine with central fuel injection
27 Place the transmission in Park or Neutral, A/C in the Off position.
28 Connect an inductive timing light and a hand- held tachometer according to the manufacturer's instructions.
29 Disconnect the single white* wire connector near the distributor.
30 Start the engine and let it reach operating temperature.
31 With the engine at timing RPM, check and adjust the ignition timing to specification (refer to the emissions decal).
32 Reconnect the single white* wire connector.
* *Black connector on some models.*

7 Clutch

General information

1 There are no changes in the clutch on late model vehicles, but an automatic adjusting clutch cable has been added. This system automatically adjusts the clutch release bearing lever to compensate for movement of the release lever as the clutch disc wears.
2 On 1984 models a new safety device has been added called a starter/clutch interlock switch. It is connected to the top of the clutch pedal, designed to prevent the engine from starting unless the clutch is depressed to the floor.

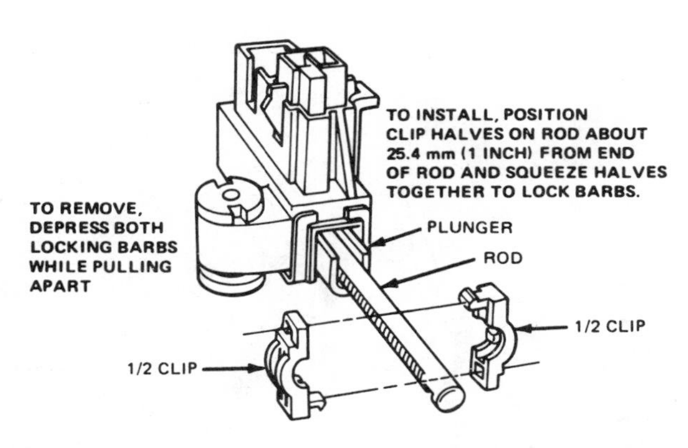

Fig. 13.68 Starter/clutch interlock switch (1984 models) (Sec 7)

Starter/clutch interlock switch

Testing

3 Disconnect the wiring connector by reaching around the A/C duct and flexing the retaining tab on the connector.

4 Using a test light or continuity tester, check that the switch is open (no continuity) with the clutch pedal up. The switch should have continuity with the clutch pedal approximatly 1.0-in from the floor.

5 If the switch does not operate as outlined in Step 4, check to see if the self-adjusting clip is out of position on the rod. It should be near the end.

6 If the self-adjusting clip is out of position, remove and reposition it about 1.0-in from the end of the rod.

7 Reset the switch by pressing the pedal to the floor.

8 Repeat Step 4. If the switch is damaged replace it.

Replacement

9 Disconnect the wiring connector.

10 Remove the retaining pin from the clutch pedal.

11 Remove the switch bracket retaining screws.

12 Lift the switch and the bracket assembly upward to disengage its tab from the pedal support.

13 Move the switch assembly outward to disengage the actuating rod eyelet from the clutch pedal pin.

14 Remove the entire switch assembly from the vehicle.

15 Installation is the reverse of removal. **Note:** *Always install the switch with the self-adjusting clip about 1.0-in from the end of the rod. The clutch pedal must be fully up or the switch could be maladjusted.*

Clutch pedal — removal and installation

16 Remove the starter/clutch interlock switch (refer to Steps 9 through 15).

17 Remove the clutch pedal attaching nut.

18 Pull the clutch pedal off the clutch pedal shaft.

19 Align the square hole of the clutch pedal with the clutch pedal shaft and install the clutch pedal.

20 Tighten the attaching nut to 40 ft-lb.

21 Reinstall the starter/clutch interlock switch.

Clutch cable — removal and installation

22 Lift the clutch pedal to its upwardmost position to disengage the pawl and quadrant. Push the quadrant forward and unhook the cable from the quadrant. Allow the quadrant to slowly swing rearward.

23 Open the hood and remove the retaining screw that holds the cable to the dash panel.

24 Raise the vehicle and support it on jackstands.

25 Remove the dust cover from the bellhousing.

26 Remove the clip retainer holding the cable to the bellhousing.

27 Slide the ball on the end of the cable through the hole in the clutch release lever and remove the cable.

28 Installation is the reverse of removal with the following notes:

a) To install the cable into the adjusting assembly, lift the clutch pedal to disengage the pawl and quadrant. Then, pushing the quadrant forward, hook the cable over the rear of the quadrant.

b) Depress the clutch pedal several times to adjust the cable.

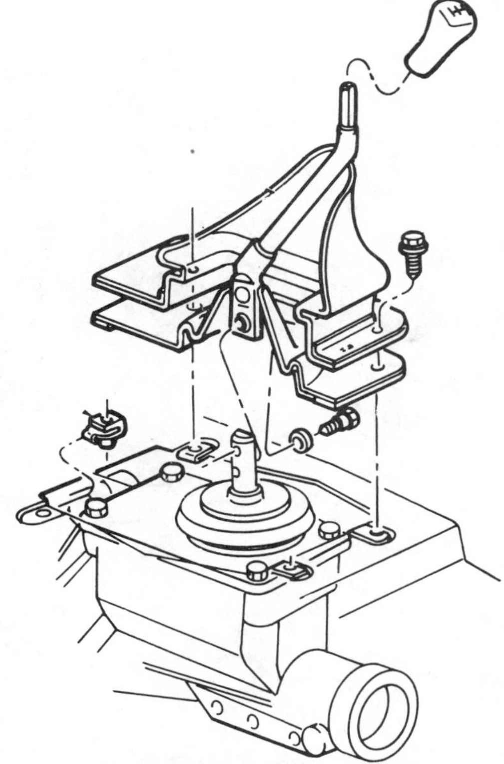

Fig. 13.69 Shifter and boot installaton (Sec 8)

8 Transmission

1 Three transmissions have been added to the list of available transmissions on the late model Mustang/Capri. The first is a 5-speed manual transmission (T5OD). The other two transmissions are automatics. The first is a conventional automatic (C-5) with a lock-up torque converter. The second is an automatic overdrive transmission with a lock-up torque converter (AOD).

2 The T5OD transmission is a 5-speed transmission with 5th speed an overdrive gear. All gears except reverse are synchronized and helical cut for smooth, quiet operation. The case is aluminum and all of the fasteners are meteric.

3 90% of the T5OD transmission can be disassembled with basic hand tools. The removal of the countergear and disassembly of the main shaft will require the use of a press and the necessary holding fixtures. This work can be easily done at your local machine shop.

Transmission — (T5OD)

Removal and installation

4 Disconnect the battery ground lead.

5 Remove the four bolts holding down the shift boot.

6 Remove the two bolts securing the shift lever to the transmission and remove the shift lever.

7 Raise the vehicle high enough to allow sufficient clearance for the removal of the transmission and support it on jackstands.

8 To avoid spilling the transmission fluid it can be drained at this point, but is not necessary for the removal procedure.

9 Mark the driveshaft so it can be reinstalled in the same position. Disconnect the driveshaft from the rear U-joint flange and remove it from the vehicle.

10 Remove the four bolts to the catalytic converter and remove the converter.

11 Remove the two bolts attaching the transmission to the rear crossmember.

12 Support the transmission and engine with a suitable jack.

13 Disconnect the wires from the back-up light switch.

14 Remove the speedometer retainer bolt and remove the speedometer drive gear from the transmission.

15 Remove the two bolts from the rear crossmember, raise the

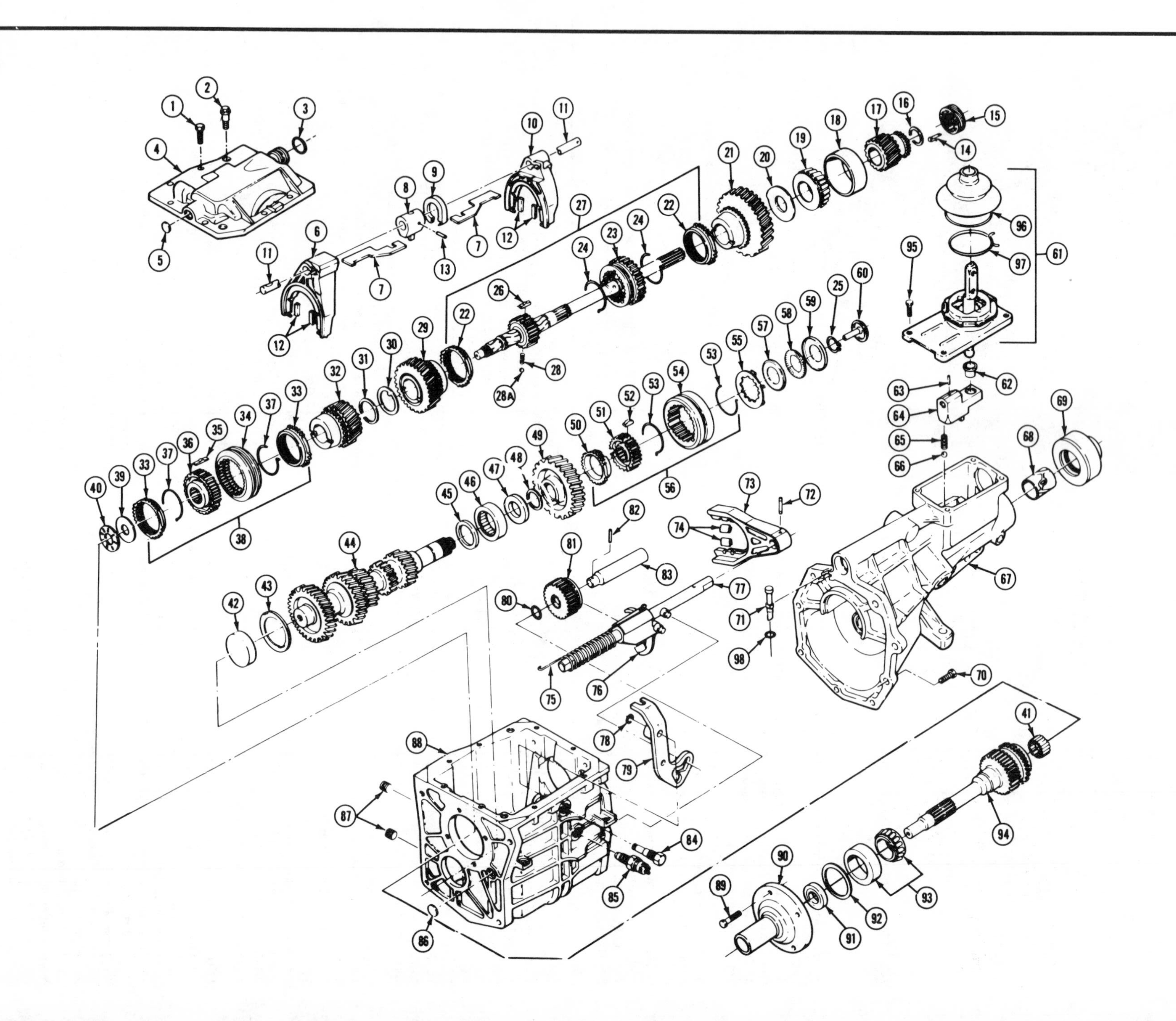
1
2
3
4
5
6
7
8
9
10
11
12
13
14
15
16
17
18
19
20
21
22
23
24
25
26
27
28
28A
29
30
31
32
33
34
35
36
37
38
39
40
41
42
43
44
45
46
47
48
49
50
51
52
53
54
55
56
57
58
59
60
61
62
63
64
65
66
67
68
69
70
71
72
73
74
75
76
77
78
79
80
81
82
83
84
85
86
87
88
89
90
91
92
93
94
95
96
97
98

Fig. 13.70 T50D manual transmission — exploded view (Sec 8)

1 Bolt — cover attaching
2 Bolt — cover attaching dowel
3 Seal — O-Ring (cover to extension housing)
4 Cover — case
5 Plug — 3/4'' diameter expansion
6 Fork — 3rd & 4th gearshift
7 Plate — gearshift selector arm (2 required)
8 Arm assembly -- control selector
9 Plate — gear selector interlock
10 Fork — 1st & 2nd gearshift
11 Shaft — shifter
12 Insert — gearshift fork
13 Pin — control selector arm attaching
14 Clip — speedometer drive gear retaining
15 Gear — speedometer drive
16 Snap ring — 5th gear retaining
17 Gear — 5th speed
18 Cup — output shaft rear bearing
19 Cone and roller assembly — output shaft
20 Washer — 1st gear thrust
21 Gear — 1st speed
22 Ring — synchronizer blocking
23 Sleeve/gear — 1st-2nd
24 Spring — synchronizer retaining
25 Snap ring — 5th speed synchronizer retaining
26 Insert — synchronizer hub
27 Shaft assembly — output
28 Spring — detent
29 Gear — 2nd speed
30 Washer — 2nd gear thrust
31 Snap ring — 2nd gear retaining
32 Gear — 3rd speed
33 Ring — synchronizer blocking
34 Sleeve — 3rd-4th synchronizer
35 Insert — synchronizer hub
36 Hub — 3rd-4th synchronizer
37 Spring — synchronizer retaining (2 required)
38 Synchronizer assembly — 3rd-4th speed
39 Race — input shaft thrust bearing
40 Bearing assembly — input shaft thrust
41 Bearing — input shaft roller (15)
42 Bearing assembly — countershaft front
43 Washer — countershaft gear thrust
44 Gear — countershaft
45 Spacer — countershaft rear bearing (front)
46 Bearing assembly — countershaft rear
47 Spacer — countershaft rear bearing (rear)
48 Snap ring — 5th gear retaining
49 Gear — 5th speed
50 Ring — synchronizer blocking
51 Hub — 5th speed sychronizer
52 Insert — synchronizer hub
53 Spring — synchronizer retaining
54 Sleeve — 5th speed sychronizer
55 Retainer — 5th speed sychronizer insert
56 Sychronizer assembly — 5th speed
57 Race — countershaft thrust bearing (front)
58 Bearing assembly — countershaft thrust (rear)
59 Race — countershaft thrust bearing (rear)
60 Funnel — lubrication
61 Lever assembly — gearshift lower
62 Bushing — gearshift damper
63 Pin — offset lever attaching
64 Lever assembly — gearshift offset
65 Spring — offset lever detent
66 Ball — offset lever detent
67 Housing — extension
68 Bushing — extension housing
69 Seal — extension housing O.L.
70 Bolt — extension housing attaching
71 Vent — breather
72 Pin — 5th speed shift fork attaching
73 Fork — 5th speed shift
74 Insert — gearshift fork
75 Spring — gearshift lever return
76 Fork — reverse gearshift
77 Rail —5th speed shift
78 Ring — 7/16'' retaining (C-clip)
79 Lever — gearshift
80 O-ring — reverse idler gear overtravel stop
81 Gear/bushing assembly — reverse idler
82 Pin — reverse idler shaft attaching
83 Shaft — reverse idler gear
84 Pin — Gearshift lever pivot
85 Switch assembly — back-up lamp
86 Plug — 3/4'' diameter expansion
87 Plug — drain/refill
88 Case assembly
89 Bolt — bearing retainer attaching
90 Retainer — input shaft bearing
91 Seal — input shaft
92 Shim — input shaft front bearing (geartrain endplay)
93 Bearing assembly — input shaft
94 Shaft — input
95 Bolt — gearshift lever attaching
96 Boot — gearshift lower
97 Clamp — gearshift boot
98 O-ring — bearing vent seal

transmission slightly and remove the crossmember.

16 Remove the four bolts that hold the transmission to the flywheel cover.

17 Move the transmission rearward to let the input shaft clear the flywheel housing, then lower the transmission out of the vehicle. **Caution:** *Do not depress the clutch pedal when the transmission is out of the vehicle.*

18 Apply a small amount of light grease to the transmission input splines and install the transmission using the reverse of the removal procedure. **Note:** *It may be necessary to rotate the engine a small amount to align the clutch disc and input splines.*

Disassembly (1983 and 1984)

19 Place the transmission on a firm work bench or in a suitable holding device. In addition to the normal hand tools, you will need the following:

a) Snap ring pliers, one expanding and one contracting.
b) Brass-headed hammer, at least 2 pounds.
c) Brass drift.
d) Small containers for parts.

20 Read the entire section before starting work.

21 If the transmission fluid was not drained during removal use a 3/8-in. extension to remove the drain plug and drain out all the fluid.

22 With the transmission in neutral, remove the turret cover attaching bolts with a 13mm socket. Carefully pry the turret cover loose and remove it.

23 With a 3/16-inch pin punch remove the roll pin attaching the offset lever to the shifter shaft. Remove the damper sleeve. **Caution:** *Do not try to remove the offset lever with the transmission extension housing bolted in place. A lug on the bottom of the offset lever prevents enough rearward movement of the offset lever to allow removal.*

24 Remove the extension housing bolt.

25 Using a pry bar, loosen the extension housing from the case.

26 Remove the extension housing and the offset lever as an assembly by sliding it away from the case.

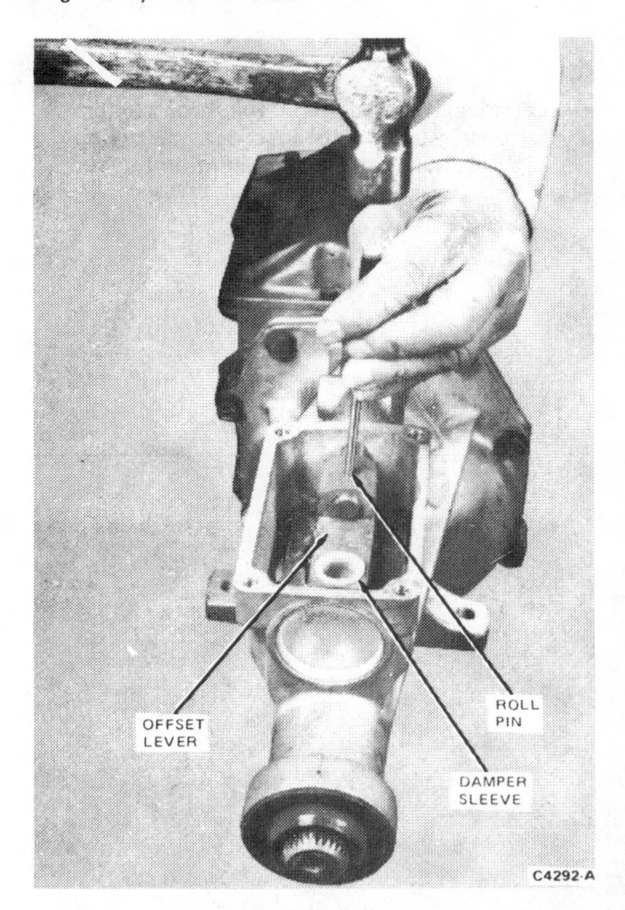

Fig. 13.71 Use a 3/16-inch punch to remove the damper sleeve roll pin (Sec 8)

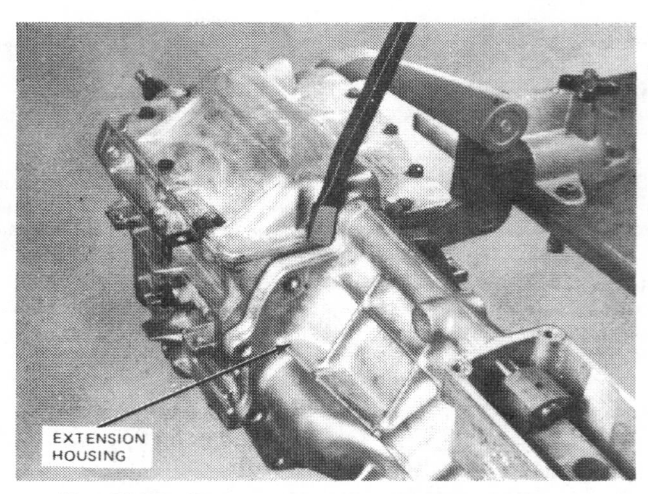

Fig. 13.72 Use a pry bar to separate the extension housing from the main case (Sec 8)

27 Remove the offset lever, roll pin, detent ball, and the detent spring from the extension housing detent plate.

28 Remove the plastic funnel, bearing race and thrust bearing from the end of the countershaft.

29 Remove the cover attaching bolts with a 10mm socket.

30 After carefully breaking the cover loose, lift it slightly and slide it to the filler plug side of the transmission. When the shift mechanism clears the groove in the 5th/reverse shift lever, remove the cover.

31 Remove the C-clip attaching the 5th/reverse shift lever to the pivot pin.

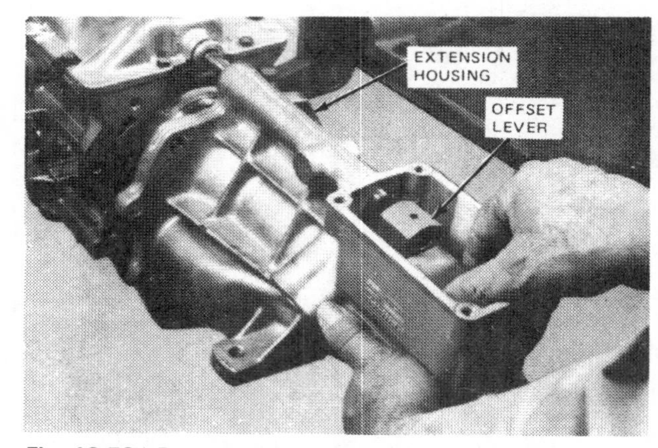

Fig. 13.73 Remove the offset lever and extension housing as an assembly (Sec 8)

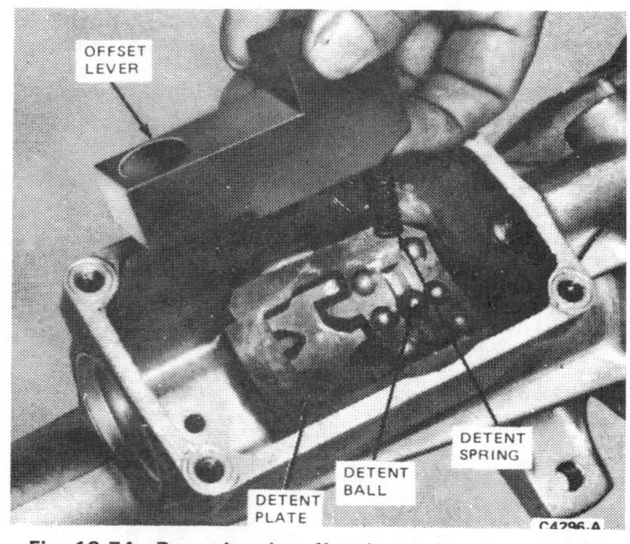

Fig. 13.74 Removing the offset lever, detent spring and detent plate (Sec 8)

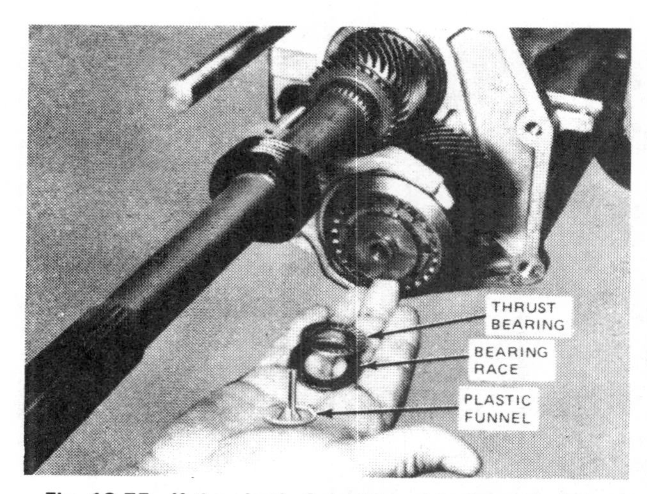

Fig. 13.75 If the plastic funnel is not in the end of the countershaft it could be in the extension housing (Sec 8)

Fig. 13.76 Use needle nose pliers to remove the C-clip on the 5th/reverse shift lever (Sec 8)

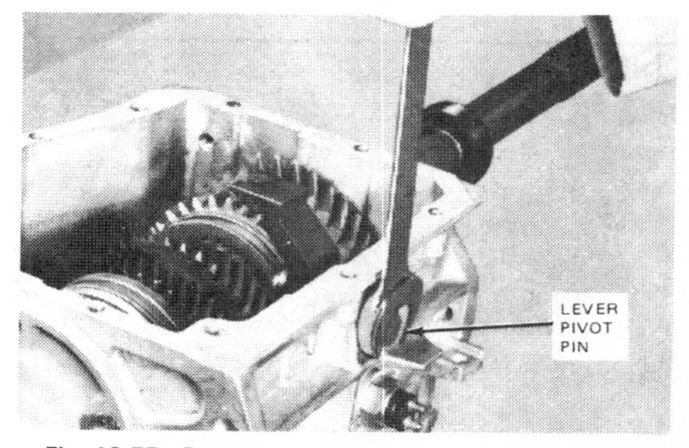

Fig. 13.77 Remove the 5th/reverse pivot pin, but leave the shift lever in the case (Sec 8)

32 Remove the 5th/reverse pivot pin, but do not remove the shift lever at this time.
33 Using long needle nose pliers, unhook the gearshift lever return spring from the front spring anchor.
34 With snap ring pliers, remove the 5th gear synchronizer snap ring and spacer from the rear of the countershaft.
35 Remove the 5th gear, synchronizer, shift fork and shift rail as an assembly by pulling it back away from the case.
36 While pressing down on the speedometer gear retaining clip, slide the gear off the output shaft. Remove the retaining clip.
37 Remove the front bearing retainer.
38 Rotate the input shaft until the flat on the synchronizer teeth aligns with 1st gear on the countershaft. With the input shaft in the proper position, remove it, being careful not to drop the 15 roller bearings, thrust bearing and race from the rear of the input shaft.
39 Remove the 4th gear blocking ring from the 3rd/4th synchronizer.
40 Remove the output shaft bearing race from the rear of the case. To partially remove the bearing race, pull back on the output shaft until 1st gear stops against the case. **Note:** *If the race sticks it is probably misaligned in the case bore. To free the race work the shaft back and forth in the case.*

Fig. 13.78 Use needle nose pliers to unhook the lever return spring (Sec 8)

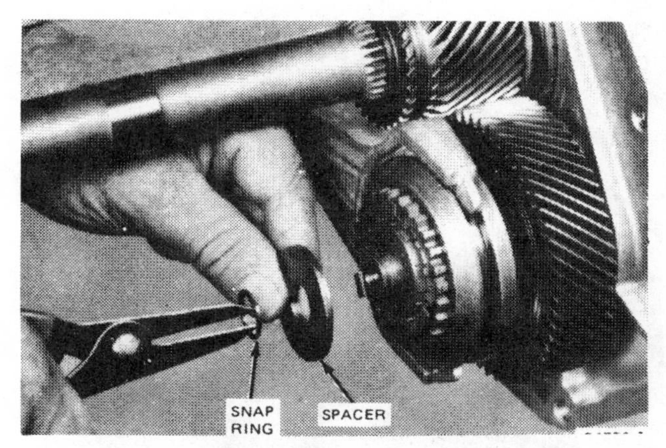

Fig. 13.79 Removing the 5th gear synchronizer snap ring (Sec 8)

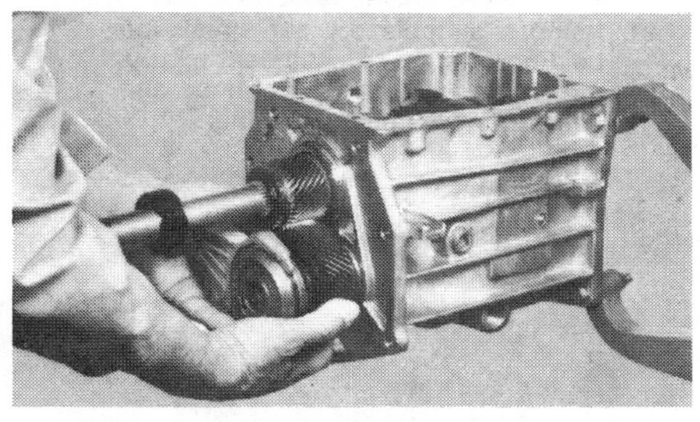

Fig. 13.80 Remove the 5th gear, synchronizer, shift fork and rail as an assembly (Sec 8)

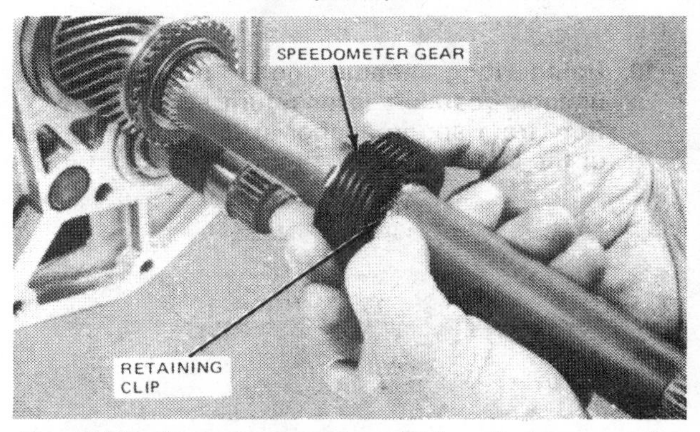

Fig. 13.81 Press down on the retaining clip to remove the speedometer gear (Sec 8)

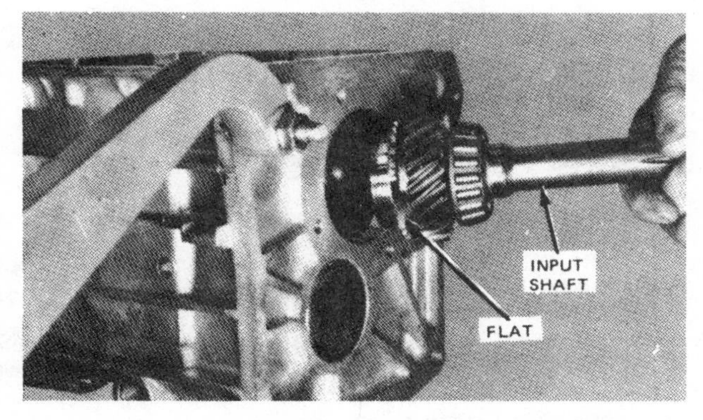

Fig. 13.82 Align the flat on the input shaft with first gear to remove it (Sec 8)

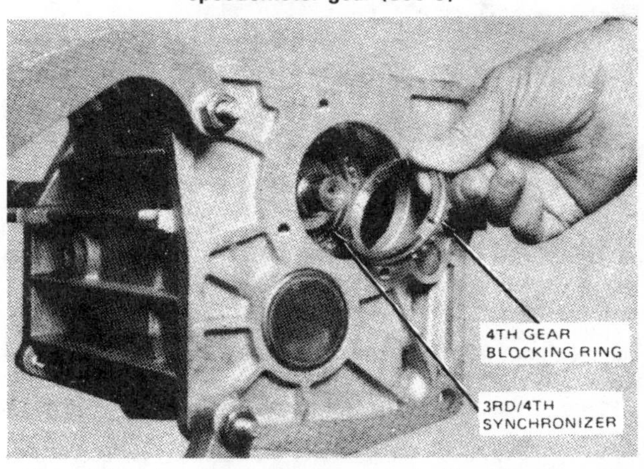

Fig. 13.83 Removing the 4th gear blocking ring (Sec 8)

Fig. 13.84 Remove the output shaft bearing race from the rear of the case (Sec 8)

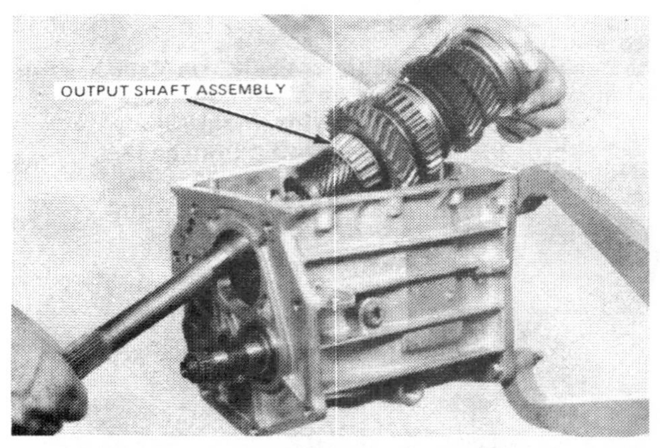

Fig. 13.85 Tilt the output shaft assembly upward to remove it from the case (Sec 8)

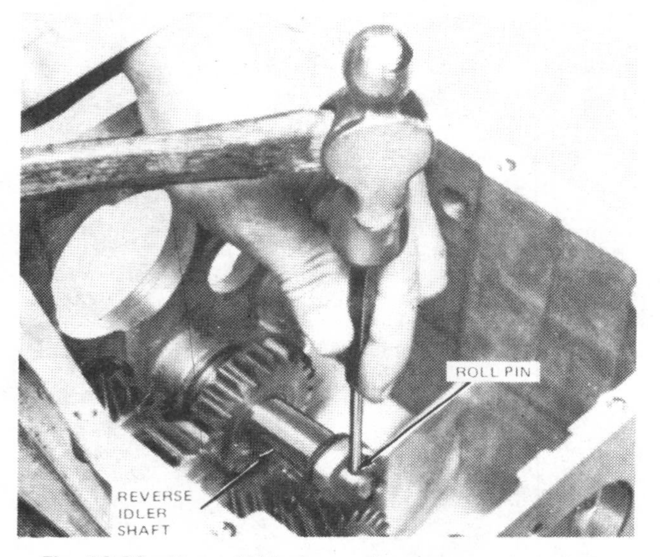

Fig. 13.86 Use a 3/16 pin punch to remove the roll pin from the reverse idler shaft (Sec 8)

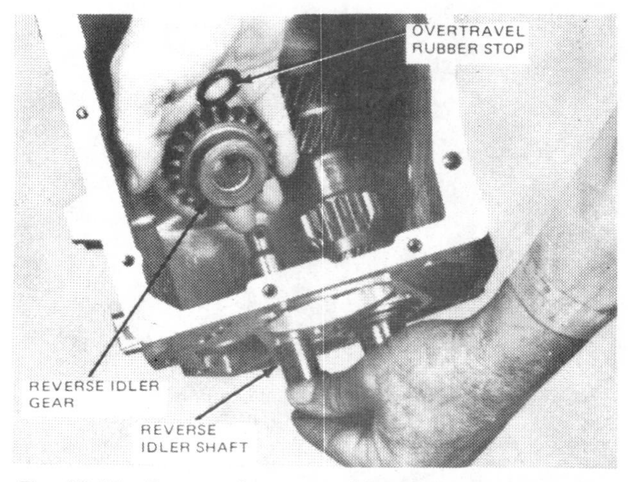

Fig. 13.87 Remove the reverse idler shaft out the back of the case (Sec 8)

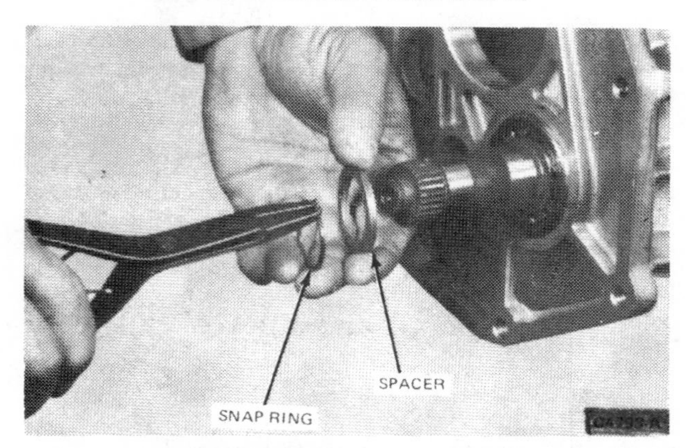

Fig. 13.88 Remove the snap ring and spacer from the countershaft (Sec 8)

Fig. 13.89 Use a brass drift and press to remove the countershaft (Sec 8)

41 Tilt the output shaft assembly upward and lift it out of the case.
42 Remove the 5th/reverse shift lever, reverse shift fork and spring from the case.
43 Use a 3/16 pin punch to remove the roll pin from the reverse idler shaft.
44 Remove the reverse idler shaft out the back of the case. Remove the reverse idler gear and the overtravel rubber stop from the case. **Note:** *To proceed any further in the disassembly process will require the use of a press.*
45 After removing the rear countershaft snap ring and spacer from the end of the countershaft, use a press and a brass drift to remove the rear countershaft bearing by placing the brass drift against the edge of the countershaft and pressing the bearing from the case.
46 Move the countershaft through the rear bearing bore and tilt it up-

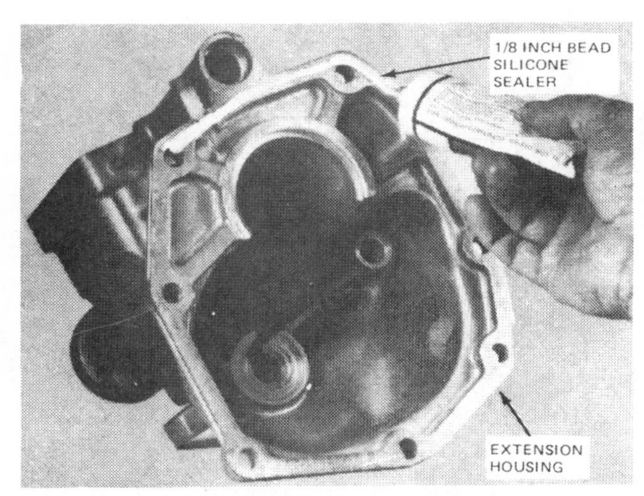

Fig. 13.90 Use a 1/8-in bead of silicone sealer to seal the extension housing (Sec 8)

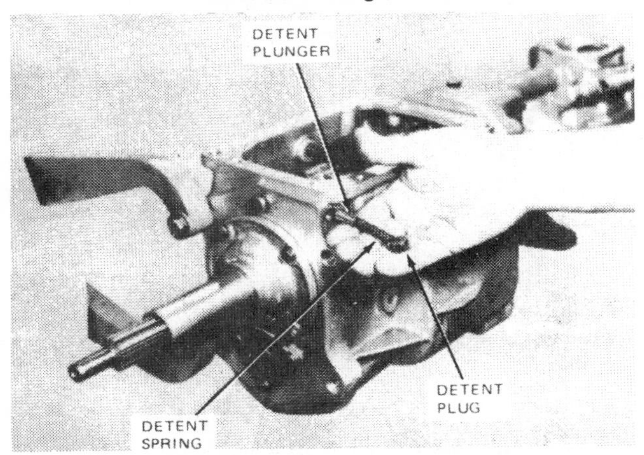

Fig. 13.92 Removing the detent plug, plunger and spring (Sec 8)

ward to remove the assembly from the case.
47 Remove the countershaft thrust washer from the case.
48 Remove the spacer from the rear of the countershaft. **Note:** *Disassembly of the output shaft and other transmission subassemblies requires the use of special equipment and is best left to a professional.*

Inspection and overhaul

49 Carefully clean and inspect all parts for wear, distortion, looseness of fit or damage to machined faces and threads.
50 Inspect the gears for excessive wear or chipping of the teeth. Replace with new gears as necessary.
51 Inspect the countershaft for signs of wear or chipping of the teeth.
52 If the synchro-rings are badly worn it is a good idea to replace them. New rings will improve the smoothness and speed of gear changes.
53 The roller bearing located between the front of the output shaft and the rear of the input shaft is likely to wear and should be replaced.
54 If the synchro-hubs are worn they must be replaced as complete assemblies.
55 The nylon insert in the offset lever should be replaced even if it appears to be in good condition.
56 If the bush bearing in the extension housing is badly worn it should be replaced.

Assembly (1983 and 1984)

57 Reassembly is the reverse of the disassembly procedure with the exception of the following details:
58 Prior to installation the countershaft thrust washer, 15 input shaft roller bearings, 4th gear blocking ring, and 5th gear thrust bearing and race should be lubricated with polyethylene grease or equivalent.
59 After installing the countershaft thrust washer in the case, make sure the thrust washer tab engages the groove in the case.

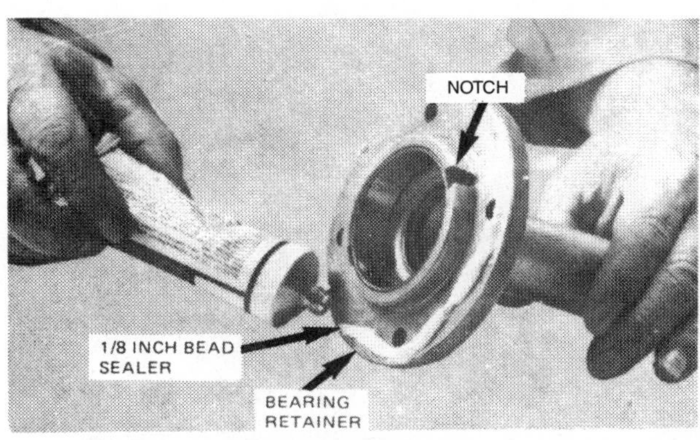

Fig. 13.91 When sealing the front bearing retainer do not cover notch (Sec 8)

60 Use a press, bearing installer, and a driver handle to install the countershaft rear bearing. **Note:** *When correctly installed the countershaft rear bearing will extend 0.125 to 0.129 in. above the case surface.*
61 Make sure that the reverse idler gear is installed with the shift lever groove facing the rear of the case. Position the overtravel stop between the gear and the shaft support.
62 Before installing the input shaft, align the flat on the synchonizer teeth with the countershaft.
63 If necessary, use a plastic-tipped hammer to install the output shaft rear bearing race.
64 When installing the lever return spring, the long end of the spring must face the rear of the case.
65 Use a thread sealant on the threads of the 5th/reverse shift lever pivot pin. **Note:** *Before installing the pivot pin, make sure the shift fork pin and 5th gear shift rail pin are engaged with the shift lever. If output shaft geartrain end play is to be adjusted, the front bearing retainer should be installed without sealer to allow easy removal.*
66 Petroleum jelly should be used on the lubrication funnel and the detent spring to help hold them in position.
67 Lubricate the detent plate and install the detent ball in the neutral position on the plate. Position the offset lever in the extension housing with the spring over the detent ball.
68 Install the offset lever and extension housing on the transmission as an assembly.
69 Seal the transmission cover with a silicone sealer.
70 Torque all the bolts to the proper specification (refer to Specifications).

Checking end play (1983 and 1984)

71 Rotate the transmission to a vertical position with the extension housing facing up.
72 Mount a dial indicator on the extension housing with the indicator stylus contacting the output shaft.
73 Rotate the input and output shafts. Zero the dial indicator.
74 Using a block of wood, push upward on the input shaft and note the reading on the dial indicator.
75 Adjust the end play shims to achieve a .000 end play measurement. **Caution:** *Although zero end play is the ideal specification, 0.002-in is an acceptable tolerance. Do not overload the bearings with too thick of a shim.*
76 To adjust end play, rotate the transmission to the horizontal position and remove the front bearing retainer. Remove the bearing race from the retainer to install the necessary shim(s).

Disassembly (1981 and 1982)

77 Place the transmission on a firm work bench or in a suitable holding device. In addition to the normal hand tools you will need the following:

a) Snap ring pliers, one expanding and one contracting.
b) Brass-headed hammer, at least 2 pounds.
c) Brass drift.
d) Small containers for parts.

78 Read the entire section before starting work.
79 If the transmission fluid was not drained during removal use a 3/8-in extension to remove the drain plug and drain out all the fluid.
80 Remove the ten cover bolts and remove the cover.
81 Remove the shift rail detent plug, spring and plunger from the front

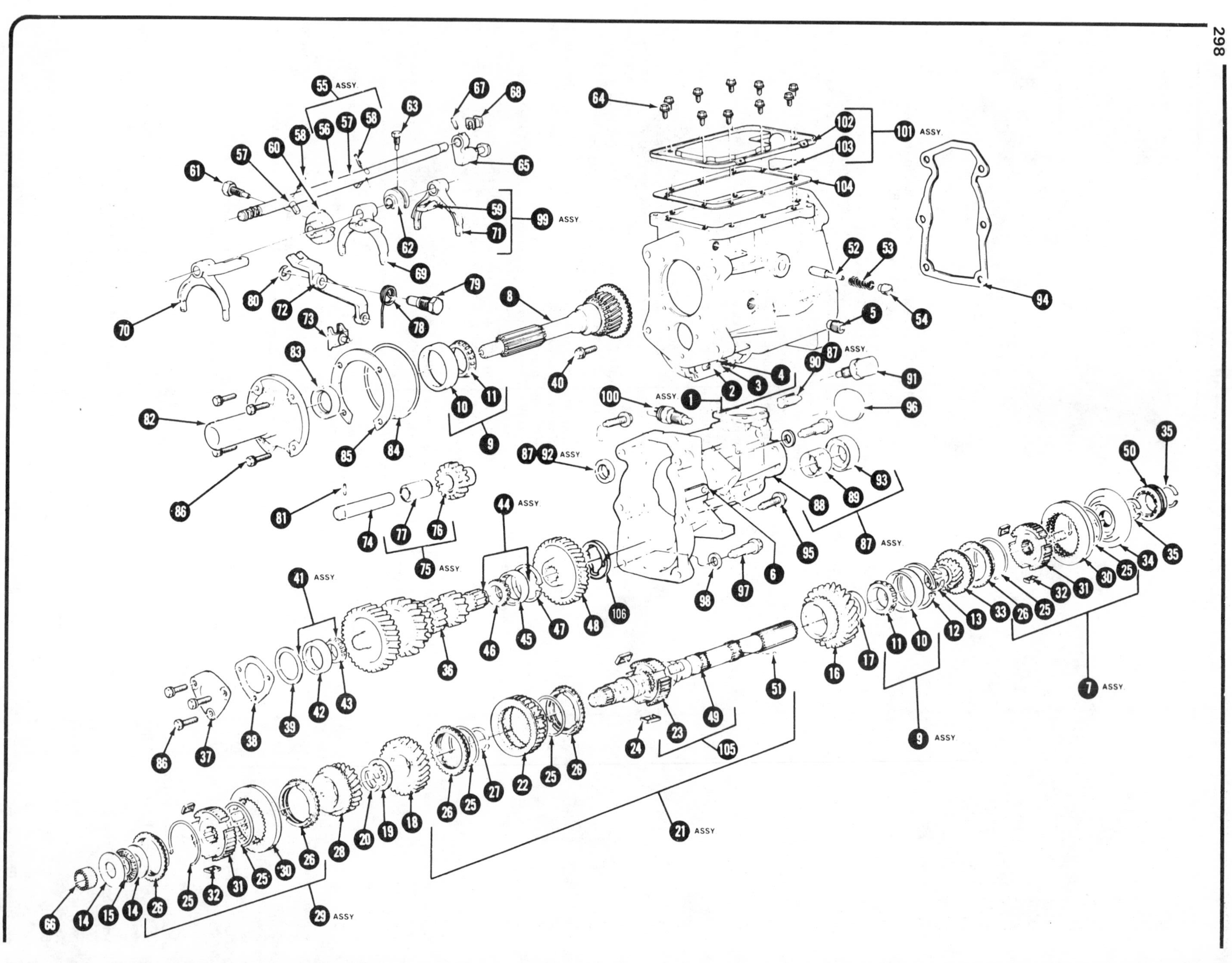

Fig. 13.93 Exploded view of the 1981 and later T5OD (Sec 8)

1 Transmission case assembly
2 Transmission case
3 Transmission case chip magnet
4 Spring push on nut
5 Transmission filler plug
6 Transmission service identification tag
7 5th gear synchronizer assembly
8 Input shaft
9 Input shaft tapered roller bearing
10 Bearing cup
11 Bearing cone and roller assembly
12 65mm internal snap ring
13 35mm external select snap ring
14 Input shaft thrust washer
15 Needle thrust bearing assembly
16 1st speed gear
17 1st gear thrust washer
18 2nd speed gear
19 2nd gear thrust washer
20 35mm external snap ring
21 Output shaft and sliding gear assembly
22 Reverse sliding gear
23 1st & 2nd gear clutch hub
24 1st & 2nd synchronizer insert
25 Synchronizer retaining spring
26 Synchronizer blocking ring
27 39.4mm external snap ring
28 3rd speed gear
29 3rd & 4th speed gear synchronizer assembly
30 3rd & 4th speed gear clutch hub sleeve
31 3rd & 4th speed gear clutch hub
32 3rd & 4th speed synchronizer insert
33 5th speed maindrive gear
34 5th speed synchronizer retaining spacer
35 26mm external snap ring
36 Countershaft gear
37 Countershaft gear front bearing retainer
38 Countershaft gear front bearing retainer gasket
39 Countershaft bearing select fit shim
40 Screw and washer assembly
41 Countershaft gear front bearing assembly
42 Bearing cup
43 Bearing cone and roller assembly
44 Countershaft gear rear bearing assembly
45 Bearing cup
46 Bearing cone and roller assembly
47 58mm internal snap ring
48 5th speed cluster gear
49 Output shaft
50 Speedometer drive gear
51 1/4-inch diameter ball
52 Meshlock plunger
53 Shifter interlock spring
54 Detent spring plug
55 Shifter shaft and pin assembly
56 Shifter shaft
57 Gearshift selector pin
58 Spring pin (3mm x 12mm)
59 5th gear fork pin
60 Gear selector interlock sleeve
61 Hex head pilot bolt
62 5th gear selector interlock sleeve
63 Hex head pilot bolt
64 Hexagon screw
65 Gearshift shaft offset lever
66 Mainshaft roller bearing
67 Hex head spring pin
68 Gearshift damper bushing
69 1st & 2nd gearshift fork
70 3rd & 4th gearshift fork
71 5th gearshift fork
72 Reverse gearshift relay lever
73 Reverse gearshift fork
74 Reverse idler gear shaft
75 Reverse idler sliding gear bushing assembly
76 Reverse idler gear
77 Reverse idler gear bushing
78 Reverse relay lever spring
79 Reverse gear selector fork pivot pin
80 Retaining ring
81 Spring pin
82 Input shaft gear bearing retainer
83 Input shaft oil seal
84 O-ring seal
85 Input shaft front bearing select fit shim
86 Screw and washer assembly
87 Transmission extension assembly
88 Transmission extension
89 Extension bushing
90 Gearshift lever reverse stop
91 5th gear inhibitor assembly
92 Gearshift rail seal
93 Extension yoke oil seal
94 Extension gasket
95 Hex head screw and washer assembly
96 Extension access plug
97 Hex head shoulder bolt
98 Washer
99 5th gearshift fork assembly
100 Backup light switch
101 Case access cover assembly
102 Case access cover
103 Vent hole cover plate
104 Case access cover gasket
105 1st & 2nd speed hub and output shaft assembly
106 Ring 1.0 — split-internal

left side of the case. It may be necessary to use a pencil-size magnet to remove the spring and plunger.
82 Remove the access plug from the rear of the extension housing with a punch and hammer.
83 Shift the transmission into reverse, then remove the gear shift shaft offset lever roll pin. Then, using a screwdriver, slide the offset lever and bushing off the shaft.
84 Remove the 5th-gear interlock pilot bolt from the front top of the extension housing.
85 After removing the extension housing attaching bolts, slide the extension housing off the output shaft.
86 Remove the snap ring, speedometer drive gear and drive ball from the output shaft.
87 Remove the snap ring that holds the 5th-gear synchonizer on the output shaft, then slide the retaining spacer off the shaft.
88 Shift the transmission into first gear.
89 Remove the shifter shaft, 5th-gear, shift fork and 5th-gear synch-

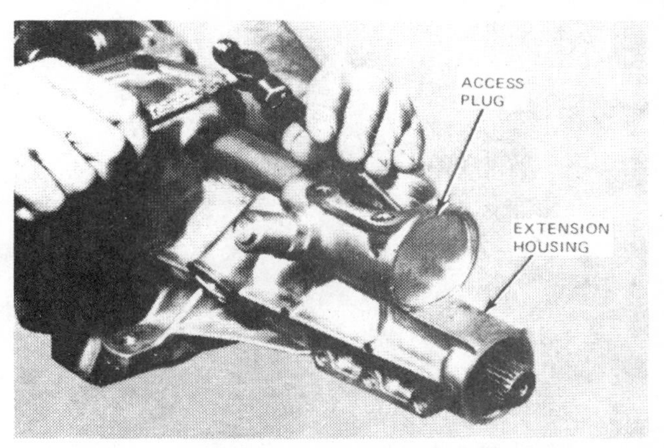

Fig. 13.94 Use a brass drift to remove the access plug from the rear of the transmission (Sec 8)

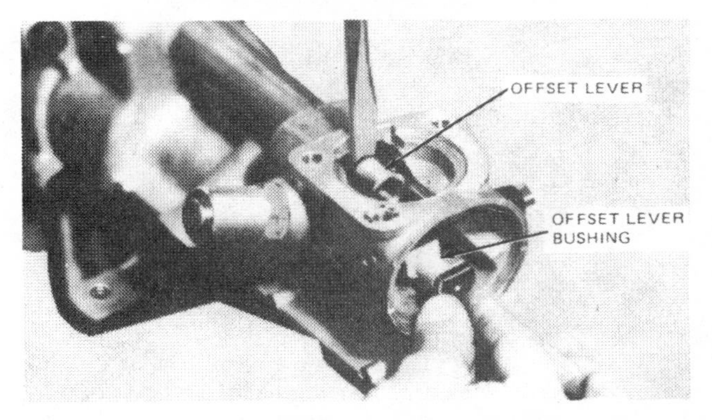

Fig. 13.95 Removing the offset lever (Sec 8)

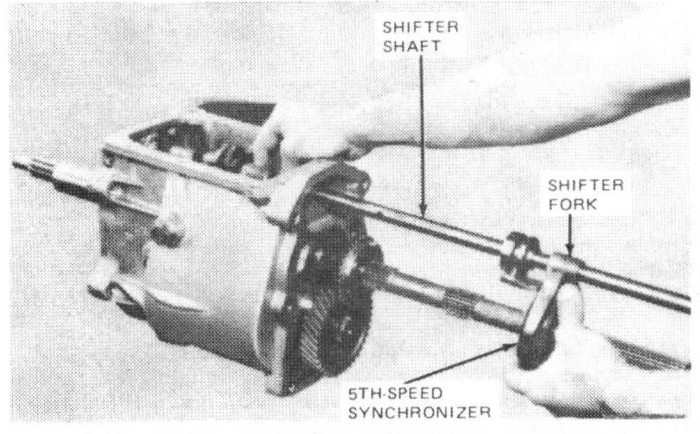

Fig. 13.96 Remove the 5th-gear shaft, fork and synchronizer as an assembly (Sec 8)

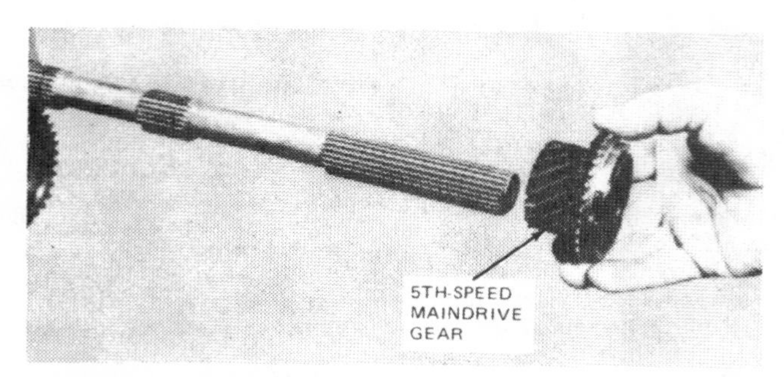

Fig. 13.97 Slide the main drive gear off the output shaft (Sec 8)

Fig. 13.99 Removing the input shaft bearing retainer (Sec 8)

Fig. 13.101 Lift the mainshaft out of the top of case (Sec 8)

ronizer from the output shaft as an assembly.

90 Remove the interlock sleeve bolt from the right side of the transmission case.

91 Lift the interlock sleeve, 3rd/4th gear shift fork and 1st/2nd gear shift fork from the case.

92 From inside the transmission case, remove the C-clip from the reverse gear selector fork pivot pin, then remove the pivot pin and lift the reverse gear selector fork relay lever, the spring and the reverse gearshift fork from the transmission case.

93 After sliding the main drive 5th-gear off the output shaft remove the two piece snap ring located at rear of the 5th-gear cluster gear.

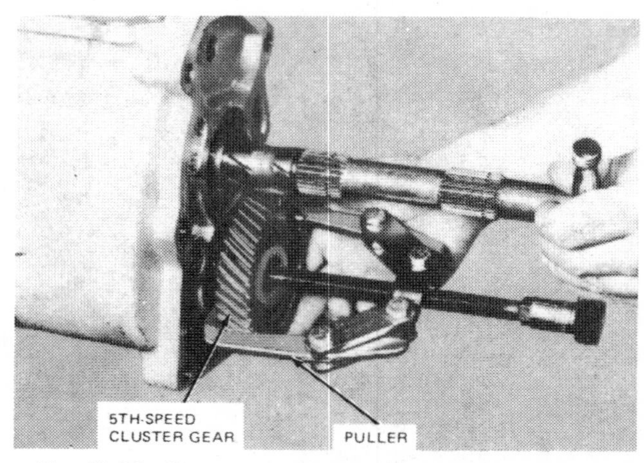

Fig. 13.98 Use a gear puller to remove the cluster gear (Sec 8)

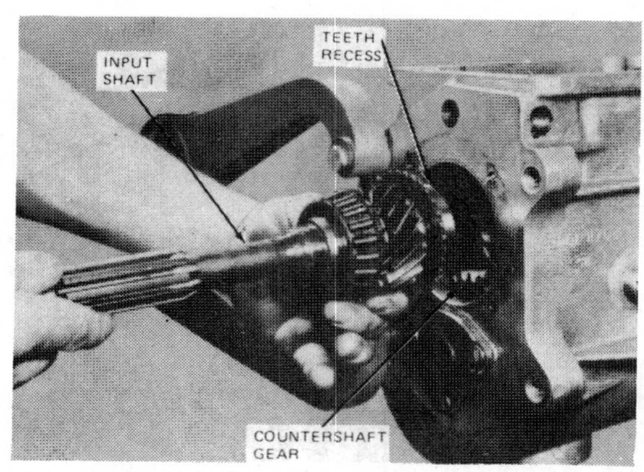

Fig. 13.100 Align the recess on the input shaft with the counter gear to remove it (Sec 8)

94 Using a gear puller remove the 5th-gear cluster gear.

95 Remove the snap ring from the output shaft rear bearing and remove the bearing cup from the transmission case.

96 Remove the bolts that attach the input shaft bearing retainer to the transmission case, then remove the bearing retainer and seal, the shim and the O-ring from the case.

97 Rotate the input shaft to position the teeth recess toward the countershaft gear to provide clearance. Then lift the input gear from the transmission case. **Note:** *Do not lose the roller bearings, the thrust washers and the thrust bearing when removing the input shaft.*

98 Lift the output shaft assembly out through the top of the transmission case.

99 Remove the snap ring from the back of the transmission and remove the countershaft gear rear bearing cup from the case.

100 Remove the countershaft front bearing retainer, gasket, shim and the front bearing cup from the case.

101 Lift the countershaft gear out of the transmission case.

102 Remove the roll pin from the reverse idler gear shaft. Remove the reverse idler gear shaft, gear and thrust washers.

Inspection and overhaul (1981 and 1982)

103 Refer to Steps 49 thru 56.

Assembly (1981 and 1982)

104 Reassembly is the reverse of the disassembly procedure with the addition of the following:

105 All bolts and plugs used throughout the transmission case, except where used in blind holes, should be coated with a sealant to prevent leakage.

106 While tightening the countershaft front bearing retainer cap

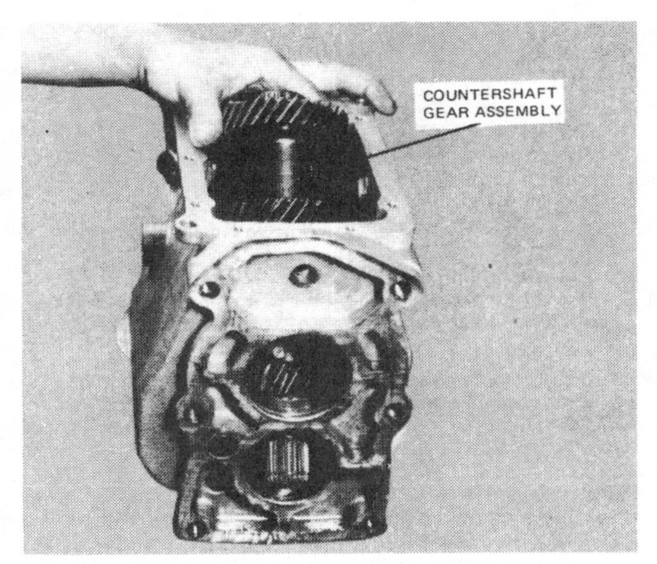

Fig. 13.102 Tilt the countershaft up to remove it out of the top of the case (Sec 8)

Fig. 13.104 Be sure to align the slot with the hole before installing the roll pin into the reverse idler shaft (Sec 8)

screws slowly rotate the gear. If the gear rotating effort increases while tightening the bearing retainer, replace the shim with a thinner one.
107 Apply a liberal coat of polyethylene grease to all of the thrust washers and the thrust bearings.
108 Carefully install the input shaft assembly in the transmission case with a blank portion of teeth toward the countershaft gear to provide the proper clearance. **Note:** *When inserting the input shaft, care must be taken not to disturb the roller bearings in the input shaft nor the thrust washers and thrust bearing on the 3rd/4th synchronizer hub.*
109 Coat the new input shaft O-ring with polyethylene grease before positioning it in the bearing retainer groove.
110 While installing the front bearing retainer to the case slowly rotate the input shaft. If the turning effort increases when tightening bearing retainer bolts, replace the shim with a thicker one.
111 Install the shifter shaft, the 5th-gear shift fork and the 5th-gear synchronizer as an assembly. Make sure that the 5th-gear synchronizer thrust surface is facing toward the rear of the output shaft.
112 When installing the extension housing access plug in the rear of the extension housing, the flare of the access plug should be restored. This is done by tapping the lip of the plug outward with a hammer. If this is not practical a new plug should be installed. Using a screwdriver or chisel and a hammer, stake two notches in the rear of the extension housing access hole behind the plug.

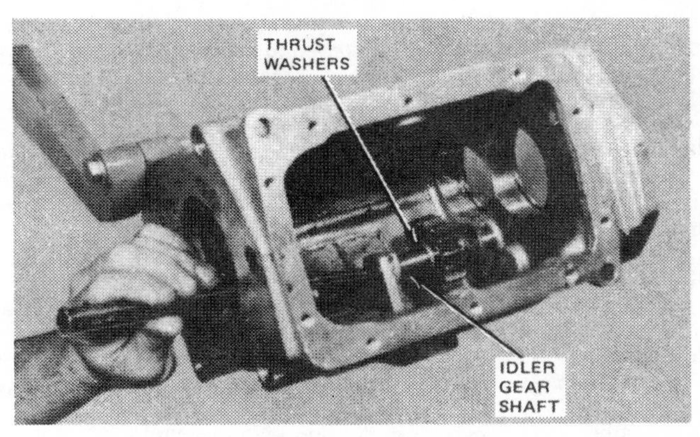

Fig. 13.103 Use a punch to remove the roll pin in the idler gear shaft (Sec 8)

Fig. 13.105 5th-gear synchronizer assembly installed (Sec 8)

Transmission (AOD)

Removal and installation

113 Raise the vehicle on jackstands.
114 Place a drain pan under the transmission fluid pan. Starting at the rear of the pan and working toward the front, loosen the attaching bolts and allow the fluid to drain. Finally remove all of the pan attaching bolts, except two at the front, to allow the fluid to further drain. With the fluid drained, install two bolts on the rear side of the pan to temporarily hold it in place.
115 Remove the converter drain plug access cover from the lower end of the converter housing.
116 Remove the converter-to-flywheel attaching nuts. Place a wrench on the crankshaft pulley attaching bolt to turn the converter to gain access to the nuts.
117 Place a drain pan under the converter to catch the fluid. With the wrench on the crankshaft pulley attaching bolt, turn the converter to gain access to the converter drain plug and remove the plug. After the fluid has been drained reinstall the plug.
118 Disconnect the driveshaft from the rear axle and slide the shaft rearward from the transmission (refer to Chapter 8).
119 Disconnect the cable from the terminal on the starter motor.
120 Remove the three attaching bolts and remove the starter motor.
121 Disconnect the neutral start switch wires at the plug connector.
122 Remove the rear mount-to-crossmember attaching bolts and the two crossmember-to-frame attaching bolts.
123 Remove the two engine rear support-to-extension housing attaching bolts.
124 Disconnect the TV linkage rod from the transmission TV lever.
125 Carefully disconnect the manual rod from the transmission manual lever at the transmission.
126 Remove the two bolts securing the bellcrank bracket to the converter housing.
127 Raise the transmission with a transmission jack to provide

clearance to remove the crossmember. Remove the rear mount from the crossmember and remove the crossmember from the side supports. **Note:** *Disconnect and remove any interfering exhaust system hardware.*

128 Lower the transmission to gain access to the oil cooler lines.

129 Disconnect the oil cooler lines from the fittings on the transmission.

130 Disconnect the speedometer cable from the extension housing.

131 Remove the bolt that secures the transmission fluid filler tube to the cylinder block. Lift the filler tube and the dipstick from the transmission.

132 Secure the transmission to the jack with a chain.

133 Remove the converter housing-to-cylinder block attaching bolts.

134 Carefully move the transmission and converter assembly away from the engine and, at the same time, lower the jack to clear the underside of the vehicle.

135 Installation is the reverse of the removal procedure with the following notes:

a) Tighten the converter drain plug to 11-38 Nm (8-28 ft-lb).
b) Lubricate the converter pilot with chassis grease.
c) Align the orange balancing marks on converter stud and flywheel bolt hole if balancing marks are present.
d) When moving the converter and transmission assembly forward into position, use care not to damage the flywheel and the converter pilot. The converter face must rest squarely against the flywheel. This indicates that the converter pilot is not binding in the engine crankshaft. **Caution:** *Before installing the torque converter to the flywheel attaching nuts, check to ensure that the converter is properly seated. The converter should move freely with respect to the flywheel. Grasp a stud. Movement back and forth should result in a metallic clanking noise if the converter is properly seated. If the converter will not move, the transmission must be removed and the converter repositioned so that the impeller hub is properly engaged in the pump gear.*

Linkage adjustment — general instructions

136 Before any engine TV linkage adjustment can be done the throttle lever at the fuel charging assembly must be positioned at its minimum idle stop with the following procedure:

Without idle speed control (ISC)

137 Check/adjust the engine curb idle speed to specification (refer to Section 5).

138 Shut the engine off and remove the air cleaner.

139 De-cam the fast idle cam on the carburetor so that the throttle lever is against the idle stop or throttle solenoid positioner stop.

With idle speed control (ISC)

Note: When the engine is shut off, the ISC plunger automatically extends and moves the throttle lever to fast idle in preparation for the next time the engine is started. The TV linkage cannot be correctly adjusted in this position. The ISC plunger will retract only if this procedure is followed in the exact sequence.

140 Locate the Self Test Connector and Self Test Input Connector in the engine compartment. These two connectors are located next to each other (Fig. 13.106).

141 Connect a jumper wire between the STI connector and the Signal Return Ground on the Self Test Connector.

142 Turn the ignition key to the Run position but do not start the engine. The ISC plunger will retract. Wait until the plunger is fully retracted (about 10 seconds).

143 Turn off the key and remove the jumper wire.

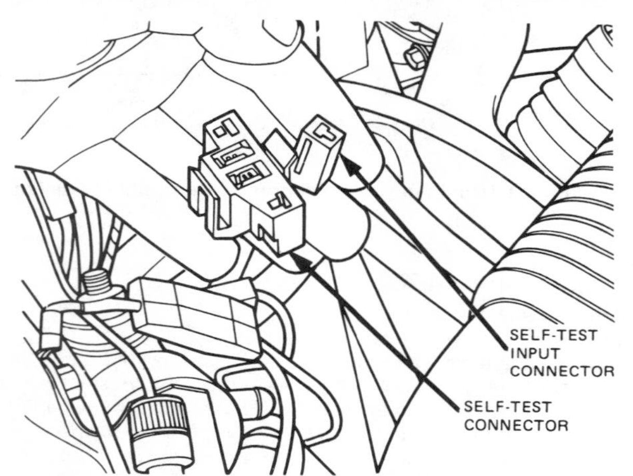

Fig. 13.106 The two self-test connectors will be next to each other in the engine compartment (Sec 8)

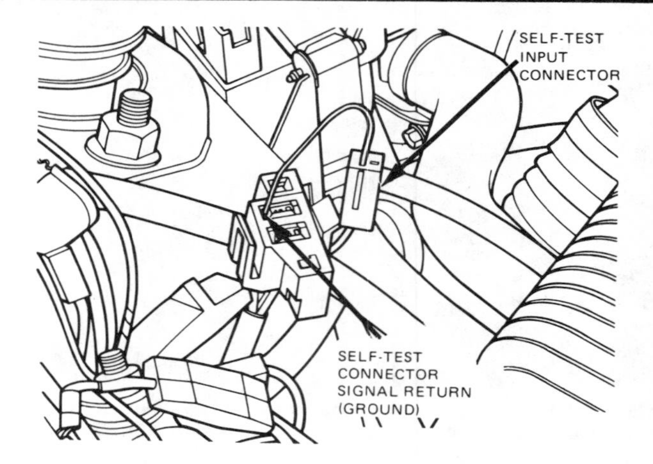

Fig. 13.107 Use a jumper wire to connect the STI connector to the self-test connector (Sec 8)

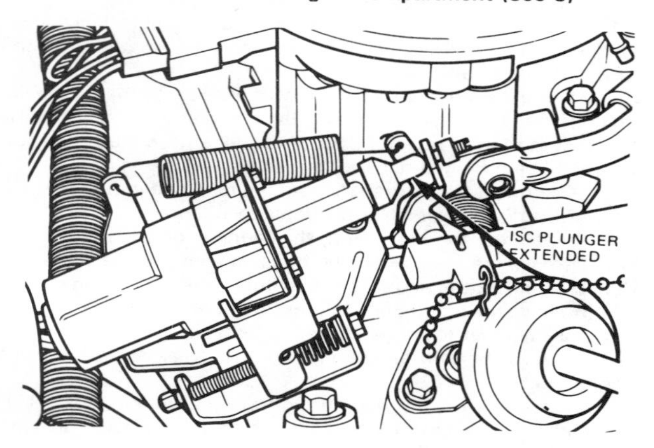

Fig. 13.108 View of the ISC plunger extended (Sec 8)

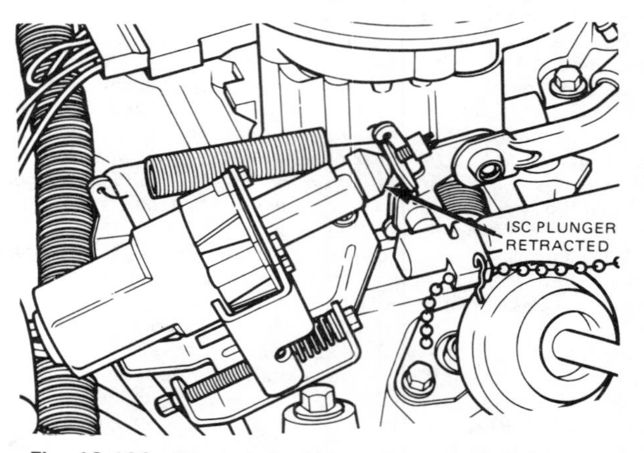

Fig. 13.109 View of the ISC plunger retracted (Sec 8)

Linkage adjustment at transmission

144 This procedure requires placing the vehicle on jackstands to give access to the linkage components at the transmission TV control lever.
145 Set the carburetor at its minimum idle stop as described in steps 137 through 143. Place the shift lever in Neutral and set the parking brake. **Note:** *The transmission selector must be in Neutral.*
146 Set the linkage lever adjustment screw at approximately mid-range.
147 If a new TV control rod assembly is being installed, connect the rod to the linkage lever at the carburetor. **Caution:** *The following steps involve working in proximity to the exhaust system. Allow the exhaust system to cool before proceeding.*
148 Raise the vehicle and suppport it on jackstands.
149 Loosen the bolt on the sliding trunnion block on the TV control rod assembly. Remove any corrosion from the control rod and free-up the trunnion block so that it slides freely on the control rod.
150 Push up on the lower end of the control rod to ensure that the linkage lever at the carburetor is firmly against the throttle lever. Release the force on the rod. The rod must stay up.
151 Push the TV control lever on the transmission up against its internal stop with a firm force (approximately 5 lbs) and tighten the bolt on the trunnion block. Do not relax force on the lever until the bolt is tightened.
152 Lower the vehicle and verify that the throttle lever is still against the minimum idle stop or throttle solenoid positioner stop. If not, repeat Steps 137 through 143.

Transmission (C-5)

Removal and installation

153 Disconnect the battery negative cable.
154 On vehicles equipped with a 3.8L engine remove the air cleaner assembly.
155 Remove the fan shroud attaching bolts and position the shroud back over the fan.
156 On vehicles equipped with a 3.8L engine, loosen the clamp and disconnect the thermactor air injection hose at the catalytic converter check valve. The check valve is located on the right side of the engine compartment near the dash panel.
157 On vehicles equipped with a 3.8L engine remove the two transmission-to-engine attaching bolts located at the top of the transmission bellhousing. **Note:** *These bolts are accessible from the engine compartment.*
158 Raise the vehicle high enough to allow removal of the transmission from under the vehicle and support it on jackstands.
159 Remove the driveshaft (refer to Chapter 8).
160 Disconnect the muffler inlet pipe from the catalytic converter outlet pipe.
161 Support the muffler/pipe assembly by wiring it to a convenient underbody bracket.
162 Remove the nuts attaching the exhaust pipe(s) to the exhaust manifold(s).
163 Pull back on the catalytic converters to release the converter hangers from the mounting bracket.
164 Remove the speedometer clamp bolt and pull the speedometer out of the extension housing.
165 Disconnect the neutral start switch harness connector.
166 Disconnect the kick down rod at the transmission lever.
167 Disconnect the shift linkage at the linkage bellcrank. On vehicles equipped with floor mounted shift, remove the shift cable routing bracket attaching bolts and disconnect the cable at the transmission lever.
168 Remove the converter dust shield.
169 Remove the torque converter to drive plate attaching nuts. **Note:** *To gain access to the converter nuts turn the crankshaft and drive plate using a ratchet handle and socket on the crankshaft pulley attaching bolt.*
170 Remove the starter attaching bolts and remove the starter.
171 Loosen the nuts attaching the rear support to the No.3 crossmember.
172 Position a transmission jack under the transmission oil pan and secure the transmission to the jack with a safety chain.
173 Remove the through bolts attaching the No.3 crossmember to the body brackets.
174 Lower the transmission enough to allow access to the oil cooler line fittings.
175 Disconnect the oil cooler lines.
176 On vehicles with 3.8L engine, remove the 4 remaining transmission-to-engine attaching bolts (2 each side). On all other models, remove the 6 transmission-to-engine attaching bolts.
177 Pull the transmission back to disengage the converter studs from the drive plate.
178 Lower the transmission out of the vehicle.
179 Installation is the reverse of removal with the following notes:
180 Lubricate the converter pilot with chassis grease.
181 As the transmission is being slowly raised into position, rotate the torque converter until the studs and drain plug are aligned with the holes in flywheel. **Note:** *Some vehicles may have an orange balancing mark on one converter stud and one flywheel bolt hole. If these marks are present, make sure they are aligned.*
182 Make sure the converter studs engage the drive plate and that the transmission dowels on the back of the engine engage the bolt holes in the bellhousing.
183 Before installing the torque conveter to flywheel attaching nuts a check should be made to ensure that the converter is properly seated. The converter should move freely with respect to the flywheel. Grasp a stud. Movement back and forth should result in a metallic clanking noise if the converter is properly seated. If the converter will not move the transmission must be removed and the converter repositioned so that the impeller hub is properly engaged in the pump gear.
184 Install the catalytic converter(s) using new seal(s) at the pipes(s) to exhaust manifold connection(s).
185 Check and if necessary adjust the shift linkage. Refer to step 186.

Selector linkage — adjustment (C-5)

186 Refer to Chapter 7, section 14.

Intermediate band — adjustment (C-5)

187 Refer to Chapter 7, section 16.

Low and reverse band — adjustment (C-5)

188 Refer to Chapter 7, section 17.

---

9 Suspension

General information

1 There are three possible modifications to the rear suspension, depending on the model and engine combination.

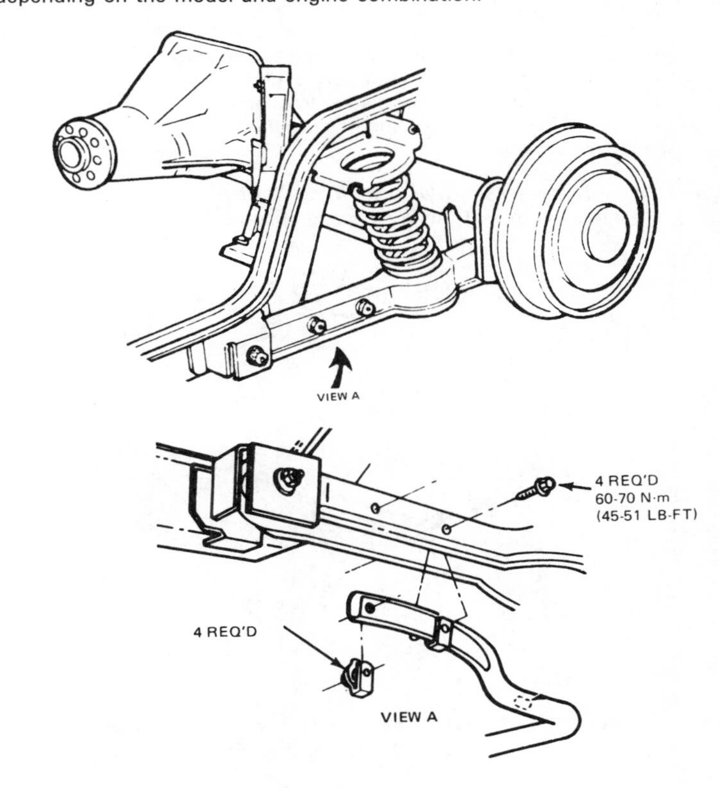

Fig. 13.110 Typical sway bar installation (Sec 9)

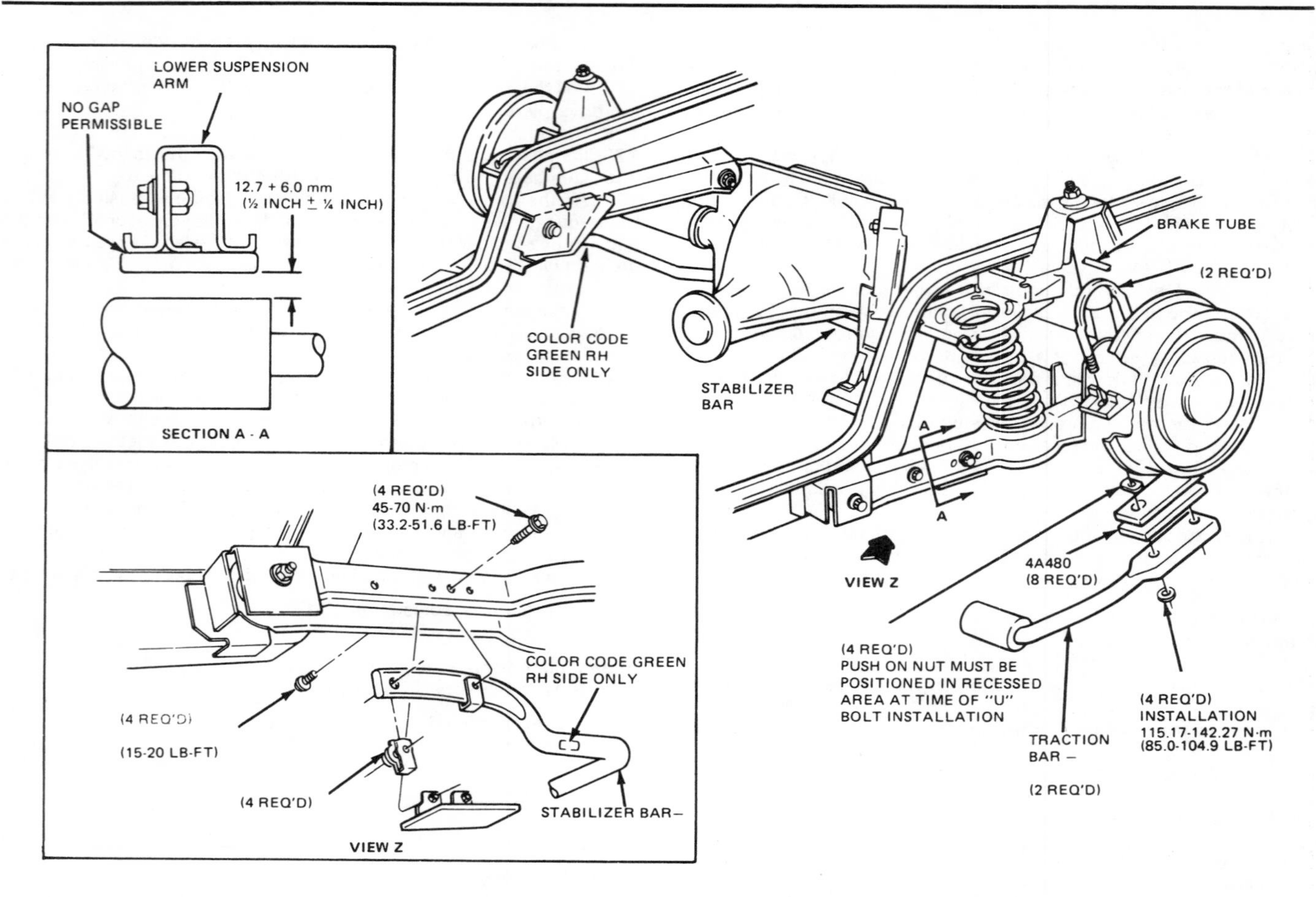

Fig. 13.111 Typical rear suspension with sway bar and traction bars (Sec 9)

2 A rear sway bar and/or traction bars have been added as part of the suspension package. They are used to improve cornering stability and reduce wheel hop during heavy acceleration.
3 On later production models the traction bars have been replaced by a pair of hydraulic axle dampers to further reduce wheel hop during heavy acceleration.

Sway bar – removal and installation

4 Raise the rear of the vehicle and support it on jackstands.

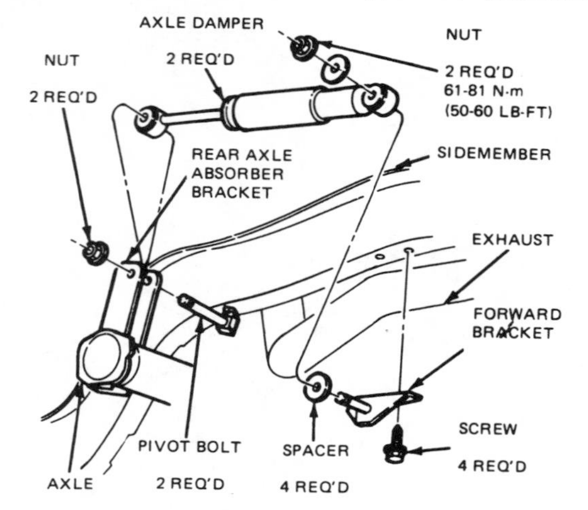

Fig. 13.112 Axle damper installation on late models with 5.0L engine (Sec 9)

5 Remove the four bolts attaching the sway bar to the lower control arm.
6 Remove the sway bar from the vehicle.
7 Installation is the reverse of removal.
8 After the sway bar is installed in the vehicle be sure that there is sufficient clearance between the sway bar and the lower control arm.
9 Tighten the four bolts to specification.

Traction bar – removal and installation

10 Raise the rear of the vehicle and support it by the body at the rear crossmember.
11 Remove the two nuts that hold the traction bar to the U-bolt and remove the traction bar, U-bolt and adjusting shim(s).
12 Installation is the reverse of the removal procedure.

Axle dampers – removal and installation

13 Raise the vehicle and support the rear axle with jackstands.
14 Remove the wheel on the side to be worked on.
15 Remove the axle damper attaching nut and pivot bolt.
16 Remove the axle damper and spacer(s).
17 Installation is the reverse of the removal procedure.

10 Electrical system

Wiring diagrams

Note that wiring diagrams for later model years have been included at the end of this Chapter. Due to space limitations we are not able to provide every diagram for all years; however, the diagrams included are typical for all years covered.

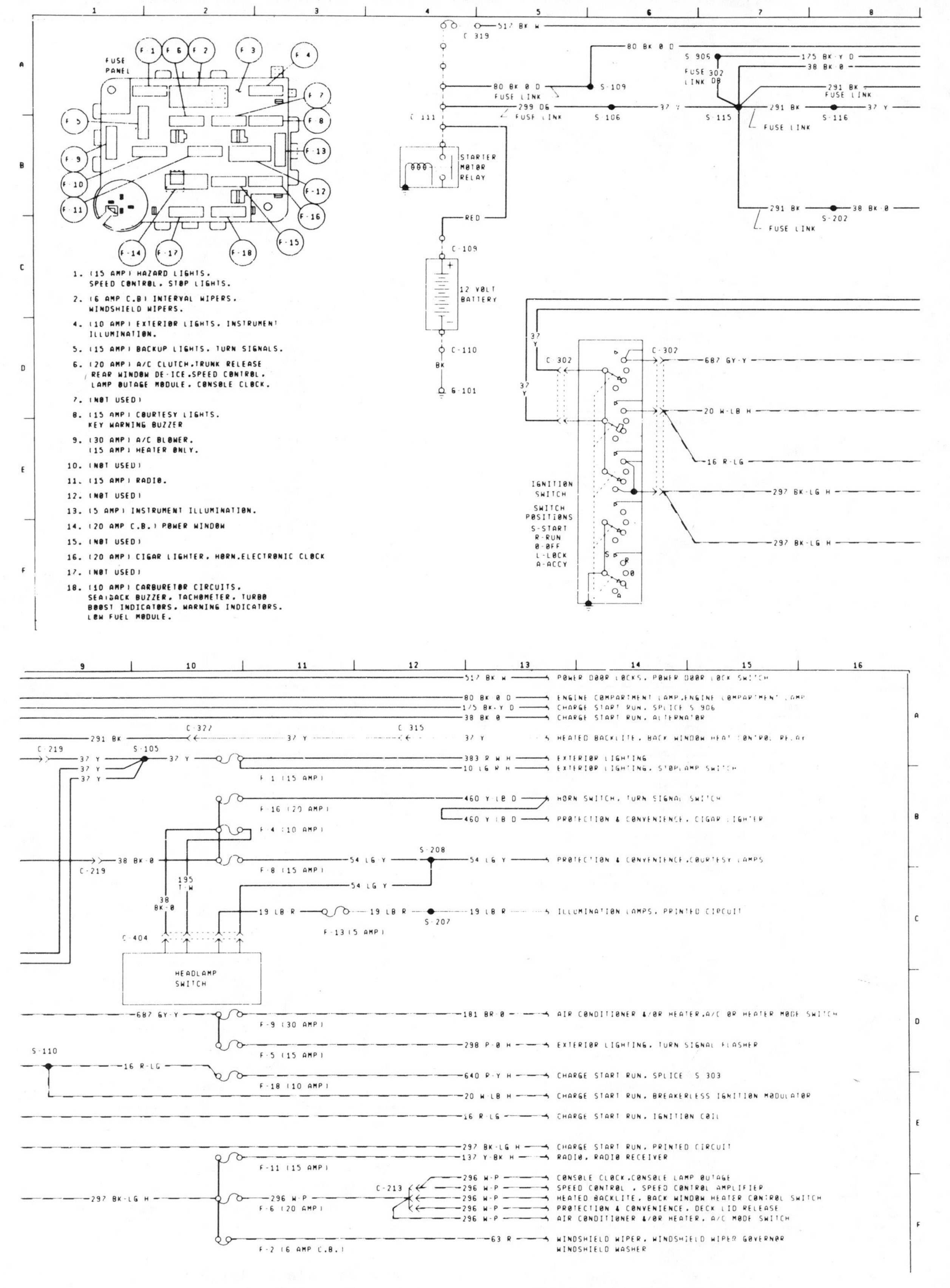

Wiring diagram — Power distribution (1) late model

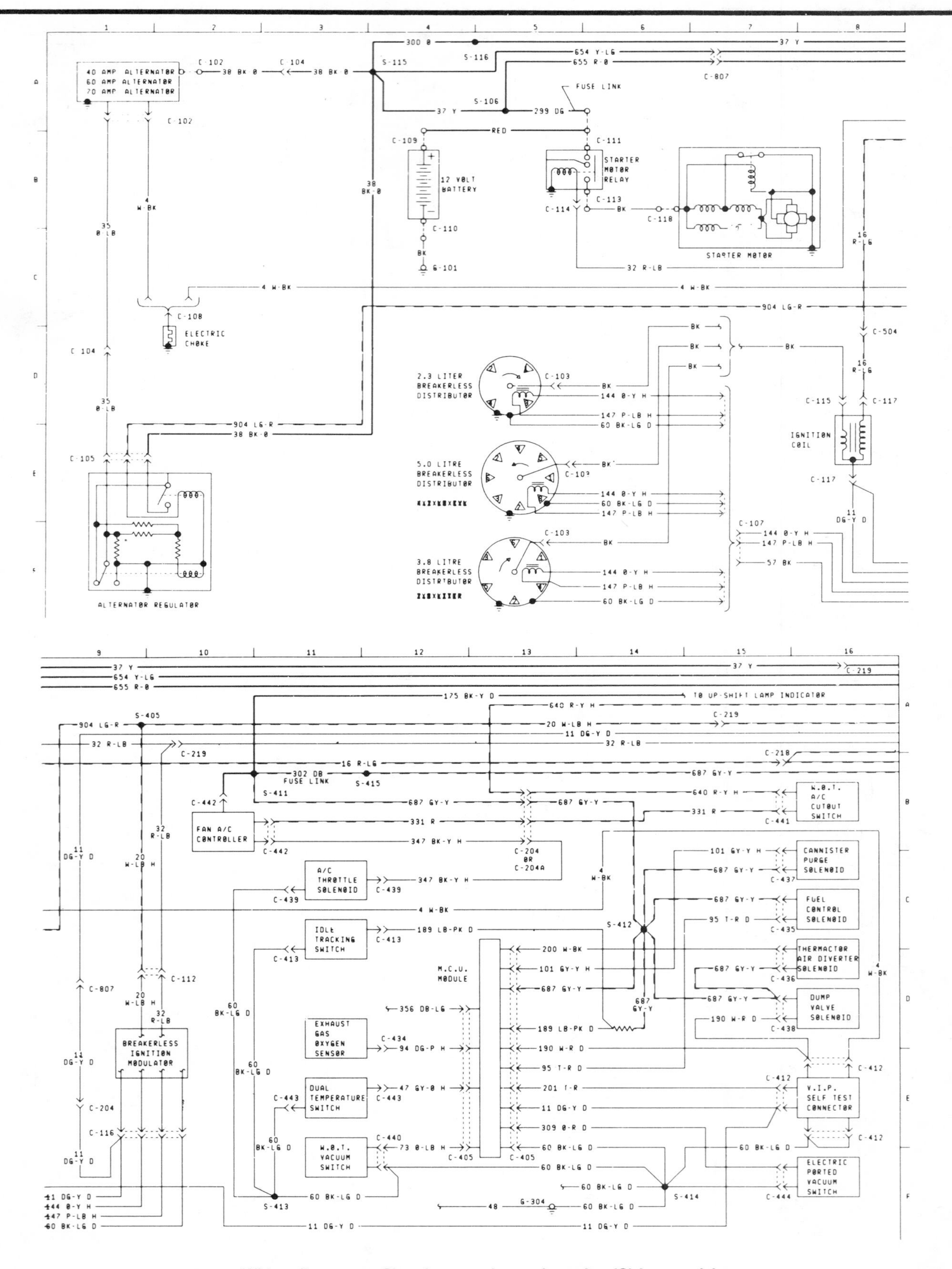

Wiring diagram — Charging, starting and running (2) late model

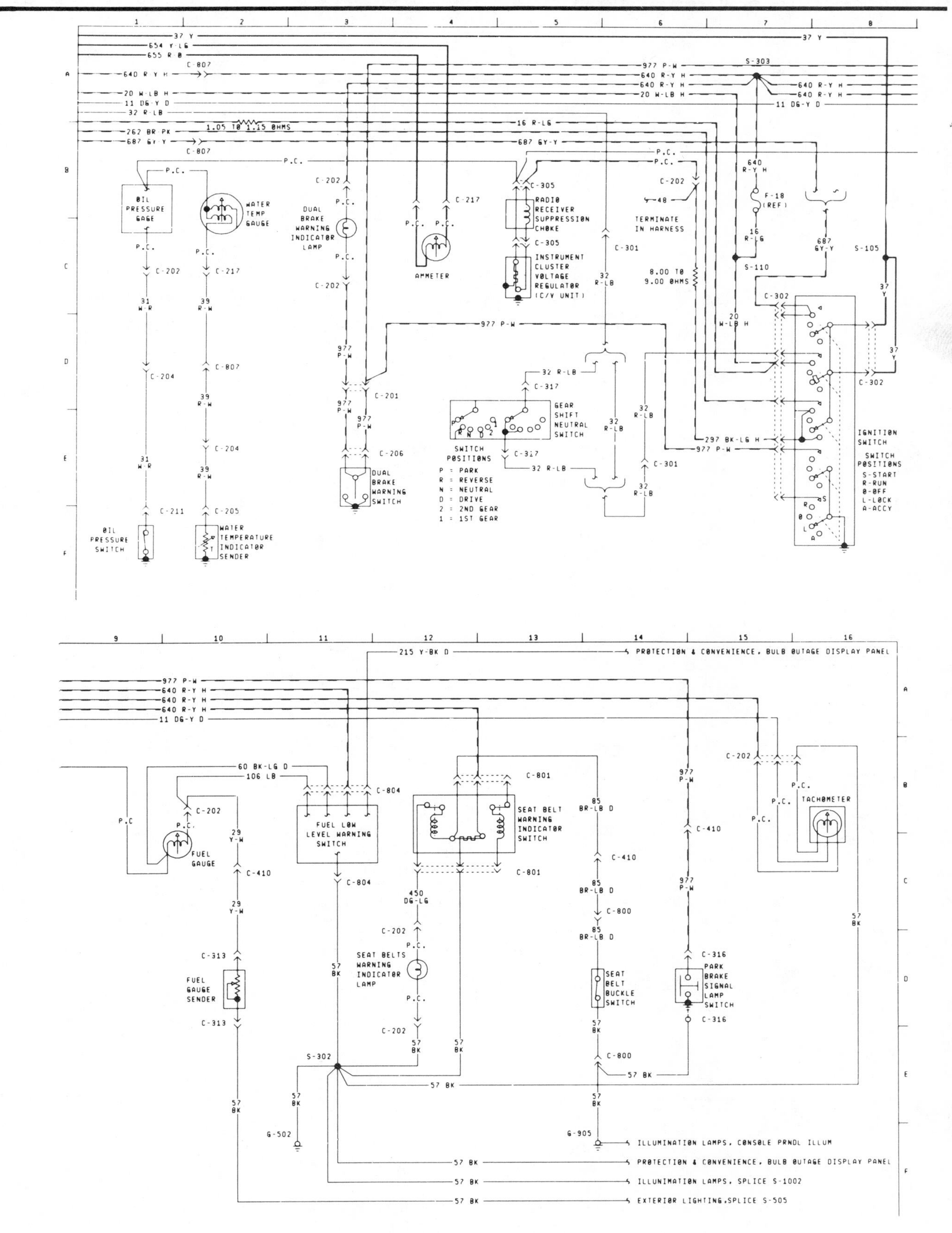

Wiring diagram — Charging, starting and running (3) late model (cont.)

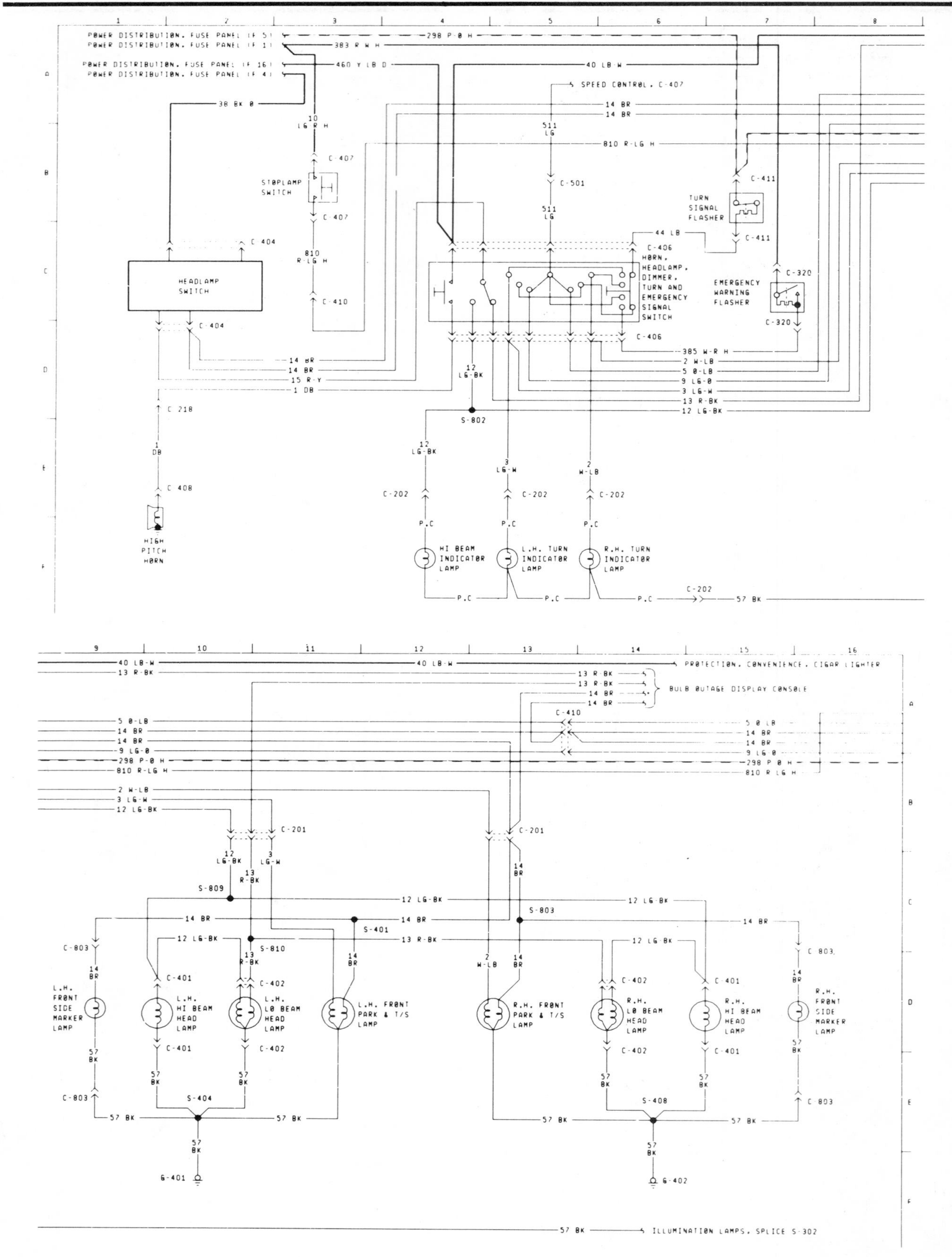

Wiring diagram — Exterior lighting (4) late model

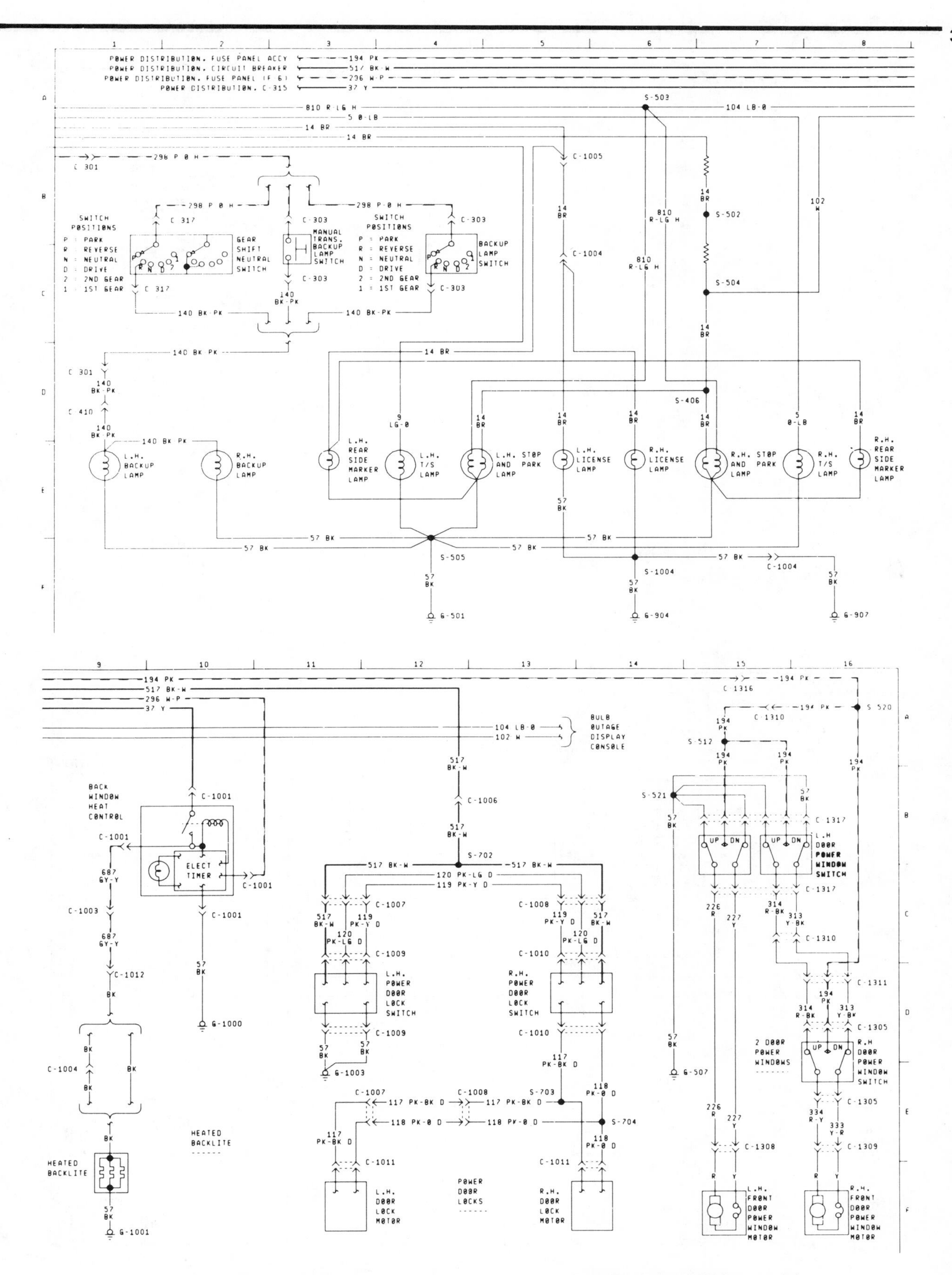

Wiring diagram — Heated rear window, power door locks and windows (5) late model

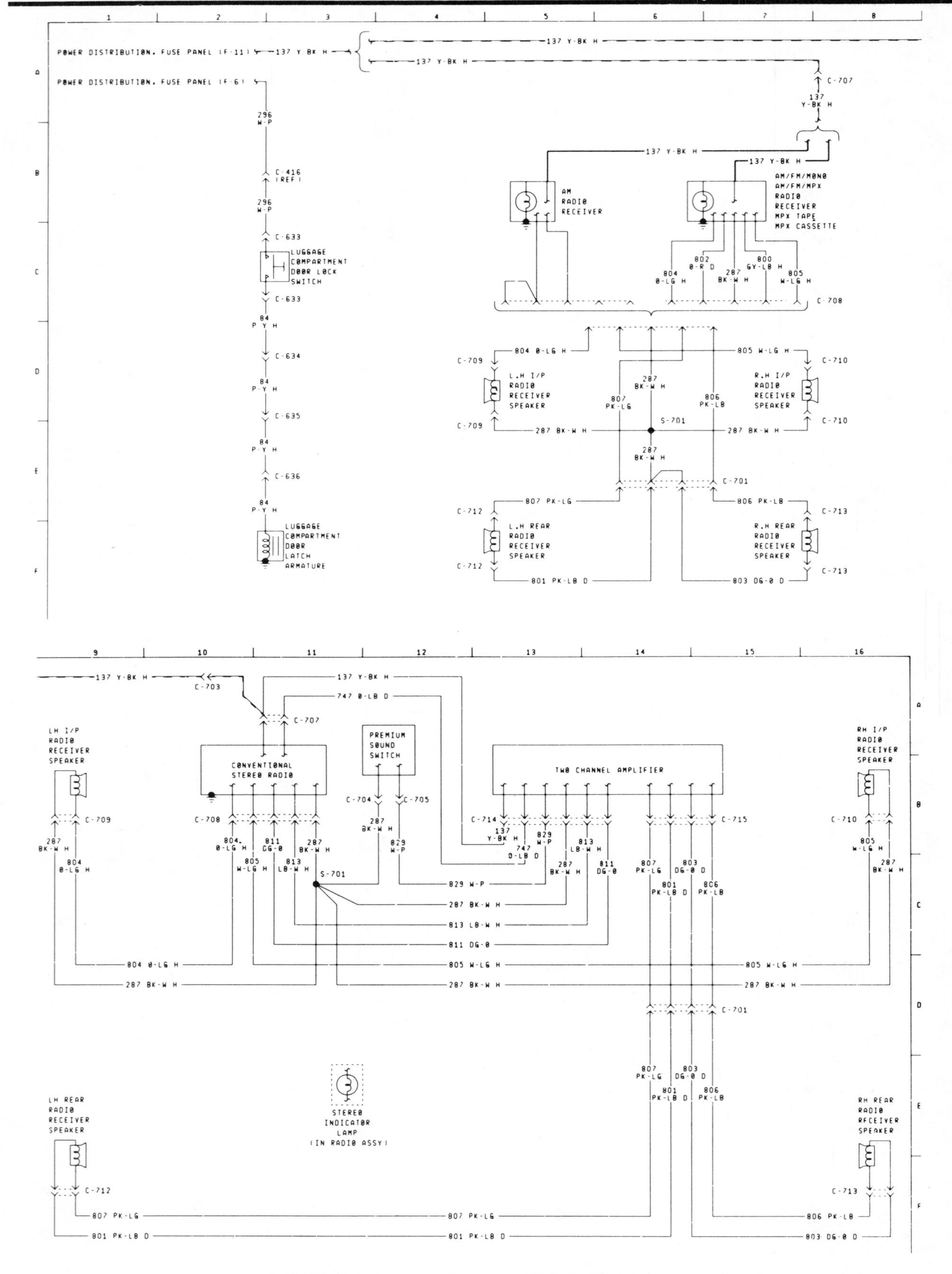

Wiring diagram — Radio and trunk release (6) late model

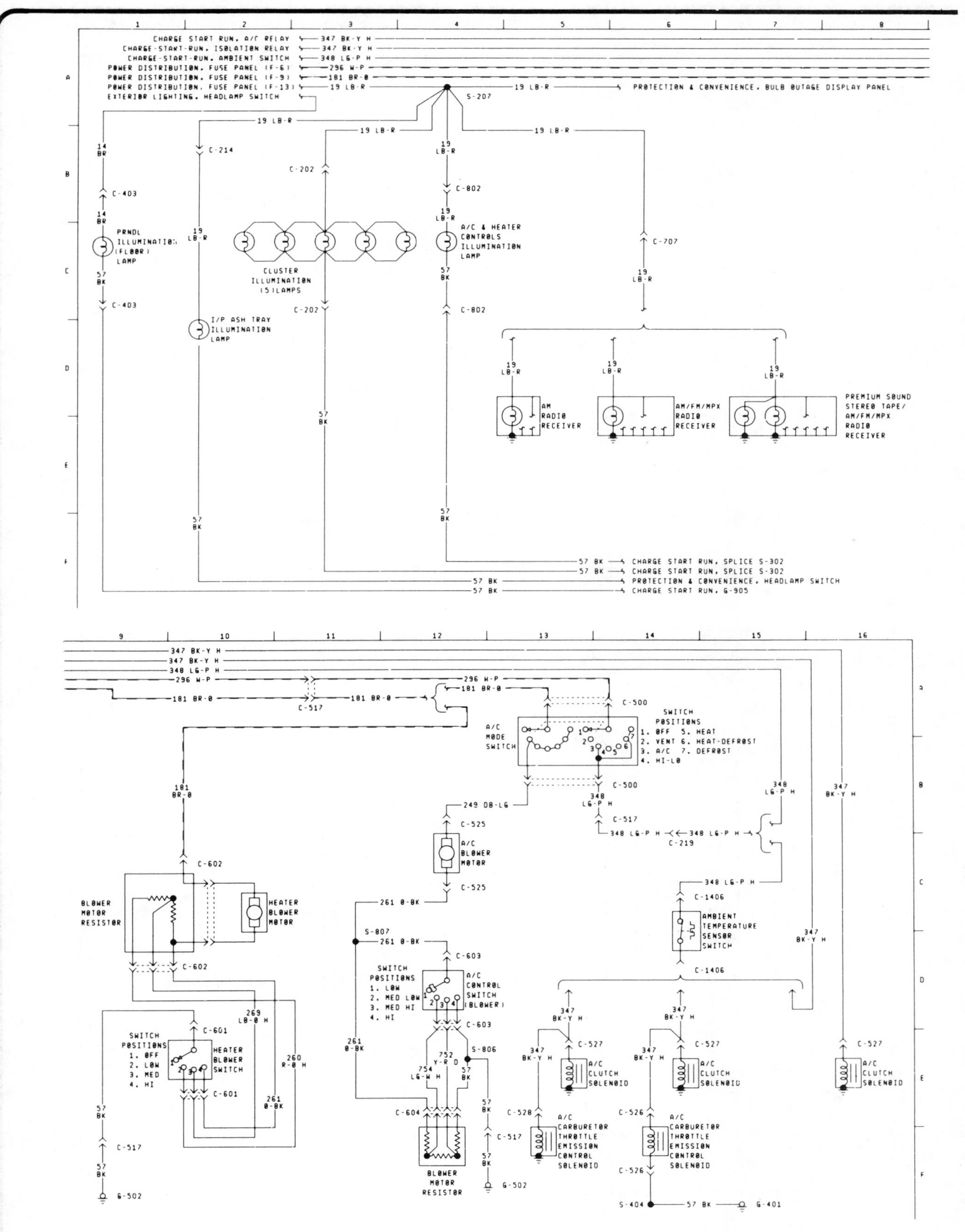

Wiring diagram — Illumination lamps and air conditioning (7) late model

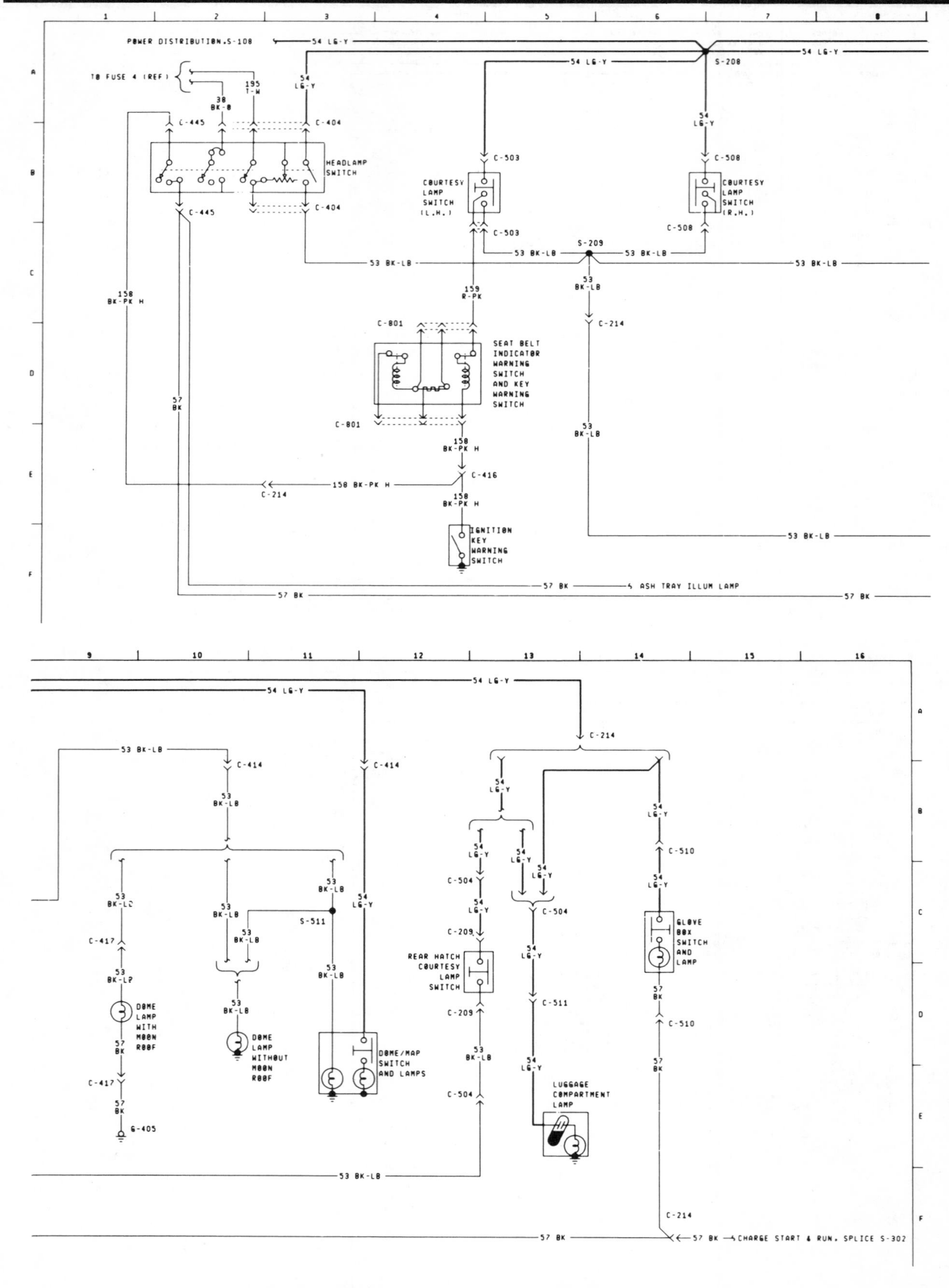

Wiring diagram – Protection and convenience (8) late model

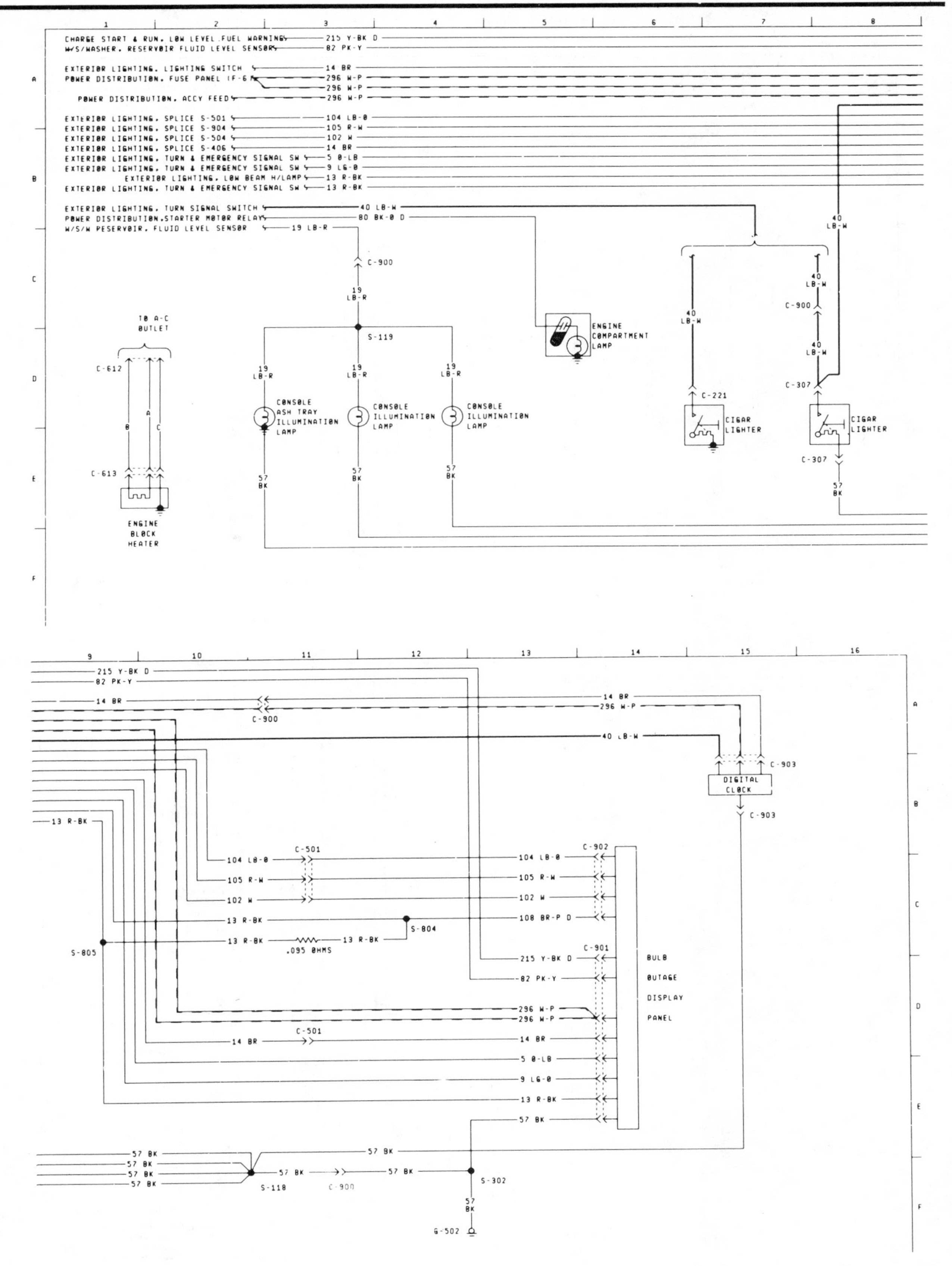

Wiring diagram — Illumination lamps, engine compartment lamp and protection and convenience (9) late model

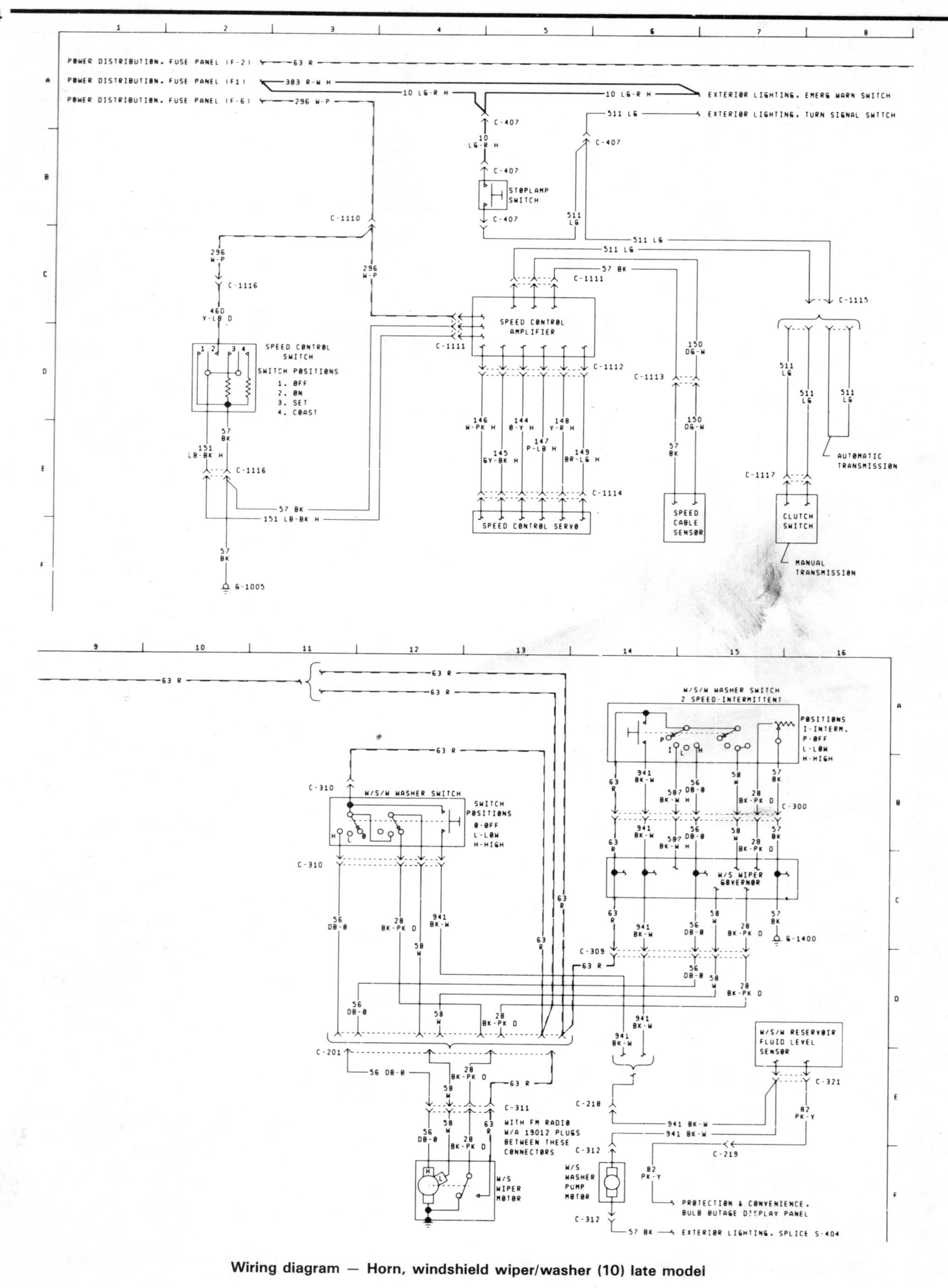

Wiring diagram — Horn, windshield wiper/washer (10) late model

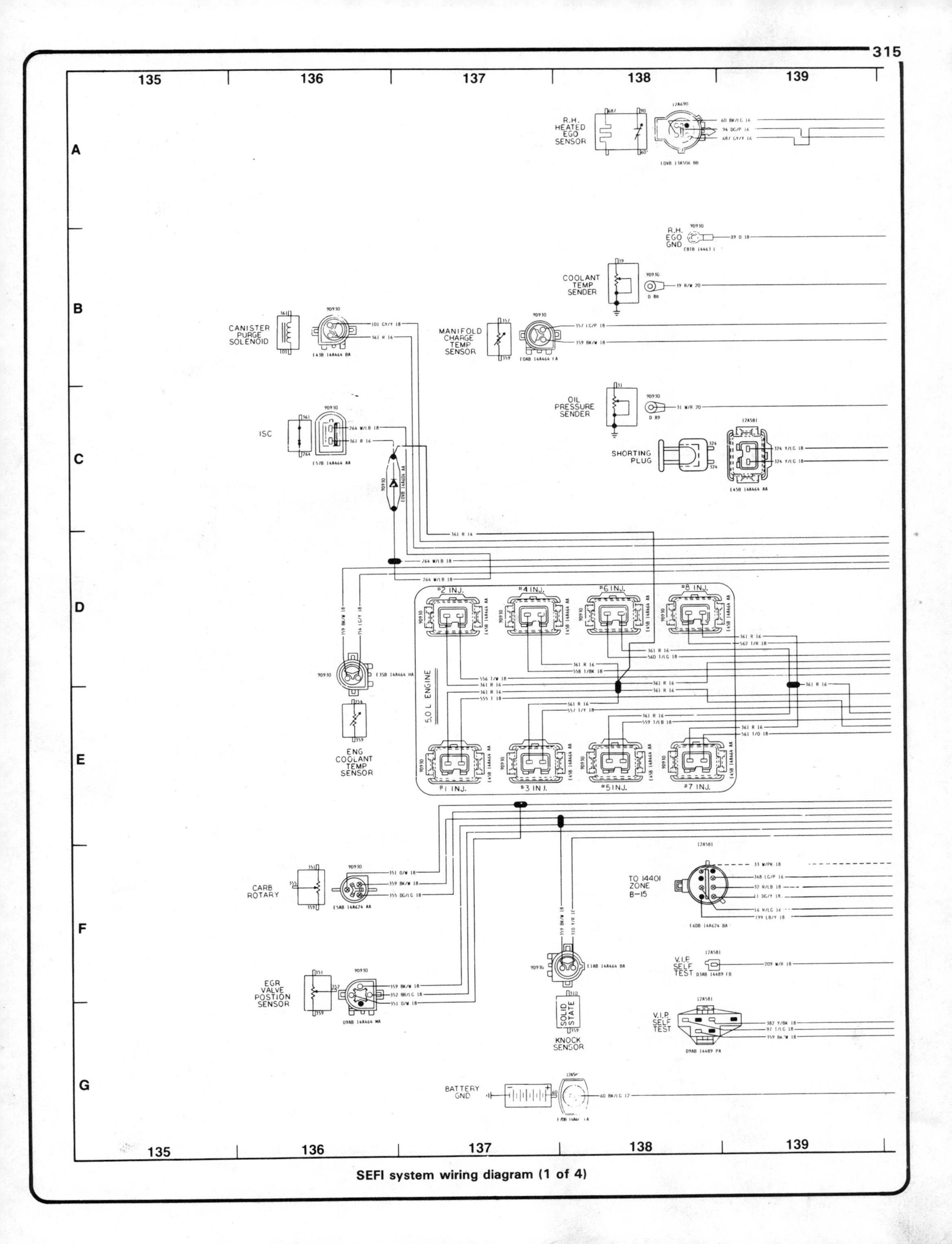

SEFI system wiring diagram (1 of 4)

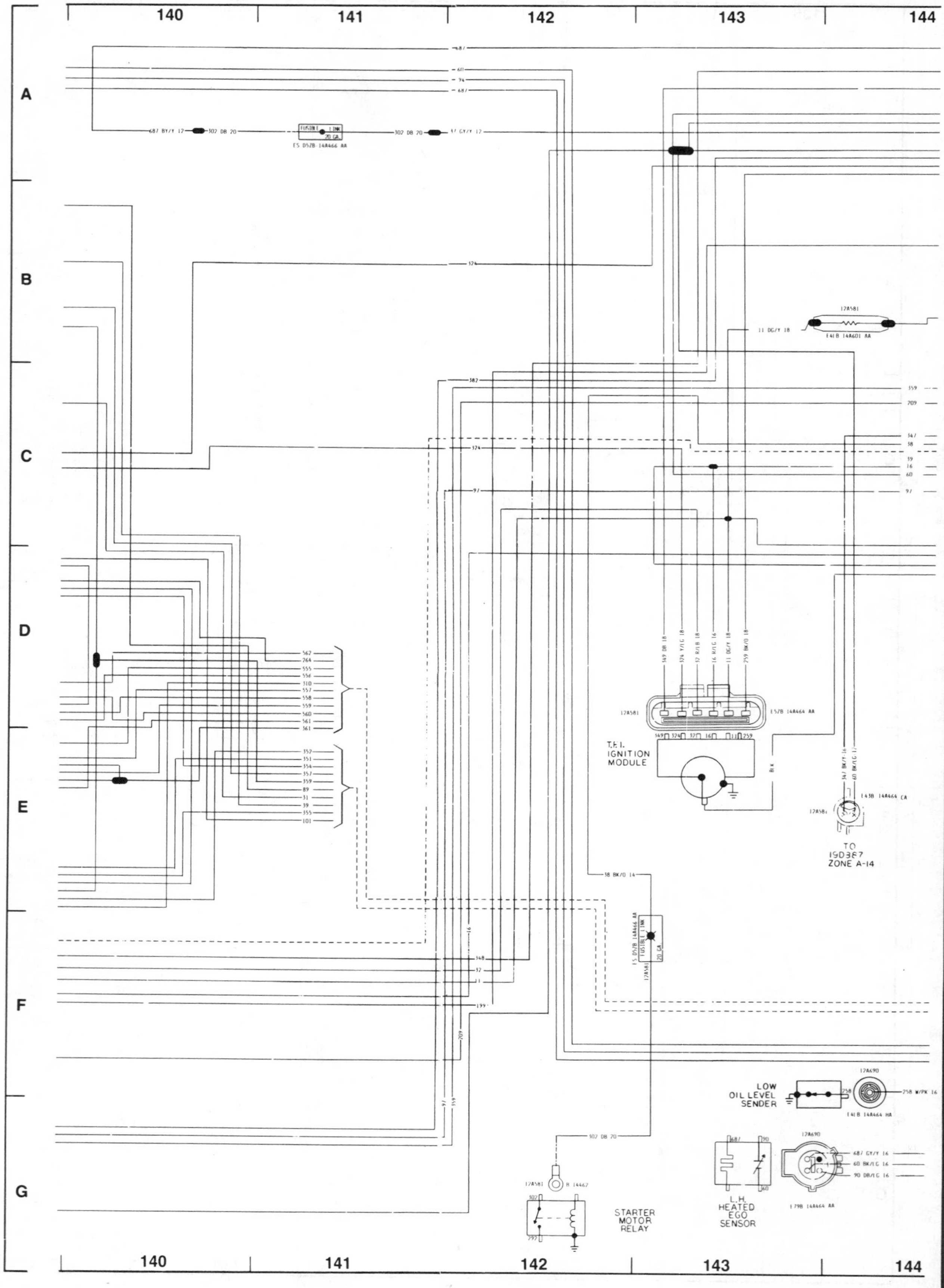

SEFI system wiring diagram (2 of 4)

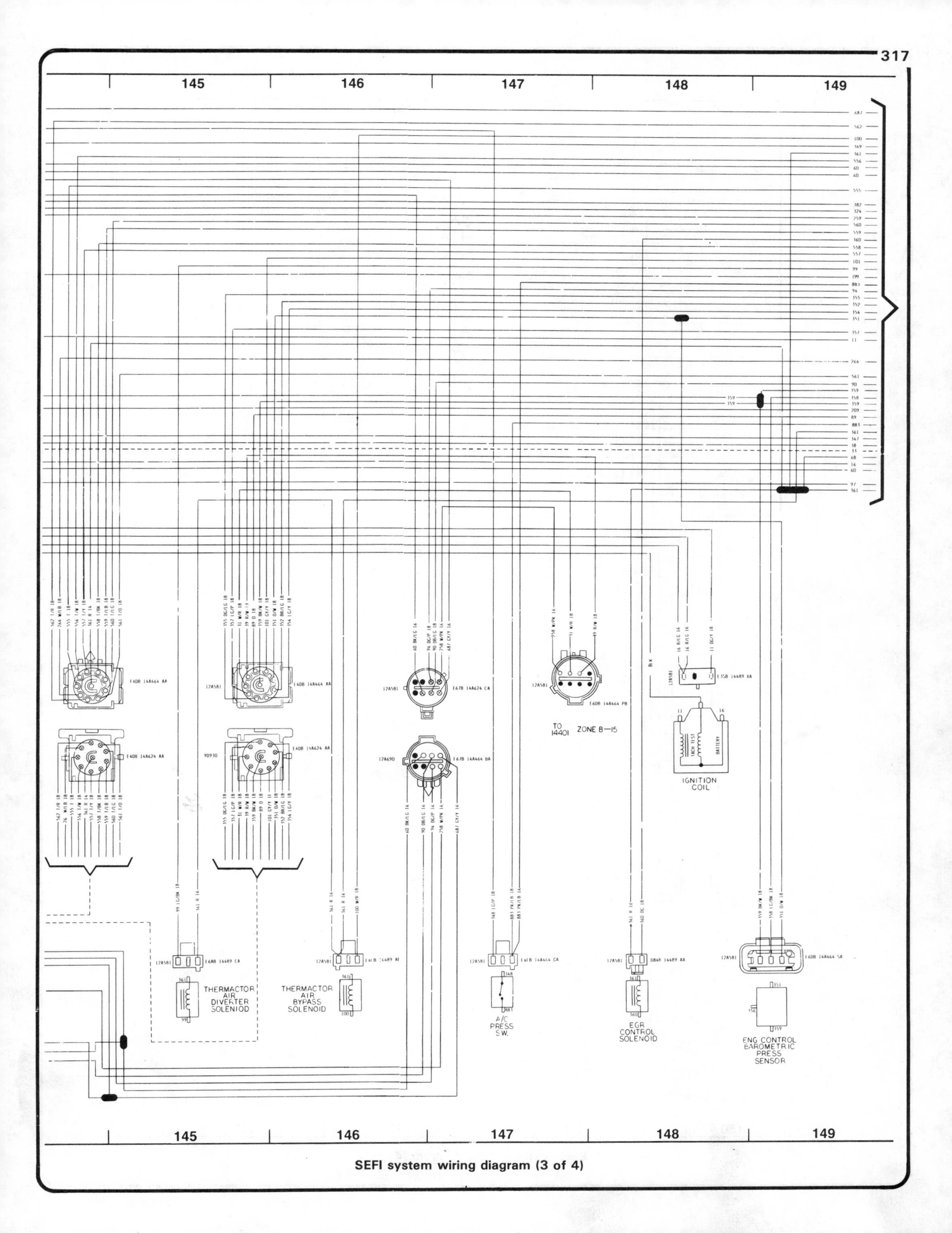

SEFI system wiring diagram (3 of 4)

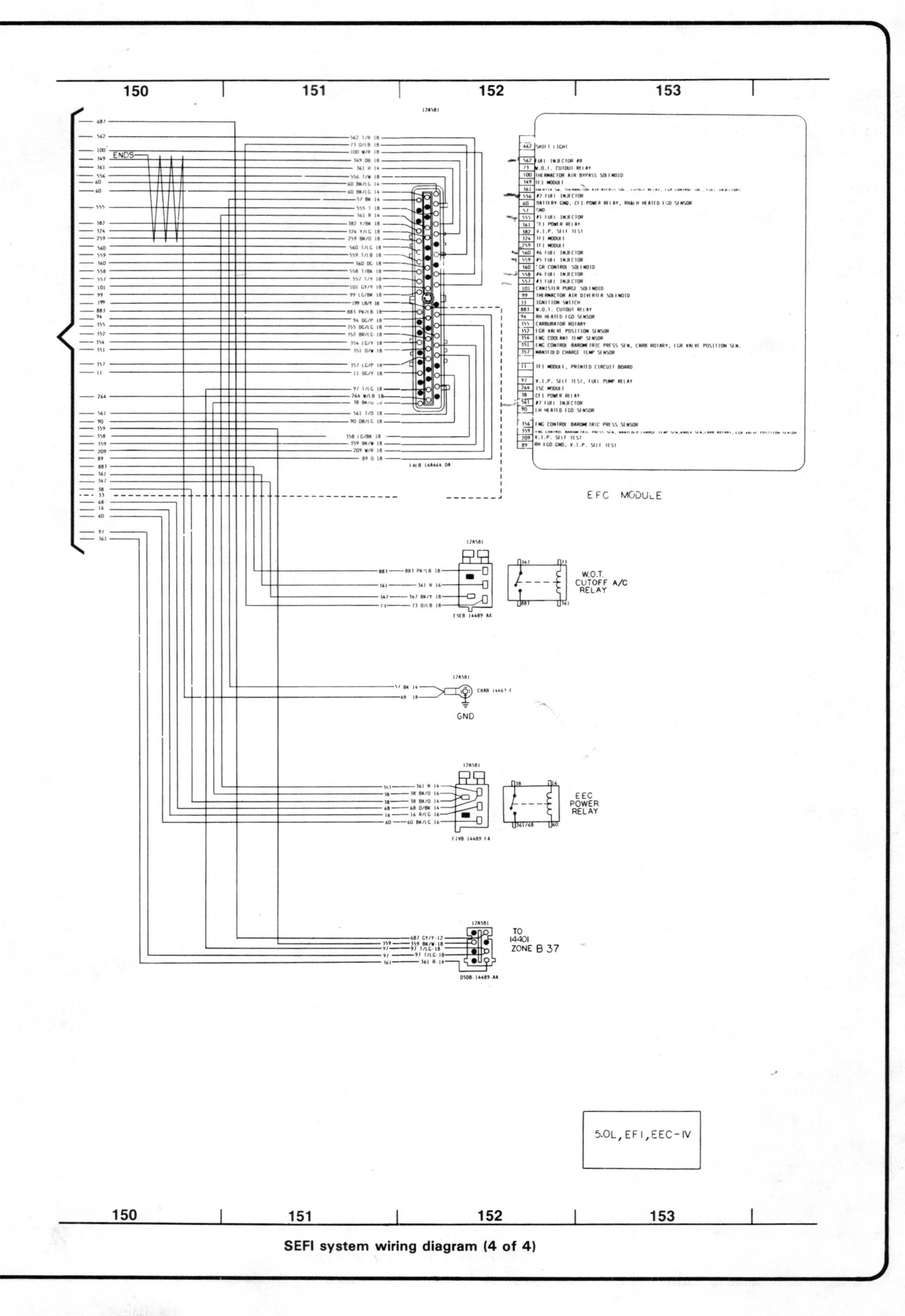

SEFI system wiring diagram (4 of 4)

Conversion factors

Length (distance)					
Inches (in)	X	25.4	= Millimetres (mm)	X 0.0394	= Inches (in)
Feet (ft)	X	0.305	= Metres (m)	X 3.281	= Feet (ft)
Miles	X	1.609	= Kilometres (km)	X 0.621	= Miles
Volume (capacity)					
Cubic inches (cu in; in^3)	X	16.387	= Cubic centimetres (cc; cm^3)	X 0.061	= Cubic inches (cu in; in^3)
Imperial pints (Imp pt)	X	0.568	= Litres (l)	X 1.76	= Imperial pints (Imp pt)
Imperial quarts (Imp qt)	X	1.137	= Litres (l)	X 0.88	= Imperial quarts (Imp qt)
Imperial quarts (Imp qt)	X	1.201	= US quarts (US qt)	X 0.833	= Imperial quarts (Imp qt)
US quarts (US qt)	X	0.946	= Litres (l)	X 1.057	= US quarts (US qt)
Imperial gallons (Imp gal)	X	4.546	= Litres (l)	X 0.22	= Imperial gallons (Imp gal)
Imperial gallons (Imp gal)	X	1.201	= US gallons (US gal)	X 0.833	= Imperial gallons (Imp gal)
US gallons (US gal)	X	3.785	= Litres (l)	X 0.264	= US gallons (US gal)
Mass (weight)					
Ounces (oz)	X	28.35	= Grams (g)	X 0.035	= Ounces (oz)
Pounds (lb)	X	0.454	= Kilograms (kg)	X 2.205	= Pounds (lb)
Force					
Ounces-force (ozf; oz)	X	0.278	= Newtons (N)	X 3.6	= Ounces-force (ozf; oz)
Pounds-force (lbf; lb)	X	4.448	= Newtons (N)	X 0.225	= Pounds-force (lbf; lb)
Newtons (N)	X	0.1	= Kilograms-force (kgf; kg)	X 9.81	= Newtons (N)
Pressure					
Pounds-force per square inch (psi; lbf/in^2; lb/in^2)	X	0.070	= Kilograms-force per square centimetre (kgf/cm^2; kg/cm^2)	X 14.223	= Pounds-force per square inch (psi; lbf/in^2; lb/in^2)
Pounds-force per square inch (psi; lbf/in^2; lb/in^2)	X	0.068	= Atmospheres (atm)	X 14.696	= Pounds-force per square inch (psi; lbf/in^2; lb/in^2)
Pounds-force per square inch (psi; lbf/in^2; lb/in^2)	X	0.069	= Bars	X 14.5	= Pounds-force per square inch (psi; lbf/in^2; lb/in^2)
Pounds-force per square inch (psi; lbf/in^2; lb/in^2)	X	6.895	= Kilopascals (kPa)	X 0.145	= Pounds-force per square inch (psi; lbf/in^2; lb/in^2)
Kilopascals (kPa)	X	0.01	= Kilograms-force per square centimetre (kgf/cm^2; kg/cm^2)	X 98.1	= Kilopascals (kPa)
Torque (moment of force)					
Pounds-force inches (lbf in; lb in)	X	1.152	= Kilograms-force centimetre (kgf cm; kg cm)	X 0.868	= Pounds-force inches (lbf in; lb in)
Pounds-force inches (lbf in; lb in)	X	0.113	= Newton metres (Nm)	X 8.85	= Pounds-force inches (lbf in; lb in)
Pounds-force inches (lbf in; lb in)	X	0.083	= Pounds-force feet (lbf ft; lb ft)	X 12	= Pounds-force inches (lbf in; lb in)
Pounds-force feet (lbf ft; lb ft)	X	0.138	= Kilograms-force metres (kgf m; kg m)	X 7.233	= Pounds-force feet (lbf ft; lb ft)
Pounds-force feet (lbf ft; lb ft)	X	1.356	= Newton metres (Nm)	X 0.738	= Pounds-force feet (lbf ft; lb ft)
Newton metres (Nm)	X	0.102	= Kilograms-force metres (kgf m; kg m)	X 9.804	= Newton metres (Nm)
Power					
Horsepower (hp)	X	745.7	= Watts (W)	X 0.0013	= Horsepower (hp)
Velocity (speed)					
Miles per hour (miles/hr; mph)	X	1.609	= Kilometres per hour (km/hr; kph)	X 0.621	= Miles per hour (miles/hr; mph)
*Fuel consumption**					
Miles per gallon, Imperial (mpg)	X	0.354	= Kilometres per litre (km/l)	X 2.825	= Miles per gallon, Imperial (mpg)
Miles per gallon, US (mpg)	X	0.425	= Kilometres per litre (km/l)	X 2.352	= Miles per gallon, US (mpg)

Temperature

Degrees Fahrenheit = (°C x 1.8) + 32

Degrees Celsius (Degrees Centigrade; °C) = (°F - 32) x 0.56

**It is common practice to convert from miles per gallon (mpg) to litres/100 kilometres (l/100km), where mpg (Imperial) x l/100 km = 282 and mpg (US) x l/100 km = 235*

Index

C

D

E

F

H

I

L

M

O

P

R

S